Data Security and Cryptography

Data Security and Cryptography

Edited by
Gina Simpson

www.willfordpress.com

Published by Willford Press,
118-35 Queens Blvd., Suite 400,
Forest Hills, NY 11375, USA

ISBN: 978-1-68285-650-5

Cataloging-in-Publication Data

Data security and cryptography / edited by Gina Simpson.
p. cm.
Includes bibliographical references and index.
ISBN 978-1-68285-650-5
1. Data protection. 2. Cryptography. 3. Computer security.
4. Computer networks--Security measures. I. Simpson, Gina.
QA76.9.A25 D38 2019
005.8--dc23

For information on all Willford Press publications
visit our website at www.willfordpress.com

Contents

Preface

This book was inspired by the evolution of our times; to answer the curiosity of inquisitive minds. Many developments have occurred across the globe in the recent past which has transformed the progress in the field.

Data security is the practice of protecting digital data from unauthorized access and unwanted actions such as cyber attack or data breach. Various technologies are used for ensuring data security. These include disk encryption, software-based security, hardware-based security, data masking, backups and data erasure. Securing communication in the presence of third parties is under the domain of cryptography. Diverse aspects of data confidentiality, integrity, non-repudiation and authentication are fundamental considerations of cryptography. The areas of study in cryptography include symmetric-key cryptography, public-key cryptography, cryptanalysis, cryptosystems, etc. This domain is crucial in the areas of electronic commerce, digital currencies, military communications and chip-based payment cards. This book contains some path-breaking studies in the field of data security and cryptography. It elucidates the concepts and innovative models around prospective developments with respect to these fields. It is a complete source of knowledge on the present status of these important fields.

This book was developed from a mere concept to drafts to chapters and finally compiled together as a complete text to benefit the readers across all nations. To ensure the quality of the content we instilled two significant steps in our procedure. The first was to appoint an editorial team that would verify the data and statistics provided in the book and also select the most appropriate and valuable contributions from the plentiful contributions we received from authors worldwide. The next step was to appoint an expert of the topic as the Editor-in-Chief, who would head the project and finally make the necessary amendments and modifications to make the text reader-friendly. I was then commissioned to examine all the material to present the topics in the most comprehensible and productive format.

I would like to take this opportunity to thank all the contributing authors who were supportive enough to contribute their time and knowledge to this project. I also wish to convey my regards to my family who have been extremely supportive during the entire project.

Editor

New Linear Cryptanalysis of Chinese Commercial Block Cipher Standard SM4

Yu Liu,[1,2] Huicong Liang,[1] Wei Wang,[1] and Meiqin Wang[1]

[1]*Key Laboratory of Cryptologic Technology and Information Security, Ministry of Education, Shandong University, Jinan, China*
[2]*Weifang University, Weifang, China*

Correspondence should be addressed to Meiqin Wang; mqwang@sdu.edu.cn

Academic Editor: Jesús Díaz-Verdejo

SM4 is a Chinese commercial block cipher standard used for wireless communication in China. In this paper, we use the partial linear approximation table of S-box to search for three rounds of iterative linear approximations of SM4, based on which the linear approximation for 20-round SM4 has been constructed. However, the best previous identified linear approximation only covers 19 rounds. At the same time, a linear approximation for 19-round SM4 is obtained, which is better than the known results. Furthermore, we show the key recovery attack on 24-round SM4 which is the best attack according to the number of rounds.

1. Introduction

SMS4 [1], issued in 2006 by Chinese government, serves the WAPI (WLAN Authentication and Privacy Infrastructure) as the underling block cipher for the security of wireless LANs. In 2012, SMS4 was announced as the Chinese commercial block cipher standard, renamed SM4 [2].

SM4 receives more attention from the cryptographic community and a lot of cryptanalytic results for SM4 have been produced. In [3], the rectangle and boomerang attacks on 18-round SM4 and the linear and differential attacks on 22-round SM4 have been presented. Using multiple linear attack, Etrog and Robshaw gave an attack on 23-round SM4 in [4]. Besides these, the differential attack and the multiple linear attack on 22-round SM4 have been introduced in [5, 6]. Till now, the best differential attack for 23-round SM4 is given in [7]. Cho and Nyberg proposed a multidimensional linear attack on 23-round SM4 in [8]. The best linear attack on 23-round SM4 is provided by Liu and Chen in [9]. Bai and Wu proposed a new lookup-table-based white-box implementation for SM4 which could protect the large linear encodings from being cancelled out in [10]. Moreover, related-key differential attack on SM4 has been given in [11] and the lower bound of the number of linear active S-boxes for SMS4-like ciphers has been analyzed in [12].

Linear cryptanalysis [13] is one of the most important techniques in the analysis of symmetric-key cryptographic primitives. The linear cryptanalysis focuses on the linear approximation between plaintext, ciphertext, and key. If a cipher behaves differently from a random permutation for linear cryptanalysis, this can be used to build a distinguisher or even a key recovery attack through adding some rounds. The subkeys of appended rounds are guessed and the ciphertexts are decrypted and/or plaintexts are encrypted using these subkeys to calculate intermediate state at the ends of distinguisher. If the subkeys are correctly guessed, then the distinguisher should hold. Otherwise, it will fail. Linear cryptanalysis has been used to analyze many ciphers such as [14–17].

Our Contributions. In terms of the number of rounds that all the previous attacks for SM4 can work, the best key recovery attacks on SM4 are linear cryptanalysis and differential cryptanalysis, and both of them are based on 19-round distinguishers. Whether we can get a better distinguisher is our first motivation to improve the attacks on SM4. Therefore, we focus on searching the linear approximation for SM4 to improve the attacks on SM4. The contributions of this paper are summarized as follows.

The best previous linear attacks work on the 19-round linear approximations. We design a new search algorithm for the

TABLE 1: Summary of linear approximations of SM4.

Rounds	Bias	Reference
19	$2^{-62.27}$	[9]
19	2^{-58}	Section 3
20	2^{-61}	Section 3

iterative linear approximations for small rounds of SM4 by gradually expanding the partial linear approximation table of S-box. Firstly, it is proved that there is no one-round or two-round iterative linear approximation for SM4, and then some properties are obtained for the iterative linear approximations of 3-round SM4. Based on these properties, we utilize our searching algorithm to get an 19-round linear approximation with bias 2^{-58} and a 20-round linear approximation with bias 2^{-61}. The results about our identified linear approximations with the previous ones are depicted in Table 1. It can be seen that our linear approximations are the best ones so far.

The best previous attacks can work on 23-round SM4. Utilizing our identified 20-round linear approximation of SM4, we give a key recovery attack on 24-round SM4, which is the best attack according to the number of rounds for SM4. Moreover, the new 19-round linear approximation is used to attack 23-round SM4. As a result, the best previous linear attack on 23-round SM4 is improved. A summary of our attacks and the previous attacks on SM4 is listed in Table 2.

The paper is organized as follows. Section 2 briefly describes the notations used in this paper and introduces the SM4 block cipher. Section 3 shows how to search the better linear approximations for SM4. In Section 4, we use the 19-round and 20-round linear approximations to attack 23-round and 24-round SM4, respectively. Section 5 concludes this paper.

2. Preliminaries

2.1. Notations. In this subsection, we will present the notations used in this paper as follows:

   (i) $\oplus$: a bitwise XOR operation

   (ii) $\|$: concatenation of two words

   (iii) $\lll$: left cyclic shift operation

   (iv) $\circ$: multiplication of two vectors, matrix and vector, or two matrices

   (v) $\cdot$: bitwise inner product

   (vi) &&: logical AND operation

   (vii) $X[i]$: the ith bit of X

   (viii) $X[i-j]$: a bit string starting from the ith bit to the jth bit of X.

2.2. Brief Description of SM4. SM4 is a Chinese national standard block cipher used in WAPI for WLAN. It has 128-bit block size and the key size is also 128 bits. The design of SM4 is based on the unbalanced generalized Feistel structure and the number of rounds is 32. We denote the plaintext

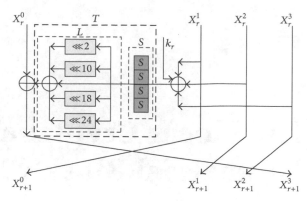

FIGURE 1: The round function of SM4.

as $(P_0, P_1, P_2, P_3) = (X_0^0, X_0^1, X_0^2, X_0^3) \in (\mathbb{F}_2^{32})^4$, and the encryption procedure is described as follows:

$$
\begin{aligned}
X_{r+1}^3 &= X_r^0 \oplus T\left(X_r^1 \oplus X_r^2 \oplus X_r^3 \oplus k_r\right) \\
&= X_r^0 \oplus L \circ S\left(X_r^1 \oplus X_r^2 \oplus X_r^3 \oplus k_r\right),
\end{aligned}
\tag{1}
$$

$$
\text{for } r = 0, \ldots, 31,
$$

where k_r is the rth round's subkey ($0 \le r \le 31$). The ciphertext $(C_0, C_1, C_2, C_3) = (X_{32}^3, X_{32}^2, X_{32}^1, X_{32}^0)$. The decryption procedure is the same as the encryption procedure with the reverse order of subkeys.

One round of SM4 is shown in Figure 1. It can be known from Figure 1 that T is composed of the nonlinear layer S and the linear transformation L. Layer S has four 8×8 S-boxes used in parallel. The specification of the S-box could be referred to [1]. Let $X \in \mathbb{F}_2^{32}$ and $Y \in \mathbb{F}_2^{32}$ be the 32-bit input and output words of the linear transformation L. Then

$$
\begin{aligned}
Y &= L(X) \\
&= X \oplus (X \lll 2) \oplus (X \lll 10) \oplus (X \lll 18) \\
&\quad \oplus (X \lll 24).
\end{aligned}
\tag{2}
$$

The key schedule of SM4 is similar to the encryption procedure but the only difference between them is that the linear transformation in the key schedule is

$$
L'(X) = X \oplus (X \lll 13) \oplus (X \lll 23).
\tag{3}
$$

The 128-bit master key (MK_0, MK_1, MK_2, MK_3) is first masked with the constants FK_0, FK_1, FK_2, FK_3 and then input to the key schedule function.

$$
\begin{aligned}
(K_0, K_1, K_2, K_3) &= (MK_0 \oplus FK_0, MK_1 \oplus FK_1, MK_2 \\
&\quad \oplus FK_2, MK_3 \oplus FK_3),
\end{aligned}
\tag{4}
$$

where $FK_0 = 0xa3b1bac6$, $FK_1 = 0x56aa3350$, $FK_3 = 0x677d9197$, and $FK_3 = 0xb27022dc$. And then k_r is computed as follows:

$$
k_r = K_{r+4} = K_r \oplus L' \circ S\left(K_{r+1} \oplus K_{r+2} \oplus K_{r+3} \oplus CK_r\right),
\tag{5}
$$

where CK_r, $r = 0, 1, \ldots, 31$, is the constant.

TABLE 2: Summary of attacks on SM4.

Rounds	Attack type	Data	Time	Memory	Source
13	Integral	2^{16}	2^{114}	—	[6]
16	Impossible differential	$2^{107.9}$	$2^{87.7}$	$2^{107.9}$	[18]
18	Rectangle	2^{124}	$2^{112.8}$	2^{128}	[3]
18	Boomerang	2^{120}	$2^{116.8}$	2^{123}	[3]
22	Multiple linear	2^{112}	$2^{119.8}$	$2^{118.8}$	[19]
23	Differential	2^{118}	$2^{126.7}$	—	[7]
23	Multidimensional linear	$2^{122.6}$	$2^{122.7}$	$2^{120.6}$	[9]
23	Linear	$2^{126.5}$	2^{122}	2^{116}	[9]
23	Linear	$2^{120.3}$	$2^{121.7}$	2^{85}	Section 4
24	Linear	$2^{126.6}$	$2^{126.6}$	2^{85}	Section 4

3. Search for the Linear Approximations of SM4

In terms of the number of rounds, all previous attacks for SM4 can work. One of the best key recovery attacks on SM4 is linear and differential cryptanalysis, and both of them are based on 19-round distinguishers. Whether we can get a better distinguisher is our first motivation to improve the attacks on SM4. Therefore, the key point is to search for the linear approximation of SM4. As far as we know, some methods to search for linear approximations of SM4 have been considered in [3, 4, 9, 19].

The search method in [3] is to construct linear approximations for reduced-round SM4 by identifying a one-round linear approximation with the same input and output masks for the T function. In this way, the number of active T functions can be minimized. As a result, an 18-round linear approximation with bias $2^{-57.28}$ for SM4 has been found.

In [4], Etrog and Robshaw derived a 5-round iterative linear approximation where only the last two rounds are active, and then they concatenated three five-round iterative linear approximations to construct an 18-round linear approximation with bias $2^{-56.2}$.

In [19], Liu et al. used the branch-and-bound algorithm in [20] to obtain a series of 5-round iterative linear approximations, which are utilized to construct an 18-round linear approximation with bias $2^{-56.14}$.

In order to get a better linear approximation for SM4, Liu and Chen gave a more dedicated search algorithm in [9]. They firstly used an MILP-based method to search the mode for the linear approximation with the minimum number of active S-boxes for reduced-round SM4; then based on the identified mode they found the 19-round linear approximation with bias $2^{-62.27}$.

It is obvious that even if the number of active S-boxes for a linear approximation is minimized, the absolute of its bias might not be maximum. From this point, we focus on searching for better linear approximations with a few more active S-boxes.

At CT-RSA 2014, Biryukov and Velichkov extended the branch-and-bound algorithm to search for the differential characteristics of ARX ciphers where the partial differential distribution table for modular addition is used in order to improve the search efficiency [21]. Inspired from this idea, we will use the partial linear approximation table to search for linear approximations of SM4.

At first, some properties for basic operations such as the XOR operation, the three-forked branching operation, and the linear map will be introduced.

Lemma 1 (XOR operation [22]). *Let $f(x_0, x_1) = x_0 \oplus x_1$; the input mask vector and output mask are $\Gamma = (\Gamma_0, \Gamma_1)$ and Λ, respectively. Then $\Pr(\Lambda \cdot f(x_0, x_1) = \Gamma_0 \cdot x_0 \oplus \Gamma_1 \cdot x_1) \neq 1/2$ if and only if $\Gamma_0 = \Gamma_1 = \Lambda$.*

Lemma 2 (three-forked branching operation [22]). *Let $f(x) = (x, x)$; the input mask and output linear mask vector are Γ and $\Lambda = (\Lambda_0, \Lambda_1)$, respectively. Then $\Pr(\Gamma \cdot x = \Lambda \cdot f(x)) \neq 1/2$ if and only if $\Gamma = \Lambda_0 \oplus \Lambda_1$.*

Lemma 3 (linear map [23]). *Let $f(x) = M \circ x$ with the input mask vector $\Gamma = (\Gamma_0, \Gamma_1, \ldots, \Gamma_{n-1})$ and output mask vector $\Lambda = (\Lambda_0, \Lambda_1, \ldots, \Lambda_{n-1})$; then $\Pr(\Gamma \cdot x = \Lambda \cdot f(x)) \neq 1/2$ if and only if $\Gamma = M^T \circ \Lambda$, where M^T is the transposed matrix of M and M is an $n \times n$ invertible binary matrix.*

Biases in the linear approximation table for S-box of SM4 take the values $l/2^8$ ($2 \leq l \leq 16$). If we put all the linear approximation table into the search program, the program will be too slow to get a better linear approximation. Thus, the partial linear approximation table is used in the search algorithm. The basic idea is that linear approximations of S-box with higher bias are utilized first. If no better linear approximation is output, then we can expand the partial linear approximation table by appending more linear approximations of S-box with less bias successively till a better linear approximation is output.

In order to get a better linear approximation, one common method is to find iterative linear approximations for short rounds first based on which long rounds of linear approximations could be produced directly. Thus, we will focus on searching for iterative linear approximations of SM4.

Now three properties for iterative linear approximations of SM4 are shown as follows.

Property 4. There is no one-round iterative linear approximation with active S-boxes on SM4.

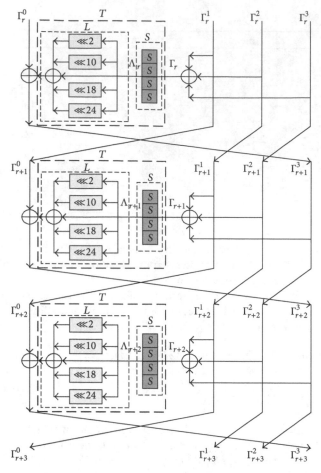

FIGURE 2: Linear approximation of 3-round SM4.

Proof. From Figure 2, if there is an iterative linear approximation for the first round, we have

$$\begin{aligned}
\Gamma_r^0 &= \Gamma_{r+1}^0, \\
\Gamma_r^1 &= \Gamma_{r+1}^1, \\
\Gamma_r^2 &= \Gamma_{r+1}^2, \\
\Gamma_r^3 &= \Gamma_r^0.
\end{aligned} \tag{6}$$

Using the property of three-forked branch, we have

$$\begin{aligned}
\Gamma_r^1 &= \Gamma_{r+1}^0 \oplus \Gamma_r, \\
\Gamma_r^2 &= \Gamma_{r+1}^1 \oplus \Gamma_r, \\
\Gamma_r^3 &= \Gamma_{r+1}^2 \oplus \Gamma_r.
\end{aligned} \tag{7}$$

From (6) and (7), we get

$$\begin{aligned}
\Gamma_{r+1}^1 &= \Gamma_r^0 \oplus \Gamma_r, \\
\Gamma_r^0 \oplus \Gamma_r \oplus \Gamma_r &= \Gamma_{r+1}^2, \\
\Gamma_r^3 = \Gamma_r^0 \oplus \Gamma_r \oplus \Gamma_r \oplus \Gamma_r &= \Gamma_r^0 \oplus \Gamma_r = \Gamma_r^0,
\end{aligned} \tag{8}$$

which implies $\Gamma_r = 0$ and all the S-boxes in this round are passive. Thus, there is no one-round iterative linear approximation for SM4. □

Property 5. The iterative linear approximation for two rounds of SM4 does not exist.

Proof. If there is an iterative linear approximation for the first two rounds in Figure 2, then we have

$$\begin{aligned}
\Gamma_r^0 &= \Gamma_{r+2}^0, \\
\Gamma_r^1 &= \Gamma_{r+2}^1, \\
\Gamma_r^2 &= \Gamma_{r+2}^2, \\
\Gamma_r^3 &= \Gamma_{r+1}^0.
\end{aligned} \tag{9}$$

With the property of three-forked branch, we have

$$\begin{aligned}
\Gamma_r^1 &= \Gamma_{r+1}^0 \oplus \Gamma_r, \\
\Gamma_r^2 &= \Gamma_{r+2}^0 \oplus \Gamma_r \oplus \Gamma_{r+1}, \\
\Gamma_r^3 &= \Gamma_{r+2}^1 \oplus \Gamma_r \oplus \Gamma_{r+1}, \\
\Gamma_{r+2}^2 &= \Gamma_r^0 \oplus \Gamma_{r+1}.
\end{aligned} \tag{10}$$

According to (9) and (10), we derive

$$\begin{aligned}
\Gamma_r^2 &= \Gamma_r^0 \oplus \Gamma_r \oplus \Gamma_{r+1}, \\
\Gamma_r^3 &= \Gamma_r^1 \oplus \Gamma_r \oplus \Gamma_{r+1}, \\
\Gamma_r^2 &= \Gamma_r^0 \oplus \Gamma_{r+1}.
\end{aligned} \tag{11}$$

Thus,

$$\Gamma_r^0 \oplus \Gamma_{r+1} = \Gamma_r^0 \oplus \Gamma_r \oplus \Gamma_{r+1} \implies \Gamma_r = 0, \tag{12}$$

which means that $\Gamma_r^0 = \Gamma_{r+2}^0 = 0$. Substitute the terms Γ_r in the above formulas and we have

$$\begin{aligned}
\Gamma_r^1 &= \Gamma_{r+1}^0 = \Gamma_{r+2}^1, \\
\Gamma_r^2 &= \Gamma_{r+1}, \\
\Gamma_r^3 &= \Gamma_{r+2}^1 \oplus \Gamma_{r+1} = \Gamma_{r+1}^0 \oplus \Gamma_{r+1} = \Gamma_{r+1}^0,
\end{aligned} \tag{13}$$

so $\Gamma_{r+1} = 0$, which means that all S-boxes in the first two rounds are passive. Therefore, 2-round iterative linear approximation for SM4 does not exist. □

Property 6. For the iterative linear approximation of 3-round SM4, the minimum number of active S-boxes is 3. Meanwhile, each round has one active S-box and the active S-boxes are located in the same positions of three rounds.

TABLE 3: Linear approximation for 19-round SM4.

Round	i	Γ_i^0	Λ_i	Γ_i	Bias	Γ_i^1	Γ_i^2	Γ_i^3
1	0	028A0828	002A0000	00950000	2^{-4}	021F0828	028B0828	028A0828
2	1	028A0828	002A0000	00940000	2^{-4}	021E0828	021F0828	028A0828
3	2	028A0828	002A0000	00010000	2^{-4}	028B0828	021E0828	028A0828
4	3	028A0828	002A0000	00950000	2^{-4}	021F0828	028B0828	028A0828
5	4	028A0828	002A0000	00940000	2^{-4}	021E0828	021F0828	028A0828
6	5	028A0828	002A0000	00010000	2^{-4}	028B0828	021E0828	028A0828
7	6	028A0828	002A0000	00950000	2^{-4}	021F0828	028B0828	028A0828
8	7	028A0828	002A0000	00940000	2^{-4}	021E0828	021F0828	028A0828
9	8	028A0828	002A0000	00010000	2^{-4}	028B0828	021E0828	028A0828
10	9	028A0828	002A0000	00950000	2^{-4}	021F0828	028B0828	028A0828
11	10	028A0828	002A0000	00940000	2^{-4}	021E0828	021F0828	028A0828
12	11	028A0828	002A0000	00010000	2^{-4}	028B0828	021E0828	028A0828
13	12	028A0828	002A0000	00950000	2^{-4}	021F0828	028B0828	028A0828
14	13	028A0828	002A0000	00940000	2^{-4}	021E0828	021F0828	028A0828
15	14	028A0828	002A0000	00010000	2^{-4}	028B0828	021E0828	028A0828
16	15	028A0828	002A0000	00950000	2^{-4}	021F0828	028B0828	028A0828
17	16	028A0828	002A0000	00940000	2^{-4}	021E0828	021F0828	028A0828
18	17	028A0828	002A0000	00010000	2^{-4}	028B0828	021E0828	028A0828
19	18	028A0828	002A0000	00950000	2^{-4}	021F0828	028B0828	028A0828
20	19	028A0828	002A0000	*	*	021E0828	021F0828	028A0828

Proof. If there is an iterative linear approximation for three rounds in Figure 2, then we have

$$\Gamma_r^1 \oplus \Gamma_r \oplus \Gamma_{r+2} = \Gamma_r^2,$$

$$\Gamma_r^3 = \Gamma_r^2 \oplus \Gamma_r \oplus \Gamma_{r+1},$$

$$\Gamma_r^3 \oplus \Gamma_r \oplus \Gamma_{r+1} \oplus \Gamma_{r+2} = \Gamma_r^0, \qquad (14)$$

$$\Gamma_r^0 \oplus \Gamma_{r+1} \oplus \Gamma_{r+2} = \Gamma_r^1.$$

So

$$\Gamma_{r+1} = \Gamma_r \oplus \Gamma_{r+2},$$

$$\Gamma_r^0 = \Gamma_r^3. \qquad (15)$$

We focus on the linear approximation with less active S-boxes. From (15), it is impossible for a three-round iterative linear approximation to have only one active S-box. If there are two active S-boxes, then $\Gamma_r = 0$ or $\Gamma_{r+1} = 0$ or $\Gamma_{r+2} = 0$. Hence, all S-boxes in the three-round linear approximation are passive. Take $\Gamma_r = 0$ as an example.

If $\Gamma_r = 0$, then $\Lambda_r = 0$, which implies $\Gamma_r^0 = 0$. Then

$$\Gamma_r^3 = \Gamma_{r+3}^0 = \Gamma_{r+3}^3 = \Gamma_r^0 = 0,$$

$$\because \Gamma_{r+2}^0 = \Gamma_{r+3}^3 \qquad (16)$$

$$\therefore \Gamma_{r+2}^0 = 0.$$

Thus, $\Lambda_{r+2} = 0$; we have $\Gamma_{r+2} = 0$.

$$0 = \Gamma_r^3 \oplus \Gamma_r = \Gamma_{r+1}^2 = \Gamma_{r+1} \oplus \Gamma_{r+2}^1 = \Gamma_{r+1} \oplus \Gamma_{r+2} \oplus \Gamma_{r+3}^0 \qquad (17)$$

$$= \Gamma_{r+1}.$$

In the cases $\Gamma_{r+1} = 0$ and $\Gamma_{r+2} = 0$, we can also obtain that there is no active S-box in the three-round linear approximation by the similar way of the case $\Gamma_r = 0$. Therefore, the iterative linear approximation for three-round SM4 has at least three active S-boxes. From (15), it is clear that each round has one active S-box and these active S-boxes are located in the same positions of three rounds. □

From Property 6, we will try to search for the iterative linear approximation of 3-round SM4 where each round has only one active S-box. The search algorithm is listed in Algorithm 1. In Algorithm 1, the following notations are used. $\Gamma_r = \Gamma_{r,0} \| \Gamma_{r,1} \| \Gamma_{r,2} \| \Gamma_{r,3}$ and $\Lambda_r = \Lambda_{r,0} \| \Lambda_{r,1} \| \Lambda_{r,2} \| \Lambda_{r,3}$ are input and output masks of S-layer in the rth round. $\Gamma_{r,j}$ and $\Lambda_{r,j}$ are input and output mask of the jth S-box of the rth round. T^l is a partial linear approximation table of S-box which consists of linear approximations with bias no less than $l/2^8$ ($2 \le l \le 16$).

After proceeding the search algorithm, we identify 12240 3-round iterative linear approximations with bias 2^{-10}. With any 3-round iterative linear approximation, we can construct linear approximations for 19-round and 20-round SM4 with bias 2^{-58} and 2^{-61}, respectively. Compared with the best previous 19-round linear approximation in [9], the bias has been improved from $2^{-62.27}$ to 2^{-58}. In Tables 3 and 4, we give linear approximations for 19-round and 20-round SM4, respectively, where all masks are denoted as hexadecimal values and "*" is undecided.

4. Key Recovery Attacks for SM4

4.1. Linear Attack on 24-Round SM4. We append two rounds to the bottom and the top of the 20-round linear

```
(1)  for l ← 16 to 2 do
(2)      for j ← 0 to 3 do
(3)          for all Λ_{0,j} ≠ 0, Λ_{1,j} ≠ 0, Λ_{2,j} ≠ 0, Λ_{0,j'} = Λ_{1,j'} = Λ_{2,j'} = 0, (0 ≤ j' ≠ j ≤ 3) do
(4)              Γ_{0,j'} = Γ_{1,j'} = Γ_{2,j'} = 0, (0 ≤ j' ≠ j ≤ 3)
(5)              find all m_0 input masks indexed by Λ_{0,j} from T^l, and store in R_j[m_0]
(6)              for k_0 ← 0 to m_0 − 1 do
(7)                  Γ_{0,j} ← R_j[k_0]
(8)                  find all m_1 input masks indexed by Λ_{1,j} from T^l, and store in R_j[m_1]
(9)                  for k_1 ← 0 to m_1 − 1 do
(10)                     Γ_{1,j} ← R_j[k_1]
(11)                     find all m_2 input masks indexed by Λ_{2,j} from T^l, and store in R_j[m_2]
(12)                     for k_2 ← 0 to m_2 − 1 do
(13)                         Γ_{2,j} ← R_j[k_2]
(14)                         for i ← 0 to 2 do
(15)                             Γ_i^0 = L^T ∘ (Λ_{i,0} ‖ Λ_{i,1} ‖ Λ_{i,2} ‖ Λ_{i,3}) = L^T ∘ (Λ_i)
(16)                         end for
(17)                         for i ← 0 to 2 do
(18)                             Γ_i = Γ_{i,0} ‖ Γ_{i,1} ‖ Γ_{i,2} ‖ Γ_{i,3}
(19)                         end for
(20)                         Γ_3^0 = Γ_0^0
(21)                         Γ_3^1 = Γ_0^0 ⊕ Γ_1 ⊕ Γ_2
(22)                         Γ_3^2 = Γ_1^0 ⊕ Γ_2
(23)                         Γ_0^3 = Γ_0^0 ⊕ Γ_0 ⊕ Γ_1 ⊕ Γ_2
(24)                         Γ_0^1 = Γ_1^0 ⊕ Γ_0
(25)                         Γ_0^2 = Γ_2^0 ⊕ Γ_0 ⊕ Γ_1
(26)                         if Γ_0^3 = Γ_2^0 && Γ_0^1 = Γ_3^1 && Γ_0^2 = Γ_3^2 then
(27)                             return Γ_0^0, Γ_1^0, Γ_2^0, Γ_3^0, Γ_0, Γ_1, Γ_2
(28)                             // 3-round iterative linear approximation
(29)                         else
(30)                             continue.
(31)                         end if
(32)                     end for
(33)                 end for
(34)             end for
(35)         end for
(36)     end for
(37)     l = l − 2
(38) end for
```

ALGORITHM 1: Search algorithm for iterative linear approximation of 3-round SM4.

approximation in Table 4, respectively. Then a linear attack on 24-round SM4 is presented. The partial sum technique [24] is used in the partial encryption and decryption procedures. See Figure 3.

According to the linear approximation in Figure 3, we denote $\Gamma_2^0 = \Gamma_2^3 = \Gamma_{22}^0 = \Gamma_{22}^3 = 0x8808A228$, $\Gamma_2^1 = 0x8808C228$, $\Gamma_2^2 = \Gamma_{22}^1 = 0x88080828$, $\Gamma_{22}^2 = 0x88086828$, $\Lambda_1 = \Lambda_{22} = 0x00008200$, and $\Lambda_{1,2} = \Lambda_{22,2} = 0x82$. From the linear approximation, we have

$$\Gamma_2^0 \cdot X_2^0 \oplus \Gamma_2^1 \cdot X_2^1 \oplus \Gamma_2^2 \cdot X_2^2 \oplus \Gamma_2^3 \cdot X_2^3 \oplus \Gamma_{22}^0 \cdot X_{22}^0 \oplus \Gamma_{22}^1 \cdot X_{22}^1 \oplus \Gamma_{22}^2 \cdot X_{22}^2 \oplus \Gamma_{22}^3 \cdot X_{22}^3 = \kappa. \quad (18)$$

Consider the partial encryption and decryption; the left side of the above equation can be written as follows:

$$\Gamma_2^0 \cdot P_2 \oplus \Gamma_2^1 \cdot P_3 \oplus \Gamma_2^2 \cdot (P_0 \oplus XX_0) \oplus \Gamma_2^0 \cdot (P_1 \oplus XX_1)$$
$$\oplus \Gamma_2^0 \cdot (C_2 \oplus XX_{22}) \oplus \Gamma_2^2 \cdot (C_3 \oplus XX_{23}) \oplus \Gamma_{22}^2$$

$$\cdot C_0 \oplus \Gamma_2^0 \cdot C_1$$
$$= \Gamma_2^0 \cdot P_2 \oplus \Gamma_2^1 \cdot P_3 \oplus \Gamma_2^2 \cdot P_0 \oplus \Gamma_2^0 \cdot P_1 \oplus \Gamma_2^0 \cdot C_2 \oplus \Gamma_2^2$$
$$\cdot C_3 \oplus \Gamma_{22}^2 \cdot C_0 \oplus \Gamma_2^0 \cdot C_1 \oplus \Gamma_2^2 \cdot XX_0 \oplus \Gamma_2^0 \cdot XX_1$$
$$\oplus \Gamma_2^0 \cdot XX_{22} \oplus \Gamma_2^2 \cdot XX_{23},$$

$$(19)$$

where XX_r is the state after transformation T and XS_r is the state after layer S in the rth round.

Since

$$\Gamma_2^0 \cdot XX_{22} = \Lambda_{22} \cdot XS_{22} = \Lambda_{22,2} \cdot XS_{22} [16\text{–}23]$$
$$= \Lambda_{1,2} \cdot S\left(\left(X_{22}^1 \oplus X_{22}^2 \oplus X_{22}^3 \oplus k_{22}\right)[16\text{–}23]\right)$$
$$= \Lambda_{1,2} \cdot S\left(\left(C_3 \oplus C_0 \oplus C_1\right)[16\text{–}23]\right)$$

TABLE 4: Linear approximation for 20-round SM4.

Round	i	Γ_i^0	Λ_i	Γ_i	Bias	Γ_i^1	Γ_i^2	Γ_i^3
1	0	$8808A228$	00008200	00006000	2^{-4}	$8808C228$	88080828	$8808A228$
2	1	$8808A228$	00008200	$0000CA00$	2^{-4}	88086828	$8808C228$	$8808A228$
3	2	$8808A228$	00008200	$0000AA00$	2^{-4}	88080828	88086828	$8808A228$
4	3	$8808A228$	00008200	00006000	2^{-4}	$8808C228$	88080828	$8808A228$
5	4	$8808A228$	00008200	$0000CA00$	2^{-4}	88086828	$8808C228$	$8808A228$
6	5	$8808A228$	00008200	$0000AA00$	2^{-4}	88080828	88086828	$8808A228$
7	6	$8808A228$	00008200	00006000	2^{-4}	$8808C228$	88080828	$8808A228$
8	7	$8808A228$	00008200	$0000CA00$	2^{-4}	88086828	$8808C228$	$8808A228$
9	8	$8808A228$	00008200	$0000AA00$	2^{-4}	88080828	88086828	$8808A228$
10	9	$8808A228$	00008200	00006000	2^{-4}	$8808C228$	88080828	$8808A228$
11	10	$8808A228$	00008200	$0000CA00$	2^{-4}	88086828	$8808C228$	$8808A228$
12	11	$8808A228$	00008200	$0000AA00$	2^{-4}	88080828	88086828	$8808A228$
13	12	$8808A228$	00008200	00006000	2^{-4}	$8808C228$	88080828	$8808A228$
14	13	$8808A228$	00008200	$0000CA00$	2^{-4}	88086828	$8808C228$	$8808A228$
15	14	$8808A228$	00008200	$0000AA00$	2^{-4}	88080828	88086828	$8808A228$
16	15	$8808A228$	00008200	00006000	2^{-4}	$8808C228$	88080828	$8808A228$
17	16	$8808A228$	00008200	$0000CA00$	2^{-4}	88086828	$8808C228$	$8808A228$
18	17	$8808A228$	00008200	$0000AA00$	2^{-4}	88080828	88086828	$8808A228$
19	18	$8808A228$	00008200	00006000	2^{-4}	$8808C228$	88080828	$8808A228$
20	19	$8808A228$	00008200	$0000CA00$	2^{-4}	88086828	$8808C228$	$8808A228$
21	20	$8808A228$	00008200	$*$	$*$	88080828	88086828	$8808A228$

$$\oplus XX_{23}[16\text{–}23] \oplus k_{22}[16\text{–}23]),$$

$$\Gamma_2^0 \cdot XX_1 = \Lambda_1 \cdot XS_1 = \Lambda_{1,2} \cdot XS_1[16\text{–}23] = \Lambda_{1,2}$$
$$\cdot S\left(\left(X_1^1 \oplus X_1^2 \oplus X_1^3 \oplus k_1\right)[16\text{–}23]\right) = \Lambda_{1,2}$$
$$\cdot S\left((P_0 \oplus P_2 \oplus P_3)[16\text{–}23] \oplus XX_0[16\text{–}23]\right.$$
$$\left.\oplus k_1[16\text{–}23]\right),$$

$$(20)$$

then, (19) can be transformed into

$$\Gamma_2^0 \cdot P_2 \oplus \Gamma_2^1 \cdot P_3 \oplus \Gamma_2^2 \cdot P_0 \oplus \Gamma_2^0 \cdot P_1 \oplus \Gamma_2^0 \cdot C_2 \oplus \Gamma_2^2 \cdot C_3$$
$$\oplus \Gamma_{22}^2 \cdot C_0 \oplus \Gamma_2^0 \cdot C_1 \oplus \Gamma_2^2 \cdot T(P_1 \oplus P_2 \oplus P_3 \oplus k_0)$$
$$\oplus \Lambda_{1,2} \cdot S\left((P_0 \oplus P_2 \oplus P_3)[16\text{–}23] \oplus XX_0[16\text{–}23]\right.$$
$$\left.\oplus k_1[16\text{–}23]\right) \oplus \Lambda_{1,2} \cdot S\left((C_3 \oplus C_0 \oplus C_1)[16\text{–}23]\right.$$
$$\left.\oplus XX_{23}[16\text{–}23] \oplus k_{22}[16\text{–}23]\right) \oplus \Gamma_2^2 \cdot T(C_0 \oplus C_1$$
$$\oplus C_2 \oplus k_{23}).$$

$$(21)$$

Let $\mathcal{O} = \Gamma_2^0 \cdot P_2 \oplus \Gamma_2^1 \cdot P_3 \oplus \Gamma_2^2 \cdot P_0 \oplus \Gamma_2^0 \cdot P_1 \oplus \Gamma_2^0 \cdot C_2 \oplus \Gamma_2^2 \cdot C_3 \oplus \Gamma_{22}^2 \cdot C_0 \oplus \Gamma_2^0 \cdot C_1$. The attack process is given as follows:

(1) Collect N plaintext/ciphertext pairs.

(2) Initialize 2^{81} counters $\mathcal{V}_0[0], \ldots, \mathcal{V}_0[2^{81}-1]$ to zero.

(3) For every plaintext/ciphertext pair, calculate $w = \mathcal{O} \parallel (P_0 \oplus P_2 \oplus P_3)[16\text{–}23] \parallel (C_3 \oplus C_0 \oplus C_1)[16\text{–}23] \parallel C_0 \oplus$ $C_1 \oplus C_2 \parallel P_1 \oplus P_2 \oplus P_3$. Then increase the counter $\mathcal{V}_0[w]$ by one.

(4) Guess the 32-bit k_{23}. Allocate 2^{49} counters $\mathcal{V}_1[0], \ldots, \mathcal{V}_1[2^{49}-1]$ to zero.

(5) For every $0 \leq w \leq 2^{81}-1$, calculate $\mathcal{O} \Leftarrow \mathcal{O} \oplus \Gamma_2^2 \cdot T(C_0 \oplus C_1 \oplus C_2 \oplus k_{23})$, XX_{23} and $x = \mathcal{O} \parallel (P_0 \oplus P_2 \oplus P_3)[16\text{–}23] \parallel (C_3 \oplus C_0 \oplus C_1)[16\text{–}23] \oplus XX_{23}[16\text{–}23] \parallel P_1 \oplus P_2 \oplus P_3$. $\mathcal{V}_1[x] += \mathcal{V}_0[w]$.

(6) Guess the 8-bit $k_{22}[16\text{–}23]$. Allocate 2^{41} counters $\mathcal{V}_2[0], \ldots, \mathcal{V}_2[2^{41}-1]$ to zero.

(7) For every $0 \leq x \leq 2^{49}-1$, calculate $\mathcal{O} \Leftarrow \mathcal{O} \oplus \Lambda_{1,2} \cdot S((C_3 \oplus C_0 \oplus C_1)[16\text{–}23] \oplus XX_{23}[16\text{–}23] \oplus k_{22}[16\text{–}23])$ and $y = \mathcal{O} \parallel (P_0 \oplus P_2 \oplus P_3)[16\text{–}23] \parallel P_1 \oplus P_2 \oplus P_3$. $\mathcal{V}_2[y] += \mathcal{V}_1[x]$.

(8) Guess the 32-bit k_0. Allocate 2^9 counters $\mathcal{V}_3[0], \ldots, \mathcal{V}_3[2^9-1]$ to zero.

(9) For every $0 \leq y \leq 2^{41}-1$, calculate $\mathcal{O} \Leftarrow \mathcal{O} \oplus \Gamma_2^2 \cdot T(P_1 \oplus P_2 \oplus P_3 \oplus k_0)$, XX_0 and $z = \mathcal{O} \parallel (P_0 \oplus P_2 \oplus P_3)[16\text{–}23] \oplus XX_0[16\text{–}23]$. $\mathcal{V}_3[z] += \mathcal{V}_2[y]$.

(10) Guess the 8-bit $k_1[16\text{–}23]$. Initialize 2^{80} counters $\mathcal{V}_{\text{key}}[0], \ldots, \mathcal{V}_{\text{key}}[2^{80}-1]$ to zero.

(11) For every $0 \leq z \leq 2^9-1$, calculate $\mathcal{O} \Leftarrow \mathcal{O} \oplus \Lambda_{1,2} \cdot S((P_0 \oplus P_2 \oplus P_3)[16\text{–}23] \oplus XX_0[16\text{–}23] \oplus k_1[16\text{–}23])$. If $\mathcal{O} = 0$, increase the counter $\mathcal{V}_{\text{key}}[k_0 \parallel k_1[16\text{–}23] \parallel k_{22}[16\text{–}23] \parallel k_{23}]$ by $\mathcal{V}_3[z]$; otherwise, decrease it by $\mathcal{V}_3[z]$.

(12) We set the advantage a to be 47 which implies that the top 2^{33} absolute values in $\mathcal{V}_{\text{key}}$ are kept. For each

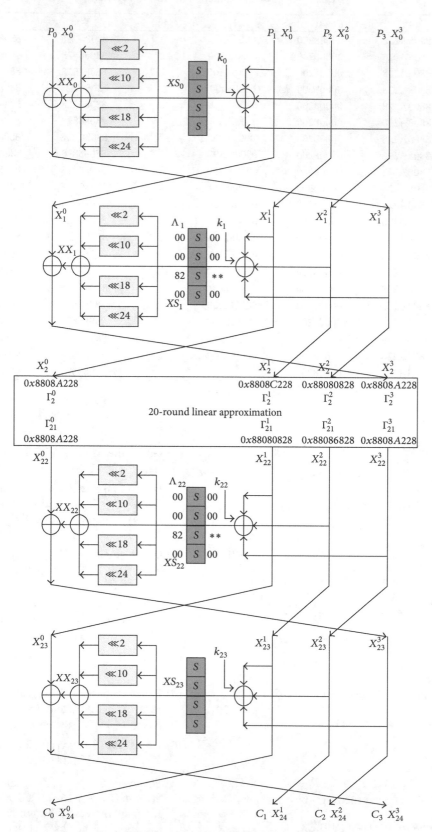

FIGURE 3: Key recovery attack on 24-round SM4.

kept subkey value, we guess the remaining 88 bits of $k_1[0\text{–}15, 24\text{–}31] \parallel k_2 \parallel k_3$ (the master key can be gotten from the key schedule) and test the key by trail encryptions.

The time complexity of Step (3) is about $2^{126.6}$ operations which is equivalent to $2^{126.6}/24 = 2^{122.0}$ 24-round encryptions. Both Steps (5) and (9) need 2^{113} one-round decryptions or encryptions. Steps (7) and (11) take 2^{89} one-round decryptions or encryptions. The complexity of Step (12) is 2^{121} 24-round encryptions. So the total time complexity is about $2^{122.6}$ encryptions.

The memory complexity of Step (2) is about $2^{81} \times 8 = 2^{84}$ bytes and the counter $\mathcal{V}_{\text{key}}$ requires $2^{80} \times 16 = 2^{84}$ bytes, so the total memory complexity is about $2^{84} + 2^{84} = 2^{85}$ bytes.

If we set the data complexity $N = 2^{126.6}$, the success rate $P_S - \Phi(2\sqrt{N}|\epsilon| - \sqrt{1 + N/2^n}\Phi^{-1}(1 - 2^{-a-1})) = 76.1\%$ by [25]. The time complexity is $2^{126.6}$ 24-round encryptions.

4.2. Linear Attack on 23-Round SM4. Two rounds are added to the bottom and the top of the 19-round linear approximation in Table 3, respectively. The key recovery attack on 23-round SM4 is similar to the attack procedure of 24-round SM4, so we omit details of the process.

If we set the data complexity $N = 2^{120.3}$ and the advantage a to be 47, the time complexity is $2^{120.3} + 2^{121} = 2^{121.7}$ 23-round encryptions, and the memory complexity is 2^{85} bytes. The success rate $P_S = 85.9\%$ is computed with the method in [25].

5. Conclusions

In this paper, it is firstly shown that there is no one-round or two-round iterative linear approximation for SM4 and the property for the 3-round iterative linear approximation. On the basis of the property, we search for the iterative linear approximation of 3-round SM4 by the partial linear approximation table. Next the 20-round linear approximation is constructed by 3-round iterative linear approximations. The best previous distinguishers only cover 19 rounds. Then the key recovery attack on 24-round SM4 is provided, which is the best known attack on SM4 so far. Moreover, we also get a better 19-round linear approximation, used to improve the linear attack on 23-round SM4. As for future work, we hope to use the similar technique to search for a better differential characteristic for SM4.

Acknowledgments

This work is supported by 973 Program (no. 2013CB834205), NSFC Projects (nos. 61133013 and 61572293), and Program for New Century Excellent Talents in University of China (NCET-13-0350).

References

[1] W. Diffie and G. Ledin, "SMS4 Encryption Algorithm for Wireless Networks," Cryptology ePrint Archive 2008/329, 2014, http://eprint.iacr.org/2008/329.pdf.

[2] "Office of State Commercial Cryptography Administration: Specification of SMS4, block cipher for WLAN products-SMS4" (Chinese), http://www.oscca.gov.cn/UpFile/200621016423197990.pdf.

[3] T. Kim, J. Kim, S. Hong, and J. Sung, "Linear and Differential Cryptanalysis of Reduced SMS4 Block Cipher," IACR Cryptology ePrint Archive 2008/281, 2008, https://eprint.iacr.org/2008/2811.pdf.

[4] J. Etrog and M. J. B. Robshaw, "The Cryptanalysis of Reduced-Round SMS4," in *Selected Areas in Cryptography*, vol. 5381 of *Lecture Notes in Computer Science*, pp. 51–65, Springer, Berlin, Germany, 2008.

[5] W. Zhang, W. Wu, D. Feng, and B. Su, "Some New Observations on the SMS4 Block Cipher in the Chinese WAPI Standard," in *Information Security Practice and Experience*, vol. 5451 of *Lecture Notes in Computer Science*, pp. 324–335, Springer, Berlin, Germany, 2009.

[6] F. Liu, W. Ji, L. Hu et al., "Analysis of the SMS4 Block Cipher," in *Information Security and Privacy*, vol. 4586 of *Lecture Notes in Computer Science*, pp. 158–170, Springer, Berlin, Germany, 2007.

[7] B.-Z. Su, W.-L. Wu, and W.-T. Zhang, "Security of the SMS4 block cipher against differential cryptanalysis," *Journal of Computer Science and Technology*, vol. 26, no. 1, pp. 130–138, 2011.

[8] J. Cho and K. Nyberg, "Improved Linear Cryptanalysis of SMS4 Block Cipher," *Symmetric Key Encryption Workshop*, pp. 1–14, 2011.

[9] M.-J. Liu and J.-Z. Chen, "Improved linear attacks on the Chinese block cipher standard," *Journal of Computer Science and Technology*, vol. 29, no. 6, pp. 1123–1133, 2014.

[10] K. Bai and C. Wu, "A secure white-box SM4 implementation," *Security and Communication Networks*, vol. 9, no. 10, pp. 996–1006, 2016.

[11] J. Zhang, W. Wu, and Y. Zheng, "Security of SM4 Against (Related-Key) Differential Cryptanalysis," in *Proceedings of the International Conference on Information Security Practice and Experience*, vol. 10060 of *Lecture Notes in Computer Science*, pp. 65–78, Springer, Berlin, Germany, November 2016.

[12] B. Zhang and C. Jin, "Practical security against linear cryptanalysis for SMS4-like ciphers with SP round function," *Science China Information Sciences*, vol. 55, no. 9, pp. 2161–2170, 2012.

[13] T. Helleseth, "Linear cryptanalysis method for des cipher," in *Advances in Cryptology—EUROCRYPT*, vol. 765 of *Lecture Notes in Computer Science*, pp. 386–397, Springer, Berlin, Germany, 1993.

[14] F. Sano, K. Ohkuma, H. Shimizu, and S. Kawamura, "On the security of nested SPN cipher against the differential and linear cryptanalysis," *IEICE Transactions on Fundamentals of Electronics, Communications and Computer Sciences*, vol. E86-A, no. 1, pp. 37–46, 2003.

[15] G. Jakimoski and L. Kocarev, "Differential and linear probabilities of a block-encryption cipher," *IEEE Transactions on Circuits and Systems. I. Fundamental Theory and Applications*, vol. 50, no. 1, pp. 121–123, 2003.

[16] Y. Sun, "Linear Cryptanalysis of Light-Weight Block Cipher ICEBERG," in *Advances in Electronic Commerce, Web Application and Communication*, vol. 149, pp. 529–532, Springer Berlin Heidelberg, Berlin, Germany, 2012.

[17] Y. Liu, K. Fu, W. Wang, L. Sun, and M. Wang, "Linear cryptanalysis of reduced-round SPECK," *Information Processing Letters*, vol. 116, no. 3, pp. 259–266, 2016.

[18] D. Toz and O. Dunkelman, "Analysis of two attacks on reduced-round versions of the SMS$_4$," in *Information and Communications Security*, vol. 5308 of *Lecture Notes in Computer Science*, pp. 141–156, Springer Berlin Heidelberg, Berlin, Heidelberg, 2008.

[19] Z. Liu, D. Gu, and J. Zhang, "Multiple linear cryptanalysis of reduced-round SMS4 block cipher," *Chinese Journal of Electronics*, vol. 19, no. 3, pp. 389–393, 2010.

[20] M. Matsui, "On correlation between the order of S-boxes and the strength of DES," in *Advances in cryptology—EUROCRYPT*, vol. 950 of *Lecture Notes in Comput. Sci.*, pp. 366–375, Springer, Berlin, Germany, 1994.

[21] A. Biryukov and V. Velichkov, "Automatic search for differential trails in ARX ciphers," in *Topics in Cryptology—CT-RSA 2014*, vol. 8366 of *Lecture Notes in Comput. Sci.*, pp. 227–250, Springer, Berlin, Germany, 2014.

[22] E. Biham, "On Matsui's linear cryptanalysis," in *Advances in Cryptology*, vol. 950 of *Lecture Notes in Comput. Sci.*, pp. 341–355, Springer, Berlin, Germany, 1994.

[23] J. Daemen, R. Govaerts, and J. Vandewalle, "Correlation matrices," in *Fast Software Encryption*, vol. 1008 of *Lecture Notes in Computer Science*, pp. 275–285, Springer, Berlin, Germany, 1994.

[24] N. Ferguson, J. Kelsey, S. Lucks et al., "Improved Cryptanalysis of Rijndael," in *Fast Software Encryption*, vol. 1978 of *Lecture Notes in Computer Science*, pp. 213–230, Springer, Berlin, Germany, 2000.

[25] A. Bogdanov and E. Tischhauser, "On the Wrong Key Randomisation and Key Equivalence Hypotheses in Matsui's Algorithm 2," in *Fast Software Encryption*, vol. 8424 of *Lecture Notes in Computer Science*, pp. 19–38, Springer, Berlin, Germany, 2013.

2

A Cloud-User Protocol Based on Ciphertext Watermarking Technology

Keyang Liu, Weiming Zhang, and Xiaojuan Dong

School of Information Science and Technology, University of Science and Technology of China, Anhui, China

Correspondence should be addressed to Weiming Zhang; zhangwm@ustc.edu.cn

Academic Editor: Kim-Kwang Raymond Choo

With the growth of cloud computing technology, more and more Cloud Service Providers (CSPs) begin to provide cloud computing service to users and ask for users' permission of using their data to improve the quality of service (QoS). Since these data are stored in the form of plain text, they bring about users' worry for the risk of privacy leakage. However, the existing watermark embedding and encryption technology is not suitable for protecting the Right to Be Forgotten. Hence, we propose a new Cloud-User protocol as a solution for plain text outsourcing problem. We only allow users and CSPs to embed the ciphertext watermark, which is generated and embedded by Trusted Third Party (TTP), into the ciphertext data for transferring. Then, the receiver decrypts it and obtains the watermarked data in plain text. In the arbitration stage, feature extraction and the identity of user will be used to identify the data. The fixed Hamming distance code can help raise the system's capability for watermarks as much as possible. Extracted watermark can locate the unauthorized distributor and protect the right of honest CSP. The results of experiments demonstrate the security and validity of our protocol.

1. Introduction

1.1. Problem Background. Right to Be Forgotten (RTBF) is a kind of people's right that was proposed for protecting people's privacy and has been mentioned as early as 1995 in Data Protection Directive of EU [1]. The 17th article of General Data Protection Regulation (GDPR) [2], which was passed by EU in 2012 to strengthen data protection for individuals in EU, defined RTBF as the right that people deserve to obtain or erase the data expired or related to their privacy from the data controller. In 2013, Senate Bill 568 of California [3] was signed to protect the RTBF of children. In 2014, the European Court of Justice compelled Google to delete the links about a Spanish man's bankruptcy from its searching results, which confirmed that the RTBF is a basic right for people living in EU. Since then, Google, Facebook, and YouTube have erased tens of thousands of links based on the request of EU citizens [4]. However, the erasure of data cannot be technically confirmed by users if they do not believe their Cloud Service Providers (CSPs). Moreover, cloud computing becomes more and more powerful and economic. Companies like Amazon, Alibaba, and Microsoft have provided cloud computing service to help people manipulating their data more cheaply and easily. If users want to lodge their data in cloud servers to lower the expenses, they need to think carefully about the risk of data leakage. As a result, confirmed deletion and several related ideas can be introduced to deal with this problem, which is also the target of our protocol.

1.2. Related Works. There are two kinds of methods used in confirmed deletion. First comes the encryption. User (U) encrypts his data and transfers it to CSP for storing [5–7]. Once U wants to delete his data, he just needs to abandon the encryption key and inform CSP that related data are useless. The management of key can be authorized to several Third Parties and use secret sharing technology to prevent conspiracy [8]. Encryption can protect the privacy of data and RTBF in ideal circumstance though it destroys the value of data. When U uses encryption technology, he can only use the storage space of CSP while wasting their ability of computation.

To solve this dilemma, homomorphic encryption (HE) [9] was introduced into this field [10]. Once the data is encrypted by HE algorithm, CSP can calculate data as user ordered while knowing nothing about it. However, HE has some other flaws. For example, it requires user to have the knowledge about what operations they want to do on data before knowing their results. What is more, the full-HE, which can do both addition and multiplication on ciphertext, is unbearably slow and costs a lot. The semi-HE, which is faster, faces the problem of restricted operations. In a word, it is not convenient and economic for using encryption to protect RTBF so far. In our solution, data will be stored as plain text in cloud servers so that U can use the ability of computation completely to manage U's data.

Other than confirming deletion, not deleted is more easy to be confirmed, which suggests the second way, tracing the unauthorized distribution of data. To the best of our knowledge, watermarking is used in copy deterrence and tracing down the distribution of illegal copies [11–13]. This fact indicates watermark can be used to protect RTBF by proving the crimes of CSP. As the successful cases have shown, Google and Facebook were forced to delete [4] those links infringing people's privacy once U reports them and proves the infringement. But this method faces a new problem that user can use his data to fraud CSP if he can get benefit from lawsuit like defaming the specific CSP or diddling indemnity. If CSP requires embedding another watermark so that he can identify whether the copy is stored in his server, CSP can leak the copy with both watermarks to avoid being charged. Once the embedding process is outsourced to a Third Party, it will raise the risk of information leak from TP. In a word, watermark technology cannot be used to protect RTBF directly.

In this paper, we design a new Cloud-User protocol as the solution based on the work of buyer-seller protocol [14, 15]. We generate and embed the watermark in ciphertext to make sure the watermark can be erased during downloading. By using only one watermark, we increase the SNR of data. Moreover, we introduce the idea of feature-extraction function (FEF), a fixed Hamming distance code into protocol to reduce the cost of searching and increase the capacity of system while maintaining the robustness of watermark system.

The rest of this paper is organized as follows. In Section 2, we will give a brief introduction to the problem models, design goals, and the threat models. Preliminaries will be introduced in Section 3. The proposed solution is described in Section 4 and the security of the scheme is analyzed in Section 5. Section 6 will explain the design of experiment as well as the subalgorithm we used for building demo. The results of each experiment will be analyzed in Section 7. The last section contains the conclusions and future work.

2. Problem Formulation

2.1. Problem Model. The problem model in this paper involves three parties: User (U), Cloud Service Provider (CSP), and the Trusted Third Party (TTP).

User. U possesses large quantities of data and wishes to store it in the CSP's server. In addition, those data are valuable and need enough computing power to dig out their value.

As a result, U wants to store his data on CSP's server and requires CSP to do some complex operations for him. In our scheme, only U and CSP can touch and manipulate these data. According to RTBF, U has the right to retrieve his data and require CSP to delete it at any time. Once U finds his data that should be deleted, U can suspect that a CSP has distributed his data illegally for interests and require TTP to verify where it comes from. Once confirmed, U can sue CSP for being guilty and ask for a compensation.

Cloud Service Provider. CSP controls piles of servers which have large storage space and powerful computing ability. U can store, manipulate, and delete his data on CSP's servers only if he pays for it according to contract. Although CSP controls all the data in his servers, he does not have the ownership of data and should take responsibility for their security. CSP can never distribute data whether U cares or not and needs to backup it in case of servers' crash.

Trusted Third Party. TTP is an arbitration agency who is responsible for generating a valid watermark for every single trade between U and CSP. TTP should be trusty so that his verification can be used as evidence. Besides, TTP should know nothing about U's data unless U requires TTP to verify whether a specific copy has been marked to be deleted.

Our solution is designed to make sure any one of the three can only know what they allowed to know and do what they required to do. Whoever disobeys the contract will suffer loss.

2.2. Threat Model. In the proposed solution, we assume TTP is selected by U and CSP, so we do not consider TTP will conspire with any one and no one can get payment from him. So there is no conspiracy among our solutions. We should consider the threat that CSP or U can get benefit while offending the other one.

CSP's Attack. CSP controls all data stored in his servers; he should obey U's order to manipulate U's data according to contract. But it may copy U's data as a backup even after U requires CSP to delete it. Since CSP has a full access to these data in plain text, we can do nothing about his analysis on data and that should be considered in contract. On one hand, CSP may not delete the data as required, and those data are leaked for CSP's careless management. On the other hand, CSP may deliberately sell these data after U's delete requirement and even try to adjust it so that U and TTP cannot trace it.

U's Attack. U possesses the ownership of data. The benefit U that can be gained from CSP is the compensation. On one hand, if CSP is innocent, U can only use the retrieved data and original data to create a copy. On the other hand, once CSP has leaked a part of U's data files, U may use them to guess other data files' watermark and forge CSP's loss.

2.3. Design Goals. This paper aims to design a solution among CSP, U, and TTP that allows U to store his data in CSP's servers as plain text while providing the remote control according to contract. In particular, we formally detail the goals as follows.

Data Privacy. As claimed in problem model, TTP is responsible for generating watermarks for giving data while TTP should have no access to data's content. Hence, we carefully design our solution so that TTP can embed the identity watermark directly in the encrypted data.

Nonrepudiation. Any copy of unauthorized data must be identifiable to find the illegal distributor.

Fairness. The proposed solution is secure and fair to all parties. Nobody can frame an honest party.

The Right to Be Forgotten. Acceptable deletion requires no information about the data remaining in servers of CSP. Once CSP does not follow requirements and the bad behavior can be proved by U (i.e., the unauthorized copy is detected). U can require TTP to verify the watermark of leaked copy and provide it as evidence which cannot be denied based on contract.

3. Preliminaries

In our solution, there are four kinds of technology we will use. Each technical method can be adjusted to fit all kinds of data (D). To simplify the declaration, we use image data as an example to introduce our solution and complete our experiment. Here is a simple introduction to these technologies and the restriction our solution required.

3.1. Feature-Extraction Function (FEF). FEF is used to identify the content of data while getting no detail about it. FEF is an important part of our solution which is used to define the validity of data for U. FEF's input is data file and the output is a feature (Fea). Once a data file A and its adjusted copy B satisfied FEF(A) = FEF(B), we call B a derivative copy (DC) of A. The set of DC is derivative set (DS).

In our solution, FEF must fit the following requirement.

(1) One-Way Function. For B = FEF(A), no one can create a DC of A if he only has the knowledge about B. This is because Fea of the stored data is shared among all three parties in our solution. This property can make sure only U and CSP can distribute DC of data.

(2) Content-Based. For no digital watermark algorithm can promise that it can resist all attacks, we use FEF as a restriction of watermark extraction algorithm so that our solution can get balance between validity and security. In our solution, U should carefully select FEF to make sure all the valuable copies of original data belong to a DS.

(3) Equiprobability. The set of possible value for Fea must be large enough, and the possibility of each value is equal. This property protects the efficiency of searching process.

3.2. Digital Watermark. Digital watermark (W) is a signal embedded into data to identify some attributions of the data (i.e., ownership). According to the domain embedded, digital watermark embedding algorithms are divided into time-spatial embedding, which is fast and relatively easy to operate

but is easy to be erased by geometrical attack, and transform domain embedding [16–19], which is good at resisting geometrical attack but is fragile facing filtering. Moreover, according to the preknowledge related to data before embedding, we classify the embedding method into preknowledge dependent embedding and preknowledge independent embedding. In most cases, dependent embedding is more robust than independent one. In our solution, we recommend to use the preknowledge dependent transform embedding method to enhance the security of our solution. Furthermore, our solution requires the following properties that digital watermark embedding algorithm should have.

(1) Markov Property. For a given $W = w_i \mid 1 < i < L$ of length L, the embedding and extracting process of w_i has no effect on the process of w_{i+1}.

(2) Predictability. Predictability means the embedding positions can be determined only by the length of embeddable positions and the bit length of watermark.

(3) Robustness. Based on the requirement of U, the watermark algorithm should guarantee that the watermark can be extracted from the DS of embedded data.

3.3. Homomorphic Encryption (HE). Encryption is the most famous method in information security. Homomorphic encryption [18] can translate some operations on plain text into other operations on ciphertext. In our solution, we require that data should be encrypted during transferring and embedding process. For full-HE is slow and costly, we decide to use semi-HE as a compromise that give the consideration to both efficiency and security. We list the requirement of our solution for the semi-HE as follows ($E()$ is encryption function, KEY is the encryption key, and S_i is the target information).

(1) Addition Homomorphism

$$E\left(KEY, S1 + S2\right) = E\left(KEY, S1\right) \odot E\left(KEY, S2\right). \quad (1)$$

(2) Multimap. The absolute value of each of the encryption results depends on the random number it used in different times:

$$E\left(KEY, S1 : t_1\right) \neq E\left(KEY, S1 : t_2\right). \quad (2)$$

4. Solution Framework

Our solution contains three protocols based on Public-Key Infrastructure (PKI) that is used for distributing public and private key pair combining to each registered ID. The notation used in protocols has been listed at the end of the paper.

4.1. Uploading Stage. In this subsection, we describe the details about uploading stage, including watermark's generating and embedding.

Input: D, L
Output: the threshold of watermark matching μ
(1) **if** $L < 2$ **then**
(2)   **return** 100
(3) **end**
(4) **if** *embed* $\{1\}_L$ *or* $\{0\}_L$ *will change Fea* **then**
(5)   **return** 100
(6) **end**
(7) $TESTD = EW(D, \{1 \mid 0\}_L)$
(8) $\mu \longleftarrow 0$
(9) **while** *there is attack method has not been tested* **do**
(10)   AD = attacked TESTD

$$\mu = \max(\mu, 100 * \frac{sum(xor(DW(AD), DW(TSETD)))}{L})$$

(11) **end**

ALGORITHM 1: Generating μ.

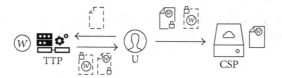

FIGURE 1: Data flow of updating process.

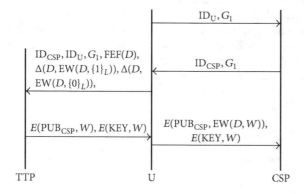

FIGURE 2: Details of updating process.

Before outsourcing data are transferred to CSP, U needs to embed watermark into his data as shown in Figure 1.

All transferred data are encrypted by CSP's public key or TTP's special key. The details of each process are presented by Figure 2 and introduced in the following steps.

Step 1. U sends CSP his ID and service contract to apply for storing and computing his data. The first contract (G_1) details the responsibilities and obligations of U and CSP and the subalgorithm, including parameters which CSP needs to know, used in the whole solution. The contract is signed by PRI_U to make sure of its integrity. Once CSP does not admit the contract, CSP can reject U's request and the protocol is finished.

Step 2. CSP sends ID_{CSP} and G_1 to U, which is signed by PRI_{CSP}. This step means U's request has been permitted. G_1 has been signed twice to make sure that its content has not been changed and will be used as an evidence in the future.

Step 3. U selects a watermark algorithm matching the requirements declared before and threshold μ according to Algorithm 1, which will be signed and attached behind G_1, to embed $\{1\}_L$ and $\{0\}_L$ into his data, where L is the watermark capacity of D and calculates the differences between original data and embedded data as δ_1 and δ_0 according to (3). TESTD is the data embedded with a random sequence of length L, which is used to test the robustness of watermark algorithm; the test round can be done more than 1 time for security purpose. U should make sure that the production of embedding process still belongs to DS(D).

$$\delta_1 = \left\{ \delta_{1i} \mid 1 < i < L \right\} = \Delta\left(D, E\left(D, \{1\}_L\right)\right)$$
$$\delta_0 = \left\{ \delta_{0i} \mid 1 < i < L \right\} = \Delta\left(D, E\left(D, \{0\}_L\right)\right).$$
(3)

Then, U sends IDs, G_1, FEF(D), δ_1, and δ_0 to TTP for recording and generating watermark W.

Step 4. TTP generates W according to existing data of U that share the same Fea. We present Algorithm 2 as an example for generating watermark here. TTP creates δ_2 by δ_1, δ_0, and W like Algorithm 3.

According to Markov property and predictability, Algorithm 3 guarantees that TTP can create an additive watermark δ_2 based on δ_1 and δ_0. δ_2 is the same as the difference between original data and its copy embedded with W by the selected watermark algorithm. Then, TTP sends the encrypted δ_2 to U as well as signature. Here, we suggest that TTP use two keys to encrypt δ_2. PUB_{CSP} encrypted copy is for embedding, and TTP's KEY encrypted copy is for

---

Input: SW(Set of exist watermark of U with same
Fea), μ, L(Capacity of File)
Output: A new watermark
(1) $flag = 1$
(2) **while** $flag$ **do**
(3)   randomly generate a sequence t shorter than $\dfrac{L}{2}$. **for**
    All item x in SW **do**
(4)   **if** $sum(xor(x,t)) < \mu$ **then**
(5) $flag = 0$ break
(6)   **end**
(7)   **end**
(8) $flag = 1 - flag$
(9) **end**
(10) **return** t

ALGORITHM 2: Generating W.

Input: δ_1, δ_0, W
Output: δ_2
(1) n← length of W;
(2) $step \leftarrow round(L/n)$;
(3) embedding positions ←random sequence
from[1,2,...step] of length $step/2$
(4) **for** $i = 1$ **to** $n + 1$ **do**
(5)   **for** $j = 1$ **to** $step$ **do**
(6)   **if** $2(i-1)step + j > L$ **then**
(7)   Break;
(8)   **end**
(9)   **else**
(10)   **if** j *is in embedding positions* **then**
(11)   **if** $w_i == 1$ **then**
(12) $\delta_{2((i-1)step+j)} = \delta_{1((i-1)step+j)}$
(13)   **end**
(14)   **else**
(15) $\delta_{2((i-1)step+j)} = \delta_{0((i-1)step+j)}$
(16)   **end**
(17)   **end**
(18)   **else**
(19) $\delta_{2((i-1)step+j)}$ is equal to
                 $\delta_{(1-w_i)((i-1)step+j)}$
(20)   **end**
(21)   **end**
(22)   **end**
(23) **end**
(24) **return** δ_2

ALGORITHM 3: Generating $\delta 2$.

---

erasing in the future which will release the storage burden of TTP.

Step 5. U verifies TTP's signature to make sure that W is valid. Then U uses PUB_{CSP} to encrypt D and embeds W into D according to the addition homomorphism of encryption algorithm as the following proof has shown, which will get the encrypted file (ED) that contains W.

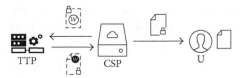

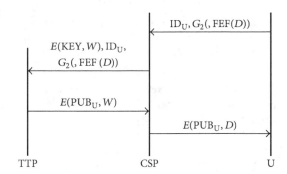

FIGURE 3: Data flow of downloading process.

$$E(KEY, W), ID_U,$$
$$G_2(, FEF(D))$$

$$ID_U, G_2(, FEF(D))$$

$$E(PUB_U, W)$$

$$E(PUB_U, D)$$

TTP   CSP   U

FIGURE 4: Details of downloading process.

Proof.

$$\begin{aligned}
ED &= E\left(PUB_{CSP}, \delta_2\right) \odot E\left(PUB_{CSP}, D\right) \\
&= E\left(PUB_{CSP}, \delta_2 + D\right) \\
&\because \delta_2 = \Delta\left(D, EW\left(D, W\right)\right) \qquad\qquad (4) \\
&\therefore ED = E\left(PUB_{CSP}, \Delta\left(D, EW\left(D, W\right) + D\right)\right) \\
&= E\left(PUB_{CSP}, EW\left(D, W\right)\right).
\end{aligned}$$

$\square$

U sends δ_2 encrypted by TTP's KEY and ED to CSP. CSP decrypts ED and stores it. Then, the uploading stage is finished.

4.2. Downloading Stage. The downloading stage is much simpler than the uploading protocol, for δ_2 has been stored encrypted in CSP's servers. The data flows are shown in Figure 3.

All data are still encrypted. Details of downloading stage are presented by Figure 4 and introduced as follows.

Step 1. U sends G_2 and ID_U to CSP. G_2 contains the requirement of retrieving or deletion which need erasing W from ED. U can use FEF(D) to help CSP and TTP search the exact data that he wants.

Step 2. After verifying U's signature, CSP sends G_2 and ID_U along with encrypted δ_2 to CSP so that CSP can create reversed watermark to erase W from ED.

Step 3. TTP verifies all the information stored in his database. If the information is correct, TTP first decrypts δ_2 and creates the reversed watermark $-\delta_2$. Then TTP encrypts it by PUB_U and sends it back to CSP.

Step 4. CSP embeds encrypted $-\delta_2$ into ED and then sends it to U. U decrypts receiving file to get his data according to the following proof.

Proof.

$$E\left(\mathrm{PUB_U}, \mathrm{EW}\left(D, W\right)\right) \odot E\left(\mathrm{PUB_U}, -\delta_2\right)$$
$$\longrightarrow E\left(\mathrm{PUB_U}, \mathrm{EW}\left(D, W\right) - \delta_2\right)$$
$$\longrightarrow E\left(\mathrm{PUB_U}, \mathrm{EW}\left(D, W\right) - \Delta\left(D, \mathrm{EW}\left(D, W\right)\right)\right) \quad (5)$$
$$\longrightarrow E\left(\mathrm{PUB_U}, D\right). \qquad \square$$

Once G_2 requires CSP to delete U's data, U cannot download that data in future again, and TTP will create the log of this data and abandon the KEY of δ_2.

4.3. Arbitration Stage. When U finds an unauthorized file L that belongs to DS(D), U can identify the illegal distributor and bring a suit against it.

U should first execute FEF function to get Fea about the leaked data (L) and then provide the L, FEF(L) as well as $\mathrm{ID_U}$ to TTP. After verifying the information about U, TTP searches the data based on FEF(L) and $\mathrm{ID_U}$ to get logs of possible leaked data as set S. If S is empty, TTP tells U that this data is not recorded in his database. Otherwise, TTP executes DW(L) according to watermark algorithm and embedding positions of each item of S and calculates the bit error ratio (BER) of DW(L) and W as δ_3. If there is any δ_3 below μ declared in G_1 of that data, TTP believes the CSP signed G_1 violate U's RTBF or privacy. TTP will provide a proof with digital signature to U as a legal evidence.

5. Solution Analysis

Our solution proposed above can solve the problem we mentioned in problem model. The safety of our solution relies critically on the security of subalgorithms like watermarking and encryption algorithm. In this section, we will analyze properties we described in design goals and requirement to each party.

5.1. Effectiveness. Our solution can solve the problem of RTBF as we have mentioned. Once CSP want to violate U's RTBF, he needs to distribute DC(D) to others. If U finds that copy, he can send it to TTP and ask for arbitration, and CSP's crime will be proved. Once U wants to fraud an innocent CSP, U should create a copy that belongs to DS(D) and contains W. However, U has no information about W in plain text. It is technically impossible for CSP to do that if the encryption algorithm is secure enough.

5.2. Security. The security of our solution is based on the fact that U and CSP cannot get information about W. We assume all the subprotocols can satisfy the property we required.

CSP possesses embedded data (ED), δ_2 and $-\delta_2$ encrypted by KEY or $\mathrm{PUB_U}$. CSP wants to create a copy of ED-δ_2, which is impossible if the encryption algorithm is strong enough. Besides, CSP can try to attack ED so that δ_3 are larger

than μ. In this case, the robustness of watermark algorithm and FEF function is tested. With the help of μ and FEF, CSP cannot create a useful copy while maintaining the validity of data for distributing.

U possesses D, δ_1 and δ_0 in plain text, δ_2, ED encrypted by $\mathrm{PUB_{CSP}}$, δ_2 encrypted by KEY. According to the multimap property, U cannot use δ_1 and δ_0 to create δ_2 in polynomial time. Besides, embedding positions will make it harder for both U and CSP to get information about W, though it sacrifices the robustness to some extent. Moreover, considering CSP may leak a part of data and be found by U, U can get a message containing W. U may try to use it to guess other watermarks. The watermark generation is completely random and each watermark shares different length and embedding positions. The possibility of creating a DC to match the watermark is P. Here, we neglect the possibility that a extract watermark can be recognized as two embedded water marks.

$$P \approx \frac{\sum_{i=1}^{\mu L}\binom{L}{i}}{2^L - \sum_{i=1}^{\mu L}\binom{L}{i}}. \quad (6)$$

In conclusion, our solution can make sure that U and CSP cannot get DC of the other one's copy. The robustness of watermark is controlled by U according to the FEF function and watermark algorithm.

5.3. Consumption

U. U outsources local data to CSP for reducing the local data storage space and the cost of complex computing. In our scheme, after uploading data, U can reserve FEF(D) for reducing the cost of searching. U should also do some computation for encrypting and decrypting data.

TTP. TTP has enough storage space for keeping the records of contracts, IDs, Fea, and watermarks for arbitration parts. In this paper, TTP is designed with memory and some necessary computing powers. TTP can take some fee for arbitration requirement so that it will not be annoyed by unsure request and balance the expenses.

CSP. CSP provides large storage space and strong computing power as service. It is reasonable to put the burden of storing outsourced data as well as encrypted δ_2 on CSP.

6. System Design

In this section, we will introduce the experiment we used for verifying the validity and security of our solution. We choose image as U's data to finish our experiment because it is the most popular kind of data used in outsourcing service. Before introducing experiment, we first clarify the subalgorithms we used in our solution.

6.1. Watermark Algorithm. The watermark scheme we used for experiment is Dither Modulation-Quantization Index Modulation (DM-QIM) [20]. It is a classical watermarking scheme and easy for use. Although it has been proved not safe enough [21, 22], it satisfies the requirements we proposed for watermark algorithm.

Generate n = q * p where p and q are both random large prime;
Generate g as a random number of $\mathbb{Z}_n^*$
$\lambda = LCM(p - 1, q - 1)$
Public key $\leftarrow$ (n,g), Private key $\leftarrow$ (p,q)
#encryption:
randomly select r < n
$C = g^m * r^n \bmod n^2$
return C
#decryption:
calculate λ
$m = \dfrac{(c^\lambda \bmod n^2) - 1}{(g^\lambda \bmod n^2) - 1} \bmod n^2$
return m
#addition:
$C_3 = C_1 * C_2 = g^{m1+m2} * (r_1 r_2)^n$
return C_3

ALGORITHM 4: Paillier.

DM-QIM embeds watermark into transforming domain. It adjusts the value of some coefficients, which is the pre-knowledge, to embed the message according to (7) where step is the quantizer and d is the dither.

$$EW(D_i, W_i)$$
$$= \begin{cases} \text{round}\left(\dfrac{D_i - d}{\text{step}}\right) * \text{step} + d & W_i == 1, \\ \text{round}\left(\dfrac{D_i + d}{\text{step}}\right) * \text{step} - d & W_i == 0. \end{cases} \quad (7)$$

In the extracting process, we use ED_i to reprensent the ouput of $EW(D_i, W_i)$. According to (8), we can find that different judgments (Jud), which are guessed result before extracting, will lead to different extracting processes and extract different values because of the quantizer. We can add up all $DW(ED_i)$ that embed same bit of watermark to measure whether Jud is equal to W_i. In any case, we will get the watermark embedded in the picture.

$$DW(ED_i) = \begin{cases} \text{round}\left(\dfrac{ED_i - d}{\text{step}}\right) * \text{step} + d - ED_i & \text{Jud} == 1, \ W_i == 1, \\ \text{round}\left(\dfrac{ED_i - d}{\text{step}}\right) * \text{step} + d - ED_i & \text{Jud} == 1, \ W_i == 0, \\ \text{round}\left(\dfrac{ED_i + d}{\text{step}}\right) * \text{step} - d - ED_i & \text{Jud} == 0, \ W_i == 1, \\ \text{round}\left(\dfrac{ED_i + d}{\text{step}}\right) * \text{step} - d - ED_i & \text{Jud} == 0, \ W_i == 0, \end{cases}$$

$$= \begin{cases} 0 & \text{Jud} == 1, \ W_i == 1, \\ \left(\text{round}\left(\dfrac{ED_i - d}{\text{step}}\right) * \text{step} + d\right) - ED_i & \text{Jud} == 1, \ W_i == 0, \\ \left(\text{round}\left(\dfrac{ED_i + d}{\text{step}}\right) * \text{step} - d\right) - ED_i & \text{Jud} == 0, \ W_i == 1, \\ 0 & \text{Jud} == 0, \ W_i == 0. \end{cases} \quad (8)$$

This watermark scheme embeds 1 or 0 into each selected coefficient as Algorithm 3 which means it satisfies the Markov property. In our solution, we split image into several 8×8 nonoverlapping blocks firstly and use DCT to transform these blocks into transform domain, which means all the coefficients can be placed in a meaningful place so that TTP can determine which position to embed. Thus, this scheme has predictability.

In our solution, DCT coefficients below 0.4 are chosen for watermarks. Embedding positions are selected according to the value of $(i + j) \bmod 2$, where i and j are the coordinates of the coefficient. In our demo, the step is 100 and the dither is 25.

6.2. Encryption. In our system, we use AES and Paillier [23] as encryption algorithm that can fit solution's requirements. AES is a famous symmetric encryption algorithm [24] which

is fast and safe. Paillier is a semi-HE that supports additive operations in ciphertext according to Algorithm 4 where $L(x) = (x - 1)/n$.

Although Paillier allows user to do addition, negative numbers and decimals are not allowed to calculate. Because δ_2 and $-\delta_2$ always need to encrypt negative numbers and decimals, we suggest U and CSP do as shown in Algorithms 5 and 6 which can solve this problem.

Besides, δ_0 and δ_1 may leak some information about the image; we recommend that U adds a mark to δ_0 and δ_1 which can be subtracted after decrypting δ_2.

6.3. Perceptual Hash Algorithm (PHA). We choose PHA as FEF function for it can reflect the content about image in its low frequency coefficients which is also used in searching engine [25]. Algorithm 7 shows pHash we used as FEF function.

(a)   (b)   (c)

FIGURE 5: The retrieved picture (a), embedded picture (b), and the original picture (c).

Input: message m, amp (integer amplifier which
    decides the accuracy of data)
Output: pretreated m, balance
(1) $m_1 = round(m * amp)$
(2) **if** m_1 *contains negative* **then**
(3)   balance = round($\frac{\max(-\min(m_1), \max(m_1))}{10}$) $* 100$
(4) **end**
(5) **else**
(6)   balance = round($\frac{\max(m_1)}{10}$) $* 100$
(7) **end**
(8) **for** $i = 1$ **to** L **do**
(9) $m_{2i} = m_{1i} + balance$
(10) **end**
(11) **return** m_2, balance, amp

ALGORITHM 5: Pretreatment: before encryption.

Input: I
Output: hash
(1) $h_r = $ Resize(I, $[32, 32]$)
(2) $h_t = $DCT($h_r$)
(3) sum=0
(4) **for** $i, j = 1$ **to** 8 **do**
(5) $h_{lij} = h_{tij}$
(6) $sum = sum + h_{tij}$
(7) **end**
(8) mid=$\frac{sum}{64}$
(9) **for** $i, j = 1$ **to** 8 **do**
(10) $h_{lij} = sgn(h_{lij} - mid)$
(11) **end**
(12) **return** h_l

ALGORITHM 7: PHA.

Input: decrypted dm, amp, balances
Output: message m
(1) FB=sum(balances)
(2) **for** $i = 1$ **to** L **do**
(3) $m_{1i} = dm_i - FB$
(4) **end**
(5) $m = round(m_1/amp)$ **return** m

ALGORITHM 6: Pretreatment: after encryption.

7. Tolerance about System

We first evaluate the tolerance about system. We assume U that has uploaded a large number of images to CSP that have been registered in TTP. One of his images, which has been required to delete, is attractive that CSP wants to distribute it for benefits. CSP needs to erase the watermark embedded in image while he knows nothing about the watermarks'

algorithm. So CSP could only use some basic function to attack it. Geometric attacks are not in considered for user that can get the information about watermark by recovering it in most cases, which is dangerous for CSP because U can use this information to create a copy of ED easily. We will consider three types of attack means: JPEG compression (JC), Gaussian filter (GF), and White Gaussian Noise (WGN) to represent the loss compression, filter, and noise attack in the following parts.

We use peak signal-to-noise ratio (PSNR) and bit error ratio (BER) as two indicators that evaluate the performance about our solution. In this section, we will evaluate DC of watermarked Lena provided by each attack mean of different parameters. To compare, the retrieved image's (Figure 5) PSNR maintains 313 dB in our solution.

7.1. JPEG Compression Test. JPEG compression is one of the most popular compression ways that is used for maintaining the main information in smaller size. We want to examine whether CSP can distribute a compressed version data illegally.

TABLE 1: Watermark's tolerance to GF.

Scale	σ									
	0.1	0.2	0.3	0.5	0.8	1	2	4	8	10
	BER									
2	0.11	0.11	0.11	0.11	0.11	0.11	0.11	0.11	0.11	0.11
4	0.11	0.11	0.11	0.11	0.01	0.01	0.32	0.46	0.48	0.48
8	0.12	0.12	0.12	0.12	0.01	0.01	0.28	0.46	0.48	0.48
10	0.12	0.12	0.12	0.12	0.01	0	0.28	0.46	0.48	0.48

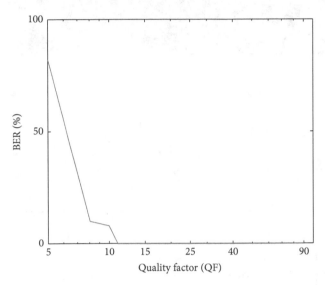

FIGURE 6: Watermark tolerance to JPEG compression.

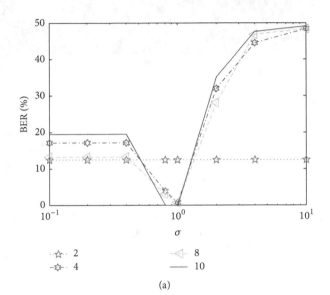

(a)

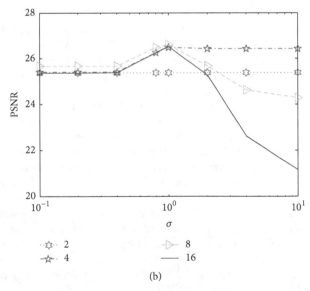

(b)

FIGURE 7: BER (a) and PSNR (b) change according to the watermark.

Figure 6 shows that the BER decreased rapidly as the quality factor (QF) grows. When QF is 5, which is not a normal choice for compression, Fea of the attacked picture (Figure 8) has changed. This means that our solution can be against the JPEG compression if $\mu > 10\%$.

7.2. Gauss Filter. Filter is the riskiest attack for DM-QIM, since it erases the details within each block of selected scale by adjusting DCT coefficients. As σ grows, picture will become more and more smooth. The mid one in Figure 8 is attacked by GF with scale = 8 and $\sigma = 2$. It suggests that PHA we have used is not the best way to represent the content of image.

Table 1 and Figure 7 show the PSNR and BER affected by GF in different scales and σ. We can notice that GF with scale of 2 has no risk to our solution. When σ is close to 1, BER of attacked image decreases to nearly 0 and the PSNR grows. We consider this as a kind of tolerance to GF. As σ grows continually, BER grows rapidly and the watermark and the detail of picture are erased.

To be against these attacks means that we can change the watermark algorithm or amplify the step as well as dither, which will introduce more noise to embedded picture. This is completely a trade-off between security and the validity of data. The restriction to μ in this experiment is 30%.

7.3. White Gaussian Noise (WGN). Noise is another kind of attack, which will quickly decrease PSNR of image. We use Gaussian noise to attack our picture. GF and compression will erase the details of images. This will help the attacker decrease the noise watermark introduced in and raise the PSNR of picture in some degree. However, WGN introduces more noise into picture (Figure 8) to cover the watermark which will decrease PSNR quickly and change the Fea.

(a)   (b)   (c)

FIGURE 8: Pictures attacked by JC (a), GF (b), and WGN (c).

TABLE 2: Watermark's tolerance to WGN.

PSNR	23.35	17.94	16.8	16.24	15.88	14.69	13.64	12.93
BER	0	0	0.09	0.26	0.39	0.51	0.52	0.52

Table 2 shows the change of BER according to WGN. The PSNR of Figure 8 is 15.88 which suggests that μ should be at least 26% so that they can defend WGN to some extent in our solution.

8. Capacity of System

In this section, we will take the arbitration stage into consideration. We assume that U finds a picture Y which may be a DC of his deleted data. For U may have not backed up his data, U uploads Y, FEF(Y), and ID_U to TTP so that TTP can determine which CSP may leak his data. In this experiment, we will test the capacity of our solution, which is the number of watermarks that are embedded into user's data with same Fea. There are several ways to generate a secure watermark [26]. For simplicity, we choose Algorithm 8 to generate our watermark easily. We named the result of Algorithm 8 as fixed Hamming distance codes, the Hamming distance of each element within answer is no less than the input limits μ. Fixed Hamming distance code allows us to identify the log about data as well as its contracts. And the watermark will be able to defend the attacks as long as U has to test μ according to Algorithm 1.

The final capacity of a TTP will be calculated by (9) where cap(D) means the span of D's value.

$$N = \left(\sum_{i=L_{min}}^{L_{max}} \text{Len}\left(watermarks^i\right) \right) * \text{cap (FEA)}$$
$$* \text{cap (ID)}. \tag{9}$$

8.1. Result. We first use 30% as threshold, 10 seconds as time limit and 128 bits as the length of watermark. We get at least 1000 watermarks. we select the 500th watermark as the embedded watermark and do attacks as Table 3 presents.

```
Input: μ, L
Output: watermarks^L
(1)  watermarks^L = empty set
(2)  threshold=μL
(3)  flag=1
(4)  while not reach time-limit do
(5)      random generate a temp watermark t of length L
(6)      flag=1
(7)      for each w in watermarks^L do
(8)          if sum(XOR(w, t)<threshold) then
(9)              flag=0
(10)             break
(11)         end
(12)     end
(13)     if flag then
(14)         Add t into watermarks^L
(15)     end
(16) end
(17) return watermarks^L
```

ALGORITHM 8: Fixed Hamming distance coding.

The results are presented by Figure 9 (The y-axis represents BER and x-axis represents sequence number of images). It suggests that our protocol can identify the certain data of it within our database and charge the CSP successfully under the predicted attacks. Fixed Hamming distance code makes sure that the robustness of this protocol is only determined by watermark algorithm and encryption method. The third picture in each line of Figure 9 shows that if the picture is overattacked, we cannot determine the source of the picture from watermark.

TABLE 3: Test attacks.

JPEG compression	QF = 25	QF = 8	QF = 5
GF	sigma = 0.3	sigma = 1	sigma = 4
WGN	PSNR = 18	PSNR = 16.75	PSNR = 16.41

(a) JPEG compression for QF of 25, 8, and 5

(b) GF for sigma of 0.3, 1, and 4

(c) WGN for PSNR of 18, 16.75, and 16.41

FIGURE 9: Test for $\mu = 0.3$.

In addition, we raise the threshold to 40% which results in a quickly decreasing of capacity. We can only get 60 watermarks within 10 seconds. We select the 30th watermark for embedding and do the same tests. The results are shown in Figure 10 (The y-axis represents BER and x-axis represents sequence number of images). It suggested that raising up threshold is not economic to increase the robustness of watermark algorithm for it decreases the number of watermarks largely.

9. Conclusion

In this paper, we propose a Cloud-User protocol as a solution to solve the Right to Be Forgotten problem technically. Our solution supports confirmed deletion of plain data that is stored in CSP's servers. To achieve security goals, our solution combines the existing homomorphic cryptography, watermark techniques, minimum Hamming coding, and the content-based feature extraction so that the innocent party

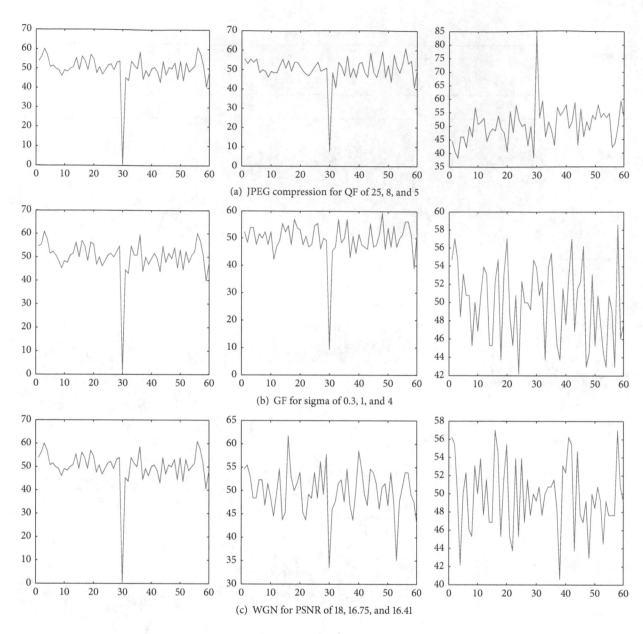

(a) JPEG compression for QF of 25, 8, and 5

(b) GF for sigma of 0.3, 1, and 4

(c) WGN for PSNR of 18, 16.75, and 16.41

FIGURE 10: Test for $\mu = 0.4$.

will not suffer losses by the other one's attack. We implement a prototype of our solution to demonstrate its availability and practicality.

10. Future Work

For future work, there are still some aspects worth thinking. Firstly, the algorithms we used in prototype are not the best ones that fit our solution. Choosing a better encryption algorithm and watermark scheme may decrease the cost of communication and computation for U and TTP.

Secondly, a better FEF can help protecting U's right and raise the robustness of our protocol. We treat the combination of FEF and watermark scheme as the most challenging question for our solution.

Thirdly, every time user retrieves his data will cost a lot for all three parties. Designing a better drawing back protocol can raise the efficiency of our solution.

Finally, as a large pile of data is plain text in CSP's server, how to provide preview of data base on its content like existing systems [27] in low cost while not leaking the information of watermarks is waiting to be solved.

Notations

CSP: Cloud Service Provider
U: User
TTP: Trusted Third Party
D: Data
W: Digital watermark

$DC(D)$: Derivative copy of D

$DS(D)$: Derivative set of D

$DW(D)$: Watermark extraction function that extracts watermark from D

$EW(D, M)$: Watermark embedding function that embeds M into D

$FEF(D)$: Feature of D

G_i: The ith round contract

ID_x: Identity of x

KEY: Key for symmetric cryptography

PUB_x: Public key of x

PRI_x: Private key of x

a_n: A string generated by combination of a that has length n

$D(KEY/PUB, D/M)$: Decryption function for D/M while key is KEY/PUB

$E(KEY/PUB, D/M)$: Encryption function for D/M while key is KEY/PUB

$\Delta(D_1, D_2)$: The difference between D_1 and D_2 as $\{D_{1i} - D_{2i} \mid 1 < i < \text{Len}(D_1)\}$.

Acknowledgments

This work was supported in part by the Natural Science Foundation of China under Grants U1636201 and 61572452.

References

[1] Directive, EU,95/46/EC of the European Parliament and of the Council of 24 October 1995 on the protection of individuals with regard to the processing of personal data and on the free movement of such data,Official Journal of the EC, 23(6), 1995.

[2] Proposal for a Regulation of the European Parliament and of the Council on the Protection of Individuals with Regard to the Processing of Personal Data and on the Free movement of Such Data (General Data Protection Regulation), 2012.

[3] Steinberg, An act to add Chapter 22.1 (commencing with Section 22580) to Division 8 of the Business and Professions Code, relating to the Internet,California senate, 2013.

[4] Google, *European privacy requests for search removals*, 2017, https://www.google.com/transparencyreport/removals/euro-peprivacy.

[5] Z. Xia, X. Wang, L. Zhang, Z. Qin, X. Sun, and K. Ren, "A privacy-preserving and copy-deterrence content-based image retrieval scheme in cloud computing," *IEEE Transactions on Information Forensics and Security*, vol. 11, no. 11, pp. 2594–2608, 2016.

[6] Y. Tang, P. P. C. Lee, J. C. S. Lui, and R. Perlman, "Secure overlay cloud storage with access control and assured deletion," *IEEE Transactions on Dependable and Secure Computing*, vol. 9, no. 6, pp. 903–916, 2012.

[7] R. Geambasu, T. Kohno, A. A. Levy et al., "Vanish: Increasing Data Privacy with Self-Destructing Data," in *Proceedings of the USENIX Security Symposium*, pp. 299–316, 2009.

[8] G. Roxana, K. Tadayoshi, A. Amit et al., "Increasing data privacy with self-destructing data," in *Proceedings of the USENIX Security09*, pp. 299–316, Berkeley, CA, USA, 2009.

[9] C. Gentry, "Fully Homomorphic Encryption Using Ideal Lattices," in *Proceedings of the 41st Annual ACM Symposium on Theory of Computing, STOC '09*, pp. 169–178, June 2009.

[10] R. Rivest L, L. Adleman, and L. Dertouzos M, "On data banks and privacy homomorphisms," *Foundations of Secure Computation*, vol. 4, no. 11, pp. 169–180, 1978.

[11] Z. Fu and X. Cao, "An Outsourcing Data Storage Scheme Supporting Privacy Preserving and Data Hiding Based on Digital Watermarking," in *Proceedings of the International Conference on Cloud Computing and Security*, pp. 468–474, Springer, 2016.

[12] J. Long, D. Zhang, C. Zuo, J. Duan, and W. Huang, "A robust low-overheadwatermarking for field authentication of intellectual property cores," *Computer Science and Information Systems*, vol. 13, no. 2, pp. 609–622, 2016.

[13] T. Bianchi and A. Piva, "Secure watermarking for multimedia content protection: a review of its benefits and open issues," *IEEE Signal Processing Magazine*, vol. 30, no. 2, pp. 87–96, 2013.

[14] N. Memon and P. W. Wong, "A buyer-seller watermarking protocol," *IEEE Transactions on Image Processing*, vol. 10, no. 4, pp. 643–649, 2001.

[15] C.-L. Lei, P.-L. Yu, P.-L. Tsai, and M.-H. Chan, "An efficient and anonymous buyer-seller watermarking protocol," *IEEE Transactions on Image Processing*, vol. 13, no. 12, pp. 1618–1626, 2004.

[16] B. Chen and G. W. Wornell, "Quantization index modulation: a class of provably good methods for digital watermarking and information embedding," *Institute of Electrical and Electronics Engineers Transactions on Information Theory*, vol. 47, no. 4, pp. 1423–1443, 2001.

[17] P. Tao and A. M. Eskicioglu, "A robust multiple watermarking scheme in the Discrete Wavelet Transform domain," in *Proceedings of the Internet Multimedia Management Systems V*, pp. 133–144, October 2004.

[18] J. Molina-Garcia, R. Reyes-Reyes, V. Ponomaryov, and C. Cruz-Ramos, "Watermarking algorithm for authentication and self-recovery of tampered images using DWT," in *Proceedings of the 9th International Kharkiv Symposium on Physics and Engineering of Microwaves, Millimeter and Submillimeter Waves, MSMW 2016*, pp. 1–4, June 2016.

[19] O. Wahballa, A. Abdalla, K. Hamdnaalla, M. Ramadan, and C. Xu, "An efficient and secure certificateless public key watermarking scheme based on 1VD-DWT," in *Proceedings of the 2016 IEEE International Conference on Cloud Computing and Big Data Analysis, ICCCBDA 2016*, pp. 183–188, July 2016.

[20] B. Chen and G. Wornell, "Digital watermarking and information embedding using dither modulation," in *Proceedings of the 1998 IEEE Second Workshop on Multimedia Signal Processing*, pp. 273–278, Redondo Beach, CA, USA.

[21] P. Bas and J. Hurri, "Security of DM quantization watermarking schemes: a practical study for digital images," in *Proceedings of the International Workshop on Digital Watermarking*, pp. 186–200, Springer, 2005.

[22] B. Matam and D. Lowe, "Watermark-only security attack on DM-QIM watermarking: Vulnerability to guided key guessing," in *Proceedings of the Crime Prevention Technologies and Applications for Advancing Criminal Investigation*, pp. 85–106, IGI Global, 2012.

[23] P. Paillier, "Public-key cryptosystems based on composite degree residuosity classes," in *Proceedings of the International Conference on the Theory and Applications of Cryptographic Techniques*, pp. 223–238, 1999.

[24] C.-C. Lu and S.-Y. Tseng, "Integrated design of AES (Advanced Encryption Standard) encrypter and decrypter," in *Proceedings*

of the IEEE International Conference on Application-Specific Systems, Architectures, and Processors, ASAP 2002, pp. 277–285, July 2002.

[25] E. Klinger, "pHash The open source perceptual hash library," 2017, http://www.phash.org/.

[26] D. Boneh and J. Shaw, "Collusion-secure fingerprinting for digital data," *Institute of Electrical and Electronics Engineers Transactions on Information Theory*, vol. 44, no. 5, pp. 1897–1905, 1998.

[27] S. Pandey, P. Khanna, and H. Yokota, "A semantics and image retrieval system for hierarchical image databases," *Information Processing & Management*, vol. 52, no. 4, pp. 571–591, 2016.

Noninteractive Verifiable Outsourcing Algorithm for Bilinear Pairing with Improved Checkability

Yanli Ren,[1] **Min Dong,**[1] **Zhihua Niu,**[2] **and Xiaoni Du**[3]

[1]*School of Communication and Information Engineering, Shanghai University, Shanghai 200444, China*
[2]*School of Computer Engineering and Science, Shanghai University, Shanghai 200444, China*
[3]*College of Mathematics and Information Science, Northwest Normal University, Lanzhou 730070, China*

Correspondence should be addressed to Yanli Ren; renyanli@shu.edu.cn

Academic Editor: Rémi Cogranne

It is well known that the computation of bilinear pairing is the most expensive operation in pairing-based cryptography. In this paper, we propose a noninteractive verifiable outsourcing algorithm of bilinear pairing based on two servers in the one-malicious model. The outsourcer need not execute any expensive operation, such as scalar multiplication and modular exponentiation. Moreover, the outsourcer could detect any failure with a probability close to 1 if one of the servers misbehaves. Therefore, the proposed algorithm improves checkability and decreases communication cost compared with the previous ones. Finally, we utilize the proposed algorithm as a subroutine to achieve an anonymous identity-based encryption (AIBE) scheme with outsourced decryption and an identity-based signature (IBS) scheme with outsourced verification.

1. Introduction

Outsourcing computation has received widespread attention with the development of cloud computing and the proliferation of mobile devices [1]. Despite of the huge benefits, it also encounters some security concerns and challenges. Firstly, the computation tasks often include some private information that should not be disclosed to the cloud servers, since the servers are not fully trusted. Secondly, the cloud servers may return an invalid result, but the outsourcer fails to detect the error [1]. Therefore, two main security challenges of the outsourcing computation are privacy and checkability: (1) the cloud servers cannot learn anything about the private inputs and the outputs of the computation outsourced to them; (2) the outsourcer can detect any failure if the cloud servers return a wrong computation result.

Verifiable computation (VC) allows a client with limited computation capability to outsource evaluation of a function on some inputs to a powerful but semitrusted server [2, 3]. The client in this model first executes a lot of off-line computation and encrypts the function which will be evaluated and then sends the encrypted function to the server. The server then performs the computation on the encoded function and responds with a result and a proof that the result is correct. Finally, the client verifies whether the computation has been carried out honestly based on the server's proof. During the whole process, the computation cost of the client is less than computing the function directly itself.

Our Contributions. In this paper, we propose a noninteractive verifiable outsourcing algorithm of bilinear pairing in the one-malicious model of two untrusted servers, which improves the checkability of the outsourcer without any interactive operation between the outsourcer and the server. In the proposed algorithm, the outsourcer could detect any failure with a probability close to 1 if one of the servers returns the false result. The proposed algorithm improves the checkability at the expense of only a little efficiency when compared with previous algorithms. Finally, we utilize the proposed algorithm as a subroutine to achieve an AIBE scheme with outsourced decryption and an IBS scheme with outsourced verification.

1.1. Related Works. In the cryptographic community, outsourcing expensive operations to a semitrusted device is widely studied. Chaum and Pedersen [4] introduced the concept of "wallets with observers" that allows installing a piece of hardware on the client's device to execute some operations for each transaction. Hohenberger and Lysyanskaya formalized this model [5] and presented algorithms for the computation of modular exponentiations (MExps) based on two noncolluding servers. Further, Chen et al. [1] proposed a new outsourcing algorithm for MExps with improved efficiency and checkability based on the same model as [5]. However, it is still possible for the outsourcer to be cheated by the server. Ren et al. then constructed a verifiable outsourcing scheme of MExps, where the outsourcer can detect the error with a probability of 1 if the server misbehaves [6]. Lai et al. [7] proposed an attribute-based encryption (ABE) scheme with verifiable outsourcing decryption, which guaranteed that an outsourcer can efficiently detect the wrong results. Qin et al. [8] then proposed new ABE scheme with outsourced decryption, where the outsourcer could verify the outsourcing results with a high efficiency at the expense of minimal overhead. Chen et al. first considered the problem of outsourcing computation in attribute-based signature (ABS) schemes and delegated the verification of signature to an untrusted server [9]. Yu et al. [10] proposed a secure and efficient cloud storage auditing scheme with verifiable outsourcing of key updates. The process of key updates is outsourced to the third party auditor (TPA), and the TPA only knows the encrypted secret key. Meanwhile, the outsourcer could verify the effectiveness of encrypted secret keys when uploading new files to the cloud server. Also, Wang et al. [11] proposed a privacy-preserving public auditing system for data storage security and extended it to handle the problem of multiple auditing, where the TPA could learn nothing about data and the integrity of data could be verified publicly. Other works target specific classes of functions, such as revocable identity-based encryption [12], solution of linear equations [13], and image features extraction [14].

In recent years, bilinear pairings have various applications in constructing new cryptographic primitive, for example, identity-based encryption [15], short signature [16], and key agreement protocol [17]. In pairing-based cryptography, the computation of bilinear pairing is the most expensive operation and it has important effects on efficiency of these schemes or protocols. Thus, a lot of research work has been done to compute bilinear pairing efficiently [18, 19].

Chevallier-Mames et al. [20] presented the first algorithm for secure outsourcing of bilinear pairings based on an untrusted server, where the outsourcer could detect any failure with probability of 1 if the server returns an incorrect result. However, the outsourcer must execute some other expensive operations such as scalar multiplications and modular exponentiations, where these computations are even comparable to those of bilinear pairings in some scenarios [19, 21]. Subsequently, other works on delegation of bilinear pairings [22, 23] also suffer from the same problems. Chen et al. proposed the first efficient outsourcing algorithm of bilinear pairing in the one-malicious version of two untrusted program models [24], where the outsourcer only carried out 5 point additions and 4 multiplications without any expensive operations, which is suitable for the computation-limited client. However, the checkability of the algorithm in [24] is only 1/2, and the outsourcer may accept a false result returned by a malicious server with probability of 1/2. Tian et al. presented two outsourcing algorithms of bilinear pairing based on two servers [25]. One is more efficient than the algorithm of [24], and the outsourcer needs to execute 4 point additions and 3 multiplications with the same checkability. The other algorithm is more flexible based on two untrusted servers with improved checkability. As we know, it is also possible for the outsourcer to be cheated by the server and the error cannot be detected successfully. Recently, Ren et al. presented a new outsourcing algorithm of bilinear pairing, which improves the checkability of the outsourcer to 1, and it is impossible for the server to cheat the outsourcer to accept a false outsourcing result [26]. However, it needs two interactive rounds between the outsourcer and the server and increases the communication cost, though the checkability is improved to 1.

1.2. Organization. The rest of this paper is organized as follows. In Section 2, we introduce the definition of bilinear pairing and security model of the outsourcing scheme. A noninteractive verifiable outsourcing algorithm of bilinear pairing is presented and its security analysis is given in Section 3. In Section 4, we introduce two applications of the proposed outsourcing scheme: an AIBE scheme with outsourced decryption and an IBS scheme with outsourced verification. The performance evaluation of the proposed scheme is presented in Section 5. In Section 6, we conclude the paper.

2. Definitions

In this section, we introduce the properties of bilinear pairings, security definition, and model of the proposed outsourcing algorithms.

2.1. Bilinear Pairings. Let q be a large prime, $G, \widehat{G}$ are two cyclic addition groups of order q, and G_T is a cyclic multiplicative group of order q. P, Q are generators of $G, \widehat{G}$, respectively. $e : G \times \widehat{G} \to G_T$ is a bilinear map with the following properties [15, 16, 21]:

1. Bilinear: $e(a_0 R, b_0 V) = e(R, V)^{a_0 b_0}$ for any $R \in G$, $V \in \widehat{G}$, and $a_0, b_0 \in Z_q^*$

2. Nondegenerate: there exist $R_0 \in G$, $V_0 \in \widehat{G}$ such that $e(R_0, V_0) \neq 1$

3. Computable: there is an efficient algorithm to compute $e(R, V)$ for any $R \in G$, $V \in \widehat{G}$

The bilinear map and the bilinear pairing can be realized by supersingular elliptic curves or hyperelliptic curves over finite groups and Weil or Tate pairings, respectively [15, 16, 21].

2.2. Security Definition and Model. Now we review the formal security definition of an outsourcing algorithm introduced by [5]. An algorithm *Alg* includes a trusted part T and an untrusted program U, and T^U denotes the works carried out by T invoking U. An adversary A is simulated by a pair of algorithms (E, U'), where E denotes the adversarial environment that submits adversarial inputs for *Alg* and U' represents adversarial software written by E. As described in [5], we assume that the two adversaries (E, U') can only make direct communication before the execution of T^U, and, in other cases, they can only communicate with each other by passing messages through the outsourcer T.

Definition 1 (algorithm with outsource I/O). An algorithm *Alg* takes five inputs and generates three outputs. The first three inputs are chosen by an honest party, and the last two inputs are generated by the environment E. The first input is honest and secret, which is unknown for both E and U'; the second is honest and protected, which may be public for E but is private for U'; the third is honest and unprotected, which may be public for both E and U'; the fourth is adversarial and protected, which is public for E but is protected from U'; and the last one is adversarial and unprotected, which is public for E and U'. Similarly, the first output is secret, which is protected from E and U'; the second is protected, which may be public for E but not U'; and the third is unprotected, which may be public for both E and U'.

The following security definition ensures that both E and U' cannot obtain any information about the private inputs and outputs of T^U, even if T uses the malicious software U' written by E.

Definition 2 (outsource-security). Let *Alg* be an algorithm with outsource I/O. T^U is called an outsource-secure implementation of *Alg* if the following conditions hold:

(1) *Correctness*: T^U is a correct implementation of *Alg*
(2) *Security*: for all probabilistic polynomial-time (PPT) adversaries $A = (E, U')$, there exist two PPT simulators (S_1, S_2) such that the following pairs of random variables are computationally indistinguishable

Pair One. $EVIEW_{real} \sim EVIEW_{ideal}$, which means that the malicious environment E cannot gain anything interesting about the private inputs and outputs during the execution of T^U. The detailed definitions of the real process and the ideal process are omitted because of limited space; please see [5] for the details.

Pair Two. $UVIEW_{real} \sim UVIEW_{ideal}$, which means that the untrusted software U' written by E learns nothing about the inputs and outputs during the execution of T^U. Please also see [5] for the detailed definitions.

Assume that T^U is a correct implementation of *Alg*; we have the following definitions.

Definition 3 (α-efficient, secure outsourcing). A pair of algorithms (T, U) are α-efficient if the running time of T is not more than an α-multiplicative factor of that of *Alg* for any input x.

Definition 4 (β-checkable, secure outsourcing). A pair of algorithms (T, U) are β-checkable if T detects any deviation of U' from its advertised functionality during the implementation of $T^{U'(x)}$ with probability not less than β for any input x.

Definition 5 ((α, β)-outsource-security). A pair of algorithms (T, U) are called an (α, β)-outsource-secure implementation of *Alg* if they are both α-efficient and β-checkable.

The proposed algorithms are executed based on two untrusted program models introduced by [5]. In this model, the adversarial environment E writes two programs $U' = (U_1', U_2')$, and T installs these programs in a manner such that all subsequent communication between any two of E, U_1', and U_2' must pass through T. The new adversary attacking T is $A = (E, U_1', U_2')$. We assume that at most one of the programs misbehaves, but we do not know which one. It is named as the one-malicious version of two untrusted models. In the real world, it is equivalent to buying two copies of the untrusted software from different vendors and achieving the outsource security as long as one of them is honest [1].

3. Verifiable Secure Outsourcing of Bilinear Pairing

As [5], a subroutine named Rand is used to speed up the computations. The inputs for Rand are a prime q, two cyclic addition groups $G, \widehat{G}$ of order q, and a bilinear map $e : G \times \widehat{G} \to G_T$, where G_T is a cyclic multiplicative group of order q and the output for each invocation is a random, independent vector of the following form:

$$
\begin{aligned}
\big(& t_1, t_2, a_1 P + a_2 P, a_3 P, a_4 P, b_1 P + b_2 P, b_3 P, \\
& - (a_1 P + a_2 P + b_3 P), - (t_2 a_1 P + a_2 P), \\
& - (a_1 P + t_2 a_2 P), a_1 Q + a_2 Q, a_3 Q, b_1 Q + b_2 Q, b_3 Q, \\
& b_4 Q, - (b_1 Q + b_2 Q + a_3 Q), - (t_1 b_1 Q + b_2 Q), \\
& - (b_1 Q + t_1 b_2 Q), e(a_3 P, a_3 Q), e(b_3 P, b_3 Q), \\
& e(a_4 P, b_1 Q + b_2 Q)^{t_1+1}, e(a_1 P + a_2 P, b_4 Q)^{t_2+1}, \\
& e(a_1 P + a_2 P, b_1 Q + b_2 Q)^{-1} \big),
\end{aligned}
\tag{1}
$$

where $a_1, a_2, a_3, a_4, b_1, b_2, b_3, b_4 \in_R Z_q^*$, $t_1, t_2 \in [2, 3, \ldots, s]$, and s is a small number.

We can use the table-lookup method to implement this functionality. First, a trusted server computes a table of random, independent vectors in advance and then stores it into the memory of T. For each invocation of i, T needs to retrieves a new vector in the table.

3.1. Verifiable Outsourcing Algorithm. We propose a noninteractive verifiable outsourcing algorithm *NIVBP* for bilinear pairing in the one-malicious model. In *NIVBP* algorithm, T outsources its bilinear pairing computations to U_1 and U_2 by invoking the subroutine Rand. A requirement for *NIVBP* is that the adversary A cannot know any useful information about the inputs and outputs of *NIVBP*.

Let q be a large prime. The input of *NIVBP* is $A \in G$ and $B \in \widehat{G}$, and the output is $e(A, B)$. A and B are both computationally blinded to U_1 and U_2. The proposed *NIVBP* algorithm is described as follows:

(1) T firstly runs Rand one time to create a blinding vector as (1).

(2) T queries U_1 in random order as follows:

$$U_1(A + a_1P + a_2P, B + b_1Q + b_2Q) \longrightarrow$$

$$\alpha_{11} = e(A + a_1P + a_2P, B + b_1Q + b_2Q),$$

$$U_1(A + b_1P + b_2P, a_3Q) \longrightarrow$$

$$\alpha_{12} = e(A + b_1P + b_2P, a_3Q),$$

$$U_1(-b_3P - a_1P - a_2P, B + b_3Q) \longrightarrow$$

$$\alpha_{13} = e(-b_3P - a_1P - a_2P, B + b_3Q),$$

$$(2)$$

$$U_1(A + a_4P, -t_1b_1Q - b_2Q) \longrightarrow$$

$$\alpha_{14} = e(A + a_4P, -t_1b_1Q - b_2Q),$$

$$U_1(-t_2a_1P - a_2P, B + b_4Q) \longrightarrow$$

$$\alpha_{15} = e(-t_2a_1P - a_2P, B + b_4Q).$$

Similarly, T queries U_2 in random order as follows:

$$U_2(A + a_1P + a_2P, B + b_1Q + b_2Q) \longrightarrow$$

$$\alpha_{21} = e(A + a_1P + a_2P, B + b_1Q + b_2Q),$$

$$U_2(A + a_3P, -a_3Q - b_1Q - b_2Q) \longrightarrow$$

$$\alpha_{22} = e(A + a_3P, -a_3Q - b_1Q - b_2Q),$$

$$U_2(b_3P, B + a_1Q + a_2Q) \longrightarrow$$

$$\alpha_{23} = e(b_3P, B + a_1Q + a_2Q),$$

$$(3)$$

$$U_2(A + a_4P, -b_1Q - t_1b_2Q) \longrightarrow$$

$$\alpha_{24} = e(A + a_4P, -b_1Q - t_1b_2Q),$$

$$U_2(-a_1P - t_2a_2P, B + b_4Q) \longrightarrow$$

$$\alpha_{25} = e(-a_1P - t_2a_2P, B + b_4Q).$$

(3) T verifies whether U_1 and U_2 generate the correct outputs, which means that (4)–(6) hold.

(a)

$$\alpha_{11} = \alpha_{21} \tag{4}$$

(b)

$$(\alpha_{12} \cdot \alpha_{22} \cdot e(a_3P, a_3Q))^{t_1+1}$$

$$= \alpha_{14} \cdot \alpha_{24} \cdot e(a_4P, b_1Q + b_2Q)^{t_1+1} \tag{5}$$

(c)

$$(\alpha_{13} \cdot \alpha_{23} \cdot e(b_3P, b_3Q))^{t_2+1}$$

$$= \alpha_{15} \cdot \alpha_{25} \cdot e(a_1P + a_2P, b_4Q)^{t_2+1}. \tag{6}$$

If not, T outputs "error"; otherwise, T outputs

$$\alpha_{12} \cdot \alpha_{22} \cdot e(a_3P, a_3Q) = e(A, b_1Q + b_2Q)^{-1},$$

$$\alpha_{13} \cdot \alpha_{23} \cdot e(b_3P, b_3Q) = e(a_1P + a_2P, B)^{-1}, \tag{7}$$

$$e(A, B)$$

$$= \alpha_{11} \cdot e(A, b_1Q + b_2Q)^{-1} \cdot e(a_1P + a_2P, B)^{-1} \tag{8}$$

$$\cdot e(a_1P + a_2P, b_1Q + b_2Q)^{-1}.$$

Correctness. It is obvious that formula (4) holds if two servers are all honest. In addition,

$$\alpha_{12} \cdot \alpha_{22} \cdot e(a_3P, a_3Q)$$

$$= e(b_1P + b_2P, a_3Q)e(A + a_3P, -b_1Q - b_2Q) \tag{9}$$

$$= e(A, b_1Q + b_2Q)^{-1},$$

$$\alpha_{13} \cdot \alpha_{23} \cdot e(b_3P, b_3Q)$$

$$= e(-a_1P - a_2P, B + b_3Q)e(b_3P, a_1Q + a_2Q) \tag{10}$$

$$= e(a_1P + a_2P, B)^{-1},$$

$$(\alpha_{12}\alpha_{22}e(a_3P, a_3Q))^{t_1+1}$$

$$= \alpha_{14}\alpha_{24}e(a_4P, b_1Q + b_2Q)^{t_1+1}$$

$$= e(A + a_4P, b_1Q + b_2Q)^{-(t_1+1)}e(a_4P, b_1Q + b_2Q)^{t_1+1} \tag{11}$$

$$= e(A, b_1Q + b_2Q)^{-(t_1+1)},$$

$$(\alpha_{13}\alpha_{23}e(b_3P, b_3Q))^{t_2+1}$$

$$= \alpha_{15}\alpha_{25}e(a_1P + a_2P, b_4Q)^{t_2+1}$$

$$= e(a_1P + a_2P, B + b_4Q)^{-(t_2+1)}e(a_1P + a_2P, b_4Q)^{t_2+1} \tag{12}$$

$$= e(a_1P + a_2P, B)^{-(t_2+1)}.$$

Therefore, formulas (4)–(6) hold according to the above analysis. Finally, T obtains $e(A, B)$ as (8).

Remark 6. If one of the servers is dishonest, the results could be verified successfully with a probability close to 1 except that the dishonest server knows the values of $\alpha_{11}, \alpha_{12}, \alpha_{13}, \alpha_{14}, \alpha_{15}$ (or $\alpha_{21}, \alpha_{22}, \alpha_{23}, \alpha_{24}, \alpha_{25}$) and t_1, t_2. As we know, five queries sent to U_1 and U_2 are submitted in random order and $t_1, t_2 \in [2, 3, \ldots, s]$. So, the dishonest server could guess the values of $\alpha_{11}, \alpha_{12}, \alpha_{13}, \alpha_{14}, \alpha_{15}$ (or $\alpha_{21}, \alpha_{22}, \alpha_{23}, \alpha_{24}, \alpha_{25}$) and t_1, t_2 with the probabilities of $1/5!$ and $1/(s-1)^2$, respectively. Therefore, the checkability of the *NIVBP* algorithm is

$$1 - \frac{1}{5! \, (s-1)^2} = 1 - \frac{1}{120 \, (s-1)^2} \approx 1. \tag{13}$$

Remark 7. The proposed algorithm *NIVBP* is also applicative in the condition where $G, \widehat{G}$ are two cyclic multiplication groups. Let $g, \widehat{g}$ be generators of $G, \widehat{G}$, respectively. $e : G \times \widehat{G} \to G_T$ is a bilinear map. In this case, the inputs of *NIVBP* are also $A \in G$ and $B \in \widehat{G}$, and the output is also $e(A, B)$. The details are also omitted because of limited space.

3.2. Security Analysis

Theorem 8. *In the one-malicious model, the proposed algorithm $(T, (U_1, U_2))$ is an outsource-secure implementation of NIVBP, where the input (A, B) may be honest and secret or honest and protected or adversarial and protected.*

Proof. Let $A = (E, U_1', U_2')$ be a PPT adversary that interacts with a PPT algorithm T in the one-malicious model.

First, we prove that $\text{EVIEW}_{\text{real}} \sim \text{EVIEW}_{\text{ideal}}$, which means that the environment E learns nothing during the execution of $(T, (U_1, U_2))$. If the input (A, B) is honest and protected or adversarial and protected, it is obvious that the simulator S_1 behaves the same as in the real execution. Therefore, we only need to prove the case where (A, B) is an honest, secret input.

So, suppose that (A, B) is an honest, secret input. The simulator S_1 in the ideal experiment behaves as follows. On receiving the input on round i, S_1 ignores it and instead makes five random queries of the form (α_j, β_j) to both U_1' and U_2'. Finally, S_1 randomly checks one output $e(\alpha_j, \beta_j)$ from each program. If an error is detected, S_1 saves all states and outputs $Y_p^i =$ "error," $Y_u^i = \varnothing$, $\text{rep}^i = 1$, and thus the final output for ideal process is $(\text{estate}^i, \text{"error,"} \varnothing)$. If no error is detected, S_1 checks the remaining four outputs. If all checks pass, S_1 outputs $Y_p^i = \varnothing$, $Y_u^i = \varnothing$, $\text{rep}^i = 0$; that is, the final output for ideal process is $(\text{estate}^i, y_p^i, y_u^i)$; otherwise, S_1 selects a random element r and outputs $Y_p^i = r, Y_u^i = \varnothing, \text{rep}^i = 1$, and the output for ideal process is $(\text{estate}^i, r, \varnothing)$. $\square$

In addition, we need to show that the inputs to (U_1', U_2') in the real experiment are computationally indistinguishable from those in the ideal one. In the ideal experiment, the inputs are selected uniformly at random. In the real one, each part of all five queries that T makes to any program is generated by invoking the subroutine Rand and thus is computationally indistinguishable from random numbers. Therefore, we consider three possible conditions. If (U_1', U_2') both are honest in round i, $\text{EVIEW}_{\text{real}}^i \sim \text{EVIEW}_{\text{ideal}}^i$, since the outputs of *NIVBP* are not replaced and $\text{rep}^i = 0$;

if one of (U_1', U_2') is dishonest in round i, the fault must be detected by both T and S_1 with a probability close to 1, resulting in an output of "error"; otherwise, the output of *NIVBP* is corrupted with a probability of $1/120(s - 1)^2$. In the real experiment, the five outputs generated by (U_1', U_2') are multiplied together along with a random value. Thus, $\text{EVIEW}_{\text{real}}^i \sim \text{EVIEW}_{\text{ideal}}^i$ even when one of (U_1', U_2') misbehaves, so we conclude that $\text{EVIEW}_{\text{real}} \sim \text{EVIEW}_{\text{ideal}}$.

Second, we prove that $\text{UVIEW}_{\text{real}} \sim \text{UVIEW}_{\text{ideal}}$, which means that the untrusted software (U_1', U_2') learns nothing during the execution of $(T, (U_1', U_2'))$. In the ideal experiment, the simulator S_2 always behaves as follows: when receiving the input on round i, S_2 ignores it but submits five random queries of the form (α_j, β_j) to U_1' and U_2'. Then S_2 saves its states and those of (U_1', U_2'). Since the honest, secret or honest, protected or adversarial, protected inputs are all private for (U_1', U_2'), the simulator S_2 is applicable to all those conditions. As shown in Pair One, the inputs to (U_1', U_2') in the real experiment are computationally indistinguishable from those in the ideal one randomly chosen by S_2. Thus, $\text{UVIEW}_{\text{real}}^i \sim \text{UVIEW}_{\text{ideal}}^i$ for each round i, and so $\text{UVIEW}_{\text{real}} \sim \text{UVIEW}_{\text{ideal}}$.

Theorem 9. *In the one-malicious model, the proposed algorithm $(T, (U_1, U_2))$ in Section 3.1 is verifiable; that is, the outsourcer can test the error with a probability close to 1 if one of the servers outputs the false result.*

Proof. Assume that U_1 is an honest server and U_2 is a malicious server. At the end of the algorithm, the outsourcer verifies the results by formulas (4)–(6). It is obvious that U_2 must generate the correct value of α_{21}; otherwise, formula (4) cannot pass the verification with a probability of 1. Thus, the only possibility of U_2 cheating T is returning the false value of $\alpha_{21}, \alpha_{22}, \alpha_{23}, \alpha_{24}, \alpha_{25}$, which is denoted by $\overline{\alpha_{21}}, \overline{\alpha_{22}}, \overline{\alpha_{23}}, \overline{\alpha_{24}}, \overline{\alpha_{25}}$, respectively.

Assume that $\overline{\alpha_{21}}, \overline{\alpha_{22}}, \overline{\alpha_{23}}, \overline{\alpha_{24}}, \overline{\alpha_{25}}$ could pass the verification of formulas (5) and (6); that is,

$$\left(\alpha_{12} \cdot \overline{\alpha_{22}} \cdot e\left(a_3 P, a_3 Q\right)\right)^{t_1+1}$$
$$= \alpha_{14} \cdot \overline{\alpha_{24}} \cdot e\left(a_4 P, b_1 Q + b_2 Q\right)^{t_1+1},$$
$$\left(\alpha_{13} \cdot \overline{\alpha_{23}} \cdot e\left(b_3 P, b_3 Q\right)\right)^{t_2+1} \tag{14}$$
$$= \alpha_{15} \cdot \overline{\alpha_{25}} \cdot e\left(a_1 P + a_2 P, b_4 Q\right)^{t_2+1},$$

which means that

$$\frac{\overline{(\alpha_{22})}^{t_1+1}}{\overline{\alpha_{24}}} = \frac{\alpha_{14} \cdot e\left(a_4 P, b_1 Q + b_2 Q\right)^{t_1+1}}{\alpha_{12}^{t_1+1} \cdot e\left(a_3 P, a_3 Q\right)^{t_1+1}},$$
$$\frac{\overline{(\alpha_{23})}^{t_1+1}}{\overline{\alpha_{25}}} = \frac{\alpha_{15} \cdot e\left(a_1 P + a_2 P, b_4 Q\right)^{t_2+1}}{\alpha_{13}^{t_2+1} \cdot e\left(b_3 P, b_3 Q\right)^{t_2+1}}. \tag{15}$$

Since U_1 is an honest server, $\alpha_{11}, \alpha_{12}, \alpha_{13}, \alpha_{14}, \alpha_{15}$ must be correct. In addition, $e(a_3 P, a_3 Q)$, $e(b_3 P, b_3 Q)$, $e(a_4 P, b_1 Q + b_2 Q)^{t_1+1}$, $e(a_1 P + a_2 P, b_4 Q)^{t_2+1}$ are generated randomly by Rand subroutine, and so these values must be true. Thus, the

TABLE 1: Comparison of the outsourcing algorithms for bilinear pairing.

Algorithm	Pair [24]	TZR1 [25]	TZR2 [25] ($s = 4$)	VBP [26]	NIVBP ($s = 4$)
PA (T)	5	4	11	8	8
M (T)	4	3	9	11	19
Invoke (Rand)	3	1	2	2	1
Pair (U)	8	6	6	6	10
MExp (U)	0	0	0	4	0
Interactive	No	No	No	Yes	No
Servers	Two	Two	Two	Two	Two
Checkability	0.5	0.5	0.84	1	0.999

values of $\overline{(\alpha_{22})}^{t_1+1}/\overline{\alpha_{24}}$ and $\overline{(\alpha_{23})}^{t_2+1}/\overline{\alpha_{25}}$ should be true even if $\overline{\alpha_{21}}, \overline{\alpha_{22}}, \overline{\alpha_{23}}, \overline{\alpha_{24}}, \overline{\alpha_{25}}$ are incorrect; otherwise, they could not pass the verification of formulas (5) and (6).

In order to obtain the true values of $\overline{(\alpha_{22})}^{t_1+1}/\overline{\alpha_{24}}$ and $\overline{(\alpha_{23})}^{t_2+1}/\overline{\alpha_{25}}$, U_2 must guess the values of $\alpha_{21}, \alpha_{22}, \alpha_{23}, \alpha_{24}, \alpha_{25}$ and t_1, t_2. As shown in Section 3.1, the probabilities of guessing the true values of $\alpha_{21}, \alpha_{22}, \alpha_{23}, \alpha_{24}, \alpha_{25}$ and t_1, t_2 are $1/5!$ and $1/(s-1)^2$, respectively. Therefore, the outsourcer can test the error with a probability of $1 - 1/5!(s-1)^2 = 1 - 1/120(s-1)^2 \approx 1$. □

Theorem 10. *In the one-malicious model, the proposed algorithm $(T, (U_1, U_2))$ is an $(O(s/m), \approx 1)$-outsource-secure implementation of NIVBP, where s is a small positive integer and m is the bit length of q and q is the order of $G, \widehat{G}$.*

Proof. The proposed algorithm *NIVBP* makes one call to Rand and 8 point additions (PA) in G or $\widehat{G}$ and $O(s)$ multiplication in G_T in order to compute $e(A, B)$. As shown in [24], it takes roughly $O(m)$ multiplications in resulting finite field to compute the bilinear pairing, where m is the bit length of q. Thus, the proposed algorithm is an $O(s/m)$-efficient implementation of *NIVBP*. On the other hand, it must be detected with a probability close to 1 if U_1 or U_2 fails during any execution of *NIVBP* from Theorem 9. □

3.3. Comparison. We compare the outsourcing algorithms for bilinear pairing with input privacy in Table 1, where s is a small positive integer and "PA" and "M" denote the operation of point addition in G or $\widehat{G}$ and multiplication in G_T, respectively.

From Table 1, we conclude that the *NIVBP* algorithm increases checkability of the outsourcer, though a little computation cost is appended compared with Pair and TZR1 algorithms. In addition, the *NIVBP* algorithm improves computation efficiency and checkability of the outsourcer simultaneously compared with TZR2 algorithm for the same parameter: $s = 4$. The efficiency and checkability of the *NIVBP* algorithm are nearly the same as those of VBP algorithm, but it decreases the communication cost, since it is noninteractive while the VBP algorithm is interactive. Therefore, the *NIVBP*

algorithm increases checkability and decreases communication cost of the outsourcer, although a little computation cost is appended.

4. Applications

In this section, we introduce two applications of the proposed *NIVBP* algorithm: anonymous identity-based encryption (AIBE) scheme [27] and identity-based signature (IBS) scheme [28].

Let $G, \widehat{G}, G_T$ be three cyclic multiplication groups of order q, and let $g, \widehat{g}$ be generators of $G, \widehat{G}$, respectively. $e : G \times \widehat{G} \to G_T$ is a bilinear map. In the following schemes, $G = \widehat{G}$.

4.1. Boyen-Waters AIBE Scheme with Outsourcing Decryption. The proposed outsource-secure AIBE scheme consists of the following algorithms.

Setup. It chooses a random generator $g \in G$, random group elements $g_0, g_1 \in G$, and random exponents $\omega, t_1, t_2, t_3, t_4 \in Z_q$. The master key MSK $= \{\omega, t_1, t_2, t_3, t_4\}$, and the public parameters PK are as follows:

$$\left\{ e(g, g)^{t_1 t_2 \omega}, g, g_0, g_1, v_1 = g^{t_1}, v_2 = g^{t_2}, v_3 = g^{t_3}, v_4 = g^{t_4} \right\}. \tag{16}$$

Extract (MSK, ID). To issue a private key for identity ID, it chooses two random exponents $r_1, r_2 \in Z_q$ and computes the private key SK$_{\text{ID}} = \{d_0, d_1, d_2, d_3, d_4\}$ as follows:

$$d_0 = g^{r_1 t_1 t_2 + r_2 t_3 t_4},$$
$$d_1 = g^{-\omega t_2} \left(g_0 g_1^{\text{ID}} \right)^{-r_1 t_2},$$
$$d_2 = g^{-\omega t_1} \left(g_0 g_1^{\text{ID}} \right)^{-r_1 t_1}, \tag{17}$$
$$d_3 = \left(g_0 g_1^{\text{ID}} \right)^{-r_2 t_4},$$
$$d_4 = \left(g_0 g_1^{\text{ID}} \right)^{-r_2 t_3}.$$

Encrypt (PK, ID, M). To encrypt a message $M \in G_T$ for an identity ID, it chooses random $s, s_1, s_2 \in Z_q$ and creates the ciphertext CT $= \{C', C_0, C_1, C_2, C_3, C_4\}$ as follows:

$$\left\{ Me(g, g)^{t_1 t_2 \omega s}, \left(g_0 g_1^{\text{ID}} \right)^s, v_1^{s-s_1}, v_2^{s_1}, v_3^{s-s_2}, v_4^{s_2} \right\}. \tag{18}$$

Decrypt (PK, ID, CT). The outsourcer T executes the *NIVBP* algorithm for five times and obtains

$$e(C_i, d_i) = NIVBP(C_i, d_i), \quad i = 0, 1, 2, 3, 4 \tag{19}$$

and then computes $C' \prod_{i=0}^{4} e(C_i, d_i) = M$.

4.2. Paterson-Schuldt IBS Scheme with Outsourcing Verification. The detailed scheme is shown as follows.

Setup. It picks $\alpha \in Z_q$, $g_2 \in G$, and computes $g_1 = g^{\alpha}$. Further, choose $u', m' \in G$ and vectors $U = (u_i)$, $M = (m_i)$ of length n_u and n_m, respectively, where u_i, m_i are random elements from G. The public parameters are PK = $\{g, g_1, g_2, u', U, m', M, e(g_2, g_1)\}$ and the master secret key is g_2^{α}.

Extract. Let u be a bit string of length n_u representing an identity and let $u[i]$ be the i-th bit of u. Set $U \subset \{1, 2, \ldots, n_u\}$ as the set of index i such that $u[i] = 1$. To construct the private key d_u of the identity u, pick $r_u \in Z_q$ and compute

$$d_u = \left(g_2^{\alpha} \left(u' \prod_{i \in U} u_i \right)^{r_u}, g^{r_u} \right). \tag{20}$$

Sign. Let $M \subset \{1, \ldots, n_m\}$ be the set of index j such that $m[j] = 1$, where m is a message and $m[j]$ is the j-th bit of m. To generate a signature σ for the message m, randomly choose $r_m \in Z_q$ and compute

$$\sigma = \left(g_2^{\alpha} \left(u' \prod_{i \in U} u_i \right)^{r_u} \left(m' \prod_{j \in M} m_j \right)^{r_m}, g^{r_u}, g^{r_m} \right). \tag{21}$$

Verify. Given a signature $\sigma = (V, R_u, R_m)$ of an identity u for a message m, the outsourcer T executes the *NIVBP* algorithm and obtains

$$e(V, g) = NIVBP(V, g),$$

$$e\left(u' \prod_{i \in U} u_i, R_u \right) = NIVBP\left(u' \prod_{i \in U} u_i, R_u \right),$$

$$e\left(u' \prod_{i \in U} u_i, R_u \right) = NIVBP\left(m' \prod_{j \in M} m_j, R_m \right). \tag{22}$$

And verify

$$e(V, g)$$

$$= e(g_2, g_1) e\left(u' \prod_{i \in U} u_i, R_u \right) e\left(u' \prod_{i \in U} u_i, R_u \right). \tag{23}$$

It is obvious that the two outsourcing schemes are verifiable and secure, since the *NIVBP* algorithm is verifiable with input privacy as described in Section 3.

5. Performance Evaluation

In this section, we provide an experimental evaluation of the proposed outsourcing algorithms. Our experiment is simulated on two machines with Intel Xeon Processor running at 3.4 GHz with 32 G memory (cloud server) and Intel Celeron Processor running at 1.2 GHz with 2 G memory (the

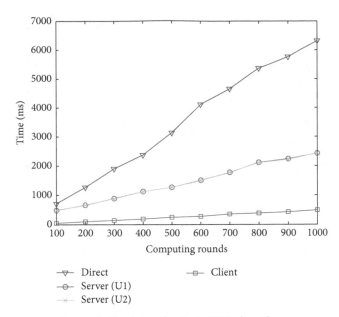

FIGURE 1: Simulation for the NIVBP algorithm.

outsourcer), respectively. The programming language is Java, using Java Pairing-Based Cryptography (JPBC) Library. The parameter q is a 160-bit prime that is randomly generated.

In Figure 1, we provide the simulation of *NIVBP* algorithm, which means that the fault can be found with a probability close to 1 if one of the servers misbehaves. It is obvious that the time cost for the outsourcer T is much smaller than that for directly computing bilinear pairing, since a number of computations have been delegated to two servers. Therefore, the proposed *NIVBP* algorithm is the implementation of secure and verifiable outsourcing for bilinear pairing.

In Figure 2, we compare the evaluation times of the outsourcing algorithms for bilinear pairing proposed in [24–26] and this paper, respectively. From Figure 2, we conclude that, for the outsourcer T, the *NIVBP* algorithm is superior to TZR2 algorithm in efficiency, and it appends small computation cost to improve the checkability compared with Pair and TZR1 algorithms. In addition, the *NIVBP* algorithm is nearly the same as VBP algorithm in efficiency, but it is noninteractive and decreases the communication cost of the outsourcer. Thus, the proposed *NIVBP* algorithm improves the checkability and decreases communication cost for the outsourcer simultaneously based on two servers in the one-malicious model.

6. Conclusions

In this paper, we propose a noninteractive verifiable out-source-secure algorithm for bilinear pairing. The security model of our proposed algorithm is based on two noncolluding servers, and the outsourcer can detect any failure with a probability close to 1 if one of the servers misbehaves. Compared with the previous ones, the proposed algorithm improves the checkability and communication efficiency simultaneously for the outsourcer.

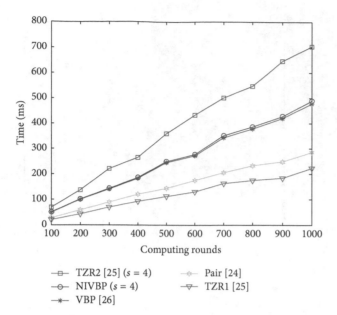

FIGURE 2: Efficiency comparison of the outsourcing algorithms for bilinear pairing.

Acknowledgments

The work described in this paper was supported by the National Natural Science Foundation of China (Grant no. 61572309), Natural Science Foundation of Shanghai (no. 16ZR1411200), and Program for New Century Excellent Talents in University (NCET-12-0620).

References

[1] X. F. Chen, J. Li, J. Ma, Q. Tang, and W. Lou, "New algorithms for secure outsourcing of modular exponentiations," *IEEE Transactions On Parallel And Distributed Systems*, vol. 25, no. 9, pp. 2386–2396, 2014.

[2] R. Gennaro, C. Gentry, and B. Parno, "Non-interactive verifiable computing: outsourcing computation to untrusted workers," in *Advances in cryptology—CRYPTO 2010*, vol. 6223 of *Lecture Notes in Comput. Sci.*, pp. 465–482, Springer, Berlin, Germany, 2010.

[3] K.-M. Chung, Y. Kalai, and S. Vadhan, "Improved delegation of computation using fully homomorphic encryption," in *Advances in cryptology—CRYPTO 2010*, vol. 6223 of *Lecture Notes in Comput. Sci.*, pp. 483–501, Springer, Berlin, Germany, 2010.

[4] D. Chaum and T. Pedersen, "Wallet databases with observers," in *Advances in Cryptology—CRYPTO' 92*, vol. 740 of *Lecture Notes in Computer Science*, pp. 89–105, Springer, Berlin, Germany, 1993.

[5] S. Hohenberger and A. Lysyanskaya, "How to securely outsource cryptographic computations," in *Proceedings of the TCC 2005*, vol. 3378 of *Lecture Notes in Computer Science*, pp. 264–282, Springer.

[6] Y. Ren, N. Dingy, X. Zhang, H. Lu, and D. Gu, "Verifiable outsourcing algorithms for modular exponentiations with improved checkability," in *Proceedings of the 11th ACM Asia Conference on Computer and Communications Security, ASIA CCS 2016*, pp. 293–303, ACM, June 2016.

[7] J.-Z. Lai, R. H. Deng, C. Guan, and J. Weng, "Attribute-based encryption with verifiable outsourced decryption," *IEEE Transactions on Information Forensics and Security*, vol. 8, no. 8, pp. 1343–1354, 2013.

[8] B. Qin, R. H. Deng, S. Liu, and S. Ma, "Attribute-based encryption with efficient verifiable outsourced decryption," *IEEE Transactions on Information Forensics and Security*, vol. 10, no. 7, pp. 1384–1393, 2015.

[9] X. Chen, J. Li, X. Huang, J. Li, Y. Xiang, and D. S. Wong, "Secure outsourced attribute-based signatures," *IEEE Transactions on Parallel and Distributed Systems*, vol. 25, no. 12, pp. 3284–3294, 2014.

[10] J. Yu, K. Ren, and C. Wang, "Enabling cloud storage auditing with verifiable outsourcing of key updates," *IEEE Transactions on Information Forensics and Security*, vol. 11, no. 6, pp. 1362–1375, 2016.

[11] C. Wang, Q. Wang, K. Ren, and W. Lou, "Privacy-preserving public auditing for data storage security in cloud computing," in *Proceedings of the IEEE INFO-COM*, pp. 525–533, San Diego, Calif, USA, March 2010.

[12] Y. Ren, N. Ding, X. Zhang, H. Lu, and D. Gu, "Identity-based encryption with verifiable outsourced revocation," *Computer Journal*, vol. 59, no. 11, pp. 1659–1668, 2016.

[13] X. Chen, X. Huang, J. Li, J. Ma, W. Lou, and D. S. Wong, "New algorithms for secure outsourcing of large-scale systems of linear equations," *IEEE Transactions on Information and Forensics Security*, vol. 10, no. 1, pp. 69–78, 2015.

[14] Y. Ren, X. Zhang, G. Feng, Z. Qian, and F. Li, "How to Extract Image Features based on Co-occurrence Matrix Securely and Efficiently in Cloud Computing," *IEEE Transactions on Cloud Computing*, 2017.

[15] D. Boneh and M. Franklin, "Identity-based encryption from the Weil pairing," in *Advances in Cryptology—CRYPTO 2001*, vol. 2139 of *Lecture Notes in Computer Science*, pp. 213–229, Springer, Berlin, Germany, 2001.

[16] J. C. Cha and J. H. Cheon, "An identity-based signature from gap Diffie-Hellman groups," in *Proceedings of the PKC*, vol. 2567 of *Lecture Notes in Computer Science*, pp. 18–30, Springer.

[17] A. Joux, "A one round protocol for tripartite Diffie-Hellman," in *Proceedings of the ANTS*, vol. 1838 of *Lecture Notes in Computer Science*, pp. 385–393, Springer, 2000.

[18] M. Scott, N. Costigan, and W. Abdulwahab, "Implementing cryptographic pairings on smartcards," in *Proceedings of the CHES*, vol. 4249 of *LNCS*, pp. 134–147, 2006.

[19] P. S. Barreto, S. D. Galbraith, C. Heigeartaigh, and M. Scott, "Efficient pairing computation on supersingular abelian varieties," *Designs, Codes and Cryptography*, vol. 42, no. 3, pp. 239–271, 2007.

[20] B. Chevallier-Mames, J.-S. Coron, N. McCullagh, D. Naccache, and M. Scott, "Secure delegation of elliptic-curve pairing," in *Proceedings of the CARDIS 2010*, vol. 6035 of *LNCS*, pp. 24–35, 2010.

[21] S. D. Galbraith, K. G. Paterson, and N. . Smart, "Pairings for cryptographers," *Discrete Applied Mathematics*, vol. 156, no. 16, pp. 3113–3121, 2008.

[22] P. Tsang, S. Chow, and S. Smith, "Batch pairing delegation," in *Proceedings of the IWSEC 2007*, 90, 74 pages, 2007.

[23] S. S. M. Chow, M. H. Au, and W. Susilo, "Server-aided signatures verification secure against collusion attack," in *Proceedings of the 6th International Symposium on Information, Computer and Communications Security, ASIACCS 2011*, pp. 401–405, March 2011.

[24] X. Chen, W. Susilo, J. Li et al., "Efficient algorithms for secure outsourcing of bilinear pairings," *Theoretical Computer Science*, vol. 562, pp. 112–121, 2015.

[25] H. Tian, F. Zhang, and K. Ren, "Secure bilinear pairing outsourcing made more efficient and flexible," in *Proceedings of the 10th ACM Symposium on Information, Computer and Communications Security, ASIACCS 2015*, pp. 417–426, April 2015.

[26] Y. Ren, N. Ding, T. Wang, H. Lu, and D. Gu, "New algorithms for verifiable outsourcing of bilinear pairings," *Science China Information Sciences*, vol. 59, no. 9, Article ID 99103, 2016.

[27] X. Boyen and B. Waters, "Anonymous hierarchical identity-based encryption (without random oracles)," in *Advances in cryptology—CRYPTO 2006*, vol. 4117 of *Lecture Notes in Computer Science*, pp. 290–307, Springer, Berlin, Germany, 2006.

[28] K. G. Paterson and J. C. N. Schuldt, "Efficient identity-based signatures secure in the standard model," in *Proceedings of the ACISP 2006*, vol. 4058 of *Lecture Notes in Computer Science*, pp. 207–222, Springer.

4

Strongly Unforgeable Certificateless Signature Resisting Attacks from Malicious-But-Passive KGC

Wenjie Yang, Jian Weng, Weiqi Luo, and Anjia Yang

College of Information Science and Technology/College of Cyber Security, Jinan University, Guangzhou 510632, China

Correspondence should be addressed to Jian Weng; cryptjweng@gmail.com and Weiqi Luo; lwq@jnu.edu.cn

Academic Editor: Salvatore D'Antonio

In digital signature, strong unforgeability requires that an attacker cannot forge a new signature on any previously signed/new messages, which is attractive in both theory and practice. Recently, a strongly unforgeable certificateless signature (CLS) scheme without random oracles was presented. In this paper, we firstly show that the scheme fails to achieve strong unforgeability by forging a new signature on a previously signed message under its adversarial model. Then, we point out that the scheme is also vulnerable to the malicious-but-passive key generation center (MKGC) attacks. Finally, we propose an improved strongly unforgeable CLS scheme in the standard model. The improved scheme not only meets the requirement of strong unforgeability but also withstands the MKGC attacks. To the best of our knowledge, we are the first to prove a CLS scheme to be strongly unforgeable against the MKGC attacks without using random oracles.

1. Introduction

In 1984, Shamir brought in the notion of identity-based public key cryptography [1] to avert the heavy certificate management problem in traditional certificate-based public key systems. In this scenario, a fully trusted key generation center (KGC) takes care of deriving the secret key from an entity's public identity information (e.g., personal identity number) which is directly used as the corresponding public key. From then on, lots of efforts have been made in this area [2–4]. However, these identity-based schemes are subject to the key escrow problem; that is, the KGC owns any entity's secret key and, therefore, can do anything on behalf of the entity whereas not being detected.

In order to avoid this problem, Al-Riyami and Paterson introduced a new notion named certificateless public key cryptography (CL-PKC) and formalized its security model [5], in which the KGC is considered as a semitrusted third party and only produces a partial secret key for an entity using its own master secret key, and each entity independently picks an extra secret value for themselves. As a consequence, the entity's secret key consists of the partial secret key and the secret value, which make an attacker not do anything instead of the entity if the attacker just has one of the two parts.

In this scenario [5], the attacks only knowing the entity's secret value are denoted by public key replacement (PKR) attacks while the others merely obtaining the master secret key are denoted by honest-but-curious key generation center (HKGC) attacks. Before long, Au et al. addressed a malicious-but-passive key generation center (MKGC) attacks [6], in which an attacker can set some trapdoors in the system parameters adaptively rather than only being told the master secret key like in HKGC attacks. So far, CL-PKC has received many attention under those adversarial models.

As an important branch in certificateless settings, many studies have focused on certificateless signature (CLS) schemes [7–13]. Nevertheless, most of these early CLS schemes are only provably secure in the random oracle model [14], whose security may not be able to remain when the random oracle is instantiated with a concrete hash function. To fill the gap, Liu et al. proposed the first CLS scheme secure in the standard model [15] and then some modified schemes were put forward in [16–23]. Nevertheless, all of them only were proven to be secure against PKR attacks and HKGC attacks. Although some of them like [19, 22, 23] have been indicated to be secure against MKGC attacks, the authors do not provide a formal security proof under MKGC attacks without random oracles. Therefore, it is still an unresolved problem to construct a concrete CLS scheme provably secure against MKGC attacks in the standard model.

Recently, Hung et al. gave a certificateless signature scheme (HT scheme, for short) [21] and discussed its security under PKR attacks and HKGC attacks. They claimed that no attacker can forge a valid signature on a message, even given some previous signatures on the message. In other words, they stated that their scheme is strongly unforgeable under their security model. In this paper, we firstly illustrate that the HT scheme does not meet strong unforgeability as they claimed, by forging a new valid signature on any previously signed message. Further, we show that the HT scheme suffers from MKGC attacks by giving a concrete attack. At last, we propose an improved certificateless signature scheme which not only is strongly unforgeable but also resists MKGC attacks in the standard model.

This paper is organized as follows. In Section 2, we give some preliminaries. In Section 3, we review the HT scheme and present our attacks. In Section 4, we describe two building blocks based on which we then construct an improved strongly secure certificateless signature scheme in the standard model. Finally, the conclusion is given in Section 5.

2. Preliminaries

2.1. Bilinear Pairings and Complexity Assumption. In this paper, we adopt the standard term about bilinear pairings described in [21]. Here, $(q, \mathbb{G}_1, \mathbb{G}_2, \hat{e}, g)$ is a concrete instance, where q denotes a big prime, $\mathbb{G}_1$ and $\mathbb{G}_2$ denote two q order cyclic groups, $\hat{e}$ denotes an admissible bilinear mapping $\mathbb{G}_1 \times \mathbb{G}_1 \rightarrow \mathbb{G}_2$, and g denotes a generator in $\mathbb{G}_1$.

Discrete Logarithm (DL) Assumption. Given $\langle \mathbb{G}_1, g, h \rangle$, the DL problem is to find the integer a such that $h = g^a$. If the DL problem cannot be solved in polynomial time, the DL assumption holds.

Computational Diffie-Hellman (CDH) Assumption. Given $\langle \mathbb{G}_1, g, g^a, g^b \rangle$, the CDH problem is to compute group element g^{ab}. If the CDH problem cannot be solved in polynomial time, the CDH assumption holds.

2.2. Collision-Resistant Hash Function (CRHF) Assumption. Let $\mathcal{H} = \{H_k\}$ be a keyed hash family of functions $H_k : \{0,1\}^* \rightarrow \{0,1\}^n$ indexed by $k \in \mathcal{K}$. We say that algorithm $\mathcal{A}$ has advantage ϵ in breaking the collision resistance of $\mathcal{H}$ if

$$\Pr\left[\mathcal{A}(k) = (m_0, m_1) : m_0 \neq m_1, H_k(m_0) = H_k(m_1)\right] \tag{1}$$
$$> \epsilon,$$

where the probability is taken over the random choice of $k \in \mathcal{K}$ and the random bits of $\mathcal{A}$. Here, a hash family $\mathcal{H}$ is (t, ϵ)-collision-resistant if no t-time adversary has advantage at least ϵ in breaking the collision resistance of $\mathcal{H}$.

2.3. Framework and Security Model. The five algorithms below which can be run in polynomial time comprise a certificateless signature scheme:

(i) *Setup*: when receiving a security parameter ψ, the algorithm outputs the master secret key msk and system parameters sp. sp is available for all the other algorithms.

(ii) *PSKExt*: when receiving the master secret key msk and an entity e, the algorithm outputs the partial secret key psk_e and sends it over a secure channel to the entity.

(iii) *SetUKey*: when receiving an entity e, this algorithm outputs the secret key sk_e and public key pk_e. Note that sk_e is composed of sv_e and psk_e, where sv_e denotes the secret value and is picked by the entity itself independently.

(iv) *Sign*: when receiving an entity's secret key sk_e and a message m, this algorithm outputs a signature σ.

(v) *Verify*: when receiving a signature σ, a message m, and an entity public key pk_e, this algorithm outputs either "accept" or "reject" relying on the signature validity.

Like [11, 21], two types of adversaries are taken into account in the above CLS definition. The first is a public key replacement (PKR) attacker who knows the targeted entity secret value but cannot request the entity partial secret key. The other is an honest-but-curious KGC (HKGC) attacker that is allowed to obtain the master secret key but cannot know the targeted entity secret value. Here, the strong security of a CLS scheme is captured by means of Games 1 and 2 between a challenger $\mathcal{C}$ and an attacker $\mathcal{A} \in \{\mathcal{A}_1, \mathcal{A}_2\}$.

Game 1 (for PKR attacker)

(i) *Init*: given a security parameter ψ, $\mathcal{C}$ invokes *Setup* to produce the master secret key msk and system parameters sp. sp is given to $\mathcal{A}$ and msk is kept by itself.

(ii) *Queries*: in this phase, $\mathcal{A}$ runs the following queries adaptively:

$\mathcal{O}^{pk}(e)$: receiving an entity e, $\mathcal{C}$ invokes *SetUkey* to obtain the entity public key pk_e and returns it to $\mathcal{A}$.

$\mathcal{O}^{rep}(e, pk_e')$: receiving a new entity public key pk_e', $\mathcal{C}$ finds and updates the corresponding item for the entity e.

$\mathcal{O}^{psk}(e)$: receiving an entity e, $\mathcal{C}$ invokes *PSKExt* to obtain the entity partial secret key psk_e and returns it to $\mathcal{A}$.

$\mathcal{O}^{sk}(e)$: receiving an entity e, $\mathcal{C}$ invokes *SetUkey* to obtain the entity secret key sk_e and returns it to $\mathcal{A}$. Here, $\mathcal{C}$ returns $\perp$ if the entity e has already appeared in $\mathcal{O}^{rep}(e, pk_e')$.

$\mathcal{O}^{sign}(e, m)$: receiving an entity e and a message m, $\mathcal{C}$ invokes *SetUkey* to obtain sk_e and then performs *Sign* to generate the signature σ for m under sk_e. At last, $\mathcal{C}$ returns it to $\mathcal{A}$.

(iii) *Forgery*: $\mathscr{A}$ returns (σ^*, e^*, m^*) and wins if the following conditions hold:

(1) σ^* is a valid signature of m^* on e^*.

(2) e^* is not requested in $\mathcal{O}^{psk}(e)$ and $\mathcal{O}^{sk}(e)$.

(3) (σ^*, e^*, m^*) is not an output in $\mathcal{O}^{sign}(e, m)$.

Game 2 (for HKGC attacker)

(i) *Setup*: given a security parameter ψ, $\mathscr{C}$ invokes *Setup* to produce the master secret key *msk* and system parameters *sp*. Both *msk* and *sp* are given to $\mathscr{A}$.

(ii) *Queries*: here, $\mathscr{A}$ may request any oracles defined in *Game 1*, except for $\mathcal{O}^{rep}(e, pk'_e)$ and $\mathcal{O}^{psk}(e)$, in an adaptive manner. Note that it is unreasonable to ask $\mathscr{C}$ to respond to the signing queries if pk_e has been replaced.

(iii) *Forgery*: $\mathscr{A}$ outputs (σ^*, e^*, m^*) and wins if the following conditions hold:

(1) σ^* is a valid signature of m^* on e^*.

(2) e^* is not requested in $\mathcal{O}^{rep}(e, pk'_e)$ and $\mathcal{O}^{sk}(e)$.

(3) (σ^*, e^*, m^*) is not an output in $\mathcal{O}^{sign}(e, m)$.

Au et al. illustrated the definition about malicious-but-passive KGC (MKGC) attacker, which is a stronger and more realistic security requirement. This MKGC may embed extra trapdoors in their system parameters before running *PSKExt*. To capture MKGC attacks, the following *Setup* algorithm is adopted in *Game 2*.

(i) *Setup*: $\mathscr{C}$ invokes $\mathscr{A}$ to initialize the system public/secret parameters (sp, msk). Here, to mount an attack more easily, $\mathscr{A}$ is allowed to set some trapdoors during the initialization phase.

Definition 1. If none of the adversaries can win the above two games with a nonnegligible advantage, in a probabilistic polynomial time (PPT), the signature scheme in certificateless settings is strongly unforgeable against adaptive chosen message attacks.

3. Analysis of HT Scheme

3.1. Review on HT Scheme. Here, we restate HT scheme [21] by the following five algorithms:

(i) *Setup*: given an instance $(q, \mathbb{G}_1, \mathbb{G}_2, \hat{e}, g)$, KGC firstly picks $\alpha \in \mathbb{Z}_p^*$ at random and computes $g_1 = g^\alpha \in \mathbb{G}_1$ and then sets the master secret key $msk = g_2^\alpha$, where $g_2 \in \mathbb{G}_1$. Furthermore, KGC randomly chooses $e_1, e_2, \ldots, e_{n_e}, e', s_1, s_2, \ldots, s_{n_v}, s', t_1, t_2, \ldots, t_{n_v}, t', w_1, w_2, \ldots, w_{n_w}, w' \in \mathbb{G}_1$ and sets four vectors $\vec{e} = \{e_i\}_{i=1}^{n_e}$, $\vec{s} = \{s_j\}_{j=1}^{n_v}$, $\vec{t} = \{t_j\}_{j=1}^{n_v}$, and $\vec{w} = \{w_k\}_{j=k}^{n_w}$, respectively. Next, KGC selects five classical collision-resistant hash functions $H_1 : \{0, 1\}^* \to \{0, 1\}^{n_e}$, $H_2, H_3 :$

$\mathbb{G}_1 \times \mathbb{G}_1 \to \{0, 1\}^{n_v}$, $H_4 : \{0, 1\}^* \to \{0, 1\}^{n_w}$, and $H_5 : \{0, 1\}^* \to \mathbb{Z}_p^*$, where n_e, n_v, and n_w are fixed lengths. Finally, KGC publishes $sp = (\mathbb{G}_1, \mathbb{G}_2, \hat{e}, g, g_1, g_2, e', \vec{e}, s', \vec{s}, t', \vec{t}, w', \vec{w}, H_1, H_2, H_3, H_4, H_5)$.

(ii) *PSKExt*: let $\vec{ve} = H_1(e) = (ve_1, ve_2, \ldots, ve_{n_e})$ be a bit string from hashing an entity e. Next, KGC randomly picks r_e from $\mathbb{Z}_p^*$ and computes $psk_e = (psk_{e1}, psk_{e2}) = (g_2^\alpha E^{r_e}, g^{r_e})$, where $E = e' \prod_{i=1}^{n_e} e_i^{ve_i}$. Finally, KGC secretly transmits psk_e to the entity.

(iii) *SetUkey*: given an entity e, this algorithm firstly chooses two random secret values $\theta_1, \theta_2 \in \mathbb{Z}_p^*$, generates the entity public key $pk_e = (pk_{e1}, pk_{e2}) = (g^{\theta_1}, g^{\theta_2})$, and then computes $\vec{vs} = H_2(pk_{e1}, pk_{e2}) = (vs_1, \ldots, vs_{n_v})$ and $\vec{vt} = H_3(pk_{e1}, pk_{e2}) = (vt_1, \ldots, vt_{n_v})$, where $\vec{vs}$ and $\vec{vt}$ are two bit strings of length n_v. Finally, the entity secret value is set to $sv_e = g_2^{\theta_1} S^{\theta_1} T^{\theta_2}$, where $S = s' \prod_{j=1}^{n_v} s_j^{vs_j}$ and $T = t' \prod_{j=1}^{n_v} t_j^{vt_j}$. Here, $sk_e = (sv_e, psk_e)$.

(iv) *Sign*: given a message m, an entity public key pk_e, and an entity secret key sk_e, this algorithm randomly selects $r_w \in \mathbb{Z}_p^*$, and computes $\vec{vw} = H_4(m) = (vw_1, vw_2, \ldots, vw_{n_w})$ and $h = H_5(m \parallel g^{r_w})$. Then, the signature σ is set by computing $(\sigma_1, \sigma_2, \sigma_3) = (psk_{e1}^h (sv_e)^h W^{r_w}, psk_{e2}^h, g^{r_w})$, where $W = (w' \prod_{k=1}^{n_w} w_k^{vw_k})$.

(v) *Verify*: given σ on m under e with pk_e, this algorithm can verify σ's validity by the following equation:

$$\hat{e}(\sigma_1, g) \overset{?}{=} \hat{e}(g_1, g_2)^h \hat{e}(\sigma_2, E) \hat{e}(pk_{e1}, g_2 S)^h$$
$$\cdot \hat{e}(pk_{e2}, T)^h \hat{e}(\sigma_3, W), \tag{2}$$

where $h = H_5(m \parallel \sigma_3)$, $E = e' \prod_{i=1}^{n_e} e_i^{ve_i}$, $S = s' \prod_{j=1}^{n_v} s_j^{vs_j}$, $T = t' \prod_{j=1}^{n_v} t_j^{vt_j}$, and $W = (w' \prod_{k=1}^{n_w} w_k^{vw_k})$.

3.2. Attacks on HT Scheme

3.2.1. Strong Forgery Attack. Here, we indicate that an attacker $\mathscr{A}$ generates a new forgery σ' from an existing signature σ on m by interacting with the challenger $\mathscr{C}$.

Stage 1. $\mathscr{C}$ normally invokes the *Setup* algorithm to produce $msk = g_2^\alpha$ and $sp = (\mathbb{G}_1, \mathbb{G}_2, \hat{e}, g, g_1, g_2, e', \vec{e}, s', \vec{s}, t', \vec{t}, w', \vec{w}, H_1, H_2, H_3, H_4, H_5)$. Here, $\mathscr{C}$ sends sp to $\mathscr{A}$ and keeps *msk* by itself.

Stage 2. Given a target entity e and a message m, $\mathscr{C}$ first invokes the *PSKExt* and *SetUkey* algorithms to generate the entity secret key $(psk_{e1}, psk_{e2}, sv_e) = (g_2^\alpha E^{r_e}, g^{r_e}, g_2^{\theta_1} S^{\theta_1} T^{\theta_2})$ and then invokes the *Sign* algorithm to obtain a signature σ of m on e. Obviously, the signature concrete forms are $(\sigma_1, \sigma_2, \sigma_3) = (psk_{e1}^h (sv_e)^h W^{r_w}, psk_{e2}^h, g^{r_w})$, where $h = H_3(m \parallel g^{r_w})$.

Stage 3. In order to generate σ' for m under e, $\mathscr{A}$ randomly picks $r'_e \in \mathbb{Z}_p^*$ and sets $\sigma'_1 = \sigma_1 E^{r'_e h} = g_2^{\alpha h} E^{(r_e + r'_e)h} s v_e^h W^{r_w}$, $\sigma'_2 = \sigma_2 g^{r'_e h} = g^{(r_e + r'_e)h}$, and $\sigma'_3 = \sigma_3$.

It is clear that σ' is a new valid signature for m on e with pk_e since

$$
\begin{aligned}
\widehat{e}\left(\sigma'_1, g\right) &= \widehat{e}\left(g_2^{\alpha h} E^{(r_e + r'_e)h} s v_e^h W^{r_w}, g\right) = \widehat{e}\left(g_2^{\alpha h}, g\right) \\
&\cdot \widehat{e}\left(E^{(r_e + r'_e)h}, g\right) \widehat{e}\left(\left(g_2 S\right)^{\theta_1 h} T_e^{\theta_2 h}, g\right) \widehat{e}\left(W^{r_w}, g\right) \\
&= \widehat{e}\left(g_1, g_2\right)^h \widehat{e}\left(E, \sigma'_2\right) \widehat{e}\left(pk_{e1}, g_2 S\right)^h \widehat{e}\left(pk_{e2}, T\right)^h \\
&\cdot \widehat{e}\left(W, \sigma'_3\right).
\end{aligned}
\tag{3}
$$

Remark 2. We notice that there is a flaw in Hung et al.'s security proof. More specifically, when receiving a signing query on (m, e), $\mathscr{C}$ first picks $r_w \in \mathbb{Z}_p^*$ at random and then sets the hash value $h = H_5(m \,\|\, g^{r_w})$ to successfully compute the simulated signature $\sigma = (\sigma_1, \sigma_2, \sigma_3)$. According to Hung et al.'s simulation process, we know that $\sigma_3 = g^{r_w}$, where $r'_w = r_w - \theta_1 h Q(\vec{vs})/K(\vec{vw})$, $r_w - (ah + \theta_1 h Q(\vec{vs}))/K(\vec{vw})$, or $r_w - ah/K(\vec{vw})$. Obviously, the verification equation $\widehat{e}(\sigma_1, g) \overset{?}{=} \widehat{e}(g_1, g_2)^{h'} \widehat{e}(\sigma_2, E) \widehat{e}(pk_{e1}, g_2 S)^{h'} \widehat{e}(pk_{e2}, T)^{h'} \widehat{e}(\sigma_3, W)$ is always not true since $h \neq h'$, where $h' = H_5(m \,\|\, \sigma_3)$. That is to say, $\mathscr{C}$ cannot always give a valid response to a signing query required by an attacker $\mathscr{A}$ with nonnegligible probability.

3.2.2. MKGC Attack. Here, we will show that the HT scheme cannot capture MKGC attacks by an interaction between $\mathscr{C}$ and $\mathscr{A}$ as follows.

Stage 1. Here, $\mathscr{A}$ is responsible for initializing the system parameters and sends them to $\mathscr{C}$. In particular, $\mathscr{A}$ adaptively sets the parameters $g_2 = g^\beta$, $s' = g^{x'}$, $s_1 = g^{x_1}, \ldots, s_n = g^{x_{n_v}}$, $t' = g^{y'}$, $t_1 = g^{y_1}, \ldots, t_n = g^{y_{n_v}}$, where $\beta, x', x_1, \ldots, x_{n_v}, y', y_1, \ldots, y_{n_v} \in \mathbb{Z}_p^*$.

Stage 2. In the queries phase, $\mathscr{A}$ can obtain the target entity public key $pk_e = (pk_{e1}, pk_{e2}) = (g^{\theta_1}, g^{\theta_2})$. Next, $\mathscr{A}$ derives the corresponding secret value $sv_e = g_2^{\theta_1} S^{\theta_1} T^{\theta_2}$ by computing $g_2^{\theta_1} = pk_{e1}^\beta$, $S^{\theta_1} = pk_{e1}^{x' \sum_{j=1}^{n_k} x_j^{vs_j}}$, and $T^{\theta_2} = pk_{e2}^{y' \sum_{j=1}^{n_k} y_j^{vt_j}}$, where $\vec{vs} = H_2(pk_{e1}, pk_{e2}) = (vs_1, \ldots, vs_{n_k})$ and $\vec{vt} = H_3(pk_{e1}, pk_{e2}) = (vt_1, \ldots, vt_{n_k})$.

Stage 3. Now, $\mathscr{A}$ can recover the entity full secret key (psk_e, sv_e) and sign any message m instead of the targeted entity.

Remark 3. In MKGC attacks, the KGC can adaptively set some trapdoor in the system parameters during the setup phase which may enhance its attack success probability. Obviously, in the security proof [21], the attacker passively received the master secret key and public parameters generated by the challenger like all the previous schemes [15–23], which did not consider how to capture the MKGC attacks.

4. Our CLS Scheme

In this section, we construct an improved strongly unforgeable certificateless signature scheme and demonstrate its security on the condition that both [3, 24] are secure, and DL and CRHF assumptions hold.

4.1. Building Blocks

Paterson and Schuldt's Identity-Based Signature Scheme (PIBS) [3]

(i) *Setup:* let $(q, \mathbb{G}_1, \mathbb{G}_2, \widehat{e}, g)$ be an instance described in Section 2. First, pick a random element α from $\mathbb{Z}_p^*$ and compute $g_1 = g^\alpha$. Then, choose random elements g_2, e', w' from $\mathbb{G}_1$ and two vectors $\vec{e} = \{e_k\}_{k=1}^{n_e}, \vec{w} = \{w_l\}_{l=1}^{n_w}$ of lengths n_e and n_w, respectively, whose entries are random elements from $\mathbb{G}_1$. Finally, the master secret key is $msk = g_2^\alpha$ and the system parameter is $sp = (\mathbb{G}_1, \mathbb{G}_2, \widehat{e}, g, g_1, g_2, e', \vec{e}, w', \vec{w})$.

(ii) *Extract:* let $E = H_e(e)$, where e is an entity. Set $\mathscr{E} = \{k \mid E[k] = 1, k = 1, 2, \ldots, n_e\}$. To construct e's secret key sk_e, pick a random number r_e from $\mathbb{Z}_p^*$ and compute

$$
sk_e = (sk_{e1}, sk_{e2}) = \left(g_2^{\alpha_1}\left(e' \prod_{k \in \mathscr{E}} e_k\right)^{r_e}, g^{r_e}\right). \tag{4}
$$

(iii) *Sign:* let $\mathscr{W} \subset \{1, 2, \ldots, n_m\}$ be the set of indices l such that $W[l] = 1$, where $W[l]$ is the lth bit of message m. σ is constructed by picking a random element r_w from $\mathbb{Z}_p^*$ and computing

$$
\sigma = \left(g_2^\alpha\left(e' \prod_{k \in \mathscr{E}} e_k\right)^{r_e}\left(w' \prod_{l \in \mathscr{W}} w_l\right)^{r_m}, g^{r_e}, g^{r_w}\right). \tag{5}
$$

(iv) *Verify:* given a signature $\sigma = (\sigma_1, \sigma_2, \sigma_3)$ of m under e, a verifier accepts σ if the following equality holds:

$$
\begin{aligned}
&\widehat{e}(\sigma_1, g) \\
&\overset{?}{=} \widehat{e}(g_1, g_2) \widehat{e}\left(e' \prod_{k \in \mathscr{E}} e_k, \sigma_2\right) \widehat{e}\left(w' \prod_{l \in \mathscr{W}} w_l, \sigma_3\right).
\end{aligned}
\tag{6}
$$

Output 1 if it is valid. Otherwise, output 0.

Boneh et al.'s Signature Scheme (BSW) [24]

(i) *SetUKey:* let $(q, \mathbb{G}_1, \mathbb{G}_2, \widehat{e}, g)$ be an instance described in Section 2. First, pick a random number β from $\mathbb{Z}_p^*$ and set $g_{e1} = g^\beta$. Then, choose three random values g_{e2}, h_e, v'_e from $\mathbb{G}_1$ where $\log_g h_e$ is known and a random n_w-length vector $\vec{v}_e = \{v_{ei}\}_{i=1}^{n_w}$ whose elements are also chosen from $\mathbb{G}_1$. In addition, choose two random collision-resistant hash functions $H : \{0,1\}^* \rightarrow \mathbb{Z}_p^*$ and $H_w : \mathbb{G}_1 \rightarrow \{0,1\}^{n_e}$. Finally, output the secret key $sk_e = g_{e2}^\beta$ and the public key $pk_e = (\mathbb{G}_1, \mathbb{G}_2, \hat{e}, g, g_{e1}, g_{e2}, h_e, v_e', \vec{v}_e)$.

(ii) *Sign*: given a message m, first, pick two random numbers r_w, s from $\mathbb{Z}_p^*$ and compute $W = H_w(g^t h_e^s)$, where $t = H(m \parallel g^{r_w})$. Then, set $\mathscr{W} = \{i \mid W[i] = 1, i = 1, 2, \ldots, n_w\}$. At last, σ is constructed by computing

$$\sigma = (\sigma_1, \sigma_2, \sigma_3) = \left(g_{e2}^\beta \left(v_e' \prod_{i \in \mathscr{W}} v_{ei} \right)^{r_w}, g^{r_w}, s \right). \quad (7)$$

(iii) *Verify*: given σ of m under pk_e, first, compute $W = H_m(g^t h_e^{\sigma_3})$, where $t = H(m \parallel \sigma_2)$. Then, set $\mathscr{W} = \{i \mid N[i] = 1, i = 1, 2, \ldots, n_m\}$. Finally, verify the following equation:

$$\hat{e}(\sigma_1, g) \stackrel{?}{=} \hat{e}(g_{e1}, g_{e2}) \hat{e}\left(v_e' \prod_{i \in \mathscr{W}} v_{ei}, \sigma_2 \right). \quad (8)$$

4.2. Our Concrete Scheme. Let $(q, \mathbb{G}_1, \mathbb{G}_2, \hat{e}, g)$ be an instance described in Section 2. In our scheme, three classic hash functions, $H : \{0,1\}^* \times sp \times pk_e \times e \times \mathbb{G}_1^2 \rightarrow \mathbb{Z}_p^*$, $H_w : \mathbb{G}_1 \rightarrow \{0,1\}^{n_w}$, and $H_e : \{0,1\}^* \rightarrow \{0,1\}^{n_e}$, are adopted from $\mathscr{H}$ to handle arbitrary messages and identities. Note that the cyclic groups and hash functions are publicly confirmed by all interested parties.

(i) *Setup*: first, choose random elements $\alpha_1, \alpha_2, \varphi, x', x_1, x_2, \ldots, x_{n_e}, y', y_1, y_2, \ldots, y_{n_w}$ from $\mathbb{Z}_p^*$. Then, compute $g_1 = g^{\alpha_1}$, $g_2 = g^{\alpha_2}$, $h = g^\varphi$, $e' = g^{x'}$, $\vec{e} = \{e_k\}_{k=1}^{n_e} = \{g^{x_k}\}_{k=1}^{n_e}$, $w' = g^{y'}$, $\vec{w} = \{w_l\}_{l=1}^{n_w} = \{g^{y_l}\}_{l=1}^{n_w}$. Finally, the master secret key is $msk = (\alpha_1, \alpha_2, \varphi, x', x_1, x_2, \ldots, x_{n_e}, y', y_1, y_2, \ldots, y_{n_w})$ and system parameter is $sp = (\mathbb{G}_1, \mathbb{G}_2, g, g_1, g_2, h, e', \vec{e}, w', \vec{w})$.

(ii) *PSKExt*: let $E = H_e(e)$ where e is an entity. Set $\mathscr{E} = \{k \mid E[k] = 1, k = 1, 2, \ldots, n_e\}$. To construct e's partial secret key psk_e, pick a random number r_e from $\mathbb{Z}_p^*$ and compute

$$psk_e = (psk_{e1}, psk_{e2}) = \left(g_2^{\alpha_1} \left(e' \prod_{k \in \mathscr{E}} e_k \right)^{r_e}, g^{r_e} \right). \quad (9)$$

(iii) *SetUKey*: first, choose random elements $\beta_{e1}, \beta_{e2}, \phi_e, z_e', z_{e1}, z_{e2}, \ldots, z_{en_w}$ from $\mathbb{Z}_p^*$. Then, compute $g_{e1} = g^{\beta_{e1}}$, $g_{e2} = g^{\beta_{e2}}$, $h_e = g^{\phi_e}$, $v_e' = g^{z_e'}$, $\vec{v}_e = \{v_{ei}\}_{i=1}^{n_w} = \{g^{z_{ei}}\}_{i=1}^{n_w}$. At last, let the public key be $pk_e = (g_{e1}, g_{e2}, h_e, v_e', \vec{v}_e)$ and the secret values be $sv_e = (\beta_{e1}, \beta_{e2}, \phi_e, z_e', z_{e1}, z_{e2}, \ldots, z_{en_w})$. Note that $sk_e = (sv_e, psk_e)$.

(iv) *Sign*: given m, pk_e, and sk_e, the signer selects two random numbers $r_w, s \in \mathbb{Z}_p^*$, computes $t = H(m \parallel$

$sp \parallel pk_e \parallel e \parallel psk_{e2} \parallel g^{r_w})$, and sets $\mathscr{E} = \{k \mid E[k] = 1, k = 1, 2, \ldots, n_e\}$, where $E = H_e(e)$, $\mathscr{W} = \{l \mid W[l] = 1, l = 1, 2, \ldots, n_w\}$, where $W = H_w(g^t h^s)$, and $\mathscr{W}' = \{i \mid W'[i] = 1, i = 1, 2, \ldots, n_w\}$, where $W' = H_w(g^t h_e^s)$, respectively. At last, σ is constructed by computing

$$\sigma = \left(g_{e2}^{\beta_{e1}} \left(v_e' \prod_{i \in \mathscr{W}'} v_{ei} \right)^{r_w}, g_2^{\alpha_1} \left(e' \prod_{k \in \mathscr{E}} e_k \right)^{r_e} \right.$$
$$\left. \cdot \left(w' \prod_{l \in \mathscr{W}} w_l \right)^{r_w}, g^{r_e}, g^{r_w}, s \right). \quad (10)$$

(v) *Verify*: given σ of m under e, any verifier first computes $E = H_e(e)$, $W = H_w(g^t h^{\sigma_5})$ and $W' = H_w(g^t h_e^{\sigma_5})$, where $t = H(m \parallel sp \parallel pk_e \parallel e \parallel \sigma_3 \parallel \sigma_4)$. Then, the verifier sets $\mathscr{E} = \{k \mid E[k] = 1, k = 1, 2, \ldots, n_e\}$, $\mathscr{W} = \{l \mid W[l] = 1, l = 1, 2, \ldots, n_w\}$, and $\mathscr{W}' = \{i \mid W'[i] = 1, i = 1, 2, \ldots, n_w\}$, respectively. Finally, the equalities are checked as follows:

$$\hat{e}(\sigma_1, g) \stackrel{?}{=} \hat{e}(g_{e1}, g_{e2}) \hat{e}\left(v_e' \prod_{i \in \mathscr{W}'} v_{ei}, \sigma_4 \right),$$

$$\hat{e}(\sigma_2, g) \quad (11)$$

$$\stackrel{?}{=} \hat{e}(g_1, g_2) \hat{e}\left(e' \prod_{k \in \mathscr{E}} e_k, \sigma_3 \right) \hat{e}\left(w' \prod_{l \in \mathscr{W}} w_l, \sigma_4 \right).$$

Output 1 if the equations hold. Otherwise, output 0.

For simplicity, we may set $msk = \alpha_1$ and $sv_e = \beta_{e1}$ because the others called implicit master secret keys/secret values are not used during its execution. Here, they are explicitly listed to easily prove its security as follows.

4.3. Security Analysis. In this subsection, we introduce two lemmas to demonstrate that our scheme is strongly unforgeable against PKR attacks and MKGC attacks based on the CDH, DL and CRHF assumptions defined in Section 2.

Lemma 4. *Our scheme is strongly secure against PKR attacks launched by the attacker $\mathscr{A}_1$ assuming PIBS is weakly secure [3], the discrete log problem is intractable in $\mathbb{G}_1$, and finding concrete collisions is difficult in $\mathscr{H}$.*

Analysis. Given any PPT adversary $\mathscr{A}_1$ trying to break our CLS scheme in an adaptive chosen-message attack, we can forge a PPT adversary $\mathscr{B}_1$ producing a weak forgery on the *PIBS* scheme/solving discrete log in $\mathbb{G}_1$/finding concrete collision of $\mathscr{H}$. Moreover, to consistently answer $\mathscr{A}_1$'s queries, $\mathscr{B}_1$ keeps a table T which is initially empty in our security proofs.

Init. First, if $\mathscr{B}_1$ attempt to break the *PIBS* scheme, $\mathscr{B}_1$ randomly picks a number φ from $\mathbb{Z}_p^*$ and sets $h = g^\varphi$, else $\mathscr{B}_1$ directly picks a random value h from $\mathbb{G}_1$. Then, $\mathscr{B}_1$ chooses three hash functions H, H_e, and H_w from a classic hash family $\mathcal{H}$. Finally, $\mathcal{B}_1$ returns (PIBS.$params, h, H, H_e, H_w$) to $\mathcal{A}_1$ as the system parameters sp. Here, in order to make the initialization appropriate, we flip a coin to predict the forgery type launched by $\mathcal{A}_1$.

Queries. In the query phase, $\mathcal{B}_1$ responds to $\mathcal{A}_1$'s all queries defined in their security model as follows:

$\mathcal{O}^{psk}(e)$: $\mathcal{B}_1$ runs *PIBS.Extract* on $H_e(e)$ to obtain the partial secret key psk_e and returns it to $\mathcal{A}_1$.

$\mathcal{O}^{sk}(e)$: $\mathcal{B}_1$ searches T to find the entity e and get the entity secret value $sv_e = (\beta_{e1}, \beta_{e2}, \phi_e, z'_e, z_{e1}, z_{e2}, \ldots, z_{en_w})$. If it does not exist, $\mathcal{B}_1$ first picks $n_w + 4$ random values $(\beta_{e1}, \beta_{e2}, \phi_e, z'_e, z_{e1}, z_{e2}, \ldots, z_{en_w})$ from $\mathbb{Z}_p^*$ and stores them in T. Finally, $\mathcal{B}_1$ returns (sv_e, psk_e) to $\mathcal{A}_1$ as the secret key for e.

$\mathcal{O}^{pk}(e)$: $\mathcal{B}_1$ searches T to discover the entity e and returns $(g_{e1}, g_{e2}, v'_e, v_{e1}, \ldots, v_{en_w})$ to $\mathcal{A}_1$. Otherwise, $\mathcal{B}_1$ first picks $n_w + 4$ random values $(\beta_{e1}, \beta_{e2}, \phi_e, z'_e, z_{e1}, z_{e2}, \ldots, z_{en_w})$ from $\mathbb{Z}_p^*$ and then stores those values in L. At last, $(g^{\beta_{e1}}, g^{\beta_{e2}}, \phi_e, g^{z'_e}, g^{z_{e1}}, \ldots, g^{z_{en_w}})$ is returned to $\mathcal{A}_1$ as the entity public key.

$\mathcal{O}^{rep}(e, pk'_e)$: $\mathcal{B}_1$ searches T to find the entity e and update its public key using a new public key pk'_e. If it does not exist, $\mathcal{A}_1$ directly sets the entity public key to be pk'_e.

$\mathcal{O}^{sign}(e, m)$: for a signature of a message m on the entity public key pk_e,

(i) if $\mathcal{B}_1$ attempts to break *PIBS* by means of $\mathcal{A}_1$'s ability, $\mathcal{B}_1$ picks a random value λ from $\mathbb{Z}_p$ and runs *PIBS.Sign*$(H_e(e), H_m(g^\lambda))$ to produce $(\sigma'_1, \sigma'_2, \sigma'_3)$. Moreover, $\mathcal{B}_1$ computes $t = H(m \parallel sp \parallel pk_e \parallel e \parallel \sigma'_2 \parallel \sigma'_3)$ to recover $s = (\lambda - t)/\varphi$.

(ii) Otherwise, $\mathcal{B}_1$ invokes *PPKExt*$(H_e(e))$ to generate e's partial secret key (psk_{e1}, psk_{e2}). Then, $\mathcal{B}_1$ picks two random values r_w, s from $\mathbb{Z}_p$ and simulates *PIBS.Sign*$(H_e(e), H_w(g^t h^s))$ to produce $(\sigma'_1, \sigma'_2, \sigma'_3)$ where $t = H(m \parallel sp \parallel pk_e \parallel e \parallel \sigma'_2 \parallel \sigma'_3)$.

Next, $\mathcal{B}_1$ computes $W' = H_w(g^t h^s_e)$ and sets $\sigma_1 = g^{\beta_{e1}\beta_{e2}}(\sigma'_3)^{\sum_{i \in \mathscr{W}'} z_{ei}}$ where $\mathscr{W}' = \{i \mid W'[i] = 1, i = 1, 2, \ldots, n_w\}$. At last, $\mathcal{B}_1$ sets $\sigma = (\sigma_1, \sigma_2, \sigma_3, \sigma_4, \sigma_5) = (\sigma_1, \sigma'_1, \sigma'_2, \sigma'_3, s)$ and returns it to $\mathcal{A}_1$.

Forgery. If $\mathcal{A}_1$ outputs σ^* on m^* for e^* with pk_e^* such that

(i) $H_w(g^{t^*} h^{s^*}) \neq H_w(g^t h^s)$, $\mathcal{B}_1$ can succeed in breaking the *PIBS* scheme by forging a valid signature $(\sigma_2^*, \sigma_3^*, \sigma_4^*)$ on the message $H_w(g^{t^*} h^{s^*})$;

(ii) $H_w(g^{t^*} h^{s^*}) = H_w(g^t h^s)$ but $g^{t^*} h^{s^*} \neq g^t h^s$, $\mathcal{B}_1$ can succeed in finding a concrete collision to hash function H_w;

(iii) $g^{t^*} h^{s^*} = g^t h^s$ but $t^* \neq t$, $\mathcal{B}_1$ can succeed in solving the discrete logarithm problem by computing $d = (t - t^*)/(s^* - s)$;

(iv) $g^{t^*} h^{s^*} = g^t h^s$, $t^* = t$ but $m^* \parallel sp \parallel pk_e^* \parallel e^* \parallel \sigma_3^* \parallel \sigma_4^* \neq m \parallel sp \parallel pk_e \parallel e \parallel \sigma_3 \parallel \sigma_4$, $\mathcal{B}_1$ can succeed in finding a concrete collision to hash function H.

Here, s, t, and $m \parallel sp \parallel pk_e \parallel e \parallel \sigma_3 \parallel \sigma_4$ denote those elements queried/involved during the query phase.

Lemma 5. *Our scheme is strongly secure against MKGC attacks launched by $\mathcal{A}_2$ assuming BSW is strongly existential unforgeable.*

Analysis. Given a PPT adversary $\mathcal{A}_2$ breaking our CLS scheme in an adaptive chosen-message attack, we simulate a PPT adversary $\mathcal{B}_2$ producing a strong forgery on the *BSW* scheme. Moreover, to consistently answer $\mathcal{A}_2$'s queries, $\mathcal{B}_2$ keeps a table T which is initially empty in our security proofs.

Init. $\mathcal{B}_2$ invokes $\mathcal{A}_2$ to initialize the master secret key $msk = (\alpha_1, \alpha_2, \varphi, x', x_1, x_2, \ldots, x_{n_e}, y', y_1, y_2, \ldots, y_{n_w})$ and the system parameters $sp = (\mathbb{G}_1, \mathbb{G}_2, g, h, g_1, g_2, e', \vec{e}, w', \vec{w})$. Here, in order to launch MKGC attacks more easily, $\mathcal{A}_2$ is allowed to set some trapdoors during the initialization phase.

Queries. In the query phase, $\mathcal{B}_2$ responds to $\mathcal{A}_2$'s all queries involved in their security model as follows:

$\mathcal{O}^{sk}(e)$: $\mathcal{B}_2$ searches T to find the entity e and get the entity secret value $sv_e = (\beta_{e1}, \beta_{e2}, \phi_e, z'_e, z_{e1}, z_{e2}, \ldots, z_{en_w})$. If it does not exist, $\mathcal{B}_2$ first picks $n_w + 4$ random values $(\beta_{e1}, \beta_{e2}, \phi_e, z'_e, z_{e1}, z_{e2}, \ldots, z_{en_w})$ from $\mathbb{Z}_p^*$ and stores them in T. Finally, $\mathcal{B}_2$ returns (sv_e, psk_e) to $\mathcal{A}_2$ as the secret key for e.

$\mathcal{O}^{pk}(e)$: Analogously, $\mathcal{B}_2$ looks up T to find the entity e and returns $(g_{e1}, g_{e2}, v'_e, v_{e1}, \ldots, v_{en_w})$ to $\mathcal{A}_2$. If e is not found, $\mathcal{B}_2$ first picks $n_w + 4$ random elements $(\beta_{e1}, \beta_{e2}, \phi_e, z'_e, z_{e1}, z_{e2}, \ldots, z_{en_w})$ from $\mathbb{Z}_p^*$ and then stores those values in T. At last, $\mathcal{B}_2$ sets $g_{e1} = g^{\beta_{e1}}$, $g_{e2} = g^{\beta_{e2}}$, $h_e = \phi_e$, $v'_e = g^{z'_e}$, $v_{e1} = g^{z_{e1}}, \ldots, v_{en_w} = g^{z_{en_w}}$ and returns these elements to $\mathcal{A}_2$.

$\mathcal{O}^{rep}(e, pk'_e)$: $\mathcal{B}_2$ searches T to find the entity e and updates the entity public key using a new public key pk'_e. If it does not exist, $\mathcal{B}_2$ directly sets the entity public key to be pk'_e provided by $\mathcal{A}_2$.

$\mathcal{O}^{sign}(e, m)$: for a signature query on a message m under an entity e with the public key pk_e, $\mathcal{B}_2$ first invokes *PPKExt*$(H_e(e))$ to get the entity partial secret key psk_e and then runs *BSW.Sign*$(psk_e, m \parallel sp \parallel pk_e \parallel e \parallel psk_{e2})$ to generate $(\sigma'_1, \sigma'_2, \sigma'_3)$. Next, $\mathcal{B}_2$ computes $t = H(m \parallel sp \parallel pk_e \parallel e \parallel psk_{e2} \parallel \sigma'_2)$ and sets $\sigma_2 = psk_{e1}(\sigma'_2)^{\sum_{l \in \mathscr{W}} y_l}$, where $\mathscr{W} = \{l \mid W[l] = 1, l = 1, 2, \ldots, n_w\}$ and $W = H_w(g^t h^{\sigma'_3})$. At last, $\mathcal{B}_2$ sets $\sigma = (\sigma_1, \sigma_2, \sigma_3, \sigma_4, \sigma_5) = (\sigma'_1, \sigma_2, D_2, \sigma'_2, \sigma'_3)$ and returns it to $\mathcal{A}_2$.

Forgery. If $\mathcal{A}_2$ eventually returns $\sigma^* = (\sigma_1^*, \sigma_2^*, \sigma_3^*, \sigma_4^*, \sigma_5^*)$ for m^* under e^* with pk_e^*, $\mathcal{B}_1$ can succeed in breaking the *BSW* scheme by forging a valid signature $(\sigma_1^*, \sigma_4^*, \sigma_5^*)$ on the message $H_e(g^{t^*} h^{s^*}_e)$ where $t^* = H(m^* \parallel sp \parallel pk_e^* \parallel e^* \parallel \sigma_3^* \parallel$

σ_4^*). Note that H and H_e are two types of classic hash in the *BSW* scheme.

In general, we demonstrate that our CLS scheme is strongly unforgeable against PKR attacks and MKGC attacks in the standard model by combining Lemmas 4 and 5.

4.4. Discussion. Although our scheme has more parameters compared with the existing schemes, it not only overcomes the weakness of those previous schemes but also is proven to be secure under our stronger security model. In Lemma 5, the KGC can set some trapdoors in the system parameters adaptively rather than passively receiving the master secret key and the corresponding public parameters from the challenger like in the previous schemes, which is consistent with the actual situation in a concrete scheme. To the best of our knowledge, we are the first to prove a CLS scheme to be strongly secure against the MKGC attacks without random oracles.

5. Conclusion

In this paper, we firstly showed that Hung et al.'s scheme cannot meet the requirements of strong unforgeability as they claimed. Then, we pointed out that their construction does not withstand the MKGC attacks and gave a concrete forgery to break it. Finally, we constructed an improved strongly unforgeable certificateless signature scheme and proved its security under the MKGC attacks in the standard model.

Acknowledgments

This work was supported by National Science Foundation of China (Grants nos. 61373158, 61472165, 61732021, and 61702222), Guangdong Provincial Engineering Technology Research Center on Network Security Detection and Defence (Grant no. 2014B090904067), Guangdong Provincial Special Funds for Applied Technology Research and Development and Transformation of Important Scientific and Technological Achieve (Grant no. 2016B010124009), Guangzhou Key Laboratory of Data Security and Privacy Preserving, and Guangdong Key Laboratory of Data Security and Privacy Preserving.

References

[1] A. Shamir, "Identity-based cryptosystems and signature schemes," in *Proceedings of the 4th International Conference on the Theory and Application of Cryptographic Techniques (CRYPTO '84)*, pp. 47–53, Santa Barbara, Calif, USA, 1987.

[2] D. Boneh and M. Franklin, "Identity-based encryption from the Weil pairing," in *Advances in Cryptology—CRYPTO 2001*, vol. 2139 of *Lecture Notes in Computer Science*, pp. 213–229, 2001.

[3] K. G. Paterson and J. C. N. Schuldt, "Efficient identity-based signatures secure in the standard model," in *Information Security and Privacy*, vol. 4058 of *Lecture Notes in Computer Science*, pp. 207–222, 2006.

[4] C. Sato, T. Okamoto, and E. Okamoto, "Strongly unforgeable ID-based signatures without random oracles," *International Journal of Applied Cryptography*, vol. 2, no. 1, pp. 35–45, 2010.

[5] S. S. Al-Riyami and K. G. Paterson, "Certificateless public key cryptography," in *Advances in Cryptology-ASIACRYPT*, vol. 2894 of *Lecture Notes in Computer Science*, pp. 452–473, Springer, 2003.

[6] M. H. Au, J. Chen, J. K. Liu, Y. Mu, D. S. Wong, and G. Yang, "Malicious KGC attacks in certificateless cryptography," in *Proceedings of the 2nd ACM Symposium on Information, Computer and Communications Security (ASIACCS '07)*, pp. 302–311, Singapore, Singapore, March 2007.

[7] D. H. Yum and P. J. Lee, "Generic construction of certificateless signature," in *Information Security and Privacy*, vol. 3108 of *Lecture Notes in Computer Science*, pp. 200–211, 2004.

[8] W. Yap, S. Heng, and B. Goi, "An Efficient Certificateless Signature Scheme," in *Emerging Directions in Embedded and Ubiquitous Computing*, vol. 4097 of *Lecture Notes in Computer Science*, pp. 322–331, 2006.

[9] Z. Zhang, D. S. Wong, J. Xu, and D. Feng, "Certificateless public-key signature: security model and efficient construction," in *Applied Cryptography and Network Security*, vol. 3989 of *Lecture Notes in Computer Science*, pp. 293–308, 2006.

[10] W. Yap, S. S. M. Chow, S. Heng, and B. Goi, "Security mediated certificateless signatures," in *Proceedings of the 5th International Conference on Applied Cryptography and Network Security (ACNS '07)*, pp. 459–477, Zhuhai, China.

[11] X. Huang, Y. Mu, W. Susilo, D. S. Wong, and W. Wu, "Certificateless signature revisited," in *Proceedings of the 12th Australasian Conference on Information Security and Privacy (ACISP '07)*, pp. 308–322, Townsville, Australia, 2007.

[12] S. Chang, D. S. Wong, Y. Mu, and Z. Zhang, "Certificateless threshold ring signature," *Information Sciences*, vol. 179, no. 20, pp. 3685–3696, 2009.

[13] Z. Wan, J. Weng, and J. Li, "Security mediated certificateless signatures without pairing," *Journal of Computers*, vol. 5, no. 12, pp. 1862–1869, 2010.

[14] R. Canetti, O. Goldreich, and S. Halevi, "The random oracle methodology, revisited," *Journal of the ACM*, vol. 51, no. 4, pp. 557–594, 2004.

[15] J. K. Liu, M. H. Au, and W. Susilo, "Self-generated-certificate public key cryptography and certificateless signature/encryption scheme in the standard model," *ACR Cryptology ePrint Archive*, vol. 2006, article 373, 2006.

[16] H. Xiong, Z. Qin, and F. Li, "An improved certificateless signature scheme secure in the standard model," *Fundamenta Informaticae*, vol. 88, no. 1-2, pp. 193–206, 2008.

[17] Y. Yuan, D. Li, L. Tian, and H. Zhu, "Certificateless signature scheme without random oracles," in *Proceedings of the 3rd International Conference and Workshops on Advances in Information Security and Assurance (ISA '09)*, pp. 31–40, 2009.

[18] Y. Yu, Y. Mu, G. Wang, Q. Xia, and B. Yang, "Improved certificateless signature scheme provably secure in the standard model," *IET Information Security*, vol. 6, no. 2, pp. 102–110, 2012.

[19] Y. Yuan and C. Wang, "Certificateless signature scheme with security enhanced in the standard model," *Information Processing Letters*, vol. 114, no. 9, pp. 492–499, 2014.

[20] L. Cheng and Q. Wen, "Provably secure and efficient certificateless signatur in the standard model," *International Journal of Information and Communication Technology*, vol. 7, no. 2-3, pp. 287–301, 2015.

[21] Y.-H. Hung, S.-S. Huang, Y.-M. Tseng, and T.-T. Tsai, "Certificateless signature with strong unforgeability in the standard

model," *Informatica*, vol. 26, no. 4, pp. 663–684, 2016.

[22] L. Pang, Y. Hu, Y. Liu, K. Xu, and H. Li, "Efficient and secure certificateless signature scheme in the standard model," *International Journal of Communication Systems*, vol. 30, no. 5, Article ID e3041, 2017.

[23] S. Canard and V. C. Trinh, "An Efficient Certificateless Signature Scheme in the Standard Model," in *The Journal of Information System Security*, vol. 10063 of *Lecture Notes in Computer Science*, pp. 175–192, 2016.

[24] D. Boneh, E. Shen, and B. Waters, "Strongly unforgeable signatures based on computational Diffie-Hellman," in *Public Key Cryptography—PKC 2006*, vol. 3958 of *Lecture Notes in Computer Science*, pp. 229–240, Springer, Berlin, Germany, 2006.

Digital Implementation of an Improved LTE Stream Cipher Snow-3G Based on Hyperchaotic PRNG

Mahdi Madani,[1,2] **Ilyas Benkhaddra,**[2] **Camel Tanougast,**[2] **Salim Chitroub,**[1] **and Loic Sieler**[2]

[1]*LISIC Laboratory, Electronics and Computer Science Faculty, University of Science and Technology of Houari Boumediene (USTHB), Algiers, Algeria*
[2]*LCOMS, Universite de Lorraine, Metz, France*

Correspondence should be addressed to Mahdi Madani; mmadani49@gmail.com

Academic Editor: Angel M. Del Rey

SNOW-3G is a stream cipher used by the 3GPP standards as the core part of the confidentiality and integrity algorithms for UMTS and LTE networks. This paper proposes an enhancement of the regular SNOW-3G ciphering algorithm based on HC-PRNG. The proposed cipher scheme is based on hyperchaotic generator which is used as an additional layer to the SNOW-3G architecture to improve the randomness of its output keystream. The objective of this work is to achieve a high security strength of the regular SNOW-3G algorithm while maintaining its standardized properties. The originality of this new scheme is that it provides a good trade-off between good randomness properties, performance, and hardware resources. Numerical simulations, hardware digital implementation, and experimental results using Xilinx FPGA Virtex technology have demonstrated the feasibility and the efficiency of our secure solution while promising technique can be applied to secure the new generation mobile standards. Thorough analysis of statistical randomness is carried out demonstrating the improved statistical randomness properties of the new scheme compared to the standard SNOW-3G, while preserving its resistance against cryptanalytic attacks.

1. Introduction

Nowadays, the security of communications becomes more and more important to meet the demand for real-time secure data transmission over the open networks [1]. Indeed, in our modern life, all our daily transactions and communications are more made over mobile networks. The Universal Mobile Telecommunications System (UMTS) [2], Long Term Evolution (LTE), and LTE-advanced standards are the 3rd- and 4th-generation mobile networks that enable mobile migrations of Internet applications like Voice over IP (VoIP), video streaming, music downloading, mobile TV, and so on. The security of these mobile standards is based principally on the SNOW-3G stream cipher [3] which is considered as the kernel of the 128-EEA1 confidentiality and 128-EIA1 integrity algorithms of the 4G LTE security [4] replacing the f8 and f9 algorithms of UMTS security [5, 6]. Thereafter, the Third-Generation Partnership Project (3GPP) has already standardized two other kernel algorithms for LTE confidentiality and integrity protection [7]. These algorithms

are the Advanced Encryption Standard (AES) in its CounTeR mode (CTR mode) [8] which is composed of 10 rounds processing essentially on the Substitution-Diffusion Network (SDN) principle [9] and the ZUC stream cipher specifically designed for use in China [10, 11].

However, AES algorithm has a long computational time [12]; ZUC stream cipher is recently designed and requires more security analysis to prove its robustness and efficiency [13]. However, several analyses have proved that SNOW-3G encryption algorithm is weak. In particular, improvements to guard against the following:

(i) The short keystream data set attack: this attack discovers a weakness in the initialization process of SNOW-3G stream cipher when 8 from the 15 NIST (National Institute of Standards and Technology) tests fail the short keystream data set test [14].

(ii) The improved Heuristic Guess and Determine (IHGD) attack which reduces the complexity from $O(2^{320})$ to $O(2^{160})$ and the size of guessed basis from

10 to 5: this attack exploits the weakness of main linear feedback polynomials of the cipher [15].

(iii) The fault attack which recovers the secret key with only 22 fault injections on the Linear Feedback Shift Register (LFSR): the attack model assumes that the attacker is able to modify a 32-bit value of one state of the LFSR (S_i^t) during the keystream generation, where i is chosen by the attacker, but he has no full control about t [16].

(iv) The cache-timing attack which is capable of recovering the full cipher state from empirical timing data in a matter of seconds: the attack exploits the cipher using the output from a S-box as input to another S-box [17].

(v) The multiset collision attack on reduced-round: this attack analyzes the resynchronization mechanism of SNOW-3G using multiset collision attacks. This technique has proved itself useful against AES [18]. This technique can be applied to SNOW-3G since its Finite State Machine (FSM) is essentially a 96-bit AES-like cipher in which the LFSR plays a role of a key-schedule. This attack is complicated by the fact that there is a feedback from the FSM to the LFSR during the setup phase (a feature never present in block ciphers) and the attacker sees only 32 bits of output at a time, while the internal state keeps changing constantly [19].

(vi) The sliding property attack of stream ciphers: this attack is used to find sets of related keys. This attack is applicable due to the nature of the initialization process of SNOW-3G; such related keys do not generate slid keystreams, but only keystreams that have several equal words. However, this still allows distinguishing the produced keystream from random keystreams [20].

Consequently, we remark that the majority of the cited attacks exploit mainly the weakness of the initialization process based on the LFSR polynomials and the FSM S-box. Therefore, we can not improve all the cited weaknesses, but we focus in this paper on the improvement of the statistical properties analyzed in [14], and we propose updating the SNOW-3G stream cipher in order to enhance its robustness and being able to resist against new cryptanalysis attacks based on the considered weaknesses.

During the last decade, the use of chaos to design digital chaotic stream ciphers has become a part of cryptography and very important topic of research [21]. With regard to the characteristics of a chaotic dynamical system these are as follows: a deterministic system, ergodic, sensitive to initial conditions and control parameters, and having a random-like behaviour. In addition, these characteristics are related to confusion and diffusion concepts usually used in traditional cryptosystems which allow the application of chaos in cryptography. Considering the possibility for the self-synchronization of chaotic systems, this concept has become a focal topic for research [22]. Therefore, several schemes have been developed to exploit this property of chaotic systems

for secure communications. Encryption based chaos has been suggested as a new and efficient way to deal with the problem of fast and highly secure mobile communications. Similarly, several works are proposed to exploit the hyperchaotic (HC) systems providing the nonlinearity and the good randomness. Among them, we can cite the *Rössler*'s hyperchaotic systems [23, 24], *Chen*'s hyperchaotic systems [25, 26], *Lu*'s hyperchaotic system [27], and *Lorenz*'s hyperchaotic systems [28–30].

This paper proposes a new architecture which combines the regular SNOW-3G cipher with a Hyperchaotic Pseudo-Random Number Generator (HC-PRNG) in order to design a hyperchaotic SNOW-3G stream cipher providing good randomness, infinite period, and unpredictability on long term while increasing the complexity of a cryptanalysis attack from the weakness in the initialization mode of the regular SNOW-3G cipher [14]. The considered HC-PRNG is based on a four-dimensional (4D) Lorenz's chaotic system which is used as an additional layer to the regular SNOW-3G while maintaining its standard properties. Contrariwise of the previous simulated system adding one simple linear chaotic map with the FSM layer of the regular SNOW-3G algorithm [31], we propose an enhancement of initialization process and complexity and randomness of output keystream. The main purpose of this added layer is the perturbation of both the digital LFSR sequences and the FSM output. Thus, we suggest this hyperchaotic perturbation technique to investigate the encryption efficiency of LFSR based stream cipher. Consequently, the proposed architecture has the following features. First, the structure of the stream generator key is more complex having a number of variables and parameters, and the time sequence of output is nonrule and not predictable. Thereby, a large key space is provided for use as seed keys of cipher sequences. Second, the standardized core of SNOW-3G stream cipher is respected in order to facilitate the integration of our approach in the current and future mobile communication networks. Moreover, the considered system is irreversible and unpredictable and it may be extended to many other (4D) continuous chaotic systems while being suitable for digital implementation. Considering the numerical resolution of nonlinear differential equations to get a digital implementation, our proposed approach has been designed and verified using a VHDL (VHSIC Hardware Description Language) description with a fixed-point representation of all data on 48 bits leading to a successful hardware implementation targeted to FPGA technology (Field-Programmable Gate Array). The obtained implementation results provide good performance in terms of hardware area and throughput. Finally, the sturdiness of our proposed architecture has been tested using security analyses and statistical tests. Consequently, the experimental results presented in this paper prove that the added HC generator enhances the randomness and robustness of SNOW-3G algorithm against different analyses and statistical attacks.

The rest of this paper is organized as follows. Section 2 briefly reminds the reader with the architecture of the regular SNOW-3G stream cipher. Section 3 details the processing steps and architecture of the enhanced SNOW-3G stream cipher including a Lorenz's HC generator as PRNG to perturb

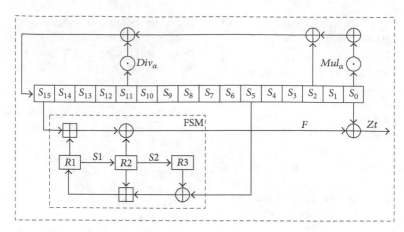

FIGURE 1: Architecture of the regular SNOW-3G stream cipher.

the digital output of the regular SNOW-3G stream cipher. The digital implementation results on Virtex-5 Xilinx FPGA technology and evaluations are presented in Section 4. In this section, the performance and architectural simulations prove the feasibility and the efficiency of our proposed HC SNOW-3G stream cipher. In Section 5, the robustness of our new scheme is evaluated through three security analyses: exhaustive key search, key sensitivity, and statistical tests to prove that the proposed HC SNOW-3G stream cipher resists against cryptanalysis attacks and exhibits truly random sequences suitable as cipher keys for the data encryption compared to the regular SNOW-3G cipher. Finally, Section 6 concludes this paper.

2. Regular SNOW-3G Algorithm

The SNOW-3G is a cryptographic algorithm which was originally designed as the kernel of the UMTS confidentiality and integrity functions f8 and f9 [5], respectively. After that, it has been kept as the first kernel algorithm for the LTE security functions 128-EEA1 and 128-EIA1, respectively [3, 4]. SNOW-3G is a stream cipher that generates 32-bit word keystream under the control of the 128-bit Ciphering Key (CK) and 128-bit Initialization Vector (IV). It is divided into two interacting layers. The first layer is the LFSR layer which is formed by 16 stages of 32 bits each $(S_0, S_1, \ldots, S_{15})$. The second one is the FSM layer which is formed by three registers ($R1$, $R2$, and $R3$) of 32 bits each. The detailed architecture of the SNOW-3G stream cipher is illustrated in Figure 1, where $\oplus$ represents bitwise XOR operation and $\boxplus$ is adder arithmetic operator. Considering that the regular SNOW-3G can not offer robustness against short keystream data set attacks [14], we propose enhancing its statistical properties and security level by overcoming its weaknesses through an additional layer updating the initialization and keystream modes while keeping its standard.

3. Enhanced SNOW-3G Algorithm Based on HC-PRNG

In this section, we present our designed scheme to enforce the confidentiality and integrity protection for LTE and

new generations of mobile standards. We propose adding a HC-PRNG as an additional layer to the regular SNOW-3G architecture which is based on the LFSR and FSM layers. The HC-PRNG is added to the regular SNOW-3G architecture to consolidate the complexity of the regular SNOW-3G stream cipher in order to improve the randomness of the output keystream and to ameliorate the LFSR initialization based on the perturbation effect. More precisely, the HC-PRNG output is mixed with the feedback value of the LFSR layer during the initialization process (see Figure 2), or mixed with the FSM output F and with the register S_0 during the keystream generation process (more details in Section 3.4). Finally, a specific HC SNOW-3G stream cipher is obtained. Figures 2 and 6 depict the considered enhanced architecture. The layers forming the HC SNOW-3G architecture are detailed in the following subsections.

3.1. LFSR Layer. As with the regular SNOW-3G, this layer is formed by 16 stages of 32 bits each $(S_0, S_1, \ldots, S_{15})$ (see Figures 1 and 2). The associated feedback is defined by a primitive polynomial over the finite Galois field GF(2^{32}) using bitwise XOR operations and the well-known Mul_α and Div_α main functions [3]. The LFSR component is clocked in two operating modes described as follows.

Initialization Mode. In this mode, the LFSR is performed by using three stage registers S_0, S_2, and S_{11} and one 32-bit word called F which is the output value of the FSM layer. First, the two 32-bit stage registers S_0 and S_{11} are divided into four bytes as follows:

$$S_0 = S_{0,0} \parallel S_{0,1} \parallel S_{0,2} \parallel S_{0,3},$$
$$S_{11} = S_{11,0} \parallel S_{11,1} \parallel S_{11,2} \parallel S_{11,3}, \tag{1}$$

where $\parallel$ is the concatenation operation. In this division step, the feedback value v is calculated by

$$v = \left(S_{0,1} \parallel S_{0,2} \parallel S_{0,3} \parallel 0x00\right) \oplus Mul_\alpha\left(S_{0,0}\right) \oplus S_2$$
$$\oplus \left(0x00 \parallel S_{11,0} \parallel S_{11,1} \parallel S_{11,2}\right) \oplus Div_\alpha\left(S_{11,3}\right) \oplus F. \tag{2}$$

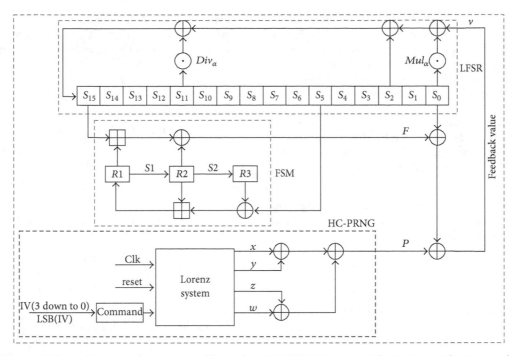

FIGURE 2: The architecture of our proposed hyperchaotic SNOW-3G stream cipher in its initialization mode.

This feedback value sets the S_{15} stage register ($S_{15} = v$) and the contents of the other stage registers are shifted as follows:

$$S_{14} = S_{15}, S_{13} = S_{14}, \ldots, S_1 = S_2, S_0 = S_1. \quad (3)$$

Keystream Mode. In this mode, the main difference with the initialization mode is that the feedback value v is calculated without using the 32-bit word F and by

$$v = (S_{0,1} \parallel S_{0,2} \parallel S_{0,3} \parallel 0x00) \oplus Mul_\alpha (S_{0,0}) \oplus S_2$$
$$\oplus (0x00 \parallel S_{11,0} \parallel S_{11,1} \parallel S_{11,2}) \oplus Div_\alpha (S_{11,3}). \quad (4)$$

All the other steps are similar to the initialization mode.

3.2. FSM Layer.

As with the regular SNOW-3G, the FSM layer is formed by three registers $R1$, $R2$, and $R3$ of 32 bits each (see Figures 1 and 2). To generate a 32-bit output keystream word named F, this component uses two substitution boxes $S1$ and $S2$, one linear bitwise XOR operation, and one nonlinear integer modulo 2^{32} adder [3]. The FSM is clocked by using two inputs provided by the two registers S_5 and S_{15} arising from the previous LFSR component (see Figure 1). Therefore, F can be expressed by

$$F = (S_{15} \boxplus R1) \oplus R2. \quad (5)$$

Thereby, an intermediate value r is calculated to set the three registers $R1$, $R2$, and $R3$ at each clock cycle as defined by

$$r = R2 \boxplus (R3 \oplus S_5),$$
$$R3 = S_2 (R2),$$

$$R2 = S_1 (R1),$$
$$R1 = r. \quad (6)$$

3.3. HC-PRNG Layer.

The added HC-PRNG layer is performed by a nonlinear dynamic generator which is very sensitive to initial conditions and presents high recurrences (see Figure 2). This system can be used in cryptography to replace the PRNG. A cryptosystem based on this HC-PRNG consists of using a chaotic nonlinear oscillator as a pseudo-random signal generator which is combined with the message before transmission. At the reception, the similar chaotic oscillator is used in order to regenerate the pseudo-random signal which is combined with the received signal through the inverse operation and in order to recover the original message [32]. Moreover, the added HC-PRNG layer must be synchronized between the emitter and the receiver to ensure encryption/decryption process like any chaotic or HC system. To realize our HC-PRNG, we have implemented the Lorenz HC system which is generated by deriving the generalized Lorenz quadratic controller system (4D) by providing a hyperchaotic behaviour. It is a four-dimensional dynamical controlled system which is characterized by the following [33]:

$$\dot{x} = a (y - x),$$
$$\dot{y} = cx - xz - y + w,$$
$$\dot{z} = xy - bz,$$
$$\dot{w} = -dx, \quad (7)$$

where a, b, c, and d are the control parameters. Note that a, b, c, and d are >0, and usually $a = 10$, $b = 8/3$, $d = 5$, and c is varied. The system exhibits one hyperchaotic behaviour for $c = 28$. The initial conditions are set as $x_0 = y_0 = z_0 = w_0 = -10$. The two principal requisites presented below must be considered to obtain hyperchaos behaviour:

(1) The minimal dimension of the phase space that embeds a HC attractor should be at least four, which requires the minimum number of coupled first-order autonomous ordinary differential equations to be four.

(2) The number of terms in the coupled equations giving rise to instability should be at least two, of which at least one should have a nonlinear function [34].

For resolving (7), we use the Runge-Kutta fourth-order resolution method (RK-4 method) [35, 36]. We present a brief review of this method.

For example, a nonlinear system is defined by

$$
\begin{aligned}
\dot{x} &= F(x, y, z, w), \\
\dot{y} &= G(x, y, z, w), \\
\dot{z} &= Q(x, y, z, w), \\
\dot{w} &= U(x, y, z, w).
\end{aligned}
\tag{8}
$$

Note that $x(t0) = x_0$, $y(t0) = y_0$, $z(t0) = z_0$, and $w(t0) = w_0$, where F, G, Q, and U are nonlinear functions. At each iteration $n + 1$, RK-4 uses four intermediate values from the iteration n. Then, (9) is used to solve (8):

$$
\begin{aligned}
x_{n+1} &= x_n + \frac{h}{6}(k_0 + 2k_1 + 2k_2 + k_3), \\
y_{n+1} &= y_n + \frac{h}{6}(m_0 + 2m_1 + 2m_2 + m_3), \\
z_{n+1} &= z_n + \frac{h}{6}(n_0 + 2n_1 + 2n_2 + n_3), \\
w_{n+1} &= w_n + \frac{h}{6}(p_0 + 2p_1 + 2p_2 + p_3).
\end{aligned}
\tag{9}
$$

Note that h is the integration step (interval). For each integration step h, four increments are defined for each function (x, y, z, and w): first increment at the beginning, then two increments at the midpoint, and a last increment at the end of the interval h, as follows.

When $t = t_0$, the first increment values are defined based on the slope at the beginning of the interval, as follows:

$$
\begin{aligned}
k_0 &= F(t_n, x_n), \\
m_0 &= G(t_n, y_n), \\
n_0 &= Q(t_n, z_n), \\
p_0 &= U(t_n, w_n)
\end{aligned}
\tag{10}
$$

and when $t = t + h/2$, the second increment values are defined based on the slope at the midpoint of the interval, using previous values (k_0, m_0, n_0, and p_0), as follows:

$$
\begin{aligned}
k_1 &= F\left(t_n + \frac{h}{2}, x_n + \frac{h}{2}k_0\right), \\
m_1 &= G\left(t_n + \frac{h}{2}, y_n + \frac{h}{2}m_0\right), \\
n_1 &= Q\left(t_n + \frac{h}{2}, z_n + \frac{h}{2}n_0\right), \\
p_1 &= U\left(t_n + \frac{h}{2}, w_n + \frac{h}{2}p_0\right)
\end{aligned}
\tag{11}
$$

and when $t = t + h/2$, the third increment values are defined based on the slope at the midpoint of the interval, using previous values (k_1, m_1, n_1, and p_1), as follows:

$$
\begin{aligned}
k_2 &= F\left(t_n + \frac{h}{2}, x_n + \frac{h}{2}k_1\right), \\
m_2 &= G\left(t_n + \frac{h}{2}, y_n + \frac{h}{2}m_1\right), \\
n_2 &= Q\left(t_n + \frac{h}{2}, z_n + \frac{h}{2}n_1\right), \\
p_2 &= U\left(t_n + \frac{h}{2}, w_n + \frac{h}{2}p_1\right)
\end{aligned}
\tag{12}
$$

and when $t = t + h$, the fourth increment values are defined based on the slope at the end of the interval, using previous values (k_2, m_2, n_2, and p_2), as follows:

$$
\begin{aligned}
k_3 &= F(t_n + h, x_n + hk_2), \\
m_3 &= G(t_n + h, y_n + hm_2), \\
n_3 &= Q(t_n + h, z_n + hn_2), \\
p_3 &= U(t_n + h, w_n + hp_2).
\end{aligned}
\tag{13}
$$

Mentioning that HC signals are real, we used the fixed-point format of 48 bits as 16Q32. The real part is encoded on 16 bits and the decimal part is encoded on 32 bits. The used arithmetic fixed-point allows achieving a good compromise between performance and cost. Equation set (8) is simulated in MATLAB platform using the numerical tool RK-4, and the results are illustrated in Figures 3 and 4. A good randomness is obtained in random HC signals (decimal part) as shown in Figure 3(b) compared to the HC signals (real and decimal parts) as shown in Figure 3(a). Similarly, the Lorenz attractor formed by the random HC signals (decimal part) and given in Figure 4(b) presents more randomness compared to the attractor obtained by the HC signals (real and decimal parts) and given in Figure 4(a). Thereafter, we used only the decimal part of hyperchaotic signals encoded on 32 bits as random perturbation signals.

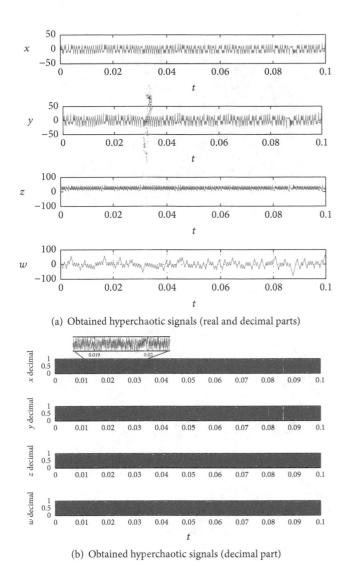

(a) Obtained hyperchaotic signals (real and decimal parts)

(b) Obtained hyperchaotic signals (decimal part)

FIGURE 3: Simulation results of the considered Lorenz hyperchaotic system.

3.3.1. Digital Implementation of the Proposed HC-PRNG. To realize the HC-PRNG component, we opt for a hardware behaviour description based on Moore's Finite State Machine [35]. This FSM system describes the numerical resolution based on Runge-Kutta method performing (7). Thereby, the RK-4 method is implemented in digital way suitable for FPGA using the FSM system coded in VHDL language and detailed in Figure 5. This figure describes the FSM system corresponding to the internal states of the HC-PRNG layer. A detailed description at each state of the FSM system is presented as follows.

State_1. It is the initialization state. All outputs are set to zero and the state variables are initialized with the initial conditions ($x_0 = y_0 = z_0 = w_0 = -10$).

State_2. In this state, we compute k_0, m_0, n_0, and p_0 and the intermediate points x_{n1}, y_{n1}, z_{n1}, and w_{n1}. RK4 signal is always set to zero. At the next rising edge of clock signal, it jumps to the next state without any condition.

State_3. The values of the intermediate points x_{n1}, y_{n1}, z_{n1}, and w_{n1} are used to update the variables α, β, γ, and δ, respectively. At the next rising edge of clock signal, it jumps to the next state without any condition.

State_4. In this state, we compute the initial slopes k_1, m_1, n_1, and p_1 and the intermediate points x_{n2}, y_{n2}, z_{n2}, and w_{n2}, respectively. RK4 signal is always set to zero. At the next rising edge of clock signal, it jumps to the next state without any condition.

State_5. The values of the intermediate points calculated in state_4 are used to update the variables α, β, γ, and δ. At the next rising edge of clock signal, it jumps to the next state without any condition.

State_6. In this state, we compute the initial slopes k_2, m_2, n_2, and p_2 and the intermediate points x_{n3}, y_{n3}, z_{n3}, and w_{n3}, respectively. RK4 signal is always set to zero. At the next rising edge of clock signal, it jumps to the next state without any condition.

State_7. The values of the intermediate points calculated in state_6 are used to update the variables α, β, γ, and δ. At the next rising edge of clock signal, it jumps to the next state without any condition.

State_8. In this state, the HC solutions x, y, z, and w of (8) are calculated, and the RK4 signal is set to one to indicate the end of the process. At the next rising edge of clock signal, it jumps to state_end without any condition.

State_End. It is the last state of the FSM, the first chaotic key values x, y, z, and w are generated to perturb SNOW-3G, and they are also used to update the variables α, β, γ, and δ, respectively, for the next chaotic key calculation. At the next rising edge of clock signal, if $Cp < N$, then it jumps to state_2 to start new generation key cycle. But if $Cp = N$, which indicates that all the required keys are generated, the FSM jumps to state_1 to wait a new order of N keystream generation. Cp is a command to control the end of output keystreams and N is the number of keystreams to be generated.

3.4. Keystream Generation. To ensure the synchronization of the enhanced SNOW-3G stream cipher parts, all its components are ordered by the same clock and reset signals. Thereby, two main 128-bit inputs CK and IV are loaded to the LFSR stages before starting the process. And then the algorithm is performed according to two operating modes (initialization and keystream modes) depending on the LFSR mode. The perturbation of the LFSR and FSM layers is ordered by a specific block command which defines the starting of perturbation (see Figures 2 and 6). This block provides one perturbation command which is defined by the 4 Least Significant Bits (LSB) of the Initial Vector (LSB(IV) = IV[3 down to 0]). The keystream generator is performed from the following processing steps.

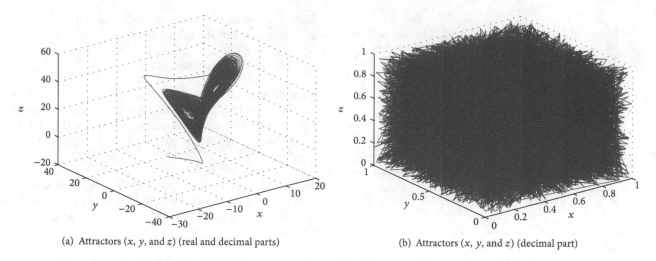

(a) Attractors (x, y, and z) (real and decimal parts)

(b) Attractors (x, y, and z) (decimal part)

FIGURE 4: Obtained attractors of the proposed Lorenz hyperchaotic system.

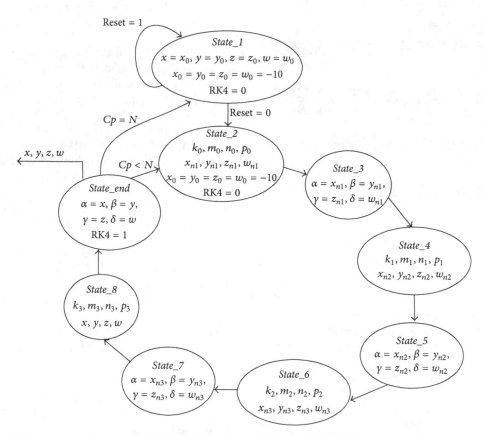

FIGURE 5: Description of the FSM system performing the RK-4 resolution of Lorenz's HC generator.

Key Loading. This step is performed before the initialization mode. First, it begins by dividing each of the two 128-bit input words CK and IV into 32-bit words as follows:

$$\text{IV} = \text{IV0} \parallel \text{IV1} \parallel \text{IV2} \parallel \text{IV3},$$

$$K = K0 \parallel K1 \parallel K2 \parallel K3. \tag{14}$$

Then, the 16 LFSR stage registers are loaded by the formed 32-bit words as follows:

$$S_{15} = K3 \oplus \text{IV0},$$

$$S_{14} = K2,$$

$$S_{13} = K1,$$

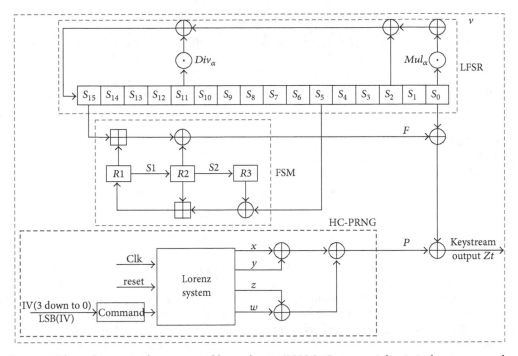

FIGURE 6: The architecture of our proposed hyperchaotic SNOW-3G stream cipher in its keystream mode.

$$S_{12} = K0 \oplus IV1,$$

$$S_{11} = K3 \oplus 1,$$

$$S_{10} = K2 \oplus 1 \oplus IV2,$$

$$S_9 = K1 \oplus 1 \oplus IV3,$$

$$S_8 = K0 \oplus 1,$$

$$S_7 = K3,$$

$$S_6 = K2,$$

$$S_5 = K1,$$

$$S_4 = K0,$$

$$S_3 = K3 \oplus 1,$$

$$S_2 = K2 \oplus 1,$$

$$S_1 = K1 \oplus 1,$$

$$S_0 = K0 \oplus 1.$$

$$(15)$$

In parallel of this key loading step, the HC-PRNG layer command is initialized by the IV as follows:

$$Command = IV (3 \; downto \; 0). \tag{16}$$

Initialization Mode. When the key loading process is completed, the FSM layer is executed using S_{15} and S_5 stage registers from LFSR layer to generate a 32-bit output word F expressed by (5). The registers of the FSM layer are set to

zero ($R1 = R2 = R3 = 0$) before computing F. At the same time, the HC-PRNG is executed to produce the 32-bit word P perturbation signal. After waiting n clock cycles, P is mixed with F by a bitwise XOR operator in order to perturb the LFSR updating. Consequently, the new feedback value is calculated from the following equation:

$$v = (S_{0,1} \| S_{0,2} \| S_{0,3} \| 0x00) \oplus Mul_\alpha (S_{0,0}) \oplus S_2$$

$$\oplus (0x00 \| S_{11,0} \| S_{11,1} \| S_{11,2}) \oplus Div_\alpha (S_{11,3}) \oplus F \tag{17}$$

$$\oplus P.$$

The number of clock cycles is defined by $n = 0, 1, \ldots, 15$, corresponding to the value contained in *Command* which depends on IV. The 16 LFSR stage registers are updated as follows:

$$S_{15} = v, S_{14} = S_{15}, S_{13} = S_{14}, \ldots, S_1 = S_2, S_0 = S_1. \tag{18}$$

The FSM and HC-PRNG layers run in the initialization mode 32 clock cycles, producing the two 32-bit words F and P, which are used by the LFSR feedback value as defined in (17). Note that the initialization mode does not produce any output keystream Zt. The detailed architecture of the proposed HC SNOW-3G stream cipher in its initialization mode is given in Figure 2.

Keystream Mode. At the end of initialization mode, the FSM is performed during one clock cycle, and the associated output word Zt is discarded. Then, the LFSR feedback value is calculated by (4), and the 16 stage registers are updated as follows:

$$S_{15} = v, S_{14} = S_{15}, S_{13} = S_{14}, \ldots, S_1 = S_2, S_0 = S_1. \tag{19}$$

TABLE 1: FPGA implementation results and comparison.

Resource	HC SNOW-3G (proposed)	Regular SNOW-3G	PLCM SNOW-3G [31]
Device	Virtex XC5vfx70t-1ff1136	Virtex XC5vfx70t-1ff1136	Virtex XC5vfx70t-1ff1136
Number of slice registers	2391	912	1131
Number of slice LUTs	7881	1108	2495
Number of fully used LUT-FFpairs	1713	881	1046
Number of bonded IOBs	56	56	56
Number of BUFG/BUFGCTRLs	1	1	1
Number of blockRAM/FIFO	10	10	10
Maximum frequency (Mhz)	28.84	287.81	13.83
Throughput (Mbps)	922.88	8264.32	442.56
Power (Watts)	1.36	1.34	1.36

For the next clock cycles, the FSM 32-bit output word F generated by (5) is mixed with the HC-PRNG 32-bit output word P and the register S_0 of the LFSR in order to produce the 32-bit keystream word Zt as defined by (20). The architecture of the proposed HC SNOW-3G stream cipher in its keystream mode is given in Figure 6:

$$Zt = F \oplus S_0 \oplus P. \tag{20}$$

Therefore, in this processing mode, the LFSR operates on keystream mode, and both FSM and HC-PRNG layers are clocked at each clock cycle to generate a 32-bit keystream word Zt as mentioned before. This mode runs j times where j is the number of 32-bit blocks to be encrypted.

4. FPGA Implantation of the Proposed Design

The proposed architecture is mainly based on three layers, as already discussed: the HC-PRNG layer and the FSM and LFSR layers of the regular SNOW-3G. The added HC-PRNG layer is used in order to perturb the LFSR synchronization in the initialization mode and the FSM output in the keystream mode, as described in Figures 2 and 6, respectively.

The RTL description of the proposed architecture has been implemented on Xilinx Virtex-5 FPGA (XC5vfx70t-1) through the ML507 Virtex Development platform [37] using VHDL structural description. ISE 13.1i of Xilinx tools have been used for this digital implementation allowing obtaining the logic resource requirements and the associated real-time constraints. The Xilinx Synthesis Technology (XST) results after place and route show the performance analysis of our implementation in Table 1. To exhibit the importance of this architecture, we also implemented the regular SNOW-3G and the PLCM (Piecewise Linear Chaotic Map) SNOW-3G proposed in [31] on the same FPGA device. The results are presented in Table 1. This table depicts comparison in terms of hardware resources, maximum time frequency, throughput, and the power consumption. Our logic implementation on a Xilinx Virtex-5 device requires only 2391 Slice registers, 56 bonded IOBs, and 10 block RAMs. In addition, the low power consumption estimated by 1.36 Watts is suitable for embedded electronic applications thanks to the considered FSM encoding algorithm and the fixed-point coding data.

To evaluate the performance of the proposed stream cipher, the throughput rate metric is considered. The throughput rate is defined as the number of bits of key in a unit of time for a keystream. In view of the performance results (see Table 1), we have achieved a maximal throughput of 922.88 Mbps for the proposed HC SNOW-3G and 422.56 Mbps for the PLCM SNOW-3G, where the regular SNOW-3G achieves a maximal throughput of 8264.32 Mbps. Thus, the proposed architecture is two times faster than PLCM SNOW-3G architecture and nine times slower than the regular SNOW-3G architecture. On the other hand, the proposed HC SNOW-3G architecture occupies greater area compared to the regular and PLCM SNOW-3G architectures. The difference in terms of hardware area is due to the following:

(1) The HC system is for order 4 where the PLCM system is for order 3.

(2) The HC system is more complex and has more nonlinearity than the PLCM system.

(3) The HC system complexity provides good randomness and security compared to the PLCM system.

Based on the obtained results and the discussed comparison, we conclude that the proposed HC SNOW-3G is better than the PLCM SNOW-3G in terms of randomness, security, and high throughput.

To ensure that the proposed architecture enhances the complexity of the standardized SNOW-3G stream cipher suitable for increasing the robustness of data encryption, security and statistical tests are performed in order to prove the high level of security obtained from our architecture.

5. Cryptographic Strength and Performance

The security and statistical analyses of our designed architecture are presented in this section. The proposed stream cipher HC SNOW-3G algorithm is subjected to two security tests: (1) key sensitivity and (2) key space and several statistical analyses such as uniformity and randomness. to demonstrate its satisfactory security and good randomness with regard to the added HC-PRNG layer.

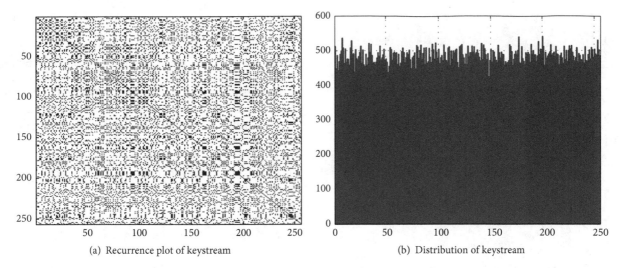

(a) Recurrence plot of keystream

(b) Distribution of keystream

FIGURE 7: Uniformity of keystream generated.

5.1. Statistical Analysis. Many statistical analyses are applied to our proposed stream cipher scheme to demonstrate its robustness such as randomness, uniformity, mixing nature, low coefficient correlation between original and encrypted data packets, and NIST tests. The simulations are done using keystreams of 125000 bytes in length which are normally distributed with a mean equal to 128 and standard deviation equal to 8.

5.1.1. Randomness and Uniformity Analysis. Any performing stream cipher should produce high random keystreams and with best uniformity representation. Therefore, a keystream of 1000000 bits produced by our design is analyzed. The recurrence plot representation (Figure 7(a)) and distribution (Figure 7(b)) of the generated keystream indicate clearly a good degree of randomness and uniformity.

The high randomness of generated keystream is also proved by the random-excursion and random-excursion-variant tests of NIST [38]. To perform these tests, we analyzed 250 keystream sequences where each sequence is composed of 50 packets of 1000000 bits. The proportion value of each sequence is shown in Figure 8. The determined range of acceptable proportion using the confidence interval is defined by

$$\widehat{P} \mp 3\sqrt{\frac{\widehat{P}\left(1 - \widehat{P}\right)}{m}}, \tag{21}$$

where m is the sample size, $\widehat{P} = 1 - \alpha$, and $\alpha = 0.01$.

In our case, the confidence interval is 0.99 $\mp$ $3\sqrt{(0.99 \times 0.01)/50}$ (i.e., the proportion value should be laid above 0.947786) which is represented in Figure 8 by the red line. The simulation results indicate clearly the high randomness of keystreams. Indeed, all random-excursion and random-excursion-variant proportion values are above the minimum proportion value and close to ideal value 1. In

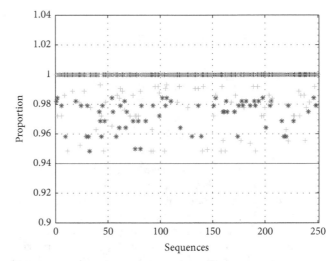

* Proportion (random-excursions test)
+ Proportion (random-excursions-variant test)
—— Confidence interval

FIGURE 8: Proportion values of random-excursion and random-excursion-variant NIST tests.

addition, other tests proving randomness and uniformity of our proposed stream cipher are presented in the following subsections.

5.1.2. Low Correlation Coefficient. The correlation is an important test to prove the independence of encrypted data from the original ones. Indeed, the encrypted data are increasingly different from the original ones when the correlation coefficient becomes as low as possible. The correlation coefficient is computed according to [39]

$$\rho_{x,y} = \frac{\operatorname{cov}\left(x, y\right)}{\sqrt{D\left(x\right) \times D\left(y\right)}}, \tag{22}$$

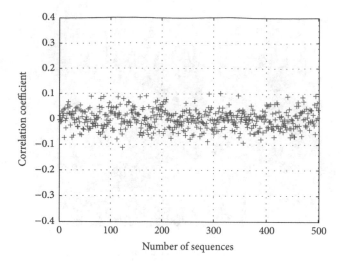

FIGURE 9: Correlation coefficient between original and encrypted packets.

where

$$\text{cov}(x, y) = E\left[\{x - E(x)\}\{y - E(y)\}\right],$$

$$E(x) = \frac{1}{n} \times \sum_{i=1}^{n} x_i, \tag{23}$$

$$D(x) = \frac{1}{n} \times \sum_{i=1}^{n} \{x_i - E[x]\}.$$

For performing this test, we have analysed 500 encrypted packets with different keys, and in each case we have calculated the correlation coefficient between original packet and its corresponding encrypted packet. The results are shown in Figure 9. The illustrated results indicate clearly that no detectable correlation exists between the original and corresponding cipher packets considering that the correlation coefficient is always close to ideal value zero.

5.1.3. Distribution and Chi-Square Uniformity. An additional statistical approach, the distribution of frequency counts which can define the uniformity of generated keystreams, is performed. Any sequence is categorized uniform if its corresponding distribution is close to a uniform distribution. In Figures 10(a) and 10(b) distributions of an original and its corresponding encrypted packet obtained by our proposed stream cipher are presented, respectively. From these results, we deduce that the contents of the encrypted packet are spread over the entire space and have a uniform distribution thanks to a good level of mixing included by our added HC-PRNG layer. To validate this uniformity, the Chi-square test is applied [40]. The Chi-square distance is computed according to

$$\chi^2_{\text{test}} = \sum_{i=1}^{l} \frac{o_i - e_i}{e_i}. \tag{24}$$

Note that l represents the number of levels (here 256), o_i represents the observed occurrence frequencies of each level of field size (0–255) in the histogram of ciphered generation contents, and e_i is the expected occurrence frequency of uniform distribution. Before applying the test, we fixed the significant level to 0.05. After test, we analyzed the result according to the χ^2_{test} value. Indeed, if $\chi^2_{\text{test}} \leq \chi^2_{\text{theory}}(255, 0.05) \approx 293$ (in our case study), and the null hypothesis is not rejected, then the distribution of the histogram is uniform. In Figure 11, the results of the Chi-square test for 500 different ciphered packets of 125000 bytes each are shown. Based on these results, we conclude that a stronger mixing property is obtained with uniform distribution exceeding ≈95% considering all values are below the value of χ^2_{theory} presented by a red line in Figure 11.

5.1.4. NIST Keystream Analysis. Various statistical tests can be used to evaluate the randomness of a sequence, for example, NIST [38], DIEHARD [41], NESSIE [42]. In our case study, the NIST statistical tests are used to evaluate our HC SNOW-3G stream cipher. To illustrate the importance of the proposed design, we repeat the three statistical tests done in [14] to evaluate the randomness of the generated keystreams. To perform comparison results with previous work [14], we have considered the usual significance level used in the NIST tests [38] and the same sample size sequences. Therefore, in all the experiments the significance level was set to 0.01 and sample size was set to 300 sequences. The tests are defined as follows:

(1) Long keystream data set test: it begins by generating 2^{20} bits for each of the 300 random CK (set IV to zero in all the cases) to obtain 300 vectors of 1048576 bits. Then, it evaluates the result vectors by the 15 NIST tests.

(2) Short keystream data set test: it begins by generating 2^{10} bits for each of the 307200 random CK (set IV to zero in all the cases). The concatenation of all the keystreams of 2^{10} bits allows obtaining 300 vectors of 1048576 bits. Then, it evaluates the result vectors by the 15 NIST tests.

(3) IV data set: it begins by generating 256 sequences of 4096 bits each for 300 random CK. Note that the first sequence of each key is generated with IV set to zero. Then, it is incremented for the following 255 sequences. As a result, we obtain 300 vectors of 1048576 bits for evaluation by the 15 NIST tests.

To perform the analysis, we compare the results of our proposed HC SNOW-3G stream cipher with results of the regular SNOW-3G done in [14]. The aim of this analysis is to prove the amelioration of the initialization process and randomness of short keystream data set. As a result, we find that both algorithms (regular SNOW-3G and our proposed design) pass in success all the fifteen NIST tests for test set 1 (long keystream data set) and test set 3 (IV data set). However, only our proposed design passes in success all the fifteen NIST tests for test set 2 (short keystream data set).

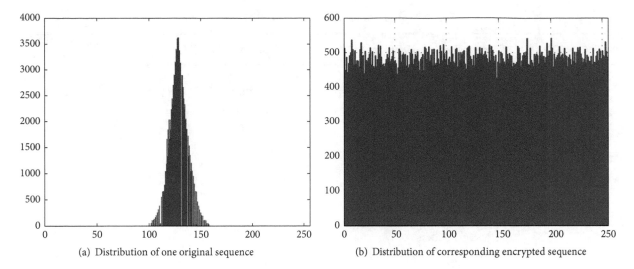

(a) Distribution of one original sequence   (b) Distribution of corresponding encrypted sequence

FIGURE 10: The distribution comparison between original and encrypted sequences.

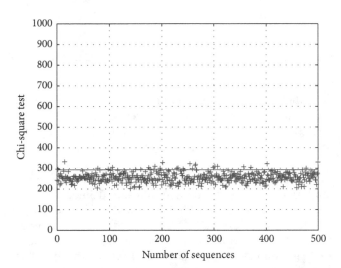

FIGURE 11: Variation of χ^2_{test} of cipher sequence versus 500 random keys.

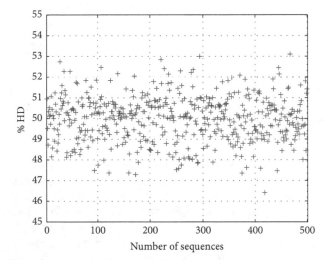

FIGURE 12: The key sensitivity analysis results.

Indeed, the regular SNOW-3G fails in the eight NIST tests as it is presented in Table 2. More precisely, this table gives a comparison of short keystream generated by the regular SNOW-3G cipher with short keystream generated by our proposed HC SNOW-3G design. We can clearly observe that all tests are passed compared to the regular SNOW-3G cipher where NIST tests based on the short keystream data set have failed [14]. Therefore, we can conclude that our proposed design present an enhanced initialization process and generates very good pseudo-random keystream, which justify its high level of security. Indeed, it is very difficult to find a plaintext masked by a sequence generated by this stream cipher which can be used in the 128-EEA1 confidentiality algorithm. Similarly, it is theoretically impossible to generate the same MAC by the 128-EEIA1 integrity algorithm based on this stream cipher without knowing original message.

5.2. Key Sensitivity Analysis. The key sensitivity analysis is one among the most important security tests of cryptosystems. In other words, an ideal cryptosystem should be sensitive with respect to the secret key. For testing the key sensitivity of the proposed architecture, we analyzed 500 random keys, where in each case a single bit in the secret key is changed. Then, the percent of Hamming Distance (HD) is calculated according to

$$\text{HD} = \frac{\sum_{k=1}^{N} C_i \oplus C_i'}{N} \times 100\%, \qquad (25)$$

where N is the length in bit level of the encrypted packet and C_i and C_i' are the corresponding ciphers packets using two secret keys different in one bit K_i and K_i', respectively. The obtained results are shown in Figure 12 in which a high sensitivity is indicated, while the average Hamming Distance

TABLE 2: Comparison results of NIST tests.

The number of test	The type of test	Regular SNOW-3G [14]	Proposed SNOW-3G based on HC-PRNG
1	Frequency (monobit) test	Success	Success
2	Frequency test with a block	Success	Success
3	Runs test	Fail	Success
4	Long runs of ones test	Fail	Success
5	Binary matrix rank test	Fail	Success
6	Discrete Fourier transform (spectral) test	Fail	Success
7	Nonoverlapping template matching test	Fail	Success
8	Overlapping template matching test	Fail	Success
9	Maurer's "universal statistical" test	Success	Success
10	Linear complexity test	Success	Success
11	Serial test	Fail	Success
12	Approximate entropy test	Fail	Success
13	Cumulative sums (Cusum) test	Success	Success
14	Random-excursion test	Success	Success
15	Random-excursion-variant test	Success	Success

percent is closer to the optimal value 50% in bit level. We conclude that a change of one bit in the secret key leads to thoroughly different keystreams with respect to the avalanche effect [43].

5.3. *Key Space Analysis.* The proposed enhanced stream cipher HC SNOW-3G has the advantage of being able to generate a usable random number while maintaining a large enough key space and high level security. The key space achieved in the present work is increased from 2^{128} in the regular SNOW-3G stream cipher to 2^{132} by addition of 2^4 through the controlling command used to perform the perturbation process which is coded in 16 bits.

Additionally, considering all the initial values ($x0, y0, z0,$ and $w0$) and control parameters ($a, b, c,$ and d) of our HC generator (defined by (7)) as internal keys, the key space of the generator is based upon those 8 parameters. First, we fix the initial values ($x0, y0, z0,$ and $w0$) and the three parameters $a, b,$ and c whereas d is considered the key of the random number generator (we change slightly the value of d) to generate a new binary sequence. The experiment is done more than 1000 times. The obtained results show that the variance ratio of each bit is approximated to 99%, even if the change of initial value or control parameter is an extremely small value 10^{-15}, which means that the system is extremely sensitive to the key changes. Consequently, the key space is larger than 10^{15} for this considered key (d). Similarly, the 4 initial values and the 3 remaining control parameters can be considered as key of our random sequence generator. Finally, the key space is defined by $(10^{15})^8 = 10^{120} \approx 2^{398}$, which is large enough to withstand attacks limited by a key space of 2^{128}.

Otherwise, the HC generator key space of 2^{398} is much better than the PLCM generator key space of 2^{124} [44]. Finally, we conclude that our HC generator is sufficiently large to make the brute-force attacks infeasible.

5.4. *Synthesis and Discussion.* In cryptography, any cipher must exhibit the confusion and diffusion defined on Shannon's theory with success to be considered secure enough and able to resist attacks [45]. Our designed cipher is resistant against the powerful attacks that are based on statistical analysis. Moreover, the avalanche effect is attained when repeating the tests several times [43], and then a significant difference is caused in the generated keystream by changing of a single bit in the Ciphering Key, which makes our cipher resistant against a special case of differential cryptanalysis. The proposed cipher is also resistant against the statistical attacks proved by the obtained statistical analysis results. Furthermore, the key space of 2^{132} is achieved, which is sufficiently large to make the brute-force attack infeasible. Finally, the added nonrevertible HC generator limits the ability of the attackers who try to break the cipher. The high randomness and security of our cipher is achieved according to the new combined HC technique with both regular LFSR and FSM layers in addition to the strength of the original SNOW-3G against contemporary cryptanalytic.

6. Conclusion

In this paper, an enhanced SNOW-3G stream cipher is proposed. The objective is the improvement of the randomness and the complexity of the regular SNOW-3G stream cipher which presents a weakness in its initialization mode leading to failure of the NIST test based on the short keystream data set. The adopted original approach is to include a HC-PRNG (Hyperchaotic Pseudo-Random Number Generator) based on 4D Lorenz system in the regular SNOW-3G cipher as an additional layer while keeping standardization and in order to generate a more robustness keystream. The proposed architecture performs the perturbation concept of digital LFSR (Linear Feedback Shift Register) sequences and the digital output of the regular SNOW-3G cipher part through one hyperchaotic generator which is used as PRNG *(Pseudo-Random Number Generator)*. The obtained statistical and security tests proved that the proposed stream cipher is more secure than the regular SNOW-3G cipher as long as it passes all analyses presented in this paper. Therefore, the proposed stream cipher can replace the regular SNOW-3G stream cipher without modification in its mechanism while respecting its standard requirements, mainly the length of input and output parameters. Consequently, this paper proposed a new digital hyperchaotic SNOW-3G stream cipher architecture which can be used as the kernel of the confidentiality and integrity algorithms used in the UMTS and LTE standards. The hardware implementation results of our proposed hyperchaotic SNOW-3G cipher provide a good trade-off between high security, performance, and hardware resources. Indeed, the proposed implemented design in FPGA Virtex-5 device consumes a low logic area cost while it achieves a throughput of 922.88 Mbps. Finally, our technique exhibits attractive performance and can be extended to enhancing the 4G security level by scrambling the plaintext for the LTE 128-EEA1 confidentiality algorithm or controlling the integrity of a signalling message for 128-EIA1 algorithm.

References

[1] K. E. Mayes and K. Markantonakis, "Mobile communication security controllers an evaluation paper," *Information Security Technical Report*, vol. 13, no. 3, pp. 173–192, 2008.

[2] C. Blanchard, "Security for the third generation (3G) mobile system," *Information Security Technical Report*, vol. 5, no. 3, pp. 55–65, 2000.

[3] Specification of the 3GPP Confidentiality and Integrity Algorithms UEA2 & UIA2; Document 2: SNOW 3G specification, Technical Specification (TS) TS 35.216 V12.0.0, 3GPP (Sep 2014-09).

[4] Specification of the 3GPP Confidentiality and Integrity Algorithms UEA2 & UIA2; Document 1: UEA2 and UIA2 specifications, Technical Specification (TS) TS 35.215 V12.0.0, 3GPP (Sep 2014-09).

[5] Tech. Rep., 3G Security; Specification of the 3GPP Confidentiality and Integrity Algorithms; Document 1: f8 and f9 specification, Technical Specification (TS) TS 35.201 V12.0.0, 3GPP (Sep 2014-09).

[6] 3G Security; Specification of the 3GPP Confidentiality and Integrity Algorithms; Document 2: KASUMI specification, Technical Specification (TS) TS 35.202 V12.0.0, 3GPP (Sep 2014-09).

[7] Digital cellular telecommunications system (phase 2+); Universal Mobile Telecommunications System (UMTS); LTE; 3GPP

[8] P. Szalachowski, B. Ksiezopolski, and Z. Kotulski, "CMAC, CCM and GCM/GMAC: advanced modes of operation of symmetric block ciphers in wireless sensor networks," *Information Processing Letters*, vol. 110, no. 7, pp. 247–251, 2010.

[9] D.-S. Kundi, A. Aziz, and N. Ikram, "A high performance ST-Box based unified AES encryption/decryption architecture on FPGA," *Microprocessors and Microsystems*, vol. 41, pp. 37–46, 2016.

[10] Specification of the 3GPP Confidentiality and Integrity Algorithms EEA3 & EIA3; Document 1: EEA3 and EIA3 specifications, Technical Specification (TS) TS 35.221 V12.0.0, 3GPP (Sep 2014-09).

[11] Specification of the 3GPP Confidentiality and Integrity Algorithms EEA3 & EIA3; Document 2: ZUC specification, Technical Specification (TS) TS 35.222 V12.0.0, 3GPP (Sep 2014-09).

[12] S. Murphy, "The advanced encryption standard (AES)," *Information Security Technical Report*, vol. 4, no. 4, pp. 12–17, 1999.

[13] F. Lafitte, O. Markowitch, and D. Van Heule, "SAT based analysis of LTE stream cipher ZUC," *Journal of Information Security and Applications*, vol. 22, pp. 54–65, 2015.

[14] P. Bohm, "Statistical Evaluation of Stream Cipher SNOW 3G," in *Proceedings of the "Constantin Brancusi" University of Targu Jiu Engineering Faculty Scientific Conference with International Participation*, Targu Jiu, Romania, 13th edition, 2008.

[15] M. S. N. Nia and T. Eghlidos, "Improved Heuristic guess and determine attack on SNOW 3G stream cipher," in *Proceedings of the 2014 7th International Symposium on Telecommunications, IST 2014*, pp. 972–976, September 2014.

[16] B. Debraize and I. M. Corbella, "Fault analysis of the stream cipher snow 3G," in *Proceedings of the 6th International Workshop on Fault Diagnosis and Tolerance in Cryptography, FDTC 2009*, pp. 103–110, Lausanne, Switzerland, September 2009.

[17] B. B. Brumley, R. M. Hakala, K. Nyberg, and S. Sovio, "Consecutive S-box lookups: a timing attack on SNOW 3G," in *Proceedings of the 12th International Conference, ICICS 2010*, pp. 171–185, Barcelona , Spain, 2010.

[18] H. Gilbert and M. Minier, "A Collision Attack on 7 Rounds of Rijndael," in *Proceedings of the AES Candidate Conference*, pp. 230–241, 2000.

[19] A. Biryukov, D. Priemuth-Schmid, and B. Zhang, "Multiset Collision Attacks on Reduced-Round SNOW 3G and SNOW 3G ⊕," in *Proceedings of the 8th International Conference, ACNS 2010*, pp. 139–153, Beijing, China, 2010.

[20] A. Kircanski and A. M. Youssef, "On the sliding property of SNOW 3G and SNOW 2.0," *IET Information Security*, vol. 5, no. 4, pp. 199–206, 2011.

[21] S. Sadoudi, C. Tanougast, and M. S. Azzaz, "First experimental solution for channel noise sensibility in digital chaotic communications," *Progress in Electromagnetics Research C*, vol. 32, pp. 181–196, 2012.

[22] M. S. Azzaz, C. Tanougast, S. Sadoudi, and A. Bouridane, "Synchronized hybrid chaotic generators: application to real-time wireless speech encryption," *Communications in Nonlinear Science and Numerical Simulation*, vol. 18, no. 8, pp. 2035–2047, 2013.

[23] O. E. Rossler, "An equation for hyperchaos," *Physics Letters A*, vol. 71, no. 2-3, pp. 155–157, 1979.

[24] S. Nikolov and S. Clodong, "Occurrence of regular, chaotic and hyperchaotic behavior in a family of modified Rossler hyper-

System Architecture Evolution (SAE); Security Architecture, Technical Specification (TS) ETSI TS 133 401 V11.5.0, 3GPP (Oct 2012-10).

chaotic systems," *Chaos, Solitons & Fractals*, vol. 22, no. 2, pp. 407–431, 2004.

[25] A. Chen, J. Lu, J. Lü, and S. Yu, "Generating hyperchaotic Lü attractor via state feedback control," *Physica A: Statistical Mechanics and its Applications*, vol. 36, no. 4, pp. 103–110, 2006.

[26] T. Gao, Z. Chen, Z. Yuan, and G. Chen, "A hyperchaos generated from Chen's system," *International Journal of Modern Physics C*, vol. 17, no. 4, pp. 471–478, 2006.

[27] Y. Li, W. K. S. Tang, and G. Chen, "Generating hyperchaos via state feedback control," *International Journal of Bifurcation and Chaos*, vol. 15, no. 10, pp. 3367–3375, 2005.

[28] G. Tiegang, C. Zengqiang, G. Qiaolun, and Z. Yuan, "A new hyper-chaos generated from generalized Lorenz system via nonlinear feedback," *Chaos, Solitons & Fractals*, vol. 35, no. 2, pp. 390–397, 2008.

[29] Q. Jia, "Hyperchaos generated from the Lorenz chaotic system and its control," *Physics Letters A*, vol. 366, no. 3, pp. 217–222, 2007.

[30] W. Xingyuan and W. Mingjun, "A hyperchaos generated from Lorenz system," *Physica A: Statistical Mechanics and its Applications*, vol. 387, no. 14, pp. 3751–3758, 2008.

[31] M. Wasi, A. Arif, and S. Windarta, "Modified SNOW 3G: Stream cipher algorithm using piecewise linear chaotic map," in *Proceedings of the AIP Conference Proceedings*, vol. 1707, Issue 1, 2016.

[32] G. Alvarez, G. P. F. Monotoya, G. Pastor, and M. Romera, "Chaotic cryptosystems," in *Proceedings of the IEEE 33rd Annual International Carnahan Conference on Security Technology*, pp. 332–338, Madrid, Spain, October 1999.

[33] E. Lorenz, "Deterministic nonperiodic flow," *Journal of Atmospheric Sciences*, no. 20, pp. 130–141, 1963.

[34] T. Tsubone and T. Saito, "Hyperchaos from a 4-D manifold piecewise-linear system," *IEEE Transactions on Circuits and Systems I: Fundamental Theory and Applications*, vol. 45, no. 9, pp. 889–894, 1998.

[35] S. Sadoudi, C. Tanougast, M. S. Azzaz, and A. Dandache, "Design and FPGA implementation of a wireless hyperchaotic communication system for secure real-time image transmission," *Eurasip Journal on Image and Video Processing*, vol. 2013, article 43, pp. 1–18, 2013.

[36] J.-P. Demailly, "Analyse numérique et équations différentielles, EDP Sciences 4," *Collection Grenoble Sciences*, 2006.

[37] Virtex 5 FPGA Configuration User Guide, ug702, Xilinx (sep 2012).

[38] A. Rukhin, J. Sota, J. Nechvatal et al., "A statistical test suite for random and pseudorandom number generators for cryptographic applications," Special Publication NIST 800-22, National Institute of Standards and Technology, 2010.

[39] J. L. Rodgers and A. W. Nicewander, "Thirteen ways to look at the correlation coefficient," *The American Statistician*, vol. 42, no. 1, pp. 59–66, 1988.

[40] C. Bates and B. Carl, "The Chi-square Test of Goodness of Fit for Bivariate Normal Distribution," Defence Technical Information Center.

[41] G. Marsaglia, "The Marsaglia Random Number CDROM, with The Diehard Battery of Tests of Randomness," Florida State University under a grant from The National Science Foundation, 1985.

[42] B. Preneel, "New European Schemes for Signature, Integrity and Encryption (NESSIE): A Status Report," in *Proceedings of the International Workshop on Public Key Cryptography (PKC) 2002: Public Key Cryptography*, pp. 297–309, 2002.

[43] D. Han, L. Min, and G. Chen, "A Stream Encryption Scheme with Both Key and Plaintext Avalanche Effects for Designing Chaos-Based Pseudorandom Number Generator with Application to Image Encryption," *International Journal of Bifurcation and Chaos*, vol. 26, no. 5, article 1650091, 2016.

[44] Y. Hu, C. Zhu, and Z. Wang, "An improved piecewise linear chaotic map based image encryption algorithm," *The Scientific World Journal*, vol. 2014, Article ID 275818, 7 pages, 2014.

[45] C. E. Shannon, "Communication theory of secrecy systems," *Bell Labs Technical Journal*, vol. 28, pp. 656–715, 1949.

6

A Novel Fuzzy Encryption Technique Based on Multiple Right Translated AES Gray S-Boxes and Phase Embedding

Naveed Ahmed Azam

Faculty of Engineering Sciences, GIK Institute of Engineering Sciences and Technology, Topi, Pakistan

Correspondence should be addressed to Naveed Ahmed Azam; naveedzm961@gmail.com

Academic Editor: Pascal Lorenz

This paper presents a novel image encryption technique based on multiple right translated AES Gray S-boxes (RTSs) and phase embedding technique. First of all, a secret image is diffused with a fuzzily selected RTS. The fuzzy selection of RTS is variable and depends upon pixels of the secret image. Then two random masks are used to enhance confusion in the spatial and frequency domains of the diffused secret image. These random masks are generated by applying two different RTSs on a host image. The decryption process of the proposed cryptosystem needs the host image for generation of masks. It is therefore, necessary, to secure the host image from unauthorized users. This task is achieved by diffusing the host image with another RTS and embedding the diffused secret image into the phase terms of the diffused host image. The cryptographic strength of the proposed security system is measured by implementing it on several images and applying rigorous analyses. Performance comparison of the proposed security technique with some of the state-of-the-art security systems, including S-box cryptosystem and steganocryptosystems, is also performed. Results and comparison show that the newly developed cryptosystem is more secure.

1. Introduction

The demand of security of digital images is increased due to extensive transmission of different image files through internet [1, 2]. Therefore, it is essential to develop some algorithms to secure secret images. Different types of image security techniques are proposed by the researchers. Cryptography and steganography are two different widely used techniques for securing the content of secret images. The basic principle of cryptography is to transform secret image (plain image) into diffused image (cipher image) by creating confusion in its information. In many cryptosystems, substitution box (S-box) is solely responsible for creation of diffusion in image [3]. Daemen and Rijmen proposed a block cipher which is used by National Institute of Standard and Technology as Advanced Encryption Standard (AES) [4]. At present, AES is commonly used cryptosystem. Due to the fundamental role of S-box in AES, many cryptographers have paid their attention to study the AES S-box. An algebraic expression for Rijndael block cipher is presented in [5]. In [6], a new simple mathematical description of the AES S-box is given.

A permutation polynomial representation of the AES S-box is presented in [7]. It is observed that the polynomial of the AES S-box has only nine nonzero terms which reveals that the security of AES is suspected against computational attacks [6, 7]. In order to remove this weakness of AES, many researchers have proposed new S-boxes (e.g., refer to [8–13]). In [8], an improved S-box is proposed. The drawback of their work is that their S-box cannot be implemented by using the existing framework of AES. The reason behind low complexity of the AES S-box is identified in [9]. Moreover, a new version of S-box is also presented in [9]. In [10], another S-box is developed based on affine mapping having 253 nonzero terms in its polynomial and reuses the existing implementation of AES. The algebraic complexity of the AES S-box is further enhanced by introducing a new S-box based on Gray codes in [11]. The improved S-box has 255 nonzero terms and reuses the whole existing framework of AES. A generalization of Gray S-box is presented in [12]. Right translation and regular representation of Galois field $GF(2^8)$ are used to generate 256 different RTSs all with high algebraic complexity and satisfying other security tests including nonlinearity, bit independence, strict avalanche, linear approximation, differential approximation, algebraic complexity, correlation, and histogram. Similar to Gray S-box, RTSs are also compatible with the existing implementation of AES S-box. Furthermore, it is claimed in [12] that the latest computational attacks, such as linear, differential, and algebraic attacks [14, 15], can be effectively encountered with a cryptosystem based on multiple S-boxes as compared to a security system relaying on single S-box.

In steganography, secret image is embedded into another image called host image. The embedding is done in such a way that unauthorized users cannot detect the presence of the secret image in the resulting image [16–19]. Recently, many scientists have developed new image security algorithms based on combination of cryptography and steganography. In [20], a steganocryptosystem is proposed by using optical encryption, phase embedding, and fixed data hiding technique for Gray scale images. In [21], an improved version of steganocryptosystem with adaptive data hiding technique is presented. Chaotic S-boxes are used to improve the security of secret image after embedding it into a host image in [22]. In [23], secret image is first encrypted by AES and then embedded into host image by using least significant bit (LSB) embedding technique. Similarly, many other researchers proposed steganocryptosystems (e.g., refer to [24–27]).

In this paper, we propose a novel image security system based on variable multiple RTSs and steganography. The proposed technique uses four different RTSs and phase embedding technique. Fuzzy approach is used for the selection of RTSs which depends upon pixels of the secret image. The proposed algorithm also utilizes spatial and frequency domains of the secret image for confusion purpose. The aim of this technique is to develop a security system which can efficiently resist the computational attacks as compared to single S-box security techniques and steganocryptosystems. Several tests are applied on the proposed cryptosystem to evaluate its security strength. The experimental results show that the proposed security technique has high resistance against computational attacks as compared to some of the well-known existing security algorithms. Rest of the paper is organized as follows: Section 2 consists of preliminaries. Novel encryption technique is presented in Section 3. Section 4 consists of analyses and comparisons. Finally, conclusion and future directions are given in Section 5.

2. Preliminaries

2.1. Fuzzy Set.
A fuzzy set is a pair (f, X), where X is a set and f is a function from set X to the interval $[0, 1]$. The function f is called membership function and it indicates the grade of membership of elements of X in (f, X). Nowadays, fuzzy theory is widely used in many cryptosystems (e.g., refer to [28–30]).

2.2. Right Translated AES Gray S-Boxes (RTSs).
A technique for the generation of multiple S-boxes is introduced in [12]. This technique uses the regular representation of Galois field $GF(2^8)$ and Gray codes [31]. The main advantage of this technique is that it generates an algebraically complex S-box

corresponding to each element of $GF(2^8)$. Since there are 256 elements in $GF(2^8)$, therefore there are 256 different RTSs. The mathematical expression for the generation of RTSs is given below:

$$\xi(g) = S_{AES} \circ \rho_g \circ G, \qquad (1)$$

where g is an element of $GF(2^8)$, S_{AES} is the AES S-box, ρ_g is a permutation representation of g, G is the Gray code mapping, and $\xi(g)$ is the resultant RTS corresponding to g.

3. The Proposed Security System

In this section, we presented a new security system based on RTSs and steganography. Let I be a secret image and J a host image. Both I and J are Gray scale images of same dimensions $M \times N$. The main steps of the proposed encryption and decryption algorithms are given below.

3.1. The Encryption Algorithm

Step 1. Fuzzy selection criterion for RTS:

(a) Define a fuzzy set $(f, GF(2^8))$ by

$$f(g) = \frac{\#(g)}{M \times N}, \qquad (2)$$

where $\#(g)$ is the frequency of g in I. This fuzzy set gives the grade of membership of each element of Galois field $GF(2^8)$ in the secret image.

(b) Suppose l is the supremum of the range of f; that is, $l = \sup\{f(g)\}$.

(c) Now, calculate preimages $g_1, g_2, g_3, \ldots, g_n$ of l. The infimum g of the preimages is the minimum element of $GF(2^8)$ which has maximum grade of membership in the secret image I.

(d) Diffuse I with $\xi(g)$, RTS corresponding to g, to get I_g.

Step 2. Generation of random masks and confusion in spatial and frequency domains:

(a) Fix an element c of $GF(2^8)$ and select three RTSs $\xi(S_1)$, $\xi(S_2)$, and $\xi(S_3)$ by using (1) and following three equations:

$$\begin{aligned} S_1 &= g + c, \quad (\text{mod } 256), \\ S_2 &= S_1 + c, \quad (\text{mod } 256), \\ S_3 &= S_2 + c, \quad (\text{mod } 256). \end{aligned} \qquad (3)$$

(b) Apply $\xi(S_1)$ and $\xi(S_2)$ on the host image J to get its two different diffused versions J_1 and J_2.

(c) Now generate two random masks R_1 and R_2 for creation of confusion in spatial and frequency domains of the diffused secret image I_g. The mathematical expressions of these masks are given below:

$$R_1 = \exp\left(\frac{i\pi J_1}{128}\right),$$
$$R_2 = \exp\left(\frac{i\pi J_2}{128}\right). \tag{4}$$

The random noise is then generated in the content of I_g by using

$$I_R = F^{-1}\left[F\left(I_g \times R_1\right) \times R_2\right], \tag{5}$$

where F is the Fourier transformation and F^{-1} is the inverse Fourier transformation.

Step 3. Securing the host image and embedding process:

The process of decryption cannot be completed until R_1 and R_2 are known. Traditionally, R_1 and R_2 can be retrieved by embedding them in I_R. But, this process increases the size of encrypted image and affects the quality of decrypted image [20–22]. Despite this, we embed I_R in the host image because R_1 and R_2 can be regenerated by J. The host image is secured from third party by diffusing J with RTS corresponding to S_3, that is, $\xi(S_3)$. Finally, I_R and g are embedded in the phase terms of the diffused host image J_3. The following is the mathematical equation of embedding process:

$$I_S = J_3 \exp\left(i\frac{\pi}{2}I_R\right). \tag{6}$$

The proposed encryption process is elaborated in Figure 1(a).

3.2. The Decryption Algorithm

Step 1. In the decryption process, first of all J_3, I_R, and g are extracted by calculating complex modulus and argument of I_S:

$$J_3 = |I_S|,$$
$$I_R = \frac{2}{\pi}\arg(I_S). \tag{7}$$

Step 2. Apply inverse of $\xi(S_3)$ on J_3 to generate random masks R_1 and R_2 by using Step 2 of the proposed encryption technique. Now, calculate their complex conjugates $\overline{R_1}$ and $\overline{R_2}$ because they can cancel the effect of random masks as shown below:

$$R_1 \times \overline{R_1} = \exp\left(\frac{i\pi J_1}{128}\right) \times \exp\left(-\frac{i\pi J_1}{128}\right)$$
$$= \exp\left(\frac{i\pi J_1}{128} - \frac{i\pi J_1}{128}\right) = \exp(0) = 1. \tag{8}$$

Step 3. Next, random masks are removed by using the following equation:

$$I_g = F^{-1}\left[F\left(I_R\right) \times \overline{R_2}\right] \times R_1. \tag{9}$$

Step 4. Finally, inverse of RTS corresponding to g is applied on I_g to restore the secret image I.

The flowchart of the proposed decryption process is shown in Figure 1(b).

4. Security Analyses and Comparison

We implemented the proposed technique and other security systems, presented in [10–12, 23, 24, 32–34], with the help of Matlab on 31 Gray scale images of dimensions 225×225. These test images were taken from [35]. We used image of Lena as host image for our experiments. The aim of this section is to investigate and compare the strength of the proposed security algorithm with some of the existing cryptosystems based on single S-box and combination of S-box and steganography.

4.1. Objective Fidelity Criteria. The purpose of this experiment is to measure the amount of error in the reconstructed image and original image. A cryptosystem is good if the value of error is high and if the value of error is small then the security of cryptosystem is suspicious. Root mean square error (RMSE) and peak signal to noise ratio (PSNR) are the two commonly used parameters to measure the level of fidelity [36–38]. RMSE and PSNR are given by the equations:

$$\text{RMSE} = \sqrt{\frac{\sum_{x=1}^{M}\sum_{y=1}^{N}\left(I(x,y) - I'(x,y)\right)^2}{M \times N}},$$

$$\text{PSNR} = 10\log_{10}\left[\frac{(255)^2}{\sum_{x=1}^{M}\sum_{y=1}^{N}\left(I(x,y) - I'(x,y)\right)^2}\right.$$
$$\left.\times M \times N\right], \tag{10}$$

where I denotes plain image and I' denotes cipher image.

We applied fidelity analysis on the proposed technique and other security systems. A comparison of the experimental results is given in Figures 2(a) and 2(b). It is clear from Figures 2(a) and 2(b) that the proposed cryptosystem is creating maximum value of RMSE and minimum value of PSNR as compared to other security techniques. Hence, the proposed technique is satisfying objective fidelity criterion efficiently more than that of other cryptosystems.

4.2. Sensitivity Analysis. Generally, a cryptanalyst uses differential attack to steal the information from the ciphered image. In this attack a slight change is produced in the pixels of the image to analyze the extent of change in the resultant image. Unified average changing intensity (UACI) is used to measure the level of security of a cryptosystem against differential

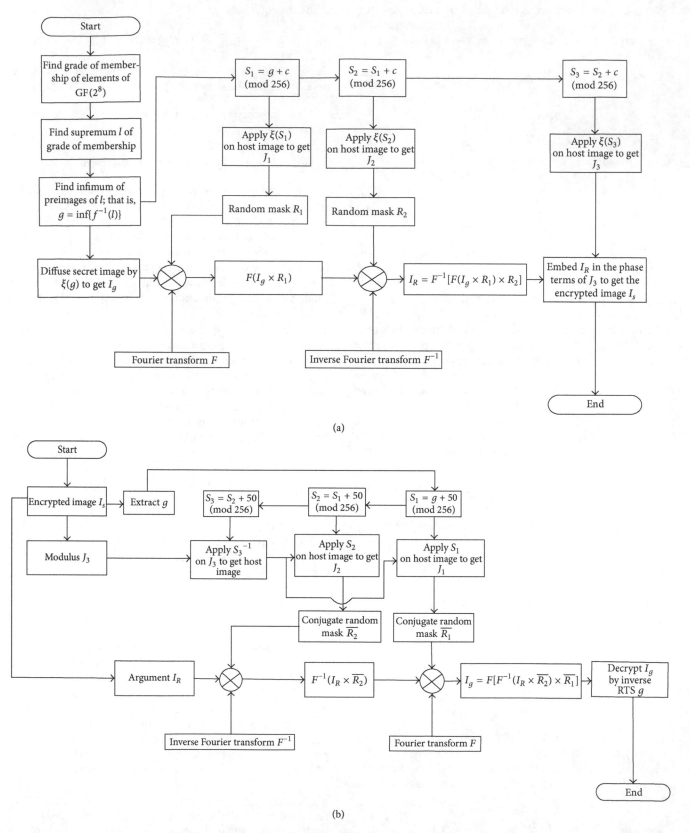

Figure 1: (a) Flowchart of encryption algorithm. (b) Flowchart of decryption algorithm.

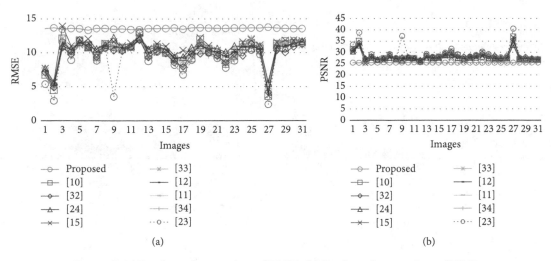

FIGURE 2: (a) Results and comparison of RMSE. (b) Results and comparison of PSNR.

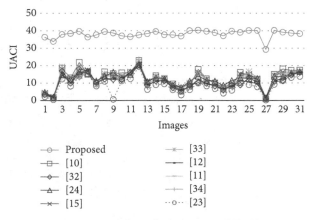

FIGURE 3: Results and comparison of UACI.

attack [32, 39]. The mathematical expression for calculation of UACI is given below:

$$\text{UACI} = \frac{1}{M \times N} \left[\frac{\sum_{x=1}^{M} \sum_{y=1}^{N} \left| I(x, y) - I'(x, y) \right|}{255} \right] \times 100. \tag{11}$$

The results of this experiment are shown in Figure 3. It is evident from Figure 3 that the proposed technique generates maximum value of UACI. Hence it resists differential attack efficiently as compared to other techniques.

4.3. Correlation and Contrast Analysis.
The pixels of plain image are highly correlated in horizontal, vertical, and diagonal directions. A cryptosystem is secure if it can reduce correlation and increase contrast between pixels significantly.

The correlation coefficient r_{xy} is calculated by the following expression:

$$r_{xy} = \frac{\text{cov}(x, y)}{\sqrt{H(x)} \sqrt{H(y)}}, \tag{12}$$

where

$$\text{cov}(x, y) = \frac{1}{M} \sum_{i=1}^{M} (x_i - E(x))(y_i - E(y)),$$

$$H(x) = \frac{1}{M} \sum_{i=1}^{M} (x_i - E(x))^2, \tag{13}$$

$$E(x) = \frac{1}{M} \sum_{i=1}^{M} x_i.$$

We calculated the correlation of pixels in vertical, horizontal, and diagonal directions and their results are plotted in

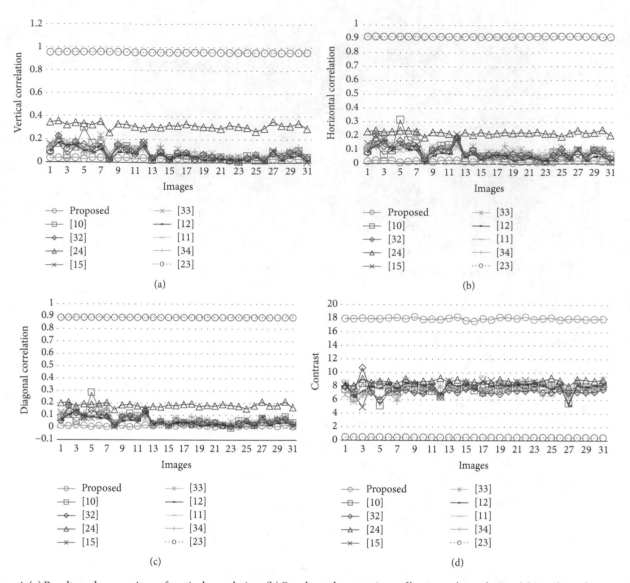

FIGURE 4: (a) Results and comparison of vertical correlation. (b) Results and comparison of horizontal correlation. (c) Results and comparison of vertical correlation. (d) Results and comparison of contrast analysis.

Figures 4(a)–4(c). The results of contrast analysis are shown in Figure 4(d). These figures indicate that the proposed security technique produces minimum correlation and maximum contrast.

4.4. Spectrum Magnitude Analysis. In an image, the frequency spectrum is not uniformly distributed. A cryptosystem is said to be good if it distributes frequency uniformly and creates significant difference between the spectrums of plain image and cipher image. We have applied this test on all 31 images. Three encrypted images and their frequency spectrums are shown in Figures 5(g)–5(i) and Figures 5(j)–5(l), respectively. Figures 5(d)–5(f) show frequency spectrums of the secret images. Note that the frequency distribution in Figures 5(d)–5(f) is concentrated in a small region located in the middle of each image. Usually, this small region suffers from security attacks. It is evident from Figures 5(j)-5(i)

that the frequency is distributed uniformly in the encrypted images. Hence, encrypted images by the proposed scheme are secure against statistical attacks.

5. Conclusion

In this study, we proposed a Gray scale image encryption technique based on RTSs and steganography. The proposed cryptosystem uses multiple RTSs and phase embedding technique for the generation of confusion in spatial and frequency domains of secret image. Fuzzy approach is used for the selection of RTSs. Analyses and comparison showed that the proposed security system is more secure as compared to some of the well-known cryptosystems based on single S-box and combination of S-box and steganography. In future, the newly developed algorithm can be used for the encryption of color image and data hiding purpose with some modifications.

FIGURE 5: (a) Secret image. (b) Secret image. (c) Secret image. (d) Frequency spectrum of (a). (e) Frequency spectrum of (b). (f) Frequency spectrum of (c). (g) Encryption of (a). (h) Encryption of (b). (i) Encryption of (c). (j) Frequency spectrum of (g). (k) Frequency spectrum of (h). (l) Frequency spectrum of (i).

Competing Interests

There is no conflict of interests regarding publication of this article.

Acknowledgments

The author thanks Shahid Ahmad for proofreading this paper.

References

[1] A. Philip, "A generalized pseudo-Knight's tour algorithm for encryption of an image," *IEEE Potentials*, vol. 32, no. 6, pp. 10–16, 2013.

[2] J. Liu, H. Jin, L. Ma, Y. Li, and W. Jin, "Optical color image encryption based on computer generated hologram and chaotic theory," *Optics Communications*, vol. 307, pp. 76–79, 2013.

[3] C. E. Shannon, "Communication theory of secrecy systems," *Bell System Technical Journal*, vol. 28, no. 4, pp. 656–715, 1949.

[4] J. Daemen and V. Rijmen, *The Design of RIJNDAEL: AES—The Advanced Encryption Standard*, Springer, Berlin, Germany, 2002.

[5] N. Ferguson, R. Schroeppel, and D. Whiting, "A simple algebraic representation of Rijndael," in *Selected Areas in Cryptography SAC '01*, vol. 2259 of *Lecture Notes in Computer Science*, pp. 103–111, Springer, 2001.

[6] S. Murphy and M. J. Robshaw, "Essential algebraic structure within the AES," in *Advances in Cryptology—CRYPTO 2002: 22nd Annual International Cryptology Conference Santa Barbara, California, USA, August 18–22, 2002 Proceedings*, vol. 2442 of *Lecture Notes in Computer Science*, pp. 1–16, Springer, Berlin, Germany, 2002.

[7] J. Rosenthal, "A polynomial description of the Rijndael advanced encryption standard," *Journal of Algebra and Its Applications*, vol. 2, no. 2, pp. 223–236, 2003.

[8] J. Liu, B. Wei, X. Cheng, and X. Wang, "An AES S-box to increase complexity and cryptographic analysis," in *Proceedings of the 19th International Conference on Advanced Information Networking and Applications (AINA '05)*, pp. 724–728, Taipei, Taiwan, March 2005.

[9] L. Jingmei, W. Baodian, and W. Xinmei, "One AES S-box to increase complexity and its cryptanalysis," *Journal of Systems Engineering and Electronics*, vol. 18, no. 2, pp. 427–433, 2007.

[10] L. Cui and Y. Cao, "A new S-box structure named affine-power-affine," *International Journal of Innovative Computing, Information and Control*, vol. 3, no. 3, pp. 751–759, 2007.

[11] M.-T. Tran, D.-K. Bui, and A.-D. Duong, "Gray S-box for advanced encryption standard," in *Proceedings of the International Conference on Computational Intelligence and Security (CIS '08)*, pp. 253–258, December 2008.

[12] M. Khan and N. A. Azam, "Right translated AES gray S-boxes," *Security and Communication Networks*, vol. 8, no. 9, pp. 1627–1635, 2015.

[13] M. Khan and N. A. Azam, "S-boxes based on affine mapping and orbit of power function," *3D Research*, vol. 6, article 12, 2015.

[14] T. Jakobsen and L. R. Knudsen, "The interpolation attack on block ciphers," in *Fast Software Encryption: 4th International Workshop, FSE'97 Haifa, Israel, January 20–22 1997 Proceedings*, Lecture Notes in Computer Science, pp. 28–40, Springer, Berlin, Germany, 1997.

[15] N. T. Courtois and J. Pieprzyk, "Cryptanalysis of block ciphers with overdefined systems of equations," in *Advances in Cryptology—ASIACRYPT 2002: 8th International Conference on the Theory and Application of Cryptology and Information Security Queenstown, New Zealand, December 1–5, 2002 Proceedings*, vol. 2501 of *Lecture Notes in Computer Science*, pp. 267–287, Springer, Berlin, Germany, 2002.

[16] T.-S. Chen, C.-C. Chang, and M.-S. Hwang, "A virtual image cryptosystem based upon vector quantization," *IEEE Transactions on Image Processing*, vol. 7, no. 10, pp. 1485–1488, 1998.

[17] Y.-C. Hu, "High-capacity image hiding scheme based on vector quantization," *Pattern Recognition*, vol. 39, no. 9, pp. 1715–1724, 2006.

[18] C.-C. Chang, C.-Y. Lin, and Y.-Z. Wang, "New image steganographic methods using run-length approach," *Information Sciences*, vol. 176, no. 22, pp. 3393–3408, 2006.

[19] W.-Y. Chen, "Color image steganography scheme using set partitioning in hierarchical trees coding, digital Fourier transform and adaptive phase modulation," *Applied Mathematics and Computation*, vol. 185, no. 1, pp. 432–448, 2007.

[20] G.-S. Lin, H. T. Chang, W.-N. Lie, and C.-H. Chuang, "Public-key-based optical image cryptosystem based on data embedding techniques," *Optical Engineering*, vol. 42, no. 8, pp. 2331–2339, 2003.

[21] C.-H. Chuang and G.-S. Lin, "Optical image cryptosystem based on adaptive steganography," *Optical Engineering*, vol. 47, no. 4, Article ID 047002, 2008.

[22] I. Hussain, N. A. Azam, and T. Shah, "Stego optical encryption based on chaotic S-box transformation," *Optics & Laser Technology*, vol. 61, pp. 50–56, 2014.

[23] R. Manoj, N. Hemrajani, and A. K. Saxena, "Secured steganography approach using AES," *International Journal of Computer Science Engineering and Information Technology Research*, vol. 3, no. 3, pp. 185–192, 2013.

[24] H. Sharma, "Secure image hiding algorithm using cryptography and steganography," *IOSR Journal of Computer Engineering*, vol. 13, no. 5, pp. 1–6, 2013.

[25] H. Al-Assam, R. Rashid, and S. Jassim, "Combining steganography and biometric cryptosystems for secure mutual authentication and key exchange," in *Proceedings of the 2013 8th International Conference for Internet Technology and Secured Transactions (ICITST '13)*, pp. 369–374, IEEE, London, UK, March 2013.

[26] D. Bloisi and L. Iocchi, "Image based steganography and cryptography," in *Proceedings of the 2nd International Conference on Computer Vision Theory and Applications (VISAPP '07)*, pp. 127–134, Barcelona, Spain, March 2007.

[27] K. Challita and H. Farhat, "Combining steganography and cryptography: new directions," *International Journal of New Computer Architectures and their Applications*, vol. 1, no. 1, pp. 199–208, 2011.

[28] P. Xu, H. Jin, Q. Wu, and W. Wang, "Public-key encryption with fuzzy keyword search: a provably secure scheme under keyword guessing attack," *IEEE Transactions on Computers*, vol. 62, no. 11, pp. 2266–2277, 2013.

[29] C. Kuo, S. Wang, J. Lin, C. Wang, and J. Yan, "Image encryption based on fuzzy synchronization of chaos systems," in *Proceedings of the IEEE 37th Annual Computer Software and Applications Conference (COMPSAC '13)*, Kyoto, Japan, July 2013.

[30] A. Sahai and B. Waters, "Fuzzy identity-based encryption," in *Advances in Cryptology—EUROCRYPT 2005*, vol. 3494 of *Lecture Notes in Computer Science*, pp. 457–473, 2005.

[31] M. Gardner, "The binary Gray code," in *Knotted Doughnuts and Other Mathematical Entertainments*, chapter 2, W. H. Freeman, New York, NY, USA, 1986.

[32] X.-Y. Wang, S.-X. Gu, and Y.-Q. Zhang, "Novel image encryption algorithm based on cycle shift and chaotic system," *Optics and Lasers in Engineering*, vol. 68, pp. 126–134, 2015.

[33] I. Hussain, T. Shah, M. A. Gondal, W. A. Khan, and H. Mahmood, "A group theoretic approach to construct cryptographically strong substitution boxes," *Neural Computing and Applications*, vol. 23, no. 1, pp. 97–104, 2013.

[34] J. Kim and R. C.-W. Phan, "Advanced differential-style cryptanalysis of the NSA's Skipjack block Cipher," *Cryptologia*, vol. 33, no. 3, pp. 246–270, 2009.

[35] http://sipi.usc.edu/database/database.php.

[36] H. Bahjat and M. A. Salih, "Speed image encryption scheme using dynamic Galois field GF(P) matrices," *International Journal of Computer Applications*, vol. 89, no. 7, pp. 7–12, 2014.

[37] C. H. Chuang and G. S. Lin, "Data steganography for optical color image cryptosystems," *International Journal of Image Processing*, vol. 3, no. 6, pp. 318–327, 2010.

[38] O. M. Olaniyi, O. T. Arulogun, E. O. Omidiora, and O. O. Okediran, "Enhanced stegano-cryptographic model for secure electronic voting," *Journal of Information Engineering and Applications*, vol. 5, no. 4, 2015.

[39] S. Som and S. Sen, "A non-adaptive partial encryption of grayscale images based on chaos," *Procedia Technology*, vol. 10, pp. 663–671, 2013.

7

An SDN-Based Authentication Mechanism for Securing Neighbor Discovery Protocol in IPv6

Yiqin Lu, Meng Wang, and Pengsen Huang

South China University of Technology, Guangzhou, China

Correspondence should be addressed to Meng Wang; w.m15@mail.scut.edu.cn

Academic Editor: Jesús Díaz-Verdejo

The Neighbor Discovery Protocol (NDP) is one of the main protocols in the Internet Protocol version 6 (IPv6) suite, and it provides many basic functions for the normal operation of IPv6 in a local area network (LAN), such as address autoconfiguration and address resolution. However, it has many vulnerabilities that can be used by malicious nodes to launch attacks, because the NDP messages are easily spoofed without protection. Surrounding this problem, many solutions have been proposed for securing NDP, but these solutions either proposed new protocols that need to be supported by all nodes or built mechanisms that require the cooperation of all nodes, which is inevitable in the traditional distributed networks. Nevertheless, Software-Defined Networking (SDN) provides a new perspective to think about protecting NDP. In this paper, we proposed an SDN-based authentication mechanism to verify the identity of NDP packets transmitted in a LAN. Using the centralized control and programmability of SDN, it can effectively prevent the spoofing attacks and other derived attacks based on spoofing. In addition, this mechanism needs no additional protocol supporting or configuration at hosts and routers and does not introduce any dedicated devices.

1. Introduction

IPv6 is a protocol designed as the successor to IPv4 protocol [1]. It is used to solve the problems faced by IPv4 in today's Internet, such as IP address space limitation, security, and scalability. Compared with the 32-bit length of the IP address in IPv4, the IPv6 address comprises 128 bits. This is absolutely enough in the foreseeable future as it supports an address space of $O(2^{32})$. The NDP is an auxiliary protocol for IPv6, and it comprises two RFCs (Requests for Comments): Neighbor Discovery for IPv6 [2] and IPv6 stateless address autoconfiguration (SLAAC) [3]. The former is used for discovery of the IPv6 nodes on the same link, and the latter allows the hosts to automatically configure the IPv6 address without the outside help like DHCP (Dynamic Host Configuration Protocol) server. As the IPv6 address is long and its address space is huge, SLAAC is a very convenient function and makes the IPv6 network become plug-and-play. For the normal operation of IPv6, NDP also provides other functions including router/prefix/parameter discovery, address resolution, next-hop determination, neighbor unreachability detection (NUD), duplicate address detection

(DAD), and redirection. All of these functions are based on the transmission of NDP messages, which are encapsulated in ICMPv6 (Internet Control Message Protocol version 6) packets. Meanwhile, the NDP messages are confined to a link and only transmitted in the scope of a LAN. This means any router will not forward NDP messages from one network to another. According to [2], NDP uses five kinds of ICMPv6 messages as follows.

Router Solicitation (RS). Hosts send RS messages to find the default router and request for the network information from routers.

Router Advertisement (RA). RA message is sent by routers periodically or responses to the RS message.

Neighbor Solicitation (NS). Nodes send NS message to resolve a neighbor node's IPv6 address to its MAC (Media Access Control) address or to detect the reachability of a neighbor.

Neighbor Advertisement (NA). A node sends NA message to answer solicited NS message or sends unsolicited NA

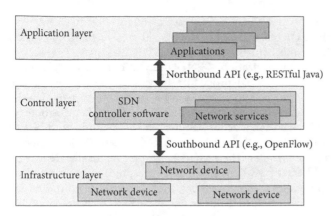

FIGURE 1: SDN architecture.

Match fields	Priority	Counters	Instructions	Timeouts	Cookie

FIGURE 2: A flow entry.

message to propagate its changed information, such as the MAC address variation.

Redirect Message (RM). Routers send redirect packets to inform a host of a better first-hop node on the path to a destination.

Here, we introduce two procedures of the functions to show how the NDP messages are used. The first is address resolution. When a node wants to communicate with another node using IPv6 address without knowing the corresponding MAC address, it will firstly send a multicast NS message to ask all nodes in the LAN who has this IPv6 address. Then, the node occupying this address will send back a unicast NA message to advise its MAC address. The second is DAD procedure. When a node autoconfigures itself with an IPv6 address, it will firstly verify the uniqueness of this address. It orderly sends several NS messages with setting the destination as solicited-node multicast address. Then, if it receives any NA message in response to this solicitation, this address is already used. Otherwise, this address could be issued on the network by this node. From these two examples, we could find that they are vulnerable to be attacked through spoofing. A fake reply to address resolution may lead to MITM (man-in-the-middle) attacks, and forged NAs to DAD will result in DoS (denial-of-service) attacks. Therefore, an effective authentication mechanism is very important for securing the NDP.

SDN is a different network architecture compared with the traditional distributed network. In SDN architecture, the control plane and data plane are decoupled [4], and SDN is designed to have a logical centralized controller and distributed forwarding devices. The whole architecture can be divided into three layers: application layer, control layer, and infrastructure layer, as depicted in Figure 1. The application layer is composed of various applications that are programmed by developers, and the control layer abstracts the underlying infrastructure to provide programmability to the upper layer through northbound API (Application Program Interface). The infrastructure layer contains the physical and virtual network devices, which are conducted by the controller through southbound API. This way, SDN presents many benefits (e.g., the programmability of network, the rise of virtualization, device configuration, and

troubleshooting) to solve the problems and challenges faced in legacy distributed networks [5]. According to the survey of [6], the ability to programmatically control network behavior and view global network state in real time gives SDN exciting possibilities for the network security. For example, the applications in SDN can have a "god view" ability profited from the global view of the controller, but, in traditional networks, the distributed control components only have local information, and it is very difficult to build a global view because of the distribution and autonomy of many network devices. Therefore, we are inspired to think about securing NDP in SDN environment.

OpenFlow (OF) is one of the many southbound API specifications. It is based on an Ethernet switch, with an internal flow table and a standardized interface to add and remove flow entries [7]. The OF specification defines how the packets are processed in OF-enabled switches, and Figure 2 gives an example of a flow entry in a flow table [8]. When the switch receives a packet, it matches the packet header with the flow entries in a flow table. If the packet matches a flow entry, it will be processed according to the actions specified in the entry. Otherwise, it will be sent to the controller as a packet-in message, and the controller will handle it according to the strategies implemented by control components and applications. Then, the controller will send a packet-out message to command the switch to continue processing this packet. According to [8], a packet can trigger a packet-in message through the "send to controller" action, and this packet can be included in the data portion of this packet-in. After the controller handled this packet-in message, a packet-out message will be sent to the switch, and then the switch processes this packet according to the action field of this packet-out. The packet included in packet-in is also included in the data portion of this packet-out. We use this feature to capture the NDP packets transmitted in a LAN and extract the header of these packets from the packet-in messages to authenticate and then send the packets back to switch through packet-out messages.

The rest of this paper is organized as follows. In Section 2, we analyse the security issues in NDP and the existing solutions. Section 3 describes the details of our proposed mechanism. Then, we give a validation experiment and discussion in Section 4. At last, we draw a conclusion and talk about the future works in Section 5.

2. Security Issues and Solutions in NDP

In IPv6 network, NDP is an essential component in a LAN. However, there are many security issues that can be used by attackers to impact the legitimate communication of users. This section analyses the common security issues and talks about the existing solutions.

2.1. Security Issues in NDP. Although the NDP defined many rules for the nodes to send or receive NDP messages legitimately, there is no compulsive method to guarantee the node behaves normally. Therefore, malicious nodes can launch attacks through illegally using NDP messages. Referring to the work of [2, 9–12], we conclude that there are mainly six basic kinds of attacks in NDP as follows.

Spoofing. This attack is executed by using a forged address and may cause a false entry in a node's neighbor cache. Meanwhile, spoofing is often used to leverage other attacks, such as MITM attacks, DoS attacks, and redirect attacks.

MITM Attack. This attack hijacks the communication between two nodes. When node A sends a NS message to resolve the MAC address of node B, the attacker can pretend to answer this NS with spoofed NA. Then, the attacker will receive the subsequent packets from node A and forward them to node B also using spoofed packets. This way, although nodes A and B seem to be normally communicating with each other, the attacker has taken over all the traffic flows between them without being perceived.

DoS Attack. This attack aims to prevent the nodes from normally running the functions provided by NDP. For example, when a node executes the DAD, an attacker can snoop the NS messages sent by this procedure and send back forged NA saying "I have occupied this address." Hence, the victim cannot finish the DAD to get an IPv6 address for the following communication. Similarly, an attacker can send forged RA and NA messages to create DoS attacks on router/prefix/parameter discovery and NUD procedure.

Redirect Attack. An attacker can fabricate RMs to redirect the packets away from the correct path and take over the packets transmitted to a router. Then, the attacker can act as MITM or hinder the normal communication to a remote node.

Replay Attack. The attackers can capture the multicast packets and then resend these packets on the link to confuse the hosts or routers with false information. All neighbor/router discovery messages are prone to replay attacks.

Rogue Router. In this attack, a malicious node can pretend to be a router and send fake RA messages. If a node selects it as default router, it can siphon off the traffic of this node or act as MITM. An attacker can also inject rogue information to poison the routing tables in a good router to prevent victims from accessing the desired network.

Some other sophisticated attacks are the combination of the above attacks. From the above content, we conclude that all attacks rely on the spoofing or abusing of the NDP messages. If there is a perfect authentication mechanism to verify the NDP messages, this protocol can be protected fundamentally and have strong resistibility to various attacks. Many works of securing NDP are making efforts toward this direction, and several related works will be talked about next.

2.2. Existing Solutions of Securing NDP. The SEND (SEcure Neighbor Discovery) protocol [13] is developed by the IETF (Internet Engineering Task Force) to specify security mechanisms for NDP. Actually, NDP intended to use IPsec (IP security) to protect itself through IP layer authentication, but IPsec is not suited for the autoconfiguration in SLAAC, as there is a bootstrapping problem. Therefore, SEND proposed three mechanisms to protect NDP messages. The first is router authorization. SEND uses authorization delegation discovery (ADD) procedure to validate and authorize the IPv6 routers. This is based on a trusted third party, called trust anchor, to issue the certifications. Only after the router is authorized can it act as a router, and every node must certify the router via the trust anchor before setting the router as a default router. The second is Cryptographically Generated Addresses (CGA). A node cryptographically generates IPv6 address by using a one-way hash function from the node's public key and some other parameters. CGA is used to make sure that the sender of NDP packets is the "owner" of the claimed address. The third mechanism aims to protect the integrity of the messages and authenticate the identity of their sender. These three mechanisms consume vast computation resources for computing the cryptographic algorithm. Moreover, the new options add more than one Kbyte to each NDP packet. SEND also introduced some new vulnerabilities and attacks, such as CGA verification vulnerability and DoS attacks on router authorization. In a word, SEND has many limitations including computation, deployment, and security.

The paper [14] proposed an attack detection mechanism for the spoofing of NS and NA messages. The mechanism aims to ensure the genuineness of the IP-MAC pairing through an active verification procedure. It defines six data tables to maintain the information obtained from an IDS (Intrusion Detection System) and uses two main modules named NS-Handler and NA-Handler to handle the NS and NA messages, respectively. For example, when a host sends a NA message to another host, the NA will be checked by the authenticated bindings table, which records the IP-MAC bindings that have been verified by IDS, and if the IP-MAC pair of this message exists in the table, it is judged as genuine. Otherwise, the IDS will send a NS probe packet to verify the source MAC address claimed by this message, and then it will judge the address as genuine or spoofed according to the response. Although this mechanism can prevent the spoofing of NS and NA messages, it still has some drawbacks. On the one hand, the probe analyser module can only detect the existence of spoofing when it receives more than one response but cannot find out which one is genuine. On the other hand, a smart attacker may poison the authenticated binding table through sophisticated spoofing, which will result in false negatives and positives. In addition, it introduces a new IDS device which is connected to a mirror port to monitor all traffic on the network. This is costly and needs the device to have high performance.

The paper [15] proposed a rule-based mechanism to detect the DoS attacks in the DAD process. This method introduced a trusted controller scheme machine to execute the detection rules to verify the generated IPv6 address. It firstly screens out NS/NA packets through ip6tables rules and then uses the control scheme to do detection. For example, when a new host sends NS messages to perform DAD, it will wait for the controller machine to verify the uniqueness of the address, and the host only uses the address after receiving the verification reply from the controller machine. The paper [16]

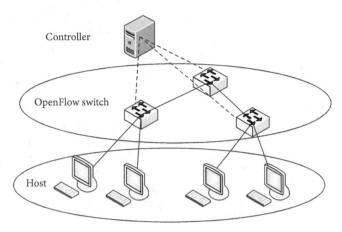

FIGURE 3: Deployment scenario.

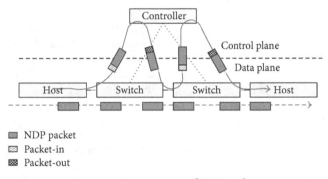

■ NDP packet
▨ Packet-in
▩ Packet-out

FIGURE 4: Transmission of NDP packet.

proposed a pull model to improve the reliability and security of DAD by changing the solicitation model. This proposal reduces the overhead of DAD and enhances the flexibility in address generation, but it is vulnerable to brute force and inverting attacks.

From the above related works, we could see that it is most important to build an effective authentication mechanism to verify the identity of NDP packets for defending the attacks on NDP. SEND and [16] build this mechanism through cryptography and hash algorithm. References [14, 15] introduce a trust component to monitor NDP packets and execute authentication. All of these methods either proposed new protocols that need to be supported by all nodes or built defense mechanisms that require the cooperation of all nodes. This is inevitable in the traditional networks because of the distribution and autonomy of network devices. Moreover, these kinds of methods are usually difficult and costly to deploy in a network. Nevertheless, the SDN provides a new perspective to think about how to build the authentication mechanism. In SDN environment, we can realize the authentication mechanism as a program based on the APIs provided by the controller. It has a global view of the network. Meanwhile, as the network is centralized and controlled, it does not need any new protocol support on distributed devices. Furthermore, the interactive communication of authentication is at the control plane of SDN, which means the mechanism is transparent to all nodes and does not need any additional configuration on the hosts and routers,

totally satisfying the fundamental goal of zero configuration indicated in RFC 3756 [17].

3. The Proposed Mechanism

This section describes the details of the proposed mechanism. We start with an overview of the workflow and then talk about the module and algorithm.

3.1. Workflow Overview. Our proposed mechanism is deployed in an OpenFlow-based SDN network, as depicted in Figure 3. When a switch receives a NDP packet, it will be included in a packet-in message and sent to the controller. Meanwhile, the mechanism listens to packet-in messages and extracts the NDP packet from desired packet-in. Then, it verifies the identity of this packet according to the global information of the network. After this, the NDP is encapsulated in a packet-out message and resent to the switch. At last, the switch will process this packet according to the action specified in packet-out. If the packet successfully passed the verification, the action is to output the packet to the suitable port based on the global topology; otherwise, the action is to drop this packet. The transmission of the NDP packets is depicted in Figure 4; we could see that the mechanism is transparent to the nodes at data plane.

3.2. Module and Algorithm. The whole mechanism contains five modules as depicted in Figure 5. The function of every

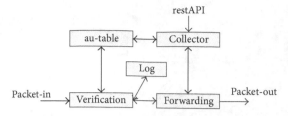

FIGURE 5: Modules of the mechanism.

```
{
  "entityClass":"DefaultEntityClass",
  "mac":[
    "00:00:00:00:00:03"
  ],
  "ipv4": [],
  "ipv6": [
    "fe80::200:ff:fe00:3"
  ],
  "vlan":[
    "0x0"
  ],
  "attachmentPoint": [
    {
      "switchDPID": "00:00:00:00:00:00:00:01"
      "port": 3,
      "errorStatus":null
    }
  ],
  "lastSeen": 1472470896206
},
```

FIGURE 6: JSON data of device information.

module and the details of the algorithm are presented as follows.

Collector. This module is responsible for invoking the restAPIs provided by the controller to get the global information of the network, including device information, global topology, and routing path. Then, it sends the returned JSON (JavaScript Object Notation) data to the module that has sent the invoking command. The device information lists all devices tracked by the controller and their details including MAC, IP, and attachment point. Figure 6 gives an example of the JSON data of this information.

au-Table. This module builds and maintains an authentication table through processing the JSON data of device information returned from the collector. The items of this table comprise MAC address, IPv6 address, and attachment point, as depicted in Table 1. The attachment point item has two subitems named DPID (datapath ID) and port: the former identifies a switch and the latter indicates the accessing port of a device. This item points out the location of a node in the network topology. This table is indexed by the MAC address item, so that it is not allowed to have repetitive entries in this item. Strictly speaking, the duplication of IPv6 address item is

TABLE 1: Authentication table.

MAC	IPv6	Attachment point	
		DPID	Port

also not allowed, but this is the IP conflict problem, which is out of the scope of this paper. In addition, this table is updated periodically every t_0 seconds. This parameter determines the sensitivity to the topology changing, such as a mobile node moving from an attachment point to another one, and this parameter is configured by the administrator according to the experience.

Verification. This module is responsible for verifying the NDP packets and is the core component of this mechanism. At the initial stage, this module sends a flow entry to all switches to capture the ICMPv6 packets. According to [8], this flow entry is configured with the OXM_OF_ETH_TYPE match field setting to match $0x86dd$ (IPv6 type), the OXM_OF_IP_PROTO field setting to match 58 (ICMPv6 type), the *priority* field setting to a high value, and the *instructions* field setting as "send to controller" action. This way, every ICMPv6 packet will be included in a packet-in message and sent to the controller. Here, why we do not capture the NDP packets directly through the OXM_OF_ICMPV6_TYPE match field is because this field is not a required match field, which means it may not be supported by the switch. This module listens to the packet-in messages and screens out the NDP packets according to the value of type field of ICMPv6 packet. If it is between 133 and 137, which means a NDP packet, the process will build an entry according to the packet-in constructed as [sMAC,sIPv6,DPID,port], where sMAC and sIPv6 mean source MAC address and source IPv6 address, respectively. Then, this entry is checked to match the entries in the au-table to finish verification. If the packet is not NDP, this module will do nothing with it, and it will be processed by other default modules of the controller. The pseudocode of the algorithm is shown in Algorithm 1.

According to the algorithm, the process will first check whether the entry [sMAC,sIPv6] exists in re-table. This table records the historical authentication and path-finding and is used to avoid unnecessary cost in look-up and path-finding when a NDP packet passes multiple switches (the following paragraphs will give more details). If the entry [sMAC,sIPv6] exists in re-table, then this NDP packet will be sent to forwarding module immediately. Only when the entry is not in re-table will the process turn to look up in au-table and continue the authentication. The IPv6 address 0:0:0:0:0:0:0:0 is the uncertain address used to specify the default of address when a node is at the initial stage and does not have an address. In this situation, the *ipv6* value of the entry in au-table mapped to this node will be *null*, and we regard these two values as matching. At last, the process executes the forwarding function according to the verification result flagged by the value of *flag*. If *flag* equals two, which means fail, the process also invokes *add_log()* function and adds this event to log module.

```
procedure verification (packet-in,au-table,re-table)
extract information from packet-in
DPID := dpid of the switch sent this packet-in
port := OFPXMT_OFB_IN_PORT {ingress port
of the ICMPv6 packet}
packet := data[] {data field of
packet-in which contains the packet}
header := packet.header
type := header.ICMPv6Header.type
flag := 0
if (type ∉ {133, 134, 135, 136, 137})
    exit
else
    sMAC:=header.sourceMAC
    sIPv6:=header.sourceIPv6
    dMAC:=header.destinationMAC
    dIPv6:=header.destinationIPv6
    if ([sMAC,sIPv6] exists in re-table)
      flag := 0
    else if (sMAC exists in au-table)
      read entry [sMAC,ipv6,dpid,p] from au-table
      if ([sIPv6,DPID,port]==[ipv6,dpid,p])
          flag := 1
      else if (sIPv6==0:0:0:0:0:0:0:0 && ipv6==null
      && [DPID,port]==[dpid,p])
          flag := 1
      else
          flag := 2
    else
        flag := 2
comb:=[sMAC,sIPv6,dMAC,dIPv6,DPID,port]
if (flag == 2)
    add_log ([sMAC,sIPv6,DPID,port])
execute forwarding (packet-in,comb,flag,re-table)
```

ALGORITHM 1

Forwarding. This module processes the packet-in messages according to the verification result. It also maintains a table called re-table to simplify the process of verification and forwarding when the NDP packets traverse multiple switches. Because these packets will be verified and forwarded repeatedly, we record the verification result and path in re-table when a packet is firstly verified and forwarded, and when this packet is sent to the controller again, it will be verified and forwarded immediately according to the information stored in re-table. So it reduces the time cost compared to look-up in au-table, which is usually much bigger than re-table, and avoids repeatedly finding path to the destination. Every entry in this table is constructed as ([smac,sipv6],([dmac,dipv6],path)), where smac/sipv6 and dmac/dipv6 represent the source and destination MAC/IPv6 address, respectively, and *path* indicates the path from the source to the destination node. This table is indexed by the key [smac,sipv6], and every key can map to multiple values because a node may send different NPD packets to different destinations. When the au-table updates an entry (e.g., host changes its connection to another attachment point), the re-table will look up all values of [dmac,dipv6] to examine

whether a value related to the changed entry, and if it does exist, the re-table will find a new path to update the value of *path*. Besides, every entry in re-table only lasts for t_1 seconds, which controls the size of this table. Here, we firstly give the pseudocode of the forwarding algorithm and then explain the details with an example (see Algorithm 2).

Suppose a network is as the topology as shown in Figure 7, and the au-table and re-table have been initialized. Assume all hosts have run for a certain time so that the au-table has three entries and the re-table is empty. The three entries are denoted as [mac1,ip1,s1,p1], [mac2,ip2,s1,p3], and [mac3,ip3,s2,p1]. If host 1 wants to send a NA response packet to host 3, the steps are as follows:

(1) Host 1 sends this packet to port 1 of switch 1.

(2) The packet matches the flow entry and is sent to the controller through a packet-in message.

(3) Verification module verifies this packet. Because the re-table is empty, it looks up in au-table. Then, the packet is matched to the entry [mac1,ip1,s1,p1] and passes the verification with the value of *flag* being one.

```
procedure forwarding (packet-in,comb,flag,re-table)
sMAC:=comb.sMAC
sIPv6:=comb.sIPv6
dMAC:=comb.dMAC
dIPv6:=comb.dIPv6
DPID:=comb.DPID
port:=comb.port
if (flag == 2) {authentication failed}
    send packet-out with drop action
else if (flag == 1)
    path:=collector_find_path ([sMAC,sIPv6,dMAC,dIPv6])
    add ([sMAC,sIPv6],([dMAC,dIPv6],path)) to re-table
    determine action based on path
    send packet-out with the action
else if (flag == 0)
    if ([dMAC,dIPv6] exists in re-table.([sMAC,sIPv6])
    && [DPID,port] exists in path)
        determine action based on stored path
    else
        path:=collector_find_path ([sMAC,sIPv6,dMAC,dIPv6])
        add ([dMAC,dIPv6],path) to re-table.([sMAC,sIPv6])
        determine action based on path
        send packet-out with the action
else
    error value of flag
```

ALGORITHM 2

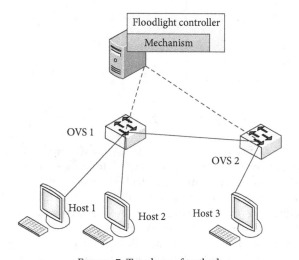

FIGURE 7: Topology of testbed.

(4) Forwarding module invokes function to find a path for the NDP packet, and, according to the topology, the value of *path* is denoted as [(s1,p1),(s1,p2),(s2,p2), (s2,p1)]. The entry ([mac1,ip1],([mac3,ip3],[(s1,p1), (s1,p2),(s2,p2),(s2,p1)])) is added to the re-table. Then, this packet is sent out through port 2 of switch 1 (corresponding to (s1,p2)).

(5) Switch 2 receives the packet at its port 2 and sends it to the controller again.

(6) Verification module firstly looks up in re-table and finds a matching entry. So the process does not check in au-table and executes the forwarding function immediately with the value of *flag* being zero.

(7) Forwarding module firstly checks whether [mac3,ip3] and (s2,p2) both exist in the entry related to the [mac1,ip1] in re-table. As we can see in step (4), they do exist and the next point on the path is (s2,p1), so that the packet is sent out to port 1 of switch 2 immediately. If either of them does not exist in re-table, which may be because host 1 sent a new packet to a new destination or host 3 moved to another attachment point or the link between switches on the path changed, the module will invoke the function to find a new path and update it to the re-table.

(8) Host 3 receives the packet at port 1 of switch 2.

The steps of transmitting other kinds of NDP packets are similar to the above. The main difference is when the NDP packet is a multicast packet; the process will use a special value of *path* to direct the transmission of this packet, and here we do not give more details of the process.

Log. This module is used to record the event of false verification. When the verification module invokes *add_log()* function, this module searches the au-table according to the value of [MAC,DPID,port], and if it finds that an entry in the table is the same as this value, it will regard the device owning this MAC address at attachment point [DPID, port] as a suspicious node. When this situation happens, log module will alarm the administrator to take further actions, such as informing the owner to scan for viruses or set an ACL (Access Control List) for this device.

TABLE 2: Testing result.

Number of packets		Host 1		Host 3		Detection %	False %
Legitimate	Spoofed	Sent NS	Received NA	Received NS	Sent NA		
10	0	10	10	10	10	100%	0
20	10	30	20	20	20	100%	0
200	100	300	200	200	200	100%	0

4. Validation Experiment and Discussion

In this section, we give some results of the experiment to validate the effectiveness of the proposed mechanism. And then we discuss some problems of it.

4.1. Validation Experiment. In this experiment, we use Floodlight [18] as a controller. The topology of the testbed is depicted in Figure 6. The testbed is deployed based on Open vSwitch (OVS) [19] and VirtualBox [20] installed in two servers, respectively. The OVS is virtual OpenFlow-enabled switch software and VirtualBox is virtual machine (VM) software. One server is installed with two OVS VMs and a controller VM, and the other one is installed with three host VMs. Both servers possess 8 CPUs of Intel Core i7-4790 at 3.60 GHz, 32 GB RAM, and multiple NICs (Network Interface Cards).

We use the THC-IPv6 toolkit [21] to generate NDP packets and Wireshark to capture the packets on host 1 and host 3. We send legitimate and spoofed NS packets in different rates from host 1 to host 3 to simulate the address resolution procedure and then check the captured packets to assess the detection rate. The result is shown in Table 2. From this result, we could see that the proposed mechanism filtered all spoofed packets and successfully transmitted the legitimate packets, so it is effective to verify the NDP packets. As the NDP packets belong to the tiny traffic in a LAN, here we do not take stress testing with thousands of NDP packets.

4.2. Discussion. Strictly speaking, this experiment only validates the effectiveness of the proposed mechanism. Its performance and scalability greatly depend on the performance of the controller. As far as we know, some benchmark results of Floodlight show that it can handle more than 30,000 flows every second with 3 switches and more than 7,000 flows every second with 200 switches. As the number of NDP packets sent per unit time is very small, the controller is fully competent to handle the NDP packets timely in a common LAN. In addition, there is a significant problem that we should discuss: why do we not push flow entry to process the subsequent NDP packets at switches but choose to process all of them at the controller? There are two main reasons. Firstly, because the flow entry we used to capture the NDP packets has a very high priority and the action is "send to controller," if we push a new flow entry to process subsequent NDP packets after verification, the packet will be processed starting at the first flow table, so that the packets will match the prior flow entry and will be sent to the controller again. According to

[8], this may lead to a controller-to-switch loop and make the new flow entry and the proposed mechanism invalid. Secondly, the memory resource of the switch is small and precious but the memory of the controller server is sufficient and cheap. Suppose there are m switches and n hosts; in order to process the packet at the granularity that could identify every NDP packet from a host to another host, the number of the flow entries in a switch is $O(n^2 - n)$, but in our solution it is a constant one, which saves much more memory resource of the switch. The size of au-table is determined by the active hosts in a network and is no more than n, and the size of re-table is much smaller than au-table because it only records NDP packets lately sent in t_1 seconds. So the proposed solution takes very little memory resource and the time cost of verification is small. If we do not consider the transition from traditional network to SDN, this mechanism, compared with the mechanism in [13–16], is very easy to deploy and has a low cost, and it is totally transparent to the hosts/routers and does not introduce any dedicated devices.

Actually, this mechanism made an assumption that the controller and switch are trusted and the network global information obtained from the controller is credible and reliable. As the network of switches and controller is usually a separate dedicated network and the connection between switch and controller is through security channel such as TLS connection, this assumption is reasonable and acceptable in real network. If the controller is trusted, all nodes at data plane can be verified by this controller to act as a trustworthy node. This way, we transfer the trust problems at data plane to the control plane. According to the analysis of [8], many threats are not a concern if NDP works in the trust model that all authenticated nodes trust each other to behave correctly at the IP layer and not send spoofed NDP packets. So, if the controller can authenticate the nodes to trust each other, it could provide an ideal trust model for the NDP to work as supposed. As the controller is logically centralized, the security policies for it are easy to be realized by the administrator compared with the complicated configuration and deployment in traditional distributed networks. The problem of single point of failure can be solved by the solutions like master/slave method, which is out of the scope of this paper. In addition, the network that connects the controller and switches is usually physically isolated from the outside networks, and this prevents the compromise from the Internet. In a word, transferring the authentication problems of NDP to the controller provides us with a new perspective to secure the NDP in a way with zero configuration and transparent to hosts and routers.

5. Conclusion and Future Works

In this paper, we proposed an authentication mechanism to verify the source of NDP packets for securing the NDP protocol. This mechanism is based on the functions of SDN controller, and it handles the NDP packets based on the global view of the network. Compared with the solutions in traditional networks, our mechanism does not need any new protocol support or configuration on hosts and routers. This is because we transfer the trust problem in data plane to the control plane, and, with the help of the logical centralization of SDN, we could solve this problem at a single point. The programmability of SDN also makes it easy to realize the solution, and we believe SDN can provide more exciting possibilities for solving the IPv6 security issues.

In the future, we mainly consider three problems. The first problem is the detection of attacks that use the real IPv6 address, such as flooding DoS attacks on address resolution. Secondly, the potential vulnerabilities of this mechanism also need to be researched, and, for example, this mechanism may incur DoS attacks on the controller. At last, as different applications may adopt different strategies for the packet-in messages, the rules or actions conflict should be treated carefully.

Competing Interests

The authors declare that there are no competing interests regarding the publication of this paper.

Acknowledgments

This work is supported by the CERNET Innovation Project NGII20150401.

References

[1] S. Deering and R. Hinden, *Internet Protocol Version 6 (IPv6) Specification*, Internet rfc 2460 edn, 1998.

[2] T. Narten, E. Nordmark, W. Simpson, and H. Soliman, "Neighbor Discovery for IP version 6 (IPv6)," Internet rfc 2461 edn. 2007.

[3] S. Thomson, T. Narten, and T. Jinmei, "IPv6 stateless address autoconfiguration," Internet rfc 4862, 2007.

[4] Open Networking Foundation(ONF), *Software-Defined Networking: The New Norm for Networks*, 2012.

[5] M. Jammal, T. Singh, A. Shami, R. Asal, and Y. Li, "Software defined networking: state of the art and research challenges," *Computer Networks*, vol. 72, pp. 74–98, 2014.

[6] S. T. Ali, V. Sivaraman, A. Radford, and S. Jha, "A survey of securing networks using software defined networking," *IEEE Transactions on Reliability*, vol. 64, no. 3, pp. 1086–1097, 2015.

[7] N. McKeown, T. Anderson, H. Balakrishnan et al., "OpenFlow: enabling innovation in campus networks," *ACM SIGCOMM Computer Communication Review*, vol. 38, no. 2, pp. 69–74, 2008.

[8] Open Networking Foundation(ONF), *OpenFlow Switch Specification Version 1.3.0*, 2012.

[9] F. Xiaorong, L. Jun, and J. Shizhun, "Security analysis for IPv6 neighbor discovery protocol," in *Proceedings of the 2nd International Symposium on Instrumentation and Measurement (IMSNA '13)*, pp. 303–307, Toronto, Canada, December 2013.

[10] A. AlSa'deh and C. Meinel, "Secure neighbor discovery: review, challenges, perspectives, and recommendations," *IEEE Security and Privacy*, vol. 10, no. 4, pp. 26–34, 2012.

[11] C. E. Caicedo, J. B. D. Joshi, and S. R. Tuladhar, "IPv6 security challenges," *Computer*, vol. 42, no. 2, pp. 36–42, 2009.

[12] A. S. Ahmed, R. Hassan, and N. E. Othman, "Improving security for IPv6 neighbor discovery," in *Proceedings of the International Conference on Electrical Engineering and Informatics (ICEEI '15)*, pp. 271–274, IEEE, Denpasar, Indonesia, August 2015.

[13] J. Arkko, J. Kempf, B. Zill, and P. Nikander, "Secure Neighbor Discover (SEND)," Internet rfc 3971 edn. 2005.

[14] F. A. Barbhuiya, S. Biswas, and S. Nandi, "Detection of neighbor solicitation and advertisement spoofing in IPv6 neighbor discovery protocol," in *Proceedings of the 4th International Conference on Security of Information and Networks (SIN '11)*, pp. 111–118, November 2011.

[15] S. U. Rehman and S. Manickam, "Rule-based mechanism to detect Denial of Service (DoS) attacks on Duplicate Address Detection process in IPv6 link local communication," in *Proceedings of the 4th ICRITO (Trends and Future Directions)*, pp. 1–6, 2015.

[16] G. Yao, J. Bi, S. Wang, Y. Zhang, and Y. Li, "A pull model IPv6 duplicate address detection," in *Proceedings of the 35th Annual IEEE Conference on Local Computer Networks (LCN '10)*, pp. 372–375, Denver, Colo, USA, October 2010.

[17] P. Nikander, J. Kempf, and E. Nordmark, "IPv6 Neighbor Discovery (ND) Trust Models and Threats," Internet rfc 3756 edn. 2004.

[18] floodlight, http://www.projectfloodlight.org/.

[19] OpenvSwitch, http://openvswitch.org/.

[20] Virtualbox, https://www.virtualbox.org/.

[21] THC-IPv6, https://www.thc.org/thc-ipv6/.

8

Research on Secure Localization Model Based on Trust Valuation in Wireless Sensor Networks

Peng Li,[1,2] Xiaotian Yu,[1] He Xu,[1,2] Jiewei Qian,[1] Lu Dong,[1] and Huqing Nie[1]

[1]School of Computer Science, Nanjing University of Posts and Telecommunications, Nanjing 210003, China
[2]Jiangsu High Technology Research Key Laboratory for Wireless Sensor Networks, Jiangsu Province, Nanjing 210003, China

Correspondence should be addressed to Peng Li; lipeng@njupt.edu.cn

Academic Editor: Qing Yang

Secure localization has become very important in wireless sensor networks. However, the conventional secure localization algorithms used in wireless sensor networks cannot deal with internal attacks and cannot identify malicious nodes. In this paper, a localization based on trust valuation, which can overcome a various attack types, such as spoofing attacks and Sybil attacks, is presented. The trust valuation is obtained via selection of the property set, which includes estimated distance, localization performance, position information of beacon nodes, and transmission time, and discussion of the threshold in the property set. In addition, the robustness of the proposed model is verified by analysis of attack intensity, localization error, and trust relationship for three typical scenes. The experimental results have shown that the proposed model is superior to the traditional secure localization models in terms of malicious nodes identification and performance improvement.

1. Introduction

WSNs (wireless sensor networks) are composed of a large number of static or mobile sensors. Positioning technologies based on WSN [1] estimate the current location of unknown nodes using the cooperation of position nodes and localization algorithm. In the locating, the nodes whose positions are known are called anchor nodes, while the nodes whose positions are unknown are called unknown nodes. The information on distance of anchor nodes and unknown nodes can be obtained via cooperation. Afterwards, that information and the localization algorithm are used to determine the positions of unknown nodes.

Due to random deployment and network topology dynamicity, the locating in the WSN is more vulnerable to various attacks [2, 3]. On this basis, the secure localization algorithms are widely used. Namely, they can be divided into three categories [4]: (1) secure localization algorithms based on robust observation; (2) secure localization algorithms based on isolation of malicious beacon node; and (3) secure localization algorithms based on localization verification. In the first group, the upper-bound limitation of the nodes'

distance disables the attack node to reduce the measure distance. In the second group, the beacon nodes are used as checkpoints for mutual monitoring, in order to prevent the false localization. In the third group, a predetermined deployment location combined with a set of neighbor nodes is used to determine whether the localization process is attacked or not. However, these algorithms have different shortcomings [5]. The first group's algorithms are unable to resist to the attack, which causes the increase of the measured distance. In addition, the algorithms can only roughly confirm whether the unknown node is in certain area or not. The second group relies too much on the base station node, which might cause the base station overload during the processing of a large amount of node information. Namely, the base station becomes the bottleneck of algorithm performance. The third group's defense capability is greatly influenced by deployment of the nodes. In order to compensate the inadequacy of the above algorithms and to improve their resistance to various attacks, a secure localization model based on trust valuation is designed.

The remainder of the paper is organized as follows. Section 2 introduces related work. In Section 3, we detail the secure localization model and give the formal description. Section 4 makes some simulation and analysis on secure localization model based on trust valuation. Section 5 concludes the paper.

2. Related Works

According to the usage of distance in the positioning, the positioning technologies can be divided into two main categories: distance-based (range-based) positioning technologies and distance-independent (range-free) positioning technologies. In the distance-based positioning algorithms, the absolute distance, or angle, between anchor node and unknown node is required. On the other hand, in distance-independent localization algorithms, there is no need to obtain the exact distance between anchor and unknown nodes. The distance-based localization algorithms usually consist of two steps: firstly, the distance (or angle) is measured, and, secondly, the measured distance is used to calculate the coordinates of unknown node. The distance measurement methods can be divided into following categories: methods based on time, methods based on signal arrival angle, and methods based on received signal strength.

The principle of distance-independent localization is simple and easy to implement, and it has advantages in terms of cost and power consumption. Besides, its performance is not affected by environmental factors. These algorithms can be divided into four categories: APTI algorithm, DV-Hop algorithm [6], Amorphous algorithm [7], and N-hop algorithm.

In the WSN, the localization algorithm can be attacked in many ways. The attacks can be divided into two categories: internal attacks and external attacks. Four types of external attacks are concerned: Sybil attack [8], selective forwarding attack, wormhole attack, and node capture attack [9–11].

Due to limitation on sensor nodes, it is impossible to have a well-integrated defense system in the traditional WSN. The secure localization algorithms intended for WSN need to balance availability and integrity. According to that, the security localization algorithms can be divided into three categories: secure localization algorithms based on robust observation, secure localization algorithms based on isolation of malicious beacon node, and secure localization algorithms based on localization verification.

The gradual application of WSN localization caused the appearance of various attack methods [12]. Nowadays, the main secure localization algorithm in the WSN has no ability to deal with the internal attacks and to identify the malicious nodes. Moreover, in the case of nodes compromising, the secure localization cannot be achieved. Thus, the trust management, which has been widely studied in various network environments, is considered as an effective complement to the traditional localization.

In 1994, Marsh proposed a model of trust and cooperation for the first time, which has been regarded for a long time as a scope of sociology and psychology. In addition, Marsh introduced the concept of trust relationship formalization. In 1996, Blaze et al. proposed the concept of trust model in order to solve the complex security problems in the Internet [13].

The trust management models can be roughly divided into two categories: objective trust management models and subjective trust management models. The objective trust management models abstract the trust value into Boolean value; thus, there are only two possibilities for trust value. Due to the aforementioned, the commonly used trust management models are subjective trust management models. The most popular subjective trust management models are presented in the following.

(1) Pervasive Trust Management. Pervasive Trust Management (PTM) represents a subresearch project of the UBISEC project, which defines a dynamic trust model based on a pervasive environment. The method of average weight is used for trust evaluation, and the evaluation result for two interactive entities can be expressed as

$$R(A, B) = \alpha, \quad \alpha \in [0, 1],$$

$$\exists R(A, B) = \alpha \mid G(\alpha^+ \longrightarrow R(A, B) \geq \alpha) \tag{1}$$

$$\wedge G(\alpha^- \longrightarrow R(A, B) < \alpha),$$

where α represents the trust value, α^+ indicates that trust increases when feedback is positive, and α^- indicates that trust decreases when feedback is negative.

The disadvantage of this model is that the arithmetic mean is used to calculate the indirect trust degree. In addition, this method processes data roughly and cannot accurately reflect the characteristics of the fuzzy trust value.

(2) Hassan's Model. Hassan's model is based on vector mechanism. If there are n entities, namely, $Q_1, Q_2, Q_3, \ldots, Q_n$, then, the relationship between entity Q_i and other entities can be represented as a trust vector: $\vec{Q_i} = (t_{Q_i Q_1}, t_{Q_i Q_2}, \ldots, t_{Q_i Q_{i-1}}, t_{Q_i Q_{i+1}}, t_{Q_i Q_n})$.

The disadvantage of this model is that it is not resistant to the collusion attacks. Namely, malicious nodes can give each other a high trust value.

(3) Sun's Model. Sun's model is based on entropy; namely, it uses T to express trust relationship, while P represents the probability that the agent nodes take action to the target nodes. The calculation process of trust value used in Sun's model is shown as

$$T = \begin{cases} 1 - H(p), & 0.5 \leq p \leq 1, \\ H(p) - 1, & 0 \leq p \leq 0.5, \end{cases} \tag{2}$$

where $H(p) = -p \log_2^{(p)} - (1-p) \log_2^{1-p}$ represents the entropy function. Then, the trust value is defined by

$$T_{ABC} = R_{AB} T_{BC}, \tag{3}$$

where T_{ABC} represents the trust degree of node A to node C, T_{BC} denotes direct trust value of node B to node C, and R_{AB} denotes the recommendation trust value of node A to node B.

The convergence rate of Sun's model is limited by the length of trust chain, and it is difficult to get the trust value when the trust chain length increases.

3. Secure Localization Model Based on Trust Valuation

3.1. Trust Valuation Basis. The concepts in trust valuation and roles of nodes are listed as follows.

Definition 1. Comprehensive trust value is based on the localization error and time consumption of the beacon nodes, and it refers to the adoption level of the information provided by the beacon nodes.

Definition 2. Direct trust value refers to the confidence of unknown node in the anchor node, which is directly involved in the localization process.

Definition 3. Indirect trust value refers to the confidence of unknown node in the anchor node based on recommendation from other nodes.

Definition 4. Recommended trust value refers to the confidence of unknown node in the recommended nodes.

Definition 5. Source node represents an unknown node in the localization process.

Definition 6. Target node represents an anchor node needed for the localization.

Definition 7. Recommended nodes represent all nodes used in the localization except source node and target node.

3.1.1. Trust Valuation Framework. In the WSN localization, the unknown node N sends the localization request, Loc_req, and the beacon node B, which is within communication range of node N, sends the response, Loc_ack, to node N after receiving of its request. Then, N calculates direct trust value D for node B using the valuation algorithm. Other beacon nodes, which are within the communication range of node N, form the recommended node set defined as $R = \{B_1, B_2, \ldots, B_i\}$. In order to get indirect trust value of node B, node N calculates the recommended trust value of nodes in R. Therefore, the indirect trust value of node B for node N is obtained and labeled as M. According to all mentioned, the comprehensive trust value is defined as

$$C = \alpha D + \beta M, \quad (4)$$

where α and β represent weight coefficients of direct and recommended trust values, respectively, and C represents the comprehensive trust value. The frame diagram of trust validation is shown in Figure 1.

3.1.2. Direct Trust. According to the multidimensional decision theory [14], the direct trust of source node for target node consists of n attributes that form a set of attributes $S = \{p_1, p_2, \ldots, p_i, \ldots, p_n\}$ $(0 \leq p_i \leq 1)$.

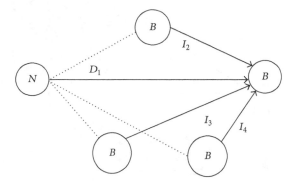

FIGURE 1: Frame diagram of trust validation.

Each attribute value has different influence on calculation of direct trust value; thus, the weight vector is defined as $V = \{v_1, v_2, \ldots, v_i, \ldots, v_n\}$ $(0 \leq v_i \leq 1, \sum_{i=1}^{n} v_i = 1)$. Moreover, the time decay function, $T(k)$, defined by (5), is used to calculate the direct trust value:

$$T(k) = \begin{cases} 0 & k = 0, \\ 1 & k = 1, \\ T(k-1) - \left(\dfrac{1}{2}\right)^{k-1} & 1 \leq k \leq n. \end{cases} \quad (5)$$

Based on the above function, the kth calculation of direct trust value is obtained. The direct trust value function is defined by

$$W_k^{(p,v)} = T(k) \times \sum_{i=1}^{n} v_i \times p_i. \quad (6)$$

All previous direct trust values are combined in order to obtain the final result:

$$D_{xy} = \prod_{k=1}^{n} W_k^{(p,v)}, \quad (7)$$

where D_{xy} indicates the direct trust value of the source node x for target node y. The difference between direct trust values of attack node and normal node is enlarged by this calculation method. In case of attack, the node is close to zero according to the calculated $W_k^{(p,v)}$ value, and the node will be abandoned.

3.1.3. Indirect Trust and Recommended Trust. The trust model is composed of three types of nodes, the source node, the target node, and the recommended node, which form the trust chain as shown in Figure 2.

In Figure 2, S, R, and O represent the source node, the recommended node, and the target node, respectively, while I and D indicate the recommended trust value and the direct trust value, respectively.

Received Signal Strength Indicator (RSSI) represents the strength of the received signal [15], with the RSSI signal attenuation model in WSN defined by

$$RSSI(d) = C_0 - 10\lambda \log_{10}^{d}, \quad (8)$$

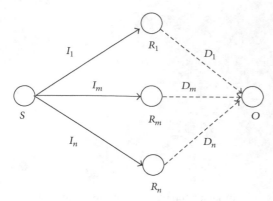

FIGURE 2: Trust chain.

where RSSI(d) represents the signal strength at distance d from the transmitter, C_0 indicates the signal strength reference value from the transmitter, and λ denotes the path loss factor.

Due to the influence of environmental noise, there may be errors when measuring RSSI. Thus, (8) can be modified to

$$\text{RSSI}(d) = C_0 - 10\lambda \log_{10}^d + E, \qquad (9)$$

where the measurement error E follows the normal distribution defined by

$$E \sim N\left(0, \sigma^2\right), \qquad (10)$$

where σ is random variable changes depending on the existing environment [16].

Some experiments were carried out in article [17], in order to describe the relationship between the RSSI error and the corresponding distance. It adopts regular pattern as the communication model, and the communication radius of the nodes is 20 m. The distance between two nodes is fixed and RSSI values are observed 100 times. It repeats the observation of RSSI value as the distance between two nodes increases; it comes to the conclusion as shown in Figure 3.

As can be seen from Figure 3, the error of RSSI gradually increases with the increasing of distance within communication range. However, the error decreases gradually when distance is beyond the scope of communication. Since the distance is calculated according to the RSSI value, the variation law of distance error is coincident with RSSI error. Thus we get Theorem 8.

Theorem 8. *The error, that is, the difference between measured and actual distance values, increases with the increase of distance between nodes [18].*

According to Theorem 8, three anchor nodes that are closest to the target node will be selected as recommended nodes and labeled as R_l, R_m, and R_n. Recommendation trust value is then defined as

$$I_{xy}(k, s, n) = \begin{cases} \dfrac{1}{2} & i = 1, \\[2mm] \dfrac{1 + \sum_{i=1}^{n} T(k) \times s_i}{2 + n} & i > 1, \end{cases} \qquad (11)$$

where n denotes the total number of nodes that participate in the trust calculation and s_i represents the Boolean value that indicates whether the node is being trusted in calculation of direct trust. The initial value of the recommended trust value is 1/2. After a certain period, the value fluctuates due to performance of recommended node.

Finally, the indirect trust value is obtained by

$$M_{xy}(k, s, n, p, v) = \frac{\left(I_{xu}(k, s, n) \times D_{uy}(p, v) + I_{xv}(k, s, n) \times D_{vy}(p, v) + I_{xw}(k, s, n) \times D_{wy}(p, v)\right)}{3}. \qquad (12)$$

3.1.4. Comprehensive Trust. Based on direct and indirect trust values, the comprehensive trust value of the source node for the target node is obtained, namely, $C = \alpha D + \beta M$. Similar to that in the ordinary trust valuation, α and β are generally considered as fixed values; thus, the trust model has no dynamic adaptability. Therefore, an adjustment method based on information entropy theory [19] is proposed.

In the calculation of comprehensive trust value, the information entropy of direct trust value is defined by

$$\begin{aligned} H_{sd} &= \sum_{i=1}^{n} p_i I_\varepsilon = -\sum_{i=1}^{n} p_i \log_2(p_i) \\ &= -D_{xy}(p, v) \times \log_2\left(D_{xy}(p, v)\right) \\ &\quad - \left(1 - D_{xy}(p, v)\right) \times \log_2\left(1 - D_{xy}(p, v)\right). \end{aligned} \qquad (13)$$

Similarly, the information entropy of indirect trust value is defined by

$$\begin{aligned} H_{sm} &= \sum_{i=1}^{n} p_i I_e = -\sum_{i=1}^{n} p_i \log_2(p_i) \\ &= -M_{xy}(k, s, n, p, v) \times \log_2\left(M_{xy}(k, s, n, p, v)\right) \\ &\quad - \left(1 - M_{xy}(k, s, n, p, v)\right) \\ &\quad \times \log_2\left(1 - M_{xy}(k, s, n, p, v)\right). \end{aligned} \qquad (14)$$

Through the calculation of direct and indirect trust values of information entropy, the certain information can be acquired. The weight distribution is obtained as

$$\begin{aligned} \alpha &= \frac{H_{sm}}{H_{sd} + H_{sm}}, \\[2mm] \beta &= \frac{H_{sd}}{H_{sd} + H_{sm}}. \end{aligned} \qquad (15)$$

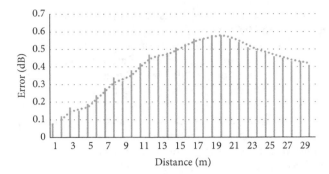

FIGURE 3: Relationship between distance and error.

3.2. Key Technologies

3.2.1. Attribute Set Selection

(1) Distance Measurement. The difference between measured and actual distances in the WSN positioning obeys to the normal distribution [20]. Therefore, the error function can be defined by

$$\sigma_N(d) = ae^{-(d-d_0)^2/b^2}, \tag{16}$$

where $\sigma_N(d)$ refers to the Gaussian function of distance d. When $d = d_0$, the measurement error reaches its maximal value. In summary, the p_1 attribute of the measured distance value is defined as

$$p_1(d) = \begin{cases} \dfrac{d}{d_0} & d \le d_0, \\[2mm] \dfrac{d - d_0}{d_0} & d > d_0. \end{cases} \tag{17}$$

(2) Localization Performance

Definition 9. The unknown node's location reference set is defined as $R = \{(x_1, y_1, d_1), (x_2, y_2, d_2), \ldots, (x_i, y_i, d_i), \ldots, (x_n, y_n, d_n)\}$, where (x_i, y_i) represents the coordinates set of the anchor node i and d_i is the distance between anchor node i and unknown node.

Definition 10. The residual represents the deviation of observed distance value and real distance value, and the total localization residual is defined as

$$\sigma_{\text{sum}} = \sum_{i=1}^{n} \left| \sqrt{(x - x_i)^2 + (y - y_i)^2} - d_i \right|, \tag{18}$$

where x and y represent the measured coordinates of unknown node, x_i, and y_i denote the coordinates of anchor node, and d_i is measured distance between beacon node i and unknown node.

In (18), the coordinates x and y are obtained by the least square method and the least squares regression model [21, 22], while the estimation function is defined by

$$d_i^2 = (x - x_i)^2 + (y - y_i)^2 + \eta,$$

$$(x, y) = \arg\min \sum_{i=1}^{n} \left(\sqrt{(x_i - x_0)^2 + (y_i - y_0)^2} - d_i \right)^2, \tag{19}$$

where η is the measurement error and $\eta \sim U(-\varepsilon, \varepsilon)$ [23], while ε is the maximal measurement error defined as

$$\max \left| d_i - \sqrt{(x_i - x)^2 + (y_i - y)^2} \right| \le \varepsilon. \tag{20}$$

The residuals are used to indicate the degree of each node's deviation from its true location. The mean residual error is defined as

$$\rho = \frac{\sigma_{\text{sum}}}{n} \le \xi, \tag{21}$$

where n represents the number of anchor nodes involved in positioning. In order to define a threshold, value of ε is needed. When the mean residual error is smaller than the threshold value, the localization result is considered as consistent. Otherwise, the presence of malicious nodes is indicated. The attribute value of localization performance p_2 is defined as

$$p_2 = \begin{cases} \dfrac{\rho}{\zeta}, & \rho \le \zeta, \\[2mm] 0, & \rho > \zeta. \end{cases} \tag{22}$$

(3) Detection of Anchor Node Position. Based on (22), the major attacks can be filtered by comprehensive trust value. Nevertheless, in the case of Sybil attack, the above attribute value is not enough to fight against the attack.

Definition 11. The concept of Sybil attack in the WSN indicates that a single node has a multiple identity.

The RSSI signal attenuation model in WSN environment is defined by (8).

According to the attenuation model, the distance ratio can be deduced as

$$\frac{d_r^i}{d_r^j} = 10^{(\text{RSSI}(d_r^i) - \text{RSSI}(d_r^j))/10\lambda}, \tag{23}$$

where d_r^i is the distance between receiver and transmitter. From (23), it can be concluded that the distance ratio is related only to the RSSI difference. Therefore, (23) can be rewritten as

$$\frac{d_r^i}{d_r^j} = f\left(\text{RSSI}\left(d_r^i\right) - \text{RSSI}\left(d_r^j\right)\right). \tag{24}$$

Based on the above analyses, we know that if the distance between receiver and transmitter is constant, the RSSI difference is stable. The positioning in the case of Sybil attack is presented in Figure 4.

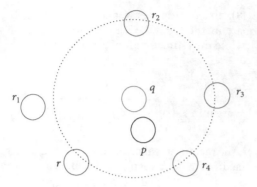

FIGURE 4: Localization in the case of Sybil attack.

In Figure 4, p is an unknown node, q is an auxiliary judgment node, and r_1, r_2, r_3, and r_4 denote the false localization information, while the anchor node r is the attacked node. The RSSI value is affected by environment; thus, the measured distance between node r and node p will change according to the RSSI fluctuation. Therefore, the auxiliary node q is introduced. According to the above analysis, the difference between RSSI(d_r^p) and RSSI(d_r^q) is stable. Thus, according to (23), the value of d_r^q/d_r^p remains stable.

The coordinates of q are (x_q, y_q), the coordinates of p are (x_p, y_p), and the coordinates of r are (x_r, y_r).

(1) When $k = \pm 1$, (26) can be simplified as (23). According to the form of (27), it can be concluded that the equation represents a straight line.

(2) When $k \neq \pm 1$, (26) can be simplified as (28).

The discriminant of circle defined as $D^2 + E^2 - 4F$ is substituted into (29).

When $k \neq \pm 1$, the result is always greater than zero. In summary, the trajectory of r is a circle or a straight line.

According to the above conclusions, the difference of RSSI is stable only when the faked nodes are distributed strictly in standard circle or straight line. Therefore the difference between RSSI(d_r^p) and RSSI(d_r^q) can be used against the witch attack.

At time moment t_1, node p is an unknown node, nodes q and r are the auxiliary nodes, and nodes s, t are the anchor nodes. In the following moments, t_2 and t_3, RSSI is detected by these values.

Definition 12.

$$\text{diff}_{t_1}(p,q,r) = \left| \text{RSSI}\left(d_r^p\right) - \text{RSSI}\left(d_r^q\right) \right|$$

when the current moment is t_1,

$$\begin{aligned}
&\text{diff}_{t_1}(p,q,r,s,t) \\
&= \max\Big(\left| \text{diff}_{t_1}(p,q,s) - \text{diff}_{t_1}(p,q,t) \right|, \\
&\quad \left| \text{diff}_{t_1}(p,q,s) - \text{diff}_{t_1}(p,q,t) \right|, \\
&\quad \left| \text{diff}_{t_1}(p,q,s) - \text{diff}_{t_1}(p,q,t) \right| \Big), \\
&\text{diff}(p,q,r,s,t) = \max\Big(\text{diff}_{t_n}(p,q,r,s,t) \Big)
\end{aligned}$$

$$1 \leq n \leq 3.$$

(25)

Thus, the definition of attribute value p_3 is defined as (30).

$$\frac{\sqrt{\left(x_r - x_q\right)^2 + \left(y_r - y_q\right)^2}}{\sqrt{\left(x_r - x_p\right)^2 + \left(y_r - y_p\right)^2}} = k \Longrightarrow$$

(26)

$$\left(x_r - x_q\right)^2 + \left(y_r - y_q\right)^2 = k^2 \left(\left(x_r - x_p\right)^2 + \left(y_r - y_p\right)^2 \right) \Longrightarrow$$

$$\left(k^2 - 1\right) x_r^2 + \left(k^2 - 1\right) y_r^2 - 2 x_r \left(x_q - k^2 x_p\right) - 2 y_r \left(y_q - k^2 y_p\right) = k^2 \left(x_p^2 + y_p^2\right) - \left(x_q^2 + y_q^2\right),$$

$$y_r = \frac{x_p - x_q}{y_q - y_p} x_r + \frac{x_q^2 + y_q^2 - x_p^2 - y_p^2}{2\left(y_q - y_p\right)},$$

(27)

$$x_r^2 + y_r^2 - \frac{2\left(x_q - k^2 x_p\right)}{k^2 - 1} x_r + \frac{2\left(y_q - k^2 y_q\right)}{k^2 - 1} y_r + \frac{\left(x_q^2 + y_q^2\right) - k^2\left(x_p^2 + y_p^2\right)}{k^2 - 1} = 0,$$

(28)

$$\frac{4\left(x_q - k^2 x_p\right)^2}{\left(k^2 - 1\right)^2} + \frac{4\left(y_q - k^2 y_p\right)^2}{\left(k^2 - 1\right)^2} - \frac{4\left(x_q^2 + y_q^2\right) - 4k^2\left(x_p^2 + y_p^2\right)}{k^2 - 1}$$

$$\Longrightarrow \frac{4x_q^2 - 8k^2 x_q x_p + 4k^4 x_p^2 + 4y_q^2 - 8k^2 y_q y_p + 4k^4 y_p^2}{\left(k^2 - 1\right)^2} - \frac{4\left(x_q^2 + y_q^2\right) - 4k^2\left(x_p^2 + y_p^2\right)}{k^2 - 1}$$

$$\implies \frac{8x_q^2 - 8k^2 x_q x_p + 8y_q^2 - 8k^2 y_q y_p - 4k^2 x_q^2 - 4k^2 y_q^2 + 4k^2 x_p^2 + 4k^2 y_p^2}{(k^2-1)^2}$$

$$\implies \frac{4k^2\left(y_p - y_q\right)^2 + 4k^2\left(x_p - x_q\right)^2 + \left(1+k^2\right)\left(8x_q^2 + 8y_q^2\right)}{(k^2-1)^2},$$

$$(29)$$

$$p_3 = \begin{cases} \dfrac{\left|\mathrm{diff}\left(p,q,r,s,t\right)\right|}{\tau} & \left|\mathrm{diff}\left(p,q,r,s,t\right)\right| \le \tau, \\ 1 & \left|\mathrm{diff}\left(p,q,r,s,t\right)\right| > \tau. \end{cases} \tag{30}$$

(4) Transit Time Detection. As it is well known, there are many attacks in the WSN [24, 25], which mainly consist of replayed attacks, Sybil attacks, and wormhole attacks. In these attacks, the certain time is needed to tamper the information. As a result, the time used for positioning will increase. Figure 5 represents the node communication process.

Node p is the source node, while node q is the target node. The observation time of the target node is $T = t_3 - t_2$. Before positioning, the n group of experiment were conducted. In the experiments, a set of times T was obtained. The maximum value T_{max} was selected from the set.

Based on the experimental results, the definition of attribute value p is obtained by

$$p_4 = \begin{cases} 0 & T > T_{max}, \\ \dfrac{T}{T_{max}} & T \le T_{max}. \end{cases} \tag{31}$$

3.2.2. Discussion on Threshold. In Section 3.2.1, the attribute set selection and calculation processes are presented. Equations (20), (21), and (26) are all crucial for the threshold. According to (20), the threshold ε and the maximal measurement error should be discussed.

In the environment without obstacles, according to Definition 9, the localization error follows the normal distribution defined by

$$d_E \sim N\left(0, \sigma^2\right). \tag{32}$$

The second parameter of normal distribution is determined in the literature [26]. The relationship between parameter σ and the distance d can be fitted into the Gaussian function shown as

$$\sigma(d) = ae^{-(d-d_0)^2/b^2}. \tag{33}$$

According to the above analysis, when distance between unknown node and anchor node is d_0, the standard deviation of the distance error reaches the maximum. Therefore, the maximal deviation value between measured and calculated distances can be used as a threshold. The positioning in the presence of obstacles is presented in Figure 6.

In Figure 6, M represents an obstacle between the anchor node p_3 and the unknown node q. According to the trilateral localization algorithm principle, when the RSSI is much smaller than the normal value, the localization fails.

In the case of localization failure, the RSSI values of the nodes are RSSI$(p_1 q)$, RSSI$(p_2 q)$, RSSI$(p_3 q)$, RSSI$(p_1 p_2)$, RSSI$(p_2 p_3)$, and RSSI$(p_1 p_3)$. Because RSSI$(p_3 q)$ is much smaller than the normal value, the distance calculated by the distance attenuation model is larger than distance of $p_3 q$.

If $p_3 q > p_1 p_3 + p_1 q$ and $p_3 q > p_2 p_3 + p_2 q$, there is a barrier between node q and node p_3. In the environment with obstacles, the distance between two nodes, which are affected by the obstacles, is the maximal distance between the obstacles. The maximal measurement error can be obtained by derivations as

$$\cos\left(\angle p_3 p_1 p_2\right) = \frac{p_1 p_3^2 + p_1 p_2^2 - p_2 p_3^2}{2 p_1 p_3} \times p_1 p_2,$$

$$\cos\left(\angle q p_1 p_2\right) = \frac{p_1 q^2 + p_1 p_2^2 - p_2 q^2}{2 p_1 q} \times p_1 p_2. \tag{34}$$

At the same time, (35) can be obtained:

$$\cos\left(\angle p_3 p_1 q\right) = \cos\left(\angle p_3 p_1 p_2\right)\cos\left(\angle q p_1 p_2\right)$$
$$+ \sin\left(\angle p_3 p_1 p_2\right)\sin\left(\angle q p_1 p_2\right). \tag{35}$$

According to the values of $\cos(\angle p_3 p_1 q)$, $p_1 p_3$ and $p_1 q$, $p_3 q$ can be obtained by

$$p_3 q = \sqrt{p_1 q^2 + p_1 p_3^2 - 2 p_1 q \times p_1 p_3 \times \cos\left(p_3 p_1 q\right)}. \tag{36}$$

In an environment with obstacles, $\varepsilon = d_{p_3 q} - p_3 q$. $d_{p_3 q}$ is the distance value obtained by distance attenuation model.

In (21), $\rho = \sigma_{\mathrm{sum}}/n \le \xi$, and threshold ξ is a mean residual.

Definition 13. In the WSN positioning, the reference node set is *Loc_refer* = $\{l_1, l_2, l_3, l_4, l_n\}$, and the information frame format of each reference node is $(x_i, y_i, d_{\mathrm{rssi}_i})$, wherein (x_i, y_i) are the reference node coordinates, and d_{rssi_i} is the distance between reference node and unknown node.

According to Definition 13, the localization error of each reference node in the security localization can be obtained by

$$e_i = \left| d_{\mathrm{rssi}_i} - \sqrt{\left(x_i - x\right)^2 + \left(y_i - y\right)^2} \right|, \tag{37}$$

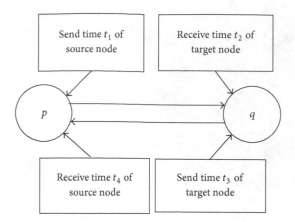

FIGURE 5: Communication process between nodes.

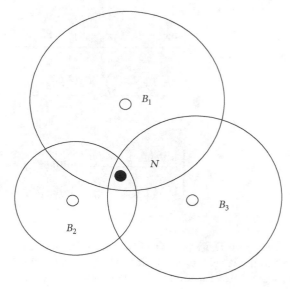

FIGURE 7: Trilateral-centroid localization.

Based on the above conclusions, (40) can be obtained:

$$\lim_{n\to\infty} P\left(p \le \xi\right) = \lim_{n\to\infty} P\left(q_n \le n\xi\right)$$

$$= \lim_{n\to\infty}\left(\frac{q_n - \mu_0}{\sigma_0} \le \frac{n\xi - \mu_0}{\sigma_0}\right) \qquad (40)$$

$$= \Phi\left(\frac{n\xi - \mu_0}{\sigma_0}\right).$$

According to (40), the standard normal distribution can be obtained. Therefore, the standard normal distribution table can be used to set the appropriate threshold ξ in different environments.

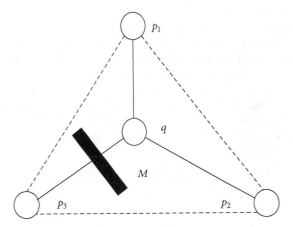

FIGURE 6: Localization in the presence of obstacles.

3.2.3. Localization Process. According to the trust valuation model, the trust value of each anchor node can be obtained in the communication range of the unknown node. Three anchor nodes with the largest value of trust are used for computing.

Trilateral-centroid localization [28] is used for unknown node localization. The unknown node is N, and the three beacon nodes are B_1, B_2, B_3. Trilateral-centroid localization is shown in Figure 7.

The coordinates of three anchor nodes are (x_1, y_1), (x_2, y_2), and (x_3, y_3). Unknown node coordinate is (x, y). Measurement distance values are d_1, d_2, and d_3. Equation (41) can be listed according to Figure 7:

where e_i is the localization error of each reference node, and (x, y) refers to the actual position of the unknown node.

$$p_n = \frac{\sum_{i=1}^{n} e_i}{n}. \qquad (38)$$

In (38), p_n represents the average localization error, and e_i obeys the normal distribution; thus p_n also obeys the normal distribution. In the experimental environment, the mean μ and the variance σ of the p_n were obtained by the actual measurement.

According to the central limit theorem [27], when $n \to \infty$, the distribution function of $Y_n = (\sum_{k=1}^{n} P_k - n\mu_0)/n\sigma_0$ obeys the standard normal distribution, where $\mu_0 = \mu$, $\sigma_0 = \sqrt{n}\sigma$. If q_n is equal to $n * p_n$, then we may get

$$\sqrt{(x - x_1)^2 + (y - y_1)^2} = d_1,$$

$$\sqrt{(x - x_2)^2 + (y - y_2)^2} = d_2, \qquad (41)$$

$$\sqrt{(x - x_3)^2 + (y - y_3)^2} = d_3.$$

$$\lim_{n\to\infty} p\left(\frac{q_n - \mu_0}{\sigma_0} \le x\right) = \Phi(x). \qquad (39)$$

According to (38) and the least square method, unknown node coordinates can be obtained as follows [29]:

$$\begin{bmatrix} x \\ y \end{bmatrix} = \begin{bmatrix} 2\left(x_1 - x_3\right) 2\left(y_1 - y_3\right) \\ 2\left(x_2 - x_3\right) 2\left(y_2 - y_3\right) \end{bmatrix}^{-1}$$
$$\cdot \begin{bmatrix} x_1^2 - x_3^2 + y_1^2 - y_3^2 + d_3^2 - d_1^2 \\ x_2^2 - x_3^2 + y_2^2 - y_3^2 + d_3^2 - d_2^2 \end{bmatrix}. \tag{42}$$

In addition, due to the presence of measurement errors, in some cases, the equations may not be solvable (as shown in Figure 7). In this case, the center of triangle is formed by the intersection of all circles, taken as the coordinates of the unknown point.

There are six intersections among three circles in Figure 8. The coordinates of the three intersection points which are close to the unknown nodes are (x_1, y_1), (x_2, y_2), and (x_3, y_3). The coordinates of the estimated position of the unknown node are (x, y). Thus we can calculate (x, y) via

$$(x, y) = \left(\frac{x_1 + x_2 + x_3}{3}, \frac{y_1 + y_2 + y_3}{3} \right). \tag{43}$$

4. Simulation and Analysis

4.1. Experiment of Environment Selection and Parameter Setting. Matlab7.0 experimental platform is used as the simulation environment. In this simulation environment, 100 nodes are randomly deployed in the range of 100 m * 100 m [30]. The number of anchor nodes and unknown nodes is 40 and 60, respectively. The communication radius of the nodes is 20 m, and the communication model is the regular pattern. The path loss factor is $\eta = 2.5$ and the range standard deviation is $\sigma = 0.5$.

4.2. Simulation Experiment. In the simulation experiment, three types of nodes are listed as follows: attack node, anchor node, or unknown node. First of all, three groups of experiments are carried out under different environments. The experimental conditions are listed as follows: nonexisting attack nodes, attack nodes existing, and attack nodes existing under trust valuation model.

According to Figures 9, 10, and 11, it can be concluded that the localization error increases with the increasing of attack nodes. When the trust valuation model is added in the localization process, the localization error recovers to normal level.

In addition, the robustness of the model is also investigated. One is attack power and the other is the number of attack nodes.

As can be seen from Figure 12, when the number of attack nodes is less than 20, the localization error of secure localization model is much smaller than normal localization algorithm. However, when the number of attack nodes exceeds 20, the localization error increases sharply, since the attack node produces much fake information with consistency. The system cannot distinguish between malicious nodes and normal nodes through the consistency of the given information.

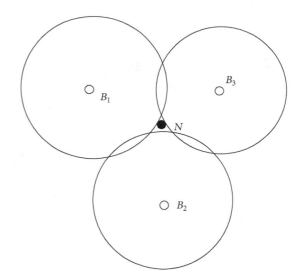

FIGURE 8: Trilateral-centroid localization.

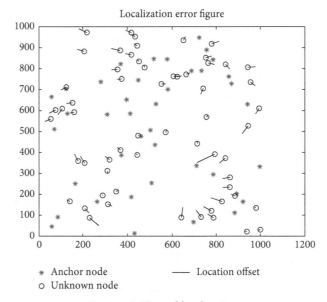

* Anchor node —— Location offset
o Unknown node

FIGURE 9: Normal localization.

As can be seen from Figure 13, the localization error of secure localization model remains in a very low level and the localization error of normal localization algorithm increases with the increasing of attack power. The localization error of secure localization model increases with the increasing of attack power, in case the attack power is under 5, with the performance of malicious nodes being similar to normal nodes. However, the system can distinguish between malicious nodes and normal nodes from the values of each attribute with the increasing of attack power. Thus the localization error remains in a low level.

In addition, this algorithm is compared with other secure localization algorithm in localization error.

As can be seen from Figure 14, the overall localization error of this algorithm is smaller than AR-MMSE algorithm. In the AR-MMSE algorithm [31], the localization error

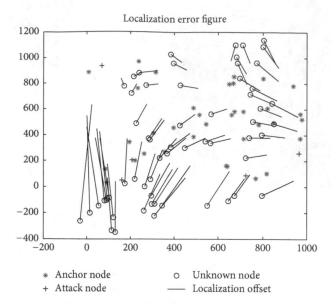

FIGURE 10: Localization under attack node.

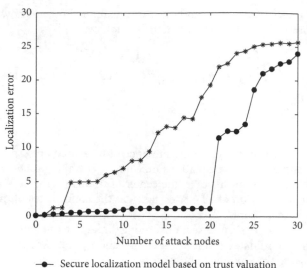

FIGURE 12: Localization algorithms comparison.

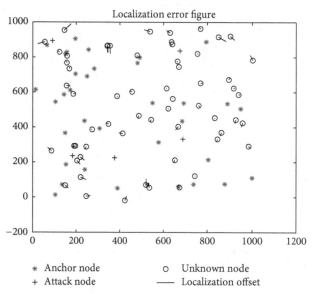

FIGURE 11: Localization under trust valuation model.

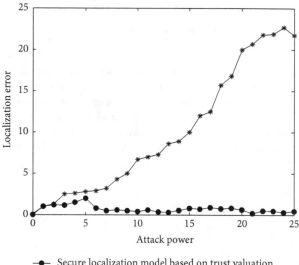

FIGURE 13: Localization algorithms comparison.

becomes large when the number of malicious nodes exceeds 14. After that, with the increasing of the number of malicious nodes, the localization error is also growing. The algorithm proposed in this paper gets much larger localization error when the number of malicious nodes exceeds 20. AR-MMSE algorithm determines malicious nodes just by the consistency of the location information, while the proposed algorithm is capable of identifying malicious nodes via some additional attributes, such as distance measurement, detection of anchor node position, and detection of transition time.

As can be seen from Figure 15, the trust relationship network becomes tighter as the density of anchor nodes increases. Normal node does not build trust relationship with attack node, so the attack node is removed from the secure localization model.

5. Conclusion

The problem of secure localization is closely related to the structure characteristics and application background in WSN. Traditional security algorithms in WSN are constrained by the limited resources of sensor nodes. Trust management can improve the security and reliability of the localization system with low system overhead. In this paper, a number of attributes related to the localization are adopted and the threshold of the attribute value is discussed to ensure that the method can deal with the internal attacks and a certain degree of collusion attack. This model is superior to the traditional secure localization algorithm based on WSN in the success rate of identifying malicious nodes and performance overhead.

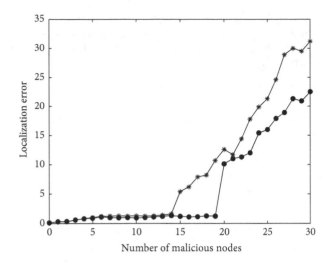

Figure 14: Localization algorithms comparison.

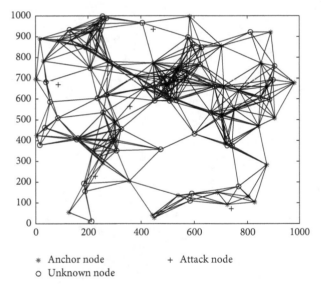

Figure 15: Trust relationship.

Competing Interests

The authors declare that they have no competing interests.

Acknowledgments

The subject is sponsored by the National Natural Science Foundation of China (no. 61373017, no. 61572260, no. 61572261, no. 61672296, and no. 61602261), the Natural Science Foundation of Jiangsu Province (no. BK20140886 and no. BK20140888), Scientific & Technological Support Project of Jiangsu Province (no. BE2015702 and no. BE2016777, BE2016185), China Postdoctoral Science Foundation (no. 2014M551636 and no. 2014M561696), Jiangsu Planned Projects for Postdoctoral Research Funds (no. 1302090B and no. 1401005B), Jiangsu High Technology Research Key Laboratory for Wireless Sensor Networks Foundation (no. WSNLBZY201508).

References

[1] M. Jadliwala, S. Zhong, S. J. Upadhyaya, C. Qiao, and J.-P. Hubaux, "Secure distance-based localization in the presence of cheating beacon nodes," *IEEE Transactions on Mobile Computing*, vol. 9, no. 6, pp. 810–823, 2010.

[2] P. R. Vamsi and K. Kant, "Trust and location-aware routing protocol for wireless sensor networks," *IETE Journal of Research*, vol. 62, no. 5, pp. 634–644, 2016.

[3] S. Nandhakumar and N. Malmurugan, "ETIDS: an effective trust based intrusion detection system for wireless sensor networks," *Journal of Computational and Theoretical Nanoscience*, vol. 13, no. 3, pp. 1791–1797, 2016.

[4] N. Labraoui, M. Gueroui, and M. Aliouat, "Secure DV-Hop localization scheme against wormhole attacks in wireless sensor networks," *European Transactions on Telecommunications*, vol. 23, no. 4, pp. 303–316, 2012.

[5] W.-W. Chang, T.-J. Sung, H.-W. Huang et al., "A smart medication system using wireless sensor network technologies," *Sensors and Actuators*, vol. 172, no. 1, pp. 315–321, 2011.

[6] J. Wang, R. K. Ghosh, and S. K. Das, "A survey on sensor localization," *Journal of Control Theory and Applications*, vol. 8, no. 1, pp. 2–11, 2010.

[7] K. Jeril, V. Amruth, and N. N. Swathy, "A survey on localization of Wireless Sensor nodes," in *Proceedings of the International Conference on Information Communication and Embedded Systems (ICICES '14)*, pp. 1–6, Chennai, India, February 2014.

[8] M. M. Patel and A. Aggarwal, "Security attacks in wireless sensor networks: a survey," in *Proceedings of the International Conference on Intelligent Systems and Signal Processing (ISSP '13)*, pp. 329–333, Anand, India, March 2013.

[9] A. Ahmed, K. Abu Bakar, M. I. Channa, K. Haseeb, and A. W. Khan, "A trust aware routing protocol for energy constrained wireless sensor network," *Telecommunication Systems*, vol. 61, no. 1, pp. 123–140, 2016.

[10] E. Goldoni, A. Savioli, M. Risi, and P. Gamba, "Experimental analysis of RSSI-based indoor localization with IEEE 802.15.4," in *Proceedings of the European Wireless Conference (EW '10)*, pp. 71–77, IEEE, Pavia, Italy, April 2010.

[11] R. Garg, A. L. Varna, and M. Wu, "An efficient gradient descent approach to secure localization in resource constrained wireless sensor networks," *IEEE Transactions on Information Forensics and Security*, vol. 7, no. 2, pp. 717–730, 2012.

[12] P. Guo, J. Wang, X. H. Geng, C. S. Kim, and J.-U. Kim, "A variable threshold-value authentication architecture for wireless mesh networks," *Journal of Internet Technology*, vol. 15, no. 6, pp. 929–935, 2014.

[13] M. Blaze, J. Feigenbaum, and J. Lacy, "Decentralized trust management," in *Proceedings of the IEEE Symposium on Security and Privacy*, vol. 30, pp. 164–173, 1996.

[14] S. Guo, V. Leung, and Z. Qian, "A permutation-based multipolynomial scheme for pairwise key establishment in sensor networks," in *Proceedings of the IEEE International Conference on Communications (ICC '10)*, pp. 1–5, Cape Town, South africa, May 2010.

[15] D. Dong, M. Li, Y. Liu, X.-Y. Li, and X. Liao, "Topological detection on wormholes in wireless ad hoc and sensor networks," *IEEE/ACM Transactions on Networking*, vol. 19, no. 6, pp. 1787–1796, 2011.

[16] M. Ye and Y.-P. Wang, "A new malicious nodes attack-resistant security location method in wireless sensor network," *Chinese Journal of Computers*, vol. 36, no. 3, pp. 532–545, 2013.

[17] Y. Guo and X. Liu, "A research on the localization technology of wireless sensor networks employing TI's CC2530 instrument," in *Proceedings of the 11th International Conference on Computational Intelligence and Security (CIS '15)*, pp. 446–449, Shenzhen, China, December 2015.

[18] A. Lewandowski and C. Wietfeld, "A comprehensive approach for optimizing ToA-localization in harsh industrial environments," in *Proceedings of the IEEE/ION Position, Location and Navigation Symposium (PLANS '10)*, pp. 516–525, Indian Wells, Calif, USA, May 2010.

[19] F. G. Mármol and G. M. Pérez, "TRMSim-WSN, trust and reputation models simulator for wireless sensor networks," in *Proceedings of the IEEE International Conference on Communications (ICC '09)*, pp. 1–5, IEEE, Dresden, Germany, June 2009.

[20] M. Bshara, U. Orguner, F. Gustafsson, and L. Van Biesen, "Fingerprinting localization in wireless networks based on received-signal-strength measurements: a case study on wimax networks," *IEEE Transactions on Vehicular Technology*, vol. 59, no. 1, pp. 283–294, 2010.

[21] S. M. Lasassmeh and J. M. Conrad, "Time synchronization in wireless sensor networks: a survey," in *Proceedings of the Energizing Our Future, IEEE Southeast Con (SOUTHEASTCON '10)*, pp. 242–245, Charlotte-Concord, NC, USA, March 2010.

[22] S. Mohammad Ali and W. Tat-Chee, "Message passing based time synchronization in wireless sensor networks: a survey," *International Journal of Distributed Sensor Networks*, vol. 12, no. 4, pp. 1–21, 2016.

[23] E. Kim and K. Kim, "Distance estimation with weighted least squares for mobile beacon-based localization in wireless sensor networks," *IEEE Signal Processing Letters*, vol. 17, no. 6, pp. 559–562, 2010.

[24] J. Shen, H. Tan, J. Wang, J. Wang, and S. Lee, "A novel routing protocol providing good transmission reliability in underwater sensor networks," *Journal of Internet Technology*, vol. 16, no. 1, pp. 171–178, 2015.

[25] J. Hwang, T. He, and Y. Kim, "Secure localization with phantom node detection," *Ad Hoc Networks*, vol. 6, no. 7, pp. 1031–1050, 2008.

[26] X. Chen, N. C. Rowe, J. Wu, and K. Xiong, "Improving the localization accuracy of targets by using their spatial–temporal relationships in wireless sensor networks," *Journal of Parallel and Distributed Computing*, vol. 72, no. 8, pp. 1008–1018, 2012.

[27] J. Lee, W. Chung, and E. Kim, "A new kernelized approach to wireless sensor network localization," *Information Sciences*, vol. 243, no. 1, pp. 20–38, 2013.

[28] S. Bohidar, S. Behera, and C. R. Tripathy, "A comparative view on received signal strength (RSS) based location estimation in WSN," in *Proceedings of the IEEE International Conference on Engineering and Technology (ICETECH '15)*, pp. 2–5, IEEE, Coimbatore, India, March 2015.

[29] L. Mu, X. Qu, and Z. Zhou, "SARL: a flexible simulation architecture of range-based location in WSN," in *Proceedings of the 35th Chinese Control Conference (CCC '16)*, pp. 8412–8417, Chengdu, China, July 2016.

[30] S. Ganeriwal and M. B. Srivastava, "Reputation-based framework for high integrity sensor networks," *ACM Transactions on Sensor Networks*, vol. 4, no. 4, pp. 66–77, 2004.

[31] D. Liu, P. Ning, A. Liu, C. Wang, and W. K. Du, "Attack-resistant location estimation in wireless sensor networks," *ACM Transactions on Information and System Security*, vol. 11, no. 4, article 22, 2008.

9

A Fusion of Multiagent Functionalities for Effective Intrusion Detection System

Dhanalakshmi Krishnan Sadhasivan[1] and Kannapiran Balasubramanian[2]

[1]*Department of ECE, Kalasalingam University, Krishnankoil, Tamil Nadu 626126, India*
[2]*Department of Instrumentation & Control Engineering, Kalasalingam University, Krishnankoil, Tamil Nadu, India*

Correspondence should be addressed to Dhanalakshmi Krishnan Sadhasivan; dhanalakshmi.jai3@gmail.com

Academic Editor: Zheng Yan

Provision of high security is one of the active research areas in the network applications. The failure in the centralized system based on the attacks provides less protection. Besides, the lack of update of new attacks arrival leads to the minimum accuracy of detection. The major focus of this paper is to improve the detection performance through the adaptive update of attacking information to the database. We propose an Adaptive Rule-Based Multiagent Intrusion Detection System (ARMA-IDS) to detect the anomalies in the real-time datasets such as KDD and SCADA. Besides, the feedback loop provides the necessary update of attacks in the database that leads to the improvement in the detection accuracy. The combination of the rules and responsibilities for multiagents effectively detects the anomaly behavior, misuse of response, or relay reports of gas/water pipeline data in KDD and SCADA, respectively. The comparative analysis of the proposed ARMA-IDS with the various existing path mining methods, namely, random forest, JRip, a combination of AdaBoost/JRip, and common path mining on the SCADA dataset conveys that the effectiveness of the proposed ARMA-IDS in the real-time fault monitoring. Moreover, the proposed ARMA-IDS offers the higher detection rate in the SCADA and KDD cup 1999 datasets.

1. Introduction

Nowadays, security reports show that the increase of real-time applications such as government and commercial network systems leads to an increase of the new type of attacks sequentially. The prediction of malicious or anomaly behavior is called intrusion detection. In general, the intrusion detection depends on the availability and confidentiality of information resources, and it is crucial due to high dimensionality and dynamic nature of distributed systems. The systems that detect the intrusions effectively are known as Intrusion Detection Systems (IDS). Research area categorizes the IDS approaches into two, namely, multiagent based and data mining based. Multiagent-based IDS can resist the attacks themselves and improve the detection accuracy, speed, and security. But the rise in the network complexities requires the data mining approaches. The extraction of useful information from large datasets refers to data mining. Data mining approaches deal with the protection of system against new and complex attacks.

The data mining techniques that are employed in IDS are outlier prediction, classification, and clustering. Among these, the employment of different clustering algorithms, namely, partition-based, fuzzy clustering (FCM, K-means) in anomaly based IDS, discovers the groupings and populations in the datasets. Classification governs the identification of instance label categories, which define the features present in the dataset. Several classifiers such as fuzzy logic, Hidden Markov Model (HMM), and Bayesian analysis are used in data mining applications to detect the intrusions. Even though the data mining approaches achieved an effective detection of intrusions, the high complexity and their energy consumption are more. High detection rate is the major constraint of the design of an efficient IDS. The nonadaptive nature of parameter adjustment in game theoretic-based IDS limits the detection rate.

The process of the identification of understandable patterns with high rate refers to Knowledge Discovery and Data (KDD). The reckoning of KDD models subjects to the efficiency limitations. Nowadays, most of the researchers utilize the Supervisory Control and Data Acquisition (SCADA) which is an alternate to the KDD models. The assurance of effective isolation between the normal and abnormal is the major requirement for intrusion detection in SCADA. The design of suitable detection algorithm considers the following issues:

(i) the definition of criterion for an algorithm selection;

(ii) choosing the algorithm with the minimum selection criteria;

(iii) comparing the merits/demerits of selected and existing algorithms.

The presence of correlations between the parameters in dataset 1 (water and gas) and the sequential nature of dataset 2 (electric power transmission) leads to the unsuitability of IDS and machine learning algorithms, respectively. A quantitative measure to validate the effectiveness of extracted patterns refers to interestingness. Clustering and rule-based algorithms are effective to handle the multiagent-based systems. The lack of sequential update of the attack information on the dataset in traditional models leads to less detection accuracy. This paper focuses on the improvement of detection accuracy by using the multiagent framework. This paper proposes the new Adaptive Rule-Based Multiagent IDS (ARMA-IDS) for a secure data transfer in a network. The proposed ARMA-IDS integrates the density-based clustering with the rule formation for multiagents (Sniffer, Filter, Rule Mining Agent (RMA), Anomaly Detection Agent (ADA), and Rule-Based Agent (RBA)) under certain policies to define or isolate the anomaly and misuse. Density-based clustering uses the combination of distance measurement and Fuzzy C-Means (FCM) for detection of unknown intrusions. Rules in RBA review the connections between the networks and categorize them as either the normal or the anomalous behavior in the network. The lack of database update reduces the detection rate of intrusions for practical large size datasets. Hence, this paper proposes the ARMA-IDS to improve the detection performance with an adaptive update of attack information to the dataset. The ARMA-IDS validates the performance of two datasets KDD cup'99 and SCADA to show better detection rate.

The organization of the paper is as follows: Section 2 reviews some of the existing works related to Intrusion Detection Systems (IDSs) in data mining in WSNs. Section 3 gives the detailed description of the proposed Multiagent-based Intrusion Detection System in WSNs. Section 4 presents the performance results of both the existing and proposed techniques. Finally, Section 5 states the conclusion, and the future work to be carried out.

2. Related Works

The rise of extensive applications performed in real-time opened the platform to new attacks. The introduction of cyber security threads on smart grid degraded the overall network performance. Zhang et al. [1] proposed an Analyzing Module (AM) for the detection of intrusions in the distributed environment. They utilized the Support Vector Machine (SVM) for outlier detection. The problems addressed in Network IDS (NIDS) were the correlation of attacks, hiding of attack information, and nondetection of new arrival attacks. The evolution of Computer Intelligence (CI) techniques made the IDS better. Shamshirband et al. [2] discussed the traditional multiagent-based IDS with the help of CI techniques. They also analyzed the significance, limitations of various IDS, and prevention mechanisms. Lui et al. [3] enhanced the strength of NIDS against the new attacks by using the agents model. The data mining algorithms extracted the useful patterns from the large size dataset and reduced the complexities of manual computation of intrusion. Chauhan et al. [4] reported the various data mining algorithms for detection of intrusions present in the distributed environment. The limitations of distributed environment such as high false positives and low efficiency lead to low detection rates. Davis and Clark [5] proposed a data preprocessing technique for anomaly based network intrusion detection. Time-based statistics were derived to predict network scans, warm behavior, and Denial of Service (DoS) attacks.

The variance and bias are high in the traditional NIDS due to the availability of large dataset. Joshi and Pimprale [6] simultaneously used binary classifier and multiboosting to reduce the variance and bias. The binary classifier utilization in feature selection increased the efficiency against the new attack arrival. Ferreira et al. [7] designed a wavelet and artificial neural networks based IDS for Knowledge Discovery and Data (KDD) dataset. Nadiammai and Hemalatha [8] utilized four algorithms, namely, EDADT, hybrid IDS, and semisupervised and varying HOPERRA algorithms on KDD dataset to solve the issues in WSN. The distributed network environment like smart grid composed of various components such as sensors, digital meters, and digital controls. Reliable IDS design requires the security assurance mechanism for sensors due to the changes in node behaviors. Singh et al. [9] constructed an effective sensor activity detection system adaptive to the behavioral changes of the nodes. The analysis of the skeptical behavior of nodes supports an efficient malicious behavior detection. The existence of attacks hides the useful information in the network. The utilization of spatial data decreased the clustering efficiency. Advanced Metering Infrastructure (AMI) is responsible for collection, measurement, and transmission of data from the smart meter to data center. The security of the AMI is the major concern during its deployment to the smart grid. Faisal et al. [10] proposed the reliable IDS architecture that includes the individual IDS and AMI components such as AMI head end, smart meter, and data concentrator.

Shrivastava and Gupta [11] analyzed the spatial data by using density-based clustering algorithms. The elimination of noisy objects and outliers increased the efficiency of network effectively. But the computation of cluster centroid is difficult in that approach. The ineffective cluster center degraded the efficiency and made the global minimum computation difficult. Ganapathy et al. [12] identified proper cluster center by using fuzzy rules based clustering model. Global optimum value is the gain factor which is derived from the maximum classification and detection rate values. The use of single classifier in IDS failed to create the best attack prevention system. Panda et al. [13] suggested an intelligent hybrid technique for an intrusion detection. The authors used 2-class classification strategy along with 10-fold cross-validation method for better classification results. Govindarajan and Abinaya [14] provided simultaneous outlier detection and classification to assure the effectiveness compared to traditional approaches. Sivatha Sindhu et al. [15] performed the redundancy removal by discussing the IDS for removal of redundancies that lead to unbiased nature of feature selection algorithms and improvement of detection accuracy by the construction of neurotree.

The design of IDS, extension of MANET IDS to Wireless Sensor Network (WSN), is required in intrusion analysis. Butun et al. [16] surveyed the IDS techniques, MANET based IDS, and the application of IDS to WSN. They opened research issues in WSN IDS. The fast utilization of networks in environmental monitoring, weather forecasting, and disaster management raised the assurance of security. Xu et al. [17] proposed the intrusion detection policy specifically for WSN. The monitoring of overall communication process predicted the abnormal working of nodes. Sometimes, in an IDS, the features were also used to predict the unknown attacks. Less awareness of network operators caused the degradation in prediction accuracy. Louvieris et al. [18] presented the anomaly based detection technique to increase the operator awareness against the new attacks in the network. They combined Naïve Bayesian feature selection, K-means clustering, and C4.5 decision tree for intrusion detection. The integration of multiagent features and high accuracy of data mining techniques were required to enhance the IDS behavior. The data mining techniques governed the extraction of used patterns from a large dataset. Alrajeh et al. [19] discussed the problems that occurred due to various attacks in WSN. Limited computational energy and resources in WSN makes it vulnerable to several unknown attacks. Coppolino et al. [20] utilized both anomalous and misuse based IDS to improve the efficiency of NIDS.

The lighter anomalous detection system used a central agent and some local agents. Biswas et al. [21] used the multiagent concept in multilevel IDS. They stored the various types of attacks in the database and analyzed the dependency of new arrival type with the database. The analysis of subject behavior over the unlabeled HTTP streams is required in IDS. Wang et al. [22] employed Affinity Propagation (AP) algorithm to learn the subject's behavior in dynamic clustering. The data classification, human interaction, deficiency in labeled data were the important issues in NIDS. The classification of network activities into normal and abnormal minimized the misclassification problem effectively. Recently, the modern control systems are integrated with the functional process of physics to create test bed. A test bed makes the research process into the discovery of vulnerabilities in a controlled manner. Morris et al. [23] described the Mississippi State University SCADA Security Laboratory in which model

control system was combined with the physical functions. They proposed the cyber security mitigations for SCADA dataset. The penetration of control systems into food, agricultural, and chemical applications governed by the potential vector derived from the deployment of industrial radios. The arrival of high-speed networks in power system made the intrusions in the integration. Pan et al. [24] proposed an innovative approach for the development of specification-based IDS that performed the graphical encoding of relations by using Bayesian network. The identification and transmission of fault or cyber attack quicker operators reacted immediately to avoid the unnecessary loss. Pan et al. [25] proposed sequential pattern mining approach for accurate extraction of power system disturbances and attacks. The introduction of automatic discovery of common paths from the labeled data logs. Pan et al. [26] presented the systematic approach for the design of hybrid IDS and learned the temporal based specifications. They proposed the common path mining algorithms for the learning. From the study, the preservation of specific information from these attacks was an active research area in the network. Guarantee of integrity and availability of resources were the investigating parameters in the research field to provide better detection rate for attacks. The major observation is that the creation of agent-based IDS for the detection and prevention of attacks in real-time datasets by using the combination of clustering with the multiagent rules was the major research area in IDS. Also, the provision of necessary update of attacks in the original database required improving the detection accuracy.

3. ARMA-IDS: Adaptive Rule-Based Multiagent Intrusion Detection System

The Adaptive Rule-based Multiagent Intrusion Detection System (ARMA-IDS) implemented on KDD cup 1999 and SCADA datasets to convey that the intrusion detection performance in SCADA is better than the KDD cup'99. The overall flow of the proposed Adaptive Rule-Based Multiagent Intrusion Detection System is shown in Figure 1.

3.1. Training Data. The proposed ARMA-IDS uses two datasets, namely, KDD cup 1999 and SCADA datasets, in the training phase. For KDD cup'99, the training data includes seven different network traffic patterns in the form of TCP dump data, approximately 5 million connection records with the size of each record as 100 bytes. A list of 41 features for KDD cup'99 is presented in Table 1.

The objective of this research is to show the better intrusion detection rate in SCADA and KDD cup'99. The typical SCADA architecture as shown in Figure 2 comprises the following units: corporate infrastructure, SCADA master, network, Remote Terminal Unit (RTU), sensor, actuators, and plant. SCADA includes the laboratory readings of water tower, gas pipeline, and electric transmission system. All three readings containing preprocessed network transaction and lower strip transaction data are organized as shown in Table 2.

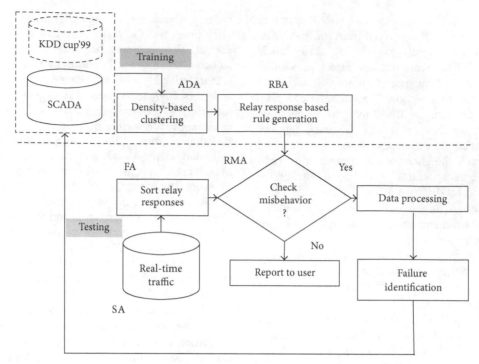

FIGURE 1: Flow of the proposed Adaptive Rule-Based Multiagent Intrusion Detection System.

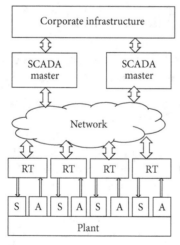

FIGURE 2: SCADA architecture.

The detailed description of gas and water parameters and the electrical system parameters is listed in Tables 3 and 4, respectively.

3.2. Testing Data: Attack Model.

The proposed method takes the real-time data for the testing process. This section investigates the existence of various attacks on KDD cup 1999 and SCADA dataset. Table 5 illustrates the different types of attacks present in the KDD cup 1999 dataset.

The testing attacks models for SCADA include eight attack vectors for gas and water datasets as shown in Table 6.

The scenarios in SCADA electrical transmission system are short circuit fault, line maintenance, remote tripping command injection, and changes in relay settings and data injection. Among these, the last three scenarios are identified as attack vectors in an electric transmission system under real-time scenario.

(1) Remote Tripping Command Injection. An attack in the relay sends the command to the breaker to be open.

(2) Relay Setting Changes. Distance protection scheme is responsible for the configuration of relay design. The arrival of attacker changes the settings leading to a poor response to the fault.

(3) Data Injection. The changing parameters of voltage, current, and sequence components aimed to handle the block-out by the operator.

The existence of correlation between the gas pipeline or water storage parameters and the attacks makes the SCADA system unsuitable in IDS research. Hence, they must be avoided to extend the applicability of the system. The group of these attack models is analyzed in this proposed agent-based IDS. The rule formation for analysis of intrusions is based on the response of relays. The misbehavior of real attack models compared to SCADA dataset is identified, and the feedback report sent to the user and database.

3.3. Multiagent-Based Intrusion Detection System.

The collection and analysis of massive data traffic are governed by using the distributed Multiagent IDS (MA-IDS). The gathering and

TABLE 1: List of 41 features in KDD cup'99.

S. number	Feature name
(1)	duration
(2)	protocol_type
(3)	service
(4)	Flag
(5)	Src_bytes
(6)	Dst_bytes
(7)	land
(8)	Wrong_fragment
(9)	urgent
(10)	hot
(11)	Num_failed_logins
(12)	Logged.in
(13)	Num_compromised
(14)	Root_shell
(15)	Su_attempted
(16)	Num_root
(17)	Num_file_creations
(18)	Num_shells
(19)	Num_access_files
(20)	Num_outbound_cmds
(21)	Is_hot_login
(22)	Is_guest_login
(23)	count
(24)	Srv_count
(25)	Serror_rate
(26)	Srv_serror_rate
(27)	Rerror_rate
(28)	Srv_rerror_rate
(29)	Same_srv_rate
(30)	Diff_srv_rate
(31)	Srv_diff_host_rate
(32)	Dst_host_count
(33)	Dst_host_srv_count
(34)	Dst_host_same_srv_rate
(35)	Dst_host_diff_srv_rate
(36)	Dst_host_same_src_port_rate
(37)	Dst_host_srv_diff_host_rate
(38)	Dst_host_serror_rate
(39)	Dst_host_srv_serror_rate
(40)	Dst_host_rerror_rate
(41)	Dst_host_srv_rerror_rate

TABLE 2: SCADA dataset details.

S. number	Dataset	Number of entries	Unique parameters
(1)	Gas pipeline	100,000	27
(2)	Water tower	200,000	24
(3)	Electric transmission system	5,000,000	132

analysis of real-time data model called KDD includes five different agents as follows:

(1) Sniffer Agent (SA);

(2) Filter Agent (FA);

(3) Anomaly Detection Agent (ADA);

(4) Rule Mining Agent (RMA);

(5) Rule-Based Agent (RBA) (association rule-based and sequential rule-based agent).

The reasons to adapt the multiagent IDS are listed as follows:

(i) collection of packets between the components;

(ii) extraction of relevant packets requires filtering process.

(iii) the prediction of abnormal instances or connections in both KDD and SCADA that requires Anomaly Detection Agent;

(iv) the rules governing the abnormal instances prediction that require rule-based agent.

The selection of specified agents for KDD and SCADA is dependent on the functionalities which are discussed in the following section.

3.3.1. Multiagent Functionalities in KDD. This section describes the functions performed by each agent in KDD dataset in detail.

Sniffer Agent. The first agent that can capture the packets and investigates the contents presented in the captured packets. The sniffing operation performed by this agent provides various advantages, namely,

(i) an efficient analysis of network problems;

(ii) easy detection of intrusion attempts;

(iii) compliance documentation by using regular monitoring.

SA records the captured packets in memory in the sequential intervals. The distribution of packets throughout the network and the duplication process in SA limit the charge assigned to the network. The packets captured from the SA are passed to the next agent that is called Filter Agent (FA) to isolate the irrelevant packets from large size packets.

Filter Agent. The distributed framework collects the large number of events from the different nodes in a network. FA received the captured packets from the SA and performed the following actions to know the fields and categories:

(i) the destination address and protocol used for packet transfer are identified;

(ii) by using packets category (TCP, UDP, and ICMP), FA arranges the packets in ascending order to find the type of intrusions.

TABLE 3: Gas and water parameters.

S. number	Parameter	S. number	Parameter
(1)	command address	(1)	command address
(2)	response address	(2)	response address
(3)	command memory	(3)	command memory
(4)	response memory	(4)	response memory
(5)	command_memory_count	(5)	command_memory_count
(6)	response_memory_count	(6)	response_memory_count
(7)	comm_read_function	(7)	comm_read_function
(8)	comm_write_function	(8)	comm_write_function
(9)	resp_read_function	(9)	resp_read_function
(10)	resp_write_function	(10)	resp_write_function
(11)	sub_function	(11)	sub_function
(12)	command_length	(12)	command_length
(13)	resp_length	(13)	resp_length
(14)	gain	(14)	HH
(15)	reset	(15)	HH
(16)	deadband	(16)	L
(17)	cycletime	(17)	LL
(18)	rate	(18)	control_mode
(19)	setpoint	(19)	control_scheme
(20)	control_mode	(20)	pump
(21)	control_scheme	(21)	crc_rate
(22)	pump	(22)	Measurement
(23)	solenoid	(23)	Time
(24)	crc_rate	(24)	result
(25)	Measurement		
(26)	Time		
(27)	result		

Anomaly Detection Agent (ADA). The ADA in MA-IDS utilized the clustering mechanisms to identify the intrusions in the network. K-means and density-based algorithms are the predominant algorithms for clustering process. Even though the K-means algorithm offered the fast clustering performance, noise occurrence and dependency were more. Hence, this paper utilizes the density-based clustering to limit the cluster dependency, noise. The density-based clustering-(DBC-) based ADA (DBC-ADA) contains the following steps to detect the anomaly behavior. The DBC algorithm implementation depends on the following parameters: instances for the data arrival (f_i), cluster center (c_i), threshold value (α), and minimum number of neighbors N_{min}. There are two metrics governing the DBC processes and they are listed as follows.

(i) Reachability. The instance for data arrival is density-reachable from the cluster center and the center has the sufficient neighbors within the threshold value.

(ii) Connectivity. The instances f_i and c_i are density connected only if there exist a new instance f_{new} that has the sufficient number of minimum neighbors and both f_i and c_i are within threshold value.

(1) Let the data records $D = \{D_1, D_2, D_3, \ldots, D_N\}z$ arrive at instance f_i.

(2) The data is mapped to the density grid $g(x) = \{j_1, j_2, j_3, \ldots, j_d\}$ and density coefficient (depending on the instances) is greater than the threshold value.

(3) Calculate the Euclidean distance between the cluster center and the instance of the closest cluster. The distance between the instance and the cluster center is considered as the basic parameter in the density-based clustering process and defined by

$$\text{distance}\ (f_i, c_i) = \sqrt{\sum_{i=1}^{n} (f_i - c_i)^2}. \quad (1)$$

(4) The distance between the instances is recorded and the cluster center that is less than the threshold value (α) is regarded as the neighbor of cluster center.

(5) If the size of neighbors is less than the minimum number of neighbors N_{min}, then the corresponding data is regarded as noise.

(6) If the size of neighbors is more than the value of N_{min}, then the corresponding data is added to the

TABLE 4: Parameters of electric data.

Network/other	Features
data	Voltage Phase Angle (R1-PA1 to R4-PA1)
timestamp	Voltage Phase Magnitude (R1-PM1 to R4-PM1)
control_panel_log1	Voltage Phase Angle (R1-PA2 to R4-PA2)
control_panel_log2	Voltage Phase Magnitude (R1-PM2 to R4-PM2)
control_panel_log3	Voltage Phase Angle (R1-PA3 to R4-PA3)
control_panel_log4	Voltage Phase Magnitude (R1-PM3 to R4-PM3)
realy1_log	Current Phase Angle (R1-PA4 to R4-PA4)
realy2_log	Current Phase Magnitude (R1-PM4 to R4-PM4)
realy3_log	Current Phase Angle (R1-PA5 to R4-PA5)
realy4_log	Current Phase Magnitude (R1-PM5 to R4-PM5)
snort_log1	Current Phase Angle (R1-PA6 to R4-PA6)
snort_log2	Current Phase Magnitude (R1-PM6 to R4-PM6)
snort_log3	Pos.-Neg. – Zero Voltage Phase Angle (R1-PA7 to R4-PA7)
snort_log4	Pos.-Neg. – Zero Voltage Phase Magnitude (R1-PM7 to R4-PM7)
marker	Pos.-Neg. – Zero Voltage Phase Angle (R1-PA8 to R4-PA8)
fault_loc	Pos.-Neg. – Zero Voltage Phase Magnitude (R1-PM8 to R4-PM8)
load_con1	Pos.-Neg. – Zero Voltage Phase Angle (R1-PA9 to R4-PA9)
load_con2	Pos.-Neg. – Zero Current Phase Angle (R1-PA(10–12) to R4-PA(10–12))
load_con3	Pos.-Neg. – Zero Current Phase Magnitude (R1-PM(10–12) to R4-PM(10–12))
Status flag	S

TABLE 5: Attack types on the KDD Cup'99 dataset.

Class	Attacks in the training data
DOS	Back, Land, Smurf, Pod, Neptune, and Teardrop
Probe	IPsweep, Portsweep, Nmapr, and Satan
U2R	Load module, Rootkit, Perl, and Buffer_overflow
R2L	Guess_passwd, Multihop, Ftp_write, Spy, Phf, Imap, Warezclient, and Warezmaster

cluster and it is regarded as normal cluster. Table 7 presents the features selected for clustering process for different categories.

Table 8 describes the variables used in density-based clustering and associated description.

TABLE 6: Attack model for SCADA.

Attack name	Abbreviation
Normal	Normal(0)
Naïve Malicious Response Injection	NMRI(1)
Complex Malicious Response Injection	CMRI(2)
Malicious State Command Injection	MSCI(3)
Malicious Parameter Command Injection	MPCI(4)
Malicious Function Code Injection	MFCI(5)
Denial Of Service	DOS(6)
Reconnaissance	Recon(7)

The algorithm of density-based clustering by an Euclidean distance is described as follows.

Density-Based Clustering

Inputs. Instances (f_i), cluster center (c_i).

Output. Clusters (C_{new}, C_{int}).

Step 1. Extract the instances and center and initialize the cluster as $C = 0$.

Step 2. Calculate the Euclidean distance by using (1).

Step 3. Estimate the neighborhood.

Step 4. Extract two most similar clusters.

Step 5. Merge the similar clusters.

If (size of neighbor > α)

Add the data to the cluster

Else

Extracted cluster is considered as noise.

Step 6. Calculate the distance between instance and cluster center in merged clusters.

Step 7. Classify the instance according to nearest cluster

If (neighbors < N_{min})

C_{new} = normal instances;

Else

C_{int} is intruder.

Initially, the algorithm extracts the instances and the cluster center. The Euclidean distance between the candidate cluster center and the instances estimated and assigned to the nearest cluster. The granularity of density-based clustering is defined by the minimal number of neighborhood instances. The minimization of some instances to the overall instance by the iterative process of merging of similar clusters. The establishment of clusters is too high for a small value of t'.

The formulation of reallocated instances decomposes the clusters. The iterative process of density-based clustering

TABLE 7: Features for clustering process.

Categories	Features selected			
Cluster TCP	Number of unique ports accessed	Mean packet size	Number of RST packets	Time range covered by frame
Cluster UDP	Number of unique ports accessed	Mean packet size	Number of ICMP packets	Time range covered by frame
Cluster SYN flood	Number of unique ports accessed	Number of open connections attempted	Number of RST packets	Time range covered by frame

TABLE 8: Notations used in density-based clustering.

Symbols	Descriptions
f_i	Instances
c_i	Cluster center
C	Cluster
$N_{\min}$	Minimum number of clusters
α	Minimum number of neighbors required

is performed for nonempty clusters. The merging of similar clusters is performed according to the relationship of instances after the removal of outliers. After the merging, the distance between the new instance and the cluster center is calculated and assigned to the nearest neighbor (NN). The categories of the nearest cluster have a major role in merging process. The estimation of the shortest distance between new instance and cluster center is categorized as normal and intrusion.

If the neighborhood for a particular instance is lesser than α, then a new cluster is formed. Otherwise, the present instance is assigned to noise. The resultant cluster is a candidate for initial cluster centers. The algorithm estimates the distance between the center of the candidate centers and instances. Moreover, the algorithm automatically divides or merges the clusters to estimate the value of the initial cluster centers k. At last, a new set of initial cluster centers are retrieved, and C-Means algorithm is used to classify the instances according to normal and abnormal behavior. The summarization of the anomalous connections is required to construct the anomalous behavior provided by Rule Mining Agent (RMA). The proposed ARMA-IDS in this paper efficiently handles the noise and cluster dependency problems by density-based clustering. The Rule-Based Agent (RBA) initiated the rule generation for designated network connections.

Parameter Selection. $N_{\min}$ is the minimum number of neighbors depending on the data dimensions such as $N_{\min} > N + 1$. The low values of $N_{\min}$ (1 and 2) have no meaning in better cluster formation. Hence, the minimum value is selected as more than 2.

α is the threshold value that is computed from the k-distance graph. The small values of α result in large part of the data being not clustered and the large values of threshold lead to the merging. The reasonable similarity measurement via distance formulation has the great impact on the threshold value.

Rule Formations for Intrusion Detection (RBA). Two rules are defined in this paper for MA-IDS by RBA as follows:

(1) association rules;

(2) sequential rules.

Association Rule-Based Agent. The identification of a relationship between the selected features and traffic characteristics is considered as the major role in rules formation. The association rule-based agents testing the features are as follows:

(1) accessing of unique ports (large if attack);

(2) average packet size in frame (smaller than normal traffic);

(3) number of ICMP destination unreachable packets in frame (large due to the victim response)

(4) time range covered by packets (port scan normally depicts the burst in short time range).

The formulation of rules in this paper is in the form of $A \Rightarrow B$, which satisfy the user-specified minimum support and minimum confidence thresholds. The identified anomalous connections by RMA are large. Hence, the research analyst spends more time for inspection of each connection in the records. The utilization of association rules provided the high summary of connection records and eliminated the infrequent occurring patterns based on minsup value. The low value minsup increases the number of rules that degraded the performance. The increase in rule size affected the operational speed of IDS and caused the redundancy. The assurance of an adequate protection effectively improves the operational speed and redundancy removal with the periodical update of the signature database.

Sequential Rule-Based Agent. The usual and unusual patterns in the connection stages of normal traffic governed by sequential rules are defined by RBA. The generation of rules is based on the categorization of normal or an intruder traffic. The depreciation percentage with the minimum support between the reports is used to define the rules. The minimum support is reduced by a stated depreciation percentage (dep) described by

$$\text{Support}_k\,(\%) = \text{dep}\,(\%) * \text{Support}_{k-1}\,(\%). \tag{2}$$

Here, k denotes k-item set. For each frame, when the number of abnormal occurrences matched within the time frame is greater than the threshold, the packet is declared as intrusion; otherwise it will be regarded as normal.

TABLE 9: Features for clustering process.

Categories	Features selected			
Gas	Comm_read_fun	Resp_read_fun	Control mode	Measurement
Water	Comm_read_fun	Resp_read_fun	Control mode	Measurement
Electrical data	Line current magnitude	Snort log	Relay log	Control log

TABLE 10: Ranges for selected features.

Feature Name	Ranges
Line current magnitude	(High, Warning, Normal, Zero)
Sbort log	(True, False)
Relay log	(True, False)
Control log	(True, False)
Comm_read_function	(3 or 1)
Resp_read_function	(3 or 1)
Control mode	(0 or 1 or 2)
Measurement	6 to 11 or 1 to 100

TABLE 11: Notations used in density-based clustering.

Rules	Report status	Output
r_1	Relay reports (R_1, R_2, R_3, and R_4)	Normal
r_2	R_2 lacks time stamp t_2 and delayed to t_3	Delay
r_3	R_3 behavior instead of R_2	Misbehavior
r_4	Interchange of relay reports	Modified
r_5	Absence of any report	Error

3.3.2. Multiagent Functionalities in SCADA.

The hierarchical tree structure in the multiagent system for SCADA contains three agents, namely, monitor, decision, and an action. Each agent performs the corresponding tasks.

Monitor Agent (MA). The first agent collects information about the network traffic in gas, water pipeline, and electric transmission system. The extraction of the independent features effectively reduced the noise and irrelevant data.

Decision Agent (DA). The DA utilized the density-based clustering to cluster the normal and abnormal patterns into a group. DA highlighted the action and coordinated agents if the abnormal actions are detected. Table 9 lists the selected features for clustering.

For both gas and water types in SCADA, the features are comm_read_fun, resp_read function, control mode, and measurement. For SCADA electrical system, the features and their ranges are described as shown in Table 10.

The proposed ARMA-IDS integrates distance and density-based measures (Table 11) in the clustering techniques for detection of abnormal packets.

Action Agent. Based on the notification, the AA issued the corresponding responses in such a way that a cluster is predicted with the minimum distance. The utilization of density-based clustering algorithm effectively isolated the

TABLE 12: Rules formation.

Path	Time stamps					Output
	t_1	t_2	t_3	t_4	t_5	
p_1	R_1	R_2	R_3	R_4		Ideal
p_2	R_1		R_2	R_3	R_4	Delay
p_3	R_1	R_3	R_2	R_3	R_4	Misbehaviors
p_4	R_2	R_1	R_3	R_4		Modified
p_5	R_1	R_2		R_4		Error

normal and abnormal behaviors and the regular database update is also provided. The rule formulation with the consideration of minimum support provided the necessary update by a feedback loop. Table 12 depicts the formulation of association rules.

Based on the number of rules, the counting of matched connection is performed. If the frequency is greater than the threshold, it is identified as the normal traffic; otherwise the traffic is affected by an intruder.

3.4. Fuzzy Based Intrusion Detection.

Fuzzy rules are formed based on training and testing rules from RBA. These rules are used to classify the behavior of a connection whether it is normal or intruder. Figure 3 shows the flow of the proposed detection blocks. Table 12 describes the final computed set of fuzzy based results. Based on the fuzzy table, the incoming connection is identified as either normal or intrusion. The rules formation for SCADA dataset is based on the paths in one scenario.

The continuous variables' existence in both KDD and SCADA dataset makes the mining algorithms not suitable. Hence, the 1-length items for each attribute are simplified by estimating the frequency of continuously variable occurrence and the frequent items are extracted based on the Support_k (%) value. The mined 1-length items (normal or noise) are stored as the vectors in the class c expressed as

$$c = [v_1, v_2, \ldots, v_i],\qquad(3)$$

where $v_i = \{f_i, \; 1 \le i \le \text{minsupport}\}$.

The comparison of items with the minimum and maximum range forms the deviation range of attributes as follows:

$$D_{v_i} = \{f_{\min}, f_{\max}\},\qquad(4)$$

where $f_{\min} = \min(f_i)$ and $f_{\max} = \max(f_i)$.

Then, comparing the deviation range with the effectiveness of attributes (normal or intrusion) decides the fuzzy rules. The compact classification of abnormal patterns depends on the two criteria such as a minimum number of

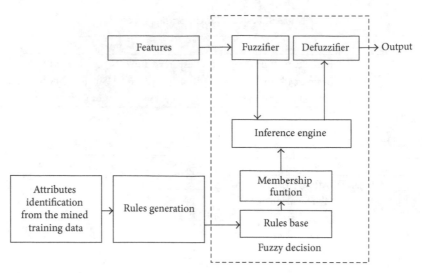

FIGURE 3: Fuzzy based intrusion detection.

fuzzy rules and short IF part. The definite rules formulation based on the criteria declares that IF part is numerical variable and THEN part is class label to predict the instances as normal and intrusion. During the testing phase, the test data from KDD and SCADA are applied to the fuzzy logic system. The test data with the attributes inclusion passes to the fuzzifier that converts the attributes to the linguistic variables by using the membership function. The state t describes the time stamps for states. The calculated minimum support value detects the variation in the output states. For 60% threshold value, the sequence of relay responses R_1, R_2, R_3, and R_4 are maximal, which refers to an optimal path. If threshold limit is 70%, then the corresponding sequences varied to update the new path. The time stamps information (t_1 to t_5) obtained from the agents (SA to RBA) participated in the fuzzy rule generation.

4. Performance Analysis

In this section, the performance of the proposed Adaptive Rule-Based Multiagent IDS (ARMA-IDS) is analyzed with the combination of density-based clustering and rules formation. The comparative analysis of ARMA-IDS and the existing random forest, JRip, AdaBoost + JRip, and common path mining algorithm is also illustrated. The proposed framework considered KDD cup 1999 and SCADA as the training dataset and the real-time traffic as a testing dataset. The simulated environment is defined by the real-time traffic in NS-2. In simulation environment of SCADA, the corporate network is modelled as NS-2 emulation (NSE). The ability of introducing the simulator into the live network refers to emulation. The objects existing in the simulator are capable of injecting the traffic to the live network. The interface between the simulator and the live network is provided by the collection of special objects referring to multiagents used in this paper.

4.1. Error Rate. The measure of how many times the base station makes an incorrect decision is referred to as error rate

Q_E. In general, the algorithm is better only if the error rate is minimum. Figures 4(a), 4(b), and 4(c) depict the variation of error rate with varying detection (P_{det})/attacking probability (P_{mal}), and the number of attackers for proposed ARMA-IDS and the random forest algorithm.

From Figures 4(a), 4(b), and 4(c), the rule-based multiagent IDS offers the minimum error rate compared to random forest algorithm. The increase in detection probability and the attacking probability gradually decreases the error rate and the up to 30 attacker nodes the error rate is minimum; when the attacker nodes are greater than the 30, the error rate is minimum compared to the existing random forest algorithm.

4.2. Recall. The evaluation of successful detection of members in one class is more significant than the other classes referred to as recall or detection rate Q_D. Figures 5(a), 5(b), and 5(c) depict the variation of detection rate with varying detection/attacking probability and the number of attackers for proposed ARMA-IDS and the random forest algorithm. The increase in probability values of detection and attacking provides the maximum detection rate due to the isolation of normal from intrusion. With an increase of attacker nodes, ARMA-IDS provided the best detection rate compared to existing random forest algorithm.

4.3. False Detection. The measure of misidentification of normal nodes as attackers is termed as false detection rate Q_F. In general, the algorithm is better only if the false detection rate is maximum. Figures 6(a), 6(b), and 6(c) depict the variation of the false positive rate with varying detection/attacking probability and the number of attackers for proposed ARMA-IDS and the random forest algorithm. With an increase of attacker nodes, ARMA-IDS provides the minimum false positive rate compared to existing random forest algorithm.

4.4. Parametric Analysis. The proposed ARMA-IDS validated the SCADA dataset performance by the exploitation

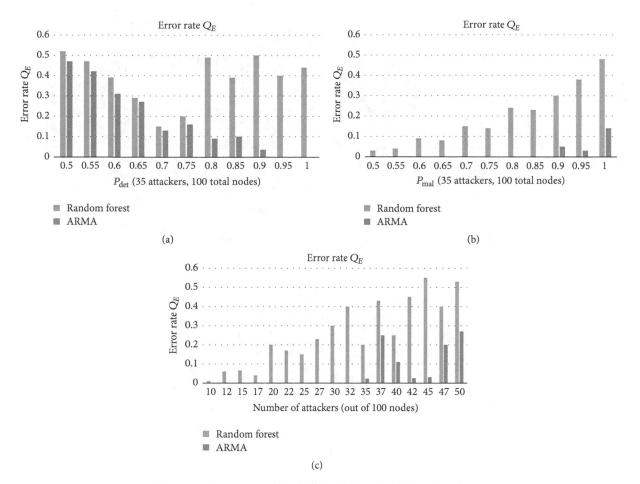

FIGURE 4: Error rate analysis with P_{det}, P_{mal} and number of attackers.

TABLE 13: Classification results of water pipeline control system.

Parameters	Scenario							
	HH alarm		Above H set point		Above L set point		LL alarm	
	NN classifier	ARMA	NN classifier	ARMA	NN classifier	ARMA	NN classifier	ARMA
FPR (%)	4.5	2.3	2.3	1.2	2.4	1.6	3.2	1.2
FNR (%)	0	0.8	3	2.4	3	2.1	0	1.3
Accuracy (%)	95.5	97.4	94.7	96.7	94.6	96.8	96.8	97.7

of different scenarios in a water tank control system. The comparative analysis of proposed method with the neural network classifier [23] is on four scenarios, namely, HH alarm, above H set point, above L set point, and LL alarm with the parameters of false positive, false negative, and accuracy as shown in Table 13. The performance comparison of proposed method and the existing neural network classifier shows that ARMA based IDS provides the accuracy compared to NN-classifier.

4.5. Comparative Analysis.
The comparison between proposed ARMA-IDS and traditional random forest, JRip, AdaBoost, and common path mining algorithms [26] on the parameters of accuracy, precision, recall, F-measure, and number of classes is as shown in Figure 7. The comparison

yields the better results of accuracy, precision, recall, and F-measure for a maximum number of classes. The rule-based detection and the feedback update of fault response to the SCADA database improve the adaptability of real-time monitoring.

4.6. Detection Rate Analysis.
The increase in connection records will increase the detection rate linearly. The sizes of connection records in both KDD and SCADA datasets increased from 1000 to 5000, and the corresponding detection rate is measured. Figure 8 depicts the graphical representation of detection rate variation on connection records for both KDD and SCADA datasets.

Figure 8 shows that the proposed ARMA-IDS provided better detection rate in SCADA compared to KDD datasets.

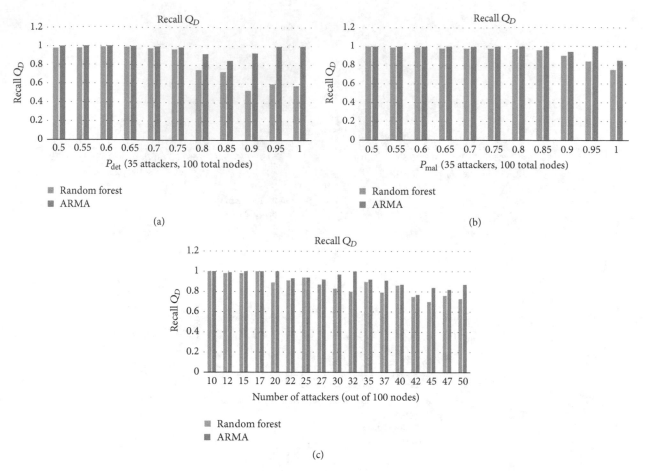

FIGURE 5: Recall analysis with various P_{det}, P_{mal} and number of attackers.

For the minimum number of records (1000), the detection rate in KDD is 62.53% and in SCADA is 78.56%. The performance of SCADA is 16.03% more than KDD. Similarly, for the maximum number of records (5000), the detection rate of KDD is 81.6% and SCADA is 95.62% that is 14.05% better. The comparison of detection rate proved that SCADA has the higher detection performance compared to KDD.

4.7. Zero-Day Attack Scenario Analysis.

In existing hybrid IDS [25], the performance validation is investigated under various attacking scenarios such as zero-day and unknown in terms of detection accuracy. Table 14 presents the variations of detection accuracy for existing hybrid IDS and proposed ARMA-IDS under zero-day attack scenario.

The simulation is performed in 10 rounds and the corresponding detection accuracy for each round is tabulated. The existing hybrid IDS and the proposed ARMA-IDS offers 76.3 and 82.89% in the first round. The detection accuracy is linearly increased with the increase in simulation rounds. For the maximum round, the hybrid IDS and the ARMA-IDS offer 99.8 and 100% accuracy. The comparative analysis between the existing hybrid IDS and ARMA-IDS shows that the proposed ARMA-IDS offers 7.95 and 0.2% improvement in minimum and maximum simulation rounds compared to hybrid IDS, respectively.

TABLE 14: Detection accuracy analysis.

Round	Detection accuracy (%)	
	Hybrid IDS	ARMA-IDS
(1)	76.3	82.89
(2)	67.3	75.51
(3)	50.5	55.59
(4)	73.3	81.25
(5)	91.8	97.18
(6)	64.7	76.64
(7)	63.8	73.58
(8)	70.7	74.45
(9)	76.3	85.84
(10)	99.8	100

4.8. Improved Dataset Analysis.

The original KDD includes the 5,209,460 network transactions and it refers to full dataset. The full version of KDD includes the redundant records and irrelevant DoS items. The inclusion of biased distribution of various attacks causes the difficulties in accurate classifications on U2R and R2L. Hence, the conventional KDD dataset is redefined with 1,48,517 network transactions

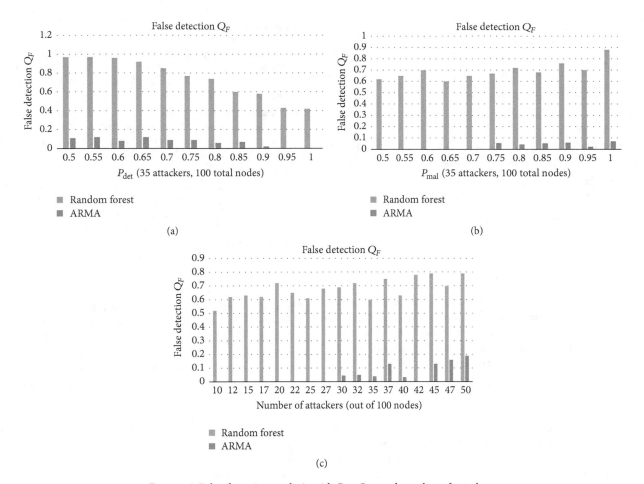

FIGURE 6: False detection analysis with P_{det}, P_{mal} and number of attackers.

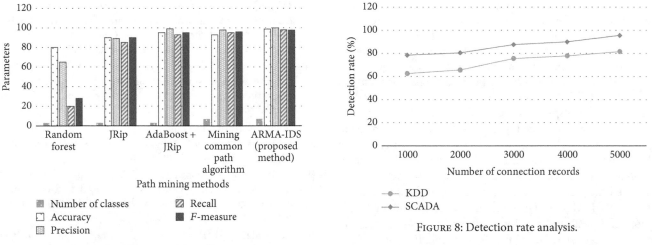

FIGURE 7: Comparative analysis.

FIGURE 8: Detection rate analysis.

and such dataset refers to improved dataset [27]. The classification performance on improved dataset is investigated with the existing and proposed ARMA-IDS regarding the accuracy, Kappa statistics, and FPR and FNR measures. Table 15 shows the variation of the above-mentioned parameters with existing methods [10] and proposed ARMA-IDS.

The comparison of proposed ARMA-IDS with the existing techniques shows the effectiveness of ARMA-IDS. The accuracy of the LimATT classifier is maximum (96.59%) among the existing methods. The integration of tree and vague space partition-based trajectory pattern mining in proposed work further improves the accuracy as 97.47% which is 0.9% improvement. The reduction in number of

TABLE 15: Improved data analysis.

Classifier	Accuracy (%)	Kappa statistics (%)	FPR (%)	FNR (%)
Accuracy Updated Ensemble	93.39	90.23	3.26	8.7
Active Classifier	89.26	84.19	4.04	15.29
Leveraging Bag	95.65	93.6	2.03	6.85
LimAtt Classifier	96.59	95.02	2.49	3.39
OzaBagAdwin	96.05	94.21	2.15	5.55
OzaBagASHT	95.6	93.58	3.17	3.92
Single Classifier Drift	93.97	91.09	2.49	8.23
ARMA-IDS	97.47	94.84	2.24	3.78

instances in the improved dataset causes the reduction in accuracy and Kappa statistics. The Leveraging bag, LimAtt, and OzaBagAdwin offer better accuracy and Kappa statistics. But the proposed ARMA-IDS improves the accuracy and Kappa statistics based on agents-based framework.

5. Conclusion

In this paper, an investigation of detection performance Adaptive Rule-Based Multiagent Intrusion Detection System (ARMA-IDS) on KDD and SCADA datasets is presented. The proposed ARMA-IDS validated its performance on KDD cup 1999 dataset and SCADA dataset. This paper combined the definition of rules and responsibilities for each agent for anomaly and misuse based detection. The proposed ARMA-IDS detected the faults in the network and provided the update in the existing database by a provision of the feedback loop. The database update improved the detection accuracy in a considerable manner. The instance based distance estimation and cluster size reduction by the fuzzy rules formulation offered better detection accuracy in SCADA and KDD datasets. The intrusions are detected by the analysis of response functions and the relay reports in corresponding gas/water pipeline and electric transmission system, respectively. Distance and density-based clustering algorithm formed the clusters of selected features. The formulation of rules in both association and sequential detected and classified the faults for each agent. The comparative analysis of proposed ARMA-IDS with the existing random forest, JRip, AdaBoost, and mining common path algorithms on the parameters of accuracy, precision, recall, F-measure, false detection, and probabilities of detection/attacking shows the effectiveness of proposed method. Moreover, the analysis of detection rate on KDD and SCADA datasets is made and proved that the proposed ARMA-IDS provided better performance in SCADA and KDD.

Competing Interests

The authors declare that they have no conflict of interests.

References

[1] Y. Zhang, L. Wang, W. Sun, R. C. Green II, and M. Alam, "Distributed intrusion detection system in a multi-layer network architecture of smart grids," *IEEE Transactions on Smart Grid*, vol. 2, no. 4, pp. 796–808, 2011.

[2] S. Shamshirband, N. B. Anuar, M. L. M. Kiah, and A. Patel, "An appraisal and design of a multi-agent system based cooperative wireless intrusion detection computational intelligence technique," *Engineering Applications of Artificial Intelligence*, vol. 26, no. 9, pp. 2105–2127, 2013.

[3] C.-L. Lui, T.-C. Fu, and T.-Y. Cheung, "Agent-based network intrusion detection system using data mining approaches," in *Proceedings of the 3rd International Conference on Information Technology and Applications (ICITA '05)*, pp. 131–136, Sydney, Australia, July 2005.

[4] A. Chauhan, G. Mishra, and G. Kumar, "Survey on data mining techniques in intrusion detection," *International Journal of Scientific & Engineering Research*, vol. 2, no. 7, pp. 1–4, 2011.

[5] J. J. Davis and A. J. Clark, "Data preprocessing for anomaly based network intrusion detection: a review," *Computers & Security*, vol. 30, no. 6-7, pp. 353–375, 2011.

[6] S. A. Joshi and V. S. Pimprale, "Network Intrusion Detection System (NIDS) based on data mining," *International Journal of Engineering Science and Innovative Technology*, vol. 2, no. 1, pp. 95–98, 2013.

[7] E. W. T. Ferreira, G. A. Carrijo, R. de Oliveira, and N. V. de Souza Araujo, "Intrusion detection system with wavelet and neural artifical network approach for networks computers," *IEEE Latin America Transactions*, vol. 9, no. 5, pp. 832–837, 2011.

[8] G. V. Nadiammai and M. Hemalatha, "Effective approach toward Intrusion Detection System using data mining techniques," *Egyptian Informatics Journal*, vol. 15, no. 1, pp. 37–50, 2014.

[9] M. Singh, G. Mehta, C. Vaid, and P. Oberoi, "Detection of malicious node in wireless sensor network based on data mining," in *Proceedings of the International Conference on Computing Sciences (ICCS '12)*, pp. 291–294, September 2012.

[10] M. A. Faisal, Z. Aung, J. R. Williams, and A. Sanchez, "Data-stream-based intrusion detection system for advanced metering infrastructure in smart grid: a feasibility study," *IEEE Systems Journal*, vol. 9, no. 1, pp. 31–44, 2015.

[11] P. Shrivastava and H. Gupta, "A review of density-based clustering in spatial data," *International Journal of Advanced Computer Research*, vol. 2, pp. 200–202, 2012.

[12] S. Ganapathy, K. Kulothungan, P. Yogesh, and A. Kannan, "A novel weighted fuzzy C-means clustering based on immune genetic algorithm for intrusion detection," *Procedia Engineering*, vol. 38, pp. 1750–1757, 2012.

[13] M. Panda, A. Abraham, and M. R. Patra, "A hybrid intelligent approach for network intrusion detection," *Procedia Engineering*, vol. 30, pp. 1–9, 2012.

[14] M. Govindarajan and V. Abinaya, "An outlier detection approach with data mining in wireless sensor network," *International Journal of Current Engineering and Technology*, vol. 4, pp. 929–932, 2014.

[15] S. S. Sivatha Sindhu, S. Geetha, and A. Kannan, "Decision tree based light weight intrusion detection using a wrapper approach," *Expert Systems with Applications*, vol. 39, no. 1, pp. 129–141, 2012.

[16] I. Butun, S. D. Morgera, and R. Sankar, "A survey of intrusion detection systems in wireless sensor networks," *IEEE Communications Surveys & Tutorials*, vol. 16, no. 1, pp. 266–282, 2014.

[17] J. Xu, J. Wang, S. Xie, W. Chen, and J.-U. Kim, "Study on intrusion detection policy for wireless sensor networks," *International Journal of Security and its Applications*, vol. 7, no. 1, pp. 1–6, 2013.

[18] P. Louvieris, N. Clewley, and X. Liu, "Effects-based feature identification for network intrusion detection," *Neurocomputing*, vol. 121, pp. 265–273, 2013.

[19] N. A. Alrajeh, S. Khan, and B. Shams, "Intrusion detection systems in wireless sensor networks: a review," *International Journal of Distributed Sensor Networks*, vol. 9, no. 5, Article ID 167575, 2013.

[20] L. Coppolino, S. D'Antonio, A. Garofalo, and L. Romano, "Applying data mining techniques to Intrusion Detection in Wireless Sensor Networks," in *Proceedings of the 8th International Conference on P2P, Parallel, Grid, Cloud and Internet Computing (3PGCIC '13)*, pp. 247–254, October 2013.

[21] A. Biswas, M. Sharma, T. Poddder, and N. Kar, "An approach towards multilevel and multiagent based intrusion detection system," in *Proceedings of the IEEE International Conference on Advanced Communication, Control and Computing Technologies (ICACCCT '14)*, pp. 1787–1790, IEEE, Ramanathapuram, India, May 2014.

[22] W. Wang, T. Guyet, R. Quiniou, M.-O. Cordier, F. Masseglia, and X. Zhang, "Autonomic intrusion detection: adaptively detecting anomalies over unlabeled audit data streams in computer networks," *Knowledge-Based Systems*, vol. 70, pp. 103–117, 2014.

[23] T. Morris, A. Srivastava, B. Reaves, W. Gao, K. Pavurapu, and R. Reddi, "A control system testbed to validate critical infrastructure protection concepts," *International Journal of Critical Infrastructure Protection*, vol. 4, no. 2, pp. 88–103, 2011.

[24] S. Pan, T. Morris, and U. Adhikari, "A specification-based intrusion detection framework for cyber-physical environment in electric power system," *International Journal of Network Security*, vol. 17, no. 2, pp. 174–188, 2015.

[25] S. Pan, T. Morris, and U. Adhikari, "Developing a hybrid intrusion detection system using data mining for power systems," *IEEE Transactions on Smart Grid*, vol. 6, no. 6, pp. 3104–3113, 2015.

[26] S. Pan, T. Morris, and U. Adhikari, "Classification of disturbances and cyber-attacks in power systems using heterogeneous time-synchronized data," *IEEE Transactions on Industrial Informatics*, vol. 11, no. 3, pp. 650–662, 2015.

[27] M. Tavallaee, E. Bagheri, W. Lu, and A. A. Ghorbani, "A detailed analysis of the KDD CUP 99 data set," in *Proceedings of the 2nd IEEE Symposium on Computational Intelligence for Security and Defense Applications (CISDA '09)*, July 2009.

10

1-Resilient Boolean Functions on Even Variables with Almost Perfect Algebraic Immunity

Gang Han,[1] Yu Yu,[2,3] Xiangxue Li,[3,4,5] Qifeng Zhou,[4] Dong Zheng,[5] and Hui Li[1]

[1]*School of Electronics and Information, Northwestern Polytechnical University, Shaanxi, China*
[2]*Department of Computer Science and Engineering, Shanghai Jiao Tong University, Shanghai, China*
[3]*Westone Cryptologic Research Center, Beijing, China*
[4]*Department of Computer Science and Technology, East China Normal University, Shanghai, China*
[5]*National Engineering Laboratory for Wireless Security, Xi'an University of Posts and Telecommunications, Xi'an, China*

Correspondence should be addressed to Yu Yu; yuyu@yuyu.hk and Xiangxue Li; xxli@cs.ecnu.edu.cn

Academic Editor: Pedro García-Teodoro

Several factors (e.g., balancedness, good correlation immunity) are considered as important properties of Boolean functions for using in cryptographic primitives. A Boolean function is perfect algebraic immune if it is with perfect immunity against algebraic and fast algebraic attacks. There is an increasing interest in construction of Boolean function that is perfect algebraic immune combined with other characteristics, like resiliency. A resilient function is a balanced correlation-immune function. This paper uses bivariate representation of Boolean function and theory of finite field to construct a generalized and new class of Boolean functions on even variables by extending the Carlet-Feng functions. We show that the functions generated by this construction support cryptographic properties of 1-resiliency and (sub)optimal algebraic immunity and further propose the sufficient condition of achieving optimal algebraic immunity. Compared experimentally with Carlet-Feng functions and the functions constructed by the method of first-order concatenation existing in the literature on even (from 6 to 16) variables, these functions have better immunity against fast algebraic attacks. Implementation results also show that they are almost perfect algebraic immune functions.

1. Introduction

Boolean functions are one of the most important cryptographic primitives for stream ciphers, block ciphers, and hash functions in cryptography [1–4]. For instance, we take Boolean functions extensively as filter and combination generators of stream ciphers based on linear feedback shift registers [3]. Cryptographic criteria for Boolean functions include balancedness, algebraic degree, nonlinearity, and correlation immunity. An overview of cryptographic criteria for Boolean functions with extensive bibliography is given in [1].

The study of the cryptographic criteria of Boolean functions is essential because of the connections between known cryptanalytic attacks and these criteria [4]. An improperly chosen Boolean function will render the system open to various kinds of attacks. Take the property of balancedness (i.e., its Hamming weight $= 2^{n-1}$), for example, the classical

cryptographic criterion for designing Boolean function is useful in preventing the system from leaking statistical information on the plaintext when the ciphertext is known.

1.1. Related Work

1.1.1. Resilient Functions. Resilient functions (see Definition 3), first studied by Siegenthaler in [5], are a special class of Boolean functions and find many interesting applications in stream ciphers.

A function f is said to be correlation-immune of the order t if the output of the function is statistically independent of the combination of any t of its inputs [6]. In 1988, Xiao and Massey introduced (by using properties of Walsh spectra) the notion of correlation immunity as an important cryptographic measure of a Boolean function with respect to its resistance against the correlation attack (which can be seen as solving a system of multivariate linear equations) [7].

In [8], Maitra and Sakar discussed the various methods for constructing resilient functions, and their results constitute a subset of a larger set of resilient functions.

1.1.2. Algebraic Attacks. In recent years, algebraic attack [9–11] has received a lot of attention in cryptography. This kind of attacks dates back to 2003 when Courtois and Meier [10] proposed algebraic attack on stream ciphers with linear feedback, which is much powerful (breaking stream ciphers satisfying the previously known design criteria in at most the square root of the complexity of the previously known generic attack). Thus the new cryptographic property of Boolean functions-algebraic immunity (AI), the minimum algebraic degree of annihilators of f or $f + 1$, was introduced by Meier et al. [11] to measure the ability of Boolean functions to resist algebraic attacks.

It was shown by Courtois and Meier [10] that maximum AI of n-variable Boolean functions is $\lceil n/2 \rceil$. The properties and constructions of Boolean functions with maximum AI are concerned in a large number of works (to name a few [9, 12–16]). The problem of efficiently constructing balanced Boolean functions with optimal algebraic immunity (and/or other cryptographic properties) is thus of great significance.

1.1.3. Fast Algebraic Attacks. Although Boolean functions with high (or optimal, ideally) algebraic immunity can effectively resist algebraic attack, it does not rule out the possibility that these functions are vulnerable to the improved algebraic attack, that is, fast algebraic attack [17, 18].

Therefore, the cryptographic community turns to address much concern on Boolean functions resisting fast algebraic attack, besides their algebraic immunity. At Asiacrypt 2012, Liu et al. [20] initiated perfect algebraic immune (PAI) functions, Boolean functions with perfect immunity against algebraic and fast algebraic attacks. Although we know that the Carlet-Feng functions [9] on $2^s + 1$ variables and the modified Carlet-Feng functions on 2^s variables are shown to be perfect algebraic immune functions [20], it is still not easy in general to explore perfect algebraic immune functions, and we do not see much successful attempt made in the literature on perfect algebraic immune functions on even variables. Thus, it is significant in both theory and practice to construct (almost) perfect algebraic immune functions on even variables with other cryptographic properties (such as resiliency) simultaneously.

We notice that Pan et al. [19] presented a construction for a class of 1-resilient Boolean functions with optimal algebraic immunity on an even number of variables by dividing them into two correlation classes, that is, equivalence classes. However, the cryptographic properties of the resulting functions are highly related to those of the initial functions we choose, and in particular, one would not expect strong resistance against fast algebraic attack in the resulting Boolean functions.

1.2. Our Contributions. In the paper, we use primitive polynomials to construct a class of Boolean functions on even variables, achieving at the same time several desirable features. For the resulting functions, we prove the properties of 1-resiliency (see Definition 3) and suboptimal algebraic immunity (see Definition 4). We also propose the sufficient condition of achieving optimal algebraic immunity.

Compared with Carlet-Feng functions [9] and the functions constructed by the method of first-order concatenation existing in the literature on even (from 6 to 16) variables [19], ours show better immunity against fast algebraic attacks. We check that our constructions are almost perfect algebraic immune functions (see Definition 5).

1.3. Roadmap. The remainder of the paper is organized as follows. Section 2 reviews some definitions related to Boolean functions and their cryptographic criteria. Section 3 presents our proposed construction of almost perfect algebraic immune resilient functions on even variables, followed by resiliency analysis in Section 4, by algebraic immunity analysis in Section 5, and by fast algebraic immunity analysis in Section 6, sequentially. Concluding remarks are located in Section 7.

1.4. Notations. We summarize in Notations the notations used in this paper.

2. Preliminaries

Let F_2^n be the vector space of dimension n over the finite field F_2. A Boolean function f on n variables is a mapping from F_2^n to F_2. By the truth table of a Boolean function on n input variables $x = (x_1, \ldots, x_n)$, we mean the 2^n length binary string $\{f(0, 0, \ldots, 0), f(0, 0, \ldots, 1), f(0, \ldots, 1, 0), \ldots, f(1, \ldots, 1, 1)\}$. The set of n-variable Boolean functions on F_2^n is denoted by $\mathbb{B}_n$.

The Hamming weight of f is the number of 1s in the binary string, denoted by $\mathrm{wt}(f)$. The support of f is the set $\{x \in F_2^n \mid f(x) = 1\}$ and is denoted by $\mathrm{supp}(f)$; that is, $\mathrm{wt}(f) = |\mathrm{supp}(f)|$. The Hamming distance $d_H(f, g)$ between two Boolean functions f and g is the Hamming weight of their difference $f + g$ (i.e., $d_H(f, g) = \mathrm{wt}(f + g)$), where $+$ is the addition on F_2.

Definition 1 (balancedness). A Boolean function f is balanced if its output is equally distributed, that is, the number of 0 elements in its truth table is equal to the number of 1 elements. In other words, an n-variable Boolean function f is balanced if and only if $\mathrm{wt}(f) = 2^{n-1}$.

For $f(x) \in \mathbb{B}_n$, it can be uniquely represented as a multivariate polynomial in the ring

$$\frac{F_2[x_1, x_2, \ldots, x_n]}{(x_1^2 - x_1, \ldots, x_n^2 - x_n)}, \tag{1}$$

and its algebraic normal form (ANF) is written as follows:

$$f(x_1, \ldots, x_n) = \sum_{I \subseteq \{1, 2, \ldots, n\}} a_I \prod_{i \in I} x_i, \quad a_I \in F_2. \tag{2}$$

Elements of a finite field can be represented in a variety of ways, depending on the choice of basis for the representation.

Let $(\alpha_1, \alpha_2, \ldots, \alpha_n)$ be a basis of F_2^n over F_2. Then, we can build an isomorphism between F_2^n and F_{2^n}:

$$(x_1, x_2, \ldots, x_n) \longmapsto x_1 \cdot \alpha_1 + x_2 \cdot \alpha_2 + \cdots + x_n \cdot \alpha_n \quad (3)$$

and we can further represent $f : F_{2^n} \to F_2$ as the polynomial

$$f(x) = \sum_{i=0}^{2^n-1} a_i x^i, \quad a_i \in F_{2^n}. \quad (4)$$

Now suppose $n = 2k$. Similarly, $f : F_{2^k} \times F_{2^k} \to F_2$ can be represented uniquely as bivariate polynomial

$$f(x, y) = \sum_{i=0}^{2^k-1} \sum_{j=0}^{2^k-1} a_{i,j} x^i y^j, \quad a_{i,j} \in F_{2^k} \quad (5)$$

and the algebraic degree of f is

$$\deg(f) = \max_{a_{i,j} \neq 0} \left\{ \mathrm{wt}(i) + \mathrm{wt}(j), \ 0 \leq i, j \leq 2^k - 1 \right\}, \quad (6)$$

where $\mathrm{wt}(i)$ is the Hamming weight of the binary string corresponding to the integer i; namely,

$$\mathrm{wt}(i) = i_1 + i_2 + \cdots + i_\tau \quad (7)$$

if $i = \sum_{l=1}^{\tau} i_l 2^l$.

Definition 2 (Walsh spectrum). Let $f : F_{2^k} \times F_{2^k} \to F_2$, $f(x, y) = \sum_{i=0}^{2^k-1} \sum_{j=0}^{2^k-1} a_{i,j} x^i y^j, a_{i,j} \in F_{2^k}$, and $(a, b) \in F_{2^k} \times F_{2^k}$. The Walsh spectrum of f (at (a, b)) is defined as

$$W_f(a, b) = \sum_{(x,y) \in F_{2^k} \times F_{2^k}} (-1)^{f(x,y) + \mathrm{Tr}_1^n(ax+by)}, \quad (8)$$

where $\mathrm{Tr}_1^n : F_{2^n} \to F_2$ is the trace function, defined as

$$\mathrm{Tr}_1^n(\alpha) = \alpha + \alpha^2 + \alpha^{2^2} + \cdots + \alpha^{2^{n-1}}, \quad \forall \alpha \in F_{2^n}. \quad (9)$$

Correlation immunity has long been recognized as one of the critical indicators of nonlinear combining functions of shift registers in stream generators [21, 22]. A high correlation immunity is generally a very desirable property, in view of various successful correlation attacks against a number of stream ciphers (see, e.g., [23]). The concept of correlation-immune functions was introduced by Siegenthaler [5]. Xiao and Massey gave an equivalent definition [7, 24].

Definition 3 (correlation immunity). A function f is called an mth-order correlation-immune function if

$$W_f(\omega) = 0, \quad \forall \omega \in F_2^n, \ 1 \leq \mathrm{wt}(\omega) \leq m, \quad (10)$$

where $\mathrm{wt}(\omega)$ is the Hamming weight of ω, that is, the number of nonzero components.

If f is also balanced, then it is called m-resilient.

Definition 4 (annihilator and algebraic immunity). Given $f \in \mathbb{B}_n$, we define

$$\mathrm{AN}(f) = \left\{ g \in \mathbb{B}_n \mid f \cdot g = 0 \right\}, \quad (11)$$

where $\cdot$ is the multiplication on F_2. Any $g \in \mathrm{AN}(f)$ is called an annihilator of f.

The algebraic immunity of f, denoted by $\mathrm{AI}(f)$, is defined as the minimum degree of nonzero annihilators of f or $f + 1$; that is,

$$\mathrm{AI}(f) = \min \left\{ \deg(g) \mid 0 \neq g \in \mathrm{AN}(f) \cup \mathrm{AN}(f+1) \right\}. \quad (12)$$

It is known [10] that $\mathrm{AI}(f) \leq \lceil n/2 \rceil$, for any $f \in \mathbb{B}_n$. If $\mathrm{AI}(f) = \lceil n/2 \rceil$, then we say the n-variable Boolean function f has optimal algebraic immunity.

At Crypto 2003, Courtois [17] proposed fast algebraic attacks (FAAs). The key idea is to decrease the degree of the equations (a multivariate polynomial system of equations over a finite field) using a precomputation algorithm. More formally, if there exists n-variable Boolean function g of low degree such that $\deg(f \cdot g)$ is somewhat not large, then one can perform fast algebraic attack on f with much confidence. To measure the resistance against fast algebraic attack, Liu et al. introduced fast algebraic immunity (FAI), which is considered as an important cryptographic property for Boolean functions used in stream ciphers:

$$\mathrm{FAI}(f) = \min \left\{ 2\,\mathrm{AI}(f), \deg(g) + \deg(f \cdot g) \right\}, \quad (13)$$

where $1 \leq \deg(g) < \mathrm{AI}(f)$.

It is folklore that $\mathrm{FAI}(f) \leq n$ [10, 25].

Almost all the symmetric Boolean functions including the functions with good algebraic immunity behave badly against FAAs [18, 25]. However, Carlet-Feng function, a class of n-variable balanced Boolean functions with the maximum algebraic immunity as well as good nonlinearity [9], was proved to have almost optimal resistance and even optimal resistance against FAAs if $n = 2^s + 1$ exactly with positive integer s [20]. Another class of even n-variable balanced Boolean functions with the maximum algebraic immunity and large nonlinearity, called Tang-Carlet function [26], was also proved to have almost optimal resistance [27]. Moreover, the immunity of some rotation symmetric Boolean functions against FAAs was also analyzed [18, 28].

The following definition provides the functionalities of both algebraic immunity and fast algebraic immunity.

Definition 5 ((almost) perfect algebraic immunity). Let f be an n-variable Boolean function. The function f is said to be perfect algebraic immune (PAI) if, for any positive integers $e < \lceil n/2 \rceil$, the product $f \cdot g$ has degree at least $n - e$ for any nonzero function g ($g \in \mathbb{B}_n$) of degree at most e.

The function f is said to be almost perfect algebraic immune if, for any positive integers $e < \lceil n/2 \rceil$, the product $f \cdot g$ has degree at least $n - e - 1$ for any nonzero function g ($g \in \mathbb{B}_n$) of degree at most e.

3. The Proposed Construction

Resilient functions (see Definition 3) are a special class of Boolean functions and find many interesting applications in stream ciphers. In [8], Maitra and Sakar discussed the various methods of creation of resilient functions, and functions constructed by these methods constitute a subset of a larger set of all resilient functions.

Pan et al. [19] presented a construction for a class of 1-resilient Boolean functions with optimal algebraic immunity on an even number of variables by dividing them into two correlation classes. More precisely, Pan et al. proposed a secondary construction (i.e., Siegenthaler's [6] construction) by concatenating two balanced Boolean functions f, g with odd variables n, where $\deg(f) = n-1$, $\mathrm{AI}(f) = (n+1)/2$. They can prove the existence of a nontrivial pair (f, g) applied in the construction. But they can only construct a part of 1-resilient Boolean functions with optimal algebraic immunity by using these pairs. Pan et al. generalized the construction to a larger class of functions with suboptimal algebraic immunity on any number (>2) of variables. However, the cryptographic properties of the resulting functions are highly related to those of the initial functions they chose as building block, and in particular, this does not rule out the possibility that these functions are vulnerable to fast algebraic attack; that is, one would not expect strong resistance against fast algebraic attack in the resulting Boolean functions. More details on the rationale of their constructions can be found in [19] where two constructions are presented and security properties are analyzed mathematically step by step. In Section 6, we also compare the properties of fast algebraic immunity between our construction and the proposal of Pan et al. [19].

This section will present our construction followed by cryptographic property analysis in the next sections.

Throughout the rest of the paper, let k, s, u, v, m be positive integers, $n = 2k$, $k \geq 3$, $0 \leq s \leq 2^k - 2$, and $2^{k-1} - 1 \leq m \leq 2^k - 2$. Let α be a primitive element of finite field F_{2^k}, and $\beta = \alpha^{(u+v)^{-1}} \in F_{2^k}$.

Set

$$
Z_{2^k-1} \triangleq \left\{0, 1, \ldots, 2^k - 1\right\},
$$

$$
\Delta_{m,s} \triangleq \left\{s, s+1, \ldots, 2^{k-1} + s - 2\right\} \cup \{m + s\},
$$

$$
P \triangleq \left\{(u, v) \mid \gcd\left((u + v) u, 2^k - 1\right) = 1, \ 0 < u, v < 2^k - 1\right\}. \tag{14}
$$

For any $(u, v) \in P$, define n-variable Boolean function f whose support $\mathrm{supp}(f)$ consists of the following four sets:

$$
\bigcup_{i=s}^{2^{k-1}+s-2} \left\{(x, y) \mid x = \alpha^i y^{-1}, \ y \in F_{2^k}^*\right\},
$$

$$
\left\{\left(\beta^{ui}, \beta^{vi}\right) \mid i \in Z_{2^k-1} \setminus \Delta_{m,s}\right\}, \tag{15}
$$

$$
\left\{\left(\beta^{ui}, 0\right) \mid i \in \Delta_{m,s}\right\},
$$

$$
\left\{\left(0, \beta^{vi}\right) \mid i \in \Delta_{m,s}\right\}.
$$

In the coming sections, we will discuss its cryptographic properties: resiliency, algebraic immunity, and fast algebraic immunity. In particular, we will show that the functions derived from our construction are 1-resilient and with almost perfect algebraic immunity.

4. Resiliency of the Proposed Construction

Nonlinear Boolean functions are generally used in symmetry cryptography. It is not surprising that the functions should have sufficiently simple scheme implementation in hardware. Besides, they must satisfy certain criteria to resist different attacks (e.g., correlation attacks suggested by Siegenthaler [29] and different types of linear attacks). One of the important factors is good correlation immunity (of order m); namely, the output should be statistically independent of combination of any m its inputs. And 1-resiliency specifies a balanced correlation-immune of order 1 Boolean function.

Theorem 6. *Suppose that f is a Boolean function derived from our construction. Then we have that f is 1-resilient.*

Proof. According to the definition of resiliency (see Definition 3), we first show that the function derived from our construction is balanced.

In fact, we have that

$$
\mathrm{wt}(f) = \left(2^{k-1} - 1\right)\left(2^k - 1\right) + \left|Z_{2^k-1} \setminus \Delta_{m,s}\right| + 2\left|\Delta_{m,s}\right| = 2^{2k-1}; \tag{16}
$$

thus, the function f is balanced as expected.

Set $\Omega = F_{2^k} \times F_{2^k}$. We know that

$$
\sum_{(x,y)\in\Omega} (-1)^{\mathrm{Tr}_1^k(ax+by)} = 0; \tag{17}
$$

then, for any $(a, b) \in \Omega \setminus \{(0, 0)\}$, it holds that

$$
\begin{aligned}
W_f(a, b) &= \sum_{(x,y)\in\Omega} (-1)^{f(x,y)+\mathrm{Tr}_1^k(ax+by)} \\
&= \sum_{(x,y)\in\Omega\setminus\mathrm{supp}(f)} (-1)^{\mathrm{Tr}_1^k(ax+by)} \\
&\quad - \sum_{(x,y)\in\mathrm{supp}(f)} (-1)^{\mathrm{Tr}_1^k(ax+by)} \\
&= -2 \sum_{(x,y)\in\mathrm{supp}(f)} (-1)^{\mathrm{Tr}_1^k(ax+by)}.
\end{aligned} \tag{18}
$$

Plugging the four sets of $\mathrm{supp}(f)$ into $\sum_{(x,y)\in\mathrm{supp}(f)}(-1)^{\mathrm{Tr}_1^k(ax+by)}$, we have that

$$
\begin{aligned}
&\sum_{(x,y)\in\mathrm{supp}(f)} (-1)^{\mathrm{Tr}_1^k(ax+by)} \\
&= \sum_{i=s}^{2^{k-1}+s-2} \sum_{y\in F_{2^k}^*} (-1)^{\mathrm{Tr}_1^k(a\alpha^i y^{-1}+by)} + \sum_{i\in\Delta_{m,s}} (-1)^{\mathrm{Tr}_1^k(a\beta^{ui})} \\
&\quad + \sum_{i\in Z_{2^k-1}\setminus\Delta_{m,s}} (-1)^{\mathrm{Tr}_1^k(a\beta^{ui}+b\beta^{vi})} \\
&\quad + \sum_{i\in\Delta_{m,s}} (-1)^{\mathrm{Tr}_1^k(b\beta^{vi})}.
\end{aligned} \tag{19}
$$

Now we consider the following two cases.

Case 1 ($a \neq 0$ and $b = 0$). We have

$$\sum_{(x,y)\in \text{supp}(f)} (-1)^{\text{Tr}_1^k(ax+by)}$$

$$= \left(2^{k-1}-1\right)(-1) + |\Delta_{m,s}|$$

$$+ \sum_{i\in Z_{2^k-1}\setminus \Delta_{m,s}} (-1)^{\text{Tr}_1^k(a\beta^{ui})} + \sum_{i\in \Delta_{m,s}} (-1)^{\text{Tr}_1^k(a\beta^{ui})} \tag{20}$$

$$= 0.$$

Case 2 ($a = 0$ and $b \neq 0$). We have

$$\sum_{(x,y)\in \text{supp}(f)} (-1)^{\text{Tr}_1^k(ax+by)}$$

$$= \left(2^{k-1}-1\right)(-1) + |\Delta_{m,s}| + \sum_{i\in Z_{2^k-1}\setminus \Delta_{m,s}} (-1)^{\text{Tr}_1^k(b\beta^{vi})} \tag{21}$$

$$+ \sum_{i\in \Delta_{m,s}} (-1)^{\text{Tr}_1^k(b\beta^{vi})} = 0.$$

Therefore, we can conclude that $W_f(a,b) = 0$, for any $(a,b) \in \Omega \setminus \{(0,0)\}$ and $ab = 0$. According to Definition 3, we know that f is 1-resilient. $\square$

5. Algebraic Immunity of the Proposed Construction

Algebraic attacks have become a powerful tool that can be used for almost all types of cryptographic systems. Algebraic immunity defined for a Boolean function measures the resistance of the function against algebraic attacks. The properties and constructions of Boolean functions with high algebraic immunity are concerned in extensive work, for example, [9, 12–16].

In this section, we will analyze the algebraic immunity of the proposed construction. First we have the following lemma.

Lemma 7 (see [30, 31]). *Suppose the integer $k \geq 3$; it holds that*

(1) for any $0 \leq t \leq 2^k - 2$ we have

$$\#\left\{(i,j) \mid 0 \leq i,j \leq 2^k - 2, \ i - j\right.$$

$$\left. \equiv t\left(\bmod 2^k - 1\right), \ \text{wt}(i) + \text{wt}(j) \leq k-1\right\} \leq 2^{k-1}; \tag{22}$$

(2) for any $1 \leq t \leq 2^k - 2$ we have

$$\#\left\{(i,j) \mid 0 \leq i,j \leq 2^k - 2, \ i - j\right.$$

$$\left. \equiv t\left(\bmod 2^k - 1\right), \ \text{wt}(i) + \text{wt}(j) \leq k-1\right\} \leq 2^{k-1} \tag{23}$$

$$- 1.$$

Theorem 8. *Let the Boolean function f be derived from the proposed construction. We have*

(1) $\text{AI}(f) \geq k - 1$;

(2) $\text{AI}(f) = k$ (i.e., f has optimal algebraic immunity) if $m + s = 2^{k-1} - 1$ or $0 \ (\bmod 2^k - 1)$.

Proof. Let h be an annihilator of f such that $f \cdot h = 0, \deg(h) < k$. Suppose that

$$h(x,y) = \sum_{i=0}^{2^k-2}\sum_{j=0}^{2^k-2} h_{i,j} x^i y^j. \tag{24}$$

For any $(x,y) \in \text{supp}(f)$, we have $h(x,y) = 0$ and

$$\bigcup_{i=s}^{2^{k-1}+s-2} \left\{(x,y) \mid x = \alpha^i y^{-1}, \ y \in F_{2^k}^*\right\} \subset \text{supp}(f). \tag{25}$$

Then, for any $s \leq l \leq 2^{k-1} + s - 2, 0 \leq s \leq 2^k - 2$, and $y \in F_{2^k}^*$, it holds that

$$0 = h\left(\alpha^l y^{-1}, y\right) = \sum_{i=0}^{2^k-2}\sum_{j=0}^{2^k-2} h_{i,j}\alpha^{li} y^{j-i} = \sum_{t=0}^{2^k-2} h_t(\alpha) y^t, \tag{26}$$

where

$$h_t(\alpha) = \sum_{0\leq i,j\leq 2^k-2, i-j\equiv t(\bmod 2^k-1)} h_{i,j}\alpha^{li}, \tag{27}$$

$$0 \leq t \leq 2^k - 2.$$

Suppose that y travels in $F_{2^k}^*$. Then the coefficients y^t in (26) will make up a coefficient matrix which is Vandermonde-like. From the invertibility property of Vandermonde matrix, we know that

$$\sum_{0\leq i,j\leq 2^k-2, i-j\equiv t(\bmod 2^k-1)} h_{i,j}\alpha^{li} = 0 \tag{28}$$

for any $0\leq t \leq 2^k - 2$ and $s \leq l \leq 2^k + s - 2$.

Now we consider the following two cases.

Case 1 ($1 \leq t \leq 2^k - 2$). From Lemma 7, we know that the number of different $h_{i,j}$ in (28) is no more than $2^{k-1} - 1$. Thus we can further assume these $h_{i,j}$ are $\{h_{i_1,j_1}, h_{i_2,j_2}, \ldots, h_{i_{2^{k-1}-1},j_{2^{k-1}-1}}\}$.

Set

$$H \triangleq \left(h_{i_1,j_1}, h_{i_2,j_2}, \ldots, h_{i_{2^{k-1}-1},j_{2^{k-1}-1}}\right)^T,$$

$$M$$

$$\triangleq \begin{pmatrix} \left(\alpha^{i_1}\right)^s & \left(\alpha^{i_2}\right)^s & \cdots & \left(\alpha^{i_{2^{k-1}-1}}\right)^s \\ \left(\alpha^{i_1}\right)^{s+1} & \left(\alpha^{i_2}\right)^{s+1} & \cdots & \left(\alpha^{i_{2^{k-1}-1}}\right)^{s+1} \\ \vdots & \vdots & \ddots & \vdots \\ \left(\alpha^{i_1}\right)^{2^{k-1}+s-2} & \left(\alpha^{i_2}\right)^{2^{k-1}+s-2} & \cdots & \left(\alpha^{i_{2^{k-1}-1}}\right)^{2^{k-1}+s-2} \end{pmatrix}; \tag{29}$$

then, we have

$$M \cdot H = 0. \tag{30}$$

Now, the invertibility property of Vandermonde matrix tells that

$$H = 0. \tag{31}$$

Namely, for any $0 \le i, j \le 2^k - 2$, and $1 \le t \le 2^k - 2$, we have

$$h_{i,j} = 0 \quad \text{if } i - j \equiv t \left(\text{mod } 2^k - 1 \right). \tag{32}$$

Therefore, for any $1 \le j \le 2^k - 2$, it holds that

$$h_{0,j} = 0. \tag{33}$$

As $(0, 1) \in \text{supp}(f)$, we have

$$h(0, 1) = 0 = \sum_{j=0}^{2^k - 2} h_{0,j}; \tag{34}$$

thus $h_{0,0} = 0$ follows.

Case 2 ($t = 0$, i.e., $i = j$). From Lemma 7, we know that the number of different $h_{i,j}$ in (28) is no more than $2^{k-1} - 1$. Thus, for any $1 \le i \le 2^k - 2$, we have

$$h_{i,i} = 0. \tag{35}$$

Putting all together, we know that

$$h \equiv 0; \tag{36}$$

namely, there is not any annihilator of degree lower than k.

Next we consider $f + 1$. Its support $\text{supp}(f + 1)$ consists of the following sets:

(i) $\bigcup_{i=2^{k-1}+s-1}^{2^{k-1}+s-2} \{(x, y) \mid x = \alpha^i y^{-1}, \ y \in F_{2^k}^* \setminus \{\beta^{vi}\}\}$

(ii) $\{(\beta^{ui}, 0) \mid i \in Z_{2^k-1} \setminus \Delta_{m,s}\}$

(iii) $\{(0, \beta^{vi}) \mid i \in Z_{2^k-1} \setminus \Delta_{m,s}\}$

(iv) $\{(0, 0), (\beta^{u(m+s)}, \beta^{v(m+s)})\}$.

Assume that h is an annihilator of $f + 1$, $\deg(h) < k$.

Without loss of generality, set

$$h(x, y) = \sum_{i=0}^{2^k-2} \sum_{j=0}^{2^k-2} h_{i,j} x^i y^j. \tag{37}$$

Denote

$$h^{(1)} \triangleq \sum_{i=0}^{2^k-3} \sum_{j=0}^{2^k-3} h_{i,j} x^i y^j$$

$$h^{(2)} \triangleq \sum_{i=0}^{2^k-2} h_{i, 2^k-2} x^i y^{2^k-2} \tag{38}$$

$$h^{(3)} \triangleq \sum_{j=0}^{2^k-2} h_{2^k-2, j} x^{2^k-2} y^j;$$

then

$$h(x, y) = h^{(1)} + h^{(2)} + h^{(3)}. \tag{39}$$

For any $(x, y) \in \text{supp}(f + 1)$, we have

$h(x, y) = 0$,

$$\bigcup_{i=2^{k-1}+s-1}^{2^k+s-2} \{(x, y) \mid x = \alpha^i y^{-1}, \ y \in F_{2^k}^* \setminus \{\beta^{vi}\}\} \tag{40}$$

$$\subset \text{supp}(f + 1).$$

Then, for any $2^{k-1} + s - 1 \le l \le 2^k + s - 2$ and $y \in F_{2^k}^* \setminus \{\beta^v\}$, it holds that

$$0 = h^{(1)} \left(\alpha^l y^{-1}, y \right) = \sum_{t=0}^{2^k-3} h_t (\alpha) y^t, \tag{41}$$

where

$$h_t (\alpha) = \sum_{0 \le i, j \le 2^k-3, i-j \equiv t (\text{mod } 2^k-1)} h_{i,j} \alpha^{li}, \tag{42}$$

$$0 \le t \le 2^k - 3.$$

Suppose that y travels in $F_{2^k}^* \setminus \{\beta^v\}$. Then the coefficients y^t in (41) will make up a coefficient matrix which is Vandermonde-like. Similarly, Lemma 7 will lead to the fact that

$$h^{(1)} = 0, \tag{43}$$

and $\text{AI}(f) \ge k - 1$ follows.

If $m + s = 2^{k-1} - 1$ or $0 \ (\text{mod } 2^k - 1)$, then (note that $\deg(h^{(2)}) < k$)

$$h^{(2)} = h_{0, 2^k-2} y^{2^k-2}. \tag{44}$$

On the other hand, we have

$$\{(0, \beta^{vi}) \mid i \in Z_{2^k-1} \setminus \Delta_{m,s}\} \subset \text{supp}(f + 1). \tag{45}$$

Thus for any $i \in Z_{2^k-1} \setminus \Delta_{m,s}$,

$$h^{(2)} (0, \beta^{vi}) = 0; \tag{46}$$

therefore

$$h_{0, 2^k-2} = 0. \tag{47}$$

Similarly, we have

$$h_{2^k-2, 0} = 0. \tag{48}$$

In a nutshell, one can conclude that $\text{AI}(f) = k$ (i.e., f has optimal algebraic immunity) if $m + s = 2^{k-1} - 1$ or $0 \ (\text{mod } 2^k - 1)$. And this completes the proof. $\qquad \square$

6. Fast Algebraic Immunity of the Proposed Construction

Algebraic attacks are based on the establishment and processing of an overdefined system of nonlinear equations involving the secret key and the keystream sequence. The system can be practically solved, and thus the secret key is compromised, only if the equations are of low degree. Courtois and Meier demonstrated that a successful algebraic attack exists when the Boolean function f (or its complement $f + 1$) has a low degree annihilator (a nonzero Boolean function g, such that $f g = 0$). At crypto 2003, Courtois [17] further generalized the standard algebraic attack to an improved version, fast algebraic attack (see also [32]), by presenting a method that allows substantially reducing the complexity of the attack. Several stream ciphers appeared to be vulnerable to the FAA, such as Toyocrypt, LILI-128, and the keystream generator that is used in E0 cipher. Fast algebraic attacks are considered to be more difficult to study than the standard algebraic attack, and thus a design with good immunity against FAA is expected.

Definition 9 (Carlet-Feng function [9]). Let f be an n-variable Boolean function, α be a primitive element in F_{2^n}, and s be an integer, $0 \le s \le 2^n - 2$. Denote

$$\Delta_s \triangleq \left\{ \alpha^s, \alpha^{s+1}, \ldots, \alpha^{s+2^{n-1}-2} \right\}. \tag{49}$$

We call f a Carlet-Feng function if $\mathrm{supp}(f) = \Delta_s$.

Theorem 10 (see [9]). *Carlet-Feng function f derived from Definition 9 has a good behavior against fast algebraic attacks.*

In particular, Carlet and Feng checked that no nonzero function g of degree at most e and no function h of degree at most d exist such that $f \cdot g = h$, when $(e, d) = (1, n-2)$ for n odd and $(e, d) = (1, n-3)$ for n even.

This has been checked for $n \le 12$ and also conjectured for every n; for $e > 1$, pairs (g, h) of degrees (e, d) such that $e + d < n - 1$ were never observed; precisely, the nonexistence of such pairs could be checked exhaustively for $n \le 9$ and $e < n/2$, for $n = 10$ and $e \le 3$, and for $n = 11$ and $e \le 2$.

This suggests that this class of functions, even if not always optimal against fast algebraic attacks, has a very good behavior.

Pan et al. presented [19] a construction for a class of 1-resilient Boolean functions with optimal algebraic immunity on an even number of variables by dividing them into two correlation classes, that is, equivalence classes. The coming result states the construction.

Theorem 11 (see [19]). *Let n be any odd integer ($n \ge 3$), f be a balanced Boolean function with maximum degree $n - 1$ and optimal algebraic immunity $(n + 1)/2$, and g be an annihilator of f. Then the following is 1-resilient Boolean function with optimal algebraic immunity:*

$$h = f \parallel g = (1 + x_{n+1}) f + x_{n+1} g \in F_2^{n+1}. \tag{50}$$

TABLE 1: Fast algebraic immunities of three classes of functions.

n	Carlet-Feng Functions [9]	Functions by [19]	The Proposed construction
6	5	5	5
8	6	6	7
10	9	9	9
12	10	10	11
14	13	12	13
16	15	14	15

Let $f \in \mathbb{B}_n$. There exist $g, h \in \mathbb{B}_n$ such that $f \cdot g = h$. Assume that $d \triangleq \deg(h)$ and $e \triangleq \deg(g)$. Following the notion of fast algebraic immunity, one may just multiply f (over F_2) by g of degree e, $1 \le e < n/2$, and get $e + d$ by enumerating all possible (e, d).

Comparatively, one can take two odd-variable Carlet-Feng functions as initial functions and construct a class of 1-resilient functions on even variables by the method proposed in [19].

Thus we can determine the appropriate values of (e, d) for the three classes of Boolean functions, the first two by Carlet-Feng method [9] and the method in [19], respectively, and the last one from the method proposed in Section 3. Implemented via Maple language, Table 1 presents the minimal values of (e, d) for the functions on even variables (from 6 to 16). In the table, the last column takes $(s, m, u, v) = (0, 2^{k-1}, 1, 2^{k-1} - 1)$.

One can check that when $n = 8, 12, 14$, and 16, the minimal values of (e, d) by the proposed method are closer to the bounds (i.e., n) than those in [19]. In fact, when $n = 8$ and 12, the results by our method are even better than those by Carlet-Feng functions [9], which makes the resistance against fast algebraic attack emerge stronger.

Moreover, one can find that, for all the (e, d) of the last column, we have $e + d \ge n - 1$. Combining this with the results in the previous section, we may expect that the functions constructed by the proposed method are almost perfect algebraic immune.

7. Conclusion

Based on bivariate representation over finite field, the paper constructed a class of 1-resilient Boolean functions on even variables with almost perfect algebraic immunity. The resulting construction can resist algebraic attack and fast algebraic attack almost perfectly along with corresponding immunity against correlation attack.

We mention that it is expected for the cryptographic community to construct Boolean function with as much cryptographic properties as possible. A natural but interesting question is how to extend the proposed construction to other important cryptographic properties such as algebraic degree and nonlinearity. We leave it as a future work.

Notations

f, g, h: Boolean functions from F_2^n to F_2

$\mathbb{B}_n$:   The set of n-variable Boolean functions on F_2^n

$\text{supp}(f)$:   Support of f

$\text{wt}(f)$:   Hamming weight of f

$d_H(f, g)$:   Hamming distance between f and g

$\deg(f)$:   Algebraic degree of f

$W_f(a, b)$:   Walsh spectrum of f at (a, b)

Tr_1^n: Trace function $\text{Tr}_1^n : F_{2^n} \to F_2$

$\text{AI}(f)$:   Algebraic immunity of f

$\text{FAI}(f)$:   Fast algebraic immunity of f

$\gcd(a, b)$:   The greatest common divisor of two positive integers a and b

F_2^n: The vector space of dimension n over the finite field F_2

F_{2^n}:   Finite field of order 2^n.

Acknowledgments

This work was supported by the National Natural Science Foundation of China (Grant nos. 61472249, 61572192, 61571191, and 61672238) and International Science & Technology Cooperation & Exchange Projects of Shaanxi Province (2016KW-038).

References

[1] C. Carlet, "Boolean functions for cryptography and error correcting codes," in *Boolean Methods And Models in Mathematics, Computer Science, And Engineering*, Y. Crama and P. Hammer, Eds., pp. 257–397, Cambridge University Press, Cambridge, UK, 2010.

[2] C. Carlet, D. K. Dalai, K. C. Gupta, and S. Maitra, "Algebraic immunity for cryptographically significant boolean functions: analysis and construction," *Institute of Electrical and Electronics Engineers. Transactions on Information Theory*, vol. 52, no. 7, pp. 3105–3121, 2006.

[3] N. T. Courtois and W. Meier, "Algebraic attacks on stream ciphers with linear feedback," in *Advances in cryptology—EUROCRYPT 2003*, vol. 2656 of *Lecture Notes in Comput. Sci.*, pp. 345–359, Springer, Berlin, 2003.

[4] T. W. Cusick and P. Stanica, *Cryptographic Boolean functions and applications*, Academic Press, San Diego, CA, USA, 2009.

[5] T. Siegenthaler, "Correlation-immunity of nonlinear combining functions for cryptographic applications," *Institute of Electrical and Electronics Engineers. Transactions on Information Theory*, vol. 30, no. 5, pp. 776–780, 1984.

[6] A. Canteaut and M. Trabbia, "Improved fast correlation attacks using parity-check equations of weight 4 and 5," in *Eurocrypt 2000, LNCS 1807*, vol. 1807, pp. 573–588, Springer-Verlag, 2000.

[7] G. Z. Xiao and J. L. Massey, "A spectral characterization of correlation-immune combining functions," *Institute of Electrical and Electronics Engineers. Transactions on Information Theory*, vol. 34, no. 3, pp. 569–571, 1988.

[8] S. Maitra and P. Sarkar, "Highly nonlinear resilient functions optimizing Siegenthaler's inequality," in *Advances in cryptology—CRYPTO '99 (SANta Barbara, CA)*, vol. 1666 of *Lecture Notes in Comput. Sci.*, pp. 198–215, Springer, Berlin, 1999.

[9] C. Carlet and K. Feng, "An infinite class of balanced functions with optimal algebraic immunity, good immunity to fast algebraic attacks and good nonlinearity," in *Advances in cryptology—ASIACRYPT 2008*, vol. 5350 of *Lecture Notes in Comput. Sci.*, pp. 425–440, Springer, Berlin, 2008.

[10] N. T. Courtois and W. Meier, "Algebraic attacks on stream ciphers with linear feedback," in *Advances in cryptology—EUROCRYPT 2003*, vol. 2656, pp. 345–359, Springer, Berlin, Germany, 2003.

[11] W. Meier, E. Pasalic, and C. Carlet, "Algebraic attacks and decomposition of Boolean functions," in *Advances in Cryptology—EUROCRYPT 2004*, vol. 3027, pp. 474–491, Springer, Berlin, Germany, 2004.

[12] D. K. Dalai, S. Maitra, and S. Sarkar, "Basic theory in construction of boolean functions with maximum possible annihilator immunity," *Designs, Codes and Cryptography*, vol. 40, no. 1, pp. 41–58, 2006.

[13] N. Li, L. Qu, W.-F. Qi, G. Feng, C. Li, and D. Xie, "On the construction of Boolean functions with optimal algebraic immunity," *IEEE Transactions on Information Theory*, vol. 54, no. 3, pp. 1330–1334, 2008.

[14] N. Li and W.-F. Qi, "Construction and analysis of Boolean functions of 2t + 1 variables with maximum algebraic immunity," in *Advances in cryptology—ASIACRYPT 2006*, vol. 4284, pp. 84–98, Springer, Berlin, Heidelberg, 2006.

[15] Z. Tu and Y. Deng, "A conjecture about binary strings and its applications on constructing Boolean functions with optimal algebraic immunity," *Designs, Codes and Cryptography. An International Journal*, vol. 60, no. 1, pp. 1–14, 2011.

[16] X. Zeng, C. Carlet, J. Shan, and L. Hu, "More balanced Boolean functions with optimal algebraic immunity and good nonlinearity and resistance to fast algebraic attacks," *Institute of Electrical and Electronics Engineers. Transactions on Information Theory*, vol. 57, no. 9, pp. 6310–6320, 2011.

[17] N. T. Courtois, "Fast algebraic attacks on stream ciphers with linear feedback," in *Advances in cryptology—CRYPTO 2003*, vol. 2729 of *Lecture Notes in Comput. Sci.*, pp. 176–194, Springer, Berlin, Germany, 2003.

[18] X. Li, Q. Zhou, H. Qian, Y. Yu, and S. Tang, "Balanced 2p-variable rotation symmetric Boolean functions with optimal algebraic immunity, good nonlinearity, and good algebraic degree," *Journal of Mathematical Analysis and Applications*, vol. 403, no. 1, pp. 63–71, 2013.

[19] S.-S. Pan, X.-T. Fu, and W.-G. Zhang, "Construction of 1-resilient Boolean functions with optimal algebraic immunity and good nonlinearity," *Journal of Computer Science and Technology*, vol. 26, no. 2, pp. 269–275, 2011.

[20] M. Liu, Y. Zhang, and D. Lin, "Perfect algebraic immune functions," in *Advances in cryptology—ASIACRYPT 2012*, vol. 7658 of *Lecture Notes in Comput. Sci.*, pp. 172–189, Springer, Heidelberg, 2012.

[21] P. Camion and A. Canteaut, "Correlation-immune and resilient functions over a finite alphabet and their applications in cryptography," *Designs, Codes and Cryptography*, vol. 16, no. 2, pp. 121–149, 1999.

[22] J. Seberry, X.-M. Zhang, and Y. Zheng, "On constructions and nonlinearity of correlation immune functions (extended abstract)," in *Eurocrypt 1993, LNCS 765*, pp. 181–199, 1994.

[23] M. Hermelin and K. Nyberg, "Correlation Properties of the Bluetooth Combiner," in *Information Security and Cryptology - ICISC'99*, vol. 1787, pp. 17–29, Springer Berlin Heidelberg, Berlin, Heidelberg, 2000.

[24] P. Camion, C. Carlet, P. Charpin, and N. Sendrier, "On correlation-immune functions," in *Advances in cryptology—CRYPTO '91*, vol. 576 of *Lecture Notes in Comput. Sci.*, pp. 86–100, Springer, Berlin, Santa Barbara, CA, USA, 1992.

[25] M. Liu, D. Lin, and D. Pei, "Fast algebraic attacks and decomposition of symmetric Boolean functions," *Institute of Electrical and Electronics Engineers. Transactions on Information Theory*, vol. 57, no. 7, pp. 4817–4821, 2011.

[26] D. Tang, C. Carlet, and X. Tang, "Highly nonlinear Boolean functions with optimal algebraic immunity and good behavior against fast algebraic attacks," *Institute of Electrical and Electronics Engineers. Transactions on Information Theory*, vol. 59, no. 1, pp. 653–664, 2013.

[27] M. Liu and D. Lin, "Almost perfect algebraic immune functions with good nonlinearity," in *Proceedings of the 2014 IEEE International Symposium on Information Theory, ISIT 2014*, pp. 1837–1841, usa, July 2014.

[28] Y. Zhang, M. Liu, and D. Lin, "On the immunity of rotation symmetric Boolean functions against fast algebraic attacks," *Discrete Applied Mathematics. The Journal of Combinatorial Algorithms, Informatics and Computational Sciences*, vol. 162, pp. 17–27, 2014.

[29] T. Siegenthaler, "Decrypting a Class of Stream Ciphers Using Ciphertext Only," *IEEE Transactions on Computers*, vol. C-34, no. 1, pp. 81–85, 1985.

[30] G. Cohen and J. P. Flori, "On a generalized combinatorial conjecture involving addition mod 2k," Tech. Rep. 1., 2011.

[31] Y. Du, F. Zhang, and M. Liu, "On the resistance of Boolean functions against fast algebraic attacks," in *Information security and cryptology—ICISC 2011*, vol. 7259 of *Lecture Notes in Comput. Sci.*, pp. 261–274, Springer, Heidelberg, 2012.

[32] P. Hawkes and G. G. Rose, "Rewriting variables: the complexity of fast algebraic attacks on stream ciphers," in *Advances in cryptology—CRYPTO 2004*, vol. 3152, pp. 390–406, Springer, Berlin, 2004.

11

Comparable Encryption Scheme over Encrypted Cloud Data in Internet of Everything

Qian Meng,[1,2] Jianfeng Ma,[2,3] Kefei Chen,[4] Yinbin Miao,[2,3] and Tengfei Yang[2,3]

[1]School of Telecommunication Engineering, Xidian University, Xi'an 710071, China
[2]Shaanxi Key Laboratory of Network and System Security, Xi'an 710071, China
[3]School of Cyber Engineering, Xidian University, Xi'an 710071, China
[4]School of Science, Hangzhou Normal University, Hangzhou 310036, China

Correspondence should be addressed to Jianfeng Ma; jfma@mail.xidian.edu.cn

Academic Editor: Shujun Li

User authentication has been widely deployed to prevent unauthorized access in the new era of Internet of Everything (IOE). When user passes the legal authentication, he/she can do series of operations in database. We mainly concern issues of data security and comparable queries over ciphertexts in IOE. In traditional database, a Short Comparable Encryption (SCE) scheme has been widely used by authorized users to conduct comparable queries over ciphertexts, but existing SCE schemes still incur high storage and computational overhead as well as economic burden. In this paper, we first propose a basic Short Comparable Encryption scheme based on sliding window method (SCESW), which can significantly reduce computational and storage burden as well as enhance work efficiency. Unfortunately, as the cloud service provider is a semitrusted third party, public auditing mechanism needs to be furnished to protect data integrity. To further protect data integrity and reduce management overhead, we present an enhanced SCESW scheme based on position-aware Merkle tree, namely, PT-SCESW. Security analysis proves that PT-SCESW and SCESW schemes can guarantee completeness and weak indistinguishability in standard model. Performance evaluation indicates that PT-SCESW scheme is efficient and feasible in practical applications, especially for smarter and smaller computing devices in IOE.

1. Introduction

With the new era of Internet of Everything (IOE) [1] and cloud computing [2, 3], smaller and smarter computing devices have begun to be integrated into our lives such as e-Health [4, 5], online shopping [6], and image retrieval [7]. Authentication is regarded as a first line of defense and has been widely used to prevent unauthorized access. Series of research efforts [8–17] have been made. User authentication can be password-based authentication [18, 19], biometric-based authentication [20, 21], and others [22–24]. However, security issues of user authentication, especially issues of data security and the availability of ciphertext data, are rather challenging tasks in IOE. When user passes the legal authentication, he/she can do comparable queries over ciphertexts. On the premise of ensuring safety, we concern how to make comparable queries over ciphertexts for authorized users.

As the cloud service provider is not a completely trusted entity, data usually utilize encryption technique by authorized users to guarantee security before being outsourced to the cloud service provider. There exist some scenes such as e-Health and stock exchange, which need to compare numeric data [25] over encrypted data. Unfortunately, what is of prime importance is how to make comparable operations over ciphertexts as well as data integrity without leaking any information.

To ensure comparable query operations over ciphertexts, series of research efforts [26–31] have been made. Among these efforts, one of popular works is a request-based comparable encryption scheme [31] which utilizes the idea of Prefix Preserving Encryption (PPE). Although this scheme can make comparable query operations over ciphertexts, it brings in high computational and storage burden. To this end, an efficient request-based comparable encryption scheme was discussed by Chen et al. [32] through utilizing sliding window method to reduce computational and storage burden. To further relief ciphertexts storage space, SCE scheme was presented by Furukawa through using PPE idea [33]. Compared with request-based comparable encryption scheme, SCE scheme encrypts each bit into 3-ary, thereby dramatically reducing ciphertexts space and improving work efficiency. As the semitrusted cloud service provider may maliciously conduct a fraction of operations and forge some ciphertexts, we should verify the correctness of outsourced data for the purpose of ensuring data integrity.

To ensure data integrity without maliciously being forged, large amount of work [34–37] aimed to verify the integrity of static and dynamic outsourced data. For example, a remote integrity checking scheme which is based on modular-exponentiation cryptographic techniques was introduced by Deswarte et al. [38] Unfortunately, the new scheme has high computing complexity. To tackle this problem, Gazzoni Filho and Barreto [39] proposed a scheme by utilizing an RSA-based secure hash function in order to achieve safe data transfer transaction through a trusted third party. However, this protocol is still vulnerable to the collusion attack in a P2P environment [39] as most of existing schemes cannot prevent the user data from being leaked to external auditors. After that, Wang et al. [36] proposed a scheme known as privacy-preserving public auditing for data storage security in cloud computing, which was the first privacy-preserving auditing protocol to support scalable and public auditing in the cloud computing. In Wang et al. protocol, computational overhead came from several time-consuming operations. Aiming at reducing high computational and storage overhead, we use position-aware Merkle tree (PMT) [40] to ensure data integrity.

Inspired by the aforementioned sliding window method and PMT, we first propose a basic scheme called SCESW scheme which is based on the sliding window method to reduce computational and storage overhead. Since the cloud service provider is a semitrusted entity which can obtain some sensitive information and then derive plaintexts, we further present an enhanced scheme named PT-SCESW scheme according to PMT to verify the stored data integrity. The main contributions of our work are listed as follows.

(i) *SCESW scheme:* inspired by sliding window method and SCE scheme, we first put forward the basic SCESW scheme to relief computational burden and storage overhead as well as enhance work efficiency.

(ii) *PT-SCESW scheme:* to further protect data integrity for authorized users, we then introduce the enhanced lightweight PT-SCESW scheme based on PMT, which allows the authorized verifier to check the correctness of stored cloud data. Table 1 shows comparisons among various schemes.

(iii) *Security and efficiency:* formal security analysis demonstrates that PT-SCESW and SCESW schemes can guarantee data security and integrity as well as weak indistinguishability in standard model and experimental results using real-world dataset show its efficiency in practice.

TABLE 1: Comparisons among various schemes.

	SCE	SCESW	PT-SCESW
S_1	Larger	Smaller	Smaller
S_2	Larger	Smaller	Smaller
S_3	Lower	Higher	Higher
S_4	×	√	√
S_5	×	×	√

Note. S_1: storage overhead; S_2: computational overhead; S_3: efficiency; S_4: sliding window method; S_5: public auditing; Yes: √; no: ×.

The reminder of this paper is organized as follows. Section 2 depicts some preliminaries which will be used in our paper. Section 3 gives a detailed description of the proposed basic and enhanced schemes. Section 4 shows security analysis and Section 5 illustrates the performance of proposed schemes.

2. Preliminaries

In this section, we will give some descriptions of sliding window method and position-aware Merkle tree.

2.1. Sliding Window Method. Sliding window method proposed by Koç [41] is one of the widely used methods for exponentiation. For example, computing x^e, we can write e using its binary code, such as $e = (b_{n-1}, \ldots, b_1, b_0)$, $b_i \in \{0, 1\}$, $i = 0, 1, \ldots, n - 1$. Based on the value of b_i, $(b_{n-1}, \ldots, b_1, b_0)$ is divided into a tuple of zero windows and nonzero windows. Sliding window technology can bring in the reduction in the amount of computation and management overhead. Algorithm 1 illustrates details of sliding window method [32].

In our schemes, numeric numbers are considered as a sequence of the binary codes. However, we suppose that all the windows have the same window size without distinguishing zero windows or nonzero windows. The fixed window size is chosen by the user's security level requirements. Hence, security and efficiency can be trade-off in practice.

2.2. Position-Aware Merkle Tree. Merkle hash tree [42] is extensively utilized in data integrity [43]. The structure of Merkle tree [44] contains a root on the top of the tree, nonleaf nodes, and leaf nodes, which is shown in Figure 1. Every nonleaf node is labeled as the hash value of its children nodes and every leaf node is defined as the hash value of a file block. $\Lambda = \{A_i \mid A_i = h(x_i), 1 \leq i \leq 15\}$, where $h(\cdot)$ represents a hash function. The root node of the Λ is regarded as A_{root}. For a node A_i, Auxiliary Authentication Information (AAI) is used to depict the smallest order node set $Y_i = \{A_1^i \gg A_2^i \gg \cdots\}$. Given a node A_i, AAI contains all the brother nodes related to A_i through root path from A_i to root node A_{root}. For example, the AAI of node A_3 is $Y_i = \{A_4 \gg A_9 \gg A_{14}\}$, as shown in Figure 1.

In the PMT structure, every node is noted as A_i. Besides, A_i is presented by a 3-tuple $A_i = (A_i \cdot p; A_i \cdot r; A_i \cdot v)$, where $A_i \cdot p$ represents node A_i's relative position to its parents node; $A_i \cdot r$ represents the number of node A_i's leaf nodes; $A_i \cdot v$ represents the value of the node A_i. We label nodes from left

---

Input: two numbers x and e where x represents base and e represents exponent
Output: $y = x^e$
(1) **for** *all* w, $w = 3, 5, 7, \ldots, 2^d - 1$ **do**
(2)   Compute and store x^w;
(3) e is divided into zero windows and non-zero windows F_i of length $T(F_i)$
    where $T(F_i)$ represents the length of windows;
(4) **for** $i = n - 1, \ldots, 0$ **do**
(5)   Compute the value of $y := x^{F_{n-1}}$;
(6)   **for** $0 \le i \le n - 2$ **do**
(7)   Compute and store $y := y^{2^{T(F_i)}}$;
(8)   **if** $f_i \ne 0$ **then**
(9)   Compute and store $y := y \cdot x^{F_i}$;
(10)   **else**
(11) F_i is a zero window.
(12) Return y;

ALGORITHM 1: The sliding window method [32].

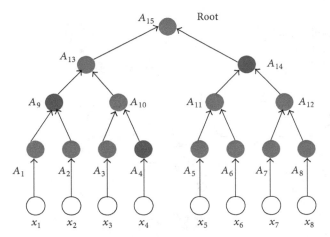

FIGURE 1: Position-aware Merkle tree.

TABLE 2: Nodes of position-aware Merkle tree in Figure 1.

Nodes	$A_i \cdot p$	$A_i \cdot r$	$A_i \cdot v$
A_1	0	1	$h(0 \parallel x_1 \parallel 1)$
A_2	1	1	$h(1 \parallel x_2 \parallel 1)$
A_3	0	1	$h(0 \parallel x_3 \parallel 1)$
A_4	1	1	$h(1 \parallel x_4 \parallel 1)$
A_5	0	1	$h(0 \parallel x_5 \parallel 1)$
A_6	1	1	$h(1 \parallel x_6 \parallel 1)$
A_7	0	1	$h(0 \parallel x_7 \parallel 1)$
A_8	1	1	$h(1 \parallel x_8 \parallel 1)$
A_9	0	2	$h(0 \parallel A_1 \cdot v \parallel A_2 \cdot v \parallel 2)$
A_{10}	1	2	$h(1 \parallel A_3 \cdot v \parallel A_4 \cdot v \parallel 2)$
A_{11}	0	2	$h(0 \parallel A_5 \cdot v \parallel A_6 \cdot v \parallel 2)$
A_{12}	1	2	$h(1 \parallel A_7 \cdot v \parallel A_8 \cdot v \parallel 2)$
A_{13}	0	4	$h(0 \parallel A_9 \cdot v \parallel A_{10} \cdot v \parallel 4)$
A_{14}	1	4	$h(1 \parallel A_{11} \cdot v \parallel A_{12} \cdot v \parallel 4)$
A_{15}	Null	8	$h(\text{null} \parallel A_{13} \cdot v \parallel A_{14} \cdot v \parallel 8)$

to right in each layer with $A_i \cdot p$, $A_i \cdot r$, and $A_i \cdot v$ defined as follows, where set Ω_l represents the set of left subtrees, set Ω_r represents the set of right subtrees, set Ω_{root} represents the root of tree, and set Θ represents the set of leaf nodes.

$$A_i \cdot p = \begin{cases} 0 & \text{if } A_i \in \Omega_l; \\ 1 & \text{if } A_i \in \Omega_r; \\ \text{null} & \text{if } A_i \in \Omega_{\text{root}}, \end{cases}$$

$$A_i \cdot r = \begin{cases} A_l^i \cdot r + A_r^i \cdot r & \text{if } A_i \notin \Theta; \\ 1 & \text{if } A_i \in \Theta, \end{cases} \tag{1}$$

$$A_i \cdot v$$
$$= \begin{cases} h\left(A_i \cdot p \parallel A_l^i \cdot v \parallel A_r^i \cdot v \parallel A_i \cdot r\right) & \text{if } A_i \notin \Theta; \\ h\left(A_i \cdot p \parallel x_i \parallel 1\right) & \text{if } A_i \in \Theta. \end{cases}$$

From Figure 1, we know that node A_3 is a leaf node that relates to the block x_3 and A_3 is located in the left of its parent

node A_{10}. According to the formula above, $A_3 \cdot p = 0$, $A_3 \cdot r = 1$, and $A_3 \cdot v = h(0 \parallel x_3 \parallel 1)$. Similarly, we can obtain $A_4 = h(1 \parallel x_4 \parallel 1)$ and $A_{10} = h(1 \parallel A_3 \cdot v \parallel A_4 \cdot v \parallel 2)$. Table 2 illustrates the value of nodes in Figure 1.

3. Proposed Basic and Enhanced Schemes

Before presenting concrete constructions of SCESW and PT-SCESW schemes outlined above, we give some notations which will be utilized in the whole paper, as shown in Notations.

3.1. System Model. We first describe the system model of PT-SCESW scheme which mainly involves four entities, namely, Data Owner (DO), cloud service provider (CSP), user, and Third-Party Auditor (TPA), as shown in Figure 2. When user passes the legal authentication, he/she can do comparable queries operations over encrypted data. First,

Input: Root node A_{root}, corresponding tag x_i, integrity authentication path Y_i, k' represents numbers of corresponding nodes in Y_i

Output: correct, $\perp$

(1) Let $p_0 = \neg A_1^i \cdot p$; $r_0 = 1$; $n_0 = 1$; $v_0 = h(p_0 \parallel x_i \parallel r_0)$;

(2) **for** *all* $1 \leq j \leq k'$ **do**

(3)   **if** $j = k'$ **then**

(4) $p_j = \text{null}$;

(5)   **else**

(6) $p_j = \neg A_{j+1}^i \cdot p$.

(7) $r_j = \neg A_{j+1}^i \cdot r + r_{j-1}$;

(8)   **if** $\neg A_j^i \cdot p = 1$ **then**

(9) $n_j = n_{j-1}$; $v_j = h(p_j \parallel h_{j-1} \parallel A_j^i \cdot v \parallel r_j)$;

(10)   **else**

(11)   **if** $\neg A_j^i \cdot p = 0$ **then**

(12) $n_j = n_{j-1} + A_j^i \cdot r$; $v_j = h(p_j \parallel A_j^i \cdot v \parallel h_{j-1} \parallel r_j)$;

(13) **if** $r_{k'} = A_{\text{root}} \cdot r$; $v_{k'} = A_{\text{root}} \cdot v$ and $n_{k'} = i$ **then**

(14)   Output correct, $n_{k'}$, $A = \{\text{null}, r_{k'}, v_{k'}\}$;

(15) **else**

(16)   Output $\perp$.

ALGORITHM 2: Integrity verification algorithm.

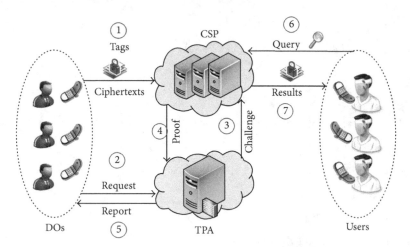

FIGURE 2: The architecture of PT-SCESW scheme.

the DO encrypts files by using SCESW scheme and finally sends the file $\mathscr{CP}$ and the corresponding φ to the CSP. When user wants to issue the search query over encrypted cloud data, he/she needs to submit a search query to CSP. The CSP returns the result of the query to the user. If the verifier wants to check the outsourced data integrity, she/he sends an auditing request to the TPA and the TPA submits the auditing challenge $\mathscr{CL}$ to the CSP. Upon receiving the auditing challenge $\mathscr{CL}$, CSP computes $\mathscr{P}_1$, $\mathscr{P}_2$ and sends the auditing proof to the TPA. Then TPA conducts the integrity verification algorithm (Algorithm 2) to check the data integrity and returns the auditing report to the verifier. Figure 2 depicts the task of each entity, with an assumption that the DO is the verifier.

(1) DO: it has twofold responsibilities. Firstly, data files are encrypted through SCESW scheme and then outsourced to the CSP, as shown in step ①. Secondly, the DO sends auditing request to the TPA in order to check ciphertexts integrity, as illustrated in step ②.

(2) CSP: it can provide infinite storage and computation resources to the DO and the user. After executing auditing challenge, the CSP sends auditing proof to the TPA, as shown in step ④.

(3) User: it has the following responsibilities. Firstly, the user submits a query to compare a pair of ciphertexts $\mathscr{CP}$ and $\mathscr{CP}^*$, as shown in step ⑥. Secondly, upon doing Cmp operation, the CSP returns the relationship of two numeric ciphertexts, as illustrated in step ⑦.

(4) TPA: it has twofold responsibilities. Firstly, the TPA submits auditing challenge to the CSP, as shown in step ③. Secondly, the TPA returns the auditing report to the verifier shown in step ⑤. If the result of auditing is correctness, system continues the Cmp step;

SCESW scheme is a tuple of algorithms including `KeyGen`, `Par`, `Der`, `Enc`, `Cmp`, which are shown as follows:

(i) $KeyGen(1^k)$: given the security parameter $k \in \mathcal{N}$, range parameter $n \in \mathcal{N}$ and master key $\mathcal{MSK}$, the DO runs the algorithm to output the master key $\mathcal{MSK}$ and public parameter $\mathcal{PP}$.

(ii) $Par(\mathbb{N})$: given the number $\mathbb{N}$, the DO runs the algorithm to output the number $\mathbb{N}'$ rewritten through its binary code by utilizing sliding window method, where t represents the window size, $m = n/t$ is the number of blocks and $\mathbb{N} = \mathbb{N}'$

$$\mathbb{N} = (b_0, \ldots, b_{n-1}) = \sum_{0 \le i \le n-1} b_i 2^i;$$

$$\mathbb{N}' = (B_0, \ldots, B_{m-1}) = \sum_{0 \le i \le m-1} B_i (2^t)^i.$$

(iii) $Der(k, n, \mathcal{MSK}, \mathbb{N})$: given the security parameter $k \in \mathcal{N}$, range parameter $n \in \mathcal{N}$, master key $\mathcal{MSK}$ and num $0 \le \mathbb{N} \le 2^n$, the DO runs the algorithm to output a token $\mathcal{TK}$.

(iv) $Enc(k, n, \mathcal{MSK}, \mathbb{N})$: given the security parameter $k \in \mathcal{N}$, range parameter $n \in \mathcal{N}$, master key $\mathcal{MSK}$ and num $0 \le \mathbb{N} \le 2^n$, the DO runs the algorithm to generate the ciphertext $\mathcal{CP}$ and submits it to the CSP.

(v) $Cmp(\mathcal{PP}, \mathcal{CP}, \mathcal{CP}^*, \mathcal{TK})$: given the public parameter $\mathcal{PP}$, two ciphertexts $\mathcal{CP}$ and $\mathcal{CP}^*$, and token $\mathcal{TK}$, the CSP outputs $-1, 0, 1$, then it returns the relevant search results to the user.

ALGORITHM 3: Definition of SCESW scheme.

otherwise, the scheme demonstrates that ciphertexts are not with integrity and system stops working.

3.2. The SCESW Scheme. Let t be the window size, which means each block file has t bits. We assume arbitrary number n is a multiple of t. If n is not a multiple of t, we make n a multiple of t by adding zero in the end of the n's binary code. SCESW scheme consists of five algorithms, namely, `KeyGen`, `Par`, `Der`, `Enc`, and `Cmp`. When user passes the legal authentication, he/she can do comparable queries operations over encrypted data. Thus, we mainly consider data security and comparable queries operations over ciphertexts. A detailed construction of SCESW scheme is depicted as follows.

(1) Definitions of SCESW Scheme. The SCESW scheme is composed of five algorithms involving `KeyGen`, `Par`, `Der`, `Enc`, and `Cmp`. SCESW system definition can be defined in Algorithm 3.

(2) Details of SCESW Scheme. Concrete construction of SCESW scheme can be defined as follows.

(i) $KeyGen(k, n) \rightarrow (\mathcal{PP}, \mathcal{MSK})$: given a security parameter $k \in \mathcal{N}$ and range parameter $n \in \mathcal{N}$, `KeyGen` first randomly chooses hash functions: $H_1(\cdot), H_2(\cdot), H_3(\cdot) : \{0,1\}^k \times \{0,1\}^* \rightarrow \{0,1\}^k$ and then returns $\mathcal{PP} = (n, H_1, H_2, H_3)$.

Finally, `KeyGen` algorithm outputs a public parameter $\mathcal{PP}$ and a master key $\mathcal{MSK}$.

(ii) $Par(\mathbb{N}, t) \rightarrow (\mathbb{N}')$: given an original number $\mathbb{N}$, the DO rewrites it through its binary code by utilizing sliding window method with (2), where t represents

the window size, $m = n/t$ is the number of blocks, and $\mathbb{N} = \mathbb{N}'$:

$$\mathbb{N} = (b_0, \ldots, b_{n-1}) = \sum_{0 \le i \le n-1} b_i 2^i;$$

$$\mathbb{N}' = (B_0, \ldots, B_{m-1}) = \sum_{0 \le i \le m-1} B_i (2^t)^i. \tag{2}$$

(iii) $Der(\mathcal{PP}, \mathcal{MSK}, \mathbb{N}) \rightarrow (\mathcal{TK})$: given $\mathcal{PP} = (n, H_1, H_2, H_3)$, master key $\mathcal{MSK}$, and number $\mathbb{N}$, `Der` algorithm outputs a token $\mathcal{TK} = (d_1, d_2, \ldots, d_m)$ with the following equations:

$$\mathbb{N} = (B_0, \ldots, B_{m-1}) = \sum_{0 \le i \le m-1} B_i (2^t)^i;$$

$$B_0 = (b_0, b_1, \ldots, b_{t-1}), \ldots,$$

$$B_{m-1} = (b_{n-t}, b_{n-t+1}, \ldots, b_{n-1}), \tag{3}$$

$$B_m = 0;$$

$$d_i = H_1(\mathcal{MSK}, B_m, \ldots, B_i), \quad i = 1, \ldots, m.$$

(iv) $Enc(\mathcal{PP}, \mathcal{MSK}, \mathbb{N}) \rightarrow (\mathcal{CP})$: given $\mathcal{PP} = (n, H_1, H_2, H_3)$, master key $\mathcal{MSK}$, and number $\mathbb{N}$, `Enc` randomly picks $\mathcal{TK} = (d_1, d_2, \ldots, d_m)$ and a random number $I \in \{0,1\}^k$, where

$$\mathbb{N} = (B_0, \ldots, B_{m-1}) = \sum_{0 \le i \le m-1} B_i (2^t)^i. \tag{4}$$

Next, `Enc` generates f_i, where

$$f_i = H_3(d_{i+1}, I) + H_2(\mathcal{MSK}, d_{i+1})$$
$$+ B_i \bmod (2^{(t+1)} - 1) \quad (i = m-1, \ldots, 0). \tag{5}$$

PT-SCESW scheme is a series of algorithms namely *Setup, Encryption, Auditing, Comparison* phases, which are shown as follows:

Setup Phase. The DO chooses a security parameter $k \in \mathcal{N}$, range parameter $n \in \mathcal{N}$ and master key $\mathcal{MSK}$ to generate a public parameter $\mathcal{PP}$. The DO runs KeyGen to produce the secret key $\mathcal{SK}$ and public key $\mathcal{PK}$. Setup phase outputs the secret key $\mathcal{SK}$, public key $\mathcal{PK}$, public parameter $\mathcal{PP}$ and master key $\mathcal{MSK}$. Setup phase contains KeyGen algorithm in SCESW scheme. The DO shares $\mathcal{PK}$ with others and preserves $\mathcal{SK}$ as a secret.

Encryption Phase

    (i) $Par(\mathbb{N})$, $Der(\mathcal{PP}, \mathcal{MSK}, \mathbb{N})$: system definitions are similar to SCESW scheme, as shown in Algorithm 3.

    (ii) $Enc(\mathcal{PP}, \mathcal{MSK}, \mathbb{N})$: given a security parameter $k \in \mathcal{N}$, range parameter $n \in \mathcal{N}$, master key $\mathcal{MSK}$, public key $\mathcal{PK}$, private key $\mathcal{SK}$ and num $0 \le \mathbb{N} \le 2^n$, the DO runs the algorithm to output a ciphertext $\mathcal{CP}$, set φ and the metadata. Then file $\mathcal{CP}$ and set φ will be sent by the DO to the CSP. The metadata might be signed and kept by the DO.

Auditing Phase

    (i) $ChalGen(s) \rightarrow (\mathcal{CL})$: given the secret parameter s, the verifier outputs auditing challenge $\mathcal{CL}$ for the query.

    (ii) $ProofGen(g_s, F, \varphi, \mathcal{CL}) \rightarrow (\mathcal{P})$: given the DO's public parameter g_s, file F, set φ and auditing challenge $\mathcal{CL}$, the TPA outputs the auditing proof $\mathcal{P}$ to verify that the CSP owns the outsourced file correctly.

    (iii) $ProofCheck(\mathcal{PK}, \mathcal{CL}, metadata, \mathcal{P}) \rightarrow (\text{correct}, \perp)$: given the DO's public key $\mathcal{PK}$, evidence $\mathcal{P}$, metadata and auditing challenge $\mathcal{CL}$, the TPA outputs correct or $\perp$. If the proof $\mathcal{P}$ passes the verification, the function outputs correct; otherwise, the function outputs $\perp$ and the system stops to work. At last, TPA sends the auditing report to the verifier.

Comparison Phase

    (i) $Cmp(\mathcal{CP}, \mathcal{CP}^*, \mathcal{TK})$: system definition is similar to SCESW scheme, as illustrated in Algorithm 3.

ALGORITHM 4: Definition of PT-SCESW scheme.

Enc finally outputs ciphertexts $\mathcal{CP} = (I, F) = (I, (f_0, f_1, \ldots, f_{m-1}))$. The DO submits $\mathcal{CP}$ to the CSP.

Here, $(f_0, f_1, \ldots, f_{m-1})$ can be encoded into F_t to reduce storage space, where

$$F_t = \sum_{0 \le i \le m-1} f_i \cdot \left(2^{(t+1)} - 1\right)^i. \tag{6}$$

(v) $Cmp(\mathcal{CP}, \mathcal{CP}^*, \mathcal{TK}) \rightarrow (\omega)$: given two ciphertexts $\mathcal{CP} = (I, (f_0, f_1, \ldots, f_{m-1}))$, $\mathcal{CP}^* = (I', F^*) = (I', (f'_0, f'_1, \ldots, f'_{m-1}))$, and a token $\mathcal{TK} = (d_1, d_2, \ldots, d_m)$, Cmp algorithm sets $j = m - 1$ and keeps producing c_j by decreasing j by 1 at each step, where

$$c_j = f_j - f'_j - H_3\left(d_{j+1}, I\right) + H_3\left(d_{j+1}, I'\right) \bmod \left(2^{(t+1)} - 1\right). \tag{7}$$

This algorithm stops when Cmp produces c_j such that $c_j \neq 0$ or when $c_j = 0$ for all $i = m - 1, m - 2, \ldots, 0$. If $\mathbb{N} > \mathbb{N}^*$, then $1 \le c_j \le 2^t - 1$ holds. If $\mathbb{N} < \mathbb{N}^*$, then

$2^t \le c_j \le 2^{(t+1)} - 2$ holds. If $\mathbb{N} = \mathbb{N}^*$, then $c_j \equiv 0$ holds. Then we have

$$\omega = \begin{cases} -1 & \text{if } 1 \le c_j \le 2^t - 1 \\ 0 & \text{if } c_j \equiv 0 \\ 1 & \text{if } 2^t \le c_j \le 2^{(t+1)} - 2. \end{cases} \tag{8}$$

3.3. The PT-SCESW Scheme

(1) Definitions of PT-SCESW Scheme. To efficiently support public auditing, we propose an enhanced SCESW scheme called PT-SCESW scheme. PT-SCESW scheme consists of four phases *Setup, Encryption, Auditing and Comparison*, defined in Algorithm 4. When user passes the legal authentication, he/she can do comparable queries operations over encrypted data. Thus, we mainly consider data security and comparable queries operations over ciphertexts.

(2) Details of PT-SCESW Scheme. Concrete construction of PT-SCESW scheme is defined as follows.

Setup Phase. This phase contains the KeyGen algorithm, which is utilized by the DO to initialize system.

The DO chooses a security parameter $k \in \mathcal{N}$, range parameter $n \in \mathcal{N}$, master key $\mathcal{MSK} \in \{0,1\}^*$, and hash functions H_1, H_2, H_3. Then he/she calculates the secret key $\mathcal{SK} = (p, q)$ and public key $\mathcal{PK} = (N = p \cdot q, g)$, where p, q are two large primes and g is the generator of a high-order cyclic group. Besides, he/she defines $\mathcal{PP} = (n, H_1, H_2, H_3)$. The DO runs KeyGen algorithm to generate the public parameter $\mathcal{PP}$ and secret key $\mathcal{SK}$. Setup phase contains KeyGen algorithm in SCESW scheme.

Setup phase outputs the secret key $\mathcal{SK}$, public key $\mathcal{PK}$, public parameter $\mathcal{PP}$, and master key $\mathcal{MSK}$.

Encryption Phase. Par algorithm is run by the DO to generate the num $\mathbb{N}$ which adopts the sliding window method. Der algorithm is used by the DO to produce the token of the num $\mathbb{N}$. Enc algorithm is run by the DO to generate ciphertexts of the num $\mathbb{N}$.

(i) $Par(\mathbb{N}) \rightarrow (\mathbb{N}')$, $Der(\mathcal{PP}, \mathcal{MSK}, \mathbb{N}) \rightarrow (\mathcal{TK})$: algorithms are similar to SCESW scheme.

(ii) $Enc(\mathcal{PP}, \mathcal{MSK}, \mathbb{N}) \rightarrow (\mathcal{CP})$: suppose that a public parameter $\mathcal{PP} = (n, H_1, H_2, H_3)$, master key $\mathcal{MSK}$, and number $\mathbb{N}$ are given, where

$$\mathbb{N} = (B_0, \ldots, B_{m-1}) = \sum_{0 \le i \le m-1} B_i \left(2^t\right)^i, \tag{9}$$

Enc algorithm randomly chooses a token $\mathcal{TK} = (d_1, d_2, \ldots, d_m)$ and a random number $I \in \{0,1\}^k$. Next Enc generates

$$\begin{aligned} f_i &= H_3\left(d_{i+1}, I\right) + H_2\left(\mathcal{MSK}, d_{i+1}\right) \\ &\quad + B_i \bmod \left(2^{(t+1)} - 1\right) \quad (i = m-1, \ldots, 0). \end{aligned} \tag{10}$$

Enc finally outputs ciphertexts $\mathcal{CP} = (I, (f_0, f_1, \ldots, f_{m-1}))$. Here, $(f_0, f_1, \ldots, f_{m-1})$ can be encoded into an integer F_t to make ciphertexts shorter, where

$$F_t = \sum_{0 \le i \le m-1} f_i \cdot \left(2^{(t+1)} - 1\right)^i. \tag{11}$$

The DO regards $F = (f_0, f_1, \ldots, f_{m-1})$ as m parts. For each file block f_i, $(i = 0, \ldots, m-1)$, the DO computes tag $x_i = g^{m_i} \bmod N$. Then the user constructs the PMT according to the data block tags $X = \{x_1, \ldots, x_m\}$ and calculates root value A_{root} as the metadata, where $A_{\text{root}} = (A_{\text{root}} \cdot p, A_{\text{root}} \cdot r, A_{\text{root}} \cdot v)$. A and $\mathcal{SK}$ can be kept by the DO, while file F and set $\varphi = \{X, \text{PMT}\}$ can be sent to the CSP.

Auditing Phase. ChalGen algorithm is run by the verifier to produce the auditing challenge $\mathcal{CL}$. ProofGen algorithm is used by the TPA to generate the auditing proof $\mathcal{P}$. ChalGen algorithm is conducted by the TPA to produce auditing results.

(i) $ChalGen(s) \rightarrow (\mathcal{CL})$: the verifier randomly chooses the secret parameter $s \in Z_N^*$ and calculates the public

parameter $g_s = g^s \bmod N$. The verifier randomly chooses c weight coefficient pairs $Q = \{i_j, a_j\}_{j=1,\ldots,c}$, where $i_j \in [1, m]$ is different from each other, $a_j \in \{0,1\}^l$. Then the verifier sends the auditing request to the TPA, and TPA sends auditing challenge $\mathcal{CL} = \{g_s, Q\}$ to the CSP.

(ii) $ProofGen(g_s, F, \varphi, \mathcal{CL}) \rightarrow (\mathcal{P})$: upon receiving the $\mathcal{CL} = \{g_s, Q\}$ sent by the verifier, the CSP computes $\mathcal{P}_1 = g_s^{\sum_c^{i=1} a_j \cdot f_{i_j}} \bmod N$, $\mathcal{P}_2 = \{x_{i_j}, \Upsilon_{i_j}\}_{j=1,\ldots,c}$. Then the CSP returns auditing proof $\mathcal{P} = (\mathcal{P}_1, \mathcal{P}_2)$ to the TPA.

(iii) $ProofCheck(PK, \mathcal{CL}, metadata, \mathcal{P}) \rightarrow (\text{correct}, \bot)$: upon receiving the auditing proof $\mathcal{P} = (\mathcal{P}_1, \mathcal{P}_2)$, the TPA conducts Algorithm 2 to verify $(A, x_{i_j}, \Upsilon_{i_j}) \rightarrow \{\text{correct}, \bot\}$, in which $j = 1, \ldots, c$. If Algorithm 2 outputs correct, it means tags corresponding to the auditing request are correct. Then, the TPA computes $\mathcal{P}_3 = \prod_{j=1}^c (x_{i_j})^{a_j} \bmod N$. If $\mathcal{P}_3^s = \mathcal{P}_1$ holds, it outputs correct, which means the auditing challenge $\mathcal{CL}$ passes the verification and the system continues the Cmp algorithm; otherwise, it outputs $\bot$, which means the outsourced file was forged at the CSP side and the system stops the Cmp algorithm.

Comparison Phase. Cmp algorithm is employed by the user to compare the relationship of the numbers $\mathbb{N}$ and $\mathbb{N}^*$ from $\mathcal{CP}$ and $\mathcal{CP}^*$.

(i) $Cmp(\mathcal{CP}, \mathcal{CP}^*, \mathcal{TK}) \rightarrow (\omega)$: Cmp algorithm is similar to SCESW scheme. Given two ciphertexts $\mathcal{CP} = (I, (f_0, f_1, \ldots, f_{m-1}))$, $\mathcal{CP}^* = (I', F^*) = (I', (f_0', f_1', \ldots, f_{m-1}'))$ and a token $\mathcal{TK} = (d_1, d_2, \ldots, d_m)$, Cmp algorithm outputs $-1, 0, 1$.

4. Security Analysis

In this section, we will give properties of completeness and weak indistinguishability in PT-SCESW scheme by theoretical analysis, which are similar to SCESW scheme.

Theorem 1. *The PT-SCESW scheme is complete as long as H_1, H_2, and H_3 are pseudorandom functions and the CSP honestly performs operations according to the auditing challenge.*

Proof. We denote that $\mathcal{CP}$ and $\mathcal{CP}^*$ are generated from $\mathbb{N}$ and $\mathbb{N}^*$, respectively.

$$\begin{aligned} \mathbb{N} &= \sum_{0 \le i \le n-1} b_i 2^i = \sum_{0 \le i \le m-1} B_i \left(2^t\right)^i; \\ \mathbb{N}^* &= \sum_{0 \le i \le n-1} \beta_i 2^i = \sum_{0 \le i \le m-1} B_i' \left(2^t\right)^i, \end{aligned} \tag{12}$$

where t is the window size; $m = n/t$ is the number of blocks via utilizing sliding window technology.

$$TK = (d_0, \ldots, d_m);$$

$$TK^* = (d_0', \ldots, d_m');$$

$$\mathscr{CP} = \left(I, \left(f_0, \ldots, f_{m-1}\right)\right);$$

$$\mathscr{CP}^* = \left(I', \left(f_0', \ldots, f_{m-1}'\right)\right). \tag{13}$$

From (3) we know that d_i and d_i' depend on B_i, B_{i+1}, B_i', B_{i+1}', and $\mathscr{MSK}$. Suppose that l is the first different block of $\mathbb{N}$ and $\mathbb{N}^*$, for $i = l+1, \ldots, m-1$; if the equation $B_{i+1} = B_{i+1}'$ holds, then $d_{i+1} = d_{i+1}'$ holds. Hence, if $\mathbb{N} = \mathbb{N}^*$, $c_i = 0$ holds for $i = 0, \ldots, m-1$, and then ω outputs 0. If $\mathbb{N} \neq \mathbb{N}^*$, for this arbitrary j,

$$c_j = f_j - f_j' - H_3\left(d_{j+1}, I\right)$$

$$+ H_3\left(d_{j+1}, I'\right) \bmod \left(2^{(t+1)} - 1\right)$$

$$= \left(f_j - H_3\left(d_{j+1}, I\right)\right) - \left(f_j'\right.$$

$$\left. - H_3\left(d_{j+1}, I'\right)\right) \bmod \left(2^{(t+1)} - 1\right)$$

$$= \left(H_3\left(d_{j+1}, I\right) + H_2\left(\mathscr{MSK}, d_{j+1}\right) + B_j \right. \tag{14}$$

$$- H_3\left(d_{j+1}, I\right)\right) - \left(H_3\left(d_{j'+1}, I\right)\right.$$

$$+ H_2\left(\mathscr{MSK}, d_{j'+1}\right) + B_j'$$

$$\left. - H_3\left(d_{j+1}, I'\right)\right) \bmod \left(2^{(t+1)} - 1\right)$$

$$= B_j - B_j' \bmod \left(2^{(t+1)} - 1\right).$$

For $j = 0, \ldots, m-1$, equation $B_j - B_j' = 0$ means $\mathbb{N} = \mathbb{N}^*$; equation $B_j - B_j' \neq 0$ means j is the first different bit. Specifically, if $1 \leq c_j \leq (2^t - 1)$, then $\mathbb{N} > \mathbb{N}^*$; if $2^t \leq c_j \leq (2^{(t+1)} - 2)$, then $\mathbb{N} < \mathbb{N}^*$.

Upon receiving $\mathscr{CL} = \{g_s, Q\}$ sent by the verifier, the CSP computes $\mathscr{P}_1 = g_s^{\sum_c^{i=1} a_j \cdot f_{i_j}} \bmod N$, $\mathscr{P}_2 = \{x_{i_j}, A_{i_j}, \Upsilon_{i_j}\}_{j=1,\ldots,c}$. According to the PMT formula, we can prove that x_{i_j} is the corresponding tag to the leaf node A_{i_j} and the result outputs correctly.

The verifier computes

$$\mathscr{P}_3 = \prod_{j=1}^c \left(x_{i_j}\right)^{a_j} \bmod N$$

$$= \prod_{j=1}^c \left(g_{f_{i_j}}\right)^{a_j} \bmod N$$

$$= g^{\sum_c^{i=1} a_j \cdot f_{i_j}} \bmod N, \tag{15}$$

$$\mathscr{P}_3^s \bmod N = \left(g^{\sum_c^{i=1} a_j \cdot f_{i_j}} \bmod N\right)^s \bmod N$$

$$= g^{s \cdot \sum_c^{i=1} a_j \cdot f_{i_j}} \bmod N = g_s^{\sum_c^{i=1} a_j \cdot f_{i_j}} \bmod N$$

$$= \mathscr{P}_1 \bmod N.$$

Hence, the PA-SCESW scheme is complete. □

TABLE 3: Comparison of computational cost in various schemes.

	PT-SCESW scheme	SCESW scheme	SCE scheme [33]
Encryption phase	$3m \cdot a + m \cdot E$	$3m \cdot a$	$4n \cdot a$
Comparison phase	$2(m - L + 1) \cdot a$	$2(m - L + 1) \cdot a$	$2(n - L + 2) \cdot a$
Auditing phase	$(2+c)E+(k'+1)a$	0	0

Note. m, n, L, a, c, k', E represent sliding window numbers of $\mathbb{N}$, original window numbers of $\mathbb{N}$, hash operations, number of windows for verification, numbers of corresponding nodes in Υ_i, and exponentiation operation, respectively.

TABLE 4: Comparison of storage overhead in various schemes.

	Ciphertext generation phase	Token generation phase
SCE scheme [33]	$(n + 1) \cdot k$	$k + (\ln 3 / \ln 2) \cdot n$
SCESW scheme	$m \cdot k$	$k + (\ln (2^{t+1} - 1) / \ln(t + 1)) \cdot m$
PA-SCESW scheme	$m \cdot k$	$k + (\ln (2^{t+1} - 1) / \ln(t + 1)) \cdot m$

Note. m, n, k represent sliding window numbers of $\mathbb{N}$, original window numbers of $\mathbb{N}$, and output bits of hash operations, respectively.

Theorem 2. *The PT-SCESW scheme is weakly indistinguishable if H_1, H_2, and H_3 are pseudorandom functions.*

Proof. Let C, C_A, and C_B represent challengers. Suppose that there exists an adversary A such that $\text{Adv}_{C,A} := |\Pr(\text{Exp}_{C,A}^k = 0) - \Pr(\text{Exp}_{C,A}^k = 1)| \geq \epsilon$ in the weak distinguishing game. Then, we know that hash function is distinguishable from the random function, which is against the assumption that they are pseudorandom functions. In particular, we consider a sequence of games by challengers C, C_A, and C_B and then prove the theorem by the hybrid argument. From literature [33], we know that $|\text{Adv}_{C,A} - \text{Adv}_{C_B,A}| < \epsilon$ as long as hash is a pseudorandom function as well as $\text{Adv}_{C_B,A} = 0$. Hence, $\text{Adv}_{C,A} < \epsilon$ and Theorem 2 is proved. □

5. Performance

In this section, we first compare our schemes with SCE scheme in *Encryption Phase, Comparison Phase*, and *Auditing Phase* in experiments, as shown in Tables 3 and 4, respectively. In *Auditing Phase*, auditing costs of [40] are almost of PT-SCESW scheme, so we just evaluate the actual performance of PT-SCESW scheme in experiments. These experiments are conducted using C on a Ubuntu Server 15.04 with Intel Core i5 Processor 2.3 GHz and Paring Based Cryptography (PBC). In Table 3, L is the L bit of numbers $\mathbb{N}_1 = (\beta_0, \ldots, \beta_{m-1})$, $\mathbb{N}_2 = (\gamma_0, \ldots, \gamma_{m-1})$ such that $(\beta_L, \ldots, \beta_{m-1}) = (\gamma_L, \ldots, \gamma_{m-1})$, $\beta_{L-1} < \gamma_{L-1}$ for two numbers. We randomly choose k and n, where $k = 160$ bits, $n = 1024$ bits in experimental simulations. Experimental tests are conducted for 100 times.

We will mainly focus on the computational and storage overhead. Due to the fact that SCESW scheme utilizes sliding window method, a comparison in computational and storage overhead between SCESW scheme and SCE scheme is made, which shows that SCESW scheme is cost-effective. Analysis can demonstrate that PT-SCESW scheme by using sliding window technology can relief the high computational and storage overhead. To largely reduce storage overhead, $(f_0, f_1, \ldots, f_{m-1})$ can be encoded into an integer F_t to make ciphertexts shorter in SCESW scheme and PT-SCESW scheme, shown in Table 4, where

$$F_t = \sum_{0 \le i \le m-1} f_i \cdot \left(2^{(t+1)} - 1\right)^i. \tag{16}$$

Considering computational costs, we just only consider several time-consuming operations, such as exponentiation operation "E" and Hash$_i$ ($i = 1, 2, 3, 4, 5$) operations. Table 3 shows the theoretical analysis of these schemes. Now we give detailed theoretical analysis of PT-SCESW scheme as an example.

(1) In *Encryption Phase*, computing $\mathcal{CP}$ and tags x_i for each block f_i can bring the exponentiation operation "E" and Hash$_i$ ($i = 1, 2, 3$) operation "h." Overall, this phase costs $3m \cdot a + m \cdot E$ operations.

(2) In *Comparison Phase*, costs mainly depends on computing c_j, with computing c_j only bringing Hash$_i$ ($i = 1, 2, 3$) operation "h." Overall, this phase costs $2(m - L + 1) \cdot a$ operations.

(3) In *Auditing Phase*, costs mainly depend on computing $g_s = g^s \bmod N$, $\mathcal{P}_1 = g_s^{\sum_c^{i=1} a_j \cdot f_{i_j}} \bmod N$, $\mathcal{P}_3 = \prod_{j=1}^{c} (x_{i_j})^{a_j} \bmod N$, and hash operations in Algorithm 2. Overall, this phase costs $(2 + c)E + (k' + 1)a$ operations.

In Figure 3, we set $n = 1024$ bits and vary numbers of sliding windows m from 4 to 512, and then we notice that the encryption time in PT-SCESW scheme approximately increases with m. For example, when we set $m = 32$, encryption costs of SCESW scheme and PT-SCESW scheme are 1.214 ms and 2.034 ms, respectively, which is much more smaller than SCE scheme. Due to using sliding window method, PT-SCESW scheme and SCESW scheme can significantly reduce encryption costs.

In Figure 4, we set $n = 1024$ bits and $m = 256$, and then we notice that the comparable time in PT-SCESW scheme approximately decreases with L. For example, when setting $L = 63$, our scheme needs 4.674 ms to compare ciphertexts. In *Comparison Phase*, the PT-SCESW scheme and SCE scheme have similar computational burden. Based on sliding window method, our PT-SCESW scheme and SCESW scheme can significantly reduce the computational overhead when these schemes are compared with SCE scheme.

In Figure 5, we set $n = 1024$ bits and vary number of windows for verification presented by c from 2 to 256, and then we notice that the auditing time in PT-SCESW scheme approximately increases with c. For example, when setting $c = 16$, our scheme needs 2.472 ms to make

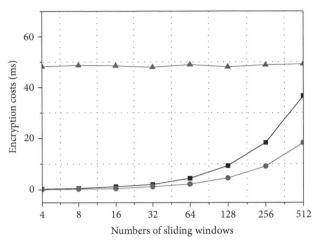

FIGURE 3: Encryption costs in PT-SCESW scheme.

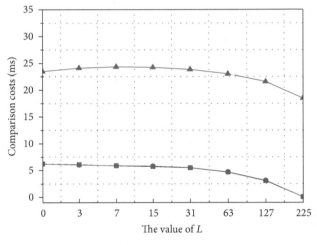

FIGURE 4: Comparison costs in PT-SCESW scheme.

auditing. Therefore, our PT-SCESW scheme is still acceptable in practice, especially for users with constrained computing resources and capacities.

In summary, actual performance results are completely in accord with the theoretical analysis shown in Tables 3 and 4. Exploring PT-SCESW scheme mainly focuses on achieving one property that is auditing. PT-SCESW scheme is feasible and efficient in practice applications, especially for users with constrained computing resources and capacities.

6. Conclusion

In this paper, a basic scheme named SCESW scheme is proposed for relief of the computational and storage overhead by using sliding window method. Furthermore, PT-SCESW scheme is presented for authorized users to support public

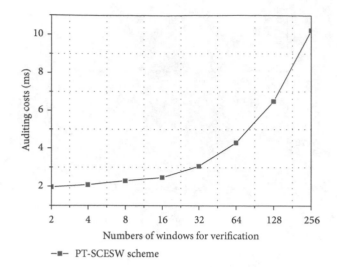

FIGURE 5: Auditing costs in PT-SCESW scheme.

auditing and reduce computational and storage overhead. Formal security analysis proves that PT-SCESW and SCESW schemes can guarantee data security and integrity as well as weak indistinguishability in standard model. Actual performance evaluation shows that, compared with SCE scheme, SCESW scheme and PT-SCESW scheme can relieve the computational and storage burden to some extent. In our future work, we will enhance PT-SCESW scheme by deducing its computational and storage overhead. Nevertheless, there exists another important problem to be solved. How to apply the PT-SCESW scheme to image retrieval field is rather a challenging task to be solved in cloud computing and artificial intelligence fields.

Notations

n: Number's length
a: Hash operations
$\mathcal{P}$: Auditing proof
$\mathcal{CL}$: Auditing challenge
I: $k$bits random number
m: Number of window blocks
H_i: Hash$_i$ ($i = 1, 2, 3$) function
Υ: Smallest order node set.

Acknowledgments

This work is supported by the National High Technology Research and Development Program (863 Program) (no. 2015AA016007.2015AA017203), the National Natural Science Foundation of China (no. 61702404), China Postdoctoral Science Foundation Funded Project (no. 2017M613080), the Fundamental Research Funds for the Central Universities (no. JB171504), the Key Program of NSFC (no. U1405255), the 111 Project (no. B16037), the Shaanxi Science & Technology Coordination & Innovation Project (no. 2016TZC-G-6-3), and the Fundamental Research Funds for the Central Universities (no. BDZ011402).

References

[1] S. Abdelwahab, B. Hamdaoui, M. Guizani, and A. Rayes, "Enabling smart cloud services through remote sensing: An internet of everything enabler," *IEEE Internet of Things Journal*, vol. 1, no. 3, pp. 276–288, 2014.

[2] M. Sookhak, A. Gani, M. K. Khan, and R. Buyya, "Dynamic remote data auditing for securing big data storage in cloud computing," *Information Sciences*, 2015.

[3] Y. Miao, J. Ma, X. Liu, X. Li, Q. Jiang, and J. Zhang, "Attribute-Based Keyword Search over Hierarchical Data in Cloud Computing," *IEEE Transactions on Services Computing*, pp. 1-1.

[4] L. Guo, C. Zhang, J. Sun, and Y. Fang, "PAAS: a privacy-preserving attribute-based authentication system for eHealth networks," in *Proceedings of the 32nd IEEE International Conference on Distributed Computing Systems (ICDCS '12)*, pp. 224–233, IEEE, Macau, June 2012.

[5] Y. Miao, J. Ma, X. Liu, J. Zhang, and Z. Liu, "VKSE-MO: verifiable keyword search over encrypted data in multi-owner settings," *Science China Information Sciences*, vol. 60, no. 12, 122105, 15 pages, 2017.

[6] R. Buyya, C. S. Yeo, S. Venugopal, J. Broberg, and I. Brandic, "Cloud computing and emerging IT platforms: vision, hype, and reality for delivering computing as the 5th utility," *Future Generation Computer Systems*, vol. 25, no. 6, pp. 599–616, 2009.

[7] Z. Xia, Y. Zhu, X. Sun, Z. Qin, and K. Ren, "Towards Privacy-preserving Content-based Image Retrieval in Cloud Computing," *IEEE Transactions on Information Forensics and Security*, vol. 11, no. 11, pp. 2594–2608, 2016.

[8] D. Wang and P. Wang, "Two Birds with One Stone: Two-Factor Authentication with Security Beyond Conventional Bound," *IEEE Transactions on Dependable and Secure Computing*, pp. 1-1.

[9] D. Wang, H. Cheng, P. Wang, X. Huang, and G. Jian, "Zipfs law in passwords," *IEEE Transactions on Information Forensics and Security*, vol. 12, no. 11, pp. 2776–2791, 2017.

[10] Y. Miao, J. Ma, X. Liu, J. Zhang, and Z. Liu, "VKSE-MO: verifiable keyword search over encrypted data in multi-owner settings," *Science China Information Sciences*, vol. 60, no. 12, 2017.

[11] Y. Miao, J. Liu, and J. Ma, "Efficient keyword search over encrypted data in multi-cloud setting," *Security and Communication Networks*, vol. 9, no. 16, pp. 3808–3820, 2016.

[12] Q. Jiang, J. Ma, Z. Ma, and G. Li, "A privacy enhanced authentication scheme for telecare medical information systems," *Journal of Medical Systems*, vol. 37, no. 1, article no. 9897, 2013.

[13] Q. Jiang, J. Ma, and Y. Tian, "Cryptanalysis of smart-card-based password authenticated key agreement protocol for session initiation protocol of Zhang et al.," *International Journal of Communication Systems*, vol. 28, no. 7, pp. 1340–1351, 2015.

[14] Q. Jiang, Z. Chen, B. Li, J. Shen, L. Yang, and J. Ma, "Security analysis and improvement of bio-hashing based three-factor authentication scheme for telecare medical information systems," *Journal of Ambient Intelligence and Humanized Computing*, vol. 12, pp. 1–3, 2017.

[15] L. Lamport, "Password authentication with insecure communication," *Communications of the ACM*, vol. 24, no. 11, pp. 770–772, 1981.

[16] R. M. Needham and M. D. Schroeder, "Using Encryption for Authentication in Large Networks of Computers," *Communications of the ACM*, vol. 21, no. 12, pp. 993–999, 1978.

[17] M.-S. Hwang and L.-H. Li, "A new remote user authentication

scheme using smart cards," *IEEE Transactions on Consumer Electronics*, vol. 46, no. 1, pp. 28–30, 2000.

[18] B.-L. Chen, W.-C. Kuo, and L.-C. Wuu, "Robust smart-card-based remote user password authentication scheme," *International Journal of Communication Systems*, vol. 27, no. 2, pp. 377–389, 2014.

[19] X. Li, J. Niu, M. Khurram Khan, and J. Liao, "An enhanced smart card based remote user password authentication scheme," *Journal of Network and Computer Applications*, vol. 36, no. 5, pp. 1365–1371, 2013.

[20] S. Ghosh, A. Majumder, J. Goswami, A. Kumar, S. P. Mohanty, and B. K. Bhattacharyya, "Swing-Pay: One Card Meets All User Payment and Identity Needs: A Digital Card Module using NFC and Biometric Authentication for Peer-To-Peer Payment," *IEEE Consumer Electronics Magazine*, vol. 6, no. 1, pp. 82–93, 2017.

[21] Y. Lu, L. Li, H. Peng, and Y. Yang, "An Enhanced Biometric-Based Authentication Scheme for Telecare Medicine Information Systems Using Elliptic Curve Cryptosystem," *Journal of Medical Systems*, vol. 39, no. 3, 2015.

[22] D. Wu, J. Yan, H. Wang, D. Wu, and R. Wang, "Social Attribute Aware Incentive Mechanism for Device-to-Device Video Distribution," *IEEE Transactions on Multimedia*, vol. 19, no. 8, pp. 1908–1920, 2017.

[23] D. Wu, Q. Liu, H. Wang, D. Wu, and R. Wang, "Socially Aware Energy-Efficient Mobile Edge Collaboration for Video Distribution," *IEEE Transactions on Multimedia*, vol. 19, no. 10, pp. 2197–2209, 2017.

[24] D. Wu, S. Si, S. Wu, and R. Wang, "Dynamic Trust Relationships Aware Data Privacy Protection in Mobile Crowd-Sensing," *IEEE Internet of Things Journal*, pp. 1-1.

[25] P. Karras, A. Nikitin, M. Saad, R. Bhatt, D. Antyukhov, and S. Idreos, "Adaptive indexing over encrypted numeric data," in *Proceedings of the 2016 ACM SIGMOD International Conference on Management of Data, SIGMOD 2016*, pp. 171–183, USA, July 2016.

[26] D. Agrawal, A. El Abbadi, F. Emekci, and A. Metwally, "Database management as a service: Challenges and opportunities," in *Proceedings of the 25th IEEE International Conference on Data Engineering, ICDE 2009*, pp. 1709–1716, China, April 2009.

[27] R. A. Popa, F. H. Li, and N. Zeldovich, "An ideal-security protocol for order-preserving encoding," in *Proceedings of the 34th IEEE Symposium on Security and Privacy, SP 2013*, pp. 463–477, USA, May 2013.

[28] H. Kadhem, T. Amagasa, and H. Kitagawa, "A secure and efficient Order Preserving Encryption Scheme for relational databases," in *Proceedings of the International Conference on Knowledge Management and Information Sharing, KMIS 2010*, pp. 25–35, esp, October 2010.

[29] D. Liu and S. Wang, "Programmable order-preserving secure index for encrypted database query," in *Proceedings of the 2012 IEEE 5th International Conference on Cloud Computing, CLOUD 2012*, pp. 502–509, USA, June 2012.

[30] R. Agrawal, J. Kiernan, R. Srikant, and Y. R. Xu, "Order preserving encryption for numeric data," in *Proceedings of the ACM SIGMOD International Conference on Management of Data (SIGMOD '04)*, pp. 563–574, ACM, Paris, France, June 2004.

[31] J. Furukawa, "Request-based comparable encryption," *Lecture Notes in Computer Science (including subseries Lecture Notes in Artificial Intelligence and Lecture Notes in Bioinformatics): Preface*, vol. 8134, pp. 129–146, 2013.

[32] P. Chen, J. Ye, and X. Chen, "Efficient request-based comparable encryption scheme based on sliding window method," *Soft Computing*, vol. 20, no. 11, pp. 4589–4596, 2016.

[33] J. Furukawa, "Short comparable encryption," in *Cryptology and network security*, vol. 8813 of *Lecture Notes in Comput. Sci.*, pp. 337–352, Springer, Cham, 2014.

[34] Y. Yu, M. H. Au, G. Ateniese et al., "Identity-Based Remote Data Integrity Checking with Perfect Data Privacy Preserving for Cloud Storage," *IEEE Transactions on Information Forensics and Security*, vol. 12, no. 4, pp. 767–778, 2017.

[35] Z. Hao, S. Zhong, and N. Yu, "A privacy-preserving remote data integrity checking protocol with data dynamics and public verifiability," *IEEE Transactions on Knowledge and Data Engineering*, vol. 23, no. 9, pp. 1432–1437, 2011.

[36] Q. Wang, C. Wang, J. Li, K. Ren, and W. Lou, "Enabling public verifiability and data dynamics for storage security in cloud computing," *Lecture Notes in Computer Science (including subseries Lecture Notes in Artificial Intelligence and Lecture Notes in Bioinformatics): Preface*, vol. 5789, pp. 355–370, 2009.

[37] Q. Wang, C. Wang, K. Ren, W. Lou, and J. Li, "Enabling public auditability and data dynamics for storage security in cloud computing," *IEEE Transactions on Parallel and Distributed Systems*, vol. 22, no. 5, pp. 847–859, 2011.

[38] Y. Deswarte, J. J. Quisquater, and A. Sadane, "Remote integrity checking," in *Integrity and internal control in information systems VI*, vol. 12, pp. 1–12, 2004.

[39] D. L. Gazzoni Filho and P. S. L. M. Barreto, "Demonstrating data possession and uncheatable data transfer," *IACR Cryptology ePrint Archive*, p. 150, 2006.

[40] J. Mao, Y. Zhang, P. Li, T. Li, Q. Wu, and J. Liu, "A position-aware Merkle tree for dynamic cloud data integrity verification," *Soft Computing*, vol. 21, no. 8, pp. 2151–2164, 2017.

[41] C. K. Koç, "Analysis of sliding window techniques for exponentiation," *Computers & Mathematics with Applications*, vol. 30, no. 10, pp. 17–24, 1995.

[42] Y. Wang, Y. Shen, H. Wang, J. Cao, and X. Jiang, "MtMR: Ensuring MapReduce Computation Integrity with Merkle Tree-based Verifications," *IEEE Transactions on Big Data*, pp. 1-1.

[43] P. Cong, Z. Ning, F. Xue, K. Xu, B. Fan, and H. Li, "Hierarchy merkle tree wireless sensor network architecture," *International Journal of Wireless and Mobile Computing*, vol. 12, pp. 341–348, 2017.

[44] M. Szydlo, "Merkle tree traversal in log space and time," in *Advances in cryptology-EUROCRYPT 2004*, vol. 3027 of *Lecture Notes in Comput. Sci.*, pp. 541–554, Springer, Berlin, Germany, 2004.

12

Multiuser Searchable Encryption with Token Freshness Verification

Dhruti Sharma[1] and Devesh C. Jinwala[2]

[1]*Sarvajanik College of Engineering and Technology, Surat, Gujarat, India*
[2]*Sardar Vallabhbhai National Institute of Technology, Surat, Gujarat, India*

Correspondence should be addressed to Dhruti Sharma; sharmadhruti77@gmail.com

Academic Editor: Sherali Zeadally

A Multiuser Searchable Encryption (MUSE) can be defined with the notion of Functional Encryption (FE) where a user constructs a search token from a search key issued by an Enterprise Trusted Authority (ETA). In such scheme, a user possessing search key constructs search token at any time and consequently requests the server to search over encrypted data. Thus, an FE based MUSE scheme is not suitable for the applications where a log of search activities is maintained at the enterprise site to identify dishonest search query from any user. In addition, none of the existing searchable schemes provides security against token replay attack to avoid reuse of the same token. In this paper, therefore we propose an FE based scheme, Multiuser Searchable Encryption with Token Freshness Verification (MUSE-TFV). In MUSE-TFV, a user prepares one-time usable search token in cooperation with ETA and thus every search activity is logged at the enterprise site. Additionally, by verifying the freshness of a token, the server prevents reuse of the token. With formal security analysis, we prove the security of MUSE-TFV against chosen keyword attack and token replay attack. With theoretical and empirical analysis, we justify the effectiveness of MUSE-TFV in practical applications.

1. Introduction

With the cloud storage infrastructure, one can easily share data with multiple users at a low cost. However, maintaining security and privacy of such data located on the untrusted remote server is nontrivial [1–3]. Therefore, a common trend is to upload the encrypted data onto a third-party cloud server. However, extraction of partial information from the stored encrypted data is indeed difficult. The notion of Searchable Encryption (SE) is used to resolve the issue. In SE, a Data Owner prepares a ciphertext by associating a list of encrypted keywords (to be searched) with an encrypted payload message and uploads it onto the Storage Server. Subsequently, a Data User asks the server to search over encrypted data by issuing a search token (of keyword(s)). The server applies a token over available ciphertexts and extracts the data containing that keyword(s) (Figure 1). However, the server learns nothing else about the data while searching. Here, a payload message is encrypted using any standard encryption algorithm, whereas keywords are encrypted with the defined Searchable Encryption algorithm.

There exist numerous Searchable Encryption schemes for a single user [4–8] as well as for multiple users [9–13]. Practically, any single-user Searchable Encryption scheme can be adapted to define a multiuser Searchable Encryption scheme at the cost of a ciphertext size linear to the number of users in the system. Formally, when a single-user searchable scheme is extended to support multiple users, its ciphertext size becomes $O(U)$ for U users that subsequently raises to $O(|D| \cdot U)$ for $D = \{d1, d2, \ldots, dm\}$ data items in the system. This ultimately outputs an impractical system with $O(|D| \cdot U)$ computational overhead at the Data Owner site and $O(|D| \cdot U)$ storage overhead at the server site. As solution, several Searchable Encryption schemes in [9, 10, 14–20] with a built-in support of multiple users are devised in recent years. Amongst them, the scheme proposed by Hwang and Lee [9] is a simple extension of a single-user Searchable Encryption with the ciphertext size $O(|D| + |W| \cdot U)$, where $|W|$ is the number of keywords to be searched. However, this scheme works for the prefixed set of users. In contrast, the schemes in [10, 14–16] support the dynamic groups of users where joining/leaving a group by a member is entirely controlled

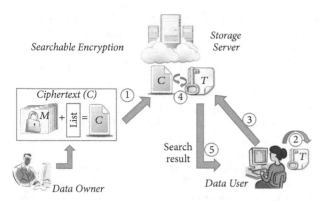

FIGURE 1: System model of Searchable Encryption (SE). Steps: (1) Data Owner uploads a ciphertext C (i.e., encrypted payload message + list of encrypted keywords) onto the Storage Server; (2) Data User constructs a search token T using a secret key; (3) Data User sends T to the server; (4) Storage Server applies T on C; (5) Storage Server returns the result to the requesting user.

by a Data Owner. In addition, the recent schemes in [17–20] provide Multiuser Searchable Encryption with the notion of Functional Encryption (FE) (Section 2.1) where an Enterprise Trusted Authority (ETA) is responsible for the System Setup and a master public key setup. The most notable characteristic of FE is that a system's master public key is utilized to prepare the searchable ciphertexts and a single ciphertext can serve multiple search tokens (may be issued by different users). Therefore, such FE based searchable schemes can support multiple users in the system with the optimal storage-computational overhead (i.e., $O(|D|)$) for the ciphertexts. Additionally, in the schemes [17–20], a separate search key (related to the master public key) is issued (either by an ETA or by a Data Owner) to each user. Subsequently, a user constructs a search token with an available search key. The downside is that once a user has a search key, he can prepare a search token at any time. As a result, a dishonest user colluding with the untrusted cloud server can maliciously search the valid data and the system administrator (i.e., ETA) is completely unaware about such adversarial activity. Moreover, with the existing Searchable Encryption mechanisms, there is no provision for the token freshness checking at the server site. As a result, if an unauthorized user masquerading as an authorized user has a valid token, he can use the token to make search queries in the future. In practice, there exist applications wherein every search query from the users should be logged to the enterprise trusted site in order to identify any dishonest activity performed by any user (authorized or unauthorized). In addition, there should be a provision against token replay attack to avoid misuse of a valid token. Let us take one of such applications as an example.

(i) Consider an Online Banking System, where the customers' transaction records are stored at the Bank's cloud Storage Server. Practically, these records are utilized by several official users (i.e., managers, officers, clerks, etc.) of the Bank. Let us assume that the Bank's centralized processing server (trusted authority) uses

any of the existing FE based searchable schemes and accordingly issues a separate search key to each authorized user of the Bank.

In such a setup, let us take a case of a manager who is responsible for generating a daily report for the ATM transactions with a specific ATM-ID. To perform this activity, every day the manager constructs a search token (using his search key) for a query, that is, "list all ATM transactions for ATM-ID today." He issues this token to the server and collects the result. In this scenario, what happens if a peon steals the search token and masquerades as an officer to send this token to the server? In any FE based searchable scheme, the server only checks the authorization of a user. In this case, since a peon impersonates an authorized officer of the Bank, he passes the authorization test conducted by the server and gets the search result. In fact, performing such token replay attack (by reusing the token) and leaking the information about ATM transactions to the intruder (outsider) on a daily basis, the peon may provoke the criminal activities near that ATM.

From the above scenario, we say that, in the Banking system, since every search result involves critical financial information, the search activity by each user should be logged at the Bank's centralized processing server. In addition, to avoid misuse of any valid token, it is desirable to prevent token replay attack in such system.

With the existing FE based searchable schemes [17–20], a user possessing a search key can ask the server to execute a search operation at any time and therefore the search activity of a user cannot be tracked. The problem can be resolved by an interactive scheme where a search token is constructed by the centralized trusted authority on request from an authorized user. However, such solution raises the demand of secure token transmission along the entire path from the trusted authority up to the server through a user. Moreover, a token replay attack should be prevented by verifying the freshness of each search token at the server site. In addition, it is desirable to have a search operation with the support of conjunctive queries in such system.

1.1. Related Work. The notion of Searchable Encryption is introduced by Song et al. in [4] where the authors consider search over encrypted keywords within a file. However, this first practical scheme leaks the search keywords to the server and suffers from the communication overhead linear to the file size. In fact, the scheme in [4] is not secure against statistical analysis across multiple queries. To resolve the problems, Goh et al. [5] and Chang and Mitzenmacher [24] in their separate work construct the secure searchable schemes by proposing an encrypted index for a document. Though the schemes in [4, 5, 24] perform efficient search operations, they introduce storage overhead linear to the size of an index for each document. Curtmola et al. [25] propose the first symmetric searchable encryption scheme with a formal security model. The first public key Searchable Encryption scheme is given by Boneh et al. [6] wherein a user with his private key can search over data encrypted with the corresponding public key. However, none of the schemes [4–6, 24] support conjunctive keyword search.

Conjunctive Keyword Searchable Schemes. To narrow down the scope of searching and get optimal results, several searchable schemes exist with conjunctive keyword search operation. In the symmetric key settings, Golle et al. [26] have constructed two schemes for a conjunctive keyword search. However, in the first construction of [26], the size of a capability (search token) is linear to the number of documents available on the server and so the scheme is impractical. On the other hand, the second construction of [26] is practical with a constant size capability. The other constructions based on the secret sharing and bilinear map are given by Ballard et al. [27] but they are still inefficient in terms of a size of a token linear to the number of documents being searched. In public key settings, a first conjunctive keyword searchable scheme is defined by Park et al. [8]. Subsequently, the schemes with the improved communication and storage efficiency are proposed in [9, 28]. Boneh and Waters have given a generalized scheme [29] for conjunction as well as for subset queries. Later on, a scheme with a refined form of a token (that is independent of specifying the keyword field position) is devised by Wang et al. [13]. Subsequently, B. Zhang and F. Zhang [21] have improved the security flaws of [13] and defined a conjunctive-subset keyword search. Other efficient constructions with the support of conjunctive keyword search operation are given in [22, 23, 30].

Multiuser Searchable Schemes. In public key settings, Hwang and Lee [9] have first introduced a storage efficient multiuser scheme. Subsequently, several other schemes [10, 11, 13, 14, 16] have proposed managing a group of users. However, a scheme in [11] supports the static groups of users, whereas the schemes discussed in [10, 13, 14] work for the dynamic groups of users. Apart from this, the scheme in [14] provides a single keyword search whereas the schemes in [10, 13] handle the conjunctive search queries. Recently, a multiuser multikeyword search scheme is proposed by Huang et al. [16] but its inverted index based construction cannot support an efficient conjunctive search. In addition, a scheme in [16] leaks user access control information to the server. Few other multiuser schemes [17–20] are based on the notion of FE wherein an ETA is responsible for the System Setup and a master public key setup. In these schemes, a ciphertext is prepared by a Data Owner using a master public key. A search token is constructed by a user with his own search key issued either by the ETA as in [18–20] or by the Data Owner as in [17]. A scheme in [17] offers a constant size ciphertext and a constant size token. However, the scheme [17] is computationally inefficient since, to encrypt an index for a document, the encryption algorithm involves a computational complexity linear to the number of authorized users for that document. In a scheme of [18], the Storage Server has a list of authorized users (U_List), and thus each enrollment/revocation of a user

is known to the server. This indeed leaks information about users (i.e., a number of users in the system, the users' activity) to the Storage Server. The other two schemes [19, 20] use CPABE (Ciphertext Policy Attribute Based Encryption) to manage access control of users. However, amongst all these schemes, only the schemes in [9, 10, 13, 16] support multi-keyword (specifically conjunctive) search and multiple users at the same time. There is no FE based scheme proposing a conjunctive keyword based search.

Secure Channel-Free Searchable Schemes. There exist searchable schemes in [7, 31, 32] with secure channel-free architecture for a token transmission. However, these schemes support a single keyword search. The most recent conjunctive search schemes [30, 33] provide a secure channel-free token transmission.

To the best of our knowledge, none of the existing schemes define a secure channel-free conjunctive keyword based Searchable Encryption that prevents token replay attack in multiuser environment.

1.2. Our Contributions. In this paper, we propose a Multiuser Searchable Encryption with Token Freshness Verification (MUSE-TFV). In MUSE-TFV, a user constructs a search token in cooperation with the ETA and thus every search activity from each user is logged at the enterprise trusted site. Moreover, each search token is one-time usable token. The server avoids reuse of the same token by verifying the freshness of the token using a verification key given by the ETA. Our main contributions are as follows.

(i) *Multiuser Support.* Utilizing the notion of FE, we devise a Searchable Encryption scheme that supports multiple users, with a constant size ciphertext (i.e., independent of the number of users). Our scheme has an optimal computational overhead at the Data Owner site and an optimal storage overhead at the server site.

(ii) *Token Freshness Verification.* We propose a token freshness verification at the server site by adapting Haller's S/Key One-Time Password System [34] and prevent token replay attack from the system.

(iii) *Conjunctive Keyword Search.* With the proposed scheme, we offer a conjunctive keyword search with a constant sized search token.

(iv) *Secure Channel-Free Architecture.* We offer a secure channel-free architecture to transfer a token securely via any public channel without channel setup overhead.

(v) *Theoretical Analysis and Empirical Evaluation.* We present a detailed theoretical analysis to show the efficiency of the proposed scheme. Additionally, with experimental evaluation of MUSE-TFV for different size system (with a different number of keywords) and different number of users, we justify its effectiveness.

1.3. Organization of the Rest of the Paper. The rest of the paper is organized as follows: In Section 2, we briefly discuss the

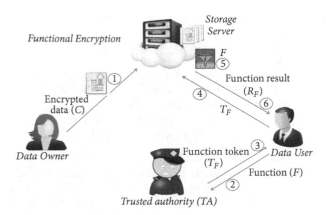

FIGURE 2: System model of Functional Encryption (FE). Steps: (1) Data Owner uploads ciphertext C onto the Storage Server; (2) Data User requests TA for a token of a function (F); (3) TA issues a token T_F to the user; (4) Data User sends T_F to the Storage Server; (5) Storage Server runs F on available C; (6) Storage Server forwards the result R_F to the user.

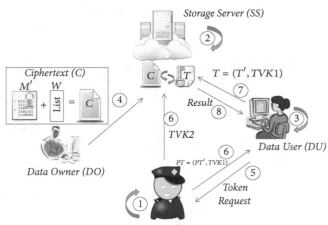

FIGURE 3: System model of MUSE-TFV.

preliminaries required for the proposed scheme. In Section 3, we define the formal model of MUSE-TFV, the proposed algorithms, and the attack model with security definition. We elaborated the algorithms with a detailed security analysis in Section 4. Further, in Section 5, we present a theoretical analysis and empirical evaluation of MUSE-TFV. Finally, we put the concluding remarks in Section 6.

2. Preliminaries

In this section, we present an overview of a Functional Encryption, a cryptographic primitive (i.e., Bilinear Map), and a hardness assumption associated with the proposed scheme.

2.1. Functional Encryption (FE). FE is a generalization of the existing access control mechanisms, namely, Identity Based Encryption (IBE) [35, 36], Attribute Based Encryption (ABE) [37–39], and Predicate Encryption (PE) [29, 40]. In FE, apart from the Data Owner, Data User, and the Storage Server, there exists an additional centralized trusted authority (TA) that is responsible for the System Setup and generation of a master public-private key pair. A Data Owner prepares the ciphertexts with a master public key and stores them to the Storage Server. To execute a predefined function at the server site, a user asks the TA for the corresponding token. In response, the TA constructs a token utilizing a master private key and issues it to the user. The server runs the function on the availability of a token from a user and sends the result to the user (Figure 2). In such a setup, any user who possesses a token can ask the server for the function execution. Since the server could use the same set of ciphertexts to execute a function with different tokens (may be from different users), we say that the FE supports multiple users in the system.

2.2. Bilinear Map. Bilinear map is a mathematical tool for pairing based cryptography. It is defined using suitable cryptographic groups. Let G_1 and G_2 be two multiplicative

cyclic groups of prime order p. For these groups, a bilinear map $e: G_1 \times G_1 \to G_2$ must satisfy the following properties:

(1) *Bilinear*: given random $P, Q \in G_1$ and $a, b \in Z_p^*$ we have $e(aP, bQ) = e(P, Q)^{ab}$.

(2) *Nondegenerate*: if P is a generator of G_1, then $e(P, P)$ is a generator of G_2.

(3) *Computable*: given $P, Q \in G_1$, there exists a polynomial time algorithm to compute $e(P, Q) \in G_2$.

2.3. Hardness Assumption

Decisional Diffie-Hellman (DDH) Assumption. Let G_1 be a cyclic group of prime order p and P is a generator of G_1. The *Decisional Diffie-Hellman* problem is to distinguish the tuple (aP, bP, abP) from (aP, bP, cP) for any random $a, b, c \in Z_p^*$. Let us assume that the DDH problem is (ϵ, t)-hard in G_1. Then there does not exist any polynomial time (t) adversary $\mathcal{A}$ that can solve the DDH problem with a nonnegligible advantage ϵ, if $|Pr[\mathcal{A}(aP, bP, abP)] - Pr[\mathcal{A}(aP, bP, cP)]| \le \epsilon$.

3. Proposed Multiuser Searchable Encryption with Token Freshness Verification (MUSE-TFV)

We list out the notations used throughout the paper in Notations section. We include a system model, the associated algorithms, and the attack model with the security definition for the proposed scheme.

3.1. System Model. The proposed MUSE-TFV involves four entities: (i) Data Owner (DO), (ii) Data User (DU), (iii) Storage Server (SS), and (iv) Enterprise Trusted Authority (ETA) (Figure 3).

The interactive actions amongst these entities are as follows:

(1) Initially, the ETA sets up the system's public parameters and a master secret key.

(2) Using public parameters, the SS computes a public-private key pair (Y, y) and publishes Y while keeping y secret.

(3) Using public parameters, the DU computes a public-private key pair (X, x) and publishes X while keeping x secret.

(4) A DO prepares a ciphertext (C) by associating an encrypted payload (M') with a list W of encrypted keywords and uploads it onto the SS. All the keywords in the list are encrypted with an *Encryption()* algorithm of proposed MUSE-TFV.

(5) To execute a search operation, the DO requests the ETA for a token of a conjunctive query.

(6) The ETA computes a token (PT') and corresponding token verification keys $(TVK1, TVK2)$. The ETA issues a partial token $PT = (PT', TVK1)$ to the DU and $TVK2$ to the SS.

(7) The DU constructs a search token (T') from PT' and issues a final token $T = (T', TVK1)$ to the SS over a public channel.

(8) The proposed *Search()* algorithm is executed on the server SS. With the available $(TVK1, TVK2)$, the SS checks the token freshness. The SS applies the fresh token T' on the available C. If C satisfies the token T, the algorithm outputs a result $R = (E_y(E_X(M')))$; otherwise it outputs $\perp$. The algorithm applies T on all available C and generates the corresponding R.

Note. Steps (2), (3), and (4) can run in parallel.

Assumptions. (i) The payload $M' = E_{key}(M)$, where E is any symmetric encryption cipher with a symmetric key *key*. (ii) All DUs are authorized by the ETA. At the time of authorization, ETA issues (pp, key) to the DU. (iii) Before issuing a partial token PT, the ETA checks the authenticity of a DU with any standard authentication protocol. (iv) The SS is a semihonest server; that is, it follows the system protocol but tries to breach data privacy. (v) There exists a secure channel between the ETA and the SS. (vi) The $TVK2$ is stored in a system table of the SS. The size of the system table is linear to the number of DUs.

3.2. Algorithms.
The proposed MUSE-TFV involves the following polynomial time algorithms:

(1) **Setup**(α, n). The *Setup* algorithm runs by the ETA. The algorithm takes a security parameters α and n as inputs. The algorithm outputs the system's public parameter pp and a master secret key *msk*. It defines a keyword space $\mathcal{KS}$ for n keywords.

(2) **SKeyGen**(pp). The *Server Key Generation* algorithm runs by the server SS. The algorithm takes the system's public parameter pp as inputs. It selects a random $y \in Z_p^*$ and computes the public-private key pair (Y, y) for the server SS.

(3) **UKeyGen**(pp). The *User Key Generation* algorithm runs by the DU. The algorithm takes the system's public parameter pp as inputs. It selects a random $x \in Z_p^*$ and computes the public-private key pair (X, x) for the Data User, DU.

(4) **Encryption**(pp, W, Y, M'). The *Encryption* algorithm runs by the DO. The algorithm constructs a ciphertext C' from the list of keywords $W = \{w_1, w_2, \ldots, w_n\}$ using pp and Y. It associates C' with an encrypted payload M' and outputs a ciphertext $C = (C', M')$.

(5) **TokGen**(pp, msk, Q, X, x, Y). The *Token Generation* is an interactive algorithm where initially a DU supplies a conjunctive query $Q = (W', I')$ to the ETA. Here, $W' = \{w_1', w_2', \ldots, w_t'\}$ is a set of keywords and $I' = \{I_1, I_2, \ldots, I_t\}$ shows their positions in $\mathcal{KS}$. For each new query, the ETA assigns a unique token identification string $(TOKID)$ in order to generate the token verification keys $(TVK1, TVK2)$. Subsequently, the ETA constructs a token PT' using *msk* and X. The ETA then issues a partial token $PT = (PT', TVK1)$ to the DU and $(TVK2)$ to the SS. With an available PT, the DU constructs T' and outputs a final token $T = (T', TVK1)$.

(6) **Search**(C, T, y). The *Search* algorithm runs by the SS. The algorithm utilizes $(TVK1, TVK2)$ to verify the freshness of T. If T is fresh, the algorithm performs a conjunctive search using (T', C', y). It returns the result $R = (E_y(E_X(M')))$ to the DU if C' satisfies the conjunctive query Q within T'; otherwise it returns $\perp$. The algorithm applies T' on all the ciphertexts. At last, the algorithm updates the system table entry of $TVK2$ for the requesting DU to prevent a token replay attack.

The algorithms involved in the verification key generation and token verification as well as system table update are discussed in Section 4.2.

3.3. Flowchart.
To show the process of the proposed MUSE-TFV, we define four phases: (i) System Setup, (ii) Data Upload, (iii) Token Generation, and (iv) Search. The sequence of the proposed algorithms utilized by the entities (i.e., ETA, DO, DU, SS) during each of these phases is given as a flowchart in Figure 4. As shown in Figure 4(a), all four entities are involved in System Setup phase where a public parameter (pp) and various keys (i.e., $msk, key, (X, x), (Y, y)$) are defined. On the other hand, Data Upload phase (Figure 4(b)) includes only DO and SS since, during this phase, a DO prepares a ciphertext C and uploads it on to the SS. The interactive steps amongst DU, ETA, and SS during Token Generation phase are shown in Figure 4(c) wherein initially a DU sends a conjunctive query Q to the ETA. In response, the ETA sends a partial token along with a token verification key (i.e., $(PT, TVK1)$) to the DU. In addition, the ETA sends a token verification key (i.e., $TVK2$) to the SS. With the available $(PT, TVK1)$, the DU prepares a final token T. During Search phase, the DU sends T to the SS as shown in Figure 4(d). In response, the SS finds the results R for the available ciphertexts and forwards these results to the DU.

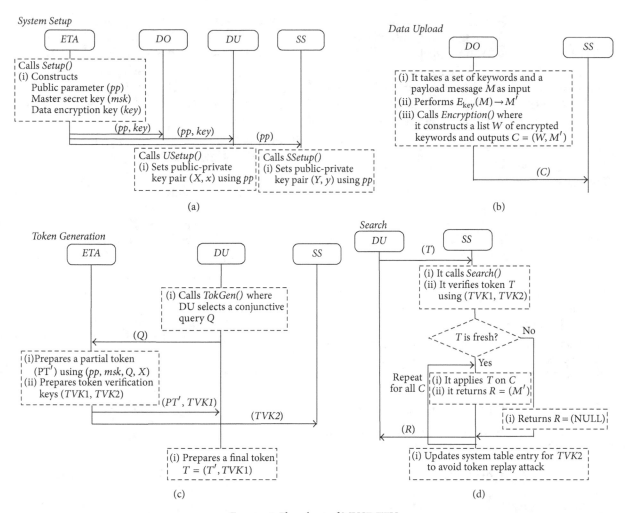

FIGURE 4: Flowchart of MUSE-TFV.

3.4. Attack Model and Security Definitions. First, we reemphasize that the principal motivation of the proposed MUSE-TFV is to overcome the limitation in the existing Searchable Encryption schemes that allow replay of tokens and thus lack verification of token freshness. Thus, MUSE-TFV is aimed at supporting a Searchable Encryption scheme with the novel provision for verification of the token freshness and thereby avoiding replay attacks. Therefore in the attack model described here we consider only token replay attacks and assume that any other attack against the scheme can be mitigated by using already existing mitigation approaches.

We assume that an adversary $\mathcal{A}$ has the capabilities to perform the following attacks:

(1) The server SS as an adversary $\mathcal{A}$ can perform chosen keyword attack to deduce the plaintext (keywords) from the available ciphertexts (lists of encrypted keywords) and tokens.

(2) The Data User, DU, as an adversary $\mathcal{A}$ can perform token replay attack to reuse the maliciously captured token.

With SS as an adversary, we define semantic security (a.k.a. indistinguishability against chosen keyword attack

(IND-CKA)) for the proposed conjunctive keyword search scheme based on the security game ICLR (Indistinguishability of Ciphertext from Limited Random) [26, 41] as follows.

Definition 1 (ICLR). Let $\mathcal{A}$ be a polynomial bounded adversary and $\mathcal{B}$ be a challenger. With ICLR, when $\mathcal{A}$ has issued a keyword set W and a subset $T \subseteq \{1, 2, \ldots, n\}$, $\mathcal{B}$ responds with two encrypted keyword sets associated with T in such a way that $\mathcal{A}$ cannot distinguish the encrypted keyword sets created with T. Thus, with this game, we achieve our security goal where we require that $\mathcal{A}$ should not be able to deduce the plaintext from other keyword sets. The following are the steps for the game ICLR [26, 41].

(1) $\mathcal{A}$ adaptively requests $\mathcal{B}$ for the Encryption (pp, W_i, Y, M') of any keyword set W_i and any search token.

(2) $\mathcal{A}$ selects a keyword set W, a subset $T \subseteq \{1, 2, \ldots, n\}$, and $t \in T$ in such a way that none of the tokens given in Step (1) are distinguishing for $Rand(W, T)$ and $Rand(W, T - \{t\})$. Here, $Rand(W, T)$ outputs a set W where the keywords indexed by T (i.e., the set $\{w_i \mid i \in T\}$) are replaced by random values. $\mathcal{A}$ then sends (W, T, t) to the challenger $\mathcal{B}$.

(3) $\mathscr{B}$ constructs two keyword sets $W_0 = Rand(W, T-\{t\})$ and $W_1 = Rand(W, T)$. $\mathscr{B}$ then randomly chooses $b \in \{0, 1\}$ and returns Encryption (pp, W_b, Y, M') to $\mathscr{A}$.

(4) $\mathscr{A}$ again makes requests for encrypted keyword sets and search tokens, with the restriction that he cannot ask for the token that is distinguishing for W_0 and W_1.

(5) $\mathscr{A}$ outputs a bit $b' \in \{0, 1\}$ and wins the ICLR game if $b' = b$.

We say that the polynomial time adversary $\mathscr{A}$ has an advantage ϵ in this attack game, if

$$Adv_{\mathscr{A}}(1^{\alpha}) = \left| Pr\left[b' = b \right] - \frac{1}{2} \right| > \epsilon. \qquad (1)$$

Additionally, we define the security against token replay attack based on the following actions performed by a Data User, DU, as an adversary $\mathscr{A}$.

(1) $\mathscr{A}$ intercepts a token $T = (T', c = E_Y(TVK1))$ transmitted from the ETA to the DU (or from a DU to the SS) and stores it.

(2) To reuse the token T, $\mathscr{A}$ replaces its verification key part, that is, $c = E_Y(TVK1)$, with c' in such a way that the SS considers a forged $T = (T', c')$ as a fresh token and returns a result R.

(3) $\mathscr{A}$ repeats Step (2) till he does not receive the result R.

We say that an adversary $\mathscr{A}$ is successful in token replay attack if he gets the result R using a forged value of c.

4. Construction of MUSE-TFV

In this section, we give the formal construction for the proposed algorithms of MUSE-TFV. We also present a token verification procedure used in the design of the MUSE-TFV. Additionally, we provide a security analysis for the proposed scheme.

4.1. Formal Construction. The concrete constructions for the proposed algorithms are as follows.

(1) **Setup**(α, n). Let G_1 and G_2 be bilinear groups of prime order p where a security parameter α defines the group size. Let $e : G_1 \times G_1 \rightarrow G_2$ be a bilinear pairing and $H_1 : \{0, 1\}^* \rightarrow Z_p^*$ is a hash function. Let $H : \{0, 1\}^* \rightarrow \{0, 1\}^b$ be any standard hash function (e.g., SHA2) that outputs a message digest of b bits. Let P be a generator of G_1. The algorithm initializes the keyword space $\mathscr{KS}$ of total n keywords. For each jth keyword, it randomly selects $k_j \in Z_p^*$ and computes $K_j = k_j P$. Finally, the algorithm sets the public parameter $pp = \{H_1, H, G_1, G_2, P, e, \{K_j\}_{1 \leq j \leq n}\}$ and a master secret key $msk = \{\{k_j\}_{1 \leq j \leq n}\}$.

(2) **SKeyGen**(pp). The algorithm selects a random $y \in Z_p^*$ and computes $Y = yP$. It sets the public-private key pair for the server SS as (Y, y).

(3) **UKeyGen**(pp). The algorithm selects a random $x \in Z_p^*$ and computes $X = xP$. It sets the public-private key pair for the user DU as (X, x).

(4) **Encryption**(pp, W, Y, M'). The algorithm takes as input a list of keywords $W = \{w_1, w_2, \ldots, w_n\}$. It chooses a random $r_1 \in Z_p^*$ and constructs a ciphertext $C' = \{C_{1j}, C_2\}_{1 \leq j \leq n}$, where $C_{1j} = r_1(H_1(w_j)P + K_j) + r_1 Y$, $C_2 = r_1 P$. Finally, it outputs a ciphertext $C = (C', M')$, where M' is an encrypted payload.

(5) **TokGen**(pp, msk, Q, X, x, Y). This interactive algorithm works in 3 phases.

(a) A DU sends a conjunctive query $Q = (W', I')$ to the ETA where $W' = \{w_1', w_2', \ldots, w_t'\}$ is a set of keywords and $I' = \{I_1, I_2, \ldots, I_t\}$ is a set of positions of keywords in $\mathscr{KS}$.

(b) In response, the ETA chooses a unique token identification string $TokID \in \{0, 1\}^{\ell}$ and a secret random integer N. The ETA uses $TokVerKey(TokID, N, H()) \rightarrow (TVK1, TVK2)$ algorithm to construct the token verification keys. The ETA selects $t_1 \in Z_p^*$ randomly. It uses msk and X to construct a token component $PT' = \{PT_1, PT_2\}$, where $PT_1 = t_1(\sum_{j=I1}^{It}(H_1(w_j) + k_j))P + t_1 X$, $PT_2 = t_1 P$. At last, the ETA sends a partial token $PT = (PT', E_Y(TVK1))$ to the DU. At the same time, it forwards $(E_Y(TVK2))$ to the SS.

(c) The DU selects a random element $a' \in Z_p^*$. Using x and Y, the DU computes $T' = \{T_1, T_2, T_3, T_4\}$ as follows:
$T_1 = \tau + a'Y$, $T_2 = PT_2 = t_1 P$, $T_3 = a'P$, $T_4 = I'$
Where $\tau = PT_1 - xPT_2 = t_1(\sum_{j=I1}^{It}(H_1(w_j) + k_j))P$.

Finally, the algorithm outputs a token $T = (T', E_Y(TVK1))$.

(6) **Search**(C, T, y). The algorithm applies $D_y(E_Y(TVK1))$ and $D_y(E_Y(TVK2))$ to get the original verification key $(TVK1, TVK2)$ from the encrypted values using a private key y of the SS. The algorithm then calls $TokVer(TVK1, TVK2)$ to verify the freshness of the input token T. If a token is fresh (i.e., $TokVer(\cdot) \rightarrow 1$), it applies T' of T on an available ciphertext C' from C as follows.

The algorithm computes

$$\tau_1 = \sum_{j=I1}^{It} \left(C_{1j} - yC2 \right)$$

$$= \sum_{j=I1}^{It} \left(r_1 \left(H_1\left(w_j \right) P + K_j \right) + r_1 Y - yr_1 P \right)$$

$$= r_1 \left(\sum_{j=I1}^{It} \left(H_1\left(w_j \right) P + K_j \right) \right),$$

$$\tau_2 = T_1 - yT_3$$

$$= t_1 \left(\sum_{j=I1}^{It} \left(H_1 \left(w_j \right) + k_j \right) \right) P + a'Y - ya'P$$

$$= t_1 \left(\sum_{j=I1}^{It} \left(H_1 \left(w_j \right) + k_j \right) \right) P. \tag{2}$$

Then, it checks the following correctness:

$$e \left(\tau_1, T_2 \right) = e \left(\tau_2, C_2 \right). \tag{3}$$

If (3) is satisfied, then the algorithm outputs the associated payload message M'; as a result $R = E_y(E_X(M'))$. Here, encryption with a public key X of DU provides confidentiality and signature with the private key y of SS maintains integrity of a result R during transit. The algorithm repeatedly applies T' on each available ciphertext at the server SS. At last, the algorithm updates the current entry of $TVK2$ in the system table with $TUpdate(TVK2, TVK1)$.

Note. (i) The algorithms $TokVerKey()$, $TokVer()$, and $TUpdate()$ are described in Section 4.2. (ii) The query Q from a DU to the ETA is in plaintext format. It does not impact the security of token as even if any unauthorized DU maliciously captures a partial token, he is unable to construct a final token unless having secret key x. (iii) The E/D for the verification keys is any standard encryption/decryption cipher. The encryption of the verification keys with the public key Y of SS prevents their modification by a malicious DU.

Correctness. LHS of (3):

$$e \left(\tau_1, T_2 \right) = e \left(r_1 \left(\sum_{j=I1}^{It} \left(H_1 \left(w_j \right) P + K_j \right) \right), t_1 P \right)$$

$$= e \left(\sum_{j=I1}^{It} \left(H_1 \left(w_j \right) P + K_j \right), P \right)^{r_1 t_1}$$

$$= e \left(\sum_{j=I1}^{It} \left(H_1 \left(w_j \right) P + k_j P \right), P \right)^{r_1 t_1} \tag{4}$$

$$= e \left(P, P \right)^{r_1 t_1 \Delta}.$$

RHS of (3):

$$e \left(\tau_2, C_2 \right) = e \left(t_1 \left(\sum_{j=I1}^{It} \left(H_1 \left(w_j \right) + k_j \right) \right) P, r_1 P \right) \tag{5}$$

$$= e \left(P, P \right)^{r_1 t_1 \Delta}.$$

Here, $\Delta = \sum_{j=I1}^{It} (H_1(w_j) + k_j)$. From (4) and (5), the correctness is proved.

4.2. Token Verification Procedure. To define a token verification procedure, we borrow the idea from Haller's S/Key One-Time Password System [34]. The S/Key scheme provides a technique to construct a one-time password at the client site and its verification at the host site. The scheme works on 3 parameters $(s, RN, H())$, where s is a secret string, RN represents the number of times the hash is applied on s, and $H()$ is any standard cryptographic hash function. We adopt similar parameters to define a token verification procedure for the proposed MUSE-TFV. The token freshness verification involves three algorithms:

(1) **TokVerKey(s, RN, H())**: the *token verification key generation* algorithm outputs two keys (K_1, K_2), where $K_1 = H^{RN}(s)$ and $K_2 = H^{RN-1}(s)$.

(2) **TokVer(K₁, K₂)**: the *token verification* algorithm verifies the freshness of a token by checking $K_1 = H(K_2)$. If condition is true, the algorithm outputs "1" otherwise "0."

(3) **TUpdate(K₁, K₂)**: the *token update* algorithm updates the current memory location of K_1 with K_2; that is, it performs $K_1 = K_2$.

The original S/Key mechanism is defined with the traditional hash function, that is, MD4. For MUSE-TFV, we prefer SHA-2 to avoid collision attack.

4.3. Security Analysis. We analyze the semantic security of MUSE-TFV against chosen keyword attack (IND-CKA) under DDH assumption. Additionally, we prove that the proposed MUSE-TFV provides security against token replay attack.

Theorem 2. *The proposed MUSE-TFV is semantically secure against a server SS as an adversary according to the game ICLR, assuming DDH is intractable.*

Proof. Let us assume a server SS as an adversary $\mathcal{A}$ can attack the proposed scheme in a polynomial time. Suppose $\mathcal{A}$ makes at most q_k token queries where $q_k < p$ and has the advantage ϵ in solving DDH problem in G_1. Let G_1 and G_2 be two groups of prime order p and P be the generator of G_1. We build a simulator $\mathcal{B}$ as a challenger that has the advantage $\epsilon' = \epsilon/e^n q_k n$ to simulate the game where e is base of natural logarithm.

Suppose an instance (aP, bP, cP) of the DDH problem in G_1 is the $\mathcal{B}$'s challenge information where $a, b, c \in Z_p^*$. The goal of $\mathcal{B}$ is to distinguish $cP = abP$ from random element in G_1. One restriction is that the random element z is independent of the location t selected in ICLR game; then the simulation game is demonstrated as follows.

(1) **Setup.** An adversary $\mathcal{A}$ randomly selects $y \in Z_p^*$ and computes $Y = yP$. $\mathcal{A}$ then defines a public-private key pair (Y, y). Let $(X = xP, x)$ be the $\mathcal{B}$'s public-private key pair.

(2) **Encryption Queries.** An adversary $\mathcal{A}$ issues the queries for the ciphertext of the keyword set $W_i = \{w_{i1}, w_{i2}, \ldots, w_{in}\}$. In response, challenger $\mathcal{B}$ simulates $Encryption(pp, W_i, Y)$ as follows.

(i) $\mathcal{B}$ selects $\gamma_j \in Z_p^*$ for each keyword $w_{ij} \in W_i$, where $1 \le j \le n$.

(ii) $\mathcal{B}$ chooses a random value $r_{1i} \in Z_p^*$ and constructs a ciphertext $C_i = \{(C_{1j})_i, (C_2)_i\}_{1 \le j \le n}$, where

$$(C_{11})_i = r_{1i}(\gamma_1 P + K_1) + r_{1i} Y$$

$$(C_{12})_i = r_{1i}(\gamma_2 P + K_2) + r_{1i} Y$$

$$\vdots$$

$$(C_{1z})_i = br_{1i}(\gamma_z P + K_z) + r_{1i} Y \qquad (6)$$

$$\vdots$$

$$(C_{1n})_i = r_{1i}(\gamma_n P + K_n) + r_{1i} Y$$

$$(C_2)_i = r_{1i} P.$$

(3) **Token Queries.** To evaluate *Search()* algorithm, $\mathcal{A}$ issues the token queries by sending $Q_i = (W_i', I_i')$, where $W_i' = \{w_{iI1}', w_{iI2}', \ldots, w_{iIt}'\}$ and $I_i' = \{I1, I2, \ldots, It\}$ to $\mathcal{B}$. $\mathcal{B}$ takes a partial token $PT' = \{PT_1, PT_2\}$ from the ETA where $PT_1 = t_1(\sum_{j=I1}^{It}(H_1(w_j) + k_j))P + t_1 X$, $PT_2 = t_1 P$. $\mathcal{B}$ then selects a random $a' \in Z_p^*$ and computes final token $T_i = \{T_{1i}, T_{2i}, T_{3i}, T_{4i}\}$ as follows.

$T_{1i} = \tau + a' Y$, $T_{2i} = t_1 P$, $T_{3i} = a' P$, $T_{4i} = I'$, where $\tau = PT_1 - x PT_2 = t_1(\sum_{j=I1}^{It}(H_1(w_j) + k_j))P$.

At last, $\mathcal{B}$ sends this token T_i to $\mathcal{A}$.

(4) **Challenge.** $\mathcal{A}$ issues a tuple (W_i, T, t) to $\mathcal{B}$ where $T \subseteq \{1, n\}$ and $t \in T$.

If $z \ne t$, $\mathcal{B}$ sends a random guess as the response to the DDH challenge.

If $z = t$, $\mathcal{B}$ responses are as follows.

(a) It first sets $h_t = c(\gamma_t P + K_t) + cY$.
(b) It sets $h_{1j} = \ell_j$, for $j \ne t$, $j \in T$, where $\ell_j \in Z_p^*$.
(c) It sets $h_{1j} = a(\gamma_j P + K_j) + aY$, for $j \ne t$, $j \notin T$.
(d) It sets $h_2 = aP$.

Finally, $\mathcal{B}$ sends $\{h_{1j}, h_2\}$ for $1 \le j \le n$ as challenge ciphertext to $\mathcal{A}$.

If $z = t$, then $\mathcal{B}$ wins the security game. The ciphertext for every position $j \notin T$ is the encryption of W and ciphertext in position t where $c = ab$ is also an encryption of W. Otherwise, for other position, it is not.

(5) **More Queries.** $\mathcal{A}$ queries encryption of other keyword sets and tokens that $\mathcal{A}$ has not asked before. $\mathcal{B}$ responds in the same way as in Step (2) and Step (3). The restriction is that $\mathcal{A}$ cannot issue the aforementioned queries for location t.

(6) **Guess.** At the end, $\mathcal{A}$ outputs the guess $b' \in \{0, 1\}$. If $b' = 1$ and B outputs "Yes," then (aP, bP, cP) is considered as a DDH tuple. Thus, for $z = t$, we can prove that (aP, bP, cP) is a DDH tuple as follows.

We know from (3) that

$$e(\tau_1, T_2) = e(\tau_2, C_2). \qquad (7)$$

This can be represented as

$$e(\tau_1, T_2) = e(br_1(\tau_z P + K_z), t_1 P)$$
$$= e(P, P)^{br_1(\tau_z + K_z)t_1},$$
$$e(\tau_2, C_2) = e(t_1 H_1(w_z + k_z)P, r_1 P)$$
$$= e(P, P)^{r_1 H_1(w_z + k_z)t_1}. \qquad (8)$$

From (8), we get

$$e(P, P)^{br_1(\tau_z + K_z)t_1} = e(P, P)^{r_1 H_1(w_z + k_z)t_1}. \qquad (9)$$

Now, from the challenge ciphertext,

$$e(\tau_1, T_2) = e(c(\tau_t P + K_t), t_1 P) = e(P, P)^{c(\tau_t + K_t)t_1},$$
$$e(\tau_2, C_2) = e(t_1 H_1(w_t + k_t)P, aP)$$
$$= e(P, P)^{aH_1(w_t + k_t)t_1}. \qquad (10)$$

From (10), we get

$$e(P, P)^{c(\tau_t + K_t)t_1} = e(P, P)^{aH_1(w_t + k_t)t_1}. \qquad (11)$$

Now, from (9) and (11)

$$\frac{e(P, P)^{br_1(\tau_z + K_z)t_1}}{e(P, P)^{r_1 H_1(w_z + k_z)t_1}} = \frac{e(P, P)^{c(\tau_t + K_t)t_1}}{e(P, P)^{aH_1(w_t + k_t)t_1}}$$

$$\therefore e(P, P)^{br_1(\tau_z + K_z)t_1} \, e(P, P)^{aH_1(w_t + k_t)t_1}$$
$$= e(P, P)^{c(\tau_t + K_t)t_1} \, e(P, P)^{r_1 H_1(w_z + k_z)t_1}$$
$$\therefore e(P, P)^{abr_1(\tau_z + K_z)t_1} \, e(P, P)^{H_1(w_z + k_z)t_1} \qquad (12)$$
$$= e(P, P)^{cr_1(\tau_z + K_z)t_1} \, e(P, P)^{H_1(w_z + k_z)t_1}$$

$$e(P, P)^{abr_1(\tau_z + K_z)t_1} = e(P, P)^{cr_1(\tau_z + K_z)t_1}$$

$$e(P, abP) = e(P, cP)$$

$$ab = c.$$

On the other hand, if $b' = 0$, we cannot prove that the challenge (cP, bP, cP) is a DDH tuple, since encryption at position j is random and it cannot confirm (12). However, the advantage of $\mathcal{A}$ to win the game ICLR is same as that of the $\mathcal{B}$ which solves the DDH challenge.

Now, the following are the two simulations of $\mathscr{B}$'s advantages.

(i) $S1$: $\mathscr{B}$ responds to the search token queries for n keyword issued by $\mathscr{A}$.

(ii) $S2$: $\mathscr{B}$ is not aborted in the challenge phase.

For large enough q_k, the probability of $S1$ and $S2$ can be defined as

$$Pr[S1] = \frac{1}{e^n},$$
$$Pr[S2] = \frac{1}{q_k n}. \tag{13}$$

Thus, the $\mathscr{B}$'s advantage ϵ' in solving the DDH problem is $\epsilon' = \epsilon \cdot Pr[S1 \cap S2] \geq \epsilon/e^n q_k n$.

According to Propositions 1 and 2 of [26], if there exists an adversary with nonnegligible advantage to win ICC game, then there exists another adversary with a nonnegligible advantage to win the ICLR game. However, as per the above proof, the advantage of $\mathscr{B}$ is $\epsilon/e^n q_k n \in [0, 1/2e^n q_k n]$ which is negligible. Thus, the proposed MUSE-TFV scheme is at least $(1 - 1/2e^n q_k n)$ secure under the ICLR game if DDH assumption is intractable. This completes the proof for Theorem 2. □

Theorem 3. *The proposed MUSE-TFV provides security against token replay attack.*

Proof. Let us assume a DU as an adversary $\mathscr{A}$ can perform a token replay attack as follows.

(1) An adversary $\mathscr{A}$ maliciously captures a valid token $T = (T', c = E_Y(TVK1))$ and stores it.

(2) To reuse the token T, an adversary $\mathscr{A}$ replaces its verification key part, that is, $c = E_Y(TVK1)$, with c' in such a way that the further execution of *TokVer()* (at the site of SS) outputs "1" and so the SS returns a result R.

If *Csize* is the size of a ciphertext generated by an encryption algorithm E, then an adversary $\mathscr{A}$ required 2^{Csize} attempts to forge a value "c." With any standard secure algorithm (i.e., 160-bit ECEL (ECC based Elgamal Encryption) (as public key Y of SS is an element from a group of points of an elliptic curve, any ECC based encryption algorithm must be used)), the probability of an adversary $\mathscr{A}$ to guess a valid ($c' = c$) is $1/(2^{160})$.

Additionally, the adversary $\mathscr{A}$ is completely unaware about the other verification key $TVK2$ available at the site of the SS. Thus, a token with the replaced verification key, that is, $T = (T', c')$, must be issued to the SS to check the output of *TokVer(TVK1, TVK2)* algorithm. Denoting CC as a communication cost (from a DU to SS) of a single message, we find $O(CC \cdot 2^{160})$ communication complexity in the system for 2^{160} attempts potentially performed by an adversary $\mathscr{A}$ to forge a value of c.

However, with a communication link of 100 Mbps and a Maximum Transmission Unit (MTU) of 1500 bytes (Ethernet), it requires about $57 \cdot 10^{30}$ years to attempt all the possible values of c. Thus, for any adversary $\mathscr{A}$, the probability of getting the result R by forging the value c is negligible.

Thus, we say that the proposed scheme MUSE-TFV is secure against token replay attack. □

TABLE 1: Comparative analysis: significant characteristics.

Schemes	MU	MKC	MKQ	SCF	TFV
Hwang and Lee 2007 [9]	√	√	√	×	×
Kiayias et al. 2016 [17]	√	×	×	×	×
Zhang et al. 2016 [18]	√	√	×	×	×
Wang et al. 2016 [19]	√	×	×	×	×
B. Zhang and F. Zhang 2011 [21]	×	√	√	×	×
Ding et al. 2012 [22]	×	√	√	√	×
Chen et al. 2012 [23]	×	√	√	×	×
MUSE-TFV	√	√	√	√	√

MU: multiuser support, MKC: multiple keywords in ciphertext, MKQ: multiple keywords in query, SCF: secure channel-free architecture, and TFV: token freshness verification.

5. Theoretical Analysis and Empirical Evaluation

In this section, we first present theoretical analysis of the proposed MUSE-TFV. Subsequently, we show the performance efficiency of MUSE-TFV with a detailed empirical evaluation.

5.1. Theoretical Analysis. We highlight the significant characteristics of MUSE-TFV in comparison with the existing multiuser searchable schemes [9, 17–19] and conjunctive search schemes [21–23] in Table 1. As the other multiuser searchable schemes [10, 11, 13, 16] utilize inverted index search structure (in inverted index based Searchable Encryption, a single common index (list of keywords) is defined for the entire set of encrypted documents), their comparison with the simple index based MUSE-TFV (in simple index searchable scheme, a separate index of keywords is associated with each encrypted document) is inapplicable here.

From Table 1, we observe that no scheme amongst the listed multiuser schemes provides a secure channel-free architecture for a token transmission. On the other hand, a conjunctive search scheme discussed in [22] offers such architecture, but it does not support multiple users in the system. In contrast, the proposed MUSE-TFV provides a conjunctive keyword based search with secure channel-free token transmission in multiuser settings. Additionally, MUSE-TFV has provision to verify the freshness of token to prevent token replay attack.

TABLE 2: Comparative analysis: storage-computational complexity.

Schemes	Storage overhead		Computational overhead		
	Ciphertext	Token	Encryption()	TokGen()	Search()
Hwang and Lee 2007 [9]	$(n + u)G_1$	$3G_1$	$(2 + 2n + u)E + P$	$2tM' + 3E$	$tM' + 3P$
Kiayias et al. 2016 [17]	$10G_1$	$5G_1$	$22E + (4 + 2u_k)M' + 2P$	$8M' + 13E$	$(1 + u_k)M' + 3P$
Zhang et al. 2016 [18]	nH	G_1	$2E + (1 + n)P$	$1E$	$E + 2P + U$
Wang et al. 2016 [19]	$(q + C)n$	$1H$	$2nE + 2nP$	$1E$	$1P + nD$
B. Zhang and F. Zhang 2011 [21]	$(1 + n)G_1 + G_2$	$(2 + t)G_1$	$(2 + 2n)E + P$	$(2 + 3t)E$	$(1 + 2t)P$
Ding et al. 2012 [22]	$(1 + n)G_1$	G_1	$(2 + 2n)M$	$M + E$	$3M + 2P$
Chen et al. 2012 [23]	$5G_1$	$4G_2$	$(4 + n)E$	$4E$	$4P$
MUSE-TFV	$\mathbf{(1 + n)G_1}$	$\mathbf{3G_1 + V}$	$\mathbf{(2 + 2n)M}$	$\mathbf{6M}$	$\mathbf{2M + 2P}$

n: number of keywords in the system, **t**: number of keywords in a query, **u**: number of users in the system, $\mathbf{u_k}$: number of users accessing an associated file, **H**: size of a message digest output by the used hash function, $\mathbf{(G_1, G_2)}$: size of an element from bilinear groups G_1 and G_2, **V**: ciphertext size of the used encryption routine, **q**: size of a random integer, **P**: pairing, **E**: exponentiation, **M**: scalar multiplication, $\mathbf{M'}$: modular multiplication, **D**: data comparison, and **U**: set union operation.

We compare the performance of MUSE-TFV with the existing schemes in terms of the storage overhead (i.e., size of a ciphertext (excluding payload) and size of a token) and computational overhead (for the proposed *Encryption()*, *TokGen()*, and *Search()* algorithms) in Table 2.

5.1.1. Storage Complexity. To show the storage overhead, we present the ciphertext/token size in terms of the size of an element from the bilinear groups (G_1, G_2). Observing Table 2, we say that the constructions given in [17, 23] are storage efficient with the constant ciphertext and token size (i.e., $O(1)$). In contrast, the proposed MUSE-TFV has a ciphertext size linear to the number of keywords in the system (i.e., $O(n)$) that is same as ciphertext storage complexity of the existing schemes [18, 19, 21, 22].

The significant characteristic of MUSE-TFV is its constant (i.e., $O(1)$) token storage complexity. This constant overhead makes the proposed scheme as efficient as the existing schemes [9, 17, 18, 22]. In fact, the actual token size for the MUSE-TFV is three times higher than the token constructed by the schemes [18, 22]. However, with such increased token size, we offer a secure token transmission over any public channel without channel setup overhead. Moreover, with an added component V to the token (where V is the size of a ciphertext for an encrypted verification key $TVK1$), we prevent the token replay attack.

5.1.2. Computational Complexity. We present the computational overhead in terms of the major operations, namely, modular multiplication (M'), scalar multiplication (M), exponentiation (E), and pairing (P) involved in the listed schemes. From our experiments, we observe that a scalar multiplication, an exponentiation, and a pairing operation are costlier (involving more CPU cycles) than a modular multiplication operation. Therefore, from Table 2, we say that the computational cost of the proposed *Encryption()* algorithm (i.e., $(2 + 2n)M$) is almost same as the encryption cost of the listed multikeyword schemes [9, 21, 22]. We note that this encryption overhead is double as compared to the encryption overhead involved in the schemes [18, 23].

On the other hand, similar to the scheme in [18], MUSE-TFV has a constant computational complexity, i.e., $(O(n))$ (independent of the number of users u), for *Encryption()* algorithm. Such computational cost is far more better than the existing schemes [9, 17] with $O(n + u)$ and $O(u_k)$ encryption overhead, respectively. Therefore, we say that with moderate computational overhead for the proposed *Encryption()* algorithm MUSE-TFV supports multiple keyword based search as well as multiple users in the system.

From Table 2, we observe that the computational complexity of the proposed *TokGen()* algorithm of MUSE-TFV is same as the token construction cost of the existing schemes [18, 22, 23], i.e., $O(1)$. With such constant computational overhead, MUSE-TFV performs better than the existing schemes [9, 21] having $O(t)$ token construction overhead. Additionally, we note that *TokGen()* algorithm of MUSE-TFV consumes more CPU cycles as compared to the Token Generation algorithm of the schemes [18, 22, 23] due to its interactive token construction steps. However, with such added overhead, MUSE-TFV supports multiple users in the system.

We also note that the computational cost of a *Search()* algorithm of MUSE-TFV (i.e., $(2M + 2P)$) is almost same as the existing schemes [18, 22, 23]. This constant search complexity (i.e., $O(1)$) is better than the search complexity (i.e., $O(t)$) involved in [9, 21]. Moreover, as a multiuser scheme, the MUSE-TFV offers constant computational cost $O(1)$ (i.e., independent from u) during search phase. This cost is much more better than the search computational overhead (i.e., $O(u_k)$) involved in the scheme [17]. It is worth noting that, with similar search complexity as the existing schemes [18, 22, 23], the proposed MUSE-TFV provides an additional token freshness verification feature.

5.1.3. Communication Complexity. In Table 3, we present the communication complexity of the proposed MUSE-TFV during *Data Upload*, *Token Generation*, and *Search* phases, as compared to the existing multiuser schemes [9, 17–19]. We note that, with S as a message, a scheme in [19] suffers with the highest communication overhead (i.e., $3cS$ for c

TABLE 3: Comparative analysis: communication complexity.

Schemes	Data Upload	Token Generation	Search
Hwang and Lee 2007 [9]	cS	—	$(1 + c)S$
Kiayias et al. 2016 [17]	cS	—	$(3 + c)S$
Zhang et al. 2016 [18]	cS	—	$2S$
Wang et al. 2016 [19]	$3cS$	—	$(1 + c)S$
MUSE-TFV	**cS**	**$2qS$**	**$(1 + c)S$**

S: a message, c: number of ciphertexts available at the server, and q: number of queries.

TABLE 4: Simulation parameters.

Parameters	Values for simulation
n	$\{50, 100, 150, 200, 250, 300\}$
u	$\{1000, 2000, 3000, 4000, 5000\}$
t	$\{10, 20, 30, 40, 50\}$

ciphertexts) during *Data Upload* phase wherein uploading of a single ciphertext involves three messages (i.e., a preindex message from a Data Owner to the server, an index parameter message from the server to the Data Owner, and a ciphertext message from the Data Owner to the server). In contrast, the proposed MUSE-TFV has an optimal communication overhead of a single message per ciphertext (i.e., cS messages for c ciphertexts) from a Data Owner to the server. With such overhead, the proposed scheme performs similar to the existing schemes discussed in [9, 17, 18].

A scheme in [17] uses two servers (S_{main} and S_{aid}) to perform a search operation where a communication overhead is $(3 + c)S$ messages (i.e., a token message from a user to S_{main}, a token message from a user to S_{aid}, an additional message from S_{aid} to S_{main}, and c result messages from S_{main} to the requesting user). In contrast, the proposed MUSE-TFV involves $(1+c)S$ messages (i.e., a token message from a user to the Storage Server and c result messages from the server to the user) during *Search* phase. The scheme of [18] has the lowest communication overhead during search operation, that is, $2S$ (a token message from a user to the server and a result message from the server to the user). However, in the scheme [18], the server suffers with the additional computational overhead (for set union operations) in order to incorporate c result messages into a single message.

Table 3 shows that the *Token Generation* phase of the proposed MUSE-TFV suffers with the communication overhead of $2qS$ for q queries. This overhead is due to the interactive Token Generation algorithm that involves two message exchanges between a DU and the ETA, that is, a Token Request message from a DU and a response message from the ETA. However, with such added communication overhead, we achieve a more secure system wherein every Token Generation activity is logged at the trusted site and thus any dishonest activity from a DU can easily be tracked. Moreover, with such interactive Token Generation algorithm, the proposed scheme provides a token freshness verification to prevent a token replay attack. Thus, MUSE-TFV is indeed an effective multiuser scheme for the applications where security of each search activity is a prime requirement.

5.2. Empirical Evaluation. To evaluate the performance, we conduct the experiments on 32-bit, 2.10 GHz Pentium Core 2 Duo CPU with Windows 7 machine using Java Pairing based Cryptographic (JPBC) Library [42]. From JPBC Library, we utilize Type A pairing (i.e., $G_1 \times G_1 \rightarrow G_2$) which is based on

an elliptic curve $E(F_q) : y^2 = x^3 + x$. Here, the group G_1 is a subgroup of $E(F_q)$, and the cyclic group G_2 is a subgroup of $E(F_q)^2$ where q is a large prime number. The group order of G_1 is 160 bits, and the base field is 512 bits.

To systematically compare the performance of the MUSE-TFV with other schemes, we consider three significant parameters, that is, (i) number of keywords in the system (n), (ii) number of keywords in a query (t), and (iii) number of users in the system (u) (Table 4). We perform experiments for different size systems with $n \in \{50, 100, 150, 200, 250, 300\}$. For each system, we simulate the *Encryption()*, *TokGen()*, and *Search()* algorithms multiple times and consider their average results. To show the efficiency of MUSE-TFV as a multiuser scheme, we consider a different number of users, that is, $u \in \{1000, 2000, 3000, 4000, 5000\}$ in the system. Additionally, during Token Generation experiments, we select the conjunctive queries with the variable number of keywords, that is, $t \in \{10, 20, 30, 40, 50\}$. As a large number of keywords in conjunction make a query complex and impractical, we select comparatively small values for t.

From Table 2, we identify that the computational cost of *Encryption()* algorithms for all multikeyword schemes (MKC) [21–23] depends upon n whereas for all multiuser schemes [9, 17, 18], it depends upon n, or u or u_k. Thus, we simulate *Encryption()* algorithms for all the listed schemes with different values of n and u separately and show their responses in Figures 5(a) and 5(b), respectively. Note that for simulation purpose we consider the worst case scenario for a scheme [17], where $u_k = u$.

From the results in Figure 5(a), we note that the encryption time of the proposed MUSE-TFV is linearly increasing with the number of keywords (i.e., n). However, this time overhead is same as the encryption time overhead of [9, 21, 22] but larger than the overhead involved in [18, 23]. Additionally, from Figure 5(b), we observe that the existence of multiple users in the system does not affect the time consumption of encryption algorithm of MUSE-TFV. This characteristic makes the MUSE-TFV more practical than the existing multiuser schemes [9, 17] where the encryption time overhead is linearly increasing with the number of users. Here, we say that with the constant encryption overhead (i.e., independent of the number of users (u)) the *Encryption()* algorithm of MUSE-TFV supports multiple keywords in a ciphertext and multiple users in the system.

We present the empirical results for *TokGen()* algorithm of MUSE-TFV and other multikeyword (MKQ) schemes in Figure 6. From these results, we say that the MUSE-TFV takes almost constant time to construct a token regardless of the number of keywords in a query. With this characteristic, MUSE-TFV resembles the schemes [22, 23] and performs

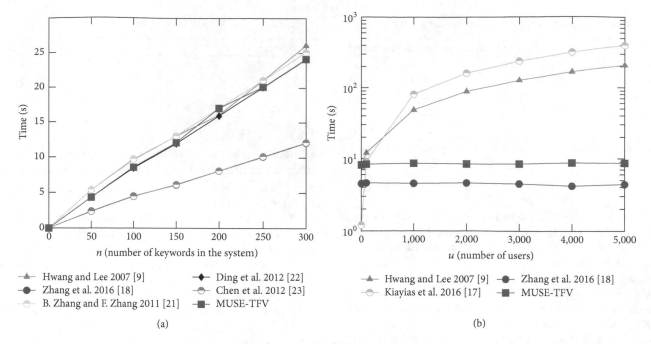

(a)

(b)

FIGURE 5: Simulation results for *Encryption()* algorithm.

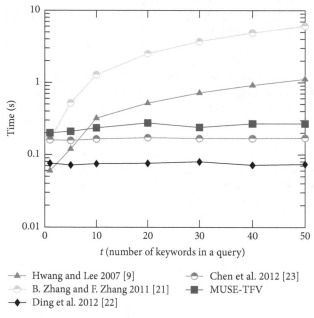

FIGURE 6: Simulation results for *TokGen()* algorithm.

Observing the results in Figure 7(a), we note that the search time overhead for MUSE-TFV is almost constant and independent of the number of keywords in a query (t). With this characteristic, the MUSE-TFV performs a conjunctive search with much less computational time as compared to the existing conjunctive search schemes [9, 21] where the search time is affected by the number of keywords in query (t). From the results in Figure 7(b), we note that, with constant search time overhead, the proposed MUSE-TFV supports multiple users in the system as efficiently as the scheme [18]. In addition, we say that with the search time linear to the number of users (u) the scheme of [17] is indeed less practical. In contrast, with the constant search time overhead, the MUSE-TFV performs a conjunctive keyword search in response to a query coming from any user in the multiuser settings.

At last we claim that our empirical results are completely in accordance with the theoretically measured computational complexity presented in Table 2. From the theoretical analysis and empirical evaluation, we conclude that, with the moderate storage-computational overhead, the proposed MUSE-TFV is an elegant multiuser searchable scheme with a provision of conjunctive keyword search and token freshness verification.

6. Concluding Remarks

In this paper, we discuss the proposed MUSE-TFV: a Multiuser Searchable Encryption with Token Freshness Verification that is based on the concept of Functional Encryption. Unlike the existing Functional Encryption based multiuser searchable schemes wherein a user generates a search token using his own search key, in the proposed MUSE-TFV, a Data User, DU, constructs a search token in cooperation with the

better than the other multikeyword schemes [9, 21] having $O(t)$ token computational overhead. However, MUSE-TFV takes more time as compared to [22, 23] because of its interactive nature.

According to Table 2, the computational overhead for the *Search()* algorithm of the listed schemes is either constant or otherwise depending upon t or u_k. Thus, we simulate the listed schemes for their *Search()* algorithm with different values of t and u separately and show their responses in Figures 7(a) and 7(b), respectively.

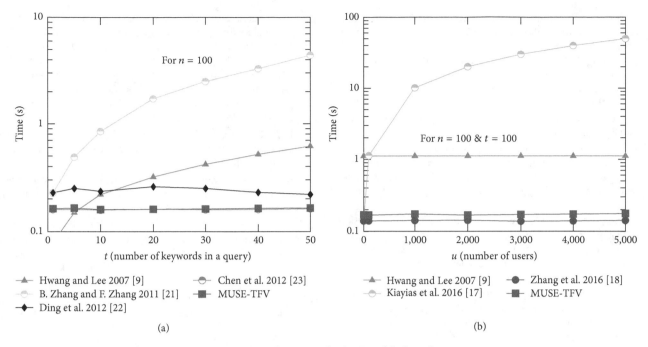

(a)

(b)

FIGURE 7: Simulation results for *Search()* algorithm.

ETA. With such interactive Token Generation mechanism, every search activity of each DU is logged at the enterprise trusted site and thus dishonest activity can be easily captured. Moreover, in the MUSE-TFV, each constructed token is valid for one-time use and its freshness is checked at the SS using a verification key issued by the ETA. Such token verification procedure prevents the reuse of the same token and so the MUSE-TFV avoids token replay attack. Additionally, we provide a secure channel-free token transmission as well as a conjunctive keyword search with the proposed scheme.

With a security analysis, we prove the correctness of the proposed MUSE-TFV against chosen keyword attack and token replay attack. With a detailed theoretical analysis, we justify the efficiency of the proposed scheme. Additionally, we evaluate the performance of the proposed scheme based on three significant parameters: number of users, number of keywords in the system, and the number of keywords in conjunctive query. Our experimental evaluation shows that, with almost same computational-storage overhead as the existing conjunctive keyword search schemes, the proposed MUSE-TFV provides the additional features of multiuser support and token freshness verification.

Notations

pp: System's public parameters
msk: Master secret key
n: Number of keywords in the system
u: Number of users in the system
$\mathcal{KS}$:   Keyword space that involves n keywords
(Y, y):   Server's public-private key pair
(X, x):   User's public-private key pair

$M' = E_{key}(M)$:   Encrypted payload message where E is any symmetric key cipher with a key key
$W = \{w_j \mid 1 \leq j \leq n\}$:   A list of n keywords associated with a ciphertext
C: A ciphertext
PT: A partial token
T: A token
t: Number of keywords in a conjunctive query
$Q' = \{W', I'\}$:   A conjunctive query that involves two sets (W', I') where $W' = \{w'_j\}_{j \in I'}$ is a list of t keywords and $I' = \{\ell_1, \ell_2, \ldots, \ell_t\}$ is a list of positions of keywords in $\mathcal{KS}$
C_i: ith ciphertext
$(TVK1, TVK2)$:   Token verification keys
R: A search result.

References

[1] M. Abdalla, M. Bellare, D. Catalano et al., "Searchable encryption revisited: consistency properties, relation to anonymous IBE, and extensions," in *Advances in cryptology—CRYPTO 2005*, vol. 3621 of *Lecture Notes in Comput. Sci.*, pp. 205–222, Springer, Berlin, 2005.

[2] S. Shin and K. Kobara, "Towards secure cloud storage," *Demo for CloudCom 2010*, vol. 2, p. 8, 2010.

[3] G. Brunette, R. Mogull, and et al., "Security guidance for critical areas of focus in cloud computing v2. 1," *Cloud Security Alliance*, pp. 1–76, 2009.

[4] D. X. Song, D. Wagner, and A. Perrig, "Practical techniques for searches on encrypted data," in *Proceedings of the in Security and Privacy, 2000 SP2000 IEEE Symposiumon. 1em plus 0.5em minus 0.4em IEEE*, pp. 44–55, 2000.

[5] E.-J. Goh, "Secure indexes," *IACR Cryptology ePrint Archive*, vol. 2003, p. 216, 2003.

[6] D. Boneh, G. Di Crescenzo, R. Ostrovsky, and G. Persiano, "Public key encryption with keyword search," in *Advances in Cryptology—EUROCRYPT 2004*, vol. 3027 of *Lecture Notes in Computer Science*, pp. 506–522, Springer, Berlin, Germany, 2004.

[7] J. Baek, R. Safavi-Naini, and W. Susilo, "Public key encryption with keyword search revisited," in *Proceedings in Computational Science and Its Applications–ICCSA International Conference, Part I 2008. 1em plus 0.5em minus 0.4em*, vol. 30, pp. 1249–1259, Springer, Perugia, Italy, 2008.

[8] D. J. Park, K. Kim, and P. J. Lee, "Public Key Encryption with Conjunctive Field Keyword Search," in *Information Security Applications*, vol. 3325 of *Lecture Notes in Computer Science*, pp. 73–86, Springer Berlin Heidelberg, Berlin, Heidelberg, 2005.

[9] Y. H. Hwang and P. J. Lee, "Public key encryption with conjunctive keyword search and its extension to a multi-user system," in *Pairing-based cryptography—Pairing 2007*, vol. 4575 of *Lecture Notes in Comput. Sci.*, pp. 2–22, Springer, Berlin, 2007.

[10] P. Wang, H. Wang, and J. Pieprzyk, "Common secure index for conjunctive keyword-based retrieval over encrypted data," *Secure Data Management*, pp. 108–123, 2007.

[11] P. Wang, H. Wang, and J. Pieprzyk, "Threshold privacy preserving keyword searches," in *Proceedings of the International Conference on Current Trends in Theory and Practice of Computer Science. 1em plus 0.5em minus 0.4em , 2008, pp. 646–658*, pp. 646–658, Springer, 2008.

[12] P. Wang, H. Wang, and J. Pieprzyk, "An Efficient Scheme of Common Secure Indices for Conjunctive Keyword-Based Retrieval on Encrypted Data," in *Information Security Applications*, vol. 5379, pp. 145–159, Springer, Berlin, Heidelberg, 2009.

[13] P. Wang, H. Wang, and J. Pieprzyk, "Keyword Field-Free Conjunctive Keyword Searches on Encrypted Data and Extension for Dynamic Groups," in *Cryptology and Network Security*, vol. 5339, pp. 178–195, Springer, Berlin, Heidelberg, 2008.

[14] F. Bao, R. H. Deng, X. Ding, and Y. Yang, "Private query on encrypted data in multi-user settings," in *Information security practice and experience*, vol. 4991 of *Lecture Notes in Comput. Sci.*, pp. 71–85, Springer, Berlin, 2008.

[15] J. Li and X. Chen, "Efficient multi-user keyword search over encrypted data in cloud computing," *Computing and Informatics*, vol. 32, no. 4, pp. 723–738, 2013.

[16] H. Huang, J. Du, H. Wang, and R. Wang, "A multi-keyword multi-user searchable encryption scheme based on cloud storage," in *Proceedings of the Joint 15th IEEE International Conference on Trust, Security and Privacy in Computing and Communications, 10th IEEE International Conference on Big Data Science and Engineering and 14th IEEE International Symposium on Parallel and Distributed Processing with Applications, IEEE TrustCom/BigDataSE/ISPA 2016*, pp. 1937–1943, August 2016.

[17] A. Kiayias, O. Oksuz, A. Russell, Q. Tang, and B. Wang, in *Proceedings of the European Symposium on Research in Computer Security. 1em plus 0.5em minus 0.4em*, pp. 173–195, Springer, 2016.

[18] Y. Zhang, L. Liu, and S. Wang, "Multi-User and Keyword-Based Searchable Encryption Scheme," in *Proceedings of the 2016 12th International Conference on Computational Intelligence and Security (CIS)*, pp. 223–227, Wuxi, China, December 2016.

[19] S. Wang, X. Zhang, and Y. Zhang, "Efficiently multi-user searchable encryption scheme with attribute revocation and grant for cloud storage," *PLoS ONE*, vol. 11, no. 11, Article ID e0167157, 2016.

[20] J. Ye, J. Wang, J. Zhao, J. Shen, and K.-C. Li, "Fine-grained searchable encryption in multi-user setting," *Soft Computing*, pp. 1–12, 2016.

[21] B. Zhang and F. Zhang, "An efficient public key encryption with conjunctive-subset keywords search," *Journal of Network and Computer Applications*, vol. 34, no. 1, pp. 262–267, 2011.

[22] M. Ding, F. Gao, Z. Jin, and H. Zhang, "An efficient public key encryption with conjunctive keyword search scheme based on pairings," *Proceedings in 2012 3rd IEEE International Conference on Network Infrastructure and Digital Content. 1em plus 0.5em minus 0.4em IEEE*, pp. 526–530, 2012.

[23] Z. Chen, C. Wu, and D. Wang, "Conjunctive keywords searchable encryption with efficient pairing, constant ciphertext and short trapdoor," *PAISI*, pp. 176–189, 2012.

[24] Y.-C. Chang and M. Mitzenmacher, "Privacy Preserving Keyword Searches on Remote Encrypted Data," in *Applied Cryptography and Network Security. 1em plus 0.5em minus 0.4em*, vol. 3531, pp. 442–455, Springer, Berlin, Heidelberg, 2005.

[25] R. Curtmola, J. Garay, S. Kamara, and R. Ostrovsky, "Searchable symmetric encryption: improved definitions and efficient constructions," *Journal of Computer Security*, vol. 19, no. 5, pp. 895–934, 2011.

[26] P. Golle, J. Staddon, and B. Waters, "Secure conjunctive keyword search over encrypted data," in *Applied Cryptography and Network Security: Second International Conference, ACNS 2004, Yellow Mountain, China, June 8–11, 2004. Proceedings*, vol. 3089 of *Lecture Notes in Computer Science*, pp. 31–45, Springer, Berlin, Germany, 2004.

[27] L. Ballard, S. Kamara, and F. Monrose, "Achieving efficient conjunctive keyword searches over encrypted data," *Lecture Notes in Computer Science (including subseries Lecture Notes in Artificial Intelligence and Lecture Notes in Bioinformatics): Preface*, vol. 3783, pp. 414–426, 2005.

[28] J. W. Byun, D. H. Lee, and J. Lim, "Efficient Conjunctive Keyword Search on Encrypted Data Storage System," in *Public Key Infrastructure. 1em plus 0.5em minus 0.4em*, vol. 4043, pp. 184–196, Springer, Berlin, Heidelberg, 2006.

[29] D. Boneh and B. Waters, "Conjunctive, subset, and range queries on encrypted data," in *Theory of Cryptography Conference: TCC 2007. 1em plus 0.5em minus 0.4em*, pp. 535–554, Springer, Berlin, Germany, 2007.

[30] M.-S. Hwang, S.-T. Hsu, and C.-C. Lee, "A new public key encryption with conjunctive field keyword search scheme," *Information Technology and Control*, vol. 43, no. 3, pp. 277–288, 2014.

[31] H. S. Rhee, J. H. Park, W. Susilo, and D. H. Lee, "Trapdoor security in a searchable public-key encryption scheme with a designated tester," *The Journal of Systems and Software*, vol. 83, no. 5, pp. 763–771, 2010.

[32] Y. Zhao, H. Ma, X. Chen, Q. Tang, and H. Zhu, "A new trapdoor-indistinguishable public key encryption with keyword search," *Journal of Wireless Mobile Networks, Ubiquitous Computing, and Dependable Applications*, vol. 3, no. 1-2, pp. 72–81, 2012.

[33] Y. Miao, J. Ma, F. Wei, Z. Liu, X. A. Wang, and C. Lu, "VCSE: Verifiable conjunctive keywords search over encrypted data without secure-channel," *Peer-to-Peer Networking and Applications*, vol. 10, no. 4, pp. 995–1007, 2017.

[34] N. Haller, "The S/KEY One-Time Password System," RFC Editor RFC1760, 1995.

[35] D. Boneh and M. Franklin, "Identity-based encryption from the Weil pairing," in *Advances in Cryptology—CRYPTO 2001*, vol. 2139 of *Lecture Notes in Computer Science*, pp. 213–229, 2001.

[36] A. Shamir, "Identity-based cryptosystems and signature schemes," in *Advances in Cryptology: Proceedings of (CRYPTO '84)*, vol. 196 of *Lecture Notes in Computer Science*, pp. 47–53, Springer, Berlin, Germany, 1985.

[37] J. Bethencourt, A. Sahai, and B. Waters, "Ciphertext-policy attribute-based encryption," in *Proceedings of the IEEE Symposium on Security and Privacy (SP '07)*, pp. 321–334, May 2007.

[38] V. Goyal, O. Pandey, A. Sahai, and B. Waters, "Attribute-based encryption for fine-grained access control of encrypted data," in *Proceedings of the 13th ACM Conference on Computer and Communications Security (CCS '06)*, pp. 89–98, November 2006.

[39] A. Sahai and B. Waters, "Fuzzy identity-based encryption," in *Advances in Cryptology – EUROCRYPT 2005*, vol. 3494 of *Lecture Notes in Computer Science*, pp. 457–473, Springer, Berlin, Germany, 2005.

[40] J. Katz, A. Sahai, and B. Waters, "Predicate encryption supporting disjunctions, polynomial equations, and inner products," in *Advances in Cryptology—EUROCRYPT 2008*, vol. 4965 of *Lecture Notes in Computer Science*, pp. 146–162, Springer, Berlin, Germany, 2008.

[41] C.-C. Lee, S.-T. Hsu, and M.-S. Hwang, "A study of conjunctive keyword searchable schemes," *IJ Network Security*, vol. 15, no. 5, pp. 321–330, 2013.

[42] A. de Caro and V. Iovino, "jPBC: Java pairing based cryptography," in *Proceedings of the 16th IEEE Symposium on Computers and Communications (ISCC '11)*, pp. 850–855, July 2011.

13

Protecting Private Data by Honey Encryption

Wei Yin,[1] Jadwiga Indulska,[2] and Hongjian Zhou[1]

[1]*North China Institute of Computing Technology, Beijing, China*
[2]*School of ITEE, The University of Queensland, Brisbane, QLD, Australia*

Correspondence should be addressed to Wei Yin; yinwei168@gmail.com

Academic Editor: Leandros Maglaras

The existing password-based encryption (PBE) methods that are used to protect private data are vulnerable to brute-force attacks. The reason is that, for a wrongly guessed key, the decryption process yields an invalid-looking plaintext message, confirming the invalidity of the key, while for the correct key it outputs a valid-looking plaintext message, confirming the correctness of the guessed key. Honey encryption helps to minimise this vulnerability. In this paper, we design and implement the honey encryption mechanisms and apply it to three types of private data including Chinese identification numbers, mobile phone numbers, and debit card passwords. We evaluate the performance of our mechanism and propose an enhancement to address the overhead issue. We also show lessons learned from designing, implementing, and evaluating the honey encryption mechanism.

1. Introduction

Most people in China (as in any other country) are annoyed by junk text messages. The Internet users can also be affected by identity theft when criminals are using someone's identity. This can occur because some sensitive private data was not well protected and was then maliciously used by other parties causing damage to finances and reputation of the data owner.

When purchasing a product online, we are asked to provide our mobile phone number for the delivery purpose. When buying a train ticket in China, we need to fill in the identification card number. The commercial parties gather such sensitive private data. Some store them in a plaintext format. Some employ password-based encryption (PBE) [1]. However, the robustness of encryption depends on the key length. Although current encryption algorithms are considered secure, given enough time and computing power, they will be vulnerable to brute-force attacks. Also, the existing encryption mechanisms have a vulnerability; that is, when decrypting with a wrongly guessed key, they yield an invalid-looking plaintext message, while when decrypting with the right key, they output a valid-looking plaintext message, confirming that the ciphertext message is correctly decrypted.

Juels and Ristenpart [2] proposed the honey encryption concept to address this vulnerability and make the PBE encryption more difficult to break by brute-force. The honey

term in the information security terminology describes a false resource. For example, honeypot [3] is a false server that attracts attackers to probe and penetrate. Honeyword [4] is a false username and password in the database. Once used for login, an intrusion is detected. Honey encryption can also address the previously mentioned vulnerability. Even when a wrong key is used for decryption, the system can yield a valid-looking plaintext message; therefore, the attacker cannot tell whether the guessed key is correct or not.

The innovation of honey encryption is the design of the distribution-transforming encoder (DTE). According to the probabilities of a message in the message space, it maps the message to a seed range in a seed space, then it randomly selects a seed from the range and XORs it with the key to get the ciphertext. For decryption, the ciphertext is XORed with the key and the seed is obtained. Then DTE uses the seed location to map it back to the original plaintext message. Even if the key is incorrect, the decryption process outputs a message from the message space and thus confuses the attacker.

The contribution of this paper is threefold. First, we design and implement the honey encryption system and apply the concept to three applications including Chinese identification numbers, mobile numbers, and passwords. These applications are based on uniformly distributed message spaces and the symmetric encryption mechanism. We also extend honey encryption to applications with nonuniformly distributed message spaces and an asymmetric encryption mechanism (RSA). Second, we evaluate the performance of our honey encryption mechanism and propose an enhancement. Third, we discuss lessons learned from implementing and evaluating the honey encryption technique.

The rest of this paper is organised as follows. Section 2 presents the related work, followed by the discussion of the honey encryption concept in Section 3. The design and implementation are described in Section 4 and the use of honey encryption in three applications is shown in Section 5. The performance evaluation is discussed in Section 6 and a performance enhancement is proposed in Section 7. Section 8 discusses applications with nonuniformly distributed message spaces and use of asymmetric encryption in honey encryption. Section 9 describes the learned lessons followed by the conclusion in Section 10.

2. Related Work

Most of the systems with encryption use password-based encryption (PBE). These systems are susceptible to brute-force guessing attacks. Honey encryption [5] aims to address this vulnerability by not allowing attackers to gain much information from password guessing. For each possible key, the system outputs a valid-looking decrypted message. So it is hard to tell which one is the correct password. This way honey encryption can protect sensitive data in many applications.

Honey encryption deceives attackers that the incorrectly guessed key is valid. Many luring technologies that also use the term honey have been proposed in the last 20 years. Honeytokens [6] are decoys distributed over a system. If any decoy is used, this means that a compromise is taking place. For example, honeywords are passwords that are rarely used by normal users. Once a login attempt using a honeyword occurs, the system rises an alarm. Honeypots [3], Honeynet [7], and Honeyfarm [8] are luring systems that present many vulnerabilities. They are likely to become the targets for attackers. The objective of setting such systems is to study attackers' motivations, tools, and techniques.

Honey encryption is also related to Format-Preserving Encryption (FPE) [9] and Format-Transforming Encryption (FTE) [10]. In FPE, the plaintext message space is the same as the ciphertext message space. In FTE, the ciphertext message space is different from the message space. Honey encryption maps a plaintext message to a seed range in the seed space. Since the message space and the seed space are different, the ciphertext message space is different from the message space.

While Vinayak and Nahala [11] apply the honey encryption concept to MANETs to prevent ad hoc networks from the brute-force attack, Tyagi et al. [5] adopt the honey encryption technique to protect credit card numbers and a simplified version of text messaging. Most of these data in [5, 11] are from uniformly distributed message spaces. However, genomic data usually has highly nonuniform probability distributions. The GenoGuard mechanism [1] incorporates the honey encryption concept to provide information-theoretic confidentiality guarantees for encrypted genomic data.

In [1, 5, 11], a fixed distribution-transforming encoder (DTE) is utilised for encryption and decryption, so it is only suitable for binary bit streams or integer sequences, not for images and videos. Yoon et al. [12] propose a visual honey encryption concept which employs an adaptive DTE so that the proposed concept can be applied to more complex domains including images and videos. Jaeger et al. [13] provide a systematic study of honey encryption in the low-entropy key settings. They rule out the ability to strengthen the honey encryption notions to allow known-message attacks when attackers can exhaust the key space.

Our paper focuses on applying the honey encryption technique to three new applications including citizens' identification numbers, mobile phone numbers, and debit card passwords. This data is vital private information that can cause serious damage to person's finance and/or reputation if stolen. Although honey encryption has been applied to a number of applications, due to the variety of message formats and probability features, the message space design needs to vary for new types of applications. The applications discussed in our paper are carefully selected, because later we will show that the protection honey encryption provides varieties for different applications: stronger for debit card passwords, weaker for mobile phone numbers.

In our comprehensive design and implementation of the honey encryption mechanisms for three different applications we cover small/large message spaces, uniformly/nonuniformly distributed message probabilities, and symmetric/asymmetric encryption mechanisms. As far as we know, our paper is the first one to study the performance of honey encryption. We discover the performance problem for large message spaces and present a performance optimisation for small message spaces. We also show that the capability of honey encryption to address the brute-force vulnerability could be lost if the message space has not been well designed and that this design needs to vary for different types of applications.

3. Honey Encryption Concept

Honey encryption protects a set of messages that have some common features (e.g., credit card numbers are such messages). A message set is called a message space. Before encrypting a message, we should determine the possible message space. All messages in the space must be sorted in some order. Then the probability of each message (PDF) that occurs in the space and the cumulative probability (CDF) of each message are needed. A seed space should be available for the distribution-transforming encoder (DTE) to map each message to a seed range in the seed space (n-bit binary string space). The DTE determines the seed range for each message according to the PDF and CDF of the message and makes sure that the PDF of the message is equal to the ratio of the corresponding seed range to the seed space. The n-bit seed space must be big enough so that each message can be mapped to at least one seed. A message can be mapped to multiple seeds and the seed is randomly selected.

Let us consider using honey encryption to encrypt the coffee types, as shown in Figure 1. The coffee message space M consists of Cappuccino, Espresso, Latte, and Mocha. These four messages are sorted alphabetically. Let us assume that 4/8

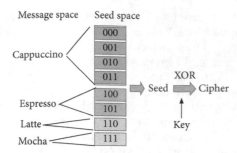

FIGURE 1: Honey encryption example.

people in Sydney like Cappuccino, 2/8 like Espresso, 1/8 like Latte and Mocha. The seed space is a 3-digit space. According to those probability statistics, we map these four messages to four ranges in the seed space. When encrypting Cappuccino, the DTE randomly selects a seed from the corresponding seed range. The seed is XORed with the key and the ciphertext is generated.

For decryption, the ciphertext is XORed with the key to obtain the seed. Then the DTE inversely maps the seed to the original plaintext message. In the encryption process, a message could have multiple mapping choices and the mapping is directional and random. However, since we sort plaintext messages in the message space and determine the seed range by the PDF and CDF of each message, it can be guaranteed that the seed ranges are arranged in the same order and the cumulative probability of the seed range in the seed space is equal to the cumulative probability of the message in the message space. Therefore, we establish an inverse_table that consists of mappings of the cumulative probability to the plaintext message. Finding the seed, we can determine the seed range. Finding the seed range, we can determine the cumulative probability shared by the seed range and the corresponding plaintext message. Then by looking up the cumulative probability in the inverse_table, we can find the original plaintext message and the ciphertext is decrypted.

In [2], Juels and Ristenpart discussed the robustness of honey encryption. First, the robustness may be compromised if the adversary has some side information about the message space. Second, if the key and message distribution are dependent or correlated, an attacker may be able to compare the decrypted message with the decryption key to identify a correct message. But even with those limitations, in the worst scenario, honey encryption security falls back to normal PBE security and therefore there is no drawback in using honey encryption.

4. Design and Implementation

We can design DTE as a common module that implements the encryption and decryption algorithms. For encryption, the DTE module takes in some parameters from the message space including the PDF and CDF probabilities of each message. Therefore, we abstract some interfaces for DTE to use when designing the message space. For decryption, the

main task for DTE is to search the inverse_table and find the correct plaintext message. Therefore, the message space implementation should provide interfaces for probabilities and the inverse_table.

4.1. Message Space APIs. DTE maps the plaintext message to a seed in a seed range. The starting point of the seed range is determined by the CDF of the message, while the end point of the seed range is determined by the PDF of the message. Therefore, we define an interface for the message space containing functions including the cumulative_probability(mesg) function and the probability(mesg) function. These two functions accept a plaintext message as the parameter and output the CDF and PDF, respectively.

In decryption, DTE finds the plaintext message from the inverse_table by looking up the cumulative probability of the seed. The inverse_table is stored in a file. We define another function as get_inverse_table_file_name() in the message space interface. The function returns the filename of the inverse_table for DTE to look up and decrypt the ciphertext. If the inverse_table is not large, we can store the content in the memory when the system initiates. Then during decryption, the binary search method can be utilised to save time. However, if the inverse_table size exceeds the available system memory, DTE needs to read the inverse_table file line by line and find the plaintext by linear search.

4.2. DTE Implementation. DTE maps the plaintext message into a seed range, randomly selects a seed from the range, and XORs the seed with the key to output the ciphertext. The beginning of the seed range is determined by the CDF and the end of the seed range is determined by the PDF. The seed is randomly selected from the range.

When decrypting a ciphertext, the ciphertext is XORed with the key to obtain the seed. Then DTE determines the location of seed in the seed range. The location is corresponding to a probability value which lies between the CDF of the message and the CDF of the next message in the message space. Every line in the inverse_table contains a cumulative probability and its corresponding plaintext message. All lines are sorted by the cumulative probability. By searching the inverse_table, the DTE can find the plaintext message given the cumulative probability determined by the seed.

5. Applications

In this section, we apply the implemented honey encryption technique to private sensitive data including Chinese identification numbers, Chinese mobile phone numbers, and passwords. The code for DTE and the message space interface can be reused. However, the message space implementation should be customised and this is the focus of this section.

5.1. Identification Numbers. Identification numbers identify citizen's personal information and are widely used for authentication. Therefore they are used and stored by many commercial organisations. Stolen/leaked identification numbers can be misused by malicious users.

$$\underbrace{1\ 3\ 1\ 1\ 2\ 1}_{\text{Location}}\ \underbrace{1\ 9\ 7\ 5\ 0\ 4\ 1\ 0}_{\text{Birth date}}\ \underbrace{8\ 5\ 9}_{\text{Seq}}\ \underbrace{2}_{\text{Checksum}}$$

FIGURE 2: Identification number format.

The identification number consists of 18 digits, as shown in Figure 2. The first 6 digits are location symbols, identifying which suburb, city, and state in which persons were born. The 7th to 14th digits represent the birth date with the format of YYYYMMDD. For example, the birth date of a person born on 11th May 1985 will be presented as 19850511. The 15th to 17th is the sequence code. It uniquely identifies people in the same suburb who were born on the same day. Specifically, the 17th digit shows that the person is a male if it is odd. The 18th digit is the checksum. In this paper, we are not concerned with how exactly it is computed because it is deterministic. When generating the message space, we neglect this bit to simplify our implementation.

By gathering statistics, we found that China has 3519 location symbols. The 11th to 14th digits have 365 choices, as a year has 365 days. The sequence code has 999 choices, but in fact, this value rarely reaches 999. So the message space has $N = 3519 * Y * 365 * 999$ messages, where Y is the number of years considered. We assume each message has the same PDF of p, then $p = 1/N$. The user identification number in a commercial database should have a uniform distribution because a person has only one unique identification number and can only register in a database once (e.g., in the Taobao website, a large e-commerce company in China). Since we cannot obtain an identification number database from any business, we construct such a database with the assumption that each identification number has the same probability.

Therefore, the probability(mesg) function returns p for each message. We sort the message space incrementally. Then the CDF of a message depends on where the message is located in the message space. As every message has the PDF of p, the CDF of the message is i/N, where i is the message location in the message space. So when implementing the cumulative_probability(mesg) function, we first determine the location of the mesg, i, and then calculate the CDF.

In this implementation, we find that the size of the message space and the inverse_table file is much larger than the available memory space if we consider 100 years and 999 sequence code. To address this problem, we divide the identification number into four parts including location, year, month-day, seq, and checksum and store their possible values in different files. Therefore the identification number without the checksum can be viewed as a $L\_6Y\_4MD\_4S\_3$, where L_6 is a location code, Y_4 is a year, and MD_4 is a month and a day. We group a month and a day together because different months may have a different number of days.

In this way, we construct a message space considering all people in China who were born between 1917 and 2016 and that the sequence code lies between 1 and 200. DTE reads these four files into the memory and stores these values in four different lists. To encrypt a message, DTE joins the four parts to make an identification number and compares it to the message to be encrypted to determine the location of the message. Then the cumulative probability is calculated and the message is encrypted. For decryption, the system XORs the ciphertext with the key to obtain the seed. Then DTE calculates the probability, P_s, dividing the seed by the seed space size. Afterwards DTE begins to make identification numbers and their cumulative probabilities. By comparing P_s with those cumulative probabilities, DTE finally finds the original plaintext message.

Although we solve the memory problem by storing the identification numbers in different files, we find that the time to honey encrypt and decrypt a message in such a large message space is very high. In addition, if taking into account a nonuniformly distributed message space, it would be more complicated, since different messages have different PDFs and CDFs that cannot be calculated by determining the message location.

5.2. Mobile Numbers. Nowadays, mobile phone numbers are combined with the debit cards for financial transaction purposes and therefore mobile numbers should be well protected. The mobile phone number consists of 11 digits. The first 3 digits represent the operator code. There are three operators, China Mobile, China Unicom, and China Telecom in China. Each operator has been assigned a number of operator codes. The 4th to 7th digits are the location code of the mobile phone. The 8th to 11th digits are random. We implement the honey encryption technique for the Beijing Unicom numbers. For Beijing Unicom, the first 7 digits have 2872 choices, and the last 4 digits have 10^4 choices, so the message space consists of $N = 2872 * 10^4$ messages. Let us assume that each number has the same PDF of p, then the probability(mesg) function returns probability $p = 1/N$. Each mobile number in a commercial database is unique for a particular telecommunication company in China. So we assume a uniform distribution of these numbers. The cumulative_probability(mesg) function returns i/N, where i stands for the location of the message in the message space.

We define the MobileNumber class and implement the mentioned three functions for the message space interface. Given a mobile number, DTE outputs a random seed, which is XORed with the key to get the ciphertext. For a specific mobile number, using the system to encrypt it multiple times, the system outputs different ciphertexts due to the randomness in the seed generation process. When the ciphertext is XORed with the key, we can obtain the seed. Then the seed is used by DTE to get the correct plaintext of the mobile number.

5.3. Passwords. Passwords usually consist of uppercase and lowercase letters, digits, and symbols. Many users use weak passwords. For example, the debit card uses a 6-digit password for withdrawing money from the ATM machine. Honey encryption can help to protect such passwords from brute-force attacks. The 6-digit password space consists of $N = 10^6$ messages, ranging from 000000 to 999999. We sort the message space incrementally and assume each message has equal probability, so the probability(mesg) function returns PDF $= 1/N$. Different people may choose the same password

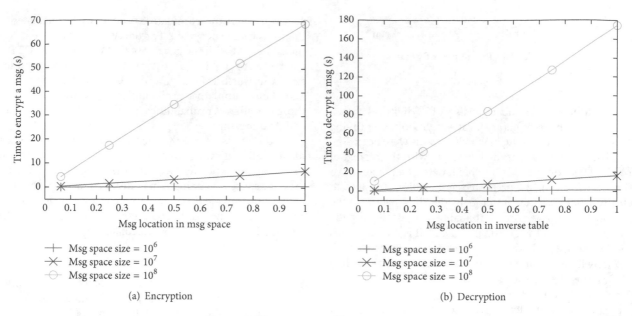

(a) Encryption

(b) Decryption

FIGURE 3: Time to encrypt/decrypt a message.

therefore the distribution may not be uniform. However, for simplicity, we assume uniformly distributed messages and therefore the cumulative_probability(mesg) function returns i/N. We will discuss nonuniformly distributed message spaces in Section 8.1.

We implement the password class by defining the three functions in the message space interface. When combined with DTE, the system can encrypt and decrypt correctly. Also when using a wrong key to decrypt a message, the system outputs a message that does not indicate that the key is not correct.

6. Evaluation

The platform for evaluating our honey encryption system is the Toshiba Portege-M800 laptop. The processor is Intel Core 2 Duo 2.0 Hz. The memory has a 3 GB RAM. The operating system is Ubuntu Kylin 16.04. The goal of experiments is to study the time taken to encrypt and decrypt a message. In order to make it easy to increase the size of the message space for multiple times, we choose the password message space for evaluation and increase the size from 10^6 to 10^8.

6.1. Time to Encrypt a Message. For encryption in a large message space, DTE should read the message space file line by line, calculate the PDF and CDF, determine the seed range, and randomly select a seed from the range. Finally, the chosen seed is XORed with the key to obtain the ciphertext.

We extend the message space size from 10^6 to 10^8 and conduct an evaluation. The time to encrypt a message is measured and displayed in Figure 3(a). The x-axis presents the message location in the message space. For example, 0.25 stands for the message that is located at 25% of the message space. The y-axis represents the time taken to

encrypt a message. It can be observed from the figure that the encryption time increases as the location of the message moves deeper. This is because the encryption algorithm reads the message space line by line until it finds the message to get the probabilities. The larger the message space, the more time it needs for encryption because the most time-consuming work in this encryption is reading and processing the message space. For the message space that contains 10^6 or 10^7 messages, the time is reasonable, but for a message space of 10^8 messages, the maximum time to encrypt a message can be as high as 70 s, which is too high.

6.2. Time to Decrypt a Message. During the decryption process, DTE first XORs the key with the ciphertext and obtains the seed. Then it determines the location of the seed in the seed space. Using the location information, it looks up the inverse_table and gets the corresponding plaintext message.

We measure the time to decrypt a message in three message spaces, ranging from 10^6 to 10^8, and display these statistics in Figure 3(b). The x-axis stands for the location of a plaintext message in the inverse_table, and the y-axis represents the time to decrypt the message. As shown from the figure, the decryption time increases as the plaintext message location in the inverse_table goes deeper. This is because the decryption algorithm reads line by line the inverse_table file until it finds the plaintext message. The larger the inverse_table, the slower the decryption process because the most time-consuming part in this decryption is to process the inverse_table file. When the inverse_table size is 10^6, the time to decrypt a message is acceptable, but when the inverse_table size is 10^8, the time can reach 160 s. Comparing Figures 3(a) and 3(b) it can be seen that the time to decrypt and encrypt a message is different because the message space file only contains a message in one line, but the inverse_table file contains a message and its cumulative probability for each line. Thus processing the latter takes more time.

7. Enhancement

For a large message space, the decryption algorithm needs to read the inverse_table file line by line and find the correct plaintext message using the calculated cumulative probability. For a small message space, we can read the whole inverse_table into the memory and use the binary search method to find the corresponding plaintext message in the decryption process.

For a large message space, the encryption algorithm needs to read the message space file and determine the message's PDF and CDF. But if the message space is incrementally sorted like the password message space, the value of the message, V, has a relationship with its location, A, in the message space; that is, $A = V + 1$. Also, the cumulative probability is related to the message location in the message space; that is, $CDF = A/N$, where N is the number of messages in the message space. Therefore, instead of searching the message space file for CDF, we can calculate the CDF. It should be noted that not all message spaces have such features. Taking the identification number, for example, the CDF of a message is not related to the value of the message itself.

We improve the encryption and decryption algorithm and evaluate their performance. Figure 4(a) shows the encryption time of the enhanced encryption algorithm. For 10^6 and 10^7 message spaces, no matter where the message is located, the encryption time is only around 136 microseconds. The lines for both 10^6 and 10^7 message spaces overlap. This means the encryption time is independent of the message space size.

Figure 4(b) shows the time taken for the enhanced decryption algorithm. No matter where the message is located in the message space, the decryption time is around 45 microseconds. The lines for both 10^6 and 10^7 message spaces overlap, which means the decryption time is independent of the message space size. This may be because the difference of the binary search algorithm in the 10^6 and 10^7 message spaces is not significant. We tried the 10^8 message spaces to verify this case, but the system fails due to memory error because the available memory is too small to hold the inverse_table file containing 10^8 messages.

8. Other Applications

We discussed honey encryption for identification numbers, mobile phone numbers, and debit card passwords in Section 5. In those applications, we assume the message space forms a uniform distribution. We also combine honey encryption with a simple symmetric encryption mechanism, XOR, for encryption and decryption. In this section we discuss the implementation of honey encryption with a nonuniformly distributed message space. We also extend honey encryption to an asymmetric encryption mechanism, RSA.

8.1. Application with Nonuniform Distribution. The coffee example in Section 3 has a nonuniform distribution. Let us consider applying honey encryption to a similar application but with a message space of 10^6 messages. We store the PDF of each message into a binary search tree and the CDF of each message into another. The probability(mesg) and cumulative_probability(mesg) functions calculate the corresponding probabilities by looking up these two trees. For decryption, another binary search tree is utilised to store the cumulative probability and plaintext message pairs. The time to encrypt and decrypt a message is shown in Figure 5. The encryption time is almost twice as the decryption time, because, for encryption, the system looks up two trees while, for decryption, it needs only one tree lookup. For the 50% location, the decryption and encryption time is almost 0. This is because the corresponding message is the root of the tree. The time increases from the center to two sides, because the message location goes deeper in the tree. This application shows that PDF and CDF probabilities can be stored in various data structures if the message space has a nonuniform distribution.

8.2. Application with Asymmetric Key Encryption. So far, we have combined a symmetric encryption mechanism, XOR, with the honey encryption technique to produce a ciphertext from a given seed. The symmetric key scheme assumes that the involved parties can store the symmetric key securely and the key is distributed to both parties by a secure channel. In this section, we extend the honey encryption mechanism to a public key encryption mechanism, RSA, to mitigate this limitation.

The encryption process can be easily integrated with RSA. The 1024-bit public and private keys are generated by the RSA algorithm. For encryption, the plaintext message is mapped to a seed by the DTE encode() process and then the seed is encrypted by an RSA public key to generate the ciphertext. For decryption, the RSA private key is used to decrypt the ciphertext to obtain the seed and then the seed goes through the DTE decode() process to obtain the plaintext message.

When decrypting with a wrong private key, RSA encounters an error instead of outputting a valid-looking seed. To solve this problem, the system captures the exception when a wrong decryption key is utilised and outputs a random seed from the seed range to confuse the attacker. If the decryption key is the correct private key, the system can call the RSA decryption function without any exception and obtain the right seed. The seed then is mapped to a cumulative probability corresponding to a plaintext message. We implemented the asymmetric key honey encryption mechanism for the debit card password application (enhanced version) with a message space size of 10^6.

We evaluate the performance of honey encryption with the RSA extension, as shown in Figure 6. It is observed from Figure 6 that the encryption time for RSA is four times higher than the symmetric key encryption mechanism and the difference is more significant for the decryption time. For the symmetric key encryption mechanism, the decryption time is only 46 microseconds. However, it is around 0.045 s for RSA. As RSA is computationally expensive, honey encryption based on RSA inherits this drawback.

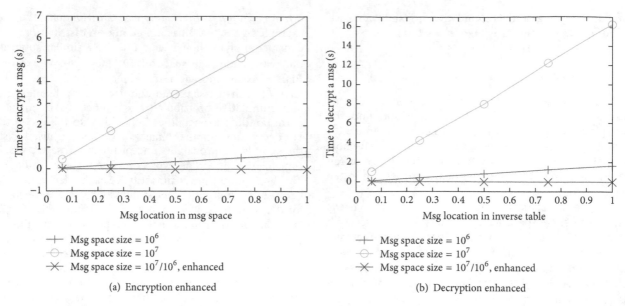

(a) Encryption enhanced

(b) Decryption enhanced

FIGURE 4: Time to encrypt/decrypt a message.

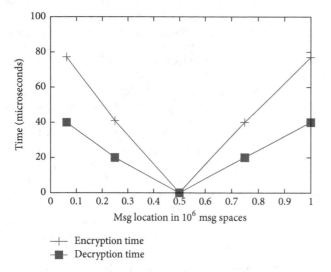

FIGURE 5: Performance in application with a nonuniform distributed message space.

9. Lesson Learned

In our research on honey encryption, we find that it is an effective countermeasure for brute-force attacks. However, we also discover the following limitations.

(1) Honey encryption is suitable for a small, not large, message space as the overhead of processing a large message space is very high. In this mechanism, DTE needs to read the message space and inverse_table file line by line for encryption and decryption if the message space is larger than the available system memory. Having these files in the memory will speed up the search (e.g., by using the binary search method) for decryption. Therefore, we claim that honey encryption is suitable for encryption/decryption with a small message space; otherwise, the encryption/decryption systems should have advanced hardware configurations.

(2) The message space should be carefully designed, or honey encryption cannot well address the brute-force vulnerability. Although a plaintext derived by DTE from a wrongly guessed key looks like a correctly decrypted ciphertext, attackers can use other methodologies to confirm whether the guessed key is incorrect if the message space has not been carefully designed. In the mobile phone number case, the attacker can dial the mobile number to check whether the number is a correct one. For the identification database in a women's hospital, the deciphered identification number should not belong to a man. Identification numbers that belong to 0-to-4-year-old babies should be less likely in a database in an e-commerce company. In a middle school, most students should not be less than 12 years old and older than 19 years old. As the decryption process outputs a message from the message space, this message should not have any fingerprint that could be used by attackers to identify the correctness of the message.

(3) The capability of protecting sensitive private data provided by honey encryption varies for different applications. The decryption process outputs a message from the message space, no matter whether the key is correct or not. This feature could leak some valid messages and this may have different impact on different applications. Taking the identification number, for example, a malicious user can still get some valid identification numbers from the system, but the attacker may not be able to get the corresponding name of the identification holder. So the possibility for the attacker to maliciously use the identification to commit crimes is limited. For text message spammers, the leakage of mobile phone numbers is enough for sending spam. For the debit card passwords, no matter what message DTE outputs, it is useless as the message is a meaningless number. Therefore, the value of honey encryption may vary for different applications.

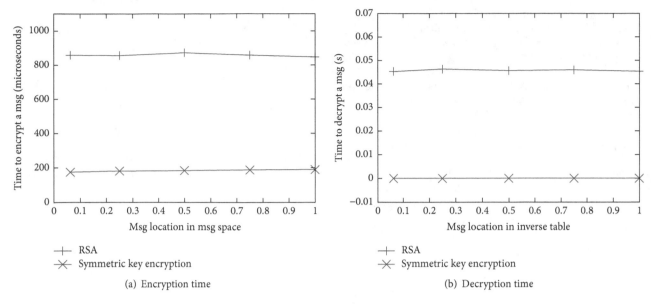

FIGURE 6: Time to encrypt/decrypt a message.

(4) The implementation of honey encryption must be customised for different applications as the message space varies. To apply honey encryption to a specific application, it requires the developer to design/customise the message space and inverse_table.

10. Conclusion

Private data should be well protected to avoid loss due to leakage and misuse. The existing password-based encryption (PBE) methods used to protect private data are vulnerable in face of brute-force attacks, as the attacker can determine whether the guessed key is correct or not by looking at the output of the decryption process. The honey encryption technique is a countermeasure for such a vulnerability. In this paper, we discussed the honey encryption concept and we also designed and implemented a honey encryption mechanism for Chinese identification numbers, mobile phone numbers, and debit card passwords. Applications with uniformly or nonuniformly distributed message spaces and with symmetric or asymmetric key encryption mechanisms are designed and implemented. The performance of our honey encryption mechanism was evaluated and an enhancement was proposed to address the overhead issue.

Finally, we discussed the lessons learned from our experience of designing, implementing, and evaluating the honey encryption mechanism. Specifically, we have the following observations. (1) Honey encryption is suitable for a small, not large, message space as the overhead of processing a large message space is very high. (2) The message space should be carefully designed for each application, or honey encryption may not properly address the brute-force vulnerability. (3) The capability of protecting sensitive private data provided by honey encryption varies for different applications. (4) The implementation of honey encryption must be customised for different applications as the message spaces vary.

Acknowledgments

The work is partially supported by the NSFC project 61702542 and the China Postdoctoral Science Foundation project 2016M603017.

References

[1] Z. Huang, E. Ayday, J. Fellay, J.-P. Hubaux, and A. Juels, "Geno-Guard: Protecting genomic data against brute-force attacks," in *Proceedings of the 36th IEEE Symposium on Security and Privacy (SP '15)*, pp. 447–462, Washington, DC, USA, May 2015.

[2] A. Juels and T. Ristenpart, "Honey encryption: security beyond the brute-force bound," in *Advances in Cryptology-EURO-CRYPT 2014*, pp. 293–310, 2014.

[3] P. Owezarski, "A near real-time algorithm for autonomous identification and characterization of honeypot attacks," in *Proceedings of the 10th ACM Symposium on Information, Computer and Communications Security, ASIACCS 2015*, pp. 531–542, Singapore, April 2015.

[4] A. Juels and R. L. Rivest, "Honeywords: making password-cracking detectable," in *Proceedings of the ACM SIGSAC Conference on Computer and Communications Security (CCS '13)*, pp. 145–160, ACM, November 2013.

[5] N. Tyagi, J. Wang, K. Wen, and D. Zuo, "Honey encryption applications," in *Computer and Network Security*, pp. 1–16, 2015.

[6] L. Spitzner, *Honeytokens: The Other Honeypot*, 2003.

[7] I. S. Kim and M. H. Kim, "Agent-based honeynet framework for protecting servers in campus networks," *IET Information Security*, vol. 6, no. 3, pp. 202–211, 2012.

[8] P. Jain and A. Sardana, "Defending against internet worms using honeyfarm," in *Proceedings of the International Information Technology Conference (CUBE '12)*, pp. 795–800, Pune, India, September 2012.

[9] B. Mihir, T. Ristenart, P. Rogaway, and T. Stegers, "Format-preserving encryption," in *Selected Area in Cryptography*, pp. 295–312, 2009.

[10] K. P. Dyer, S. E. Coull, T. Ristenpart, and T. Shrimpton, "Protocol misidentification made easy with format-transforming encryption," in *Proceedings of the ACM SIGSAC Conference on Computer and Communications Security*, pp. 61–72, ACM, November 2013.

[11] P. P. Vinayak and M. A. Nahala, "Avoiding brute force attack in manet using honey encryption," *International Journal of Science and Research*, vol. 4, no. 3, pp. 83–85, 2015.

[12] J. W. Yoon, H. Kim, H.-J. Jo, H. Lee, and K. Lee, "Visual honey encryption: application to steganography," in *Proceedings of the 3rd ACM Information Hiding and Multimedia Security Workshop*, pp. 65–74, ACM, Portland, Ore, USA, June 2015.

[13] J. Jaeger, T. Ristenpart, and Q. Tang, "Honey encryption beyond message recovery security," in *Advances in Cryptology–EUROCRYPT 2016*, pp. 758–788, 2016.

14

A New Method to Analyze the Security of Protocol Implementations Based on Ideal Trace

Fusheng Wu,[1] **Huanguo Zhang,**[1] **Wengqing Wang,**[2] **Jianwei Jia,**[2] **and Shi Yuan**[2]

[1]*Computer School of Wuhan University, Wuhan 430072, China*
[2]*Key Laboratory of Aerospace Information Security and Trusted Computing of Ministry of Education, Wuhan University, Wuhan 430072, China*

Correspondence should be addressed to Huanguo Zhang; liss@whu.edu.cn

Academic Editor: Jiankun Hu

The security analysis of protocols on theory level cannot guarantee the security of protocol implementations. To solve this problem, researchers have done a lot, and many achievements have been reached in this field, such as model extraction and code generation. However, the existing methods do not take the security of protocol implementations into account. In this paper, we have proposed to exploit the traces of function return values to analyze the security of protocol implementations at the source code level. Taking classic protocols into consideration, for example (like the Needham-Schroeder protocol and the Diffie-Hellman protocol, which cannot resist man-in-the-middle attacks), we have analyzed man-in-the-middle attacks during the protocol implementations and have carried out experiments. It has been shown in the experiments that our new method works well. Different from other methods of analyzing the security of protocol implementations in the literatures, our new method can avoid some flaws of program languages (like C language memory access, pointer analysis, etc.) and dynamically analyze the security of protocol implementations.

1. Introduction

With the fast development of the network communication, information security is becoming more and more important [1, 2]. To protect the network information from attacks, protocols are usually applied. However, general methods (e.g., formal method, computational model, and computational soundness formal) cannot guarantee the security of protocols during the process of their implementations. That is, even if protocols have been theoretically proved to be secure, some insecure factors (like the language characteristics of protocols' source codes, the operating environments of the protocol implementations) arise when implementing them at the source code level. Therefore, researchers focus on the security analysis of protocol implementations at the source code level [3].

During implementing at the source code level, it is difficult to guarantee the security of protocol specifications due to language characteristics (such as C language memory access, pointer analysis, etc.). Hence, it is more complex to analyze the security of protocol implementations at the source code

level compared to that of protocols on the theoretical level. To avoid these insecure factors that languages bring, some methods have been proposed to analyze the security of protocol implementations at the source code level. Among them are two representatives: model extraction and code generation. Model extraction is applied to avoid the problem of concrete state space explosion. During the extracting process, an abstract mapping is set up to map a concrete protocol model onto a corresponding abstract model and its properties onto corresponding abstract properties. If the security properties of the protocols on the abstract model have been proved to be sound and the abstract mapping has been proved to be reliable, then the security properties on the concrete model are proved. It guarantees the security of the protocol implementation and provides its reliability's demonstration. Related research achievements include [4–7]. Sometimes leaks arise in the process of protocol implementations due to the design imperfection, which leads protocol implementations to be insecure (such as the SSL protocol, the TLS protocol). To avoid these cases, code generation is applied. That is, protocol specifications are analyzed before

FIGURE 1: The security analysis process of protocol implementations.

implementations. After that, refined mapping and some related running choices (like concrete program languages or running environments) are applied to map a program abstract model onto a corresponding concrete model and its abstract properties onto corresponding concrete properties. If the security properties of the protocol on the abstract model have been proved to be sound and the mapping has been proved to be reliable, the properties on the concrete model are proved. Related research achievements include [8–10]. Now model extraction and code generation have been widely applied to protocol security analysis. However, neither model extraction nor code generation can guarantee the security of protocol implementations due to program language flaws, which causes the gap between the protocol security analysis on theoretical level and the security analysis of the protocol implementations at the source code level [11, 12].

The thought of our new method to analyze the security of protocol implementations at the source code level derives from a daily life phenomenon. When an object moves from A to B in an environment without any barriers (called the ideal environment), a trace will be produced by the object, which is called the ideal trace. In nonideal environments, the object will be attacked by a third party, and its trace (called nonideal trace) will deviate from the ideal trace (the detailed definitions of ideal trace and nonideal trace are given in Section 5). If the moving behavior is rectified after the object is attacked, the degree of deviation of its nonideal trace from the ideal trace will become smaller. Based on the thought above, we propose a new method to analyze the security of protocol implementations by means of the traces. The traces consist of the sets of function return values when implementing a protocol. Our new method is carried out like this: we exploit the ideal trace and the method of cluster analysis (including the degree of deviation and the similarity of the trace sequences) as the evaluated reference to analyze protocol security. To prove our new method, with strong simulation of π-calculus we refine the source codes of the Needham-Schroder protocol as an example and set up the security analysis model of protocol implementations with labelled transition systems [13]. Besides, taking the Needham-Schroder protocol and the Diffie-Hellman protocol, for example, we verify man-in-the-middle attacks on OpenSSL with our new method. To describe the specific steps of the security analysis in detail, a flow graph is drawn in Figure 1.

Our original contributions are as follows:

(1) We bring in the ideal trace as the evaluated reference of the security analysis of protocol implementations at the source code level and setting up a bijection of the mapping of events onto traces.

(2) We propose a method for analyzing the security of protocol implementations by comparing the similarity

and the deviation between nonideal traces and the ideal trace during implementing protocols at the source code level.

The remaining work of our article is as follows: a summary of related works in Section 2; the preliminaries in Section 3; building a new model in Section 4; the security analysis of protocols in Section 5; taking classical protocol implementations, for example, and doing experiments in Section 6; conclusion and future work in Section 7.

2. Related Work

It is practical and valuable to analyze the security of protocol implementations at the source code level. In recent years, researchers focus on this field and here we can find great achievements [14].

The security analysis of protocol implementations at the source code level is very complex and different from common protocol security analysis [15], for it must take program language structure and running environment into account, which adds difficulty to the security analysis of protocol implementations. To solve this problem, literature [4] has done some researches, analyzing the security of implementing the Needham-Schroeder protocol written in C language. In literature [4], C language annotations act as trust assertions, and a trust assertion model is established for protocol security analysis by means of Horn Logic. Some researchers have used some function libraries and intermediate languages, like C language, to automatically analyze the security of protocol implementations. This method has avoided the problems that C language structure brings about (like pointer operation, buffer overflow, etc.). The related literatures are [5–7, 16, 17]. Similarly, some researchers have applied the latest techniques or tools to the security analysis of protocol implementations at the source code level, which is a new direction in this field. For example, based on VCC, C language application program interface (API) has been applied to the analysis security of protocol implementations at the source code level. Literature [18] has proposed a general method for protocol security analysis, which has distinguished two different items mapped onto the same array. In literature [19], a general verifying method has been applied to practical TPM and HSMs platforms. Literature [20] has exploited interface constraint and program logic reasoning to analyze the security of protocol implementations at the source code level. To reduce the difficulty brought about by C language structure when analyzing the security of protocol implementations, researchers have exploited C language complier to analyze the security of protocol implementation. The examples are [21, 22].

Transport Layer Security (TLS) has been widely put into practice so it is a focus to analyze the security of protocol implementations on the base of TLS. For example, literature [23] has proposed that the OpenSSL crypto library can be applied to the security analysis of implementing TLS in the C language environment. Another example is literature [24], which has proposed to analyze the security of protocols on base of the control-flow integrity of the message authentication codes (MACs). This method has taken it into account that an adversary attack protocols by means of C/C++ pointer and memory leaks during the process of protocol implementations.

The methods mentioned above have promoted the research of the security analysis of protocol implementations. However, they cannot settle the security problems that are caused by the inherent flaws of program language structures. Compared with them, our new method can avoid the flaws of program language structure and dynamically analyze the security of protocol implementations at the source code level. Hence, it is helpful and valuable for protocol design, security verification, and security evaluation [25].

3. Preliminaries

For better understanding of our new method, it is necessary to have a basic knowledge of labelled transition system, strong simulation, program refinement, and so on.

3.1. Labelled Transition System and Strong Simulation. According to the automata theory, a labelled transition system is a system transferring model which consists of start point, input label, and terminal point. But a labelled transition system has no fixed start states and accepting states, which is different from automata. Therefore, any state in a labelled transition system can act as a start state. Therefore, a labelled transition system has an advantage over other systems when dynamically analyzing the security of protocol implementations at the source code level.

Definition 1 (labelled transition system [13]). A labelled transition system (LTS) over Act is a pair (Q, T) consisting of

(1) a set Q of states;

(2) a ternary relation $T \subseteq (Q \times \text{Act} \times Q)$, known as a transition relation.

If $(q, \alpha, q') \in T$, we write $q \xrightarrow{\alpha} q'$, and we call q the source and q' the target of the transition. If $q \xrightarrow{\alpha_1} q_1 \xrightarrow{\alpha_2} \cdots \xrightarrow{\alpha_n} q_n$, then we call q_n a derivate of q under $\alpha_1 \alpha_2 \cdots \alpha_n$.

Definition 2 (strong simulation [13]). Let (Q, T) be an LTS, and let S be a binary relation over Q. Then S is called a strong simulation over (Q, T); if, whenever pSq, $p \xrightarrow{\alpha} p'$ then there exists $q' \in Q$ such that $q \xrightarrow{\alpha} q'$ and $p'Sq'$.

We say that q strongly simulates p if there exists a strong simulation S such that pSq.

Definition 3 (extended strong simulation). Let (Q, T) be an LTS and (Q', T') be an LTS and S be a binary relation over $Q \times Q'$, and let $p, q \in Q$. If pSq satisfies

(1) $Q \subseteq Q', T \subseteq T'$,

(2) $p', q' \in Q'$ and $\alpha = \alpha', \alpha' \in Q'$, and if $p \xrightarrow{\alpha} p'$, then there exists q' such that $q \xrightarrow{\alpha} q'$ and $p'Sq'$. Then S is called an extended strong simulation over a 4-tuple (Q, Q', T, T').

3.2. Program Refinement. When implementing a protocol, it is very difficult to verify its properties in concrete program state space (called the state-explosion problem [26]). Program refinement is exploited to solve this problem. Program refinement, which simplifies two programs with refined relation, is an important technique of verifying programs and is useful to reduce program state space.

Definition 4 (program refinement). Let p be a concrete program, and then there exists p', a refined program of p. That is, the process from p to p' is recursive. The behaviors produced by program p' belong to the subset of the behaviors produced by program p. Therefore, p' will never produce the behaviors that p cannot produce, and wherever a program p is applied, p' can be used to replace it. Hence, p' is called a refined program of p.

According to Definition 4, many program verification problems can be reduced to refined verification. For example, the verification of a program or an algorithm is always reduced to the refined relation between programs and protocol specifications. Similarly, there exists refined relation between a protocol implementation and its specifications. To reduce refined relation and refine source codes, we design a refining algorithm of protocol implementations, shown in Algorithm 1.

The complexity analysis of the algorithm consists of two circulations. One circulation achieves the goal of choosing functions. The other labels the functions which satisfy the condition, and refines source codes. Assuming there exists N functions in the source codes, among these functions, M functions can satisfy protocol specifications ($M \leq N$). The worst case is $M = N$. Hence, the complexity of the algorithm is $O(2N) \approx O(N)$, which is polynomial time. The algorithm can be achieved.

3.3. The Program Refinement of Protocol Source Codes. In most cases, the program source codes consist of functions, such as C language source codes, Java language source codes, and F# language source codes. According to the rules of C language program execution, when implementing a protocol, called function return values, the function behaviors are decided, and the sets of called function return values decide the behavior traces of protocol interactive communications. Therefore, if the functions of source codes are refined, the difficulty of the state-explosion problem will be reduced and the security properties of the protocol will not change after refinement. Hence, we can refine a protocol to analyze its security if the refinement relation of source codes exists.

Proposition 5. *If the nonfunction part is removed from program source codes, the newly produced program source codes are the refinement of the previous program source codes.*

Step 1. IniStack(S); // *initiate a stack. Here, S represents stack.*
Step 2. Input file.c; // *input a file (protocol source codes)*
Step 3. While (judge whether the file of protocol source codes is finished)
    {if (judge whether functions are true) Push(S, f); /*functions push into the*
       stack. Here, f represents file. c./
      Continue to seek the functions of protocol source codes.
    } //*while*
Step 4. While (! StackEmpty(S)) // *judge whether the stack is empty.*
    { GetTop(S, f); // *pop the functions which are on the top of the stack.*
    if (the top functions of the stack satisfy protocol specifications) /*the functions*
      can reflect the code execution of protocol interactive communication, such as
      *send ( ) and recv ( ) of socket API. */
      {identify and reserve the functions;}
    Else {delete the functions;}
    } //*while*

ALGORITHM 1: The protocol source code refinement algorithm (written in C pseudocode).

Proof. Assume that the program running is a LTS. That is, let the LTS of the previous program source codes be (Q, T), and let the LTS of the program source codes obtained after removing the nonfunction part be (Q', T'). Let S be a binary relation over $Q \times Q'$. And there exist $Q' \subseteq Q$, $q, q' \in Q$, and $p, p' \in Q'$. Here α and α', respectively, are the input labels of two program source codes, and $\alpha = \alpha'$ (called α in the following). According to Definition 1, there exist $p \xrightarrow{\alpha} p' \in T$ and $q \xrightarrow{\alpha} q' \in T'$, as well as qSp and $q'Sp'$. According to Definition 3, the behaviors generated by LTS (Q', T') are the subset of LTS (Q, T), and (Q', T') will never produce any behaviors that (Q, T) cannot produce. That is, wherever (Q, T) is applied, it can be replaced by (Q', T'). Hence, the proposition is proved. □

4. Establishing the Model

There are always some faults in a protocol due to its imperfect design. These faults make the protocol vulnerable to malicious third-party attacks. For example, the Needham-Schroeder protocol and the Diffie-Hellman protocol cannot resist man-in-the-middle attacks. To avoid these malicious attacks, it is necessary to analyze the security of a protocol on theory level before its implementations (such as formal, computational model, the computationally sound formal). However, a protocol is not secure when implementing it at the source code level, although it has been proved to be secure on theory level. That is, it is essential to analyze the security of protocol implementations at the source code level.

In this paper, a method is proposed by us to analyze the security of protocol implementations at the source code level written in C. Our method establishes models in the following steps: ① describe a protocol symbolically; ② acquire the program source codes of the protocol; ③ refine these source codes; ④ draw the control-flow graph and the state diagram of the protocol; ⑤ establish the model of the traces of the protocol implementations. We take the classic Needham-Schroeder protocol, for example, to show how to establish a model with our new method.

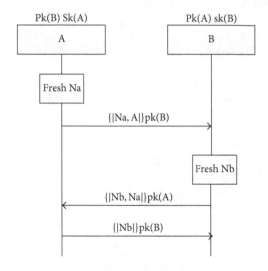

FIGURE 2: The Needham-Schroeder protocol.

4.1. The Protocol Symbolic Description. It is a basic requirement of protocol communications that at least two participants participate in an interactive communication in accordance with certain specifications. Generally, Message Sequence Charts (MSC) of protocol interactive communications are expressed by an ITU-standardized protocol specification language (ITU: International Telecommunication Union) [27] (in this paper, protocol specifications are expressed by the approaches from ITU and literature [28]). The symbolic description of the Needham-Schroeder protocol specifications is shown in Figure 2.

In Figure 2 A and B, respectively, denote two participants of a protocol; pk(A) and pk(B), respectively, denote the public keys of the participants; sk(A) and sk(B), respectively, denote the private keys of the participants; Fresh Na and Fresh Nb, respectively, denote temporary values of A and B; and ${|Na, A|}_{pk(B)}$ denotes the encryption of information ${|Na, A|}$ with the public keys of B.

4.2. The Refinement of Source Codes. Taking the Needham-Schroeder source codes written in C, for example, we illustrate the refinement of source codes with Algorithm 1 and then analyze the security of protocol implementations at the source code level. When writing protocol codes, we exploit the mechanism of RAS public key cryptography for encryption and decryption, and the functions of the OpenSSL crypto library are used while encrypting and decrypting. The protocol runs over OpenSSL. Due to the limited length of this paper, only main source codes are shown in Algorithm 2.

As is shown in Algorithm 2, the source codes of the Needham-Schroeder protocol include many redundant ones. According to Proposition 5 and Algorithm 1, the security analysis of protocol implementations will not be influenced if those redundant codes are deleted. After deletion, the left source codes of the Needham-Schroeder protocol are mainly function codes (shown in Algorithm 3). According to Definition 4, the source codes in Algorithm 3 are the refinement of the source codes in Algorithm 2. In the example of the Needham-Schroeder protocol implementations, the behaviors produced by the source codes in Algorithm 3 are the subset in those produced by the source codes in Algorithm 2. Therefore, we can exploit the traces of function return values produced by the source codes in Algorithm 3 to dynamically analyze the security of the Needham-Schroeder protocol implementations at the source code level.

According to Definition 4 and Proposition 5, the security analysis of protocol implementations after refinement is consistent with that before refinement.

4.3. Program Control-Flow Graph. To clearly see the traces of the function return values generated during the protocol implementations, taking the source codes gained after the refinement (in Algorithm 3), for example, we draw a program control-flow graph to show the process of calling functions after the refinement, shown in Figure 3.

In Figure 3, ➜ denotes the control-flow direction of program main functions; "→" denotes the control-flow direction of calling functions; and "←--" denotes the control-flow direction of function returning.

As is shown in the program control-flow graph, there are only two types of function return values: ① deterministic return values (like numerical values, alphabets, symbols, etc.); ② nondeterministic return values (such as calling functions directly or indirectly). When function return values are not deterministic, functions will continue to call other functions until the function return values become deterministic.

4.4. From the Control-Flow Graph to the State Graph. From Figure 3, we can clearly see the traces of the protocol implementations at the source code level and the state of how functions are called. According to C language grammar and program executive rules, in the normal process of program implementations every called function has a return value (deterministic or nondeterministic) and the implementation of every function is related to its return value. When a function receives its return value, the program will execute next step in order. Every function can be regarded as a state node, and function return values can be regarded as input labels. In this case, the program control-flow graph is just like an automata state graph. As mentioned above, function return values are clarified into deterministic values (like numbers, symbols, character strings, etc.) and nondeterministic values (such as functions). Here, we use {identify} to denote a deterministic value set and {unidentify} to denote a nondeterministic value set. Then after refinement, the control-flow graph of source codes is transferred into the state graph of a LTS, whose input label is {identify, unidentify}*. A LTS has no initial state and receiving state. It only has starting point and terminal point, and any state can be regarded as its starting state. Hence, let function Gene_Rand( ) be the starting point of a LTS and let Send( ) function be its terminal point. The state graph of the Needham-Schroeder protocol is obtained after refinement, shown in Figure 4.

In Figure 4 "S" denotes a state, and its subscript denotes the state of its corresponding function point. For example, S_{My} denotes the state of memcpy( ) function. If a called function does not call other functions any more, its return value is deterministic, and {identify} is written to denote its input label. If a called function continues to call other functions, then its return value is nondeterministic, and {unidentify} is written to denote its input label. Here, "unidentify = identify|unidentify" can be used to denote the constitution of nondeterministic input labels. Its final return value is deterministic {identify}. For example, the return value of the state S_{GR} is not deterministic at first, for it calls other functions, like BN_new( ) function. Then, the input label of the state S_{GR} is {unidentify}.

4.5. The Traces of Protocol Implementations. As is shown in Section 4.4, a LTS can be established on the base of the function return values in the program control-flow graph. A LTS is denoted by a 4-tuple $(S, L, \rightarrow, S_0)$. We define the LTS of protocol implementations as follows:

(1) S denotes a function node state set; S_0 denotes the starting point state of the LTS; and S_e denotes the terminal point state of the LTS.

(2) S_i denotes other functions, and there exists $S_i \in S$. $S_i \xrightarrow{\alpha} S_{i+1}$ denotes the transition relation between any two adjacent states S_i, S_{i+1}. α denotes an input label. Let $\alpha = \{identify|unidentify\}^*$. If α is unidentify, there exists a substitute function σ, and $\sigma(\alpha) = \{identify\}$. Then final function return value is deterministic.

According to the LTS of protocol implementations, after protocol implementations there exist the traces of function return values: traces = $\{identify_1, identify_2, \ldots, identify_n\}$ $n \in N$. Then the security of protocol implementations at the source code level can be dynamically analyzed on the base of these traces.

5. The Security Analysis of Protocol Implementations

Functions are an important part of the source codes of a program design language, especially C language. If the

```
1int main(int,argc,char argv[ ])
2{
3WSADATA wsaData;
4SCOKET client;
5RSA *R;
6serv.sin_family=AF_INET;
7serv.sin_port=htons(port);
8serv.sin_addr.S_un.S_addr=inet_addr("127.0.0.1");
9client=socket(AF_INET,SOCK_STREAM,0);
10connect(client,(struct sockaddr*)&serv,sizeof
(serv));
11Gene_Rand( );
12Comp_Str( );
13memcpy(plaitxt_A_E,Str_Id,1024);
14public_Encrypt(plaitxt_A_E);
15strcpy(Cipher_buf,(const char*)cipher);
16iSend=send(client,Cipher,sizeof(Cipher),0);
17iLen=recv(client,(char *)cipher,sizeof(cipher),0);
18memcpy(Tcipher_Na_Nb,cipher_Na_Nb,1024);
19Private_Dencrypt_Na_Nb(R,Tciper_Na_Nb);
20memcpy(plaitxt_Nb,StrNb,1024);
21Public_Encrypt_Nb(plaitxt_Nb);
22strcpy(Cipher,(const char*)cipher);
23iSend=send(client,Cipher,sizeof(Cipher),0);
 24}
25int Gene_Rand( )
26{
27BIGNUM *n;
28int ret,bits=128;
29char *sn;
30n=BN_new( );
31ret=BN_pseudo_rand(n,bits,1,1);
32sn=BN_bn2dec(n);
33strcpy(RandNum,sn);
34return 0;
 35}
36int Com_Str( )
37{
38strcat(Str_Id,RandNum);
39strcat(Str_Id,"|A");
40return 0;
 41}
42int Public_Encrypt(unsigned char*s)
43{
44RSA *r;
45int ret,flent,len;
46BIGNUM *bnn,*bne;
47bnn=BN_new( );
48bne=BN_new( );
49ret=BN_dec2bn(&bnn,strn);
50ret=BN_dec2bn(&bnn,stre);
51r=RSA_new( );
52r->n=bnn;
53r->e=bne;
54flen=RSA_size(r);
55len=RSA_public_encrypt(flen,s,cipher_A_E,r,3);
56return 0;
 57}
58int Private_Dencrypt_Na_Nb(RSA *r,unsigned char*s)
59{
60int len,flen;
```

ALGORITHM 2: Continued.

```
61flen=RSA_size(r);
62len=RSA_private_decrypt(flen,s,plaitxt_Na_Nb, r,3);
63return 0;
64}
65int StrDivNb(char str[ ])
66{
67int k=0,i=0,j=0;
68int strlen=0;
69int Publi_Encrypt_Nb(usigned char*s)
70{
71RSA *r;
72int ret,flen,len;
73BIGNUM *bnn,*bne;
74bnn=BN_new( );
75bne=BN_new( );
76ret=BN_dec2bn(&bnn,strn);
77ret=BN_dec2bn(&bne,strn);
78r=RSA_new( );
79r->n=bnn;
80r->e=bne;
81flen=RSA_size(r);
82len=RSA_public_encrypt(flen,s,cipher_Nb,r,3);
83return 0;
84}
```

ALGORITHM 2: The part source codes of the Needham-Schroeder protocol.

behaviors of called program functions are regarded as the events of a protocol implementation, function return values can act as the conditions for running an event during the process of protocol implementations. In this paper, operational semantics are exploited to analyze the behaviors' security of protocol implementations at the source code level.

5.1. The Operational Semantics of Function Return Values. Operational semantics clearly display the traces of function return values of a protocol implementation. That is, they display concrete behaviors of protocol implementations. Therefore, operational semantics have an advantage over other methods and are competent to analyze the security of protocol implementations.

(1) The function return values of protocol implementations is as follows.

$F = P(\text{RunFunc}) \times P(\text{Run}) \times \text{ReturnValue}$. Here $P(\text{RunFunc})$ denotes the functions of a protocol, $P(\text{Run})$ denotes running it, and ReturnValue denotes its function return values.

(2) The BNF forms of function return values (Return-Value) during protocol implementations are as follows:

ReturnValue ::= Identity|Unidentify

Unidentify ::= Function|Identify

Function ::= Self_Func|Libr_Func

Self_Func ::= Function|Identify

Libr_Func ::= Function|Identify

Identify ::= number|alphabet|string

Here, Self_Func denotes self-defined functions and Libr_Func denotes library functions. Every function has a return value (deterministic or nondeterministic). Every function return value is an element of a trace (ReturnValue ∈ Traces). After a protocol is implemented, all the function return values constitute its traces. Here is the definition of the BNF form of the traces:

Traces ::= number|alphabet|symbol

According to the relation between called function events of C language and return values, every called function has a return value, including void values. Then there exists the bijection M between called function events and return values: CallEvent|→ReturnValue. According to the traces obtained after the protocol implementations, ∀ReturnValue ∈ Trace is true. Therefore, there exists the bijection: {e|→ t,| ∀e ∈ CallEvent, ∀t ∈ Trace}. That is, every event corresponds to an element of the traces of protocol implementations.

Definition 6 (event trace). Let every event ε of protocol implementations correspond to a function return value v. There exists a set t, which consists of all the function return values. The set t denotes an event trace.

Once the bijection between called function events of protocol implementations and function return values is set up, there exists the bijection between the event set and the elements of the traces: Trace = {t | ∀e |→ ∀v ∈ t}. If the event is not secure, its trace is not secure either, which will inevitably lead to the insecurity of the protocol implementations.

```
1int main(int argc,char argc[ ])
2{
3connect(client,(struct sockaddr *)&serv,sizeof(serv));
4Gene_Rand( );
5Comp_Str( );
6memcpy(plaitxt_A_E,Str_Id,1024);
7Public_Encrypt(plaitxt_A_E);
8strcpy(Cipher_buf,(const char *)cipher);
9iSend=send(client,Cipher,sizeof(cipher),0);
10iLen=recv(client,(char *)cipher,sizeof(cipher),0);
11memcpy(Tcipher_Na_Nb,cipher_Na_Nb,1024);
12Private_Dencrypt_Na_Nb(R,Tcipher_Na_Nb);
13memcpy(plaitxt_Nb,StrNb,1024);
14Public_Encrypt_Nb(plaitxt_Nb);
15strcpy(Cipher,(const char *)cipher);
16iSend=send(client,Cipher,sizeof(Cipher),0);
17}
18int Gene_Rand( )
19{
20n=BN_new( );
21ret=BN_pseudo_rand(n,bits,1,1);
22sn=BN_bn2dec(n);
23strcpy(RandNum,sn);
24}
25int Comp_Str( );
26{
27strcat(Str_Id,RandNum);
28strcat(Str_Id,"|A");
29}
30int Public_Encrypt(unsigned char *s)
31{
32bnn=BN_new( );
33bne=BN_new( );
34ret=BN_dec2bn(&bnn,strn);
35ret=BN_dec2bn(&bne,stre);
36r=RSA_new( );
37flen=RSA_size(r);
38len=RSA_public_encrypt(flen,s,cipher_A_E,r,3);
39}
40int Private_Dencrypt_Na_Nb(RSA *r,unsigned char *s);
41{
42flen=RSA_size(r);
43len=RSA_private_decrypt(flen,s,plaitext_Na_Nb, r,3);
44}
45int Public_Encrypt_Nb(unsigned char *s)
46{
47bnn=BN_new( );
48bne=BN_new( );
49ret=BN_dec2bn(&bnn,strn);
50ret=BN_dec2bn(&bne,stre);
51r=RSA_new( );
52flen=RSA_size(r);
53len=RSA_public_encrypt(flen,s,cipher_Nb,r,3);
54}
```

ALGORITHM 3: The refined part source codes of the Needham-Schroeder protocol.

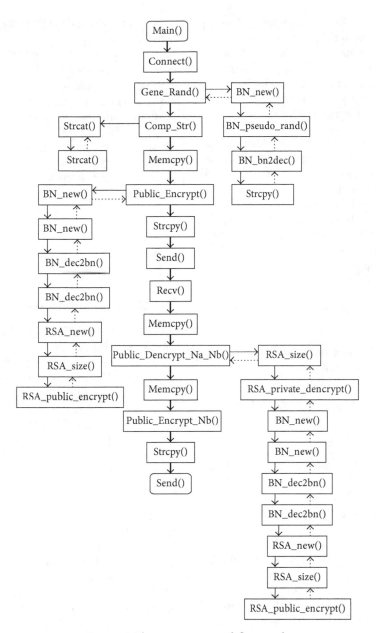

FIGURE 3: The program control-flow graph.

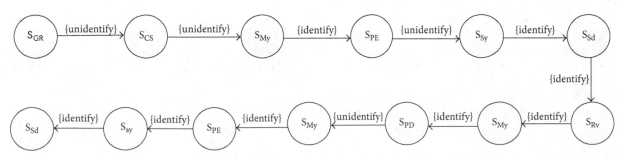

FIGURE 4: The LTS of part source codes.

5.2. *Ideal Trace and Nonideal Trace.* Generally, it depends on the Dolev-Yao model assumption to decide whether a protocol is secure or not. Equally, the trace of function return values is obtained on the base of the Dolev-Yao model assumption. We are the first to propose "the ideal trace" as the reference of protocol security evaluation for the precise security analysis of protocol implementations at the source code level.

In the following definitions, the symbol $\prec$ denotes the ordinal relation of called functions during the protocol implementations. As Definition 6 shows, $\prec$ denotes the ordinal relation of the events during the protocol implementations. $\prec$ is a binary relation over $e \times e$. $\prec$ satisfies partial ordering relation on event sequences $\{e_0, e_1, \ldots, e_n\}$: ① reflexivity (there exists $e \prec e$ for any event e); ② antisymmetry (if there exists $e_1 \prec e_2$ and $e_2 \prec e_1$ for any events e_1 and e_2, then there exists $e_1 = e_2$); ③ transmissibility (if there exists $e_1 \prec e_2$ and $e_2 \prec e_3$ for e_1, e_2, e_3, then there exists $e_1 \prec e_3$).

Definition 7 (nonideal trace). The protocols are implemented in the following environments:

(1) The environments are based on the Dolev-Yao model (adversaries have the capacity to attack actively or passively).

(2) The environments of implementing protocols are insecure.

① The environments are insecure due to the flaws of implementing program language structures, such as memory overflow and pointer operation.

② There are malicious code attacks in the environments.

The trace obtained in such environments is called a nonideal trace.

Definition 8 (ideal trace). The trace of general protocol implementations satisfies the following conditions.

(1) In an ideal communication environment (there are no adversary attacks in an ideal communication environment, passive attacks, or active attacks; i.e., there is no Dolev-Yao model assumption in the environment), all the participants of a protocol are honest. The information sent or received by these participants is protected and read by encrypting and decrypting techniques.

(2) Partial ordering relation: $e_0 \prec e_1 \prec e_2, \ldots, e_i$ $0 \leq i \leq n$. Here $\prec$ denotes that the events of protocol implementations satisfy partial order relation.

Generally, if a trace of protocol implementations satisfies both condition (1) and condition (2), it is called the ideal trace.

Definition 9 (the similarity between a nonideal trace and the ideal trace). Let α, β be ordered sequences, respectively, obtained in an ideal environment or a nonideal environment. According to the clustering method, the similarity between the ideal trace and a nonideal trace is defined as follows:

(1) Let the Euclidean distance between ordered sequences α and β be $d_{\alpha\beta}$.

(2) Let the similarity between ordered sequences α and β be $s_{\alpha\beta}$, and $s_{\alpha\beta} = \delta d_{\alpha\beta}^{-1}$. δ denotes the similarity coefficient.

The bigger $s_{\alpha\beta}$ is, the smaller the degree of deviation between α and β is. This shows that the similarity between the ideal trace and the nonideal trace is bigger, and vice versa.

According to Definitions 7, 8, and 9, the ideal trace consists of function return values obtained in an ideal environment. In practice, most communications are carried out in nonideal environments. If the trace produced in a nonideal communication environment deviates from the ideal trace, it indicates that the protocol is attacked by a third party. If the attacked protocol is improved, its trace will deviate less from the ideal trace. That is, after its improvement, the similarity between its trace and the ideal trace is bigger. It means that the improved protocol is more secure than the original protocol.

6. The Method and the Experiment

According to Algorithm 1, in the process of protocol implementations, source codes are refined. After that, labelled function return values are obtained and constitute the sequences. When analyzing the security of protocol implementations, we exploit the ideal trace as the reference of security evaluation. According to the clustering method, the sequences can be used as samples to analyze the security of protocol implementations at the source code level by means of the deviation of Euclidean distance and the similarity.

6.1. The Steps of Our New Method

(1) Supposing that source codes are executed in an ideal communication environment: after an execution, function return values are obtained and form a sequence. It is called the sequence of ideal trace data.

(2) Supposing that source codes are executed in a nonideal communication environment: after an execution, function return values are obtained and form a sequence. It is called the sequence of nonideal trace data.

(3) With the clustering method [29], the Euclidean distance [30] d_{ij} between the ideal trace and the nonideal trace is calculated. The following is the formula of the Euclidean distance:

$$d\left(x_i - x_j\right) = \left[\sum_{k=1}^{p}\left(x_{ik} - x_{jk}\right)^2\right]^{1/2}. \tag{1}$$

Let $d_{ij} = d(x_i, x_j)$, and let $D = (d_{ij})_{p \times p}$ be a distance matrix:

$$\begin{bmatrix} 0, d_{12}, \ldots, d_{1n-1}, d_{1n} \\ d_{21}, 0, \ldots, d_{2n-1}, d_{2n} \\ \vdots \\ d_{n1}, d_{n2}, \ldots, d_{nn-1}, 0 \end{bmatrix}. \tag{2}$$

Here $d_{ij} = d_{ji}$. If $d_{ij} = 0$, the nonideal trace does not deviate from the ideal trace.

TABLE 1: The trace of function return values of protocol implementations.

	1	2	3	4	5	6	7	8	9	10	11	12	13	14	15	16	17	18	19	20	21	22
INS (1)	80	1	136	216	144	176	53	5	192	128	128	128	128	208	1	168	216	16	48	53	1	192
MANS (2)	112	1	216	216	176	208	53	5	80	128	128	128	128	240	1	187	216	48	80	53	1	47
INSL (3)	80	1	136	216	144	176	53	5	192	128	128	128	128	208	1	175	216	16	48	53	1	200
MANSL (4)	112	1	240	216	176	208	53	5	80	128	128	128	128	240	1	178	216	48	80	53	1	147

	23	24	25	26	27	28	29	30	31	32	33	34	35	36	37	38	39	40	41	42	43	44
INS (1)	128	128	128	128	176	208	53	5	208	128	128	173	241	0	0	128	128	244	191	0	0	1
MANS (2)	128	128	128	208	208	240	53	5	128	128	128	128	128	0	0	0	1	216	0	0	216	0
INSL (3)	128	128	128	128	176	208	53	5	208	128	210	210	244	16	0	128	128	244	149	0	0	1
MANSL (4)	128	128	128	128	208	240	53	5	128	128	128	128	128	0	0	0	1	216	0	0	216	0

TABLE 2: Euclidean distance between protocols.

	INS	MANS	INSL	MANSL
INS	0	439	102	412
MANS	439	0	439	152
INSL	102	439	0	410
MANSL	412	152	410	0

(4) Supposing that, after implementing the protocols α and β, their sequences of trace data are obtained: let $s_{\alpha\beta}$ be the similarity between the ideal trance and a nonideal trance. The similarity between the sequence of α and the sequence of β is

$$s_{\alpha\beta} = \frac{1}{1+d_{\alpha\beta}}. \tag{3}$$

Formula (3) satisfies the following: ① If $d_{\alpha\beta} \to \infty$, $s_{\alpha\beta} \to 0$; ② if $d_{ij} \to 0$, $s_{\alpha\beta} \to 1$.

Therefore, their similarity is inversely proportional to their deviation. That is, the smaller the similarity is, the easier the protocol implementation is attacked.

With our new method, when analyzing the security of protocol implementations, there are two cases: ① If $d_{ik} > d_{ij}$, the nonideal trace $\{t_k\}$ deviates from the ideal trace $\{t_i\}$ (d_{ik} denotes the deviation between the ideal trace $\{t_i\}$ and a nonideal trace $\{t_k\}$). It means that the protocol is attacked during implementations. ② The bigger $s_{\alpha\beta}$ is, the closer the trace of the protocol α gets to the trace of the protocol β. It means that the protocol implementations are more secure.

6.2. The Experiments. We carry out experiments with classical protocols and their improvements (written in C). In the experiments, we analyze the cases in which these protocols are attacked by man-in-the-middle attacks during implementations. The running environment is Win7, Visual studio 2010, Intel(R) CPU G3240, memory 4 GB, openssl-1.0.1s. The protocols run by using the functions and the big number in OpenSSL function library. The data of the protocols are encrypted and decrypted with the mechanism of the RSA public key. Participants communicate by linking TCP of Socket API. Simulate experiments are carried out with the pattern of client/server. The function return values

are transformed into numerical values and then used as experiment data, which will not influence the result of the security analysis of protocol implementations.

(1) We analyze man-in-the-middle attacks of the Needham-Schroeder protocol implementations and the Needham-Schroeder-Lowe protocol implementations.

Experiments are carried out in two types of environments: ① the ideal environment and ② nonideal environments. In the ideal environment, the Needham-Schroeder protocol is called INS for short and the Needham-Schroeder-Lowe protocol is called INSL for short. In nonideal environments, the Needham-Schroeder protocol is called MANS for short and the Needham-Schroeder-Lowe protocol is called MANSL for short. NSL is the improvement of the Needham-Schroeder protocol. Theoretically, NSL can resist man-in-the-middle attacks. After running these protocols, their traces are obtained, shown in Table 1.

The illustration of the data in Table 1: ① the numbers in the first line are the serial numbers of the functions of the protocol implementations; ② the first row corresponds to the names of the protocols and their serial numbers; ③ the values at the intersections are the function return values of each protocol implementation. For example, INS (1) (5) = 144 means that, during the implementation of INS, the fifth function return value is 144.

As is shown in Table 1, the traces of the Needham-Schroeder protocol implementations and of the Needham-Schroeder-Lowe protocol implementations deviate from the traces of their implementations in the ideal environments. According to formula (1), we, respectively, calculate each Euclidean distance d_{ij} between INS and MANSL, INSL and MANSL, and MANS and MANSL. $d_{ij} = d_{ji}$, and $i, j \in N$, $1 \le N \le 44$. The results of calculation are shown in Table 2.

According to formula (2), we, respectively, calculate each similarity between INS and MANSL, INSL and MANSL, and MANS and MANSL. The results are shown in Table 3.

TABLE 3: Similarity between protocols.

	INS	MANS	INSL	MANSL
INS	1	2.27×10^{-3}	9.71×10^{-3}	2.41×10^{-3}
MANS	2.27×10^{-3}	1	2.27×10^{-3}	6.54×10^{-3}
INSL	9.71×10^{-3}	2.27×10^{-3}	1	2.43×10^{-3}
MANSL	2.41×10^{-3}	6.54×10^{-3}	2.43×10^{-3}	1

TABLE 4: The traces of function return values of protocol implementations.

	1	2	3	4	5	6	7	8	9	10	11	12	13	14	15	16	17	18	19	20	21	22
IDH (1)	1	1	32	1	1	0	0	77	32	128	136	0	1	1	32	1	1	0	77	32	69	8
MADH (2)	0	1	1	32	1	1	0	77	32	40	8	1	1	32	1	1	0	0	77	32	112	40
IDHS (3)	1	1	32	1	1	0	0	77	32	112	104	0	1	1	32	1	1	0	77	32	112	40
MADHS (4)	0	1	1	32	1	1	0	77	32	114	120	1	1	32	1	1	0	0	77	32	144	142

TABLE 5: Euclidean distance between protocols.

	IDH	MADH	IDHS	MADHS
IDH	0	176	64	167
MADH	176	0	135	187
IDHS	64	135	0	129
MADHS	167	187	129	0

TABLE 6: The similarity between protocols.

	IDH	MADH	IDHS	MADHS
IDH	1	5.67×10^{-3}	1.529×10^{-2}	5.59×10^{-3}
MADH	5.67×10^{-3}	1	7.40×10^{-3}	5.33×10^{-3}
IDHS	1.529×10^{-2}	7.40×10^{-3}	1	7.71×10^{-3}
MADHS	5.59×10^{-3}	5.33×10^{-3}	7.71×10^{-3}	1

As is shown in Table 2, $d_{12} = 439$ means that the trace of INS deviates from the trace of the MANS protocol implementations; $d_{34} = 410$ means that the trace of INSL deviated from the trace of MANSL. As is shown in Table 3, $2.43 \times 10^{-3} > 2.27 \times 10^{-3}$ means that the similarity between INSL and MANSL is bigger than the similarity between INS and MANS.

(2) We analyze man-in-the-middle attacks of the Diffie-Hellman protocol implementations and the Diffie-Hellman-Signature protocol implementations.

The protocols are carried out in two types of environments: ① the ideal environments and ② nonideal environments. In the ideal environment, Diffie-Hellman is called IDH for short and Diffie-Hellman-Signature is called IDHS for short; in nonideal environments, Diffie-Hellman is called MADH for short and Diffie-Hellman-Signature is called MADHS for short. DHS is the improvement of the Diffie-Hellman protocol and, theoretically, it can resist man-in-the-middle attacks. After running these protocols, their traces are obtained, shown in Table 4.

According to formula (1), we, respectively, calculate each Euclidean distance d_{ij} between IDH and MADHS, IDHS and MADHS, and MADH and MADHS. $d_{ij} = d_{ji}$, and $i, j \in N, 1 \leq N \leq 22$. The results of calculation are shown in Table 5.

According to formula (2), we, respectively, calculate the similarity between IDH and MADHS, IDHS and MADHS, and MADH and MADHS. The results are shown in Table 6.

As is shown in Table 5, $d_{12} = 176$ means that the trace of IDH deviates from the trace of MADH; $d_{34} = 129$ means that the trace of IDHS deviates from the trace of MADHS. As is shown in Table 6, $7.71 \times 10^{-3} > 5.67 \times 10^{-3}$ means that the similarity between IDHS and MADHS is bigger than the similarity between IDH and MADH.

(3) We analyze the performance of our new method.

To illustrate the performance of our new method, we only list the time overhead of each protocol implementation in the ideal environment and nonideal environments (shown in Table 7) and discuss the relation between the time overhead and the similarity (shown in Figures 5 and 6). Due to the limited length of this paper, we only list and discuss the time overhead and the similarity of each protocol implementation in the simulated experiments mentioned above.

As is shown in Table 7, the time overhead of implementing protocols in the ideal environment is less than the time overhead of implementing protocols in the nonideal environments.

We calculate the absolute values $|\Delta T|$ of the difference of the time between implementing protocols in the ideal environment and implementing protocols in the nonideal

TABLE 7: The time overhead of implementing protocols.

Name	IDH	IDHS	MADH	MADHS	INS	INSL	MANS	MANSL
Time	0.916	0.789	1.567	0.132	0.037	0.030	0.100	0.096

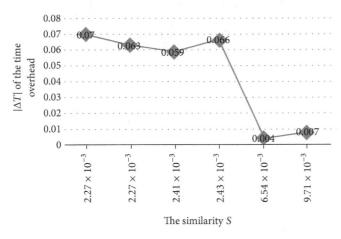

FIGURE 5: The change of similarity and $|\Delta T|$ of the time overhead.

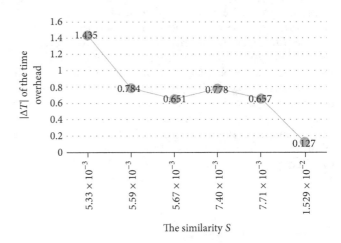

FIGURE 6: The change of similarity and $|\Delta T|$ of the time overhead.

environments. We list $|\Delta T|$ of the time overhead and $S_{\alpha\beta}$ of the Needham-Schroeder protocol and its improvement (shown in Table 3), as well as $|\Delta T|$ of the time overhead and $S_{\alpha\beta}$ of Diffie-Hellman protocol and its improvement (shown in Table 6). By comparing their changes, we can see their relation clearly, shown in Figures 5 and 6.

This shows that the relation between $S_{\alpha\beta}$ and $|\Delta T|$ tends to be in inverse proportion. It means that $S_{\alpha\beta}$ is related to the performance of protocol implementations in different environments.

As is shown in experiments (1), (2), and (3), the security of protocol implementations can be analyzed through the traces of function return values obtained when implementing the protocols in the ideal environment and in the nonideal environments. From the experiments, we can conclude the following:

① Third-party attacks can be found.

② The deviation of the improved protocols is smaller than the deviation of the original ones. This means that the improved protocols are more secure than the original ones in the process of implementations at the source code level.

③ The protocols are insecure during implementations at the source code level, even though they are proved to be secure on theory level.

④ In the ideal environment and nonideal environments, the performance of protocol implementations is related to the similarity. It is in accordance with the security thought defined by software.

This paper aims to analyze the security of protocol implementations at the source code level. With our method, attacks can be discovered by analyzing whether there are abnormal behavior characteristics when implementing protocols, such as memory overflow and malicious code (shellcode) attacks. This paper mainly analyzes man-in-the-middle attacks.

Man-in-the-middle attacks are a common type of attacks which protocols widely suffer from [31]. It is typical to analyze the security of protocol implementations which are attacked by man-in-the-middle attacks. The thought of our new method comes from life phenomena and the theory is on the base of LTS, program operational semantics, and program refinement. And we propose Algorithm 1. The purpose of analysis is to discover whether a protocol is attacked by third-party attacks, impersonation attacks, or other attacks during the implementation at the source code level. We discover that the similarity of the improved protocols, which can resist man-in-the-middle attacks, is bigger than that of the original ones. Hence, our method is competent to analyze the protocols attacked by man-in-the-middle attacks during the implementations at the source code level.

7. Conclusion and Future Work

In the paper, we have proposed a new method to dynamically analyze the security of protocol implementations at the source code level. First, we have refined protocol source codes through strong simulation relation and have established a model for the security analysis of protocol implementations. Second, when implementing protocols, we have obtained the function return values, which constitute the sequences of trace data. We propose the ideal trace as the evaluating reference for protocol security analysis. The clustering method is exploited to analyze the sequences of trace data. We propose to exploit the deviation of the Euclidean distance between the ideal trace and nonideal traces and the similarity between the ideal trace and nonideal traces to analyze the security of protocol implementations. Last, taking some classical protocols, for example, we have carried out experiments. Our experiments show that third-party attacks can be found by analyzing the deviation and similarity of the traces of the function return values obtained when implementing protocols. It is also shown through our experiments that the improved protocols are more secure than the original ones. Our method exploits the traces of protocol implementations to analyze its security and differs from other methods mentioned in the literature. It will be helpful and valuable for protocol design, security verification, and security evaluation.

The future study in this field lies in the automatic security analysis of protocol implementations [32] and the security analysis of parallel protocol implementations [33]. It requires improving existing protocol automatic analysis tools or developing new automatic tools for the security analysis of protocol implementations. On the other hand, since the flaws of language structures will make the security analysis of protocol implementations more complex, more studies should be carried out to solve these complex problems, such as C language memory access and pointer analysis. This field should be focused on.

Acknowledgments

This work was supported in part by the National Natural Science Key Foundation of China (no. 61332019) and the National Basic Research Program (NBRP) (973 Program) (no. 2014CB340601),

References

[1] H. Zhang, W. Han, X. Lai, D. Lin, J. Ma, and J. Li, "Survey on cyberspace security," *Science China Information Sciences*, vol. 58, no. 11, pp. 1–43, 2015.

[2] M. Asadzadeh Kaljahi, A. Payandeh, and M. B. Ghaznavi-Ghoushchi, "TSSL: Improving SSL/TLS protocol by trust model," *Security and Communication Networks*, vol. 8, no. 9, pp. 1659–1671, 2015.

[3] M. Backes, M. Maffei, and D. Unruh, "Computationally sound verification of source code," in *Proceedings of the 17th ACM Conference on Computer and Communications Security, (CCS '10)*, pp. 387–398, ACM, New York, NY, USA, October 2010.

[4] J. Goubault-Larrecq and F. Parrennes, "Cryptographic protocol analysis on real C code," in *Verification, model checking, and abstract interpretation*, vol. 3385 of *Lecture Notes in Computer Science*, pp. 363–379, Springer, Berlin, Germany, 2005.

[5] S. Chaki and A. Datta, "ASPIER: An automated framework for verifying security protocol implementations," in *Proceedings of the 22nd IEEE Computer Security Foundations Symposium, (CSF '09)*, pp. 172–185, IEEE, Port Jefferson, NY, USA, July 2009.

[6] M. Aizatulin, A. D. Gordon, and J. Jürjens, "Extracting and verifying cryptographic models from C protocol code by symbolic execution," in *Proceedings of the the 18th ACM conference on Computer and communications security (CCS '11)*, pp. 331–340, ACM, Chicago, Illinois, USA, October 2011.

[7] M. Aizatulin, A. D. Gordon, and J. Jürjens, "Computational verification of C protocol implementations by symbolic execution," in *Proceedings of the 2012 ACM Conference on Computer and Communications Security*, pp. 712–723, ACM, Raleigh, North Carolina, USA, October 2012.

[8] J. Almeida, E. Bangerter, M. Barbosa, K. Stephan, S. Ahmad-Reza, and T. Schneider, "A certifying compiler for zero-knowledge proofs of knowledge based on Σ- protocols," in *European Symposium on Research in Computer Security*, vol. 6345 of *Lecture Notes in Computer Science*, pp. 151–167, Springer, Berlin, Germany, 2010.

[9] S. Kiyomoto, H. Ota, and T. Tanaka, "A security protocol compiler generating C source codes," in *Proceedings of the 2nd international conference on information security and assurance, (SA '08)*, pp. 20–25, Busan, South Korea, IEEE, April 2008.

[10] C. Sarah Meiklejohn and C. Erway, "ZKPDL: A language-based system for efficient zero-knowledge proofs and electronic cash," *USENIX Conference on Security*, pp. 193–206, 2010.

[11] K. Bhargavan, C. Fournet, and A. D. Gordon, "Modular verification of security protocol code by typing," in *Proceedings of the 37th Annual ACM SIGPLAN-SIGACT Symposium on Principles of Programming Languages, (POPL '10)*, vol. 45, pp. 445–456, ACM, Madrid, Spain, January 2010.

[12] C. Sprenger and D. Basin, "Refining key establishment," in *Proceedings of the 2012 IEEE 25th Computer Security Foundations Symposium, (CSF '12)*, pp. 230–246, IEEE, Cambridge, MA, USA, June 2012.

[13] R. Milner, *Communicating and mobile systems:the π-calculus*, Cambridge University Press, Cambridge, UK, 1999.

[14] M. Avalle, A. Pironti, and R. Sisto, "Formal verification of security protocol implementations: a survey," *Formal Aspects of Computing*, vol. 26, no. 1, pp. 99–123, 2014.

[15] A. Yasinsac and J. Childs, "Formal analysis of modern security protocols," *Information Sciences*, vol. 171, no. 1-3, pp. 189–211, 2005.

[16] A. Tang, S. Sethumadhavan, and S. Stolfo, "Heisenbyte: thwarting memory disclosure attacks using destructive code reads," in *Proceedings of the 22nd ACM SIGSAC Conference on Computer and Communications Security, (CCS '15)*, pp. 256–267, Denver, Colorado, USA, October 2015.

[17] R. Corin and F. A. Manzano, "Efficient symbolic execution for analysing cryptographic protocol implementations," in *Engineering Secure Software and Systems*, vol. 6542 of *Lecture Notes in Computer Science*, pp. 58–72, Springer, Berlin, Germany, 2011.

[18] F. Dupressoir, A. D. Gordon, J. Jürjens, and D. A. Naumann, "Guiding a general-purpose C verifier to prove cryptographic protocols," *Journal of Computer Security*, vol. 22, no. 5, pp. 823–866, 2014.

[19] F. Dupressoir, *Proving C Programs Secure with General-Purpose Verification Tools [Ph.D. thesis]*, thesis Open University, 2013.

[20] L. Jia, S. Sen, D. Garg, and A. Datta, "A logic of programs with interface-confined code," in *Proceedings of the 28th IEEE Computer Security Foundations Symposium, (CSF '15)*, pp. 512–525, IEEE, Verona, Italy, July 2015.

[21] C. Fournet, C. Keller, and V. Laporte, "A certified compiler for verifiable computing," in *Proceedings of the 29th IEEE Computer Security Foundations Symposium, (CSF '16)*, IEEE, Lisbon, Portugal, July 2016.

[22] B. Mood, D. Gupta, H. Carter, K. Butler, and P. Traynor, "Frigate: A validated, extensible, and efficient compiler and interpreter for secure computation," in *Proceedings of the 1st IEEE European Symposium on Security and Privacy, (EURO S&P)*, pp. 112–127, IEEE, Saarbrucken, Germany, March 2016.

[23] B. Beurdouche, K. Bhargavan, A. Delignat-Lavaud et al., "A messy state of the union: taming the composite state machines of TLS," in *Proceedings of the 36th IEEE Symposium on Security*

and Privacy, (SP '15), pp. 535–552, San Jose, Calif, USA, May 2015.

[24] A. J. Mashtizadeh, A. Bittau, D. Boneh, and D. Mazières, "CCFI: Cryptographically enforced control flow integrity," in *Proceedings of the 22nd ACM SIGSAC Conference on Computer and Communications Security, (CCS '15)*, pp. 941–951, ACM, Denver, Colorado, USA, October 2015.

[25] R. Brooks, B. Husain, S. Yun, and J. Deng, "Security and performance evaluation of security protocols," in *Proceedings of the 8th Annual Cyber Security and Information Intelligence Research Workshop: Federal Cyber Security R and D Program Thrusts, (CSIIRW '13)*, ACM, Oak Ridge, Tennessee, USA, January 2013.

[26] E. M. Clarke, "My 27-year Quest to Overcome the State Explosion Problem," in *Proceedings of the 24th Annual IEEE Sympon Logic in Computer Science (LICS '09)*, IEEE, Los Angeles, Calif, USA, August 2009.

[27] "ITU-TS, Recommendation Z.120:Message Sequnce Chart (MSC)ITU-TS, Genva (1999)".

[28] Cas Cremers, *Sjouke Mauw.Operational Semantics and Verification of Security Protocols*, Springer, berlin, Germany, 2012.

[29] L. Kaufman and P. Rousseeuw, *Finding Groups in Data: An Introduction to Cluster Analysis*, John Wiley & Sons, Canada, 2005.

[30] M. M. Deza and E. Deza, *Encyclopedia of distances*, Springer-Verlag, Berlin, Germany, 2009.

[31] M. Conti, N. Dragoni, and V. Lesyk, "A survey of man in the middle attacks," *IEEE Communications Surveys and Tutorials*, vol. 18, no. 3, pp. 2027–2051, 2016.

[32] S. A. Menesidou, D. Vardalis, and V. Katos, "Automated key exchange protocol evaluation in delay tolerant networks," *Computers and Security*, vol. 59, pp. 1–8, 2016.

[33] A. C. Yao, M. Yung, and Y. Zhao, "Concurrent knowledge extraction in public-key models," *Journal of Cryptology. The Journal of the International Association for Cryptologic Research*, vol. 29, no. 1, pp. 156–219, 2016.

15

Two-Phase Image Encryption Scheme Based on FFCT and Fractals

Mervat Mikhail, Yasmine Abouelseoud, and Galal ElKobrosy

Department of Engineering Mathematics, Faculty of Engineering, Alexandria 21544, Egypt

Correspondence should be addressed to Mervat Mikhail; mervat.mikhail80@gmail.com

Academic Editor: Anna Cinzia Squicciarini

This paper blends the ideas from recent researches into a simple, yet efficient image encryption scheme for colored images. It is based on the finite field cosine transform (FFCT) and symmetric-key cryptography. The FFCT is used to scramble the image yielding an image with a uniform histogram. The FFCT has been chosen as it works with integers modulo p and hence avoids numerical inaccuracies inherent to other transforms. Fractals are used as a source of randomness to generate a one-time-pad keystream to be employed in enciphering step. The fractal images are scanned in zigzag manner to ensure decorrelation of adjacent pixels values in order to guarantee a strong key. The performance of the proposed algorithm is evaluated using standard statistical analysis techniques. Moreover, sensitivity analysis techniques such as resistance to differential attacks measures, mean square error, and one bit change in system key have been investigated. Furthermore, security of the proposed scheme against classical cryptographic attacks has been analyzed. The obtained results show great potential of the proposed scheme and competitiveness with other schemes in literature. Additionally, the algorithm lends itself to parallel processing adding to its computational efficiency.

1. Introduction

Multimedia communication has now become a common practice in our daily lives. Multimedia data demand both high transmission rates and security. Medical imaging systems, military image databases, and pay-per-view TV are examples of applications in which security is an essential requirement of the multimedia system [1].

Encryption is a key component for secure communication. It is the cryptographic primitive responsible for converting data into a form that is only intelligible by the intended recipient. A secret piece of information held by the recipient, the decryption key, is used to recover the original message. The proper choice of such a key is a critical component to any cryptosystem, especially in stream ciphers [2].

Image encryption is far more challenging compared to textual data encryption. The adjacent bits in an image usually show high correlation which can be used in cryptanalysis. Moreover, the image size is a major challenge requiring highly efficient algorithms that can handle such huge data size in an acceptable time frame. Furthermore, traditional symmetric encryption schemes do not work well for encrypting images. Several attempts have been made to adapt standard encryption schemes to suit the delicate nature of images [3]. The enciphered image should look random with a uniform histogram and passing well-known statistical tests of randomness in the NIST suite [4]. Moreover, the encryption scheme should be sensitive to small variations in the plain image showing a significant change in the enciphered image.

Image encryption has thus attracted the attention of many researchers, who attempt to develop new schemes representing different tradeoffs between the complexity of the algorithm and its reliability. In this paper, an image encryption algorithm is proposed employing both the finite field cosine transform [5] and fractal images [6]. Fractal images can be easily generated and they are used as a source of randomness for constructing a strong stream cipher key. The preliminary results show that the proposed scheme shows comparable performance to other schemes in literature.

The rest of the paper is organized as follows. In the following section, related work on image encryption in literature is reviewed. The finite field cosine transform, zigzag scanning idea, and fractal images are defined in Section 3. Some important characteristics of the FFCT are briefly discussed and the transform matrix to be used in our algorithm is presented. In

Section 4, evaluation techniques used to test the developed algorithm are described. Our image encryption scheme is introduced in Section 5. System key, complexity, and speed analysis are provided in Sections 6, 7, and 8, respectively. The experimental results used to illustrate and evaluate the performance of our approach are presented in Section 9. Resistance of the proposed encryption scheme to classical cryptographic attacks, like known-plaintext and chosen-plaintext attacks, is examined in Section 10. A comparative study between the proposed scheme and other schemes in literature is presented in Section 11. Finally, Section 12 concludes the paper.

2. Related Work

Much attention has been lately devoted to developing efficient and highly secure image encryption schemes. Image encryption algorithms are classified into three major categories [7]: (i) pixel position permutation based algorithms, in which a pixel is replaced by another pixel of the same image, (ii) value transformation based algorithms, in which a pixel is converted to another pixel value, and (iii) visual transformation based algorithms, in which another image is superimposed on another image such as using an image as a key or watermark-based encryption. Now, hybrid algorithms are most dominating. Different types of permutation or shuffling techniques have been successfully applied. Moreover, numerous frequency domain transforms have been considered. Furthermore, there is abundant literature on the use of chaotic maps as well as the use of fractals in image encryption.

For keystream generation, fractal geometry and chaotic maps have been extensively used in both cryptography and data hiding [8]. As for the use of chaotic function, Liu and Wang [9] used a piecewise linear chaotic map to generate a pseudorandom key stream sequence. Amin et al. [10] used a chaotic block cipher scheme to encrypt a block of bits rather than a block of pixels using cryptographic primitive operations and a nonlinear transformation function. Wang et al. in [11] encrypted images using Baker map and several one-dimensional chaotic maps. Wang et al. [12] encrypted plaintext by alternating between stream ciphering and block ciphering based on a pseudorandom number generated based on a chaotic map. On the other hand, Huang [13] used a nonlinear chaotic Chebyshev function to generate a keystream, in addition to multiple pixel permutations. In [14], Wang and Luan proposed a novel image encryption scheme based on reversible cellular automata combined with chaos.

As for the use of fractal images, the Mandelbulb set has been used in [15]. The fractal image and the fractal-compressed source image are transformed to square matrices and matrix operations are applied in encryption and decryption. The Mandelbrot set is utilized in [16] along with the Hilbert transformation to generate a random encryption key. Moreover, Abd-El-Hafiz et al. [6] introduced a novel image encryption system based on diffusion and confusion processes in which the image information is hidden inside the complex details of multiple fractal images.

The FFCT was first defined in [19] and corresponds to a finite field version of the discrete cosine transform (DCT). It exhibits interesting properties which are valuable for cryptographic purposes. In [5], a simple method for uniformizing histograms of greyscale digital images was introduced based on 8-point FFCT without any encryption mechanism. Then, a method for histogram uniformization of greyscale images integrated with a full encryption mechanism was developed in [17]. In [20], an improvement had been proposed to allow the color channels to be processed jointly by means of a single transformation round by using a 32-point FFCT over the $GF(2^{24})$ to transform blocks of the image.

The present work is based on the idea of multiphase image encryption and thus the encryption process is split over two phases: FFCT phase and encryption phase as in [18]. First, a transformation is done based on applying a recursive 8-point FFCT over $GF(2^8)$ to blocks of a color image. Since RGB images are considered, the transform is applied to each color channel separately. Application of this transformation guarantees a uniform histogram as well as decorrelation of values of adjacent pixels. This makes our method useful to provide robustness against statistical attacks in image encryption schemes. Second, encryption is based on using fractal images to generate the keystream which leads to a simple, yet secure encryption scheme.

3. Background

In this section, some important definitions are provided which are essential to the development of the proposed scheme. First, the finite field cosine transform (FFCT) is defined, and then zigzag image scanning and fractal images and their generation are described.

3.1. Finite Field Cosine Transform. In order to define the FFCT as in [5], let λ be a nonzero element in the finite field $GF(p)$, where p is an odd prime. The finite field cosine function related to λ is computed modulo p as

$$\cos_\lambda(x) := \frac{\lambda^x + \lambda^{-x}}{2}, \quad x = 0, 1, \ldots, \text{ord}(\lambda), \quad (1)$$

where $\text{ord}(\lambda)$ denotes the multiplicative order of λ.

As an advantage, the finite field cosine transform is defined over the integers modulo p and thus avoids inaccuracies associated with other real-valued transforms. A type-2 FFCT is defined in [5, 19] as follows.

Let $\lambda \in GF(p)$ be an element with multiplicative order $2N$. The finite field cosine transform of the vector $x = [x_0, x_1, \ldots, x_{N-1}]$, $x_i \in GF(p)$ is given by the vector $X = [X_0, X_1, \ldots, X_{N-1}]$, $X_k \in GF(p)$ whose elements are

$$X_k := \sqrt{\frac{2}{N}} \sum_{i=0}^{N-1} \delta_k x_i \cos_\lambda\left(k\frac{2i+1}{2}\right), \quad (2)$$

where

$$\delta_k = \begin{cases} \dfrac{1}{\sqrt{2}}, & k = 0 \\ 1, & k = 1, 2, \ldots, N-1 \end{cases}. \quad (3)$$

The inverse FFCT can be computed according to the following formula:

$$x_i := \sqrt{\frac{2}{N}} \sum_{k=0}^{N-1} \delta_i X_k \cos_\lambda \left(k \frac{1}{2} i \right). \tag{4}$$

The previous equations can be written in matrix format as $X = Tx$, where T corresponds to the transform matrix, the elements of which are obtained directly from (2). Using such a matrix notation, the FFCT can be extended to two dimensions. The two-dimensional FFCT of a matrix M with dimensions $N \times N$ can be computed by

$$C = TMT^t \pmod{p}, \tag{5}$$

where T is the transformation matrix.

In this paper, RGB color images are considered, which have three color channels red, green, and blue. Each channel has pixels values ranging from 0 to 255. As suggested by [5], the Fermat prime used in the current paper is taken to be $p = 257$. An example of a 8×8 transform matrix used for testing the scheme is the following:

$$T = \begin{bmatrix} 15 & 15 & 15 & 15 & 15 & 15 & 15 & 15 \\ 137 & 163 & 98 & 106 & 151 & 159 & 94 & 120 \\ 160 & 6 & 251 & 97 & 97 & 251 & 6 & 160 \\ 163 & 151 & 120 & 159 & 98 & 137 & 106 & 94 \\ 242 & 15 & 15 & 242 & 242 & 15 & 15 & 242 \\ 98 & 120 & 106 & 163 & 94 & 151 & 137 & 159 \\ 6 & 97 & 160 & 251 & 251 & 160 & 97 & 6 \\ 106 & 159 & 163 & 120 & 137 & 94 & 98 & 151 \end{bmatrix}, \tag{6}$$

where T is an orthogonal matrix which satisfies

$$TT^t = T^tT = I_N. \tag{7}$$

The period of the FFCT transform matrix T has great importance for the application described in this paper, since such a parameter corresponds to the least integer and positive power l giving $T^l = I$. Once the transform matrix T used has a large period l ($l = 16974594$ for the above matrix), there is not risk of returning the transformed block to its original block by the FFCT repetitive computation for a small number of times.

3.2. Zigzag Scanning of Images and Reshaping. To understand the idea of zigzag scanning of a two-dimensional matrix, see Figure 1. A two-dimensional matrix is scanned in a zigzag way to obtain a one-dimensional vector. The one-dimensional vector thus has N^2 elements, which is then to be reshaped back into an $N \times N$ two-dimensional matrix. Every N consecutive element is used to form a column of this matrix as shown in Figure 2. This method of image scanning is used in the keystream generation step mentioned in Section 5.2.

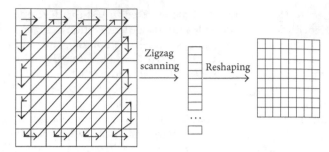

FIGURE 1: Zigzag scanning of image.

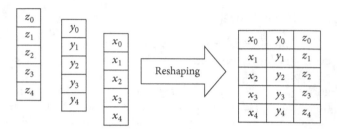

FIGURE 2: Reshaping 1D vector into 2D matrix.

3.3. Fractal Images. A fractal object [8] is a self-similar object obtained by repeating a kernel at various scales of magnification and can possess high variations. A fractal image can be generated using a mathematical equation or function that is iterated for a finite number of times. The choice of a fractal image is flexible and it depends on the level of detail and colors. Several resources are available on the Internet to generate fractals.

Many of the most popular fractal images can be obtained through Iterated Function Systems (IFS) [8]. IFS have received a lot of attention because of their appealing combination of conceptual simplicity, computational efficiency, and great ability to reproduce natural formations and complex phenomena [21]. There are miscellaneous programs, which are freely available on the Internet, for generating and rendering IFS fractals. Figure 3 shows a sample of eight fractals used in the testing phase of our scheme.

4. Encryption Evaluation Techniques

There are two main categories for performance evaluation techniques: statistical measures and sensitivity measures. In this section, the evaluation techniques used in the assessment of the performance of the proposed encryption scheme are reviewed.

4.1. Statistical Measures. The statistical means include measuring the correlation among the image pixels, histogram analysis, entropy analysis, and the NIST suite of randomness tests.

Adjacent image pixels in a plain image are highly correlated with each other and, hence, one of the encryption targets is to reduce the *correlation coefficients* for horizontal, vertical, and diagonal pixels. The correlation coefficient (ρ) between

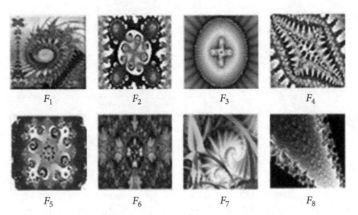

FIGURE 3: Eight fractal images used in testing the proposed system.

two N-dimensional vectors x and y is calculated using the following formula [4]:

$$\text{Cov}(x, y)$$
$$= \frac{1}{N}\sum_{i=1}^{N}\left(x_i - \frac{1}{N}\sum_{j=1}^{N}x_j\right)\left(y_i - \frac{1}{N}\sum_{j=1}^{N}y_j\right), \quad (8a)$$

$$D(x) = \frac{1}{N}\sum_{i=1}^{N}\left(x_i - \frac{1}{N}\sum_{j=1}^{N}x_j\right)^2, \quad (8b)$$

$$D(y) = \frac{1}{N}\sum_{i=1}^{N}\left(y_i - \frac{1}{N}\sum_{j=1}^{N}y_j\right)^2, \quad (8c)$$

$$\rho = \frac{\text{Cov}(x, y)}{\sqrt{D(x)D(y)}}. \quad (8d)$$

Histogram analysis is a visual test that shows the distribution of pixel color values across the whole image. For normal images, the histogram shows curves and peaks which means that some specific color values appear more than others. On the other hand, an encrypted image histogram should be flat as no specific color value should appear more than another color value.

Entropy is a measure of the predictability of a random source. Owing to the high correlation between adjacent pixels, image data is predictable and consequently has low entropy. Encrypted image data, on the other hand, should appear random to avoid any information leakage; that is, all pixel values are equally likely to occur. For a binary source producing 2^8 symbols of equal probabilities and each symbol is 8 bits long, the entropy of this source is defined as

$$\text{Entropy} = -\sum_{i=1}^{2^8} p(s_i)\log_2(p(s_i)). \quad (9)$$

This source is considered unpredictable for an entropy value of 8.

NIST SP-800-22 statistical test suite was introduced by [4], which is a group of 15 different tests designed to assess the random characteristics of a group of bits. Such bits can be the output of a random number generator or pixels of an encrypted image. The NIST tests in the second scenario examine the effectiveness of the encryption technique showing how similar the encrypted image is to a random noise based on the P value (PV) of the test and the proportion of passing sequences (PP).

4.2. Sensitivity Measures. Sensitivity tests are used in investigating the sensitivity of cryptosystems to changes in plaintext and system key. Secure cryptosystems should be very sensitive to small changes in either plaintext or system key. Sensitivity tests include differential attack measures, mean square error, and one bit change in system key.

4.2.1. Resistance against Differential Attacks. These study the statistical characteristics of the input plain image and the output enciphered image with the aim to infer any meaningful relationships when changing the input while observing the output to reveal the encryption algorithm. A strong encryption algorithm should be sensitive in the sense that small changes to the input produce a significant change in the output. Quantitatively, different measures are defined for evaluating the protection levels against differential attacks [22].

The mean absolute error (MAE) measures the absolute change between the encrypted image E and the source image P. Let W and H be the width and height of the source image, respectively; then

$$\text{MAE} = \frac{1}{W \times H}\sum_{i=1}^{H}\sum_{j=1}^{W}|P(i, j) - E(i, j)|, \quad (10)$$

where $P(i, j)$ is the original pixel value at location (i, j) and $E(i, j)$ is the encrypted pixel value at the same location.

The number of pixels change rate (NPCR) is used to measure the percentage of different pixels between two encrypted images E_1 and E_2 whose corresponding two original images are identical except for only one-pixel difference and it is calculated using

$$D(i,j) = \begin{cases} 0 : E_1(i,j) = E_2(i,j) \\ 1 : E_1(i,j) \neq E_2(i,j), \end{cases} \quad (11a)$$

$$\text{NPCR} = \frac{1}{W \times H} \sum_{i=1}^{H} \sum_{j=1}^{W} D(i,j) \times 100\%. \quad (11b)$$

The *unified average changing intensity (UACI)* measures the average intensity of differences between two encrypted images provided that their two corresponding original images are identical except for only one-pixel difference and it is calculated as

$$\text{UACI} = \frac{1}{W \times H} \sum_{i=1}^{H} \sum_{j=1}^{W} \left| \frac{E_1(i,j) - E_2(i,j)}{255} \right| \times 100\%. \quad (12)$$

4.2.2. Mean Square Error. The mean square error value gives another indication on how far the encrypted image is from the original image. As this value gets larger this implies a better encrypted image. The mean square error is calculated using the following equation:

$$\text{MSE} = \frac{\sum_{i=1}^{H} \sum_{j=1}^{W} [P(i,j) - E(i,j)]^2}{W \times H}. \quad (13)$$

Recommended values, as reported by [22], of MSE are in the order of 10^4 for (1024×1024) images.

4.2.3. One Bit Change in System Key. This test is used to test and measure the sensitivity of the system key to one bit change. The system key contains the values of the system parameters that are used to initialize the encryption process. A secure encryption process is sensitive to any slight change in any of its parameters and, hence, one bit change in the system key should lead to a totally different behavior in the encryption process. If a system is not sensitive enough to one bit change in the system key, this would lead to revealing the encryption without knowing the exact secret key, which is not acceptable in any practical cryptosystem. For one bit change in system key, two different tests are performed.

Test I. It is changing one bit in the fractals count part (S) of the key, which leads to the selection of a different number of fractals.

Test II. It is changing one bit in the fractals number part of the key, which leads to the selection of one different fractal other than the originally selected one.

4.3. Security Analysis. Security of the proposed scheme is analyzed by investigating its resistance to classical cryptographic attacks, like known-plaintext and chosen-plaintext attacks to reveal the secret parameters of the algorithm.

In *known-plaintext attack*, the attacker knows at least one sample of both the plaintext and the ciphertext. In this case, the attacker can use that to break algorithm.

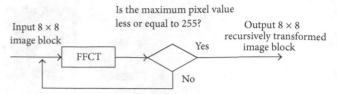

FIGURE 4: Recursive computation of the FFCT of an 8×8 image block [17].

In *chosen-plaintext attack*, the attacker can specify his own plaintext and encrypt it and then uses the result to determine the encryption key.

5. The Proposed Encryption Scheme

First, the FFCT algorithm used in the first phase is described. Next, the generation of the keystream based on multiple fractal images is described. Finally, the pseudocode for the proposed encryption algorithm is provided.

5.1. FFCT Phase. The three RGB component matrices of the source color image are separated. Each component matrix is divided into 8×8 blocks. The application of an agreed upon transform matrix T to each 8×8 image block produces a matrix (transformed version of the image block), where the elements can range from 0 to 256; this is due to the fact that modulo 257 arithmetic is being used. If any element in a transformed block is equal to 256, such a block cannot be coded using 8 bits per pixel.

The technique adopted by [17] calls for the recursive application of the transform to overcome this problem; that is, the FFCT of a block is computed repeatedly until the resulting block has no pixels with value equal to 256; see Figure 4. This process is invertible by computing the inverse transform also repeatedly until encountering the original image block, which does not contain any pixel with value equal to 256. This technique is suggested and applied in [5, 17] to encrypt greyscale images. In this paper, this technique is extended to encrypt color images by separating and treating each one of the three RGB color channels independently.

The original image block can be restored by applying the inverse finite field cosine transform (IFFCT); IFFCT of a matrix C with dimensions $N \times N$ can be computed as $M = T^{-1}C(T^t)^{-1}$ (modulo p). If T is an orthogonal matrix as in (6), its inverse is simply its transpose. This adds to the simplicity and computational efficiency of the algorithm. Another interesting characteristic of the above FFCT transform computational algorithm is that it lends itself to parallel implementation, where processing of all blocks can be done in parallel.

5.2. Pseudorandom Keystream Generation Using Fractals. Practically, assume that 2^K fractal images $F_1, F_2, \ldots F_{2^K}$ are available to both the sender and receiver, and only a subset of S fractal images are used in keystream generation, where $S \leq 2^K$. Hence, the number of fractal images used is a variable part

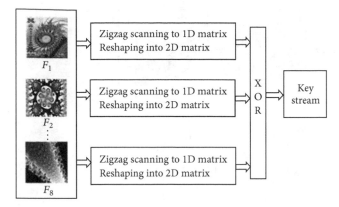

FIGURE 5: Example of key stream generation using 8 fractals.

of the system key. It is noteworthy that the selected fractals should have the same resolution as the plain image.

To generate the keystream to be used in the enciphering phase, a new method is suggested using multiple fractal images rather than the one mentioned in [6]. As shown in Figure 5, the keystream is generated by zigzag scanning each fractal image of a variable number of fractals S and then reshaping each into a matrix and finally XORing the resulting reshaped fractals. A sample of fractals used ($S = 8$) in our work is shown in Figure 3.

5.3. Pseudocode for the Proposed Scheme. Suppose a sender A wants to encrypt an image IM and send it to its recipient B; then A carries out the following steps, assuming that both A and B have agreed on the fractals to be used in the generation of the keystream as well as the transformation matrix T.

5.3.1. Encryption Process

Phase 1 (FFCT Phase)

Step 1. From the $1024 \times 1024 \times 3$ input image, extract the three red, green, and blue color channels.

Step 2. For each channel, divide the 1024×1024 image channel into 16384 blocks with each block being 8×8 in size.

Step 3. For each 8×8 block, apply FFCT recursively as in Figure 4.

Step 4. Group the transformed blocks to get the intermediate image.

Phase 2 (Encryption Phase)

Step 5 (key generation). Generate the keystream using the selected fractals agreed upon, by zigzag scanning each fractal and reshaping it and finally XORing the resulting reshaped eight fractals.

Step 6. Encrypt the image by bit XORing the intermediate image resulting from Step 3 with the keystream of Step 5.

The block diagram of the proposed encryption process is shown in Figure 6.

5.3.2. Decryption Process. The proposed decryption process proceeds as follows, with the block diagram depicted in Figure 7.

Step 1. Perform bit XORing between the ciphered image and the private keystream generated from selected fractals agreed upon to get the intermediate color image.

Step 2. From the $1024 \times 1024 \times 3$ intermediate color image, extract the three red, green, and blue color channels.

Step 3. For each channel, divide the 1024×1024 image channel into 8×8 blocks.

Step 4. For each 8×8 block, apply the IFFCT as mentioned in Section 5.1.

Step 5. Reconstruct the plain color image from 8×8 blocks of each color channel.

6. System Key Analysis

The system key is composed of the parameters, which are used in the (encryption/decryption) process. It includes the following parameters:

(i) For FFCT phase, consider the 8×8 transformation matrix T of unsigned 8-bit integers (0 to $2^8 - 1$), which is used for all 8×8 image blocks. It can be generated by specifying λ in (1); thus only 8 bits are required for generating the matrix T from λ.

(ii) K bits are required to specify the number of selected fractals, where 2^K is the maximum number of available fractals.

(iii) Consider $S \times K$ bits to specify the selected fractals' numbers, where S is the actual number of fractals selected and where $S \leq 2^K$.

Thus, the key length is variable depending on number of fractals available 2^K and the number of selected fractals S and equals $8 + K(1 + S)$ bits. In our experiment, 8 fractals are selected from 2^7 available fractals ($S = 8$, $K = 7$); hence key length used in our experiment equals 71 bits.

7. Computational Complexity Analysis

The computational complexity of the proposed encryption scheme was calculated for the two phases:

(i) For the FFCT phase, we used 8×8 matrix multiplication. Since the image resolution is $R \times R$, the number of blocks is $(R \times R)/(8 \times 8)$. Thus, the complexity of this step is $O(R^2)$.

(ii) For the encryption phase, the complexity of zigzag scanning of fractals and XORing with the source image are known to be $O(R^2)$.

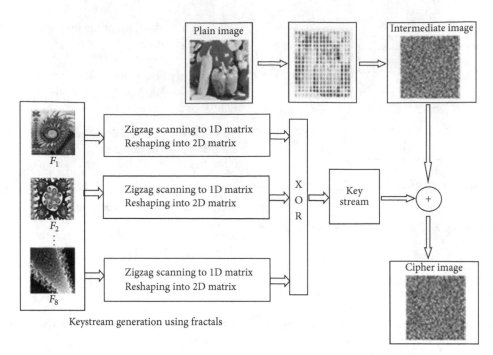

FIGURE 6: Block diagram of encryption process.

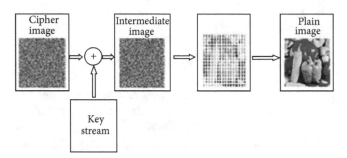

FIGURE 7: Block diagram of decryption process.

Accordingly, the computational complexity of the proposed encryption/decryption scheme is $O(R^2)$, where $R \times R$ is the source image resolution. Moreover, the computational complexity can be improved by using fast algorithms for computing the FFCT by $O(R \log R)$ as in [23].

8. Speed Analysis

After running the proposed scheme many times on different plain images, the approximate time necessary to perform encryption/decryption of a 1024 × 1024 colored image was 7 seconds; thus the average speed of our proposed scheme is approximately 0.45 MB/second. These results were obtained using an HP 250 G3 computer equipped with an Intel(R) Core (TM) i3-4005U CPU @1.70 GHz processor and 4 GB of RAM running Windows 10 64-bits. The block-by-block FFCT computation makes it possible to reduce the time required by the proposed scheme if parallel processing is employed. Moreover, there are fast algorithms for computing the FFCT as in [23].

9. Experimental Results

All the work in this paper is implemented using MATLAB. We apply our MATLAB program on 1024 × 1024 standard images available from [24]. In order to evaluate the performance of the proposed scheme, our encryption scheme has been applied to some standard images, for example, Mandrill (4.2.03), airplane (4.2.05), and peppers (4.2.07). For the fractals, 2^K Mandelbulb fractals can be readily available (from the Internet) and S fractals are chosen.

The encryption quality is evaluated using different analysis techniques including both statistical means like correlation coefficients, histogram analysis, entropy analysis, and NIST test suite. Moreover, sensitivity tests like differential attack measures, MSE, and one bit change in system key have been investigated.

It is clear from the results that the proposed scheme successfully meets various requirements for a strong image encryption scheme as detailed in the following points.

(i) As apparent in Figures 8, 9, and 10, the histogram of ciphered images is uniform with all pixel values being equally likely in the three color channels.

(ii) In Figure 11, the correlation among pixels has decreased in the encrypted image and the correlation coefficients are approximately equal to zero.

(iii) Moreover, in Figure 11, the entropy is shown to increase after applying the proposed encryption algorithm and its value approaches 8 (the ideal value).

(iv) Tables 1, 2, and 3 show that the encrypted images successfully passed the NIST suite tests. The symbol N\A in these tables means not available; that is, testing randomness according to this criterion failed.

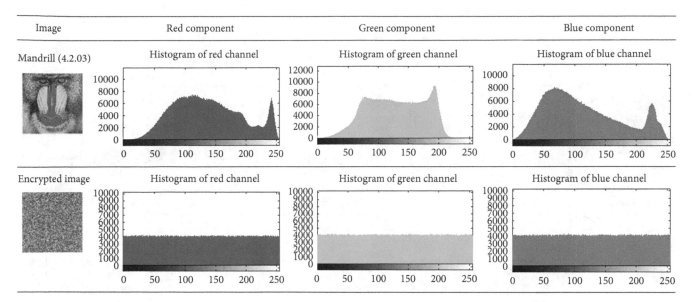

FIGURE 8: Histogram analysis of Mandrill original and encrypted image.

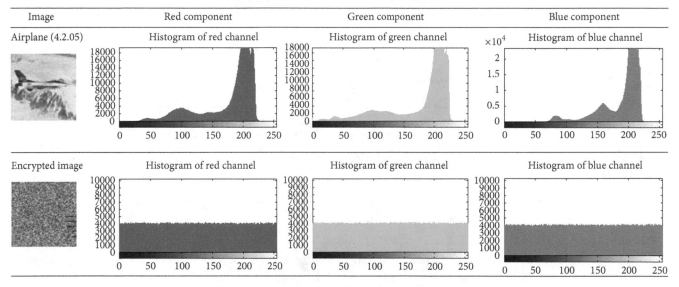

FIGURE 9: Histogram analysis of airplane original and encrypted image.

(v) From Figure 12, it is apparent that the proposed scheme is resistant to differential attacks. This is clear since the scheme is sensitive to only one pixel change in the plain image as indicated by the values of MAE, NPCR, and UACI measures.

(vi) As for MSE, from Figure 12, it is apparent that the mean square error between the original image and the encrypted image is large enough in the order of 10^4 as recommended for 1024×1024 image.

(vii) As for key sensitivity, Table 4 shows the results of the two tests. NPCR% is computed between the original plain image and the image decrypted using a wrong key in the two tests. As NCPR% approaches 100%, it is clear that the system is very sensitive to key changes.

(viii) Figure 13 shows that the encryption result is very sensitive to a change in the key, regardless of where the change occurs. All of the tests give a totally wrong image other than the peppers image.

10. Security Analysis

In this section, we analyze the security of the proposed scheme. We mount both known-plaintext attack and chosen-plaintext attack and attempt to reveal the secret parameters of the algorithm. However, it appears that the proposed scheme is resistant to both attacks.

10.1. Known-Plaintext Attack. Assume that the plain image-cipher image pair (M, C) is known to the attacker. Hence,

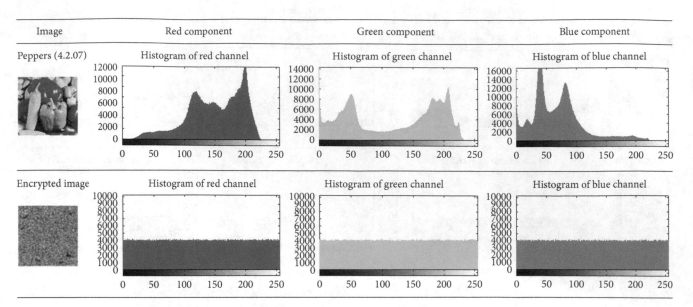

FIGURE 10: Histogram analysis of peppers original and encrypted image.

Original image		Pixel correlation coefficients			Entropy	Encrypted image		Correlation coefficients			Entropy
		Horz.	Vert.	Diag.				Horz.	Vert.	Diag.	
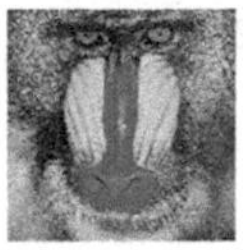	R	0.9828	0.9675	0.9549	7.6798		R	0.0013	0.0006	0.0008	7.9998
	G	0.9682	0.9408	0.9176	7.4469		G	0.0001	0.0006	0.0001	7.9998
	B	0.9776	0.9706	0.9513	7.7344		B	0.001	0.0004	0.0012	7.9998
	Avg.	0.9762	0.9597	0.9413			Avg.	0.0008	0.0006	0.0007	
	R	0.9930	0.9890	0.9824	6.7241		R	0.0029	0.0001	0.0021	7.9998
	G	0.9895	0.9918	0.9821	6.8103		G	0.0050	0.0006	0.0002	7.9999
	B	0.9910	0.9838	0.9767	6.2166		B	0.0017	0.0015	0.0003	7.9998
	Avg.	0.9912	0.9882	0.9804			Avg.	0.0032	0.0007	0.0009	
	R	0.9922	0.9929	0.9865	7.3255		R	0.0009	0.0000	0.0012	7.9998
	G	0.9956	0.9957	0.9914	7.5324		G	0.0091	0.0079	0.0058	7.9998
	B	0.9922	0.9921	0.9853	7.0896		B	0.0061	0.0059	0.0045	7.9998
	Avg.	0.9933	0.9936	0.9877			Avg.	0.0053	0.0046	0.0039	

FIGURE 11: Correlation coefficients and entropy values of some 1024 × 1024 original and encrypted test images.

TABLE 1: NIST test results for Mandrill and encrypted Mandrill.

Test	Mandrill		Encrypted Mandrill	
	PV	PP	PV	PP
Frequency	×	0.42	√	1.000
Block frequency	×	0.000	√	1.000
Cumulative sums	×	0.750	√	1.000
Runs	×	0.250	√	1.000
Longest run	×	0.000	√	1.000
Rank	×	0.000	√	1.000
FFT	×	0.000	√	1.000
Nonover. template	×	0.000	√	0.958
Overlapping template	×	0.000	√	1.000
Universal	×	0.000	√	1.000
Approximate entropy	×	0.000	√	1.000
Random excursion	N\A	N\A	√	1.000
Ran. excursion variant	N\A	N\A	√	1.000
Serial	×	0.000	√	1.000
Linear complexity	√	1.000	√	1.000
Final result	Fail		Success	

TABLE 2: NIST test results for airplane and encrypted airplane.

Test	Airplane		Encrypted airplane	
	PV	PP	PV	PP
Frequency	×	0.167	√	1.000
Block frequency	×	0.000	√	1.000
Cumulative sums	×	0.125	√	1.000
Runs	×	0.042	√	1.000
Longest run	×	0.000	√	1.000
Rank	×	0.000	√	1.000
FFT	×	0.000	√	1.000
Nonover. template	×	0.000	√	0.967
Overlapping template	×	0.000	√	1.000
Universal	×	0.000	√	1.000
Approximate entropy	×	0.000	√	1.000
Random excursion	N\A	N\A	√	1.000
Ran. excursion variant	N\A	N\A	√	1.000
Serial	×	0.000	√	1.000
Linear complexity	√	1.000	√	1.000
Final result	Fail		Success	

TABLE 3: NIST test results for peppers and encrypted peppers.

Test	Peppers		Encrypted peppers	
	PV	PP	PV	PP
Frequency	×	0.50	√	1.000
Block frequency	×	0.000	√	0.958
Cumulative sums	×	0.542	√	0.979
Runs	×	0.458	√	1.000
Longest run	×	0.000	√	1.000
Rank	×	0.000	√	1.000
FFT	×	0.000	√	1.000
Nonover. template	×	0.000	√	0.990
Overlapping template	×	0.000	√	1.000
Universal	×	0.000	√	0.958
Approximate entropy	×	0.000	√	0.997
Random excursion	N\A	N\A	√	1.000
Ran. excursion variant	N\A	N\A	√	0.997
Serial	×	0.000	√	0.959
Linear complexity	√	1.000	√	1.000
Final result	Fail		Success	

TABLE 4: Wrong decryption for the peppers image (NPCR %).

Test	NPCR %		
	R	G	B
Test I	99.79	99.74	99.77
Test II	99.79	99.75	99.78

10.2. Chosen-Plaintext Attack. Assume the attacker chooses an all zero plain image M_1 and observes the ciphertext C_1. Hence, it is easy to verify that the ciphertext $C_1 = F$, which is the keystream itself.

Again, if the attacker chooses another plain image M, hence, for each 8×8 block m, $c = TmT^t \oplus F^*$. If the same keystream is reused, the attacker can find out $T^{-1}m(T^t)^{-1}$. However, he cannot easily find out the matrix T, especially with the recursive application of the transform to various plain image blocks. But still, we suggest that the keystream is changed every time a connection is initiated between the sender and receiver; that is, we use a one-time-pad system to secure the proposed scheme against the above attack.

11. Discussion

The proposed two-phase image encryption scheme benefits from the histogram equalization capabilities of the FFCT and blends it with the success of fractal images in producing highly random keystreams. The FFCT can be computed in parallel for all 8×8 blocks of the image for efficiency. The resulting cipher image appears as random noise as clear from previous histogram analysis and application of NIST suite tests.

In our simulations, the number of recursive applications of FFCT to an image block has been investigated and the

for each 8×8 block m, $c = TmT^t \oplus F_1$, where T is the transformation matrix and F_1 is the associated block of the generated keystream by the fractals selected. Thus, going from C to M for another pair is not such an easy operation; the attacker should know the transformation matrix T and also should know number of fractals used S as well as which fractals are used. Even if the attacker knows more plain image-cipher image pairs, he could not find out the system key because the keystream is varied every run. So, the proposed scheme is robust against known-plaintext attack.

Simulation result				Differential attacks measures			MSE
				MAE	NPCR%	UACI%	
Original	Encrypted	Decrypted	R	76.0048	99.6617	33.4502	8651
			G	72.4362	99.6370	33.4866	7728
			B	79.2610	99.6235	33.4524	9508
			Avg.	75.90067	99.6407	33.4637	8629
Original	Encrypted	Decrypted	R	81.5138	99.5758	33.4640	9955
			G	84.3053	99.5449	33.4448	10670
			B	83.3591	99.5813	33.4785	10394
			Avg.	83.0594	99.567	33.4624	10340
Original	Encrypted	Decrypted	R	73.9011	99.6917	33.4720	7978
			G	86.4335	99.6500	33.4975	11208
			B	86.0157	99.7103	33.5152	11109
			Avg.	82.1168	99.684	33.4949	10098

FIGURE 12: Differential attacks and MSE of some encrypted images.

(a)   (b)

FIGURE 13: Wrong decryption of peppers image: (a) test I and (b) test II.

percentage of image blocks being subjected to a given number of recursive applications of the FFCT has been computed. Such results are shown in Table 5. In all images, for each color channel almost 80% of the blocks had to be transformed only once. A rather small percentage of blocks had to be transformed more than twice. This indicates that the extra computational effort due to the recursive application of the FFCT is minor. It has also been observed that the largest number of rounds necessary for a block was 8. An appropriate

choice of the transformation matrix T should be one with a large period l (in our experiments $l = 16974594$). Thus, there was no risk of returning the transformed block to its original block by the FFCT repetitive application.

In order to further assess the success of the proposed scheme, its performance is compared to several other schemes in literature. Table 6 shows the results obtained when encrypting the Lena (512 × 512) image using the proposed encryption scheme and compares its performance

TABLE 5: Average percentages of RGB channel blocks of test images submitted to recursive applications of the FFCT.

FFCT number of applications	Mandrill	Airplane	Peppers
1	78.2726	77.7355	78.1487
2	17.3096	17.2607	17.5293
3	3.3447	3.9795	3.4180
4	0.7812	0.8057	0.6348
5	0.2197	0.1465	0.1953
6	0.0488	0.0732	0.0488
7	0.0244	0.0000	0.0000
8	0.0000	0.0000	0.0000

TABLE 6: Comparison among the proposed scheme and other schemes in literature.

Researches	Pixel correlation			NPCR%	UACI%	Entropy
	Horz.	Vert.	Diag.			
This work	0.00069	0.0007	0.0002	99.7248	33.4647	7.9999
[6]	0.0021	0.0009	0.0018	99.740	33.470	7.9997
[9]	0.0965	0.0318	0.0362	99.633	33.458	7.9845
[10]	0.0209	0.0144	0.035	99.610	33.410	7.9998
[11]	0.0141	0.0107	0.0097	99.670	27.880	—
[12]	0.0140	0.0092	0.0051	98.563	33.081	7.9940
[13]	0.0974	0.0707	0.0484	99.684	33.439	—
[14]	0.0011	0.0193	0.0045	99.790	33.350	7.9992
[17]	−0.0049	0.0015	0.0021	99.6066	33.4758	—
[18]	0.00089	0.00170	—	—	—	7.9993

with other related recent schemes. The comparison involves correlation coefficients, some differential attacks measures, and the entropy.

Like our scheme, a colored image is encrypted in [6, 9, 10], while in other researches greyscale images are only considered [11, 12, 17, 18]. In Table 6, for a fair comparison, the averages of the performance measures for the proposed scheme for the three RGB channels are compared against the averages of other schemes. This is how we compared our technique using colored Lena image with some other techniques using a greyscale Lena image. The obtained results show great potential compared to other techniques.

12. Conclusion

In this paper, an efficient scheme for colored image encryption using image pixel value transformation is proposed. The scheme employs the finite field cosine transform FFCT to reduce correlation among adjacent pixels and to obtain a uniform histogram for the enciphered images. The FFCT does not involve any approximations inherent in other transforms as it operates on integers modulo p and results in integer sequences. Moreover, encryption is performed on the transformed image using multiple fractals to enforce more security. The experimental results show that the cipher image has entropy information close to ideal value 8 and low correlation coefficients close to ideal value 0. Thus, the analysis proves the security, correctness, effectiveness, and robustness of the proposed image encryption algorithm.

Additionally, the number of recursive applications of the FFCT to an image block has been investigated and the experiments showed that it has minor effect on the algorithm computational efficiency as it is in 80% of the cases equal to one and the FFCT algorithm can proceed on all blocks in parallel. Finally, for the scheme to resist both known-plaintext and chosen ciphertext attacks, it is suggested to refresh the keystream used in the enciphering phase per communication session and to keep the transformation matrix used in the FFCT phase as a shared secret between the communicating parties.

Competing Interests

The authors declare that they have no competing interests.

References

[1] C. Li, *Cryptanalyses of some multimedia encryption schemes [M.S. dissertation]*, Zhejiang University, Hangzhou, China, 2005.

[2] W. Stallings, *Cryptography and Network Security: Principlesand Practices*, Pearson Education India, 2006.

[3] N. Rawal and M. Dhawan, "A survey report on imageencryption techniques," *International Journal of Engineering Research and Technology*, vol. 2, no. 10, 2013.

[4] A. Rukhin, J. Soto, J. Nechvatal, M. Smid, and E. Barker, *A Statistical Test Suite for Random and Pseudorandom Number*

Generators for Cryptographic Applications, Booz-Allen and Hamilton Inc, Mclean, Va, USA, 2001.

[5] J. B. Lima and R. M. C. de Souza, "Histogram uniformization for digital image encryption," in *Proceedings of the 25th Conference on Graphics, Patterns and Images (SIBGRAPI '12)*, pp. 55–62, IEEE, Ouro Preto, Brazil, August 2012.

[6] S. K. Abd-El-Hafiz, A. G. Radwan, S. H. Abdel Haleem, and M. L. Barakat, "A fractal-based image encryption system," *IET Image Processing*, vol. 8, no. 12, pp. 742–752, 2014.

[7] K. D. Patel and S. Belani, "Image encryption using differenttechniques: a review," *International Journal of Emerging Technology and Advanced Engineering*, vol. 1, no. 1, pp. 30–34, 2011.

[8] P. S. Addison, *Fractals and Chaos: An Illustrated Course*, CRC Press, 1997.

[9] H. Liu and X. Wang, "Color image encryption based on one-time keys and robust chaotic maps," *Computers & Mathematics with Applications*, vol. 59, no. 10, pp. 3320–3327, 2010.

[10] M. Amin, O. S. Faragallah, and A. A. Abd El-Latif, "A chaotic block cipher algorithm for image cryptosystems," *Communications in Nonlinear Science and Numerical Simulation*, vol. 15, no. 11, pp. 3484–3497, 2010.

[11] X.-Y. Wang, F. Chen, and T. Wang, "A new compound mode of confusion and diffusion for block encryption of image based on chaos," *Communications in Nonlinear Science and Numerical Simulation*, vol. 15, no. 9, pp. 2479–2485, 2010.

[12] X. Wang, X. Wang, J. Zhao, and Z. Zhang, "Chaotic encryption algorithm based on alternant of stream cipher and block cipher," *Nonlinear Dynamics. An International Journal of Nonlinear Dynamics and Chaos in Engineering Systems*, vol. 63, no. 4, pp. 587–597, 2011.

[13] X. Huang, "Image encryption algorithm using chaotic Chebyshev generator," *Nonlinear Dynamics*, vol. 67, no. 4, pp. 2411–2417, 2012.

[14] X. Wang and D. Luan, "A novel image encryption algorithm using chaos and reversible cellular automata," *Communications in Nonlinear Science and Numerical Simulation*, vol. 18, no. 11, pp. 3075–3085, 2013.

[15] A. J. J. Lock, C. H. Loh, S. H. Juhari, and A. Samsudin, "Compression-encryption based on fractal geometric," in *Proceedings of the 2nd International Conference on Computer Research and Development (ICCRD'10)*, pp. 213–217, May 2010.

[16] Y.-Y. Sun, R.-Q. Kong, X.-Y. Wang, and L.-C. Bi, "An image encryption algorithm utilizing Mandelbrot set," in *Proceedings of the 3rd International Workshop on Chaos-Fractal Theories and Applications (IWCFTA '10)*, pp. 170–173, IEEE, Yunnan, China, October 2010.

[17] J. B. Lima, E. A. O. Lima, and F. Madeiro, "Image encryption based on the finite field cosine transform," *Signal Processing: Image Communication*, vol. 28, no. 10, pp. 1537–1547, 2013.

[18] S. Rakesh, A. A. Kaller, B. C. Shadakshari, and B. Annappa, "Multilevel image encryption," https://arxiv.org/abs/1202.4871.

[19] M. M. de Souza, H. M. de Oliveira, R. M. de Souza, and M. M. Vasconcelos, "The discrete cosine transform over prime finite fields," in *Telecommunications and Networking—ICT 2004: 11th International Conference on Telecommunications, Fortaleza, Brazil, August 1–6, 2004. Proceedings*, vol. 3124 of *Lecture Notes in Computer Science*, pp. 482–487, Springer, Berlin, Germany, 2004.

[20] J. B. Lima, E. S. da Silva, and R. M. de Souza, "A finite field cosine transform-based image processing scheme for color image encryption," in *Proceedings of the IEEE Global Conference on Signal and Information Processing (GlobalSIP '15)*, pp. 1071–1075, Orlando, Fla, USA, December 2015.

[21] B. Rama and J. Mishra, "Game-enabling the 3D-Mandelbulb fractal by adding velocity-induced support vectors," *International Journal of Computer Applications*, vol. 48, no. 1, pp. 1–3, 2012.

[22] Y. Wu, J. P. Noonan, and S. Agaian, "NPCR and UACIrandomness tests for image encryption," *Journal of Selected Areas in Telecommunications (JSAT)*, pp. 31–38, 2011.

[23] J. B. Lima, "Fast algorithm for computing cosine number transform," *Electronics Letters*, vol. 51, no. 20, pp. 1570–1572, 2015.

[24] The USC-SIPI Image Database, "University of Southern California, signal and image processing institute," http://sipi.usc.edu/database/.

16

CP-ABE Access Control Scheme for Sensitive Data Set Constraint with Hidden Access Policy and Constraint Policy

Nurmamat Helil[1,2] and Kaysar Rahman[1]

[1]*College of Mathematics and System Science, Xinjiang University, Xinjiang, China*
[2]*Department of Computer Science and Engineering, University of Minnesota, Minneapolis, MN, USA*

Correspondence should be addressed to Nurmamat Helil; nur924@sina.com

Academic Editor: Huaizhi Li

CP-ABE (Ciphertext-Policy Attribute-Based Encryption) with hidden access control policy enables data owners to share their encrypted data using cloud storage with authorized users while keeping the access control policies blinded. However, a mechanism to prevent users from achieving successive access to a data owner's certain number of data objects, which present a conflict of interest or whose combination thereof is sensitive, has yet to be studied. In this paper, we analyze the underlying relations among these particular data objects, introduce the concept of the sensitive data set constraint, and propose a CP-ABE access control scheme with hidden attributes for the sensitive data set constraint. This scheme incorporates extensible, partially hidden constraint policy. In our scheme, due to the separation of duty principle, the duties of enforcing the access control policy and the constraint policy are divided into two independent entities to enhance security. The hidden constraint policy provides flexibility in that the data owner can partially change the sensitive data set constraint structure after the system has been set up.

1. Introduction

With the advancement of cloud computing [1], an increasing number of organizations and individual users are willing to store their private data in cloud storage to share with others. Unlike traditional access control, the data owner reserves the right to define the access control policy for his/her data for release on the cloud. Moreover, the data owner encrypts his/her data according to his/her access control policy before putting the data on the cloud because the cloud might be compromised or untrusted. Attribute-Based Encryption [2–5] provides desirable solutions to meet the data owner's needs. Compared to KP-ABE (Key-Policy Attribute-Based Encryption) [4] and fuzzy identity-based encryption [2], CP-ABE (Ciphertext-Policy Attribute-Based Encryption) [3, 5] is more appropriate, as it enables the data owner to more freely define the access control policy. Moreover, because the access control policy itself may leak critical information, efforts have been made [6–10] to hide the access control policy by blinding the attributes within it.

However, the data owner may unavoidably release some data onto the cloud storage whereby either there may exist a conflict of interest or one can derive sensitive or confidential data from the released data. For example, the data owner may release two data objects (a data object refers to an encryption data unit in CP-ABE scenario, e.g., a file, a message) $M_{\text{company\_A}}$ and $M_{\text{company\_B}}$ to the cloud, to which the Chinese Wall security policy [11] should be applied, as company_A and company_B are competitors. Any authorized user of the two data objects can freely access either data object, but once he/she has accessed one of them, he/she can no longer access the other. In the CP-ABE scenario, it is inappropriate to split all users into two mutually disjoint sets beforehand by choosing an access structure for the two data objects. This is because an authorized user is initially supposed to be able to access either of the two data objects freely. The relations among the data released to the cloud storage are substantially more complicated. Other types of data sets exist as well. In [12, 13], we emphasized the situation in which a user's consecutive access to any k data out of

n may yield a conflict of interest or disclosure of some sensitive data. This type of data set has been studied in primary access control constraints such as SOD (Separation of Duty) of RBAC (Role-Based Access Control) [14–16] and the Chinese Wall security policy [11]; we call this kind of data set a sensitive data set in this paper. The handling of the sensitive data set problem for cloud storage should be considered. Some work has been conducted on such data sets [17, 18]. However, for cloud storage, where the access control is realized via CP-ABE, there remains no such mechanism for effectively controlling a user's successive access to data objects from a data owner's sensitive data set to prevent commercial fraud, mistakes, or the leakage of critical information.

To handle the constraint for a sensitive data set stored in cloud storage that utilizes CP-ABE, we propose a CP-ABE access control scheme for sensitive data sets with a flexible, partially hidden constraint policy; in addition, the scheme retains the features of the hidden access control policy. In this work, first, we analyze the general characteristics and structures of the sensitive data set constraint and present a formal definition of it. Second, we utilize the concept of dummy attributes [19] for the data objects in the sensitive data set, and we also introduce a semitrusted constraint monitor that is responsible for keeping track of the user's access to data objects from the sensitive data set using these dummy attributes. In our scheme, the constraint policies defined by the data owner are fully hidden from entities, except for the constraint monitor; the policies are partially hidden from the constraint monitor, and the access control policies are hidden from all entities.

The user's previous successful access to data objects in a sensitive data set constraint may affect the user's future access to other data objects in the same set. To handle the sensitive data set constraint, an entity in the system needs to know whether the user has the ability to decrypt the data objects in the sensitive data set without knowing any information about the access control policy of the data object. In addition, we choose the tree access structure with "AND," "OR," and "k OF n" gates. For the above reasons, we construct our scheme based on Hur's promising scheme [8], but our emphasis is on the constraint.

The remainder of this paper is organized as follows. Section 2 explores the essential features of a sensitive data set constraint along with its structure. The assignment of dummy attributes for the sensitive data set constraint is introduced in Section 3. Section 4 provides the system architecture, assumptions, and requirements for our scheme. The formal specification of the CP-ABE access control scheme for the constraint is presented in Section 5. A detailed scheme construction is provided in Section 6. In Section 7, we discuss extra costs due to the enforcement of the constraint, in comparison with [8]. In Section 8, security, consistency, and accessibility analyses are given. In Section 9, we survey related works. Section 10 summarizes our work.

2. Sensitive Data Set Constraint

Some data objects released to the cloud storage may be characterized by certain correlations. The combination of such data objects may induce a conflict of interest; a user may easily derive highly sensitive or confidential data that are not supposed to be disclosed to any user from other legitimately accessed but otherwise insignificant data objects. Although the data owner is aware of the hazard posed by releasing such data objects to the cloud, he/she might accept the tradeoff of information protection for sharing his/her data. We first analyze the underlying relations among the data objects released by the data owner and present the formal definition of the sensitive data set constraint.

2.1. Implicit Data. $\exists M' \notin \{M_1, M_2, \ldots, M_n\}$, if all data objects from a data set $\{M_1, M_2, \ldots, M_n\}$ are accessed by one user; then, these combined access instances are equivalent to accessing data M' by this user. $\{M_1, M_2, \ldots, M_n\}$ is the minimal set that satisfies the above condition. We call M' implicit data [12].

If the implicit data are sensitive or confidential and are not supposed to be available to any user, then we should add constraints to a user's successive access to these data objects to prevent the user's derivation of the implicit data.

2.2. Structure

(a) *Chinese Wall Structure.* For the two disjoint data sets $\{M_1, M_2, \ldots, M_s\}$ and $\{M_1', M_2', \ldots, M_t'\}$, once a user accesses a data object from one data set, he/she should no longer be authorized to access any data object from another data set [11].

(b) *(n, k) Structure.* Denoted as $(\{M_1, M_2, \ldots, M_n\}, \#k)$, $2 \leq k \leq n$, this structure requires that no user can access k or more data objects from the data set $\{M_1, M_2, \ldots, M_n\}$. This implies that the combination of any k or more data objects from $\{M_1, M_2, \ldots, M_n\}$ is sensitive or induces a conflict of interest [13].

The Chinese Wall structure is equivalent to the (n, k) structure if we set $(n, k) = (2, 2)$ and use the concept of equivalence classes. For example, two disjoint data sets $\{M_1\}$ and $\{M_2, M_3\}$ have a Chinese Wall structure. If $[M_1] = \{M_1\}$ and $[M_2] = [M_3] = \{M_2, M_3\}$, then we have $(\{[M_1], [M_2]\}, \#2)$ or $(\{[M_1], [M_3]\}, \#2)$.

Based on the aforementioned analysis, we introduce a general and formal definition of the sensitive data set constraint.

Definition 1 (SDS constraint). Define $(\{[M_1], [M_2], \ldots, [M_n]\}, \#k)$, $2 \leq k \leq n$, as a sensitive data set (SDS) constraint if any user is forbidden from accessing data objects from k or more different equivalence classes out of n classes, and $[M_i] \cap [M_j] = \emptyset$, $0 \leq i, j \leq n$, $i \neq j$.

For an SDS constraint, we say that data objects from different equivalence classes are incompatible; on the contrary, we say that data objects from the same equivalence class are compatible. For example, for $(\{[M_1], [M_2], \ldots, [M_n]\}, \#k)$, $2 \leq k \leq n$, $\forall M_1', M_2'$, if $M_1' \in [M_i]$, $M_2' \in [M_j]$, $i \neq j$, then M_1' and M_2' are incompatible; if $M'_1, M'_2 \in [M_i]$, then M'_1 and M'_2 are compatible.

A data object can be under multiple SDS constraints. Assume that $(\{[M_1], [M_2], \ldots, [M_s]\}, \#k_1)$ and $(\{[M'_1], [M'_2], \ldots, [M'_t]\}, \#k_2)$ are two SDS constraints; then, $(\bigcup_{i=1}^{s} [M_i]) \cap (\bigcup_{j=1}^{t} [M'_j]) \neq \emptyset$ is allowed.

We also have an extra rule about SDS constraints.

Rule 1. Any two compatible data objects in an SDS constraint cannot be incompatible in any other SDS constraint and vice versa.

Let us consider an example. There is a database table of an organization; the table has columns A, B, C_1, C_2, D, and E. The data of column E for each row is sensitive or confidential; however, it can be inferred from any three corresponding columns out of A, B, C_1, D or A, B, C_2, D. The organization releases this table to the cloud storage without column E. If any user is authorized to access data of any three columns out of A, B, C_1, D or A, B, C_2, D, then he/she can infer the data of column E despite the fact that he/she is not authorized to access the data of column E [12]. So, the organization should specify an SDS constraint for this case, that is, $(\{\{M_A\}, \{M_B\}, \{M_{C_1}, M_{C_2}\}, \{M_D\}\}, \#3)$.

3. SDS Constraint Specific Attributes

In CP-ABE, attributes play a key role in the enforcement of access control. Therefore, to handle the SDS constraint, additional SDS constraint specific attributes can be used. Because the additional attributes are only used to handle the SDS constraint and have no special meaning, we adopt dummy attributes [19] in our scheme.

If a data object is organized into an SDS constraint, then we need to upgrade the original access requirement for the data object. Because the data object is no longer independent, a user's access to the data object may affect later access to other data objects under the same SDS constraint. We upgrade the original access requirements with dummy attributes. Below, we first discuss the assignment of dummy attributes for the SDS constraints.

Suppose that

$$\text{SDS}_i^{(a)} = \Big(\big\{\{M_{1,1}, M_{1,2}, \ldots, M_{1,n_1}\},$$
$$\{M_{2,1}, M_{2,2}, \ldots, M_{2,n_2}\}, \ldots, \{M_{l,1}, M_{l,2}, \ldots, M_{l,n_l}\}\big\}, \quad (1)$$
$$\#k \Big)$$

is one of the SDS constraints for data owner u_a. As shown in Figure 1, we use l dummy artificial attributes $\theta_{i,1}^{(a)}, \theta_{i,2}^{(a)}, \ldots, \theta_{i,l}^{(a)}$, which are unique to $\text{SDS}_i^{(a)}$. $\theta_{i,1}^{(a)}, \theta_{i,2}^{(a)}, \ldots, \theta_{i,l}^{(a)}$ are used to distinguish between different equivalence classes. Therefore, $\theta_{i,j}^{(a)}$ corresponds to the data set $\{M_{j,1}, M_{j,2}, \ldots, M_{j,n_j}\}$ in $\text{SDS}_i^{(a)}$ in this example. We assume that these attributes do not overlap with the same data owner's other dummy attributes or with the normal attributes used in the whole system.

Consider a case in which a data object is organized into two different SDS constraints. If $\text{SDS}_{i_1}^{(a)} = (\{[M_1], [M_2], \ldots, [M_{l_1}]\}, \#k_1)$ and $\text{SDS}_{i_2}^{(a)} = (\{[M'_1], [M'_2], \ldots, [M'_{l_2}]\}, \#k_2)$, with $M \in (\bigcup_{t=1}^{l_1} [M_t]) \cap (\bigcup_{t=1}^{l_2} [M'_t])$, assume that the corresponding SDS constraint specific attributes for the two SDS constraints are $\theta_{i_1,1}^{(a)}, \theta_{i_1,2}^{(a)}, \ldots, \theta_{i_1,l_1}^{(a)}$ and $\theta_{i_2,1}^{(a)}, \theta_{i_2,2}^{(a)}, \ldots, \theta_{i_2,l_2}^{(a)}$, respectively. If $M \in [M_{j_1}]$ in $\text{SDS}_{i_1}^{(a)}$ and $M \in [M_{j_2}]$ in $\text{SDS}_{i_2}^{(a)}$, then $\theta_{i_1,j_1}^{(a)}$ and $\theta_{i_2,j_2}^{(a)}$ are both used to upgrade the access requirement for M.

4. CP-ABE Access Control System Architecture for SDS Constraint

4.1. System Architecture and Assumptions. The system architecture is as shown in Figure 2. The entities in the system are described as follows.

Cloud Storage Server. The cloud storage server provides the data sharing service.

Data Owner. The data owner owns the data objects and releases them to the cloud storage server after encryption under his/her access control policies. Furthermore, he/she defines the SDS constraints based on Definition 1 and Rule 1.

User (Consumer). The user accesses encrypted data objects on the cloud storage server.

Key Generation Center (KGC). The KGC generates public and private keys for the system. It is assumed to be semitrusted. The KGC performs legitimate tasks assigned to it by other entities, but it may peek at the data owner's data objects, access control policies, and constraint policies.

Proxy Server. The proxy server enforces access control for the data objects and performs partial decryption. It is assumed to be semitrusted. The proxy server performs legitimate tasks assigned to it by other entities, but it may peek at the data owner's data objects, access control policies, and constraint policies. Another additional assumption about the proxy server is that it does not tamper with any component of the ciphertext of the data object.

SDS Monitor. The SDS monitor enforces the SDS constraint for the data objects. It is assumed to be semitrusted. The SDS monitor performs legitimate tasks assigned to it by other entities, but it may peek at the data owner's data objects. Another critical assumption about the SDS monitor is that it will destroy the partially decrypted ciphertext if the user's accessing of the corresponding data object is about to violate any SDS constraint.

4.2. Security, Privacy, Consistency, and Accessibility Requirements

Security. Data confidentiality and collusion resistance [3, 8] should be guaranteed. Moreover, as per our contribution, the

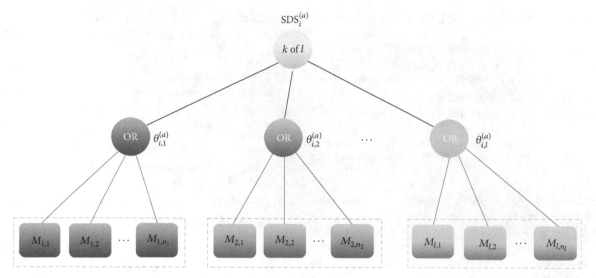

FIGURE 1: Dummy attributes corresponding to the data objects in an SDS constraint.

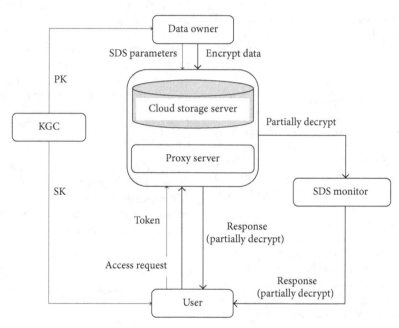

FIGURE 2: CP-ABE access control system architecture for SDS constraints.

SDS constraint in Definition 1 should also be guaranteed; accessing data objects should not cause a violation of any SDS constraint.

Policy Privacy. No entities have any information about the attributes of the access control policy. No entities, except for the SDS monitor, have any valuable information about the SDS constraint policy or its structure. The SDS monitor has limited information about the SDS constraint policy and its structure.

Consistency. Any two compatible data objects in an SDS constraint cannot be incompatible in any other SDS constraint and vice versa (Rule 1). The reason for the consistency requirement is simple: a user's access to data objects in an SDS constraint may affect his/her subsequent access to other data objects that are incompatible with the initial data objects being accessed but will not affect his/her subsequent access to other data objects that are compatible with the initial data objects being accessed. Thus, we have the consistency requirement to support the SDS constraint policy.

Accessibility. A user whose valid attributes match the tree access structure of a data object can access the data object even if it is organized into an SDS constraint unless the access violates any SDS constraint. In contrast, a user whose valid attributes do not match the tree access structure of the data object still cannot access the data object after it is organized into an SDS constraint.

5. CP-ABE Access Control Scheme for SDS Constraint

5.1. Cryptographic Background. In this section, we specify the formal definition of the CP-ABE access control scheme for the SDS constraint. Our proposal is based on [8]. We briefly review the cryptographic background on the reason for the integrity of the content.

5.1.1. Attribute Access Structure

Definition 2 (attribute access structure). Let $\{\lambda_1, \lambda_2, \ldots, \lambda_n\}$ be a set of attributes. A collection $\mathbb{A} \subseteq 2^{\{\lambda_1, \lambda_2, \ldots, \lambda_n\}}$ is monotone if $\forall B, C$: if $B \in \mathbb{A}$ and $B \subseteq C$, then $C \in \mathbb{A}$. An attribute access structure (resp., monotone attribute access structure) is a collection (resp., monotone collection) $\mathbb{A}$ of nonempty subsets of $\{\lambda_1, \lambda_2, \ldots, \lambda_n\}$, that is, $\mathbb{A} \subseteq 2^{\{\lambda_1, \lambda_2, \ldots, \lambda_n\}} \setminus \{\emptyset\}$. We call the sets in $\mathbb{A}$ the authorized sets of attributes, and the sets not in $\mathbb{A}$ are the unauthorized sets of attributes.

The attribute access structure is a monotone access structure for all data objects regardless of whether they are in the SDS constraint.

Bilinear Pairings. $\mathbb{G}_0$ and $\mathbb{G}_1$ are two multiplicative cyclic groups of prime order p. g is a generator of $\mathbb{G}_0$, and e is a bilinear map, $e : \mathbb{G}_0 \times \mathbb{G}_0 \to \mathbb{G}_1$. e has the following properties:

(i) Bilinearity: $\forall u, v \in \mathbb{G}_o$ and $\forall x, y \in \mathbb{Z}_p^*$, $e(u^x, v^y) = e(u, v)^{xy}$.

(ii) Nondegeneracy: $e(g, g) \neq 1$.

(iii) Computability: computing the bilinear map $e : \mathbb{G}_0 \times \mathbb{G}_0 \to \mathbb{G}_1$ is efficient.

Bilinear Diffie-Hellman (BDH) Assumption. Based on the aforementioned notations, given a generator g of $\mathbb{G}_0$ and elements g^x, g^y, g^z for $x, y, z \in \mathbb{Z}_p^*$, the BDH problem is to find $e(g, g)^{xyz}$.

One-Way Anonymous Key Agreement. Kate et al. [20] proposed a one-way anonymous key agreement scheme and proved that it is secure in the random oracle model under the assumption that the BDH problem in $\langle p, \mathbb{G}_0, \mathbb{G}_1, e \rangle$ is hard with respect to unconditional anonymity, session key secrecy, and impersonation.

5.2. CP-ABE Access Control Components for the SDS Constraint. The CP-ABE access control components for the SDS constraint are as follows:

(i) USERS = $\{u_1, u_2, \ldots, u_l\}$: the user set.

(ii) O_ATTR = $\{\lambda_1, \lambda_2, \ldots, \lambda_s\}$: original attributes.

(iii) SDS_ATTR$(u_j) = \{\theta_{i,1}^{(j)}, \theta_{i,2}^{(j)}, \ldots, \theta_{i,n_i}^{(j)}\}_{1 \leq i \leq m}$, $j = 1, 2, \ldots, l$: SDS constraint specific attributes for a user u_j; u_j has m different SDS constraints; m can be different for different users.

(iv) SDS_INFO$_i^{(j)} = \{\theta_{i,1}^{(j)}, \theta_{i,2}^{(j)}, \ldots, \theta_{i,n_i}^{(j)}, k_i\}$, $1 \leq i \leq m$, $j = 1, 2, \ldots, l$: SDS constraint information for user u_j's ith SDS constraint.

(v) H_Attr$(u_t, $ SDS$_i^{(j)})$: historical SDS constraint specific attribute set; it is initially an empty set; when user u_t successfully accesses data owner u_j's data object under u_j's ith SDS constraint, then the SDS constraint specific attribute that corresponds to the equivalence class the accessed data object belongs to will be put into the set.

(vi) SDS_ATTR = $\bigcup_{j=1}^{l}$ SDS_ATTR(u_j): all SDS constraint specific attributes in the system.

(vii) ATTR = O_ATTR $\cup$ SDS_ATTR, all attributes in the system, O_ATTR $\cap$ SDS_ATTR = $\emptyset$.

5.3. CP-ABE Access Control Scheme for SDS Constraint. The access control scheme for the SDS constraint with the hidden access control policy and the constraint policy includes the algorithms below. In our scheme, we omit the access control process for data objects that are not under the SDS constraints, as it is the same as the process in Hur's scheme [8].

Setup. Setup$(1^\lambda) \to$ (PK$_{KGC}$, MK$_{KGC}$), (PK$_S$, MK$_S$), (PK$_{SDS}$, MK$_{SDS}$). The KGC generates public parameters for the whole system. Then, the KGC, the proxy server, and the SDS monitor output their public key and master private key pairs (PK$_{KGC}$, MK$_{KGC}$), (PK$_S$, MK$_S$), and (PK$_{SDS}$, MK$_{SDS}$), respectively.

Key Generation. KeyGen(MK$_{KGC}$, S) $\to$ SK$_u$. The KGC takes MK$_{KGC}$ and a set of attributes $S \in 2^{O\_ATTR} \setminus \{\emptyset\}$ as input, and it outputs the private key SK$_u$ for the user u.

Data Encryption. Encrypt(PK$_{KGC}$, PK$_S$, PK$_{SDS}$, M, $\mathcal{T}$) $\to$ CT. The data owner takes PK$_{KGC}$, PK$_S$, and PK$_{SDS}$ and the tree access structure $\mathcal{T}$ as parameters to encrypt the data object M. The data owner outputs a ciphertext CT.

Token Generation. GenToken(SK$_u$, S') $\to$ TK$_{S',u}$. The user u takes SK$_u$ and the set of attributes $S' \subseteq S$ as input and outputs a token TK$_{S',u}$.

Partial Decryption

(a) *Proxy-Server-Side Partial Decryption.* SPartDecrypt(CT, TK$_{S',u}$) $\to$ CT$'$. The proxy server determines if S' matches the access control policy. If so, then the server partially decrypts CT and outputs CT$'$ for further partial decryption by the SDS monitor; otherwise, it returns $\perp$.

(b) *SDS-Monitor-Side Partial Decryption.* SDSPartDecrypt(CT$'$) $\to$ CT$''$. The SDS monitor determines if the current data access violates any SDS constraint; if so, then CT$'$ is destroyed, and $\perp$ is returned; otherwise, the monitor takes CT$'$ as input and outputs CT$''$ for the user.

Data Decryption. Decrypt(CT'', SK_u) $\rightarrow M$. The user takes CT'' and SK_u as input and outputs data object M if the decryption is successful.

6. Construction of CP-ABE Access Control Scheme for SDS Constraint

The construction of the scheme is partly based on Hur's scheme [8]. However, we add the partially hidden, flexible SDS constraint policy to his scheme. To enforce the SDS constraint, the system must have the ability to determine if the user can successfully decrypt the data object before sending it to the user. This is because the user's current and previous successful access to data objects under an SDS constraint may affect the user's future access to other data objects under the same SDS constraint. In [8], the storage server happened to have the desired ability without having any knowledge about the attributes in the access structure. Therefore, Hur's work comes in handy here. The access tree specification and satisfying the access tree are the same as in [3]; we thus omit them here.

6.1. CP-ABE Access Control Scheme Construction for the SDS Constraint. Let $\mathbb{G}_0$ be a bilinear group of prime order p, and let g be the generator of $\mathbb{G}_0$. In addition, let $e : \mathbb{G}_0 \times \mathbb{G}_0 \rightarrow \mathbb{G}_1$ denote the bilinear map. A security parameter, k, will determine the size of the groups. We use two hash functions, $H : \{0, 1\}^* \rightarrow \mathbb{G}_0$ and $H_1 : \mathbb{G}_1 \rightarrow \{0, 1\}^{\log p}$, which we will model as a random oracle. For the Lagrange coefficients $\Delta_{i,S}$ for any $i \in \mathbb{Z}_p^*$ and a set, S, of elements in $\mathbb{Z}_p^*$, we define $\Delta_{i,S}(x) = \prod_{j \in S, j \neq i}((x - j)/(i - j))$.

Setup. The KGC, proxy server, and SDS monitor produce their public and master private key pairs.

The KGC chooses $\mathbb{G}_0$ of prime order p, where g is its generator. The KGC chooses $H : \{0, 1\}^* \rightarrow \mathbb{G}_0$, $H_1 : \mathbb{G}_1 \rightarrow \{0, 1\}^{\log p}$ and the following public parameters: $(\mathbb{G}_0, g, H, H_1)$.

The KGC chooses two random exponents $\alpha, \beta \in {}_R\mathbb{Z}_p^*$, $h = g^\beta$; then, the public and private keys for the KGC are $\text{PK}_{\text{KGC}} = (h, e(g, g)^\alpha)$ and $\text{MK}_{\text{KGC}} = (\beta, g^\alpha)$, respectively.

The proxy server chooses a random exponent $\gamma \in {}_R\mathbb{Z}_p^*$; then, the public and private keys for the proxy server are $\text{PK}_S = g^\gamma$ and $\text{MK}_S = H(\text{ID}_S)^\gamma$, respectively.

The SDS monitor chooses a random exponent $\sigma \in {}_R\mathbb{Z}_p^*$; then, the public and private keys for the SDS monitor are $\text{PK}_{\text{SDS}} = g^\sigma$ and $\text{MK}_{\text{SDS}} = H(\text{ID}_{\text{SDS}})^\sigma$, respectively.

Key Generation. The KGC produces private keys for users by running the KeyGen(MK_{KGC}, S) algorithm. The algorithm takes as input MK_{KGC} and S and outputs a private key for a user that holds all attributes in S. The KGC selects two random exponents $r_t \in {}_R\mathbb{Z}_p^*$ and $r_j \in {}_R\mathbb{Z}_p^*$, where r_t is a unique secret to user u_t and r_j is a unique secret to attribute

$\lambda_j \in S$. Then, the KGC generates the following private key for the user:

$$\text{SK}_{u_t} = \Big(D = g^{(\alpha + r_t)/\beta}, \; \forall \lambda_j \in S : D_j = g^{r_t} \\ \cdot H(\lambda_j)^{r_j}, \; D'_j = g^{r_j}, \; D''_j = H(\lambda_j)^\beta \Big). \tag{2}$$

Data Encryption. Suppose that a data owner u_a has m different SDS constraints, $\text{SDS}_i^{(a)} = (\{[M_1], [M_2], \ldots, [M_{n_i}]\}, \#k_i)$, $i = 1, 2, \ldots, m$, where the corresponding dummy attributes are $\{\theta_{i,1}^{(a)}, \theta_{i,2}^{(a)}, \ldots, \theta_{i,n_i}^{(a)}\}_{1 \leq i \leq m}$. For an SDS, the data owner selects a random $a \in {}_R\mathbb{Z}_p^*$ and then computes $K_{\theta_{i,j}} = (e(g^\sigma)^a, H(\theta_{i,j}))$, $j = 1, 2, \ldots, n_i$, $i = 1, 2, \ldots, m$. These computations can be completed beforehand. The data owner only releases the SDS constraint information $\text{SDS\_INFO}_i^{(a)} = \{\theta_{i,1}, \theta_{i,2}, \ldots, \theta_{i,n_i}, k_i\}$, $1 \leq i \leq m$, to the cloud storage server.

Suppose that the data owner u_a wants to release his/her data object $M \in \mathbb{G}_1$ to the cloud storage server, $M \in [M_j]$, where $M_j \in \text{SDS}_i^{(a)} = (\{[M_1], [M_2], \ldots, [M_{n_i}]\}, \#k_i)$. Before releasing the data object, u_a encrypts the data object under an access tree $\mathcal{T}$ defined by him/her by running the Encrypt(PK_{KGC}, PK_S, PK_{SDS}, M, $\mathcal{T}$) algorithm. The algorithm first chooses a polynomial q_x for each node x, including the leaves, in the tree $\mathcal{T}$. For additional details, see the definition of access trees in [3].

Let Y be the set of leaf nodes in $\mathcal{T}$. The data owner computes $s_y = (e(g^\beta)^a, H(\lambda_y))$ for all $y \in Y$ in the leaf node of the access tree and then computes $H_1(s_y)$.

To encrypt the data object M under $\mathcal{T}$, the data owner computes a session key between the data owner and the proxy server $K_S = e((g^\gamma)^a, H(\text{ID}_S))$ as well as the session key between the data owner and the SDS monitor $K_{\text{SDS}} = e((g^\sigma)^a, H(\text{ID}_{\text{SDS}}))$. Then, the algorithm constructs a ciphertext as

$$\text{CT} = \Big(\mathcal{T}, \widetilde{C} = M \cdot K_S \cdot K_{\text{SDS}} \cdot e(g, g)^{\alpha s}, C = h^s, \; \forall y \\ \in Y : C_y = g^{q_y(0)}, \; C'_y = H(\lambda_y)^{q_y(0)}, \; H_1\big(K_{\theta_{i,j}}\big) \Big). \tag{3}$$

The data owner u_a sends (ID_a, g^a, CT) to the proxy server.

Token Generation. When a user u_t sends an access request for a data object, where the data object's owner is u_a, to the proxy server using a set of attributes $S' \subseteq S$, where S is the set of all valid attributes u_t held, user u_t obtains g^a from the proxy server first. Then, he/she generates a token TK_{S', u_t} by running the GenToken(SK_{u_t}, S') algorithm.

For all $\lambda_j \in S'$, the algorithm computes $s_j = e(g^a, D''_j) = e(g^a, H(\lambda_j)^\beta)$. Then, the algorithm selects a random $\tau \in {}_R\mathbb{Z}_p^*$ and constructs the token for S' as

$$\text{TK}_{S', u_t} = \Big(\forall \lambda_j \in S' : I_j = H_1\big(s_j\big), \big(D_j\big)^\tau, \big(D'_j\big)^\tau \Big). \tag{4}$$

If $S' \nsubseteq S$, then the algorithm outputs $\perp$.

Next, user u_t sends the token to the proxy server and a request for the partial decryption of the ciphertext with this token. Tokens can also be precomputed.

Partial Decryption

(a) Proxy-Server-Side Partial Decryption. After receiving the token from the user, the proxy server determines whether the set of attribute indices I_j in the token matches the blinded access control policy embedded in CT. If the token matches the access control policy of the data object, then it partially decrypts the ciphertext by running the SPartDecrypt(CT, TK_{S',u_t}) algorithm for user u_t.

The SPartDecrypt(CT, TK_{S',u_t}) algorithm operates in a recursive manner. We first define a recursive algorithm DecryptNote(CT, TK, x) that takes as input a ciphertext CT, a token TK, which is associated with a set of attributes S', and a node x from the tree $\mathcal{T}$. The algorithm outputs a group element of $\mathbb{G}_1$ or $\perp$.

Suppose that the proxy server runs the algorithm with a token TK_{S',u_t} provided by a user u_t. Suppose that an attribute assigned to a leaf node x is blinded as $H_1(s_x)$. Then, make the following definition: If $H_1(s_x) \in \mathcal{I}$, where $\mathcal{I}$ is a set of all attribute indices I_j associated with the token, then

$$
\begin{aligned}
\mathrm{DecryptNote}\left(\mathrm{CT}, \mathrm{TK}_{S',u_t}, x\right) &= \frac{e\left((D_x)^\tau, C_x\right)}{e\left((D'_x)^\tau, C'_x\right)} \\
&= \frac{e\left(\left(g^{r_t} \cdot H(\lambda_x)^{r_x}\right)^\tau, g^{q_x(0)}\right)}{e\left((g^{r_x})^\tau, H(\lambda_x)^{q_x(0)}\right)} = e(g,g)^{r_t \tau q_x(0)}.
\end{aligned}
\tag{5}
$$

If $H_1(s_x) \notin \mathcal{I}$, define DecryptNote(CT, TK, x) $= \perp$.

Now, consider the recursive case in which x is a nonleaf node. The DecryptNote(CT, TK_{S',u_t}, x) algorithm is executed as follows: For all nodes z that are children of x, the algorithm calls DecryptNote(CT, TK_{S',u_t}, z) and stores the output as F_z. Let S_x be an arbitrary k_x-sized set of child nodes z such that $F_z \neq \perp$; then, the algorithm computes

$$
F_x = \prod_{z \in S_x} F_z^{\Delta_{i,S'_x}(0)},
$$

where $i = \mathrm{index}(z)$, $S'_x = \{\mathrm{index}(z) : z \in S_x\}$

$$
\begin{aligned}
&= \prod_{z \in S_x} \left(e(g,g)^{r_t \cdot \tau \cdot q_z(0)}\right)^{\Delta_{i,S'_x}(0)} \\
&= \prod_{z \in S_x} \left(e(g,g)^{r_t \cdot \tau \cdot q_{\mathrm{parent}(z)}(\mathrm{index}(z))}\right)^{\Delta_{i,S'_x}(0)} \\
&= \prod_{z \in S_x} \left(e(g,g)^{r_t \cdot \tau \cdot q_x(i)}\right)^{\Delta_{i,S'_x}(0)} = e(g,g)^{r_t \cdot \tau \cdot q_x(0)}
\end{aligned}
\tag{6}
$$

and returns the result.

The algorithm begins by calling the function on the root node R of the access tree $\mathcal{T}$. If the access tree is satisfied by the token associated with the set of attributes S', then the proxy server extracts DecryptNote(CT, TK_{S',u_t}, R) $= e(g,g)^{r_t \tau s}$.

The proxy server computes $K_S = e(g^a, \mathrm{MK}_S) = e(g^a, H(\mathrm{ID}_S)^\gamma)$ and $\widetilde{C}' = \widetilde{C}/K_S = M \cdot K_{\mathrm{SDS}} \cdot e(g,g)^{\alpha s}$ in CT; then, it sends $\mathrm{CT}' = (\widetilde{C}', C = h^s, A, H_1(K_{\theta_{i,j}}))$ to the SDS monitor, where

$$
A = \mathrm{DecryptNote}\left(\mathrm{CT}, \mathrm{TK}_{S',u_t}, R\right) = e(g,g)^{r_t \tau s}. \tag{7}
$$

(b) SDS-Monitor-Side Partial Decryption. After receiving CT' from the proxy server, the SDS monitor determines if the current data access violates any SDS constraint defined by the data owner. If so, the SDS monitor destroys CT' and returns $\perp$, and the user's access request will be denied. Otherwise, the SDS monitor takes CT' as input and outputs CT'' for the user by running the SDSPartDecrypt(CT') algorithm.

Now, we give the determination process in detail. The SDS monitor precomputes all $\Theta_{i,j} = H_1(K_{\theta_{i,j}})$, $j = 1,2,\ldots,n_i$, $i = 1,2,\ldots,m$, after computing $K_{\theta_{i,j}} = e(g^a, H(\theta_{i,j})^\sigma)$, $j = 1,2,\ldots,n_i$, $i = 1,2,\ldots,m$, for $\{\theta_{i,1}, \theta_{i,2}, \ldots, \theta_{i,n_i}\}_{1 \leq i \leq m}$; and it compares $H_1(K_{\theta_{i,j}})$ in CT' to these precomputed dummy attribute indices $\Theta_{i,j}$, $j = 1,2,\ldots,n_i$, $i = 1,2,\ldots,m$. By comparison, it finds out that $\Theta_{i,j} = H_1(K_{\theta_{i,j}})$ and determines the SDS constraint information $\mathrm{SDS\_INFO}_t^{(a)} = \{\theta_{i,1}^{(a)}, \theta_{i,2}^{(a)}, \ldots, \theta_{i,n_i}^{(a)}, k_t\}$, and the threshold k_t should be applied to the current data. According to the threshold value k_t, the SDS monitor checks if $|\mathrm{H\_Attr}(u_t, \mathrm{SDS}_t^{(a)}) \cup \{\theta_{i,j}\}| = k_t$, and then it determines whether the current data access violates SDS constraint $\mathrm{SDS}_t^{(a)}$ and destroys the data immediately; otherwise, the SDS monitor performs its partial decryption. The SDS monitor first computes $K_{\mathrm{SDS}} = e(g^a, \mathrm{MK}_{\mathrm{SDS}}) = e(g^a, H(\mathrm{ID}_{\mathrm{SDS}})^\sigma)$ and then computes $\widetilde{C}'' = \widetilde{C}'/K_{\mathrm{SDS}} = M \cdot e(g,g)^{\alpha s}$.

Next, the SDS monitor updates the historical SDS constraint specific attribute set as $\mathrm{H\_Attr}(u_t, \mathrm{SDS}_t^{(a)}) = \mathrm{H\_Attr}(u_t, \mathrm{SDS}_t^{(a)}) \cup \{\theta_{i,j}\}$ and sends $\mathrm{CT}'' = (\widetilde{C}'', C = h^s, A)$ to the user.

Data Decryption. When user u_t receives the ciphertext CT'' from the SDS monitor, he/she uses the Decrypt($\mathrm{CT}'', \mathrm{SK}_{S',u_t}$) algorithm to decrypt the ciphertext by computing

$$
\begin{aligned}
&\frac{\widetilde{C}''}{\left(e(C,D)/(A)^{1/\tau}\right)} \\
&= \frac{\widetilde{C}''}{\left(e(h^s, g^{(\alpha+r_t)/\beta})/\left(e(g,g)^{r_t \tau s}\right)^{1/\tau}\right)} \\
&= \frac{\widetilde{C}''}{\left(e(g^{\beta s}, g^{(\alpha+r_t)/\beta})/e(g,g)^{r_t s}\right)} = \frac{Me(g,g)^{\alpha s}}{e(g,g)^{\alpha s}} \\
&= M.
\end{aligned}
\tag{8}
$$

6.2. A Case Study. We illustrate through an example how the SDS monitor checks whether the current data access violates any SDS constraint. Suppose a data owner *Alice* released three data objects M_1, M_2, and M_3 and defined tth SDS constraint over them; that is, $\text{SDS}_t^{(\text{Alice})} = \{\{M_1\}, \{M_2, M_3\}, \#2\}$. The corresponding SDS constraint information $\text{SDS\_INFO}_t^{(\text{Alice})} = \{\theta_{t,1}, \theta_{t,2}, 2\}$ is released to the cloud storage server. $\theta_{t,1}$ and $\theta_{t,2}$ are the two dummy attributes corresponding to $\{M_1\}$ and $\{M_2, M_3\}$, respectively. Suppose a user Bob's attributes match the access structures of data objects M_1 and M_2. When Bob sends an access request for M_1, the proxy server uses Bob's token to partially decrypt the following ciphertext:

$$\text{CT}_1 = \left(\mathcal{T}_1, \widetilde{C}_1 = M_1 \cdot K_S \cdot K_{\text{SDS}} \cdot e(g,g)^{\alpha s_1}, \, C_1 \right.$$

$$= h^{s_1}, \, \forall y \in Y_1 : C_y = g^{q_y(0)}, \, C_y' \qquad (9)$$

$$\left. = H\left(\lambda_y\right)^{q_y(0)}, \, H_1\left(K_{\theta_{t,1}}\right) \right),$$

where $\mathcal{T}_1$ is the tree access structure of M_1 and Y_1 is the set of leaf nodes in $\mathcal{T}_1$.

Since Bob's attributes match $\mathcal{T}_1$, then the partial decryption by the proxy server will be successful. The proxy server knows that M_1 is under an SDS constraint because there is $H_1(K_{\theta_{t,1}})$ in the ciphertext, and then it transfers the ciphertext $\text{CT}_1' = (\widetilde{C}_1', C_1 = h^{s_1}, A_1, H_1(K_{\theta_{t,1}}))$ to the SDS monitor. When the SDS monitor receives the partially decrypted ciphertext from the proxy server, it compares $H_1(K_{\theta_{t,1}})$ in the ciphertext to the precomputed values $\Theta_{i,j} = H_1(K_{\theta_{i,j}})$, where $K_{\theta_{i,j}} = e(g^a, H(\theta_{i,j})^\sigma)$, $j = 1, 2, \ldots, n_i$, $i = 1, 2, \ldots, m$, for $\{\theta_{i,1}, \theta_{i,2}, \ldots, \theta_{i,n_i}\}_{1 \le i \le m}$, and then it gets $\Theta_{t,1} = H_1(K_{\theta_{t,1}})$. Therefore, the SDS monitor determines that $\text{SDS\_INFO}_t^{(\text{Alice})} = \{\theta_{t,1}, \theta_{t,2}, 2\}$ is the SDS constraint information applied to the data M_1. The SDS monitor checks if $|\text{H\_Attr}(\text{Bob}, \text{SDS}_t^{(\text{Alice})}) \cup \{\theta_{t,1}\}| = 2$. Since $\text{H\_Attr}(\text{Bob}, \text{SDS}_t^{(\text{Alice})}) = \emptyset$, we have

$$\left| \text{H\_Attr}\left(\text{Bob}, \text{SDS}_t^{(\text{Alice})}\right) \cup \{\theta_{t,1}\} \right| = 1 < 2. \qquad (10)$$

Therefore, the SDS monitor knows that the current access to M_1 does not violate $\text{SDS}_t^{(\text{Alice})}$. After that, it updates $\text{H\_Attr}(\text{Bob}, \text{SDS}_t^{(\text{Alice})})$ as

$$\text{H\_Attr}\left(\text{Bob}, \text{SDS}_t^{(\text{Alice})}\right)$$
$$= \text{H\_Attr}\left(\text{Bob}, \text{SDS}_t^{(\text{Alice})}\right) \cup \{\theta_{t,1}\} \qquad (11)$$

and then sends $\text{CT}_1'' = (\widetilde{C}_1'', C_1 = h^{s_1}, A_1)$ to Bob. Bob successfully accesses M_1.

When Bob sends another access request for M_2, the proxy server uses Bob's token to partially decrypt the following ciphertext:

$$\text{CT}_2 = \left(\mathcal{T}_2, \widetilde{C}_2 = M_2 \cdot K_S \cdot K_{\text{SDS}} \cdot e(g,g)^{\alpha s_2}, \, C_2 \right.$$

$$= h^{s_2}, \, \forall y \in Y_2 : C_y = g^{q_y(0)}, \, C_y' \qquad (12)$$

$$\left. = H\left(\lambda_y\right)^{q_y(0)}, \, H_1\left(K_{\theta_{t,2}}\right) \right),$$

where $\mathcal{T}_2$ is the tree access structure of M_2 and Y_2 is the set of leaf nodes in $\mathcal{T}_2$.

Since Bob's attributes match $\mathcal{T}_2$, then the partial decryption by the proxy server will be successful. The proxy server knows that the ciphertext is under an SDS constraint because there is $H_1(K_{\theta_{t,2}})$, and then it transfers the ciphertext $\text{CT}_2' = (\widetilde{C}_2', C_2 = h^{s_2}, A_2, H_1(K_{\theta_{t,2}}))$ to the SDS monitor. When the SDS monitor receives the partially decrypted ciphertext from the proxy server, it compares $H_1(K_{\theta_{t,2}})$ in the ciphertext to the precomputed values $\Theta_{i,j} = H_1(K_{\theta_{i,j}})$, where $K_{\theta_{i,j}} = e(g^a, H(\theta_{i,j})^\sigma)$, $j = 1, 2, \ldots, n_i$, $i = 1, 2, \ldots, m$, for $\{\theta_{i,1}, \theta_{i,2}, \ldots, \theta_{i,n_i}\}_{1 \le i \le m}$, and then it gets $\Theta_{t,2} = H_1(K_{\theta_{t,2}})$. Therefore, the SDS monitor determines that $\text{SDS\_INFO}_t^{(\text{Alice})} = \{\theta_{t,1}, \theta_{t,2}, 2\}$ is also the SDS constraint information applied to the data M_2. The SDS monitor checks if $|\text{H\_Attr}(\text{Bob}, \text{SDS}_t^{(\text{Alice})}) \cup \{\theta_{t,2}\}| = 2$. Now, we have

$$\left| \text{H\_Attr}\left(\text{Bob}, \text{SDS}_t^{(\text{Alice})}\right) \cup \{\theta_{t,2}\} \right| = 2, \qquad (13)$$

so the SDS monitor knows that the current access to M_2 violates $\text{SDS}_t^{(\text{Alice})}$. It destroys the corresponding ciphertext immediately. Bob cannot access M_2.

7. Extra Costs due to the SDS Constraint and Comparison

We discuss the additional costs due to the enforcement of the SDS constraint, in comparison with [8]. We also compare our scheme with [9, 10]. We use notations in the Notations Section.

In Table 1, we compare the user's private key size, ciphertext size, public key size, and computational cost used in the whole system with those in [8–10]. Compared to [8], the user's private key size is the same, the ciphertext size is increased by the bit size of an element in $\mathbb{G}_1$ because $H_1(K_{\theta_{i,j}})$ is embedded into it, and the public key size is increased by the bit size of an element in $\mathbb{G}_0$ because $\text{PK}_{\text{SDS}} = g^\sigma$ is used as one of the public keys in the system.

In addition, we have the additional dummy attributes $\{\theta_{i,1}, \theta_{i,2}, \ldots, \theta_{i,n_i}\}_{1 \le i \le m}$ for a data owner who has m different SDS constraints. However, the obfuscation of these dummy attributes by the data owner and the computation of the attribute indices of these dummy attributes by the SDS monitor can be performed beforehand.

Compared to [8–10], our scheme has an extra network communication cost per data object if the data object is under an SDS constraint. The proxy server sends the partially decrypted ciphertext to the SDS monitor, and the SDS monitor sends the further partially decrypted ciphertext to the user.

8. Security, Consistency, and Accessibility Analysis

The security, policy privacy, consistency, and accessibility analyses are presented in this section with respect to the requirements enumerated in Section 4.2.

TABLE 1: Comparison of different schemes.

	Hur's [8]	Lai et al.'s [9]	Lai et al.'s [10]	The proposed scheme
Ciphertext size	$(2t+1)L_0 + L_1$	$(N+1)L_0 + L_1$	$(4\ell+2)L_0 + 2L_1$	$(2t+1)L_0 + 2L_1$
Private key size	$(3k+1)L_0$	$(u+1)L_0$	$(u+2)L_0$	$(3k+1)L_0$
Public key size	$2L_0 + L_1$	$(N+2)L_0 + L_1$	$(u+5)L_0 + L_1$	$3L_0 + L_1$
Encryption cost	$(3t+3)\exp + (t+1)\widehat{e}$	$(N+2)\exp$	$(8\ell+4)\exp$	$(3t+4)\exp + (t+2)\widehat{e}$
Partial decryption cost (storage server or proxy server)	$(2|R|+1)\widehat{e} + \exp$	/	/	$(2|R|+1)\widehat{e} + \exp$
Partial decryption cost (SDS monitor)	/	/	/	$\widehat{e} + \exp$
Decryption cost (user)	$\widehat{e} + 3\exp$	$(N+1)\widehat{e}$	$(4\ell+2)\widehat{e} + (2\ell+3)\exp$	$\widehat{e} + 3\exp$
Token generation cost (user)	$|R|\widehat{e} + 2|R|\exp$	/	/	$|R|\widehat{e} + 2|R|\exp$

8.1. Security

Data Confidentiality. For data objects that are not under any SDS constraint, confidentiality is guaranteed because we follow [8] for these data objects. The SDS monitor can just be regarded as an external user who does not have sufficient attributes.

Considering data objects that are under the SDS constraints, we introduced the following concepts: the SDS monitor, the SDS constraint specific dummy attributes, and additional partial decryption by the SDS monitor. Therefore, we mainly analyze the effect of the corresponding changes regarding the data confidentiality.

An external user u_t whose attributes do not match the tree access structure in the ciphertext cannot produce a valid token for partial decryption. This results in the fact that the proxy server cannot extract the expected value $e(g,g)^{r_t \tau s}$ with the invalid token without knowing r_t and τ, which are unique secrets to the user.

Assuming that the unauthorized user u_t directly fetches the ciphertext from the cloud storage server without using the token, he/she cannot compute $e(g,g)^{r_t s}$ because his/her attributes do not match the access tree. Moreover, he/she cannot cast off the session keys K_S and K_{SDS} embedded in the ciphertext component $\widetilde{C} = M \cdot K_S \cdot K_{SDS} \cdot e(g,g)^{\alpha s}$ because K_S is only shared by the data owner and the proxy server, and K_{SDS} is only shared by the data owner and the SDS monitor.

The proxy server, similar to other external unauthorized users, not only does not have sufficient attributes to decrypt the ciphertext but also cannot cast off K_{SDS} embedded in the ciphertext component $\widetilde{C} = M \cdot K_S \cdot K_{SDS} \cdot e(g,g)^{\alpha s}$ because K_{SDS} is only shared by the data owner and the SDS monitor.

The KGC cannot decrypt the ciphertext because the session keys K_S and K_{SDS} are embedded in the ciphertext component $\widetilde{C} = M \cdot K_S \cdot K_{SDS} \cdot e(g,g)^{\alpha s}$. In addition, K_S is shared only by the data owner and the proxy server, and K_{SDS} is shared only by the data owner and the SDS monitor. The KGC cannot determine K_S and K_{SDS} because of the session key secrecy property of the key agreement [20]. Assuming that the KGC can access the partially decrypted ciphertext $CT' = (\widetilde{C}', C = h^s, A, H_1(K_{\theta_{i,j}}))$, where $\widetilde{C}' = \widetilde{C}/K_S = M \cdot K_{SDS} \cdot e(g,g)^{\alpha s}$ from the proxy server, it still cannot cast off K_{SDS} because K_{SDS} is only shared by the data owner and the SDS monitor. Moreover, the KGC cannot cast off τ from

$A = e(g,g)^{r_t \tau s}$ to obtain the expected value $e(g,g)^{r_t s}$ because τ is a unique secret to the user.

The SDS monitor cannot decrypt the ciphertext for two reasons. First, it cannot cast off τ from $A = e(g,g)^{r_t \tau s}$ to obtain the expected value $e(g,g)^{r_t s}$ because τ is a unique secret to the user. Second, the SDS monitor does not know β, r_t, or g^α to obtain the expected value $g^{(\alpha + r_t)/\beta}$ because β and g^α are private keys of the KGC and because r_t is a unique secret to the user.

In addition, the SDS constraint specific dummy attributes themselves do not disclose any information about the content of the data object because they are completely independent of the content of the data object.

Collusion Resistance. For both ordinary data objects and the data objects that are under the SDS constraints, collusion resistance is guaranteed. The ciphertext component $\widetilde{C} = M \cdot K_S \cdot K_{SDS} \cdot e(g,g)^{\alpha s}$ is different from that in Hur's scheme for the data that are under an SDS constraint, but this does not affect collusion resistance. The random value r_t, which is unique to each user in the users' private keys, prevents several users from combining their private keys to produce a token to decrypt the ciphertext unless one of the users has sufficient valid attributes to produce a token to achieve $e(g,g)^{\alpha s}$.

SDS Constraint. The data object that is under an SDS constraint must pass through the SDS constraint checkpoint, the SDS monitor, because the session key K_{SDS} is embedded in the ciphertext component $\widetilde{C} = M \cdot K_S \cdot K_{SDS} \cdot e(g,g)^{\alpha s}$. Neither the proxy server, the KGC, nor the user can cast off K_{SDS} because K_{SDS} is only shared by the data owner and the SDS monitor. When the SDS monitor receives the partially decrypted ciphertext from the proxy server, the SDS monitor checks if the user's current data access violates an SDS constraint by comparing $H_1(K_{\theta_{i,j}})$ in the ciphertext to the precomputed values $\Theta_{i,j} = H_1(K_{\theta_{i,j}})$, $j = 1,2,\ldots,n_i$, $i = 1,2,\ldots,m$, where $K_{\theta_{i,j}} = e(g^\alpha, H(\theta_{i,j})^\sigma)$, $j = 1,2,\ldots,n_i$, $i = 1,2,\ldots,m$, for $\text{SDS\_INFO}_i^{(a)} = \{\theta_{i,1}^{(a)}, \theta_{i,2}^{(a)}, \ldots, \theta_{i,n_i}^{(a)}, k_i\}_{1 \le i \le m}$, and it checks if $|\text{H\_Attr}(u_t, \text{SDS}_i^{(u_a)}) \cup \{\theta_{i,j}\}| = k_i$. If the SDS monitor determines that the current data access violates an SDS constraint, the SDS monitor destroys the data immediately. We consider that the duty of access control policy enforcement and the duty of SDS constraint policy enforcement should be separated into two different entities. Therefore, we add an SDS monitor to the system architecture instead of only using the proxy server to perform both duties. Performing this separation follows the access control principle of separation of duty.

8.2. Policy Privacy

Access Control Policy Privacy. For both ordinary data object and the data objects that are under the SDS constraint, access control policy privacy is guaranteed because we follow Hur's scheme [8]. We omit the description here.

Constraint Policy Privacy. First, when the data owner only releases the SDS constraint information $\{\theta_{i,1}, \theta_{i,2}, \ldots, \theta_{i,n_i}, k_i\}_{1 \le i \le m}$ to the cloud storage server, he/she does not disclose any information about which dummy attributes are used for which data object. Initially, other entities only have knowledge that $\{\theta_{i,1}, \theta_{i,2}, \ldots, \theta_{i,n_i}, k_i\}_{1 \le i \le m}$ are used for SDS constraint and nothing else.

If the user receives the partially decrypted ciphertext from the SDS monitor, and not from the proxy server, then he/she only knows that the current data object is under an SDS constraint. The user does not know to which SDS constraint the data object belongs; the relations among this data object and other data objects received from the SDS monitor previously are also unknown to him/her.

The KGC and the proxy server know that the ciphertext is under an SDS constraint if there is a ciphertext component $H_1(K_{\theta_{i,j}})$. If they observe that several ciphertexts that belong to a data owner have the same $H_1(K_{\theta_{i,j}})$, then they only know that the corresponding data objects belong to the same equivalence class in an SDS; this does not pose a security threat. However, they still do not know other structure information of an SDS constraint, including the threshold k_i, and other data objects that are in a different equivalence class of the same SDS constraint.

The SDS monitor can observe the relations among the ciphertexts but does not know the entire SDS structure exactly. For example, it does not know how many data objects are contained in the same equivalence class. The total number of equivalence classes can vary over time as the number of corresponding dummy attributes varies. However, the SDS monitor is responsible for enforcing the SDS constraint; therefore, the SDS monitor is the entity that possesses the most knowledge about the SDS constraint structure; this situation is indispensable.

8.3. Consistency.
Any two compatible data objects under an SDS constraint cannot be incompatible under any other SDS constraint and vice versa. The data owner is required to define consistent SDS constraints. This can be achieved as follows. For each data object M, we maintain its global current incompatible set $\overline{M} = \{M' \mid \exists \text{SDS}, M, M' \in \text{SDS} \land M' \notin [M]\}$. If the data owner needs to add a new SDS constraint or add new data objects into an existing SDS constraint that includes the data object M, then he/she should ensure that data objects from $\overline{M}$ are not put into $[M]$. The details on

how to maintain SDS constraint consistency are beyond the scope of this paper. However, if we cannot guarantee this consistency, this may result in a violation of both security and accessibility requirements.

8.4. Accessibility.
A user whose valid attributes match the tree access structure of a data object can access the data object even if it is organized into an SDS constraint, unless the data access violates an SDS constraint. Access control policy enforcement is implemented by the proxy server using the user's token, which is associated with the user's valid attributes; thus, the proxy server can partially decrypt the ciphertext if the user has the valid attributes. The partially decrypted ciphertext must pass through the SDS monitor to enforce the SDS constraint. If the current data access does not violate the SDS constraint, then the SDS monitor also partially decrypts the ciphertext to send it to the user for full decryption; otherwise, the SDS monitor destroys it, and the user cannot receive the partially decrypted ciphertext. Therefore, this requirement is guaranteed to be met.

In contrast, a user whose valid attributes do not match the tree access structure of a data object still cannot access the data object after it is organized into an SDS constraint. Access control policy enforcement is performed first by the proxy server using the user's token, which is associated with the user's valid attributes. Therefore, the proxy server cannot partially decrypt the ciphertext if the user does not possess valid attributes. In that case, the proxy server does not pass the ciphertext to either the SDS monitor or the user; the user thus cannot access the data object. Therefore, this requirement is guaranteed to be met.

9. Related Work

There are quite a few research works on the formal specification of access control constraints [13, 16, 17, 21–24]. Crampton [16] analyzed and classified RBAC constraints in detail. In our previous works [13, 24], we proposed general access control constraints against similar users' successive access to permissions from a sensitive combination of permissions. Joshi et al. [21] presented the formal specification of RBAC constraints, therein considering time and location in access control decision-making. Sharifi and Tripunitara [17] proposed an approach for enforcing the Chinese Wall security policy in a least-restrictive manner compared to Brewer and Nash's specification [11]. Bijon et al. [23] first introduced ABCL (Attribute-Based Constraint Specification Language) to specify constraints in ABAC (Attribute-Based Access Control), which supports the SOD of RBAC. In contrast to these works, we intended to generalize access control constraints for data released to a cloud storage server, on which the promising CP-ABE access control mechanism is utilized; we handled the constraint in a less-restrictive manner based on accessibility requirements. Our proposal coincides as much as possible with the CP-ABE access control paradigm. The SDS constraint proposed in this paper is a compact and generalized constraint that mostly covers the SOD constraint and Chinese Wall security policy. However, we did not consider *write* actions on the data by the user (consumer); the main action described in this paper is the *read* action.

In data outsourcing environments, access control is supported by cryptographic methods [25–29]. Di Vimercati et al. [25, 26] introduced a novel approach that combines cryptography with access control. Data are placed with an honest but curious third party; therefore, their approach adopted a two-layer encryption method; the first layer of encryption is performed by the data owner, as the server is not fully trusted, and the server performs the second layer of encryption to reflect dynamic changes over the access control policy. Asghar et al. used RBAC policies for outsourced environments [28]. In their work, the actual RBAC policy is hidden via encryption from the service provider, as the service provider is honest but curious. The PDP (Policy Decision Point) can perform the policy evaluation without disclosing the contents of the requests or policies to the service provider. However, [25–28] did not consider access control constraints. Compared to [25–28], our emphasis is placed on the generalization and enforcement of access control constraints, which covers most of static SOD and Chinese Wall security policies, on outsourced data released to the cloud with the objective of achieving better synergy with the CP-ABE access control mechanism.

The privacy of the access control policy defined for the outsourced data, where CP-ABE realizes the access control, is also a nontrivial issue. Researchers have been focusing on hiding access control policies from outsiders [6–10]. Yu et al. [6] and Nishide et al. [7] proposed CP-ABE schemes with a hidden access control policy. Their schemes only used "AND" gates, which restrains the expressiveness of the policy; the key size of each user is proportional to the number of attributes. In Nishide et al.'s second scheme [7], new possible values for attributes can be added after system setup. Hur's work [8] is also a variant of CP-ABE with a hidden access control policy. In his work, the computation-intensive work, the partial decryption of the ciphertext, is completed by the storage center; the access control policy has the same expressiveness as in Bethencourt et al.'s work [3]. The main reason why we extend Hur's scheme is because the handling of the SDS constraint in our approach needs an entity, aside from the data owner, to determine if the user's attributes satisfy the access control policy of the data object before sending the data object to the user without knowing the policy; in Hur's scheme, the storage center possesses the desired ability. Lai et al. [9, 10] proposed CP-ABE with a partially hidden access policy. In their work, the attributes have two parts: the attribute name and the attribute value. The data owner hides the attribute value, and thus the access policy is partially hidden. Their schemes are fully secure in the standard model. Compared to these works, we followed CP-ABE with the hidden access control policy; however, our emphasis focused on how to handle the SDS constraint, where the SDS constraint policy structure is hidden from all entities except for the SDS monitor. The constraint policy structure is partially hidden from the SDS monitor.

Asghar et al. [29] proposed a cryptographic approach for enforcing the dynamic SOD and Chinese Wall security policy. Their proposal hides users' access histories with respect to dynamic SOD via encryption because a user's access history

might reveal critical information to the service provider, who is not fully trusted. They utilized Bethencourt et al.'s [3] access structure to describe the access control constraint. Their work is on hiding conventional constraints. Compared to their work, our work is suitable for outsourced data access control realized by CP-ABE with a hidden access control policy. In our work, the constraint policy related attributes are blinded and embedded in the ciphertext; most of the computations related to the constraint policy can be precomputed, and the SDS constraint policy can be partially changed after system setup. We can easily extend our scheme by adding a time duration to transform the SDS constraint into a time-aware dynamic constraint.

10. Conclusion

In this paper, we proposed an access control approach for generalized SDS constraints for cloud storage; the constraint originated from the SOD of RBAC and the Chinese Wall security policy. Our approach is based on CP-ABE with a hidden access control policy. We handled the SDS constraint using additional artificial attributes through the participation of an additional entity: the SDS monitor. To enforce the SDS constraint, a session key, established between the data owner and the SDS monitor, is embedded in the ciphertext component to force the proxy server to pass the initial partially decrypted ciphertext to the SDS monitor to perform the second partial decryption. The SDS constraint policy structure is hidden from the KGC, the proxy server, and the user. To prevent commercial fraud or mistakes, the duties of enforcing both the access control policy and the constraint policy are divided between the proxy server and the SDS monitor. The security, policy privacy, consistency, and accessibility analyses indicated that the approach is secure and effective. The SDS constraint policy is also extensible in that the data owner puts more data objects into the equivalence classes of an SDS constraint after system setup; the data owner can increase the total number of equivalence classes and the threshold in an SDS constraint at a lower cost following system setup. To our knowledge, the generalized concept of SDS constraints and their structure as well as the use of dummy attributes to enforce a partially hidden constraint policy represents the novelty of our work.

As our future work, we will consider how to fully hide the constraint policy structure from all entities, especially from the SDS monitor, without affecting the enforcement of the SDS constraint. To improve the expressiveness of the SDS constraint, we will also consider using "AND," "OR," and "k OF n" in the SDS constraint.

Notations

L_0: Bit-length of element in $\mathbb{G}_0$
L_1: Bit-length of element in $\mathbb{G}_1$
t: The number of attributes associated with the ciphertext
k: The number of attributes associated with the private key of a user
u: The size of original attribute universe

N: The total number of possible values of all attributes

$|R|$:   The number of user's attributes satisfying an access structure

ℓ: The number of rows in LSSS matrix

exp: Exponentiation in group operation

$\widehat{e}$:   Bilinear pairing.

Acknowledgments

The authors would like to thank Professor David Du at the Department of Computer Science and Engineering, University of Minnesota, for providing the necessary support to conduct the research and also for providing valuable suggestions. This research work was supported by the National Natural Science Foundation of China (Grants nos. 61562085, 11261057, and 11461069).

References

[1] P. Mell et al., "The NIST definition of cloud computing," 2011.

[2] A. Sahai and B. Waters, "Fuzzy Identity-Based Encryption," in *Proceedings of the Annual International Conference on the Theory and Applications of Cryptographic Techniques*, pp. 457–473, Springer, Berlin, Germany, 2005.

[3] J. Bethencourt, A. Sahai, and B. Waters, "Ciphertext-policy attribute-based encryption," in *Proceedings of the IEEE Symposium on Security and Privacy (SP '07)*, pp. 321–334, May 2007.

[4] V. Goyal, O. Pandey, A. Sahai, and B. Waters, "Attribute-based encryption for fine-grained access control of encrypted data," in *Proceedings of the 13th ACM Conference on Computer and Communications Security (CCS '06)*, pp. 89–98, November 2006.

[5] B. Waters, "Ciphertext-policy attribute-based encryption: an expressive, efficient, and provably secure realization," in *Proceedings of the International Workshop on Public Key Cryptography*, pp. 53–70, Springer, Berlin, Germany, 2011.

[6] S. Yu, K. Ren, and W. Lou, "Attribute-based content distribution with hidden policy," in *Proceedings of the 4th IEEE Workshop on Secure Network Protocols, NPSec'08*, pp. 39–44, October 2008.

[7] T. Nishide, K. Yoneyama, and K. Ohta, "Attribute-based encryption with partially hidden encryptor-specified access structures," in *Proceedings of the International Conference on Applied Cryptography and Network Security*, pp. 111–129, Springer, Berlin, Germany, 2008.

[8] J. Hur, "Attribute-based secure data sharing with hidden policies in smart grid," *IEEE Transactions on Parallel and Distributed Systems*, vol. 24, no. 11, pp. 2171–2180, 2013.

[9] J. Lai, R. H. Deng, and Y. Li, "Fully secure cipertext-policy hiding CP-ABE," in *Proceedings of the International Conference on Information Security Practice and Experience*, pp. 24–39, Springer, Berlin, Germany, 2011.

[10] J. Lai, R. H. Deng, and Y. Li, "Expressive CP-ABE with partially hidden access structures," in *Proceedings of the 7th ACM Symposium on Information, Computer and Communications Security (ASIACCS '12)*, pp. 18-19, ACM, Seoul, Republic of Korea, May 2012.

[11] D. F. C. Brewer and M. J. Nash, "The Chinese Wall security policy," in *Proceedings of the IEEE Symposium on Security and Privacy*, pp. 206–214, IEEE Computer Society Press, Los Alamitos, CA, USA, May 1989.

[12] Q. Tayir, K. Rahman, and N. Helil, "Risky permission set based access control constraint," in *Proceedings of the 2015 International Conference on Computer Science And Technology (ICCST '15)*, 517, 510 pages, 2015.

[13] N. Helil and K. Rahman, "Secret sharing scheme based approach for access control constraint against similar users' collusive attack," *JISE. Journal of Information Science and Engineering*, vol. 32, no. 6, pp. 1455–1470, 2016.

[14] R. S. Sandhu, E. J. Coyne, H. L. Feinstein, and C. E. Youman, "Role-based access control models," *Computer*, vol. 29, no. 2, pp. 38–47, 1996.

[15] D. F. Ferraiolo, R. S. Sandhu, S. Gavrila, D. R. Kuhn, and R. Chandramouli, "Proposed NIST standard for role-based access control," *ACM Transactions on Information and System Security*, vol. 4, no. 3, pp. 224–274, 2001.

[16] J. Crampton, "Specifying and enforcing constraints in role-based access control," in *Proceedings of Eighth ACM Symposium on Access Control Models and Technologies*, pp. 43–50, June 2003.

[17] A. Sharifi and M. V. Tripunitara, "Least-restrictive enforcement of the chinese wall security policy," in *Proceedings of the 18th ACM Symposium on Access Control Models and Technologies, SACMAT '13*, pp. 61–72, June 2013.

[18] R. Wu, G.-J. Ahn, H. Hu, and M. Singhal, "Information flow control in cloud computing," in *Proceedings of the 6th International Conference on Collaborative Computing: Networking, Applications and Worksharing, CollaborateCom '10*, pp. 1–7, IEEE, Ottawa, ON, Canada, October 2010.

[19] M. Chase, "Multi-authority Attribute Based Encryption," in *Proceedings of the Theory of Cryptography Conference*, pp. 515–534, 2007.

[20] A. Kate, G. Zaverucha, and I. Goldberg, "Pairing-Based Onion Routing," in *Proceedings of the International Workshop on Privacy Enhancing Technologies*, pp. 95–112, Springer, Berlin, Germany, 2007.

[21] J. B. D. Joshi, E. Bertino, U. Latif, and A. Ghafoor, "A generalized temporal role-based access control model," *IEEE Transactions on Knowledge and Data Engineering*, vol. 17, no. 1, pp. 4–23, 2005.

[22] D. Basin, S. J. Burri, and G. Karjoth, "Separation of duties as a service," in *Proceedings of the 6th International Symposium on Information, Computer and Communications Security, ASIACCS 2011*, pp. 423–429, March 2011.

[23] K. Z. Bijon, R. Krishman, and R. Sandhu, "Constraints specification in attribute based access control," *Science*, vol. 2, pp. 131–144, 2013.

[24] N. Helil and K. Rahman, "Attribute based access control constraint based on subject similarity," in *Proceedings of the 2014 IEEE Workshop on Advanced Research and Technology in Industry Applications, WARTIA '14*, pp. 226–229, IEEE, Ottawa, ON, Canada, September 2014.

[25] S. D. C. Di Vimercati, S. Foresti, S. Jajodia, S. Paraboschi, and P. Samarati, "Over-encryption: management of access control evolution on outsourced data," in *Proceedings of the 33rd International Conference on Very Large Data Bases, VLDB '07*, pp. 123–134, VLDB endowment, Washington, Wash, USA, September 2007.

[26] S. D. C. Di Vimercati, S. Foresti, S. Jajodia, S. Paraboschi, and P. Samarati, "Encryption policies for regulating access to outsourced data," *ACM Transactions on Database Systems*, vol. 35, pp. 12:1–12:46, 2010.

[27] M. R. Asghar, M. Ion, G. Russello, and B. Crispo, "ESPOON: Enforcing encrypted security policies in outsourced environments," in *Proceedings of the 2011 6th International Conference on Availability, Reliability and Security, ARES '11*, pp. 99–108, IEEE, Vienna, Austria, August 2011.

[28] M. R. Asghar, M. Ion, G. Russello, and B. Crispo, "ESPOON ERBAC: enforcing security policies in outsourced environments," *Computers and Security*, vol. 35, pp. 2–24, 2013.

[29] M. R. Asghar, G. Russello, and B. Crispo, "E-GRANT: enforcing encrypted dynamic security constraints in the cloud," in *Proceedings of the 3rd International Conference on Future Internet of Things and Cloud, FiCloud '15*, pp. 135–144, IEEE, Rome, Italy, August 2015.

17

Revocable Key-Aggregate Cryptosystem for Data Sharing in Cloud

Qingqing Gan, Xiaoming Wang, and Daini Wu

Department of Computer Science, Jinan University, Guangzhou 510632, China

Correspondence should be addressed to Xiaoming Wang; twxm@jnu.edu.cn

Academic Editor: Bruce M. Kapron

With the rapid development of network and storage technology, cloud storage has become a new service mode, while data sharing and user revocation are important functions in the cloud storage. Therefore, according to the characteristics of cloud storage, a revocable key-aggregate encryption scheme is put forward based on subset-cover framework. The proposed scheme not only has the key-aggregate characteristics, which greatly simplifies the user's key management, but also can revoke user access permissions, realizing the flexible and effective access control. When user revocation occurs, it allows cloud server to update the ciphertext so that revoked users can not have access to the new ciphertext, while nonrevoked users do not need to update their private keys. In addition, a verification mechanism is provided in the proposed scheme, which can verify the updated ciphertext and ensure that the user revocation is performed correctly. Compared with the existing schemes, this scheme can not only reduce the cost of key management and storage, but also realize user revocation and achieve user's access control efficiently. Finally, the proposed scheme can be proved to be selective chosen-plaintext security in the standard model.

1. Introduction

With the continuous development of cloud computing technology, a new kind of data storage model called cloud storage has attracted great attention. Derived from cloud computing, cloud storage can provide online storage space through the network [1]. With the advantage of low cost, easy utilizing, and high scalability, it can meet the needs of the mass data storage and provide data sharing service, which has become the important area in the data storage technology. After requesting the storage service from cloud service providers, enterprises or individuals store a large amount of data to the cloud server, greatly reducing the burden of the local hardware infrastructure and saving the local storage overhead. What is more, its function of data sharing is regarded as very important for multiuser cloud computing environment. When data owners outsource their data in the server and want to share these data with other users, they can adopt techniques to delegate permission to these users. By this way, the legitimate users can have access to corresponding data from the cloud server so as to achieve the process of data sharing.

However, when cloud storage brings great convenience for users dealing with large-scale data, it also brings new security issues and challenges [2]. Because the cloud server is not completely trusted, enterprises or individuals will lose absolute control over the data outsourced to the cloud data, which brings the worries about data security and privacy protection. So for these data, such as how to use encryption scheme to ensure the cloud security and how to protect the data privacy, realize effective data sharing, and reduce the user key management cost as much as possible, key-aggregate cryptosystem is brought forward at this moment. In such cryptosystem, user's private keys can be aggregated together to be a single key and only using the single key can user decrypt the corresponding multiple encrypted files, which simplifies the user's key management. It also grants different decryption access for different users and can be applied to the data sharing in cloud flexibly. Meanwhile, since user's access changed dynamically and frequently in the cloud environment, how to realize user's access control and revocation become vital problems to be solved. For example, when an employee leaves his company, he will no longer have permission to the company's internal data. So, in order to meet the dynamic change of user access, it is necessary to consider the problem of user revocation.

Therefore, according to the characteristics of cloud storage, the research and establishment of an efficient and secure revocable key-aggregate encryption scheme is very necessary and urgent, which has important theoretical significance and application value.

1.1. Contribution. In order to solve the key management problems and realize dynamic access control during data sharing more effectively, this paper has been focused on the study of revocable key-aggregate cryptosystem in cloud. Its main contribution shows the following:

(1) According to the characteristics of the key-aggregate cryptosystem and the needs for user revocation, this paper first makes formal definition about the revocable key-aggregate cryptosystem.

(2) Combining the subset-cover framework, this paper puts forward an efficient revocable key-aggregate encryption scheme based on multilinear maps, realizing the user's access control and revocation. Our construction not only has the characteristics of key aggregation, which simplifies the user's key management effectively, but also can delegate different users with different decryption permission and achieve revocation of user access rights, realizing the flexible access control effectively.

(3) Compared with the existing schemes, this paper analyzes the related performance for the proposed scheme. It indicates that our scheme not only keeps the users' secret key and the ciphertext in constant-size, but also reduces the length of system parameters to $O(\log N)$, where N is the maximum number of files in the system, thus saving the cost of storage and transmission efficiently. By updating ciphertext via the cloud servers, the proposed scheme realizes the user permissions revocation while legitimate users do not need to update their private keys. What is more, it provides a verification mechanism to ensure user revocation executed correctly.

(4) Lastly, security analysis shows that the proposed scheme is proved to be selective chosen-plaintext security based on Generalized DHDHE assumption in the standard model. In addition, we discuss a solution to extend our basic scheme to solve the rapid growing number of files in the cloud environment.

1.2. Related Works. In recent years, it has become a crucial problem to realize secure and effective data sharing, as well as reducing the key management costs in the cloud environment. How to reduce the number of keys that users have to save, thus simplifying the key management problems effectively, has been a hot research topic. In existing research results, they can mainly be divided into four kinds in reducing the cost of the key management: hierarchical key management scheme, key compression scheme based on symmetric encryption, identity-based key compression scheme, and other related solutions.

In cloud storage, the hierarchical key management scheme generally utilizes tree structure, where the key of each nonleaf node can generate keys of its child nodes. And users only need to save the corresponding ancestor nodes, effectively simplifying the key management. This technology was first proposed by Akl and Taylor [7] and later has been applied to the cloud environment with the rise of cloud computing [8, 9]. For example, Ateniese et al. [10] put forward a predefined hierarchical key management scheme based on the logical key tree. However, the main drawback of hierarchical key management scheme was that only under certain conditions can it achieve effective key compression. This was because the node key can only access to the subtree of the node, if authorized files were from different branches, which in turn would increase the number of users' private keys. So its key compression was limited; only when sharing all the documents from the same branch in the tree, it could achieve the effective compression of private key.

In order to solve the issue that it needs to transport a large number of keys in the broadcast encryption scenario, Benaloh et al. [11] proposed a key compression scheme based on symmetric encryption. Its basic method is to split the entire ciphertext space into finite sets and generate a constant-size key corresponding to each of these sets, so as to realize the effect of key compression. Other schemes such as [12, 13] were also symmetrical encryption schemes trying to reduce the key size. Since these schemes were set in the environment of symmetric encryption, which required to share a symmetric key through secure channel, their application scenarios were greatly limited in the cloud environment.

As Shamir [14] proposed the concept of identity-based encryption (IBE) and then Boneh and Franklin [15] put forward the first practical IBE scheme using bilinear pairings, it brought out the research of identity-based key compression scheme. Guo et al. [16] presented a multi-identity single key decryption scheme and proved its security in the random oracle model. In their scheme, when user adopted different identities as the public key in different scenarios, for example, user had more than one email address, it only needed to store a private key to decrypt multiple encrypted messages from different companies, remarkably cutting down the cost of the user key management. Then [17, 18] made improvements on the efficiency and achieved adaptive chosen-ciphertext security in the standard model. But in these schemes, key compression was restricted, which required all the keys from different identity divisions, and the length of ciphertext and public parameters were linearly related to the maximum number of keys that can be aggregated, which increased the overhead of storage and transmission. Sahai and Waters [19] proposed a fuzzy identity-based encryption (FIBE) scheme to take users' biometric information as their identities, so that user's identity was no longer a single one but was made up of several attributes. It allowed a private key to decrypt multiple ciphertexts and was proved to be secure in the standard model. However, this scheme required the ciphertext to be encrypted by identity that met certain conditions, so it could not achieve the flexible key compression.

Other relevant solutions include the attribute-based encryption (ABE) and proxy reencryption (PRE). Waters [20] presented an ABE scheme that its private key was associated with the strategy, and ciphertext was associated with attributes and could decrypt when strategy matched with attributes. In their scheme, however, the length of private key was linearly related to the leaf nodes in the strategy access tree. Li et al. [21] applied ABE to share keys in group users, but the main concern was to resist collusion attacks, rather than key compression. Canetti and Hohenberger [22] put forward PRE scheme using the thought of transformation to turn the original ciphertext into the ciphertext encrypted by the user's public key. However, such technology is essentially aimed at transferring the secure key storage to the cloud proxy server. In addition, a key management scheme based on secret sharing was proposed in [23], but it was suitable for wireless sensor networks.

Recently, Chu et al. [24] first put forward the concept of key-aggregate cryptosystem (KAC) and constructed the first key-aggregate encryption scheme applied to data sharing in the cloud environment flexibly. The scheme was set in public key cryptosystem and it could aggregate users' private key to be a single one, so that users only stored this aggregated key to decrypt multiple files. Most importantly, its aggregation could be achieved without conditions and kept the length of ciphertext in constant-size. However, the length of system parameters in their scheme was linearly related to the maximum number of files, and it did not provide a specific security proof. Soon afterwards, the thought of key-aggregate cryptosystem was adopted in [25–28], such as Dang et al. [27] who applied the key-aggregate cryptosystem in the wireless sensor network and proposed a fine-grained sharing scheme to the encrypted senor data. Sikhar et al. [3] proposed a dynamic key-aggregate encryption scheme to realize the user revocation. But one of its imitations was that once user revocation occurred, all legitimate users needed to update their private keys, which brought expensive overhead of key update.

1.3. Organization. The rest of the paper is organized as follows: Section 2 introduces some related knowledge, including multilinear maps, complexity assumption, and subset-cover framework. In Section 3 we discuss the definition, the security model, and system model of the revocable key-aggregate cryptosystem. Section 4 details our new construction and Section 5 shows the evaluation of our proposed scheme, containing performance analysis and the security analysis. Then in Section 6, we have some discussions and present an extension for our basic scheme. Finally, we conclude this paper and look forward to the future work in Section 7.

2. Preliminaries

In this section we describe some basic primitives and concepts that are used in our scheme.

2.1. Multilinear Maps. Multilinear maps were first put forward by Boneh and Silverberg [29], making the research and application of multilinear maps be more and more widely. Multilinear maps mainly consist of the following two algorithms:

(1) Setup (n): the Setup algorithm outputs an n-linear map, which contains n groups $G = (G_1, G_2, \ldots, G_n)$ with prime order p and generators $g_i \in G_i$.

(2) $e_{i,j}(g, h)$: the map algorithm takes two elements $g \in G_i$ and $h \in G_j$ as input, while $i + j \leq n$, and outputs an element in G_{i+j} satisfying $e_{i,j}(g_i^a, g_j^b) = g_{i+j}^{ab}$. We often leave out the subscripts to be written as e. The generalization of e with multiple inputs can be donated as $e(h^{(1)}, h^{(2)}, \ldots, h^{(k)}) = e(h^{(1)}, e(h^{(2)}, \ldots, h^{(k)}))$.

In the asymmetric multilinear maps [30], group is divided by a vector and the map operations make $G_{\mathbf{v}_1} \times G_{\mathbf{v}_2}$ into $G_{\mathbf{v}_1 + \mathbf{v}_2}$. The definition shows the following:

(1) Setup ($\mathbf{n}$): the Setup algorithm takes a positive integer vector $\mathbf{n} \in Z^\lambda$ as input and outputs an $\mathbf{n}$-linear map, which contains a set of groups $\{G_{\mathbf{v}}\}$ with prime order p, and generators $g_{\mathbf{v}} \in G_{\mathbf{v}}$, while $\mathbf{v}$ are nonnegative integer vectors meeting $\mathbf{v} \leq \mathbf{n}$. Assume $\mathbf{e}_i$ be the vector with 1 at the position i and 0 at else positions. Then $\{G_{\mathbf{e}_i}\}$ are the source groups, $G_{\mathbf{n}}$ is defined as the target group, and the rest of the groups are intermediate group.

(2) $e_{\mathbf{v}_1, \mathbf{v}_2}(g, h)$: the map algorithm inputs two elements $g \in G_{\mathbf{v}_1}$ and $h \in G_{\mathbf{v}_2}$ with $\mathbf{v}_1 + \mathbf{v}_2 \leq \mathbf{n}$ and outputs an element of $G_{\mathbf{v}_1 + \mathbf{v}_2}$ such that $e_{\mathbf{v}_1, \mathbf{v}_2}(g_{\mathbf{v}_1}^a, g_{\mathbf{v}_2}^b) = g_{\mathbf{v}_1 + \mathbf{v}_2}^{ab}$. Similarly, we leave out the subscripts to be written as e and also generalize e with multiple inputs as $e(h^{(1)}, h^{(2)}, \ldots, h^{(k)}) = e(h^{(1)}, e(h^{(2)}, \ldots, h^{(k)}))$.

2.2. Complexity Assumption. We introduce a new complexity assumption named Generalized DHDHE. This new assumption is the variant version of the well-known Decisional n-Hybrid Diffie-Hellman Exponent (DHDHE) proposed by Boneh et al. [30].

Assumption 1 (Generalized Decisional n-Hybrid Diffie-Hellman Exponent, Generalized DHDHE). Let params$'$ ← Setup$'(2\mathbf{n})$. Choose random $\alpha \in Z_p$; set $X_\ell = g_{\mathbf{e}_\ell}^{\alpha^{(2^\ell)}}$ for $\ell = 0, 1, \ldots, n-1$; and set $X_n = g_{\mathbf{e}_\mathbf{n}}^{\alpha^{(2^n+1)}}$ for $\ell = n$. Randomly select $t_1 \in Z_p, t_2 \in Z_p$, while $t = t_1 + t_2$, and let $Y_1 = g_{\mathbf{n}}^{t_1}$, $Y_2 = g_{\mathbf{n}}^{t_2}$. Given $\langle \{X_i\}_{i \in \{0,1,\ldots,n\}}, Y_1, Y_2, K \rangle$, the goal is to distinguish $K = g_{2\mathbf{n}}^{t\alpha^{(2^n)}}$ from a random element in $G_{2\mathbf{n}}$.

For a polynomial-time adversary A, its advantages to Generalized DHDHE problem are defined as

$$\text{Adv}_A^{\text{Weak DHDHE}}$$

$$= \left| \Pr\left[A\left(\{X_i\}_{i \in \{0,1,\ldots,n\}}, Y_1, Y_2, K = g_{2\mathbf{n}}^{t\alpha^{(2^n)}} \right) = 1 \right] \right. \quad (1)$$

$$\left. - \Pr\left[A\left(\{X_i\}_{i \in \{0,1,\ldots,n\}}, Y_1, Y_2, K = g_{2\mathbf{n}}^r \right) = 1 \right] \right|.$$

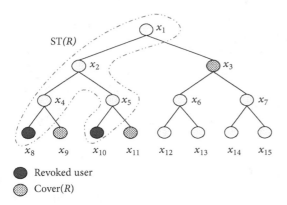

FIGURE 1: Subset-cover framework: Complete Subtree method.

From here we can see that this new assumption is the generalization of DHDHE assumption. Specifically, if we multiply Y_1 and Y_2, Generalized DHDHE assumption can be reduced to DHDHE assumption in [30].

Definition 2. We say the Generalized DHDHE assumption holds if, for any polynomial-time adversary A, A has a negligible advantage in solving the Generalized DHDHE problem.

2.3. Subset-Cover Framework. Naor et al. [4] first proposed the subset-cover framework and applied it to the broadcast encryption scheme, realizing the dynamic authorization of the user. The subset-cover framework includes complete subtree (CS) method and subset difference (SD) method. This paper mainly introduces CS method, shown as follows.

Let T be a full binary tree with depth d. Thus the number of leaf nodes in the tree is $(2^d - 1)$, representing $(2^d - 1)$ users. First, for each user u, we define a path set denoted by path(u), containing all the nodes passing through the root node to leaf node. When given a user revocation set R, let $S_{i_1}, S_{i_2}, \ldots, S_{i_m}$ be the complete subtrees in T rooted at the nodes of outdegree one in Steiner Tree ST(R), and $S_{i_1}, S_{i_2}, \ldots, S_{i_m}$ are not in the ST(R). We said that $S_{i_1}, S_{i_2}, \ldots, S_{i_m}$ cover all the nonrevoked nodes in T, denoted by cover(R). Take the example in Figure 1. Given the full binary tree T with eight leaf nodes, we get the user sets $U = \{x_8, x_9, \ldots, x_{15}\}$. Then the path set for each user can be obtained as path$(x_8) = \{x_1, x_2, x_4, x_8\}$, path$(x_{12}) = \{x_1, x_3, x_6, x_{12}\}$, and so on. Suppose the user revocation set $R = \{x_8, x_{10}\}$; then ST(R) is shown in the dotted box in Figure 1, so that cover$(R) = \{x_3, x_9, x_{11}\}$ including all the nonrevoked users.

When constructing the scheme based on the subset-cover framework, the path set is embedded in private key, while the cover set is related to the ciphertext. If and only if path$(u) \cap$ cover$(R) \neq \phi$, the user u can take the next step to the decryption. In the CS method as shown in Figure 1, only legitimate users, such as x_9, x_{12}, meet the conditions. For revoked user u, since path$(u) \cap$ cover$(R) = \phi$, then he is unable to complete the decryption, as x_8 in Figure 1.

3. Revocable Key-Aggregate Cryptosystem

Since the delegated users in cloud have the feature of dynamic change, revocable key-aggregate cryptosystem is essential for consummating the user revocation function in KAC.

3.1. Definition. Revocable key-aggregate cryptosystem (RKAC) is an extension of KAC such that a user can be revoked if his credential is expired. A revocable key-aggregate encryption scheme consists of seven polynomial-time algorithms as Setup, KeyGen, Encrypt, Extract, Update, Decrypt, and Verify, which are defined as follows:

(1) Setup($1^\lambda, n$): the Setup algorithm takes as input a security parameter 1^λ and the maximum number of files n. It outputs public parameters params.

(2) KeyGen(params): the key generation algorithm takes as input public parameters params. It generates a public key PK and a master secret key msk.

(3) Encrypt(PK, i, m, params): the encryption algorithm takes as input public key PK, an index i denoting the file, a message m, and public parameters params. It outputs a ciphertext C.

(4) Extract(msk, uid, S, params): the Extract algorithm takes as input the master secret key msk and a set S of indices corresponding to different files, user identity uid, and public parameters params. It outputs users' private key SK.

(5) Update(PK, R, C, params): the update algorithm takes as input the public key PK, the user revocation set R, a ciphertext C, and public parameters params. It outputs an updated ciphertext C'.

(6) Decrypt(C, SK, S, i, R, params): the decryption algorithm takes as input a ciphertext C, user private key SK, the set S, an index i denoting the ciphertext C, the user revocation set R, and public parameters params. If $(i \in S) \land ($uid $\notin R)$, it outputs the result m or else outputs $\perp$.

(7) Verify(C, C', PK, params): the Verify algorithm takes as input a ciphertext C, an updated ciphertext C', public key PK, and public parameters params. If the cloud server has executed the revocation honestly and updated the ciphertext correctly, it outputs 1 or else outputs 0.

3.2. Security Model. For RKAC, we present its security model through the game between a challenger Chal and a polynomial-time adversary A. The selective security property of RKAC under indistinguishable chosen-ciphertext attack (IND-CCA) is defined as follows.

Init. A initially submits a challenge file index i^* and a revoked identity set R^*.

Setup. Chal generates public parameters params and (PK, msk) by running Setup($1^\lambda, n$) and KeyGen(params). It keeps msk secretly to itself and gives params and PK to A.

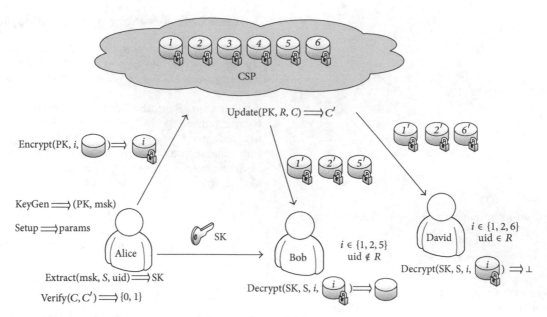

FIGURE 2: The model for RKAC.

Phase 1. A adaptively requests a series of queries. These queries are processed as follows:

(i) Step 1 (extraction query): for any file index set $S(i^* \notin S)$ and identity uid(uid $\in R^*$), Chal invokes the Extract algorithm Extract(msk, uid, S, params) and sends the generated private key SK = (K_S, K_{uid}) to A.

(ii) Step 2 (decryption query): for any ciphertext C_i, file index set $S(i^* \notin S)$, and identity uid(uid $\in R^*$), the challenger Chal executes the decryption algorithm Decrypt(C_i, SK, S, i, R, params) and sends the obtained plaintext to A.

Challenge. Once the adversary A decides to end Phase 1, it submits two challenge messages $m_0, m_1 \in M$ with equal length. Chal flips a random coin $b \in \{0, 1\}$ and sets $C =$ Encrypt(PK, i^*, m_b, params), $C^* =$ Update(C, R^*) and then gives the challenge ciphertext C^* to A.

Phase 2. A continues to request a series of adaptive queries, but with the restrictions that it cannot perform the decryption query to C^*. The challenger Chal adopts the same method as in Phase 1 to answer the queries.

Guess. Finally, A outputs a guess $b' \in \{0, 1\}$ and wins the game if $b' = b$.

The acquired advantage of the adversary A for the RKAC scheme is defined as $\text{Adv}_A^{RKAC} = |\Pr[b' = b] - 1/2|$.

Definition 3. If, for any polynomial-time t and adversary A through q queries in the above game, its advantage for RKAC scheme $\text{Adv}_A^{RKAC} \leq \varepsilon$, one said this RKAC scheme is selective (t, q, ε)-IND-CCA security.

Definition 4. If, for any polynomial-time t and adversary A through q queries in the above game without the decryption

query, its advantage for RKAC scheme $\text{Adv}_A^{RKAC} \leq \varepsilon$, one said this RKAC scheme is selective (t, q, ε)-IND-CPA security.

3.3. System Model. Applying the RKAC in a cloud environment, the model is shown in Figure 2. It consists of three entities: cloud service provider (CSP), the data owner (DO), and user.

When the data owner Alice wants to share multiple files $m_1, m_2, \ldots, m_n$ with others through the cloud server utilizing revocable key-aggregate encryption scheme, Alice first runs Setup algorithm to get the system parameters params. Then Alice executes KeyGen(params) to get a random public/master secret key-pair (PK, msk) and kept msk secretly. After that, Alice and anyone who cooperated with Alice can run the encryption algorithm Encrypt(PK, i, R, m, params) and upload the encrypted files to the cloud server. Once Alice hopes to share several of these files to user Bob, Alice will run the algorithm Extract(msk, uid, S, params) to generate a private key SK for Bob according to authorized files' indices and the user's identity. Since SK is a fixed size, it is easy for Alice to pass SK to Bob through safe channel with small communication cost. Whenever Alice wants to revoke users, Alice will send the user revocation list R to CSP. Then CSP calls the algorithm Update(PK, R, C, params) to update the corresponding ciphertext. If and only if Bob has not been revoked, Bob downloads the updated ciphertext from the cloud server and runs the algorithm Decrypt(C, SK, S, i, R, params) with the use of the private key to obtain plaintext. And if the user has been revoked, such as David in Figure 2, he will not be able to decrypt the updated ciphertext, thus withdrawing David's permission to the files. Finally, by invoking the algorithm Verify(C, C', params), Alice can achieve the verification of the updated ciphertext, to ensure that the user revocation is effectively implemented.

4. Main Construction

Our main construction of the revocable key-aggregate encryption scheme is based on multilinear maps and realizes data sharing and user revocation in cloud storage securely and efficiently.

4.1. Basic Idea. In KAC, the aggregation of file indices is embedded in the user's private key so that authorized users store the aggregate key to realize the access to multiple files. However, the access of user in system is changed dynamically, requiring KAC to support user revocation. Therefore, in order to construct a revocable key-aggregate encryption scheme, two mainly challenges are remained to be solved. One is how to construct an efficient scheme with key-aggregate function, the other is how to realize revoking users securely while not affecting the legitimate users' access to files.

For the first challenge, we are inspired by Boneh et al.'s broadcast encryption [30]. Based on this scheme, we try to construct a key-aggregate scheme to keep the users' secret key and the ciphertext in constant-size. With the multilinear maps, it can reduces the length of system parameters to $O(\log N)$, thus saving the cost of storage and transmission efficiently.

For the second challenge, our inspiration comes from Shi et al. [6] revocable key-policy ABE scheme. The scheme not only realizes the direct user revocation, but also achieves the function of ciphertext delegation by a third-party server. What is more, it provides a verification mechanism to ensure the correctness of the ciphertext delegation, which has been of great significance. However, in their scheme, the user private key is related to the access structure and path set in subset-cover framework. Besides that, Shi et al. [6] scheme is only proved to be secure under the random oracle model. So we try to combine Naor et al. [4] subset-cover framework with our scheme for user revocation. In addition, we make improvement of the complete subtree method of subset-cover framework in [4] to aggregate the path set for each user as private key, so as to realize the user's key aggregation and simplify the key management effectively.

Therefore, this paper proposes a revocable key-aggregate encryption scheme and proves its security in the standard model. The main thought of the scheme lies in constructing the ciphertext and the private key. The ciphertext of the new scheme includes not only the file index, but also the user revocation set, realizing the user revocable directly. At the same time, the private key is correspondingly divided into two parts. One is the aggregation of the file index set, and the other is the aggregation of the path set for each user, so as to realize the user's key aggregation effectively. Through the above method, only the legitimate users have access to the appropriate file, realizing the file access control function in the system effectively. This new scheme achieves the ciphertext updating through the cloud servers to save the computational overhead of data owner; when the user revocation occurs, nonrevoked user does not need to update his private key, greatly reducing the key update expensive cost and the burden of key delegate authority; because the cloud server is not completely trusted, we consider to provide a verification mechanism for the scheme, so that the data owner can validate the updated ciphertext to make sure the user revocation is carried out correctly.

4.2. Scheme Design. Let Setup$'$ be the Setup algorithm for a multilinear map, where outputs group with order p, respectively. Let T be a full binary tree with depth d ($1 \le d \le n$), where the leaf stands for user. Number all the nodes in T from one to $(2^d - 1)$; then our scheme consists of the following algorithms:

(1) Setup($1^\lambda, n$): take as input the length n of index. Let $\{0,1\}^n \setminus \{0^n\}$ be the index space. Therefore the maximum number of files in the system is $N = 2^n - 1$. Let **n** be the all-ones vector with length $(n + 1)$. Run Setup$'(2\mathbf{n})$ to obtain the public parameters params$'$ for a multilinear map of target group $G_{2\mathbf{n}}$. Select a random $\alpha \in Z_p$, and set $X_\ell = g_{\mathbf{e}_\ell}^{\alpha^{(2^\ell)}}$ for $\ell = 0, 1, \ldots,$ $n - 1$, and set $X_n = g_{\mathbf{e}_n}^{\alpha^{(2^n+1)}}$ for $\ell = n$. Lastly, let $W = g_{2\mathbf{n}}^{2\alpha^{(2^n)}}$. It outputs the public parameters params $= \langle$params$', \{X_i\}_{i\in\{0,1,\ldots,n\}}, W\rangle$.

(2) KeyGen(params): choose a random $\beta \in Z_p$, $\gamma \in Z_p$ and compute $\mu = g_{\mathbf{n}}{}^\beta$, $v = g_{\mathbf{n}}{}^\gamma$, output PK $= (\mu, v)$, msk $= (\beta, \gamma)$.

(3) Encrypt(PK, i, m, params): for a message m and an index $i \in \{1, 2, \ldots, 2^n - 1\}$, randomly pick $t_1 \in Z_p$ and compute $K = W^{t_1} = g_{2\mathbf{n}}^{t_1\alpha^{(2^n)}}$. The ciphertext is created as

$$C = \langle c_1, c_2, c_3\rangle = \left\langle g_{\mathbf{n}}^{t_1}, \left(vg_{\mathbf{n}}^{\alpha^i}\right)^{t_1}, m \cdot W^{t_1}\right\rangle. \qquad (2)$$

(4) Extract(msk, uid, S, params): given the user identity uid $\in \{0,1\}^d$, make use of the CS method in the full binary tree T to get the user's path path(uid) $= \{y_{u_0}, \ldots, y_{u_d}\}$, such that $y_{u_0} = $ root and $y_{u_d} = $ uid. Compute $P_{\text{uid}} = \prod_{y\in\text{path(uid)}} Z_{2^n-y}$; then the path aggregate key $K_{\text{uid}} = P_{\text{uid}}{}^\beta$. For the set $S \subseteq \{1, 2, \ldots, 2^n - 1\}$, the index aggregate key is computed as $K_S = \prod_{j\in S} Z_{2^n-j}^\gamma$. Since S does not include 0, $Z_{2^n-j} = g_{\mathbf{n}}^{\alpha^{2^n-j}}$ can always be retrieved from params. The user's private key is set to SK $= (K_S, K_{\text{uid}})$.

(5) Update(PK, R, C, params): for user revocation set R, compute cover(R) according to the CS method in subset-cover framework. For $x \in$ cover(R), compute $P_x = g_{\mathbf{n}}^{\alpha^x}$. Choose a random $t_2 \in Z_p$; then get $c_3' = c_3 \cdot W^{t_2} = m \cdot W^{t_1+t_2}$. Suppose that $t = t_1 + t_2$; then we have $c_3' = m \cdot W^t$. Compute $c_4 = g_{\mathbf{n}}^{t_2}, c_5 = \{(\mu P_x)^{t_2}\}_{x\in\text{cover}(R)}$. Finally get the updated ciphertext as follows:

$$C' = \langle c_1, c_2, c_3', c_4, c_5\rangle$$
$$= \left\langle g_{\mathbf{n}}^{t_1}, \left(vg_{\mathbf{n}}^{\alpha^i}\right)^{t_1}, m \cdot W^t, g_{\mathbf{n}}^{t_2}, \{(\mu P_x)^{t_2}\}_{x\in\text{cover}(R)}\right\rangle. \qquad (3)$$

(6) Decrypt(C, SK, S, i, R, params): when user receives the ciphertext C with the index i, if either the index $i \notin S$ or the user's identity uid $\in R$, then return $\perp$. Otherwise, for $x = \text{path(uid)} \cap \text{cover}(R)$, decryption can be done as follows:

$$m = c_3 \cdot \frac{e\left(K_S \cdot \prod_{j \in S, j \neq i} Z_{2^n - j + i}, c_1\right)}{e\left(\prod_{j \in S} Z_{2^n - j}, c_2\right)}$$

$$\cdot \frac{e\left(K_{\text{uid}} \cdot \prod_{y \in \text{path(uid)}, y \neq x} Z_{2^n - y + x}, c_4\right)}{e\left(P_{\text{uid}}, c_5\right)}. \tag{4}$$

(7) Verify(C, C', PK, params): to verify whether the cloud server has executed the revocation correctly and honestly, the equation $e(\mu P_x, c_4) \overset{?}{=} e(c_5, g_{\mathbf{n}})$ can be used and it returns 0 or 1. For data owner, in order to verify whether the updated ciphertext c_3' is right or not, he can use the equation $e(c_3'/c_3, g_{\mathbf{n}}) \overset{?}{=} e(W, c_4)$. If returning 1, it means right or else means wrong.

For correctness, we can see that

$$c_3 \cdot \frac{e\left(K_S \cdot \prod_{j \in S, j \neq i} Z_{2^n - j + i}, c_1\right)}{e\left(\prod_{j \in S} Z_{2^n - j}, c_2\right)}$$

$$\cdot \frac{e\left(K_{\text{uid}} \cdot \prod_{y \in \text{path(uid)}, y \neq x} Z_{2^n - y + x}, c_4\right)}{e\left(P_{\text{uid}}, c_5\right)} = c_3$$

$$\cdot \frac{e\left(\prod_{j \in S} Z_{2^n - j}^{\gamma} \cdot \prod_{j \in S, j \neq i} Z_{2^n - j + i}, g_{\mathbf{n}}^{t_1}\right)}{e\left(\prod_{j \in S} Z_{2^n - j}, \left(v g_{\mathbf{n}}^{\alpha^i}\right)^{t_1}\right)}$$

$$\cdot \frac{e\left(P_{\text{uid}}^{\beta} \cdot \prod_{y \in \text{path(uid)}, y \neq x} Z_{2^n - y + x}, g_{\mathbf{n}}^{t_2}\right)}{e\left(P_{\text{uid}}, \left(\mu g_{\mathbf{n}}^{\alpha^x}\right)^{t_2}\right)} = c_3$$

$$\cdot \frac{e\left(\prod_{j \in S} Z_{2^n - j}^{\gamma}, g_{\mathbf{n}}^{t_1}\right)}{e\left(\prod_{j \in S} Z_{2^n - j}, v^{t_1}\right)} \cdot \frac{e\left(\prod_{j \in S, j \neq i} Z_{2^n - j + i}, g_{\mathbf{n}}^{t_1}\right)}{e\left(\prod_{j \in S} Z_{2^n - j}, \left(g_{\mathbf{n}}^{\alpha^i}\right)^{t_1}\right)}$$

$$\cdot \frac{e\left(P_{\text{uid}}^{\beta}, g_{\mathbf{n}}^{t_2}\right)}{e\left(P_{\text{uid}}, \mu^{t_2}\right)} \cdot \frac{e\left(\prod_{y \in \text{path(uid)}, y \neq x} Z_{2^n - y + x}, g_{\mathbf{n}}^{t_2}\right)}{e\left(\prod_{y \in \text{path(uid)}} Z_{2^n - j}, \left(g_{\mathbf{n}}^{\alpha^x}\right)^{t_2}\right)}$$

$$= c_3 \cdot \frac{e\left(\prod_{j \in S, j \neq i} Z_{2^n - j + i}, g_{\mathbf{n}}^{t_1}\right)}{e\left(\prod_{j \in S} Z_{2^n - j}, \left(g_{\mathbf{n}}^{\alpha^i}\right)^{t_1}\right)}$$

$$\cdot \frac{e\left(\prod_{y \in \text{path(uid)}, y \neq x} Z_{2^n - y + x}, g_{\mathbf{n}}^{t_2}\right)}{e\left(\prod_{y \in \text{path(uid)}} Z_{2^n - j}, \left(g_{\mathbf{n}}^{\alpha^x}\right)^{t_2}\right)} = m \cdot W^t$$

$$\cdot \frac{e\left(g_{\mathbf{n}}^{\sum_{j \in S, j \neq i} \alpha^{(2^n - j + i)}}, g_{\mathbf{n}}^{t_1}\right)}{e\left(g_{\mathbf{n}}^{\sum_{j \in S} \alpha^{(2^n - j)}}, \left(g_{\mathbf{n}}^{\alpha^i}\right)^{t_1}\right)}$$

$$\cdot \frac{e\left(g_{\mathbf{n}}^{\sum_{y \in \text{path(uid)}, y \neq x} \alpha^{(2^n - y + x)}}, g_{\mathbf{n}}^{t_2}\right)}{e\left(g_{\mathbf{n}}^{\sum_{y \in \text{path(uid)}} \alpha^{(2^n - y)}}, \left(g_{\mathbf{n}}^{\alpha^x}\right)^{t_2}\right)} = \frac{m \cdot W^t}{\left(g_{2\mathbf{n}}^{\alpha^{2^n}}\right)^{t_1 + t_2}}$$

$$= \frac{m \cdot W^t}{\left(g_{2\mathbf{n}}^{\alpha^{2^n}}\right)^t} = m. \tag{5}$$

5. Evaluation

In this section, we evaluate the proposed scheme in two aspects, performance analysis and security analysis.

5.1. Performance Analysis. Performance analysis mainly includes the cost of computation, storage, and communication by comparison with several related schemes. In computation, since our scheme is based on asymmetric multilinear maps, $W = g_{2\mathbf{n}}^{\alpha^{(2^n)}}$ in the ciphertext is system parameter, and the value of $g_{\mathbf{n}}$, $g_{\mathbf{n}}^{\alpha^i}$ and P_x can be calculated in advance. Therefore, multilinear mapping operation in the process of encryption does not exist, which reduces the computational cost greatly. Decryption cost is linearly related to user's authorized file index set and path set in the complete subtree. In terms of storage and communication cost, this paper will compare the new scheme with [3–6], including the length of system public parameters, the length of private key, length of ciphertext, revocation manners and costs, and whether it is able to verify the correctness of revocation, as shown in Table 1.

Note that the length of ciphertext refers to the length of original ciphertext when no user has been revoked, and the revocation cost refers to the computational cost when the user revocation occurs. N stands for the maximum number of encrypted files in the system, r denotes the number of revocation users, U represents the number of legitimate users, ℓ is number for leaf node in the access tree corresponding to the user's private key, and s is on behalf of the number of attributes.

As can be seen from Table 1, the proposed scheme not only keeps the length for user's private key as $O(1)$, but also keeps the length of the ciphertext as $O(1)$, which is as well as [3, 5] and better than [4, 6]. But the length of system parameters in [3, 5] is $O(N)$, while that in the proposed scheme is $O(\log N)$. Revocation manners contain direct and indirect revocation. Direct revocation refers that the revocation list is directly embedded in the ciphertext, so that revoked users cannot decrypt any more, such as our scheme and [4, 6]; indirect revocation refers that the authorized agency or data owner distributes the updated keys for the nonrevoked users so as to realize the user revocation, such as [3, 5]. As for the revocation cost, because the indirect revocation needs to distribute updated keys to all legitimate users, computational cost for revocation is $O(U)$, while the revocation cost in our scheme and [4, 6] is mainly focused on the ciphertext update as $O(r \log U)$. In addition, our scheme and [6] also provide verification mechanism, allowing the

TABLE 1: Comparison with related schemes.

Scheme	System parameter	Private key	Ciphertext	Direct revocation	Revocation cost	Verifiability
[3]	$O(N)$	$O(1)$	$O(1)$	×	$O(U)$	×
[4]	$O(N)$	$O(\log N)$	$O(1)$	√	$O(r \log U)$	×
[5]	$O(N)$	$O(1)$	$O(1)$	×	$O(U)$	×
[6]	$O(N)$	$O(\ell)$	$O(s)$	√	$O(r \log U)$	√
Our scheme	$O(\log N)$	$O(1)$	$O(1)$	√	$O(r \log U)$	√

data owner and any trusted third-party auditor to verify the updated ciphertext, so as to ensure effective implementation of revocation, which is better than [3–5]. Above all, the proposed scheme is superior to [3–6], with less cost of storage and communication, and has ciphertext verifiability function.

5.2. Security Analysis. Our scheme is based on Generalized DHDHE assumption and is proved to be adaptive IND-CPA security under the standard model. First we analyze Generalized DHDHE assumption. Let $X_\ell = g_{\mathbf{e}_\ell}^{\alpha^{(2^\ell)}}$ for $\ell = 0, 1, \ldots, n - 1$, so as $j \in [0, 2^n - 1]$, $Z_j = g_{\mathbf{n}}^{\alpha^j}$ can be directly calculated. And given $X_n = g_{\mathbf{e}_n}^{\alpha^{(2^{n+1})}}$, when $j \in [2^n + 1, 2^{n+1}]$, Z_j can be computed out. However, from X_i, Y_1, and Y_2, it is difficult to compute $K = g_{2\mathbf{n}}^{t\alpha^{(2^n)}}$. The reason is that only the random t is related to Y_1 and Y_2. In order to obtain K, we first need to multiply Y_1 and Y_2, and let the multiplication results do the match operation with $g_{\mathbf{n}}^{\alpha^{(2^n)}}$. In other words, it is necessary to calculate $g_{\mathbf{n}}^{\alpha^{(2^n)}}$ from X_ℓ. Since $\mathbf{n}$ is a $(n + 1)$-dimensional vector composed of 1, any X_ℓ cannot match with itself, which means that we can only compute $g_{\mathbf{n}}^{\alpha^{(2^n)}}$ in the form of $e(X_0^{s_0}, X_1^{s_1}, \ldots, X_n^{s_n})$ for $s_\ell \in \{0, 1\}$ and $X_\ell^0 = g_{\mathbf{e}_\ell}$. Notice that the index of the given $X_n = g_{\mathbf{e}_n}^{\alpha^{(2^{n+1})}}$ is greater than $\alpha^{(2^n)}$, so to calculate $g_{\mathbf{n}}^{\alpha^{(2^n)}}$, it should meet $s_n = 0$ in $e(X_0^{s_0}, X_1^{s_1}, \ldots, X_n^{s_n})$. So, $g_{\mathbf{n}}^{\prod_{\ell \in L} \alpha^{(2^\ell)}}$ can be obtained for $L \subseteq [0, n-1]$. However, for all the subsets of $L \subseteq [0, n - 1]$, there are $\sum_{\ell \in L} 2^\ell < 2^n$. Therefore it is unable to calculate $g_{\mathbf{n}}^{\alpha^{(2^n)}}$; it also means that assumption is difficult.

By the following theorem, we prove the security of the proposed scheme.

Theorem 5. *If the Generalized DHDHE problem is hard to solve, then the proposed revocable key-aggregate encryption scheme is selective IND-CPA security.*

Proof. Assume there exists a polynomial-time adversary A who can break the selective IND-CPA security of the revocable key-aggregate encryption scheme; then a challenger Chal can use the adversary's ability to construct an algorithm B to solve the Generalized DHDHE problem. It is contradictory to our assumption that Generalized DHDHE problem is difficult to solve, thus proving the proposed scheme is selective IND-CPA security.

Suppose, in an asymmetric multilinear maps group system, B is given an instance of the Generalized DHDHE problem (params$'$, $\{X_i\}_{i \in \{0,1,\ldots,n\}}$, Y_1, Y_2, K) as follows:

(1) params$'$ ← Setup$'$($2\mathbf{n}$), where n is the all-ones vector of length $(n + 1)$.

(2) For $\alpha \in_R Z_p$, let $X_\ell = g_{\mathbf{e}_\ell}^{\alpha^{(2^\ell)}}$ for $\ell = 0, 1, \ldots, n - 1$; and let $X_n = g_{\mathbf{e}_n}^{\alpha^{(2^{n+1})}}$ for $\ell = n$.

(3) For $t_1 \in_R Z_p$, $t_2 \in_R Z_p$, $t = t_1 + t_2$, let $Y_1 = g_{\mathbf{n}}^{t_1}$, $Y_2 = g_{\mathbf{n}}^{t_2}$.

(4) $K = g_{2\mathbf{n}}^{t\alpha^{(2^n)}}$ or K is a random group element in $G_{2\mathbf{n}}$.

Algorithm B decides whether $K = g_{2\mathbf{n}}^{t\alpha^{(2^n)}}$; if it holds, it outputs 1 or else outputs 0. Algorithm B proceeds the following game with the adversary A. □

Init. Algorithm B initials a full binary tree T of depth d ($1 \leq d \leq n$), and all the node in T is numbered from 1 to $(2^d - 1)$. A submits an index i^*, R^* that A will challenge.

Setup. Algorithm B performs the following operations:

(i) Step 1: it chooses a random $r \in_R Z_p$ and sets $v = g_{\mathbf{n}}^r / Z_{i^*}$, of which Z_{i^*} can be calculated by X_ℓ. Therefore, $\gamma = r - \alpha^i$. Since r is randomly selected in Z_p, it is independent with α. Then, according to the principle of subset-cover framework, cover(R^*) can be obtained from R^*. For any $x_k^* \in$ cover(R^*), it chooses a random $\varphi_k \in Z_p$ and sets $\mu = g_{\mathbf{n}}^{\varphi_k} / Z_{x_k^*}$, of which $Z_{x_k^*}$ can be calculated by X_ℓ. Therefore, $\beta = \varphi_k - \alpha^{x_k^*}$. As φ_k is randomly selected in Z_p, it is independent with α. The public key is set as PK $= (\mu, v)$; note that algorithm B does not know the master secret key(β, γ).

(ii) Step 2: it computes $W' = e(g_{\mathbf{e}_0}, g_{\mathbf{e}_1}, \ldots, g_{\mathbf{e}_{n-2}}, X_{n-1}, g_{\mathbf{e}_n})$; then $W = e(W', W') = g_{2\mathbf{n}}^{\alpha^{2^n}}$.

(iii) Step 3: it sends the public parameters ($\{X_i\}_{i \in \{0,1,\ldots,n\}}$, W) and the public key PK to the adversary A.

Phase 1. A is allowed to query for private keys in this stage. For set S in condition that $i^* \notin S$, B computes the index aggregate key $K_S = \prod_{j \in S} Z_{2^n - j} / \prod_{j \in S} Z_{2^n - j + i^*}$. For user identity uid $\in R^*$, it satisfies the condition that path(uid) $\cap$ cover(R^*) $= \phi$. So for $x_k^* \in$ cover(R^*), it is bound to meet $x_k^* \notin$ path(uid). From the full binary tree T, user path is denoted as path(uid) =

$\{y_{u_0}, \ldots, y_{u_d}\}$, such that y_{u_0} = root and y_{u_d} = uid. B computes $P_{\text{uid}} = \prod_{y \in \text{path(uid)}} Z_{2^n - y}$; then the path aggregate key $K_{\text{uid}} = P_{\text{uid}}^{\varphi_k} / \prod_{y \in \text{path(uid)}} Z_{2^n - y + x_k^*}$, and SK = (K_S, K_{uid}) will be sent to A as the answer to query. Notice that

$$
\begin{aligned}
K_S &= g_{\mathbf{n}}^{\, r \sum_{j \in S} \alpha^{2^n - j} - \sum_{j \in S} \alpha^{2^n - j + i^*}} \\
&= g_{\mathbf{n}}^{\, \gamma \sum_{j \in S} \alpha^{2^n - j} + \alpha^{i^*} \sum_{j \in S} \alpha^{2^n - j} - \sum_{j \in S} \alpha^{2^n - j + i^*}} = g_{\mathbf{n}}^{\, \gamma \sum_{j \in S} \alpha^{2^n - j}} \\
&= \prod_{j \in S} Z_{2^n - j}^{\gamma},
\end{aligned}
$$

$$
\begin{aligned}
K_{\text{uid}} &= g_{\mathbf{n}}^{\, \varphi_k \sum_{y \in \text{path(uid)}} \alpha^{2^n - y} - \sum_{y \in \text{path(uid)}} \alpha^{2^n - y + x_k^*}} \\
&= g_{\mathbf{n}}^{\, \beta \sum_{y \in \text{path(uid)}} \alpha^{2^n - y} + \alpha^{x_k^*} \sum_{y \in \text{path(uid)}} \alpha^{2^n - y} - \sum_{y \in \text{path(uid)}} \alpha^{2^n - y + x_k^*}} \\
&= g_{\mathbf{n}}^{\, \beta \sum_{y \in \text{path(uid)}} \alpha^{2^n - y}} = \prod_{y \in \text{path(uid)}} Z_{2^n - y}^{\beta} = P_{\text{uid}}^{\beta}.
\end{aligned}
\tag{6}
$$

Challenge. When A ends Phase 1, it will submit two equal-length messages $m_0, m_1 \in M$ to algorithm B. B works as follows:

(i) Step 1: it flips a random coin and marks the result as b for $b \in \{0, 1\}$ and sets $c_3^* = K \cdot m_b$.

(ii) Step 2: it sets $c_1^* = Y_1 = g_{\mathbf{n}}^{t_1}$, computes $c_2^* = Y_1^{\, r}$, and observes that $c_2^* = Y_1^{\, r} = g_{\mathbf{n}}^{t_1 r} = g_{\mathbf{n}}^{t_1(\gamma + \alpha^{i^*})}$.

(iii) Step 3: it sets $c_4^* = Y_2 = g_{\mathbf{n}}^{t_2}$, computes $c_5^* = \{Y^{\varphi_k}\}_{x_k^* \in \text{cover}(R^*)}$, and notices that

$$
\begin{aligned}
c_5^* &= \{Y_2^{\varphi_k}\}_{x_k^* \in \text{cover}(R^*)} = \{g_{\mathbf{n}}^{t_2 \varphi_k}\}_{x_k^* \in \text{cover}(R^*)} \\
&= \{g_{\mathbf{n}}^{t_2(\beta + \alpha^{x_k^*})}\}_{x_k^* \in \text{cover}(R^*)}.
\end{aligned}
\tag{7}
$$

(iv) Step 4: it sets the challenge ciphertext $C^* = \langle c_1^*, c_2^*, c_3^*, c_4^*, c_5^* \rangle$ and sends C^* to A.

Phase 2. Similarly to Phase 1, A follows the constraints of the game and continues to query about private keys; algorithm B adopts the same strategy as in Phase 1 to answer the series of queries.

Guess. A outputs a bit b'. If $b' = b$, algorithm B outputs 1, which means $K = g_{2\mathbf{n}}^{t\alpha^{(2^n)}}$. Otherwise, B outputs 0 meaning that K is a random group element of $G_{2\mathbf{n}}$.

Probability analysis: when $K = g_{2\mathbf{n}}^{t\alpha^{(2^n)}}$, the challenge ciphertext $C^* = \langle c_1^*, c_2^*, c_3^*, c_4^*, c_5^* \rangle$ is encrypted of the message m_b. Otherwise, $C^* = \langle c_1^*, c_2^*, c_3^*, c_4^*, c_5^* \rangle$ is encrypted by a random element from the group $G_{2\mathbf{n}}$. In such case, the advantage of the adversary A (i.e., the probability of $b' = b$) is equal to $1/2$. Above all, the obtained advantage of A for the proposed scheme is $\text{Adv}_A^{\text{RKAC}} = |\Pr[b' = b] - 1/2| = |(1/2 \pm \varepsilon) - 1/2| = \varepsilon$; namely, the advantage of A to break the scheme is negligible, which indicates the revocable key-aggregate encryption scheme with selective IND-CPA security.

6. Extension

As is known to us, the number of files may extremely be large and grow rapidly in cloud scenario. If the number of files exceeds N, which is the maximum number of files setting in the system, the whole system should be reestablished in our basic scheme. So how to reduce such burden is an important issue. Inspired by the thought of public key extension in the scheme [24], we propose an extended scheme to solve the problem. We attempt to label every file with a two-level index $\{i, j\}$ ($1 \leq i \leq h, 1 \leq j \leq (2^n - 1)$). When the number of files is more than N, we increase i by one and run the Extend algorithm to generate a new key-pair, adding to the original key-pair (PK, msk). That is to say, the number of files is increased by N once we obtain a new key-pair. Thus we can extend our basic scheme using this technique. The details of how to extend our basic scheme is shown as below.

The Setup, KeyGen, Update, and Verify algorithm are the same as the basic scheme.

Extend($\{\mu\}_h, \{\beta\}_h$): choose a random $\gamma_{h+1} \in Z_p$ and compute $v_{h+1} = g_{\mathbf{n}}^{\gamma_{h+1}}$ and output $\{v\}_{h+1} = \{v_1, v_2, \ldots, v_{h+1}\}$ as a part of PK and $\{\gamma\}_{h+1} = \{\gamma_1, \gamma_2, \ldots, \gamma_{h+1}\}$ as a part of msk.

Encrypt(PK, $(a, b), m$, params): for a message m and an index $\{a, b\}$ ($1 \leq a \leq h, 1 \leq b \leq (2^n - 1)$), randomly pick $t_1 \in Z_p$ and compute $c_2 = (v_a g_{\mathbf{n}}^{\alpha^b})^{t_1}$ and c_1, c_3 are computed by the same way as the basic scheme.

Extract(msk, uid, S_h, params): the path aggregate key K_{uid} remains the same as the basic scheme. For the set $S_h = \{\{i, j\}\}$ ($1 \leq i \leq h, 1 \leq j \leq (2^n - 1)$), the index aggregate key is computed as $K_{S_h} = \{\prod_{\{1,j\} \in S_h} Z_{2^n - j}^{\gamma_1}, \prod_{\{2,j\} \in S_h} Z_{2^n - j}^{\gamma_2}, \ldots, \prod_{\{h,j\} \in S_h} Z_{2^n - j}^{\gamma_h}\}$, denoted as $K_{S_h} = \{k_1, k_2, \ldots, k_h\}$.

Decrypt(C, SK, S_h, $\{a, b\}$, R, params): if either the index $\{a, b\} \notin S_h$ or the user's identity uid $\in R$, then return $\perp$. Otherwise, for $x = \text{path(uid)} \cap \text{cover}(R)$, decryption can be done as follows:

$$
\begin{aligned}
m = c_3 &\cdot \frac{e\left(k_a \cdot \prod_{\{a,j\} \in S_h, j \neq b} Z_{2^n - j + b}, c_1\right)}{e\left(\prod_{\{a,j\} \in S_h} Z_{2^n - j}, c_2\right)} \\
&\cdot \frac{e\left(K_{\text{uid}} \cdot \prod_{y \in \text{path(uid)}, y \neq x} Z_{2^n - y + x}, c_4\right)}{e\left(P_{\text{uid}}, c_5\right)}.
\end{aligned}
\tag{8}
$$

The correctness of this equation can be verified after computation and therefore is omitted. The security of this extended scheme can be proved as the similar method as the basic scheme, so we do not explain it in detail here.

7. Conclusion and Future Work

In the cloud storage environment, in order to protect the security and privacy of users' data and to simplify key management in the process of data sharing more effectively, key-aggregate cryptosystem has been put forward. It is realized under the public key cryptosystem and can aggregate the user's private keys into a single one, greatly reducing the user's key management cost. At the same time, the aggregation can be achieved without constraints, realizing the flexible data sharing in cloud environment. This paper mainly studies the revocable key-aggregate cryptosystem and proposes a revocable key-aggregate encryption scheme combined with the subset-cover framework in cloud environment, realizing the key aggregation and user access control effectively. By updating ciphertext via the cloud servers, the proposed scheme realizes the user permissions revocation while legitimate users do not need to update their private keys. What is more, it provides a verification mechanism to ensure user revocation is executed correctly. Performance analysis shows that, compared with the existing schemes, the proposed scheme reduces the cost of storage and transmission and realizes the user access control effectively. Security analysis shows that the proposed scheme proved to be selective CPA security based on Generalized DHDHE assumption in the standard model. Besides, an extended scheme is proposed to adapt for the cloud scenario, where the number of files is extremely large and growing rapidly.

This paper also has limitations that it only considers to construct a CPA security scheme. Since there are a lot of solutions to transfer a scheme from CPA security to CCA security [31], how to construct an efficient CCA secure key-aggregate encryption scheme will be a concern. And the total number of users is predefined in our revocable scheme, which is not conducive to flexible extension of the system. Therefore, how to design a key-aggregate encryption scheme united the revocation and extensibility will be the future work. In addition, trying to use the theory to solve some security problems in the practical application environment, such as how to apply the idea of revocable key-aggregate cryptosystem in the privacy-preserving of data aggregation and realize the data integrity verification, will be one of the future research directions.

Competing Interests

The authors declare that they have no competing interests.

Acknowledgments

This work was partially supported by National Natural Science Foundation of China under Grants 61272415, 61070164; Natural Science Foundation of Guangdong Province, China, under Grant S2012010008767; Science and Technology Planning Project of Guangdong Province, China, under Grant 2013B010401015. This work was also supported by the Zhuhai Top Discipline-Information Security.

References

[1] J. Wu, L. Ping, X. Ge, W. Ya, and J. Fu, "Cloud storage as the infrastructure of Cloud Computing," in *Proceedings of the International Conference on Intelligent Computing and Cognitive Informatics (ICICCI '10)*, pp. 380–383, June 2010.

[2] K. Dahbur, B. Mohammad, and A. B. Tarakji, "Security issues in cloud computing: a survey of risks, threats and vulnerabilities," *Cloud Computing Advancements in Design Implementation & Technologies*, vol. 1, no. 3, pp. 1–11, 2011.

[3] P. Sikhar, S. Yash, and M. Debdeep, "Dynamic key-aggregate cryptosystem on ellipticcurves for online data sharing," *IACR Cryptology ePrint Archive*, vol. 2015, pp. 923–942, 2015.

[4] D. Naor, M. Naor, and J. Lotspiech, "Revocation and tracing schemes for stateless receivers," in *Advances in Cryptology—CRYPTO 2001. CRYPTO 2001*, J. Kilian, Ed., vol. 2139 of *Lecture Notes in Computer Science*, pp. 41–62, Springer, Berlin, Germany, 2001.

[5] S. Park, K. Lee, and D. H. Lee, "New constructions of revocable identity-based encryption from multilinear maps," *IEEE Transactions on Information Forensics & Security*, vol. 10, no. 8, pp. 1564–1577, 2015.

[6] Y. Shi, Q. Zheng, J. Liu, and Z. Han, "Directly revocable key-policy attribute-based encryption with verifiable ciphertext delegation," *Information Sciences*, vol. 295, pp. 221–231, 2015.

[7] S. G. Akl and P. D. Taylor, "Cryptographic solution to a problem of access control in a hierarchy," *ACM Transactions on Computer Systems (TOCS)*, vol. 1, no. 3, pp. 239–248, 1983.

[8] M. J. Atallah, M. Blanton, N. Fazio, and K. B. Frikken, "Dynamic and efficient key management for access hierarchies," *ACM Transactions on Information and System Security*, vol. 12, no. 3, pp. 1–43, 2009.

[9] A. R. Pais and S. Joshi, "A new probabilistic rekeying method for secure multicast groups," *International Journal of Information Security*, vol. 9, no. 4, pp. 275–286, 2010.

[10] G. Ateniese, A. De Santis, A. L. Ferrara, and B. Masucci, "Provably-secure time-bound hierarchical key assignment schemes," *Journal of Cryptology*, vol. 25, no. 2, pp. 243–270, 2012.

[11] J. Benaloh, M. Chase, E. Horvitz, and K. Lauter, "Patient controlled encryption: ensuring privacy of electronic medical records," in *Proceedings of the ACM Workshop on Cloud Computing Security (CCSW '09), Co-located with the 16th ACM Computer and Communications Security Conference (CCS '09)*, pp. 103–114, Chicago, Ill, USA, November 2009.

[12] J. Benaloh, "Key compression and its application to digital fingerprinting," Tech. Rep., Microsoft Research, 2009.

[13] B. Alomair and R. Poovendran, "Information theoretically secure encryption with almost free authentication," *Journal of Universal Computer Science*, vol. 15, no. 15, pp. 2937–2956, 2009.

[14] A. Shamir, "Identity-based cryptosystems and signature schemes," in *Advances in Cryptology*, pp. 47–53, Springer, Berlin, Germany, 1984.

[15] D. Boneh and M. Franklin, "Identity-based encryption from the weil pairing," in *Proceedings of the Annual International Cryptology Conference (CRYPTO '01)*, vol. 44, no. 3 of *Lecture Notes in Computer Science (LNCS)*, pp. 389–392, Santa Barbara, Calif, USA, 2001.

[16] F. Guo, Y. Mu, and Z. Chen, "Identity-based encryption: how to decrypt multiple Ciphertexts using a single decryption key," in *Proceedings of the Pairing-based Cryptography (Pairing '07)*, pp. 392–406, Springer, Berlin, Germany, 2007.

[17] F. Guo, Y. Mu, Z. Chen, and L. Xu, "Multi-identity single-key decryption without random oracles," in *Information security and cryptology*, vol. 4990 of *Lecture Notes in Comput. Sci.*, pp. 384–398, Springer, Berlin, Germany, 2008.

[18] Y. Ming, Y. Wang, and L. Pang, "Provably secure multi-identity single-key decryption scheme in the standard model," *Computer Science*, vol. 37, no. 3, pp. 73–75, 2010.

[19] A. Sahai and B. Waters, "Fuzzy identity-based encryption," in *Advances in Cryptology—EUROCRYPT 2005*, pp. 457–473, Springer, Berlin, Germany, 2005.

[20] B. Waters, "Ciphertext-policy attribute-based encryption: an expressive, efficient, and provably secure realization," in *Public Key Cryptography—PKC 2011. PKC 2011*, D. Catalano, N. Fazio,

R. Gennaro, and A. Nicolosi, Eds., vol. 6571 of *Lecture Notes in Computer Science*, pp. 53–70, Springer, Berlin, Germany, 2011.

[21] M. Li, S. Yu, Y. Zheng, K. Ren, and W. Lou, "Scalable and secure sharing of personal health records in cloud computing using attribute-based encryption," *IEEE Transactions on Parallel and Distributed Systems*, vol. 24, no. 1, pp. 131–143, 2013.

[22] R. Canetti and S. Hohenberger, "Chosen-ciphertext secure proxy re-encryption," in *Proceedings of the 14th ACM Conference on Computer and Communications Security (CCS '07)*, pp. 185–194, Alexandria, Va, USA, November 2007.

[23] C. Wu, S. Li, and Y. Zhang, "Key management scheme based on secret sharing for wireless sensor networks," *International Journal of Information and Communication Technology*, vol. 7, no. 2-3, pp. 126–140, 2015.

[24] C.-K. Chu, S. S. M. Chow, W.-G. Tzeng, J. Zhou, and R. H. Deng, "Key-aggregate cryptosystem for scalable data sharing in cloud storage," *IEEE Transactions on Parallel and Distributed Systems*, vol. 25, no. 2, pp. 468–477, 2014.

[25] K. Kate and S. D. Potdukhe, "Data sharing in cloud storage with key-aggregate cryptosystem," *International Journal of Engineering Research and General Science*, vol. 2, no. 6, pp. 882–886, 2014.

[26] B. Cui, Z. Liu, and L. Wang, "Key-aggregate searchable encryption (KASE) for group data sharing via cloud storage," *Institute of Electrical and Electronics Engineers. Transactions on Computers*, vol. 65, no. 8, pp. 2374–2385, 2016.

[27] H. Dang, Y. L. Chong, F. Brun et al., "Fine-grained sharing of encrypted sensor data over cloud storage with key aggregation," *IACR Cryptology ePrint Archive*, pp. 739–750, 2015.

[28] Q. Gan and X. Wang, "An efficient key-aggregate encryption scheme under cloud environment," *Computer Engineering*, vol. 42, no. 2, pp. 33–44, 2016.

[29] D. Boneh and A. Silverberg, "Applications of multilinear forms to cryptography," in *Contemporary Mathematics*, vol. 324, pp. 71–90, 2003.

[30] D. Boneh, B. Waters, and M. Zhandry, "Low overhead broadcast encryption from multilinear maps," in *Advances in Cryptology—CRYPTO 2014*, vol. 8616 of *Lecture Notes in Comput. Sci.*, pp. 206–223, Springer, Heidelberg, Germany, 2014.

[31] R. Canetti, S. Halevi, and J. Katz, "Chosen-ciphertext security from identity-based encryption," in *Advances in cryptology—EUROCRYPT 2004*, vol. 3027 of *Lecture Notes in Comput. Sci.*, pp. 207–222, Springer, Berlin, Germany, 2004.

18

Performance Evaluation of Cryptographic Algorithms over IoT Platforms and Operating Systems

Geovandro C. C. F. Pereira, Renan C. A. Alves, Felipe L. da Silva, Roberto M. Azevedo, Bruno C. Albertini, and Cíntia B. Margi

Escola Politécnica, Universidade de São Paulo, São Paulo, SP, Brazil

Correspondence should be addressed to Geovandro C. C. F. Pereira; geovandro@larc.usp.br

Academic Editor: Qing Yang

The deployment of security services over Wireless Sensor Networks (WSN) and IoT devices brings significant processing and energy consumption overheads. These overheads are mainly determined by algorithmic efficiency, quality of implementation, and operating system. Benchmarks of symmetric primitives exist in the literature for WSN platforms but they are mostly focused on single platforms or single operating systems. Moreover, they are not up to date with respect to implementations and/or operating systems versions which had significant progress. Herein, we provide time and energy benchmarks of reference implementations for different platforms and operating systems and analyze their impact. Moreover, we not only give the first benchmark results of symmetric cryptography for the Intel Edison IoT platform but also describe a methodology of how to measure energy consumption on that platform.

1. Introduction

The progressive growth of IoT applications has been broadening the spectrum of transmitted data, bringing an increasing demand of security services like data confidentiality, integrity, and source authentication. However, the attempt to employ security mechanisms that are typical of conventional networks is likely to cause undesirable effects due to hardware-related resource limitations. The most relevant overheads relate to energy consumption and/or increase of communication delays. Another concern is the relatively higher memory consumption that might be aggravated by the device's available memory and the amount of applications running on it. Therefore, one of the main challenges for deploying security mechanisms over WSN and IoT is to minimize the conflict between resource consumption and the desired security [1, 2].

In addition, with the advent of Software Defined Networking (SDN), heterogeneous networking devices can be remotely reconfigured by a central SDN controller on the fly and thus a new trend of a wider range of platforms and communication technologies has emerged, like smart homes,

autonomous cars, and many others [3]. A new requirement is thus introduced, and security solutions should take those richer environments into account while still offering acceptable performance and energy footprints among all devices within a network.

It is worth mentioning that many works in the literature concentrate their efforts either only on the evaluation of symmetric cryptographic primitives over a single microcontroller (e.g., the MSP430 embedded in TelosB motes [4, 5] or the ATmega128L embedded in MICAz motes [6]) or even on a single OS [5]. In addition, the performance evaluation is usually done by direct compilation to the target platform without an underlying OS. Even though that approach is interesting for providing a reliable benchmarking in an isolated environment, in real-world applications, an OS is required to implement its own TCP-IP protocol stack where TLS-based solutions are built on top of [7]. In practice, each OS has different energy and memory consumption footprints in addition to the delays introduced in the network communication. In the context of WSN, experiments in the literature were conducted over older versions of the operating systems [8] but many important core features have been changed since then, and thus those results do not reflect the current state of the art in terms of energy consumption among other performance metrics. One relevant example is the ContikiOS, which has been drastically reformulated recently; its 3.0 version was launched in August 2015 [9]. For example, in our experiments, typical AES operations using the SUPERCOOP implementation [10] over both most recent TinyOS 2.1.2 and ContikiOS 3.0 are 2x faster and 2x less energy consuming than the results reported by Casado and Tsigas [8].

In addition to the operating systems, many algorithm parameters and implementations were improved through time; thus an evaluation and analysis of the combined effect of them are crucial for implementors to take better decisions when security services are required.

In this work, we perform an extensive experimental evaluation of reference implementations of many cryptographic primitives for different security services over real sensor platforms. We also evaluate the influence of the most recent versions of two popular operating systems for WSN, TinyOS 2.1.2 and ContikiOS 3.0. We provide a performance and energy analysis, including a methodology, for important cryptographic operations deployed on the TI TelosB [4] and the Intel Edison [11] platforms. As far as we know, this is the first extensive benchmark of symmetric primitives for the Intel Edison platform. The implementations were obtained mostly from the original authors when possible. We preferred 16-bit implementations for TelosB and 32-bit implementations for the Intel Edison.

The paper is organized as follows. Section 2 discusses related work; Section 3 describes the scenario, platforms, and cryptographic algorithms. In Section 4 the experimental setup and methodology for the benchmarks are detailed. Section 5 introduces the results for the algorithms running over TinyOS on TelosB platform, while Section 6 presents the same evaluation for the ContikiOS. We then perform the analysis for the Intel Edison platform in Section 7. Section 8 concludes this paper and suggests future work.

2. Related Work

In 2006, Law et al. [5] evaluated eight different block ciphers and four modes of encryption over a constrained WSN platform, the Texas Instruments 16-bit RISC-based MSP430F149. They focused only on encryption operations and did not analyze primitives for other security services such as authentication, which is usually required by most of modern applications. In addition, if we think about an IoT application, an operating system will also be running over a microcontroller (like ContikiOS) and it would be interesting to measure the behavior of primitives working along with the operating system. Also, the ciphers and libraries analyzed in [5] are completely outdated, since the work is from almost a decade ago. Today sensor motes became much more energy efficient like the underlying TelosB microcontroller, that is, the MSP430F1611 which consumes a 330 μA current in active mode, while the MSP430F149 draws a nominal current of 420 μA as mentioned in [5].

In 2011, Hyncica et al. [12] evaluated the performance of 15 different block ciphers on three different microcontrollers (of 32-bit, 16-bit, and 8-bit instructions). They used the TomCrypt LTC library version 1.16 which is a general purpose cryptographic library for 32-bit platforms and thus not optimized for constrained microcontrollers. They adopted the ECB encryption mode, which allows for a clear distinction of the performance of the plain block ciphers when compared to other modes of operation, for example, CTR, CBC, and CCM. On the other hand, the ECB mode only targets confidentiality service and is considered insecure in practice today [13]. In addition to confidentiality, modern real-world secure applications must include more advanced security services such as authentication. Therefore, a performance evaluation over constrained platforms of more sophisticated modes like authenticated encryption is relevant since they present significant impact on energy consumption compared to ECB. Additionally, Hyncica et al. [12] do not provide energy measurements, which is very important in the context of battery-powered devices. They also do not address the performance behavior when operating systems also play a role.

In 2010, Margi et al. analyzed the impact of the operating systems on security applications for a single platform, that is, the TelosB. Their work is based on TinyOS 2.0.2 and Contiki 2.3. In 2013, Simplicio Jr. et al. [14] provided a comparison of message authentication code algorithms for the TelosB platform using TinyOS. They implemented the algorithms themselves and did not specify what TinyOS version was used for. The compilations were performed with GNU mspgcc version 3.2.3 and they preferred to use -Os flag to get a memory optimized result.

Regarding existing full-fledge security frameworks for WSN, the TinySec [15] and MiniSec [16] were designed only with TinyOS [17] in mind and each of them was implemented for a specific sensor device. Another popular one, ContikiSec, was planned and implemented particularly for the ContikiOS. Such differences make it impractical to compare cryptographic algorithms. Moreover, the structures within each framework can also adopt different project and implementation approaches, using different policies of processing or memory usage. Modifications in operating system components (in the case of MiniSec) are an even more complex issue.

Another difficulty is that in recent years the devices and operating systems have been updated a number of times, while the security structures have not. In this way, the structures have become unusable for a number of platforms, such as the cases of TinySec and MiniSec, which are no longer usable for series 2 of the versions of TinyOS (TinyOS2x).

In addition, the drivers are sometimes unavailable for the operating system. This was the case in the IEEE 802.15.4 security specification, which was available in certain devices, like the TelosB [4] and the MICAz [6], without certain functions required to activate the security resources in the operating systems, which made it very difficult to utilize the security structure.

All those frameworks, as explained, are highly bounded to specific platforms or operating systems, and therefore we do not evaluate them in this work.

TABLE 1: Architecture comparison.

| Class | Device | | Energy (mW) | |
	Name	Architecture	Idle	Processing
SBC	Intel Edison	Atom (x86@500 MHz dual-core)	88	340
	Intel Galileo	Quark (x86@400 MHz)	520	550
	BeagleBone Black	Cortex-A8 (ARM@1 GHz)	310	400
	Raspberry Pi A	Broadcom (ARM@700 MHz)	130	180
	Raspberry Pi B	Broadcom (ARM@700 MHz)	380	410
WSN	MICAz	ATmega128L (RISC@7.3 MHz)	26	0.025
	TelosB	TI MSP430 (RISC@8 MHz)	4.8	0.035
	Arduino Yun	ATmega32U4 (RISC@16 MHz) + Atheros (MIPS@400 MHz)	240	280

3. Scenario

Given related work discussed, the scenarios we consider for our performance evaluation must be platforms or operating systems independent. Next we present the platforms and operating systems, as well as the cryptographic algorithms we selected.

3.1. Platforms. This section presents an overview of the selected embedded devices, which are typically used in IoT and WSN applications.

Table 1 depicts a group of embedded architectures. We selected some popular embedded devices found on literature according to main usage: SBC (Single Board Computer) and WSN (Wireless Sensor Network). SBC class includes devices with general purpose computing power, for gateway or sink, and WSN includes only platforms targeting low-power communication, typically used as nodes. Data were compiled from [18–21] and updated with [22].

Considering the goal of this work, we choose Intel Edison and TelosB as representative of their respective classes. We expect that the performance behavior remain the same for a device of the same class, except for Arduino Yun, whose consumption is far from WSN nodes (built for low energy) but does not achieve enough performance to be compared with SBC class. Platforms that do not include any type of IoT communication without external support (e.g., Arduino UNO) were excluded from our evaluation.

3.1.1. TelosB. MEMSICs TelosB Mote is an open-source platform based on a low-power MSP430 16-bit 8 MHz microcontroller with 10 KB RAM and 48 KB program flash memory. TelosB has a low current consumption and is powered by two AA batteries, but it can be plugged in the USB so power is provided from the host computer [4]. TelosB has an IEEE 802.15.4 compliant RF transceiver and runs TinyOS 1.1.11 or higher and Contiki OS.

3.1.2. Intel® Edison. The Intel Edison is a low-power 32-bit x86 IoT platform, which contains a core system processing and connectivity elements: a dual-core, dual-threaded Intel Atom CPU at 500 MHz, and a 32-bit Intel Quark microcontroller at 100 MHz processor; 1 GB RAM; 4 GB eMMC internal storage; and IEEE 802.11 and Bluetooth 4.0. But it is not a self-contained, standalone device. It relies on the end-user support of input power (i.e., the computing module does not control battery recharging) [11]. The Linux distribution Yocto is its default operating system (OS), but its x86 architecture can enable a variety of OSs.

3.2. Operating Systems. This section presents a brief overview of the main operating systems involved in the performance analysis, that is, the TinyOS, ContikiOS, and Yocto.

3.2.1. TinyOS. TinyOS is an open-source operating system designed for low-power wireless devices, such as sensor networks, ubiquitous computing, personal area networks, smart buildings, and smart meters [23]. According to its authors [24], TinyOS is a tiny (less than 400 bytes), flexible operating system built from a set of reusable components that are assembled into an application-specific system and supports an event-driven concurrency model based on split-phase interfaces, asynchronous events, and deferred computation called tasks. TinyOS is implemented in the NesC language, which supports the TinyOS component and concurrency model as well as extensive cross-component optimizations and compile-time race detection. It is a programming framework and set of components for embedded systems that enable building an application-specific OS into each application [24].

TinyOS became the de facto operating system for WSN until 2012, because it combines an efficient memory footprint with an easy-to-use interface for small WSN devices like MICAz and TelosB.

3.2.2. Contiki. Contiki [25] is an open-source operating system for the Internet of Things that connects tiny low-cost, low-power microcontrollers to the Internet.

Contiki applications are written in standard C mainly using structures called *protothreads*. Applications for Contiki can be simulated using Cooja simulator to evaluate networks behavior before deployment into the hardware. ContikiOS 3.0 supports the recently standardized IETF protocols for low-power IPv6 networking, including the 6lowpan adaptation layer [26], the RPL IPv6 multihop routing protocol [27], and the CoAP RESTful application-layer protocol [25, 28, 29].

Contiki runs on a wide range of tiny platforms, ranging from 8051-powered systems on a chip through the MSP430 and the AVR to a variety of ARM devices.

3.2.3. Yocto. The Yocto Project is an open-source collaboration project that provides templates, tools, and methods to help creating custom Linux-based systems for embedded products regardless of the hardware architecture [30].

Its capabilities include a Yocto Project kernel which can cover many profiles across multiple architectures including ARM, PPC, MIPS, x86, and x86-64. It is the default OS for the Intel Edison and it is adopted in our benchmarks.

3.3. Cryptographic Algorithms. The algorithms described in this section were chosen among many other cryptographic algorithms in the literature. This choice has been made about electing algorithms that were designed to be lightweight on resource constrained platforms, where memory and processing resources are relatively scarce, but at same time providing the minimum desired security level.

3.3.1. Symmetric Ciphers. AES [31] algorithm is a symmetric block cipher capable of using cryptographic keys of 128, 192, and 256 bits to encrypt and decrypt data using blocks of 128 bits.

Curupira is a special-purpose block cipher tailored for platforms where power consumption and processing time are very constrained resources, such as sensor and mobile networks, or systems heavily dependent on tokens or smart cards. Curupira is an instance of the Wide Trail family of algorithms, which includes the AES cipher, and displays involutional structure, in the sense that the encryption and decryption modes differ only in the key schedule. Its first version, named Curupira-1 [32, 33], also presents a cyclic key schedule, meaning that the original key is recovered after a certain number of rounds, whereby allowing them to be computed in-place in any order.

Curupira-2 [34] adopts the same round structure as Curupira-1 but takes a less conservative (with a slower diffusion) key scheduling algorithm. This results in a higher performance when the round keys are computed on demand, a common situation in resource constrained networks.

Trivium is a stream cipher that takes a stream of plaintext, a secret key, and an IV as input and then operates on the plaintext with key stream generated by the key and IV, typically bit by bit. It is designed for constrained devices to generate up to 2^{64} bits of key stream from an 80-bit secret key and an 80-bit initial value (IV) [35].

Grain is another stream cipher submitted to eSTREAM [36]. This algorithm has been selected for the final eSTREAM portfolio by the eSTREAM project and is designed primarily for restricted hardware.

3.3.2. Cryptographic Hashing. Blake2 is an extremely fast hash function, yet there are no known security issues in this algorithm. Blake2 has different versions that are suitable for different situations. We chose Blake2s, because it is suitable for resource constrained platforms [37].

Keccak is the winner of SHA3 competition [38]. It consists of a family of sponge functions that hashes message texts with a high level of security. The Keccak Code Package [39] provides the implementation of the Keccak sponge function that we used. For our benchmark purposes we used the version with rate of 1088, capacity of 512, and hash output length of 256 bits.

3.3.3. Message Authentication Codes (MACs). Keyed-Hash Message Authentication Code (HMAC) is standardized in FIPS 198-1, a mechanism for message authentication using cryptographic hash functions. HMAC can be used with any iterative cryptographic hash function, in combination with a shared secret key. Additional applications of keyed-hash functions include their use in challenge-response identification protocols for computing responses, which are a function of both a secret key and a challenge message. An HMAC function is used by the message sender to produce a value (the MAC) that is formed by condensing the secret key and the message input. The MAC is typically sent to the message receiver along with the message. The receiver computes the MAC on the received message using the same key and HMAC function as used by the sender and compares the result computed with the received MAC. If the two values match, the message has been correctly received, and the receiver is ensured that the sender is a member of the community of users that share the key [40].

Marvin message authentication code [41] was proposed by Simplicio et al. and was exactly designed for resource constrained devices. Marvin explores the structure of an underlying block cipher to provide security at a small cost in terms of memory needs. Also, Marvin can be used as an authentication-only function or in an authenticated encryption with associated data (AEAD) scheme. AES, Curupira-1, or Curupira-2 can be adopted as the underlying block cipher.

3.3.4. Authenticated Encryption with Associated Data (AEAD). Counter mode (CTR) is a mode of operation that turns a block cipher into a stream cipher so it used for achieving confidentiality [42]. It generates the next keystream block by encrypting successive values of a "counter." The counter can be any function which produces a sequence which is guaranteed not to repeat for a long time, although an actual increment by one counter is the simplest and most popular. CTR mode is well suited to operate on a multiprocessor machine where blocks can be encrypted in parallel. If the IV/nonce is random, then they can be combined together with the counter using any lossless operation (concatenation, addition, or XOR) to produce the actual unique counter block for encryption. In case of a nonrandom nonce (such as a packet counter), the nonce and counter should be concatenated (e.g., storing nonce in upper 64 bits and the counter in lower 64 bits). Notice that simply adding or XORing of the nonce and counter into a single value would completely break the security under a chosen-plaintext attack.

Counter with Cipher Block Chaining-Message Authentication Code (CCM) is a two-pass patent-free AEAD. CCM is based on an approved symmetric key block cipher algorithm with 128-bit block size, such as the Advanced Encryption Standard (AES) algorithm currently specified in FIPS 197. CCM can be considered a mode of operation of the block cipher algorithm. As with other modes of operation, a single key to the block cipher must be established beforehand among the parties to the data; thus, CCM should be implemented within a well-designed key management structure. The security properties of CCM depend, at a minimum, on the secrecy of the key [43].

Offset Codebook Mode (OCB) is a one-pass authenticated encryption scheme designed by Rogaway et al. [44]. What makes OCB remarkable is that it achieves authenticated encryption in almost the same time as the fastest conventional mode, CTR mode, achieves privacy alone. This results in lower computational cost compared to using separate encryption and authentication functions. OCB performance overhead is minimal compared to classical, nonauthenticating modes like CBC. OCB does not require the nonce to be random; a counter, say, will work fine. Unlike some modes, the plaintext provided to OCB can be of any length, as well as the associated data, and OCB will encrypt the plaintext without padding it to some convenient-length string, an approach that would yield a longer ciphertext. If one is encrypting and MACing in a conventional way, like CTR-mode encryption and the CBC MAC, the cost for privacy and authenticity is going to be twice the cost for privacy alone, just counting block cipher calls. Unfortunately, OCB is patented for commercial use in the USA [45]. There are now free licenses available for OCB with unusual restrictions, which some implementors have expressed concerns over (e.g., one license only applies only to open-source software; another allows only use of OCB in OpenSSL implementation).

EAX is a two-pass AEAD; that is, encryption and authentication are done in separate operations. This makes it much slower than OCB, though unlike CCM it is "online." Still, EAX has three advantages: first, it is patent-free. Second, it is pretty easy to implement. Third, it uses only the encipher direction of the block cipher, meaning that one could technically fit it into an implementation with a very constrained code size, if that sort of thing is a concern. One possible drawback is that EAX is not entirely parallelizable due to the use of CMAC [46].

LetterSoup is a parallelizable two-pass AEAD scheme based on the Marvin for message authentication [41]. One of the main interests of using Marvin is that it follows the ALRED construction [47], meaning that each block of the message blocks is processed using a few unkeyed rounds of an underlying block cipher (the so-called Square Complete Transform, SCT) instead of a full encryption as in CMAC. LetterSoup was designed with constrained platforms in mind, one advantage being that its encryption function (the LFSRC mode) is involutional; that is, applying it twice recovers the plaintext, so the code size gets reduced since only one direction is needed. Its official implementation employs Curupira-2 as the underlying block cipher [48]. Another advantage is that the security of LetterSoup is formally analyzed giving more confidence for the algorithm. In addition, the message and the header can be processed in any desired order, and the tag can be verified before the decryption process takes place. The IVs used must be nonrepeating [41]. In the figures and tables we will refer to LetterSoup as LTS. Moreover, in our analysis the LTS implementation by Simplicio [49] utilizes Curupira-2 [50] as its underlying block cipher.

Ketje is composed of two authenticated encryption schemes with support for associated data and was designed by the inventors of Keccak, the winner of the SHA3 hash function. Ketje is a nonce-based AEAD, meaning that the encryption function is deterministic and needs a different nonce for each invocation to be secure. It supports two security levels, that is, 96 bits and 128 bits. Ketje builds on round-reduced versions of the Keccak-f permutation as primitives, that is, the Keccak-f[400] and Keccak-f[200], allowing for code reuse when Keccak is already being used. It also offers considerable side-channel protection. On the other hand, it is more memory consuming compared to the above-mentioned AEAD schemes [51]. The implementation employed Ketje v1 in this work along with Keccak-f[400] for 128-bit security. The code was obtained from the Keccak Code Package [39].

4. Experimental Setup and Methodology

As discussed in the previous section, the evaluation covers algorithms from four categories. Next we address the implementation and configuration used for each of them.

4.1. Symmetric Ciphers. The reference implementations of the underlying block ciphers Curupira and Trivium are designed for 8-bit platforms. For the case of AES operations, we used the highly optimized implementation for 16-bit CPUs with 128-bits keys (and 128-bit IVs) available at [10]. For the Trivium synchronous stream cipher [35], we used the implementation published in [52], configured with key size of 112 bits and IV size of 96 bits. For the Curupira [34] block cipher we have adopted the reference implementation [50]. This implementation is optimized for key size of 96 bits.

4.2. Cryptographic Hashing. We selected the official Blake2s implementation [53]. For the Keccak hash function we adopted the Keccak Code Package [39] which provides the implementation of the Keccak sponge function.

4.3. Message Authentication Codes (MAC). MAC algorithms can be built based on hashing or symmetric cipher algorithms. We chose one algorithm from each category.

HMAC uses a cryptographic hash function to define a MAC. Any hash function could be used by this algorithm. We used the implementation published in [54], considering the following parameters: SHA-256 hash function, 128-bit key size, and 64-byte block size.

Marvin [41] uses a symmetric cipher algorithm to ensure authenticity and integrity of a received message. It can use AES or Curupira-2 as the base cipher. We used the implementation published in [55], configured with the following parameters: Curupira-2 cipher, 96-bit key size, and 12-byte tag size.

4.4. Authenticated Encryption with Associated Data (AEAD). For EAX [56] we used the implementation published in [49], and the Curupira-2 was adopted as the underlying block cipher. For the LetterSoup [41], the default parametrization uses Curupira-2 as block cipher, which is also used in the implementation published in [48]. LetterSoup will be referred to as LTS in the next graphs and tables. OCB [57] is a patented

TABLE 2: Operations of interest for each primitive.

Symmetric ciphers	Hash	MAC	AEADs
Init	Init	Init	Init
Encryption	Update	Update	Encryption
Decryption	Final	Final	Decryption

mode of operation. Our implementation for this algorithm [49] also uses Curupira-2 as cipher algorithm. Ketje is an AEAD algorithm based on Keccak. It is designed for resource constrained platforms, and the implementation used in this report is the one at [39].

It is worth pointing out that a usual good approach for comparing performance of different algorithms is that the same implementor implements all of them since the same amount of tricks is more evenly applied. On the other hand, we think a single implementor producing tens of new nontested implementations for the different platforms is not reasonable. Actually, our goal in here is to evaluate existing already deployed and better tested implementations and their behavior in the selected platforms.

In order to evaluate algorithms for each category *(symmetric cipher, hash, MAC, AEAD)*, we calculate the run time and energy consumption of each relevant operation. The procedures considered are listed in Table 2.

The run times and energy consumption are extracted using a python script wrote by the authors, which reads the output file from the LabView setup explained next. The measurement setup for current consumption consists of an Agilent 34401A digital multimeter [58] that reads the drained current and communicates with a computer via GPIB, running LabView. The current sampling is limited to 500 Hz. The mote is powered by a fixed voltage source at 3 V. Since it is ineffective to compare cryptographic algorithms using a fixed message size, we compared all algorithms varying the sizes. Messages up to roughly 100 bytes were considered, according to the following rules:

(i) Symmetric block ciphers: Curupira-2 and AES data sizes D will be multiples of the block size

(ii) Hash: multiples of the tag size

(iii) MAC: multiples of the underlying cipher (or hash) block size

(iv) AEAD: multiples of the underlying cipher (or hash) block size

Five independent measurements are conducted in order to calculate the average, standard deviation, and confidence interval of 95%. Each operation runs N times, and N is determined by the time t of a single run of the operation. It should satisfy $N \leq (100/t)$. This is due to a limitation of a LabView internal buffer size which becomes fully loaded after 100 seconds of measurements using the maximum sampling rate of our setup.

For the *TelosB platform* the number N is defined according to the algorithm as follows:

(i) AES, Curupira-2, LetterSoup, OCB, Blake2s, Marvin, HMAC, and Trivium: $N = 100$.

(ii) EAX and Keccak: $N = 80$.

(iii) Ketje: $N = 5$.

For the Intel Edison with Yocto OS the following N is adopted for each algorithm:

(i) For execution time experiments:

(a) Symmetric ciphers: $N = 200000$.

(b) Hash: $N = 200000$.

(c) MAC: $N = 100000$.

(d) AEAD: $N = 30000$.

(ii) For energy consumption experiments:

(a) Symmetric ciphers: $N = 250000$.

(b) Hash: $N = 80000$.

(c) MAC: $N = 500000$.

(d) AEAD: $N = 40000$.

Before any test is performed, a script that stops unnecessary OS processes is executed on Yocto OS. Moreover, the run time acquisition in this case is conducted by means of the *gettimeofday* function which provides a microsecond resolution [59]. Because symmetric algorithms are very fast, one might think that *gettimeofday* may not be enough to get a precise time taking, but since we are taking a large amount of executions of the same operation we are able to get precise result, and yet the precision of microseconds is fair enough for our experiments since the fastest operation we have measured is more than 1 microsecond.

All procedures were executed N times in order to allow a statistical analysis of the experiment and defined an error margin, which was calculated with a standard error.

The compiler used for TelosB was the GNU msp430-gcc LTS 20120406 and the -O3 optimization option was set, which means optimizing for speed, since applications usually want to minimize energy consumption for the target IoT and WSN scenarios. We used GCC 5.1 for the Intel Edison.

5. Benchmarks and Results on the TelosB Platform, TinyOS

We first collect the block cipher performance results over TelosB for the *encryption operation* in Figure 1.

It is clear from the graphs in Figure 1 that run time and energy consumption are proportional in the TelosB platform. This can be explained by the fact that TinyOS is event-oriented and very lightweight operating system. When a task is to run, the operating system simply yields all the processing resources to the task. The consequence is that practically all energy consumption is due to the running algorithm in the task and energy consumption gets proportional to the running time of the algorithm.

When we compare the results in Figure 1 with the ones reported by Casado and Tsigas [8] for the AES on 16-bit MSP microcontrollers, we observe that the AES implementation SUPERCOOP combined with most recent TinyOS 2.1.2 over an MSP430 microcontroller performs 2x faster for both

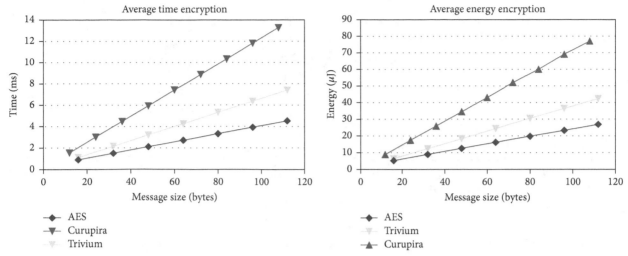

FIGURE 1: TinyOS/TelosB: average time and energy for the *encryption* operation for each block cipher.

encryption/decryption operations (1 ms per block versus >2 ms per block) and consequently spends 2x less energy for these computations. This observation gives evidence that many of the previous reports in the literature do not reflect precisely the most up-to-date energy footprints of combined best implementations and OSs for WSN.

For all the next operations with block ciphers, hash, and AEAD, energy consumption is proportional to running times; thus we provide only the time comparison for some of the next benchmarks since we can expect the same behavior for the energy comparison.

It is also worth pointing out that from Figure 1 Curupira-2 performed slower when compared to other ciphers although having smaller block size and being tailored for constrained devices. We asked the original authors about this apparent paradox and they clarified that although Curupira-2 implementation was developed with small word sizes in mind they aimed at correctness over high performance. On the other hand, a much better performance is expected if properly optimized. Moreover, from our results, the relative decryption behavior for the three algorithms is the same; thus we do not provide the detailed figures herein for conciseness.

In practice, block ciphers are used along with modes of operation. We provide the benchmarks of this combination for the AES block cipher next.

5.1. AES-CTR and AES-CBC Encryption Modes. The AES in CTR mode follows its standard specifications. For the CBC (Cipher Block Chaining) mode, the following parameters (experiments follow the same described setup) are adopted:

(i) Key size is 128 bits.

(ii) Block size is 16 bytes.

(iii) Plaintext size is 16 bytes.

(iv) Number of rounds is 10.

(v) Precomputed tables are used in AES MixColumns for run time optimization.

The run time and energy consumption for different operations from CTR and CBC modes are shown in Table 3.

TABLE 3: Time in ms for one execution in different mode AES of *init*, *encryption*, and *decryption* tasks, with message size = 16 bytes.

Mode	Init	Encryption	Decryption
CBC	1,28 ± 0,01	2,69 ± 0,02	2,82 ± 0,04
CTR	0,47 ± 0,01	0,91 ± 0,01	0,91 ± 0,01

TABLE 4: Time to execute one *init* operation for each hash algorithm. Time is in ms.

Blake2s	Keccak
0,96 ± 0,00	6,96 ± 0,02

From the results in Table 3, we notice that CTR mode is about 3x faster and less energy consuming for the encryption/decryption operations when compared to CBC.

We now provide the benchmark results for the *hash* functions.

The run time and energy consumption of the *init* operation for the different hash algorithms are relatively cheap compared to other hash operations and are shown in Table 4. But it is worth mentioning that Blake2's initialization is 7x faster than Keccak's. This operation has a roughly constant execution time for all data sizes.

Tables 5 and 6 show the comparison and the numerical differences between hash algorithms for the *update* operation.

One can check that Blake2's performance surpasses Keccak's. A better illustration of the *update* operation is provided in Figure 2.

From the results of Tables 4, 5, and 6 and Figure 2 we clearly see an advantage of Blake2s compared to Keccak. The main reason for this behavior is that Blake2s was particularly designed to run faster in smaller word processors (TelosB is embedded with a MSP430 microcontroller with 16-bit words).

Finally, Table 7 shows the execution time for the *final* operation, which is roughly constant for any data size ($12 \leq D \leq 108$), thus the time for only one input size is shown. Keccak is faster than Blake2 in this operation.

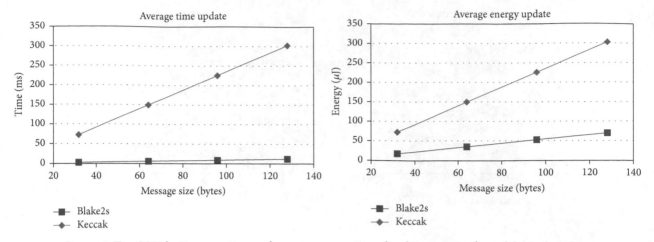

FIGURE 2: TinyOS/TelosB: average time and energy consumption of *update* operation for each hash algorithm.

TABLE 5: Time to execute one *update* operation for each hash algorithm. Time is in ms and the data size D is in bytes.

D	Blake2s	Keccak
32	3,03 ± 0,01	72,8 ± 0,2
64	6,00 ± 0,02	149,5 ± 0,4
96	8,98 ± 0,02	226,1 ± 0,6
128	11,94 ± 0,04	303,0 ± 1,0

TABLE 6: Energy to execute one *update* operation for each hash algorithm. Energy is in μJ and the data size D is in bytes.

D	Blake2s	Keccak
32	17,7 ± 0,2	410 ± 20
64	35,2 ± 0,3	840 ± 50
96	52,6 ± 0,5	1270 ± 70
128	70,0 ± 0,6	1700 ± 100

TABLE 7: Time to execute one *final* operation for each hash algorithm. Time is in ms and D is the data size in bytes.

D	Blake2s	Keccak
128	6,27 ± 0,02	4,1 ± 0,02

Notice that here we compare two *MAC* algorithms, Marvin and HMAC, which operate with different sizes of blocks. Marvin does not have exact blocks of sizes 64 bytes and 128 bytes, but it offers a range of sizes varying from 12 bytes to any multiple of it. On the other hand, HMAC works with blocks multiple of 64 bytes. For the case of 64-byte block in HMAC and 72-byte block in Marvin, Marvin is still faster and more energy efficient even when operating with large blocks.

Table 8 shows the execution time of *init* operation for each MAC algorithm. The execution time is roughly constant for every data size, and Marvin takes longer to initialize than HMAC.

Table 9 shows the execution time and energy consumption for the *update* operation for each MAC algorithm.

TABLE 8: Time to execute one *init* operation for each MAC algorithm. Time is expressed in ms.

Marvin	HMAC
5,62 ± 0,01	28,95 ± 0,04

TABLE 9: Time to execute one update operation for each MAC algorithm. Time is in ms and D is the data size in bytes.

D	Marvin	HMAC
12	1,68 ± 0,01	
36	4,88 ± 0,01	
60	8,08 ± 0,02	
84	11,28 ± 0,02	
108	14,50 ± 0,03	
128		28,37 ± 0,04

TABLE 10: Time to execute one *final* operation for each MAC algorithm. Time is expressed in ms and D is the data size in bytes.

D	Marvin	HMAC
108	7,04 ± 0,01	
128		35,43 ± 0,05

TABLE 11: Time to execute one *init* operation. Time is expressed in ms.

EAX	OCB	LetterSoup	Ketje
7,67 ± 0,01	4,88 ± 0,01	3,04 ± 0,01	18,4 ± 0,2

Benchmarks for the *update* operation are also shown in Figure 3.

Finally, Table 10 shows the time and energy performance for the *final* operation. The execution time for Marvin is roughly constant for all data sizes and thus we only plot the result for the 108-byte input size. Marvin performs about 5x faster than HMAC for the *final* operation.

Table 11 shows the execution time and energy consumption of the *init* operation for different *AEAD* algorithms.

TABLE 12: Time to execute one *encryption* operation for each AEAD algorithm (associated data size = 0). Time is expressed in ms and D is the data size in bytes.

D	EAX	OCB	LetterSoup	Ketje
12	7,85 ± 0,02	6,58 ± 0,01	4,94 ± 0,01	93,2 ± 0,2
36	15,43 ± 0,04	11,10 ± 0,01	8,66 ± 0,01	167,6 ± 0,2
60	23,00 ± 0,04	15,60 ± 0,02	12,38 ± 0,03	242,4 ± 0,2
84	30,80 ± 0,04	20,12 ± 0,03	16,08 ± 0,05	316,6 ± 0,3
108	38,18 ± 0,06	24,65 ± 0,05	19,78 ± 0,06	391,2 ± 0,3

TABLE 13: Time to execute one *encryption* operation for each AEAD algorithm (associated data size = message size). Time is expressed in ms and D is the data size in bytes.

D	EAX	OCB	LetterSoup	Ketje
12	9,86 ± 0,03	8,76 ± 0,02	4,96 ± 0,01	118,4 ± 0,2
36	21,33 ± 0,04	17,50 ± 0,03	10,30 ± 0,02	267,4 ± 0,3
60	32,8 ± 0,1	26,24 ± 0,05	14,86 ± 0,04	416,0 ± 0,6
84	44,2 ± 0,2	34,98 ± 0,06	19,40 ± 0,06	566,0 ± 3,0
108	55,7 ± 0,1	43,68 ± 0,08	23,96 ± 0,07	714,8 ± 0,7

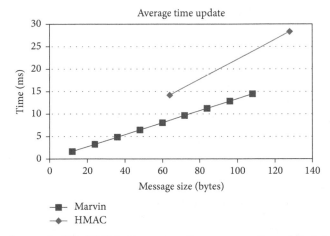

FIGURE 3: TinyOS/TelosB: average time consumption of *update* operation for each MAC algorithm.

LetterSoup initialization is the fastest AEAD with a small difference compared to OCB. Ketje has the slowest initialization which comes from the fact of managing with larger states. On the other hand, LetterSoup's better performance is influenced by the smaller state but at a penalty of a slightly smaller security level of 96 bits.

Table 12 shows the run time and energy consumption of the *encryption* operation without associated data. Note that Ketje's performance is significantly worse. Although its implementation is intended for 16-bit CPUs, the design works with 50-byte internal states which are at least 3x larger than states from other algorithms, which explains the slower behavior.

Table 13 shows the execution time of the *authenticated encryption with associated data* operation. Ketje remains the slowest algorithm in this experiment by one order of magnitude compared to others. Recall that a decision to select one of these algorithms depends on the tradeoff performance and the additional features of each algorithm.

Recall that LetterSoup is faster but comes with a slightly smaller security level and also is not standardized. EAX and OCB are standardized, and OCB has some patent issues. Ketje in turn could be reusing Keccak's code and save code memory in case a hash function is also desired in the same application.

Figure 4 shows the execution time and energy of the *encryption with associated data* operation. LetterSoup presents a better performance than others when there is associated data. Therefore it presents a better option when the combined services are desired.

The operation *decryption with associated data* presents similar performance as the encryption counterpart and is thus omitted here.

According to the results described in this section, the best performances in terms of speed and energy on TelosB with TinyOS are achieved by the following:

(i) Encryption mode: *AES-CTR*

(ii) Hash: *Blake2*

(iii) MAC: *Marvin*

(iv) AEAD: *LetterSoup*

It is worth pointing out that, for each type above, speed might not be the priority and the decision should be made taking into account all the desired features for each algorithm to have.

6. Benchmarks and Results on the TelosB Platform, ContikiOS

We first perform benchmarks for each symmetric algorithm running it along with ContikiOS 3.0 over the TelosB mote. The only exception is the Blake2s hash function. Its reference implementation consumes a large amount of flash (code) memory compared to the other analyzed algorithms and cannot be compiled along with ContikiOS 3.0 which is high code memory consuming as well. In this case, the Blake2s

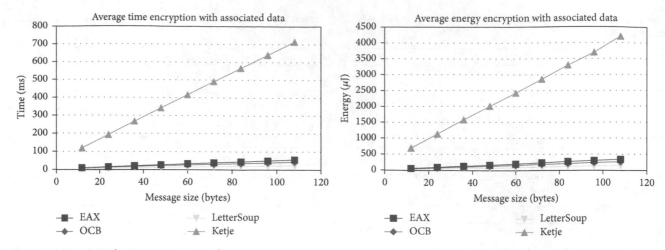

FIGURE 4: TinyOS/TelosB: average time and energy to execute one *encryption* operation for each AEAD algorithm with associated data.

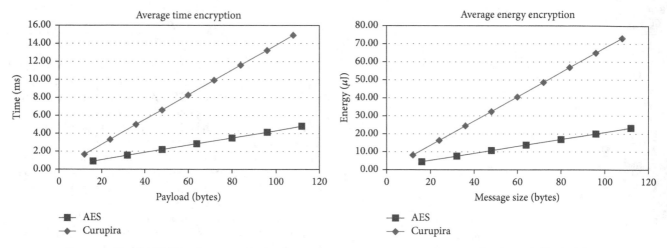

FIGURE 5: ContikiOS/TelosB: average time and energy to execute one *encryption* operation for each block cipher.

benchmarks are performed along with ContikiOS 2.7 which is less flash memory consuming. It is worth mentioning that ContikiOS 2.7 introduces some drawbacks like more current spikes which potentially leads to more energy consumption. Fortunately we were able to filter that overhead by estimating the average current of operation and considering only the area below this average current in the current versus time graph, which gives the average charge.

In the present experiments, the same methodology used for TinyOS is adopted. Same implementations are also used and same ranges of parameters are defined.

Figure 5 compares the run time of the *encryption* operation for different block ciphers. We can see a similar outcome when compared to the behavior of the ciphers on TelosB. AES is still faster than Curupira-2. It is important to point out that ContikiOS presents run times and energy consumption very close to the ones observed for TinyOS in Figure 1.

Figure 6 presents the *decryption* operation for different block ciphers.

The benchmarks for the *update* operation of MAC algorithms are shown in Figure 7 while the benchmarks for the *update* operation of *hash algorithms* are shown in Figure 8.

The *authenticated encryption with associated data* operation is shown in Figure 9.

The *decryption with associated data* displays similar behavior and thus is omitted here.

6.1. Discussion. In comparison, the performance results on TinyOS and ContikiOS are very close to one another, meaning that the overhead of those operating systems on processing-only operations is similar. This corroborates the conclusions by Margi et al. [60]. On the other hand, we also showed that even though the relative performance id comparable, the magnitude of the results of time and energy is very different from other works such as the comparison with the results in [8] already discussed in Section 5.

7. Benchmarks and Results on Intel Edison with Yocto

7.1. Ciphers. In this section we present the performance and energy results on Intel Edison platform based on the Yocto OS. Tables 14 and 15 show the execution time and energy consumption for one *init* operation. This operation has a

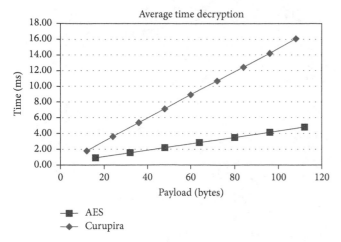

FIGURE 6: ContikiOS/TelosB: average time to execute one *decryption* operation for each block cipher.

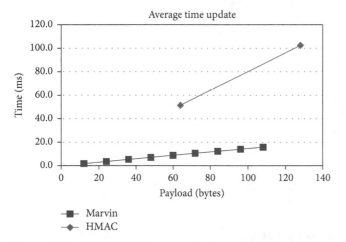

FIGURE 7: ContikiOS/TelosB: average time to execute one *update* for each MAC algorithm.

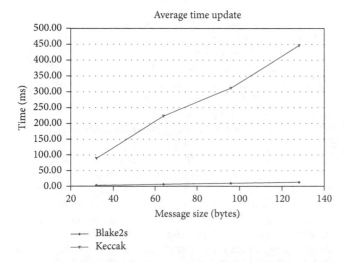

FIGURE 8: ContikiOS/TelosB: average time to execute one *update* for each hash algorithm.

TABLE 14: Time to execute one *init* operation for each block cipher. Time is in μs and D is the data size in bytes.

D	AES	Curupira	Trivium	Grain
12		13.90 ± 0.01		
16	7.33 ± 0.01		11.32 ± 0.01	8.58 ± 0.01

TABLE 15: Energy consumption to execute N *init* operations for each block cipher. The consumption is expressed in J.

AES	Curupira	Trivium	Grain
0.49 ± 0.00	1.12 ± 0.00	0.89 ± 0.00	0.62 ± 0.00

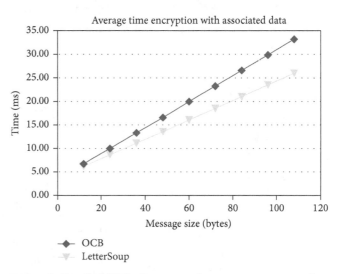

FIGURE 9: ContikiOS/TelosB: average time to execute one *authenticated encryption* with associated data operation for each AEAD algorithm.

(roughly) constant execution time that is not affected by the data size. Even though the speed of this operation cannot solely define the best algorithm, we can see that the fastest *init* operation is performed by AES, while Curupira is the slowest.

Figure 10 fully specifies the performance of the *encryption* operation for each block cipher algorithm. From the figures one can note that AES is the fastest algorithm for data size up to 32 bytes. For larger data sizes, AES is surpassed by Trivium and for even the larger messages sizes (more than $\approx$95 bytes) also by Grain.

The AES performance is expected to be more sensitive to message sizes than Trivium and Grain, since AES is a block cipher (this is also true for Curupira). Curupira in turn presented the worst performance for all data sizes, but this is due the nonfully optimized implementation.

The performance behavior observed for decryption is identical to encryption as expected and therefore the actual data is omitted.

Tables 16 and 17 show the execution time and energy consumption by the *init* operation for *hash algorithms*. Analyzing only this operation is not very meaningful for defining the best algorithm, but Blake2's initialization is much

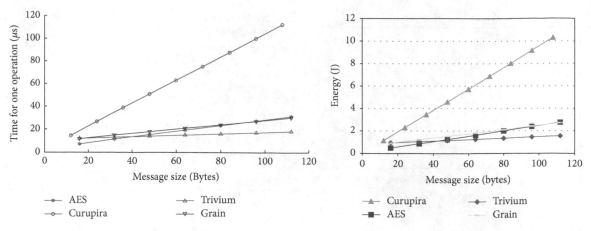

FIGURE 10: Average time and energy to execute one *encryption* operation for each block cipher.

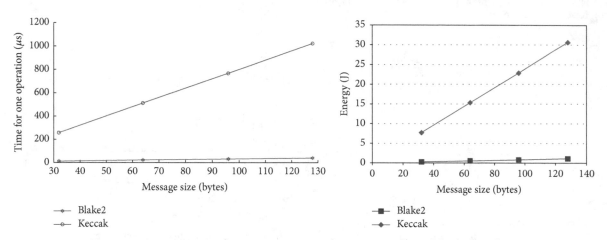

FIGURE 11: Average time and energy to execute *update* operation for each hash algorithm.

TABLE 16: Time to execute one *init* operation for each hash algorithm. Time is expressed in μs and D is the data size in bytes.

D	Blake2	Keccak
128	5.95 ± 0.01	27.23 ± 0.01

TABLE 17: Energy consumption to execute N *init* operations for each hash algorithm. The consumption is expressed in J.

Blake2	Keccak
0.12 ± 0.00	0.79 ± 0.01

TABLE 18: Time of *final* operation for each hash algorithm expressed in μs. D is the data size in bytes.

D	Blake2	Keccak
128	24.09 ± 0.01	2.13 ± 0.01

TABLE 19: Energy consumption for N *final* operations for the hash algorithms expressed in J.

Blake2	Keccak
0.59 ± 0.00	0.01 ± 0.00

faster than Keccak's. This operation has a roughly constant execution time for all data sizes.

Figure 11 illustrates the execution time and energy consumption comparisons for the *update* operation between two hash algorithms. Blake2 presents performance one order of magnitude (or even more depending on the message sizes) better than Keccak.

Finally, Tables 18 and 19 show the execution time for the *final* operation which is roughly constant for all data sizes and only results for one input size are shown. Keccak is about 11x

faster and less energy consuming than Blake2 for the analyzed operation.

It is worth observing that for smaller input sizes (<32 bytes) both algorithms have similar performance considering the combination *update + final*, but as the input length grows the Blake2 relative performance is progressively improved.

Tables 20 and 21 show the execution time of *init* operation for each *MAC algorithm*. The Marvin execution time is roughly constant for data sizes $12 \leq D \leq 108$ and only figures for $D = 108$ are shown. Marvin takes $\approx$2x longer to initialize than HMAC.

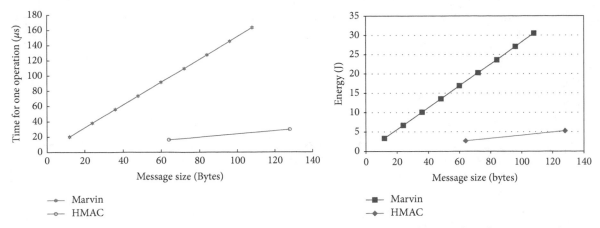

FIGURE 12: Average time and energy of the *update* operation for each MAC algorithm.

TABLE 20: Time of *init* operation for each MAC algorithm expressed in μs. *D* is the data size in bytes.

D	Marvin	HMAC
108	62.84 ± 0.20	
128		32.90 ± 0.02

TABLE 21: Energy consumption in J to execute *N init* operations for each MAC algorithm.

Marvin	HMAC
11.32 ± 0.02	5.82 ± 0.01

TABLE 22: Time of *final* operation for each MAC algorithm expressed in μs. *D* is the data size in bytes.

D	Marvin	HMAC
108	80.26 ± 0.03	
128		39.15 ± 0.05

TABLE 23: Energy consumption for *N final* operations for each MAC algorithm expressed in J.

Marvin	HMAC
14.77 ± 0.02	7.06 ± 0.01

Figure 12 compiles the benchmarks for the *update* operation for the MAC algorithms. HMAC presents a much better performance, executing this procedure for 64 bytes faster than Marvin with 12 bytes.

Finally, Tables 22 and 23 present the performance of MAC *final* operation. Marvin execution time is roughly constant for all data sizes 12 ≤ *D* ≤ 108, so only the result for *D* = 108 is shown. HMAC performs 2x faster than Marvin for the *final* operation.

Tables 24 and 25 show the execution time and energy consumption of the *init* procedure for *AEAD algorithms*. LetterSoup initialization is the fastest one with a slight difference comparing to OCB. Ketje has the slowest initialization.

TABLE 24: Time to execute one *init* operation for each AEAD algorithm. Time is expressed in μs and *D* is the data size in bytes.

D	EAX	OCB	LTS	Ketje
108	33.25 ± 0.03	20.98 ± 0.03	20.30 ± 0.03	70.98 ± 0.05

TABLE 25: Energy consumption to execute *N init* operations for each AEAD algorithm. The consumption is in J.

EAX	OCB	LTS	Ketje
0.46 ± 0.00	0.28 ± 0.00	0.27 ± 0.00	1.01 ± 0.01

Figure 13 illustrates the execution time and energy consumption of the *encryption with associated data* operation. Ketje remains the slowest algorithm in this experiment. It shows that LetterSoup presents a better performance than OCB when there is associated data.

Since the decryption operation displays similar performance for time and energy, the detailed results are also omitted here.

According to the results described in this section, the run time and energy consumption experiments agree with each other. Let *D* be the data size; the recommendation of cryptographic algorithms for the Intel Edison is as follows:

(i) Symmetric block cipher: *AES* if *D* ≤ 32, and *Trivium* if *D* > 32

(ii) Hash: *Blake2*

(iii) MAC: *HMAC*

(iv) AEAD: *OCB* when there is no associated data, and *LetterSoup* when there is associated data

8. Conclusions

We provided a detailed evaluation of symmetric cryptographic primitives providing different security services in relevant real-world platforms and operating systems, typical of IoT and WSN. We observed that some previous results in the literature only considered the (relatively) old implementations over a single platform or a single operating system.

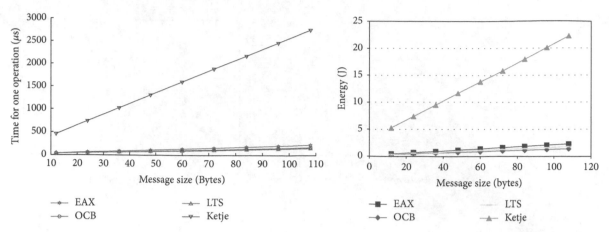

FIGURE 13: Average time and energy to execute one *encryption* operation for each AEAD algorithm with associated data.

We give some potential recommendations of algorithms depending on input data sizes. This work also provided for the first time a detailed benchmark methodology and a significant set of experiments for the Intel Edison board, a 32-bit IoT power-efficient IoT platform.

Acknowledgments

This research was supported by Fundação para o Desenvolvimento Tecnológico da Engenharia (FDTE) under Grant no. 1450. Cíntia B. Margi is supported by CNPq Research Fellowship no. 307304/2015-9.

References

[1] F. Hu and N. K. Sharma, "Security considerations in ad hoc sensor networks," *Ad Hoc Networks*, vol. 3, no. 1, pp. 69–89, 2005.

[2] J. Lee, K. Kapitanova, and S. H. Son, "The price of security in wireless sensor networks," *Computer Networks*, vol. 54, no. 17, pp. 2967–2978, 2010.

[3] C. B. Margi, R. C. A. Alves, and J. Sepulveda, "Sensing as a service: secure wireless sensor network infrastructure sharing for the internet of things," in *Proceedings of theProceedings of the International Workshop on Very Large Internet of Things (VLIoT 2017) in conjunction with the VLDB 2017*, vol. 3, Munich, Germany, 2017, https://www.ronpub.com/OJIOT_2017v3i1n08_Margi.pdf.

[4] S. Hu, X. Zhang, H. Yao, and C. She, "An Android Terminal in TelosB Wireless Sensor Networks," in *Proceedings of the 2nd International Conference on Computer and Information Applications (ICCIA '12)*, December 2012.

[5] Y. W. Law, J. Doumen, and P. Hartel, "Survey and benchmark of block ciphers for wireless sensor networks," *ACM Transactions on Sensor Networks*, vol. 2, no. 1, pp. 65–93, 2006.

[6] W. Su and M. Alzaghal, "Channel propagation characteristics of wireless MICAz sensor nodes," *Ad Hoc Networks*, vol. 7, no. 6, pp. 1183–1193, 2009.

[7] H. J. Ban, J. Choi, and N. Kang, "Fine-grained support of security services for resource constrained internet of things," *International Journal of Distributed Sensor Networks*, vol. 2016, Article ID 7824686, 2016.

[8] L. Casado and P. Tsigas, "ContikiSec: a secure network layer for wireless sensor networks under the Contiki operating system," in *Identity and Privacy in the Internet Age*, vol. 5838 of *Lecture Notes in Computer Science*, pp. 133–147, Springer, Berlin, Germany, 2009.

[9] A. Dunkels, "Contiki 3.0 released, new hardware from texas instruments, zolertia," The Official Contiki OS Blog, 2015, http://contiki-os.blogspot.ca/2015/08/contiki-30-released-new-hardware-from.html.

[10] SUPERCOP, "Mirror of SUPERCOP: System for Unified Performance Evaluation Related to Cryptographic Operations and Primitives," 2015, https://github.com/floodyberry/supercop.

[11] I. Corporation, "Intel edison product brief," 2015, http://download.intel.com/support/edison/sb/edison_pb_331179001.pdf.

[12] O. Hyncica, P. Kucera, P. Honzik, and P. Fiedler, "Performance evaluation of symmetric cryptography in embedded systems," in *Proceedings of the 6th IEEE International Conference on Intelligent Data Acquisition and Advanced Computing Systems: Technology and Applications, IDAACS'2011*, pp. 277–282, September 2011.

[13] Electronic codebook (ecb), 2016, https://en.wikipedia.org/wiki/Block_cipher_mode_of_operation#Electronic_Codebook_.28ECB.29.

[14] M. A. Simplicio Jr., B. T. De Oliveira, C. B. Margi, P. S. L. M. Barreto, T. C. M. B. Carvalho, and M. Näslund, "Survey and comparison of message authentication solutions on wireless sensor networks," *Ad Hoc Networks*, vol. 11, no. 3, pp. 1221–1236, 2013.

[15] C. Karlof, N. Sastry, and D. Wagner, "TinySec: a link layer security architecture for wireless sensor networks," in *Proceedings of the Second International Conference on Embedded Networked Sensor Systems (SenSys '04)*, pp. 162–175, November 2004.

[16] M. Luk, G. Mezzour, A. Perrig, and V. Gligor, "MiniSec: a secure sensor network communication architecture," in *Proceedings of the 2007 6th International Symposium on Information Processing in Sensor Networks*, pp. 479–488, New York, NY, USA, April 2007.

[17] J. Hill, R. Szewczyk, W. Alec, S. Hollar, D. Culler, and K. Pister, "System architecture directions for networked sensors," *ACM SIGPLAN Notices*, vol. 35, no. 11, pp. 93–104, 2000.

[18] P. Serrano, A. Garcia-Saavedra, G. Bianchi, A. Banchs, and A. Azcorra, "Per-frame energy consumption in 802.11 devices and its implication on modeling and design," *IEEE/ACM Transac-*

tions on Networking, vol. 23, no. 4, pp. 1243–1256, 2015.

[19] F. Kaup, P. Gottschling, and D. Hausheer, "PowerPi: measuring and modeling the power consumption of the raspberry Pi," in *Proceedings of the 39th Annual IEEE Conference on Local Computer Networks, (LCN '14)*, pp. 236–243, September 2014.

[20] G. De Meulenaer, F. Gosset, F. Standaert, and O. Pereira, "On the energy cost of communication and cryptography in wireless sensor networks," in *Proceedings of the 4th IEEE International Conference on Wireless and Mobile Computing, Networking and Communication (WiMob '08)*, pp. 580–585, Avignon, France, October 2008.

[21] "Embedded linux board comparison," 2014, https://learn.adafruit .com/embedded-linux-board-comparison/power-usage.

[22] "Measured power consumption of intel edison," 2016, https:// www.scivision.co/measured-power-consumption-of-intel-edison/.

[23] TinyOS, 2015, http://www.tinyos.net/.

[24] P. Levis, S. Madden, J. Polastre et al., "TinyOS: an operating system for sensor networks," in *Ambient Intelligence*, pp. 115–148, Springer, Berlin, Germany, 2005.

[25] A. Dunkels, B. Grönvall, and T. Voigt, "Contiki—a lightweight and flexible operating system for tiny networked sensors," in *Proceedings of the 29th IEEE Annual International Conference on Local Computer Networks (LCN '04)*, pp. 455–462, November 2004.

[26] N. Kushalnagar, G. Montenegro, and C. Schumacher, "IPv6 over low-power wireless personal area networks (6LoWPANs): overview, assumptions, problem statement, and goals," RFC 4919 4919, IETF, 2007, http://www.ietf.org/rfc/rfc4919.txt.

[27] T. Winter, P. Thubert, A. Brandt et al., "RPL: IPv6 routing protocol for low-power and lossy networks," RFC 6550 6550, 2012, http://www.ietf.org/rfc/rfc6550.txt.

[28] C. Bormann, A. P. Castellani, and Z. Shelby, "CoAP: an application protocol for billions of tiny internet nodes," *IEEE Internet Computing*, vol. 16, no. 2, pp. 62–67, 2012.

[29] A. Dunkels, O. Schmidt, and T. Voigt, "Using protothreads for sensor node programming in," in *In Proceedings of the REAL-WSN 2005 Workshop on RealWorld Wireless Sensor Networks*, 2005.

[30] The yocto project, 2015, https://www.yoctoproject.org/.

[31] N. F. Standard, "Announcing the advanced encryption standard (AES)," Federal Information Processing Standards Publication 197 NIST FIPS 197, 2001.

[32] P. Barreto and M. Simplicio, "Curupira, a block cipher for constrained platforms, in: Anais do 25o Simpósio Brasileiro de Redes de Computadores e Sistemas Distribuídos - SBRC'07, 2007".

[33] S. Panasenko and S. Smagin, "Lightweight cryptography: underlying principles and approaches," *International Journal of Computer Theory and Engineering*, pp. 516–520, 2011.

[34] M. Simplicio, P. Barreto, T. Carvalho, C. Margi, and M. Naslund, "The Curupira-2 block cipher for constrained platforms: Specification and benchmarking," in *Proceedings of the 1st International Workshop on Privacy in Location-Based Applications - 13th European Symposium on Research in Computer Security (ESORICS '08)*, vol. 397, 2008, http://sunsite.informatik.rwth-aachen.de/Publications/CEUR-WS/Vol-397.

[35] C. De Cannière and B. Preneel, "Trivium," in *New Stream Cipher Designs*, vol. 4986 of *Lecture Notes in Computer Science*, pp. 244–266, Springer, Berlin, Germany, 2008.

[36] M. Hell, T. Johansson, and W. Meier, "Grain: a stream cipher for constrained environments," *International Journal of Wireless and Mobile Computing*, vol. 2, no. 1, pp. 86–93, 2007.

[37] J. P. Aumasson, S. Neves, Z. Wilcox-O'Hearn, and C. Winnerlein, "BLAKE2: simpler, smaller, fast as MD5," *Applied Cryptography and Network Security*, pp. 119–135, 2013.

[38] NIST, "Announcing request for candidate algorithm nominations for a new cryptographic hash algorithm (SHA-3) family," Tech. Rep., Department of Commerce, 2007, http://csrc.nist .gov/groups/ST/hash/documents/FR_Notice_Nov07.pdf.

[39] "gvanas, Keccak code package," 2014, https://github.com/ gvanas/KeccakCodePackage.

[40] P. FIPS, "The Keyed-Hash Message Authentication Code (HMAC)," FIPS PUB 198-1 NIST FIPS 198-1, National Institute of Standards and Technology, 2008.

[41] M. A. Simplicio, B. Pedro Aquino, P. S. L. M. Barreto, T. C. M. B. Carvalho, and C. B. Margi, "The Marvin message authentication code and the LetterSoup authenticated encryption scheme," *Security and Communication Networks*, vol. 2, no. 2, pp. 165–180, 2009.

[42] H. Lipmaa, P. Rogaway, and D. Wagner, "CTR-mode encryption," *First NIST Workshop on Modes of Operation, Citeseer*, 2000.

[43] M. Dworkin, "NIST Special Publication 800-38C: The CCM Mode for Authentication and Confidentiality," US National Institute of Standards and Technology, http://csrc.nist.gov/publications/nistpubs/800-38C/SP800-38C.pdf.

[44] P. Rogaway, M. Bellare, and R. S. Ferguson, "OCB: a block-cipher mode of operation for efficient authenticated encryption," *ACM Transactions on Information and System Security (TISSEC)*, vol. 6, no. 3, pp. 365–403, 2003.

[45] P. Rogaway, "OCB: Background," 2015, http://web.cs.ucdavis .edu/rogaway/ocb/ocb-faq.htm.

[46] M. J. Dworkin, "Nist special publication 800-38b," Recommendation for Block Cipher Modes of Operation: The cmac mode for authentication NIST SP 800-38b, 2016.

[47] M. A. Simplicio Jr., B. T. De Oliveira, P. S. L. M. Barreto, C. B. Margi, T. C. M. B. Carvalho, and M. Naslund, "Comparison of authenticated-encryption schemes in wireless sensor networks," in *Proceedings of the 36th Annual IEEE Conference on Local Computer Networks, (LCN '11)*, pp. 450–457, October 2011.

[48] M. Simplicio, LetterSoup implementation, 2015, http://www .larc.usp.br/mjunior/files/algs/8%20bits/LetterSoup/LetterSoup.c.

[49] M. Simplicio, "AEAD implementations," 2015, http://www.larc .usp.br/mjunior/files/algs/8%20bits/algs8bits.zip.

[50] M. Simplicio, "Curupira-2 implementation," 2015, http://www .larc.usp.br/mjunior/files/algs/8%20bits/Curupira-2/Curupira-2 .zip.

[51] G. Bertoni, J. Daemen, M. Peeters, and G. V. Assche, CAESAR submission: Ketje v1, 2014, http://competitions.cr.yp.to/round1/ ketjev11.pdf.

[52] S. Pelissier, "Application using trivium with 16-bit microcontroller," 2009, https://github.com/tyll/tinyos-2.x-contrib/tree/ master/crypto/apps.

[53] J.-P. Aumasson, S. Neves, Z. Wilcox-O'Hearn, and C. Winnerlein, "BLAKE2: simpler, smaller, fast as MD5," *Lecture Notes in Computer Science (including subseries Lecture Notes in Artificial Intelligence and Lecture Notes in Bioinformatics)*, vol. 7954, pp. 119–135, 2013.

[54] O. Gay, "HMAC implementation," 2015, https://github.com/ ogay/hmac.

[55] M. Simplicio, Marvin implementation, 2015, http://www.larc .usp.br/mjunior/files/algs/8%20bits/Marvin/Marvin.c.

[56] M. Bellare, P. Rogaway, and D. Wagner, "The EAX mode of oper-

ation," in *Fast Software Encryption: 11th International Workshop (FSE 2004)*, B. Roy and W. Meier, Eds., pp. 389–407, Springer, Berlin, Germany, 2004.

[57] T. Krovetz and P. Rogaway, "The OCB authenticated-encryption algorithm," RFC Editor RFC7253, 2014, http://www.cs.ucdavis .edu/rogaway/papers/ocb-id.htm.

[58] Agilent, "Agilent 34401A Multimeter," 2007, http://cp.literature .agilent.com/litweb/pdf/5968-0162EN.pdf.

[59] L. P. Manual and gettimeofday., 2015, http://man7.org/linux/man-pages/man2/gettimeofday.2.html.

[60] C. B. Margi, B. T. De Oliveira, G. T. De Sousa et al., "Impact of operating systems on Wireless Sensor Networks (security) applications and testbeds," in *Proceedings of the 2010 19th International Conference on Computer Communications and Networks, (ICCCN '10)*, August 2010.

Permissions

All chapters in this book were first published in SCN, by Hindawi Publishing Corporation; hereby published with permission under the Creative Commons Attribution License or equivalent. Every chapter published in this book has been scrutinized by our experts. Their significance has been extensively debated. The topics covered herein carry significant findings which will fuel the growth of the discipline. They may even be implemented as practical applications or may be referred to as a beginning point for another development.

The contributors of this book come from diverse backgrounds, making this book a truly international effort. This book will bring forth new frontiers with its revolutionizing research information and detailed analysis of the nascent developments around the world.

We would like to thank all the contributing authors for lending their expertise to make the book truly unique. They have played a crucial role in the development of this book. Without their invaluable contributions this book wouldn't have been possible. They have made vital efforts to compile up to date information on the varied aspects of this subject to make this book a valuable addition to the collection of many professionals and students.

This book was conceptualized with the vision of imparting up-to-date information and advanced data in this field. To ensure the same, a matchless editorial board was set up. Every individual on the board went through rigorous rounds of assessment to prove their worth. After which they invested a large part of their time researching and compiling the most relevant data for our readers.

The editorial board has been involved in producing this book since its inception. They have spent rigorous hours researching and exploring the diverse topics which have resulted in the successful publishing of this book. They have passed on their knowledge of decades through this book. To expedite this challenging task, the publisher supported the team at every step. A small team of assistant editors was also appointed to further simplify the editing procedure and attain best results for the readers.

Apart from the editorial board, the designing team has also invested a significant amount of their time in understanding the subject and creating the most relevant covers. They scrutinized every image to scout for the most suitable representation of the subject and create an appropriate cover for the book.

The publishing team has been an ardent support to the editorial, designing and production team. Their endless efforts to recruit the best for this project, has resulted in the accomplishment of this book. They are a veteran in the field of academics and their pool of knowledge is as vast as their experience in printing. Their expertise and guidance has proved useful at every step. Their uncompromising quality standards have made this book an exceptional effort. Their encouragement from time to time has been an inspiration for everyone.

The publisher and the editorial board hope that this book will prove to be a valuable piece of knowledge for researchers, students, practitioners and scholars across the globe.

List of Contributors

Huicong Liang, Wei Wang and Meiqin Wang
Key Laboratory of Cryptologic Technology and Information Security, Ministry of Education, Shandong University, Jinan, China

Yu Liu
Key Laboratory of Cryptologic Technology and Information Security, Ministry of Education, Shandong University, Jinan, China
Weifang University,Weifang, China

Keyang Liu, Weiming Zhang and Xiaojuan Dong
School of Information Science and Technology, University of Science and Technology of China, Anhui, China

Yanli Ren and Min Dong
School of Communication and Information Engineering, Shanghai University, Shanghai 200444, China

Zhihua Niu
School of Computer Engineering and Science, Shanghai University, Shanghai 200444, China

Xiaoni Du
College of Mathematics and Information Science, Northwest Normal University, Lanzhou 730070, China

Wenjie Yang, Jian Weng, Weiqi Luo and Anjia Yang
College of Information Science and Technology/ College of Cyber Security, Jinan University, Guangzhou 510632, China

Salim Chitroub
LISIC Laboratory, Electronics and Computer Science Faculty, University of Science and Technology of Houari Boumediene (USTHB), Algiers, Algeria

Mahdi Madani
LISIC Laboratory, Electronics and Computer Science Faculty, University of Science and Technology of Houari Boumediene (USTHB), Algiers, Algeria
LCOMS, Universite de Lorraine, Metz, France

Ilyas Benkhaddra, Camel Tanougast and Loic Sieler
LCOMS, Universite de Lorraine, Metz, France

Naveed Ahmed Azam
Faculty of Engineering Sciences, GIK Institute of Engineering Sciences and Technology, Topi, Pakistan

Yiqin Lu, Meng Wang and Pengsen Huang
South China University of Technology, Guangzhou, China

Xiaotian Yu, Jiewei Qian, Lu Dong and Huqing Nie
School of Computer Science, Nanjing University of Posts and Telecommunications, Nanjing 210003, China

Peng Li and He Xu
School of Computer Science, Nanjing University of Posts and Telecommunications, Nanjing 210003, China
Jiangsu High Technology Research Key Laboratory forWireless Sensor Networks, Jiangsu Province, Nanjing 210003, China

Dhanalakshmi Krishnan Sadhasivan
Department of ECE, Kalasalingam University, Krishnankoil, Tamil Nadu 626126, India

Kannapiran Balasubramanian
Department of Instrumentation & Control Engineering, Kalasalingam University, Krishnankoil, Tamil Nadu, India

Gang Han and Hui Li
School of Electronics and Information, Northwestern Polytechnical University, Shaanxi, China

Yu Yu
Department of Computer Science and Engineering, Shanghai Jiao Tong University, Shanghai, China
Westone Cryptologic Research Center, Beijing, China

Xiangxue Li
Westone Cryptologic Research Center, Beijing, China
Department of Computer Science and Technology, East China Normal University, Shanghai, China
National Engineering Laboratory forWireless Security, Xi'an University of Posts and Telecommunications, Xi'an, China

Qifeng Zhou
Department of Computer Science and Technology, East China Normal University, Shanghai, China

Dong Zheng
National Engineering Laboratory forWireless Security, Xi'an University of Posts and Telecommunications, Xi'an, China

Qian Meng
School of Telecommunication Engineering, Xidian University, Xi'an 710071, China
Shaanxi Key Laboratory of Network and System Security, Xi'an 710071, China

Jianfeng Ma, Yinbin Miao and Tengfei Yang
Shaanxi Key Laboratory of Network and System Security, Xi'an 710071, China
School of Cyber Engineering, Xidian University, Xi'an 710071, China

Kefei Chen
School of Science, Hangzhou Normal University, Hangzhou 310036, China

Dhruti Sharma
Sarvajanik College of Engineering and Technology, Surat, Gujarat, India

Devesh C. Jinwala
Sardar Vallabhbhai National Institute of Technology, Surat, Gujarat, India

Wei Yin and Hongjian Zhou
North China Institute of Computing Technology, Beijing, China

Jadwiga Indulska
School of ITEE, The University of Queensland, Brisbane, QLD, Australia

Fusheng Wu and Huanguo Zhang
Computer School of Wuhan University, Wuhan 430072, China

Wengqing Wang, Jianwei Jia and Shi Yuan
Key Laboratory of Aerospace Information Security and Trusted Computing of Ministry of Education, Wuhan University, Wuhan 430072, China

Mervat Mikhail, Yasmine Abouelseoud and Galal ElKobrosy
Department of Engineering Mathematics, Faculty of Engineering, Alexandria 21544, Egypt

Kaysar Rahman
College of Mathematics and System Science, Xinjiang University, Xinjiang, China

Nurmamat Helil
College of Mathematics and System Science, Xinjiang University, Xinjiang, China
Department of Computer Science and Engineering, University of Minnesota, Minneapolis, MN, USA

Qingqing Gan, Xiaoming Wang and Daini Wu
Department of Computer Science, Jinan University, Guangzhou 510632, China

Geovandro C. C. F. Pereira, Renan C. A. Alves, Felipe L. da Silva, Roberto M. Azevedo, Bruno C. Albertini and Cíntia B. Margi
Escola Politécnica, Universidade de São Paulo, São Paulo, SP, Brazil

Index

CPSIA information can be obtained
at www.ICGtesting.com
Printed in the USA
BVHW011419240519
549249BV00004B/371/P